© Peter Morris

Peter FitzSimons is a journalist with the *Sydney Morning Herald* and *Sun-Herald*, and a busy events and motivational speaker. He is the author of twenty-seven books, including *Tobruk*, *Kokoda*, *Batavia*, *Eureka*, *Ned Kelly*, *Gallipoli* and biographies of Douglas Mawson, Nancy Wake, Kim Beazley, Nick Farr-Jones, Les Darcy, Steve Waugh and John Eales, and is one of Australia's biggest selling non-fiction authors of the last fifteen years. His latest book is *Fromelles and Pozières: In the Trenches of Hell*. He lives with his wife, Lisa Wilkinson, and their three children in Sydney.

PETER FITZSIMONS

NED KELLY

THE STORY OF AUSTRALIA'S MOST NOTORIOUS LEGEND

WILLIAM HEINEMANN: AUSTRALIA

A William Heinemann book
Published by Random House Australia Pty Ltd
Level 3, 100 Pacific Highway, North Sydney NSW 2060
www.randomhouse.com.au

First published by William Heinemann in 2013
This edition published in 2015

Random House Books is part of the Penguin Random House group of companies whose addresses can be found at global.penguinrandomhouse.com.

National Library of Australia
Cataloguing-in-Publication Entry

FitzSimons, Peter, author.
Ned Kelly/Peter FitzSimons.

ISBN 978 0 85798 814 0 (paperback)

Kelly, Ned, 1855–1880.
Kelly Gang.
Bushrangers – Australia – Biography.

364.155092

Front cover: Portrait of Ned Kelly the day before he was hanged, 1880, by Charles Nettleton; photo of Ned's helmet; 'Spot where Ned was taken' by Oswald Thomas Madeley. All photos courtesy State Library of Victoria. Back cover: Ned Kelly in chains, Old Melbourne Gaol, by Charles Nettleton, courtesy State Library of Victoria
Illustrations of ploughshare and floor plan of Glenrowan Inn by Rod McClean, Midland Typesetters, Australia
Cover design by Adam Yazxhi/MAXCO
Internal design and typesetting by Xou Creative, Australia
Printed in Australia by Griffin Press, an accredited ISO AS/NZS 14001:2004 Environmental Management System printer

Random House Australia uses papers that are natural, renewable and recyclable products and made from wood grown in sustainable forests. The logging and manufacturing processes are expected to conform to the environmental regulations of the country of origin.

To Ian Jones, the doyen of all Kelly writers, who has studied the life and times of Ned Kelly for seventy of his eighty-two years. He, more than anyone, has kept the Kelly story alive in modern Australia and was unfailingly generous to me in the course of writing this book. I salute his passion. I deeply respect his scholarship.

I do not pretend that I have led a blameless life, or that one fault justifies another, but the public in judging a case like mine should remember that the darkest life may have a bright side, and that after the worst has been said against a man, he may, if he is heard, tell a story in his own rough way that will perhaps lead them to intimate the harshness of their thoughts against him, and find as many excuses for him as he would plead for himself.

Ned Kelly, 1880

Yet who were the prophets of his day? They were sharp business men who employed missionaries, soldiers and trade representatives to subjugate the world to their will. The bravest of them would watch the Union Jack flutter to the breeze in some foreign land with tears in their eyes, or march with fire and sword through Africa without a tremor, for they believed in the machine and their mission to turn unhappy mankind into a herd of milch cows . . . But Ned Kelly was not of them and had no sympathy for them for he knew only too well what they had done to his own family, and blood and bone he was of the Australia that had shown its true colours at Eureka and was carrying on as best it knew the age-old struggle waged against the princes of Europe.

Max Brown, Australian Son

CONTENTS

Background and Acknowledgements xi

PART ONE – EARLY YEARS

Chapter One: Born a Kelly 3
Chapter Two: Troubled Times 48
Chapter Three: Working for the Man 95
Chapter Four: A Significant Visit 122

PART TWO – THE NOTORIOUS KELLY GANG

Chapter Five: Stringybark Creek 163
Chapter Six: After Stringybark 203
Chapter Seven: Euroa 250
Chapter Eight: After Euroa 287
Chapter Nine: Jerilderie 320
Chapter Ten: After Jerilderie 354

PART THREE – GLENROWAN

Chapter Eleven: Nicolson Takes Over 395
Chapter Twelve: A Plan Interrupted 434
Chapter Thirteen: Glenrowan Dances 474
Chapter Fourteen: The Siege Begins 515
Chapter Fifteen: It's a Bunyip 548

PART FOUR – RETRIBUTION

Chapter Sixteen: Trials and Tribulations 591
Chapter Seventeen: On Trial for His Life 637
Chapter Eighteen: The End Is High 661

Epilogue 694
Notes and References 728
Bibliography 797
Index 808

BACKGROUND AND ACKNOWLEDGEMENTS

The legend of Ned Kelly is the most enduring Australian one of all. There has always been something about him, what he did and how he did it that fascinated the people not only of his generation but of all generations since.

Why? What exactly is it?

In England, of course, they have long mythologised King Arthur and his knights in shining armour, while exalting those who would turn swords into ploughshares. Here in Australia, we somehow have a natural bent towards Ned Kelly and men in suits of rough iron, made out of those very ploughshares.

As to why another book on Ned, however, and why now – beyond the fact that, as I was writing it, the process of finally laying the bushranger to true rest in Greta Cemetery was in full swing – it has had a long genesis. My wife, Lisa Wilkinson, had been telling me for years that Ned was the perfect subject for me – *big, boofy bloke with a beard and strange headwear writes about another big, boofy bloke with a beard and strange headwear* – but it was only nearing the end of my book, *Eureka: The Unfinished Revolution*, that I really looked at it hard. My principal researcher for that book, Henry Barrkman, was the one who pointed out that Ned had been born within a short time and within miles of the climax of that whole saga, and that in many ways his life had been shaped by exactly the same forces that had driven the rebellion. He was insistent that there could be no better subject for me.

The more I looked at it, the more I realised that Lisa and Henry were right. It was a perfect subject as, whatever else, it really was a huge and quintessentially Australian story, and that is the subject matter that has always thrilled me the most.

A bare beginning in early research and I was hooked, not simply because Ned himself remained as fascinating a figure to me as a fifty-one-year-old professional writer as he was to me when I was four years old, heading off to the Mangrove Mountain Community Fair fancy-dress party dressed as the man himself.

What I have most enjoyed doing in recent years is not to simply tell a historical tale but to so mine that tale for details that I can have a good go at *recreating* the whole story, telling it in such a manner that – ideally – the reader's head is not with me as I spin the yarn but actually with Ned, as he has his first fight, does his first hold-up, sees the inside of a gaol cell for the first time and, yes, first spies the Glenrowan Inn in the cold moonlight.

In this sense, I have become a devotee of the approach of the great nineteenth-century German historian Leopold von Ranke, whose view was that the best way to understand the past is to tell it '*wie es eigentlich gewesen ist*' – how it essentially was – understood on its own terms and relying heavily on primary documents, with the account unburdened by the historian giving his own analysis on the material presented. Apart from some conclusions I might draw in the epilogue, in the main account I don't wish to state my views of what happened, just reconstruct the best I can what actually *did* happen. How it essentially was . . .

In the case of von Ranke, as many oft-critical historians have pointed out, it was a notably difficult exercise, for in his time 'history' was much more the study of the Big Picture than a specific episode – as exemplified by his most famous work, *Civil Wars and Monarchy in France in the Sixteenth and Seventeenth Centuries.* When writing history on that grand a scale, discovering 'how it essentially was' is extremely difficult, as there are too many complexities of cause and effect to accurately thread together and certainly too many holes in the documentary evidence. It is much more manageable, however, on the personal scale.

And here was the true joy, for me, of writing about Ned Kelly, in a way that it hasn't been done before. For, as it turns out, Ned really was so compelling to the people of the time that the historical records of what he and other people involved did and said are staggering in their width, depth and diversity – all of it rich in the wonderful detail I most crave to make a story live and breathe.

Including from Ned himself! (I defy anyone to read the Jerilderie Letter and not feel as if Ned is speaking from the grave.) Obviously, to retrieve the treasure from those millions of words of primary documents – court and Royal Commission transcripts (with just under a million words between those two sources alone), newspaper articles, letters, diaries, police reports, depositions and all the rest – would be a massive logistical exercise, but that was okay too. I had three of the best researchers in the business, and modern digital data retrieval means that sorting through that mass of words for the nuggets that lie therein is more possible than ever before.

An example of the approach that I take is the detail you will see on page 565, of how Ned was so thirsty when drops of brandy fell onto his beard that he lifted his beard up with his handcuffed hands and licked it. While that detail is likely neither here nor there to an academic historian, for me it is pure gold – as, with it, I feel as if I am in the room, *there*, as it is happening. *Wie es eigentlich gewesen ist!*

True, in terms of making the account accurate, there was a difficulty in that, just like *Eureka*, there are so many layers of mythology surrounding what actually occurred, and so many conflicting contemporary accounts, that it was frequently difficult to separate fact from folklore. When no positive determination could be made as to which of many versions of the truth was correct – just which of the *eight* possible ways that Constable Alexander Fitzpatrick came to be shot in the wrist, for example – I have tried to structure the storytelling so that the narrative still flows. In the case of Fitzpatrick, I have presented the three major versions – Alexander Fitzpatrick's, Ned Kelly's and Ned's sister Kate's – as they were presented at the time. In other disputed events, such as when *exactly* and where *precisely* Ned was born, I have gone with the version I have thought most likely, while adding an author's note in the endnotes to either explain my reasoning for my choice or to acknowledge the other versions.

In an equal effort to preserve what I hope is the novel-like feel of this account, for the sake of the storytelling I have occasionally created a direct quote from reported speech in a newspaper, diary, letter or court transcript, just as I have changed pronouns and tenses to put that reported speech in the present tense, and restored swearing words that were blanked out in the original newspaper account due to the sensitivities of the time.

I have taken a similar approach in that, even though it is only reported that a person received, say, the last rites, without detailing the actual words, I have put in the words used at the time with an author's note. Always, my goal has been to determine what were the most likely words used, and even the way those words sounded – when the accent of the person concerned is known – based on the documentary evidence presented.

For the same reason, I have stayed with the imperial form of measurement and used the spelling of the day. Equally, as an example of my approach, though there is no record of Joe Byrne's and Steve Hart's emotions in the immediate aftermath of what happened at Stringybark Creek, it is obvious to me that they would have been shocked, and I have included that shock in my account.

Though wanting to head down an entirely different path in writing this book, I was blessed, of course, to have had so many fine writers and historians preceding me, giving directions I could use to navigate. Of the modern writers, the books to which I most frequently referred were Ian Jones's *Ned Kelly: A Short Life* and Keith McMenomy's *Ned Kelly: The Authentic Illustrated History*, while Justin Corfield's *The Ned Kelly Encyclopaedia* was also a blessing. The greatest blessing of all, of course, was to be able to personally draw on the expertise and lifetime of learning of Ian Jones, in person and on the phone – and beyond my words in the dedication I will always feel privileged to have had him personally show me around and direct me to the major Kelly sites.

Time and again, when I was lost in the whirl of conflicting primary documents, I would go back to Jones, McMenomy and Corfield to find my way, and though I didn't always agree with their conclusions, just as they don't always agree with each other, whenever I found myself with Ned, lost in the Warby Ranges on a cold, dark night, they were the three stars in the night sky I constantly used to get my bearings and work out the way forward.

This way, Ned, and I think we can get you to the next major siege in time, and in shape to go again.

As to the also oft-confusing politics of the time, beyond the primary documents, both John McQuilton's book *The Kelly Outbreak* and Professor John Molony's *I Am Ned Kelly* were exceedingly helpful in getting my bearings, and both men also offered valuable advice, and vetting of certain parts, for which I warmly thank them.

I also tapped the expertise of people in particularly specialised fields, and I offer my warm thanks to: Gregory Blake, for his help in all matters to do with firearms; Bill Denheld on Stringybark Creek; Ian Shaw on Glenrowan; Sergeant Terry Claven (Curator, Historical Services, Victoria Police); Colin Nash (President of the Retired Prison Officers Association, Victoria); Warren Fahey on matters to do with Kelly ditties and poems; Michael Green of the National Trust; Peter Conole, a historian with the Western Australia Police; and Trevor Poultney of Old Melbourne Gaol, who also provided great advice on the manuscript. As to illustrations and maps, I am indebted most particularly to Bill Denheld once more, and I also thank Jane Macauley.

Beyond that, to my delight, it turns out that Australia is filled with Kelly experts, and – even though they agree with each other *less* than the aforementioned! – they are of a universally generous disposition. I cite particularly retired Sydney resident Michael Ball, who, for reasons I will never quite understand, has spent over five decades collecting books and information on Ned Kelly, and the last decade putting the distilled essence of that information into one huge document, all of which he happily sent to me to trawl through. (Nuggets! *Nuggets!* MORE nuggets!) Beyond that, Michael also broadly vetted the manuscript, looking for errors and omissions, making suggestions, and I warmly thank him. Similarly, another great help was Peter Newman, a Melbournian with a passionate interest in Australian history, who has also followed the Kelly saga since early childhood and also assisted in the vetting of the manuscript. I owe a great debt to Matt Shore, who has compiled exhibitions of Kelly artefacts and escorted Kelly tours to the key sites for many years, and was exceedingly generous in sharing his deep knowledge, including where the best Kelly photographs and illustrations could be found.

A great help throughout, from first to last, was Paul O'Keefe, the grand-nephew of Steve Hart, who has studied the Kelly Gang for most of his life and was also a fount of information and advice on the manuscript, as well as being very generous with his extensive library of Kelly books.

When all was said and done, and written, and checked and re-checked, I sent the entire manuscript to the person who is universally highly regarded in Kelly circles, Sharon Hollingsworth, who hails from the unlikely place, for a Kelly expert, of North Carolina. I am in awe of her knowledge; I am deeply indebted to her generosity.

None of this is to say that all of the aforementioned agree with my every statement of fact in this book. I learned early that, on a bad day, Kelly experts can be flat out agreeing it is Tuesday, let alone having a consensus on where *precisely* the Stringybark Creek site is – but, in my search for accuracy, I have been every bit as exhaustive as I have been exhausted by it. (And, for the record, having visited Stringybark Creek with Bill Denheld and seen the evidence with my own eyes, I am confident that he has it right, while bracing for the protest. Brace!)

In all of my historical books since *Kokoda*, I have called on my friend Dr Michael Cooper's twin passions for medicine and history to help inform me on the medical aspects of the story, and in this book he was as valuable as ever, giving me detailed advice on everything from the medical implications of a bullet wound to the wrist, to medical practices in the time of the Kelly Gang, to why being hit in the leg by shotgun pellets might make your pulse rise.

As ever, my dear friend at *The Sydney Morning Herald*, Harriet

Veitch, gave me wise counsel on every part of it and did the preliminary editing, sorting out tangled sentences, pointing out inconsistencies, and placing at my service the staggering width of her general knowledge.

Sonja Goernitz also had enormous input into this book, as with all of my last seven books, using her prodigious research skills to turn up treasure after treasure. I also thank Glenda Lynch of Canberra, who pursued leads in the National Archives, the kind and helpful staff members at the Mitchell Library of New South Wales, Charlie Farrugia at the Public Record Office Victoria, and Chris Wade and Kevin Molloy at the State Library of Victoria.

I would like to note my appreciation for the work done by the Kelly Gang and Friends Incorporated, who have set up a very helpful website that provides a wealth of information organised in a very user-friendly manner. Like Corfield, it provided an easy reference point whenever I was up King River without a paddle, and guided me safely along my way.

I most particularly deeply thank and record my enormous affection and professional admiration for Libby Effeney, a PhD Candidate in Sociology at Deakin University, who worked with me on this book from first to last, from top to bottom and back again, just as she did on *Eureka* – while also visiting the Kelly sites with me, and coordinating and collating the work of the other researchers, including her brother Patrick Effeney, who proved another great asset. As Libby and I approached Glenrowan, if I might say, I am still not sure if she was the pilot engine or I was, but she was certainly with me every mile of the way, and this book owes her intellect, work ethic and prodigious research skills a great debt.

Thank you, too, to the online digital project Trove, an initiative of the National Library of Australia, which has digitised many of the historical newspapers, in partnership with State Libraries, used in the research of this book. What a resource that is – and what a privilege to be able to instantly access contemporary accounts from journalists on the ground at the time, compare them and get ever closer to the truth.

I thank all at Random House, most particularly Nikki Christer,

Peri Wilson and, as ever, Alison Urquhart, for backing the project from the first. Alison and I have now worked together on eleven books, and she is my publishing rock.

As to my editor, Kevin O'Brien, he and I first worked together on my book *Batavia* and established a good relationship that has endured through this book, on which he has done wonderful work. His ability to spot inconsistencies missed by ten sets of expert eyes is extraordinary.

As to my wife, Lisa, she has been a Trojan, as ever, in doing so many things that allowed me the space and time I needed to get my head into Ned's life, undistracted by the quotidian duties of my own life, and, as ever, I could not have got remotely close to achieving that without her total support.

In Ned Kelly, I have been blessed firstly with one of the two most fascinating subjects I have ever worked on, and secondly with the help of so many fine professionals, and enthusiasts, to do his story justice.

I hope you enjoy it.

Peter FitzSimons
Neutral Bay, Sydney
September 2013

PART ONE

EARLY YEARS

Chapter One

BORN A KELLY

Land was life itself . . .
A summation of the view of 1840s Irish peasants
by author Cecil Woodham-Smith

Unlock the Land

Why in this sunny land of gold
Rich soil and wealth containing,
Should we from day to day behold
The unemployed complaining?

What is the cause that honest skill
Finds here no scope to ply it?
While ready hands the earth would till
Why lack they room to try it?

O, rulers wise! 'tis justice cries,
That all may share the soil;
Unlock the lands – there's willing hands
That want but room to toil . . .

This well-known Australian ballad was first published
in the 'Victorian Songster', Melbourne, in 1855,
just after Ned was born

BEVERIDGE, VICTORIA, LATE 1854, A CHILD IS BORN UNTO THEM

Such is life.

Babies born to parents whose own childhood homes are within cooee, who take food on the dinner table as the natural order of things and are raised in dwellings as stable as the era . . . have a good chance of sailing through life on much the same placid sea of content.

In such a life, there will simply be no need to make endless decisions of life and death – both your own and that of others – to take up arms against a sea of troubles and even the law. Such children will be spared the fate of having no choice but to travel on the dark side, all in the hope of finding their way back to the light.

And yet such a life is never to be Ned Kelly's.

For on the hot summer's day that Ned hits the ground in December of 1854 near the small settlement of Beveridge, just 25 miles north of Melbourne, and not far from Donnybrook, there is little in the way of stability to be found in any direction.[1]

It is certainly not to be found in the haphazard construction in which Ned takes his first cry, a shack that looks rather less half-built than already half-destroyed. Consisting of one large room of horizontal timber slabs, encasing a dirt floor, beneath a bark roof, with an open drain running through the middle, it is really a habitation in name only, and rather more a rough shelter . . . a wooden cave.[2]

Oh, certainly, other families far and wide do have grand spreads of up to 12,000 acres of the most fertile fields imaginable, but it has long been the way of the Kellys, and it long will remain, to only live on the edges of such spreads, remaining resentfully in the shadows cast by such shining splendour. After all, Ned's father, John 'Red' Kelly, had been born impoverished at Tipperary in faraway Ireland, and the thing that had first propelled him to these shores as a twenty-one-year-old in 1841 had not been following the siren call of a better life so much as the dull tones of a magistrate's judgment, sounding his punishment for stealing two pigs valued at £6: transportation to Australia for seven years.

The convict barque *Prince Regent* from Ireland had first deposited Red Kelly in Van Diemen's Land to assume the traditional position of most Irish convicts: manacled, whipped and beaten. As a poor Catholic Irishman in a land fundamentally run by the wealthy Protestant English – just as it had been back in old Ireland – it has been Red Kelly's fate to be an outsider from the first, even when granted a ticket of leave in 1845 and then being finally pardoned in 1848. At this point, he had crossed Bass Strait and been able to get his first honest work, splitting and fencing, near the Merri Creek, just north of Melbourne. Despite his harsh background, however, Red was surprisingly gentle, named for the colour of his hair and certainly not his temper, as he was known down at the public houses as 'ever prone to act the part of a peacemaker when he saw others engaged in any altercation calculated to lead to violence'.[3]

Inevitably, Red makes his way to nearby Donnybrook, the village with the most Irish name in Victoria and likely the heaviest concentration of Irish people, and it was in a public house there one night, following a hard day's work, that Red – his elbow as busy as a furious fiddler's as he knocked back drink after drink – happened to meet James Quinn, an Irish free settler with 640 acres of land rented at nearby Wallan Wallan.

The pair chatted amiably over a nobbler as the conversation turned to their mutual favourite subject: the manufacture of illicit whiskey. With the entrepreneurial spark of a man newly freed of his shackles, Red proposed that Quinn should go into partnership with him in the purchase of a 'jigger still'. Though Quinn refused to lend an ear to such a proposition, their acquaintance at least gained Red Kelly admission to the farmer's home. Before Quinn quite realised what was going on, Red was making an entirely different proposition to the Quinn's fourth of eleven children, the slim, black-haired and notably beautiful daughter Ellen, herself born in Ireland's County Antrim.

At eighteen years old, twelve years his junior, Ellen was a feisty young woman who cared little that her parents had looked askance upon her romance with the burly ex-convict, just as she had cared little about their expectations of her regularly attending school, which had left her able to read but not write. She had cared so little for prudence that, after she fell pregnant to Red Kelly in May 1850, they married on 18 November that year at St Francis's Catholic Church, Melbourne – Ellen's large baby bump marginally preceding her down the aisle – before setting up home initially in a small cottage on the Quinns' place at Wallan Wallan.

The couple's first child, Mary Jane, died in her tiny infancy, but a healthy daughter, Annie, emerged from the womb in 1853 while Red was out, over the ranges, trying his luck in the bowels of the Bendigo goldfields as a sole prospector. A month after the infant arrived, her father returned home in time for Christmas, with just enough nuggets in his pocket to impress old James Quinn, who invited the ex-convict to be a partner in his horse dealing venture.

Before long, Red had enough money to buy, for a premium price of £615, 41 acres on the southern slopes of the Big Hill – a place overlooking the small settlement of Beveridge – set in open country bursting with banksia, she-oaks, box trees and wattles, all of it a'flutter with bountiful birdlife. With Beveridge set to thrive, thanks to the surveyed Sydney Road, which bustled with life and commerce, Red was confident that in the future his land would be worth every fleck of gold . . . even if, for the moment, it was not much. But at least it could sustain a few cows for milking, he could raise some horses and make up the difference to pay the bills by selling his skills as a bush carpenter.

And now, the second surviving child is Edward – named after Red's oldest brother, back in Ireland – immediately known as 'Ned', a restless young lad from the first, born in a more than merely restless era.

In fact, Ned is born at the most politically turbulent time in the history of the continent, with the smoke from the battle of the Eureka Stockade – which had occurred just 60 miles away and taken the lives of nigh on thirty men – still not quite dissipated. From the burning issue of voting rights for the men of Victoria to ownership of land for the tens of thousands of diggers who now want to hold some against the claims of squatters who had settled on the prime land twenty years earlier, there is trouble in the air. Ah, but that part of Ned's story – the most significant force in shaping his world – will come.

For now, in his first days of life, the most important thing is to rid him of the original sin he has been born with.

It is near Christmas of 1854. Nestled in the burly arms of an enormous Augustinian priest, Charles O'Hea – himself arrived from Ireland just three years earlier, and whose other parish is Pentridge Gaol, 22 miles to the south – the infant Ned gazes up blankly as the kindly man of God breathes heavily on his face to exorcise whatever evil spirit might be in him. And now the forefinger of the priest's massive right hand is traced across his face to make the sign of the cross, before a little salt is placed in the infant's mouth so he will be 'delivered from the corruption of sin, experience a relish for good works, and be delighted with the food of divine wisdom'.[4]

And now a white veil is put on Ned's head, as the priest intones more Catholic incantations, and, after being purged of his sin, the infant is finally bidden to 'go in peace'.

And yet, just as there will be little stability in his life, so too will there be little peace – starting with the succession of squalling babies that seem always to be in the arms of his beloved mother, Ellen.

True, Red and Ellen Kelly find it extremely difficult to feed so many hungry mouths, but, whatever else, the tightly bound family have each other to depend on. The family poverty is exacerbated by the fact that, despite the cold wind blowing through the hut – just as it sometimes does in their empty bellies – Red insists on sending some of what little money he has back to his brothers and sisters in Ireland, who are stricken even worse. For Ireland is important. And *family* is important. Many a night around the sparse dinner table and in front of the fire, Red tells his children tales of the old country, the greenness of its fields, the splendour of its lakes and, yes, the bastardry of its English masters, who have taken all the best land for themselves and use their troops to keep the people down.

Of the last part, it does not take the Kelly kids an enormous leap of imagination to envision just the way it had been in the Emerald Isle, for, to their eyes, things are not so different here in this new land in which they are growing. Again, it is the British who control the government, just as most of the squatters – the first pastoralists to claim ownership of land in the new colony without reference to anyone else – who control the leases of the enormous runs of the most bountiful land are British.

True, many of the troopers are Irish, but that, too, is reflective of old Ireland, where, if well paid, my children, some of the lowest of the low will agree to take up arms against their own. And did I tell you about the way the British treated us convicts at Van Diemen's Land?

Yes, father, many times, but tell us again.

Ned takes hatred of the English with his mother's milk and his father's every rant. Such rants become all the more pointed as the 41-acre farm proves not sufficiently large to pay its way. Worse still, despite Red's hopes, progress soon passes Beveridge by as the travellers and merchants who were to secure its prosperity divert to the east and west to better built roads that avoid the dray-sized potholes that this town has become infamous for. Within fifteen months of buying the property, the lingering stench of stagnation forces Red to take out a £200 mortgage on his farm, and in 1857 it is sold for a £350 loss. The family move into a tiny shack on a quarter-acre block in town, with the one advantage, for Red, that it is much closer to either or both of Beveridge's pubs; he is not particular.

For, used up by his years as a convict, by endless labour, by the struggle to make ends meet, it sometimes seems that the only thing that can make him feel like his old self is drinking too much alcohol, which makes him weaken even further.

One thing that does not diminish is his capacity to father children, at least in the act of conception, and just a month after moving into their new shack in town Ellen gives birth to another baby girl, Margaret, to be known as Maggie.

The Kelly family keeps growing around Ned, by loins, sea and marriage. For some of the money that Red has been sending home has been put to the use of buying sea passages, and not long after Maggie is born the good ship *Maldon* brings three of Red's brothers and two of his sisters from Ireland, occasioning a tearful reunion for those newly arrived with the brother they have not seen for fifteen years. And, yes, even though Red is a near-bankrupt alcoholic ex-convict, he is still richer and more fortunate than they are.

As to Ellen's side of the family, two of her sisters, Jane and Kate, had married two brothers, Tom and Jack Lloyd, who at first settle not far away. Red and Ellen Kelly's children and the Lloyd children, thus, will all grow up as a mob together, with none closer to Ned and Maggie Kelly, particularly, as Kate and Jack Lloyd's son, Tom, born in the same year as Maggie.

As young Ned starts to strengthen to be a roaring six-year-old, the young'uns keep bursting from his mother's loins – with Jim, Dan and Kate placing ever more strain on the family budget.

All of the children are raised tough, given chores to do from when they can just walk, and help their father with everything from milking and chopping down trees to building fences and breaking in horses, not to mention helping their mother in making butter and bread, collecting firewood and feeding the animals.

Beyond that, they are encouraged to explore the areas of heavy bush that abound all around, and, as far as they know, the natural condition of shins is to be bruised, just as knees are meant to be scraped, and horses are to be ridden fast and hard. If you fall off, you simply climb back on and go again. It is not that Ned can ride before he can run, but it is close, and he proves so good at riding that it soon seems it is less that he rides a horse than the horse is an extension of him. Sometimes, he will take the horse right to the top of Big Hill and survey the mountains on all sides, bar the south, where the flat plain leads all the way to Melbourne and the sea beyond. And then it is time to gallop back down, always just as fast as he dares, 'neck or nothing', usually getting a little faster each time – and always faster than his brothers or sisters, who sometimes dare race him.

In such an environment, the Kelly kids are like the bounding kangaroo, the stoical wombat and the soaring gum tree. That is, they grow as native sons and daughters of the Australian soil: strong – and none stronger than Ned, who is notable from the first for his power, agility and sheer indomitability. Which is as well, for Ned gets tougher in sync with his family's circumstances, as Red's drinking increases and his ability to provide for his family fades away.

BIG HILL AND AVENEL, VICTORIA, EARLY 1860S, LAW AND LAWLESSNESS

The worse the Kelly family fortunes, the closer to the margins they are propelled, as they continue to move from hut to shack, from shack to back, from wooden to dirt floors, from brick and plaster to rooms created by hessian drapes, from a reasonable supply of food to sometimes having to live on fresh air and love, a hand-to-hungry-mouth existence if ever there was one . . . and, through it all, for the Kellys and their kin, the traps (police) are never far away.

Ned had been only one year old when Ellen's brother Jimmy had been charged with Possession of Stolen Cattle, and no more than five years old when Uncle Jimmy faced two charges of Assault and one charge of Horse Stealing. Uncle Jimmy had been convicted on one of the Assault charges, while Jimmy's older brother Jack only just escaped gaol in the same year on a charge of Stealing Cattle, and then the next year Robbery Under Arms. Ellen's brother-in-law Jack Lloyd has a remarkably similar arrest record, as in Donnybrook, in the first three years of the 1860s, he faces charges for Assault, Drunk and Disorderly and Larceny, even while Red's own younger brother, James, faces two charges of Stealing Cattle, but is mercifully discharged both times. And so the criminal reputation of the family grows.

In 1863, it is eight-year-old Ned who makes his way into Kilmore to face the law for the first time. Fortunately, on this occasion, he is only there trying to provide, in the company of his mother, an alibi for Uncle James, who this time is charged with stealing thirteen head of cattle. The judge does not believe the eight-year-old, nor his mother, and Uncle James is sent to gaol for three years' hard labour. Can nothing rescue the young Kellys from this despairing cycle of poverty and lawlessness into which their mob is clearly descending?

An education would clearly be a fine start . . .

As it happens, only eight weeks after Uncle James goes to gaol, young Ned goes to school for the first time when, up on Big Hill, the large bluestone building in the classic Gothic style that is the Beveridge Catholic Church and School opens its doors to students for the first time. Each morning, nine-year-old Annie, six-year-old Maggie and Ned head off to receive their lessons, following the syllabus of the Irish National School, as the gloriously dappled light of the stained-glass windows shines upon them. Bit by bit, they do indeed learn at least the rudiments of Reading, 'Riting and 'Rithmetic, courtesy of the kindly couple who are their teachers, Thomas and Sarah Wall.

Ned does not go quite as well in lessons as he goes in schoolyard games, where he excels – particularly hop, skip and jump – but he performs well enough. There seems to be a certain native, if uncultured, intelligence about him, and he is no trouble to teach. In many ways, he is just another rough young lad from a poor rough family, doing his rough best to work out what all these curious squiggles on these bits of paper actually mean.

Whatever Ned's understanding of it all, his time in this particular school lasts no longer than to the end of the year. In the summer of 1863–64, Red and Ellen Kelly decide to move the family 50 miles north to a place just outside the tiny township of Avenel, which lies on the busy Sydney Road, which they now join. Among 'bullock wagons, horse wagons, carts, coaches, jinkers, Chinese at the trot, as well as drovers with their mobs',[5] the sprawling family pushes north, eventually coming to rest in a dry, dusty, sun-bleached, quaint and busy township set on the banks of the Hughes Creek in the broad plains that stretch down from the Great Dividing Range.

Here, Red has been able to rent a 40-acre farm of unfenced grassland on the western edge of the settlement, for the price of just £14 a year, on which he intends to establish a small dairy herd. It does not take long before the Kelly patriarch – closely watched by young Ned, who is eager to do whatever he can to help – has thrown up a slab homestead with a bark roof and furnished it with whatever comes to hand, in much the same spirit as Ellen and her older daughters put whatever they can on the table for dinner.

At least at Avenel, things settle down for long enough that, at the local Common School, the Kelly kids, among forty others – at a cost of one shilling per pupil per week, to be paid promptly every Monday morning – become more than mere acquaintances of the three 'R's, and Ned manages to progress patchily. When School Inspector G. Wilson Brown arrives at the school in March 1865 to test the abilities of the pupils, fourth-class student *Edward Kelly*, who is ten years, three months, is recorded as achieving the pass level in all of Reading, 'Riting and 'Rithmetic. He seems a kid like any other – or at least there is nothing so noteworthy about him that it makes it into the inspector's notebook.

As to the fourth 'R', religion has never been in short supply in the children's lives – for Ellen, particularly, is a strong believer, insisting her offspring know the sacraments – and it is at Avenel that Father Charles O'Hea is particularly significant in their lives. A busy man, he combines his duties at this parish with being the visiting priest at now both Pentridge and Melbourne Gaols, and he gets on particularly well with Ellen Kelly, who encourages him to visit her family as often as he can.

As to Red Kelly, he worries the kindly Father O'Hea, and the priest is shocked by just how desiccated the ex-convict has become since he had first come across him around Beveridge a decade before. Young Ned, on the other hand, pleases the good father greatly. There is just something about this young fellow that he fondly warms to, and he always has an eye out for him and does his best to give strong religious instruction.

For all that, it is likely reading that remains Ned's favourite of the four 'R's, most particularly because at the time he is learning to do it and there are so many fascinating things to read about. Though, of course, it is far from certain that young Ned personally takes it up, his local paper, the *Kilmore Free Press*, carries a fascinating article that everyone is talking about at this time, with the headline 'Shooting of Hall the Bushranger':

> **A telegram from Forbes states that the body of [Ben] Hall, the bushranger, has been brought there by police, who got on his track on Friday, and during the night found his horse hobbled. Knowing that Hall must be close by, the police separated, but encircled the horse. Towards morning Hall came in view, looking for his horse, and passed close to where Inspector Davidson was concealed. He stepped out and called to Hall to stand. Hall made towards his horse, when Davidson fired. The bushranger was apparently uninjured, and Sergeant Condell fired. At the same time five troopers emerged from their hiding place, directly in front of Hall, and fired a volley. Hall fell, riddled with bullets. The corpse shows thirty bullet holes. On searching him, the police found three loaded revolvers, £70 in money, and the miniature of a female. No doubt exists of the person being Hall.**[6]

For the most part around Ned, among the common people, there is mourning at the news of the death of 'Brave Ben Hall', as he is known. Hall had only ever taken up bushranging in the first place after his wife had run away with a former policeman and he had been twice wrongfully arrested. As reported in Ned's local paper, Hall was even reputed to have said, 'That settles it . . . There's no getting out of this. May as well have the game as the blame.'[7]

He had gone on to commit over 600 robberies, without killing anyone, and had confirmed himself as a popular folk hero by doing such things as 'bailing up the entire town of Canowindra, shepherding everybody into Robinson's Hotel and instructing them to eat or drink all they wished – at the Gang's expense'.[8] That 'party' had gone on for three days.

For Ben Hall, you see, had been no ordinary bushranger but, somehow, a gentleman bushranger, as – after a persistent black-tracker had brought police to his camp, who then shot him to pieces – an obituary in the *Kilmore Free Press* movingly points out: 'Ben Hall was held in high esteem by the settlers throughout the district, not only for his generous, openhearted qualities, always showing a disposition to help his neighbours, but for the enterprise and energy he displayed in conducting his business affairs . . .'[9]

As to his body being riddled with bullets, another article in the *Kilmore Free Press*, on 25 May, points out that it was only possible because the New South Wales Government had passed a *Felons Apprehension Act*, in April, which introduced the idea of outlawry into that colony's legal system. The legislature had wanted to introduce such an Act so that a home owner, seeing a bushranger such as Ben Hall, could take aim, shoot and kill without first calling upon the outlaw to surrender or waiting for him to commit an offence, to ensure that any person who killed a bushranger was not a 'felon in law – patriot in fact – a murderer by statute, but a deliverer in morals'.[10]

In terms of local legend, even though no gentleman, there is only one man who can rival Ben Hall, and that is, of course, the bushranger who has inspired the *Felons Apprehension Act* in the first place: 'Mad Dan' Morgan.

For Mad Dan is nothing less than 'the most daring, reckless and unscrupulous of the Australian bandits',[11] whose own story has also just come to a climax at this formative time in Ned's life. Like Ben Hall, Morgan doesn't simply hold up banks and coaches, he holds up whole stations, and he loves nothing better than making the fat squatters serve their workers for a nice change, with the best food and drink that is available. Did you know that, up Burrumbuttock way – no, really, that is what it is called! – Mad Dan made the squatter Thomas Gibson, at gunpoint, write out £400 worth of cheques for his employees? And they were cashed, too! At other times, he would take tea with his captives and banter with them, and even make the mistress of the house play piano for him . . .

As to more standard fare, in early 1865, having crossed the Murray into Victoria, Morgan had been wont to position himself on a massive jutting rock of the Warby Ranges overlooking the small settlement of Glenrowan in Victoria's rugged North-East – a rock ever after known as Morgans Lookout – and, after determining just which gold-bearing stagecoaches were heading his way, and how well they were protected, he would make his moves from there.

Oh, but he was vicious, though.

On one occasion, it is said, after the man he had shot was writhing before him in agony, he leaned over him and said, 'Poor fellow – I did not mean to shoot you. I'll go and get a doctor.' An instant later, however, he turned back and, with a malicious grin, said, 'You don't want a doctor. I'll soon put an end to your troubles.'[12] And then he brought down the muzzle of his rifle to the man's chest and pulled the trigger, killing him.

On the evening of 8 April 1865, the word got out via an escaped nurse that Morgan had bailed up the Macpherson homestead at Peechelba Station, situated near the junction of the Ovens and Murray Rivers, about 20 miles from Wangaratta. There were twenty of them under his guns, she said, in just the one room at the front of the house. In response, the station's co-owner, George Rutherford, who lived just 400 yards away, rounded up five of his men and gave them arms – and they were soon joined by a second group of police and other armed civilians who had been warned by an escaped worker, 'making in all about eight and twenty men'.[13] Quietly, all of them secreted themselves in positions of cover and, with their rifles trained on the house, they waited through the night. The next day, when Mad Dan emerged with the owner Macpherson and three others to get his horse from the paddock, one of the workers, John Quinlan, simply jumped from behind a tree and shot Morgan in the back. Mad Dan dropped instantly, but he gathered strength sufficient to say, 'You might have given a fellow a chance and not acted as cowards.'[14] Five hours later, he died – meaning, of course, there was no need for the police to arrest him and go through the whole tedious process of a trial.

Though the *Felons Apprehension Act* was yet to take effect, Mad Dan was caught red-handed in the commission of a crime, with his pistol pointed at the persons he was driving before him. This meant Quinlan was justified under law in shooting and killing the bushranger. But, warned the proponents of the *Felons Apprehension Act*, what if Mad Dan hadn't been committing a crime when Quinlan saw him? Would Quinlan, a model moral citizen, be charged with murder? The editor of *The Sydney Morning Herald*, for one, thought that the facts surrounding Morgan's death clearly showed why the *Felons Apprehension Act* was a *must* in the colony. It was a case in point for why we should never let our liberal hearts bleed too much . . . 'In our tenderness for the liberty of the subject, we are endangering the life of the subject!'[15] And so, on 12 April, the government of New South Wales moved to eradicate the bushrangers once and for all, and the draconian Act was passed.

And yet the horror detail that most gripped the imagination of schoolboys like young Ned is what happened to Mad Dan Morgan after he died. As reported in the *Kilmore Free Press*, in words the schoolboys pored over:

> And when all was over, and the remains were conveyed to the Wangaratta lock-up, it is with a thrill of horror that I revert to the subsequent proceedings, by which the apartment allotted to the corpse was converted into a human shambles – a Cawnpore on a small scale. Decapitation, hacking, wrenching, cutting, skinning, fleshing and boxing up, seem to have been indulged in as a pastime or recreation; and those by whom the body should have been held as sacred, and, while in their possession, jealously guarded against any desecration, calmly looked on, or became principals in

> atrocities which make humanity shudder. The head was cut off . . . and according to the testimony of several, tossed about the room like a football . . . they pawed, turned over, twisted, and dragged the head about as fancy dictated, and no particular spot was apportioned as its resting place . . .

Oh, there was more, much more. For afterward, the Police Superintendent in charge persuaded the doctor to cut the beard off the dead man's jaw complete with the underlying skin – an act accomplished with a penknife – after which it was stretched out to dry in the sun. 'The superintendent had every intention of somehow converting the mass into a tobacco pouch'[16] – though there is another rumour that he actually wishes to do this with Mad Dan's scrotum.

The morning after the public were done playing with Mad Dan's remains, 'the actual head, swathed in thickness of hessian doused in brine, was sent off to Melbourne by coach'.[17]

Morgan's head had even been paraded through the streets of Avenel, on its way to Melbourne. Oh, the horror, the *horror*, young Ned, can you imagine?

27 MAY 1865, KILL NOT THE FATTED CALF

Father O'Hea has been right to worry about Red Kelly. Though the father of these now six children does manage to find some fencing work and timber felling to help make ends meet, and the few cows he has do allow him to sell a little milk, it is not enough. And the additional money made by setting up a still and selling a little sly grog to passers-by – which is to say the little that Red does not drink himself – amounts to a mere pittance.

So what does Red do, exactly, to feed his family?

The best he can.

On this particular day at the Kelly house, it is not just jolly swagmen whom jolly jumbucks need be wary of when wandering near billabongs. For, while the saying goes that it is as well to be hanged for a sheep as for a lamb, it truly is something else again when it comes to poddy calves . . .

The difference is that, whereas sheep by their very nature are as numerous as they are generally indistinguishable from each other – and the law is less likely to pursue you because of it – the same cannot necessarily be said for calves.

Red is just contemplating the fact that he will very shortly have another hungry mouth to feed, with his wife due in three months, when – could the good Lord be smiling on him at last? – a poddy calf from Phillip Morgan's run next door wanders across the drought-stricken creek that normally would have acted as a watery fence.

The answer to his family's hunger is there before his eyes.

Let the devil take the hindmost, for Red Kelly is soon taking the freshly slain calf's hindquarters and hanging them from a handy beam as the blood drips from the carcass. Red shows some caution for all that, to cover up what he has done. Though the risk is minimal that he will be caught – no one, with the possible exception of his kin, has seen him – he still makes the effort, after skinning the beast, to cut the identifying brand from its hide, which he then hides in the bedroom. As to the meat, one hindquarter remains strung up, the rest goes into a brine cask, as it could have come from anywhere, and Red then burns the bones in a big fire.

Surely, proof of his guilt is going up in smoke before his eyes?

Perhaps not. For, just two days later, who should arrive over the hill but an outraged Phillip Morgan himself – he has seen the hindquarters hanging from the Kelly front porch and just *knows* it is his missing calf – and who is that accompanying him? None other than the local policeman, Constable John Doxey, bearing a search warrant.

For, as would later prove to be something of a Kelly trait, Red's timing is a little off. As it happens, there has been so much stealing of cattle of late – the blame for which in the district, frequently, and sometimes unfairly, falls squarely on the shoulders of one of the Kelly/Quinn clan members – that three years earlier the Victorian Government had introduced legislation requiring all those wishing to slaughter a beast to do two things. The first is to notify the local police of their intent, and the second is to keep the brand on the hide, so they can prove the beast they have slaughtered is one that they *legally* – look it up – own. Is there any record of police applying this law to the rich squatters? Of course not. For the law is not aimed at them. It is framed specifically to apply to men like Red Kelly, and so it does now.

Did Red ask the police station for permission to slaughter a beast? As Constable Doxey is from that police station, he knows Red did not.

As to the remains of that beast, Constable Doxey has no trouble finding what is left of the calf. Not for nothing is the saying at the time 'Look for the strayed beast in the Round Swamp',[18] as in the brine cask, and, sure enough, there it is.

And where is this meat from, *Mr* Kelly?

Ah, well, you see, Constable, and Mr Morgan, it comes from an unbranded stray that has wandered onto my farm a few days earlier.

Really? And where would the unbranded hide be?

Never mind; Doxey quickly finds it.

Strange that the hide is missing the part where the brand is usually found?

Oh, that.

Red explains that he just happens to have used it to make a 'greenhide whip', made from the untanned hide of the animal.

Where is the head then?

The pigs must have dragged it away.

The bones?

. . .

Where are the bones?

Red has no satisfactory reply.

But when Constable Doxey quickly finds the remains of the bones in yonder ashes, he is satisfied – it is Red who has stolen and slain the missing calf. The only people who burn bones are those who wish to destroy evidence.

Red is arrested and, before the eyes of his horrified – perhaps terrified – family, the father of the family is led away in handcuffs to the Avenel lock-up, a rough structure of logs just behind the police station, to spend that night and subsequent nights.

It all means that, on the following Monday morning, Red Kelly finds himself in a position familiar from his former life: in the dock.

On the charge of stealing the calf, Red is found – oddly, and likely to his own amazement, unaccustomed as he is – innocent. On the charge of 'having illegally in his possession one cow hyde',[19] however, he is found guilty. No matter that this is the first time Red has been found to have broken the law in twenty-five years, since having stolen the pigs in Tipperary, and no matter that this time, just like that time, he was only trying to feed his family. No matter that, by putting him in gaol, it would be depriving a family with six kids under thirteen years of its sole bread-winner, leaving his pregnant wife all but without resources to continue to feed her family. The law takes a very dim view regardless. Red Kelly must either pay a fine of £25 or serve a sentence of six months' hard labour.

What to do? Get blood out of a stone or raise £25 to keep Red out of gaol? Well, for some it might be an option, but given Red's lack of money it is no option at all. The fine may as well be £1000 for all the chance he and Ellen have of raising it. Young Ned, all of ten years old, watches with growing outrage as his father is led away in manacles to do the better part of his time in Avenel lock-up.

Inevitably, in the absence of the man of the house, it is the oldest Kelly boy who will have to step into the breech to become that man, despite his tender years.

The adult responsibilities that go with Ned's new position are physical as much as anything. For the breezy Kelly shack is nothing if not cold, even at the best of times. The only way to keep the chill at bay is by burning copious amounts of wood, which Ned is constantly chopping, his swinging axe sending ever greater chunks of ironbark logs flying as strength flows into his arms even before the onset of puberty. His sinewy body – all muscle and gristle, just as his character is developing hustle and bristle – continues to harden. Similarly, while the small tank provides some water when there has been recent rain, most of the water must be carried in buckets up the steep hill from the creek, and it is Ned who does the bulk of it, carrying a full pail in either hand, his shoulders straining and his legs slowly pumping like a man riding a bicycle up a slope, as he makes trip after trip for his grateful mother. And even then he is just warming up, as, with his sister Annie, Ned must also feed the pigs and chooks, round up the cows and, with freezing fingers at sunup, milk them before taking the produce to town to sell, help to look after the younger kids and comfort his mother in her bitterness at the police, who have done all this to the family 'for nothing'.[20] With such a workload, it is not long after Ned learns such strange facts as there being snow on the mountains in Peru . . . that he stops going to school.

In terms of relaxing, Ned is the sort of lad who would sooner a fight than a feed – most particularly with any kid brave enough to say, 'Yah, Kelly, your Dad's a lag!'[21] – and he soon earns a reputation as a bad'un to cross in fisticuffs.

And then there is not just the horse-riding but also – to use the technical term the police give it – Horse Stealing. Ned and his mates don't really regard it like that themselves, and, indeed, many of the poor families in the area agree. It is really more just 'borrowing' the horses for a few days to have fun with them, before either hiding them in the bush until a reward is offered or cutting them loose in the knowledge that they will eventually be found and given back to the squatters.

For all the troubling nature of the times, however, it is not as if nothing good ever happens to Ned – and all the more so after a burst of wet weather makes the grass grow once more. On one particular day in 1865, just as winter is turning to spring, Ned is passing the schoolhouse he used to attend before he had to drop out and work for a living, when he happens to look up to see a seven-year-old lad, Dick Shelton, son of the local publican up at the Royal Mail Hotel, ignoring the stone bridge just up the way to cross the swollen Hughes Creek. Instead, he is going for the short cut, courtesy of a massive red gum that had fallen over a few months earlier. For the trunk of the tree has been turned into a makeshift bridge, as the branches on the upside have been chopped off, in the same manner that its rounder surface away from the water has been roughly chipped away to make a flat surface on which to get a surer footing.

Young Dick is certainly confident enough as he makes his way across, untroubled by the raging waters just below. But now what is this? On this day, Dick is wearing a new straw hat, which suddenly blows off in the fresh breeze, to catch in some of the horizontal branches. As Ned watches closely, the young lad edges out onto a branch, his right hand straining towards his hat, when there is suddenly a crack and a cry and Dick is in the swirling water!

Ned moves instinctively, and without fear, no matter that he is not a particularly strong swimmer. In an instant, he has taken a running leap and is in the water. There, in front of him, he sees the bobbing head. Several more thrashing thrusts with his arms and kicks with his legs and he is close enough to grab the young child by the collar. He pushes him upwards, to get the flailing child's head into the air.

It is, of course, far more difficult for Ned to get out of the water than it was to get into it, particularly now that he has one arm grasping this thrashing child in his iron grip. But, by simply going with the flow and steering towards one bank, in under a minute Ned has the gasping, spluttering seven-year-old lying on the bank beside him as they both wildly gasp for air, sucking in big lungfuls like half-drowned puppies.

As soon as they are able, Ned takes the lad in hand – even though they are both nominally kids, they are a world apart in maturity – and, with a protective arm around him, leads him back to his family at the hotel, the water dripping from their clothes and squelching out of their boots as they go.

Of course, when they arrive, and the story quickly comes out, Dick is instantly embraced by his anxious parents and covered in hugs and kisses, while Ned receives furious handshakes and pats on the back of enormous appreciation. He is a hero.

In fact, young Kelly is already well known to the Shelton family. Some time before, when one of the publican's horses had gone missing and he had offered a reward, he had been amazed at how quickly young Ned of the Kelly family down the way had turned up with it. 'I found it up in the bush,' the youngster had told them.[22] Even more amazing? The horse came back in better shape, and better groomed, than when it had gone missing. Rather than having roughed it, living wild in the bush, it looked very much as though the horse had been in the care of a horse-lover, which young Kelly was known to be. And yet, of course, the main thing was that it had been returned, and Esau Shelton had happily handed over the small cash reward.

And now this same lad has handed him his beloved child, whom he has rescued from a swollen creek? Well, of course, that too must be worthy of reward, even if money would be inappropriate. So it is that, just a couple of days later, the proud as punch Ned is presented with a glittering green silk sash with a golden fringe at each end – all of seven feet long by five inches wide – to drape around his torso from his right shoulder to his left hip – in reward for the courage he has displayed.

In his whole life to this point, it is the only recognition that Ned has received beyond his own family for something positive, and he is inordinately, perhaps even pathetically, proud of it. Have you seen my sash? I got it for saving the Shelton child, up by the schoolhouse, when he tumbled into the water and I dived in to save him. They gave this sash to me. Would you like to touch it?

For a short time, Ned feels like an insider, in the light, bathing in the admiration of polite society, not an outsider perpetually living his life in the shadows, to be looked upon with suspicion or rage. He belongs.

LATE 1865, AVENEL, THE MAN OF THE HOUSE

Ned's happiness might be complete if, when his father emerges from gaol with a remission of two months in October 1865, he is in good health, ready to take over the reins again, and maybe even allow Ned to go back to the Avenel School.

But, alas, it is not to be.

For even though Red is only forty-five years old, prison life has sapped the vitality from him, and it seems his only idea of how to restore it is with ever more alcohol. Day after day, night after night, all he can think is drink, and so he does – so much so that it is not long before the long arm of Constable Doxey again descends upon him, as he is arrested in early December 1865 for being Drunk and Disorderly. He is ultimately fined five shillings.

Does this stop him drinking?

It does not. Over the next twelve months, as Ned gets stronger – hauling, chopping, carrying, riding, rustling – Red gets weaker. When Ellen Kelly needs something done, it is to Ned she inevitably turns, the one who always rises to the occasion, and the bond between mother and son becomes ever tighter as Red's descent becomes ever more tragic and pathetic. He develops a terrible case of dropsy, with his heart progressively weakening. So little can he work that all of the rest of the Kelly kids drop out of school too, as even the nominal school fees are now beyond the family.

After a wretched twelve months of slow deterioration, by Christmas of 1866 all of Red's vitality has gone, as has even his will to live. For two days, the family holds a vigil around the perishing patriarch of the family as he is clearly not long for this world. Even when lucid, he does not bemoan his fate but faces it stoically.

As Red lets out his final breath, his withered, desiccated form on the bed is suddenly as still as . . . death. His one-time young bride, Ellen, now becomes a lonely widow, with no fewer than seven offspring – Annie, Ned, Maggie, Jim, Dan, Kate and the one-year-old Grace – to look after.

Ned lifts his father's body to place it in a hasty coffin that has been knocked together with spare bits of scrap wood, and Red goes beneath the sod at the hot, windy Avenel Cemetery, without even a requiem mass. Shortly afterwards, it is young Ned himself who forlornly treks to William Campion's nearby combined store/post office/registry to formally record his father's death, signing his own name as 'Edward Kelly, Son'.[23]

And yet, while Red is at last at peace, the same cannot be said for his thirty-three-year-old widow, Ellen, who, in February 1867, is brought before the courts for fighting with Red's sister, Anne Ryan. Anne had moved in with the family, and there were always tensions between the women – tensions so taut that they sometimes escalated into brawls reminiscent of two cats in a sack. On this occasion, the pair were suing each other for Assault. Ellen must have had the upper hand in a biff, as the court's judgment is that she must pay two pounds damages and five shillings costs.

A few months later, however, things are at least patched up enough between them that this time they are able to unite to take on Anne's vicious landlord, the mad pig farmer Thomas Ford, who hates the two women almost as much as he hates his own wife. Just two months earlier, he had been convicted and fined for the offence of burning her clothes and threatening to kill her,[24] and, after now being involved in a fracas with the Kelly women, is taking them to the Court of Petty Sessions for damaging his property. Ellen is separately charged with Abusive and Threatening Language. Oh, really? Well, Ellen, never one to hold back, charges Ford with Assault. In the wash-up, while both sisters-in-law are found not guilty on the charge of stealing property, Ellen is found guilty for Using Abusive Language, and Ford is found guilty for Assault. And yet, while Ford is given a heftier fine of five pounds, which he immediately pays, Ellen's fine of forty shillings is still forty shillings more than she has . . .

As meagre a provider as Red has been, without him the family is even more poverty-stricken than before, and the general rule in these parts applies: the poorer you get, the further north you must go. It is no matter that, as unpopular as Ellen had been with the police, she is popular with the community and would be remembered by the Avenel folk as 'a great horsewoman, [who] used to ride out to help anyone in trouble or needing help', just as her children are thought 'well behaved' and Ned, particularly, 'a very brave lad'.[25]

As the chill of the 1867 winter starts to take hold, Avenel slowly falls behind the Kelly family as, with all their worldly belongings in the back of Red's dray, and Ned holding the reins just as his father had done, they head further into North-Eastern Victoria, up the Old Sydney Road, which is in fact little more than a rough wagon track. After meandering through the tiny villages of Euroa and Violet Town, they come to the more substantial town of Benalla, before veering right and starting to climb the range that lies between them and their destination. From the top, they see all but trackless green hills billowing in every direction.

Their destination is the tiny settlement of Greta, which lies on the plains below, where Ellen's sisters Kate and Jane have been long established – sisters who, just like Ellen, are now living without their husbands, though they are not widowed. Just the year before, both Kate's husband, Jack Lloyd, and Jane's husband, Tom Lloyd, had been convicted of cattle stealing and sent to Beechworth Prison – where Ellen's brother Jimmy is already in residence – for an extraordinary five years. Cattle stealing has become more risky, since rich squatters have started offering substantial rewards to arrest the thieves. As one writer would comment, 'Was a bullock, which might be valued at £5, worth five years' penal servitude?'[26]

In Greta, even in this joyous reunion, the rage of the three sisters at what has befallen their husbands and families at the hands of the police is a living, breathing thing. It snarls, it spits, and a large measure of the sisters' fury is inevitably absorbed by the oldest of the male cousins, young Ned, now in his thirteenth year. And the family is far from alone in its feelings. For, all around them in Greta, and indeed through most of North-Eastern Victoria, the second stage of a land war is going on.

A small parenthesis here. The first stage of that war was fought all over Australia by the whites against the Aboriginal people, who had lived on the land for thousands of years before European occupation commenced in 1788. Claiming the land as terra nullius, the Europeans began to set out the foundations of land law, devastating the existing cultures, traditions and unwritten legal codes of the Aboriginal inhabitants.

Ned's first experience with native people was at Avenel, which was the tribal territory of hundreds of people of the Kulin Nation. For these Aboriginal people, the land was the sacred home of their gods. They were people who 'could read all the signs of the bush the way we read a newspaper', who could 'cut out a bark canoe from a tree, with a stone axe, in twenty minutes'.[27] Their land started to be sold by the Colonial Government in 1854. While the remnants of those people were still there when the Kelly family arrived, and Ned had even learned some tracking skills from some of the men – he was awestruck by their abilities – there was no doubt they had very quickly lost their land, and their way of life, at the brutal hands of the whites.

The second stage of this land war is between white men themselves, the squatters and 'selectors', and it will rage for decades. Long before, under a leasing system established in 1836, the squatters had settled and claimed most of Victoria's prime land for grazing and raising crops, paying the Colonial Government a pittance for the privilege. The government did, however, reserve the right to reclaim the land when it wanted to do so. Yet, after all, together with the Governor, the 'squattocracy' practically *was* the government, as the laws were framed such that only white men of vast wealth had the right to vote, just as it was only white men of vast wealth who were eligible to sit as members of the Legislative Council.

In the aftermath of the Eureka Stockade, however, the political ground in Victoria shifted, as the mostly English elites were obliged to loosen their stranglehold on political power and land. One of the earliest victories for the radical agitators was a preliminary move towards discarding the shackles of Mother England, with the achievement of responsible self-government in November 1855. From this time, the central role of a British imposed 'Colonial Secretary' passed over to a Victorian elected 'Chief Secretary', the Minister who acted exclusively as the head of the government.

Another outcome of the social convulsions that surrounded Eureka was that the nascent Victorian Government had been forced to recognise that even poor men had rights, including the right to vote, and there was great agitation to 'Unlock the Lands' from the squatters who controlled almost all of it. In this atmosphere, a new Land Act was instituted in 1860, recognising that all men had the right to 'select' small parcels of land from areas surveyed by the government (even including some of the squatters' runs). If successful in his application for such an allotment, the selector was bound to certain conditions, such as paying rent and improving the land through cultivation, fencing and building.

Selection was a bold new experiment in the colony, as it meant that, if all went well, for the first time the land could pass from Crown ownership to private hands. With failure to pay or improve, however, the selector's land reverted to the pastoral lease from which it had come, which usually meant back to the squatters, with crops and stock impounded by the government.

Both the impetus and the outcome of these slowly evolving laws saw a constant battle between the squatters and the selectors, with the 800 Victorian squatters controlling forty million acres of prime land bitterly resenting their monopoly on that land being challenged and using their considerable power to band together and thwart the selectors at every turn. They openly harass the poor selectors, breaking down their fences to allow their own cattle to graze on the selectors' land, do all in their power to restrict their water rights and usually are able to manipulate a compliant police force and judiciary to see things their way when it comes to securing land and legal action.

This basic conflict between the fundamentally English Establishment and the Irish upstarts seeking to get a toehold in this new land, and *on* this new land, is one of the core tensions of young Ned's world. While the English Establishment has just about everything going for it, the Irish selectors have no leadership to speak of, no collective action and not a whole lot more than the support of each other.

And that is certainly not enough to get the best land, which the squatters go to great, and often illegal, lengths to keep for themselves, especially if it is part of their own run. It means the only land the selectors usually end up with is either poor and dry or dreadfully hilly and wooded, and for many of them it proves impossible to ever gain title to that land. Most of the Irish don't even have much background in farming and, as one local newspaper would sagely note, 'The only thing the selectors seem to have, is a splendid supply of firewood, hard work, and hard times . . .'[28]

Many are the selectors who are forced to stand by and watch as their crops and stock are impounded by the authorities, for failing to pay their bills.

Far from unlocking the lands for the great unwashed, the Land Acts have simply seeded new struggles and new forms of control by the rich squatters. And the questions keep coming: 'Was it right that private individuals – the squatters – should publicly advertise, and pay cash rewards to police to obtain convictions of cattle-stealers? Such rewards encouraged perjured evidence. Should the police be allowed to accept gratuities from one section of the community, to protect its special interests?'[29]

Admittedly, one way the selectors and their kin strike back is to simply take whatever horses and cows from the squatters that come their way, just like the horse 'borrowing' that the Kelly and Lloyd kids have got up to from time to time. As a matter of fact, only a week after the Kellys had left Avenel, one of their old neighbours reported his suspicion that the twelve-year-old Ned Kelly had stolen his horse, and a notice appeared in the *Police Gazette*, describing who is being looked for:

> Edward Kelly, a Victorian native, aged 14 or 15, 5 feet 4 or 5 inches high, stout build, brown hair, light grey eyes, smooth face; wore black jumper, moleskin trousers, cloth cap and bluchers.[30]

For their first year at Greta, the Kellys lodge with the Lloyd tribe at a kind of shanty house, a derelict fourteen-room hotel, with the three sisters and seventeen cousins all mucking in together and getting on royally. No one more so than Ned and his young cousin Tom Lloyd, who are happy to be living near each other once more. Even beyond Ellen's two sisters, the whole area around Greta is awash with Kellys, Quinns and Lloyds, while the sisters' parents, James and Mary Quinn, live a day's ride away up in the lofty wilderness near the head of the King River.

Yes, there is a big problem one night when Red's brother James, known as 'Tipperary Jim', whom Ned had defended in court as an eight-year-old, turns up, drunken and keen on taking the place of his brother in Ellen's bed. Disgusted by the offer and never one to be imposed upon, especially by a pathetically drunken sod who is not half the man his brother was, she breaks a gin bottle over his head for his trouble, and he burns the place down for hers, but these things happen in the Kellys' world.

James is arrested soon enough, and the venerable Judge Redmond Barry – who, though Irish, is Protestant, so Ned already knows he can't be trusted – is as quick as he is harsh in his judgment. For, on 18 April 1868, he convicts James of Attempted Murder and sentences him to 'be hanged by the neck until you are dead'.[31] But eventually this sentence is commuted to fifteen years' hard labour.

Meanwhile, by working as a washerwoman and seamstress in Wangaratta for six months, Ellen is able to scrape together enough money to put a deposit on her own 88-acre selection at Eleven Mile Creek, just four miles west of Greta and fifteen miles from Benalla, so all is well that ends well. The place is selected under the *Grant Act 1865*, which allows seven-year leases with a rental of two shillings per acre per year.[32] She will need to pay around £9 per year, and cultivate at least ten per cent or nine acres of the selected land. Under the new Act, no purchase of the selection can be made within the first three years, nor until Mrs Kelly can prove continual residence during that period and show improvements to the land to the value of £1 per acre, usually defined in terms of housing, fencing and cultivation.

A bonus of this land is that there is already a hut on it, something significant now that her husband the bush carpenter is gone . . .

As to the homestead, positioned in a grove of wattles and willows, by a creek in the heart of the Warby Ranges, it is little more than a slab-walled hut – boasting five 'rooms' with hessian for walls, bare earth for a floor and a bark roof with enough cracks to see the stars through the top. It lies just 50 yards back from an offshoot track to Oxley, off the main track that runs from Benalla to Wangaratta. For those on horseback seeking a shortcut to Beechworth that bypasses Wangaratta, it takes them right by the Kelly hut. In truth, the main reason the family are able to get it is because there are no other families desperate enough to want it, but it is at least something, a place to make a last stand in.

It is entirely different country to Avenel. There, the land had been fertile, gently hilly and with scattered fruit orchards. Here, in the vast ranges that surround the plains on which Greta lies, it is as wild and woolly, as mountainous and as thickly forested as country gets in the entire continent. For, if the platypus was made up of every animal part that God had left over, this part of the world is its geographical equivalent. Clearly, sometime around sundown on the sixth day, God just took every gully, gulch, gorge, waterfall, mountain, marsh, hill, cave, creek, river, ravine, ragged bluff, boulder, billabong, spur, soaring summit, stream, pond and swamp he had left in the sack, and simply hurled it at this last plot of wild fecundity on earth and watched the pieces grow in extraordinary profusion. For it is a place like nowhere else. Yes, it is within Victoria, but it is also a world apart, a place no more than 150 miles from Melbourne as a truly lost crow would fly but in many ways as far from Collins Street as Bolivia.

Collins Street is smart; it is sophisticated; it is filled with powerful people. North-Eastern Victoria is rough; it is hardy; it is wild; it is, in many ways, predominantly filled with people who – the squatters apart – are just like the Kellys. Nevertheless, as rough and remote as the area is, two linear forces of modernity are beginning to have an impact upon it at the time the Kellys arrive, just as they are having an impact across the continent and the world: the telegraph line and the railway line.

Just the year before, the telegraph had been connected up across Australia so that Melbourne could send a message through to Port Denison, thousands of miles north in Queensland, and – if you can believe it – they are soon going to lay one underwater and connect us to India and then Europe. It had gone through near to Greta, as well as the rest of Victoria, by 1857.

As a writer had commented to *The Argus* at the first appearance of the invention, 'To us, old colonists who have left Britain long ago, there is something very delightful in the contemplation of this, the most perfect of modern inventions . . . as anything more perfect than this is scarcely conceivable, and we really begin to wonder what will be left for the next generation upon which to expend the restless enterprise of the human mind . . .'[33]

As to the railway, it is *the* subject of conversation when the Kellys arrive in Greta. There is enormous talk of the North-Eastern Line being built soon, to go from Melbourne to Albury, passing through Wangaratta, and around Greta everyone – squatters, farmers, selectors and townsfolk – is agitating for it to go through their town, as it would help them all.

For Ellen Kelly, it is reminiscent of Red's desperation that the Sydney Road go through Beveridge, but perhaps, this time, the family will be lucky . . .

In the meantime, one way to get money is for Ellen to provide rough lodgings and meals for those few passers-by who need a bed for the night or longer, and, of course, to go with this – in the fashion of the day – she is also able to provide sly grog that she brews on the premises. Whether or not this makes the place quite a 'shanty house' is not clear, but it does allow her to gain a small income, and in the spring of 1869 it does bring into the orbit of the family a Donnybrook lad of twenty-nine years by the name of William Skillion,[34] now trying his hand as a miner, who takes a shine to young Maggie.

The primary responsibility for working the Kelly land of course falls to Ned, including 'grubbing' – clearing out stumps – putting up the fences and looking after such livestock as there is.

EARLY FEBRUARY 1869, OF PENTRIDGE GAOL AND POWER TO THE PEOPLE

Just as the Pacific Ocean hardly needs more water, and the Nullarbor Plain requires no more sand, there are few prisoners who believe that Pentridge Gaol could possibly be in need of more walls, but of course it is not their decision. It is enough that the wardens think it needs more walls, and this particular work party is engaged in constructing one just outside the gaol proper, of course under strict surveillance.

Or *is* it that strict?

One old rogue of a prisoner, Harry Power[35] – a grey-bearded, blue-eyed Irishman of nigh on fifty years, with a loud voice and louder opinions, who, self-confessedly, 'could cooey louder than any man in the bush'[36] – is of the view that maybe it isn't as strict as he had at first thought. It is with this conviction that, by virtue of a forged pass, he manages to make his way through the first of the sentry posts, towards the work gang. Before risking the second sentry, however, he secretes himself 'in a hole just by the wall'[37] and waits until the work gang is called in for lunch, taking their guards and sentries with them.

Sure enough, the whistle blows, the warders give their orders and, bit by bit, he can hear the whole mob of them pass, until the sound of voices recedes and he is all alone. Quickly, quietly, he is on his way once more, and he is soon outside, breathing his first air as a free man since he had been put inside six years earlier for his third major stint behind bars, his most grievous offence having been stealing horses and wounding a policeman fifteen years earlier. This time, he has been in gaol for just over five years for stealing horses.

From here, it is a relatively simple matter to rise from the grass and get to the cover provided by Merri Creek, just down the gully a bit. After stripping off his prison uniform, to display the second suit he has underneath, he is soon on his way, always expecting a bullet or shout of alarm that never comes . . . Splashing his way further up the creek, using his bushcraft to ensure that he leaves neither tracks nor scent, he presently comes to a perfect spot in which to hide himself, and he waits there until nightfall. He has done it!

By the following morning, after a freezing night on the run where, as he would later recount, 'I had nothing to eat, and the only weapon I had was a little tomahawk,'[38] there is surely something of Charles Dickens's great creation Magwitch about him: 'A man with no hat, and with broken shoes, and with an old rag tied round his head. A man who had been soaked in water, and smothered in mud, and lamed by stones, and cut by flints, and stung by nettles, and torn by briars; who limped, and shivered, and glared and growled; and whose teeth chattered in his head . . .'[39]

But at least Power is still free, and that is enough to warm the cockles of his soul, if not yet his body. Now, one does not become an old rogue like Harry without learning a lot of tricks as a young rogue. As a matter of fact, Harry had been first transported to Australia for seven years for stealing a pair of shoes. This day, after stealing some clothes from a farmhouse, he knows that the next thing he must do is fashion a weapon, any weapon, with which he can trade up to other weapons. With a single blade of an old pair of sheep shears strung to a stick, he soon has a lance, which he uses to procure a real knife, and then a revolver, and then a rifle. His career as a bushranger – the most glorious career imaginable for a criminal in Australia – has begun.

Where to head now? North-Eastern Victoria is the obvious destination. In those parts, the mountains are so high, the bush so thick, the gullies so deep and hidden that a man like him can rob and disappear nearly at will, and he already has experience in the area. While in Pentridge, he had met and befriended the brothers Jack and Tom Lloyd, who had told him of a hideout to beat them all, near the Quinns' place at Glenmore. It was a spot a man like him could launch from and return to, and in which he could rest in complete safety.

AUTUMN 1869, WITH BLISTERS ON HIS BLISTERS, FOR HIS BROTHERS AND SISTERS, NED WORKS THE LAND

Acutely aware of his responsibilities to his mother and family, young Ned throws himself into enormous amounts of physical labour, including doing his best to get a fair chunk of their selection under cultivation, in the hope that one day the family will be able to afford to buy it. He makes some money by taking his sturdy axe to the many massive ironbark trees that abound, digging out the stumps and chopping up all the wood, some of which he is able to sell for firewood to the locals. It is a tough existence, and a very difficult way to make a few shillings. Perhaps there might be easier ways to bring in some money for the family, to help his mother and all his brothers and sisters who are depending on him, the way they all would have depended on Red, had he lived?

27 MAY 1869, HARRY AND THE APPRENTICE

Up Mansfield way, the Mount Battery Station is one of the most impressive squatter's runs in the colony, all 35,000 acres of it. The homestead is huge, the gardens as neat as the dozens of surrounding paddocks – all of them carefully fenced, with gates that actually swing and don't have to be dragged in the dirt. Most importantly, its horses are renowned, and that is what Harry Power and his new apprentice, Ned Kelly, have come for. The old bushranger has already pulled off many hold-ups, but with this young fellow now helping him the range of things he could accomplish is huge, so long as they have proper mounts.

So it is that, on this crisp afternoon, with their own horses tied up a little way back in the scrub, the old man and the young'un are lying on a bluff, their hardened skin immune to the prickly tufts beneath them, looking over the station and working out the best way to steal the horses once night falls – both of them entirely unaware that they have been observed by a station hand . . .

In the warm and cosy homestead a short time later, the old squatter Dr John Rowe is told about the two strange men atop yonder bluff, looking over the horse paddock, and, with his dander up, he instantly takes action. Calling for his long-range rifle, and telling his son to ready some of those horses for the pursuit, Dr Rowe carefully manoeuvres himself into a position whereby, although the strangers are within his sights, he is out of theirs . . . and squeezes the trigger.

Up on the bluff, neither Harry Power nor Ned Kelly quite knows what hits them. One instant, there is naught to hear but the call of a lost and lonely magpie and the distant whinnying of horses, and the next the gravel in front of them sprays up into their faces, followed half a second later by the almighty crack of a rifle. They are under attack!

Harry leaps to his feet, to quickly race for the horses, but Ned will not move. Petrified, never shot at before, the kid spreads himself on the ground like a dropped egg, then, as Power would later recount, 'turned deadly white, and wished to surrender'.[40]

Cuffing him to snap him out of it, Power bodily lifts Ned to his feet and, cursing him all the while, drags him crudely through the sharp scrub back to their horses. At least once in the saddle, the fourteen-year-old comes good. Though they are hotly pursued by Dr Rowe, with his son and their leading hands, Power can't help but be impressed at Ned Kelly's fearlessness and skill as he gallops full tilt, neck or nothing, down the roughest gullies, leaping fallen timber, dodging wombat holes, swerving around trees, ducking under low branches and never once flinching.

Ah, it was grand to see that mountain horseman ride.

They are able to outdistance their pursuers and then are saved from a police black-tracker who comes out after them by the rain falling . . . but it has been a close-run thing. Too close for Ned. His first taste of the bushranger's life is the taste of dust in his mouth from a bullet meant for him and he hates it. His own fragile mortality hits home, and that is precisely where he too must head. No good to his mother dead, he has already had enough, at least for the moment.

Harry Power might stop galloping, but Ned drives in the spurs and keeps going, all the way back to Eleven Mile Creek.

15 OCTOBER 1869, AT BRIGHT, NED RUNS OVER A CHINAMAN

Ned's older sister Annie no longer lives at home. Six months earlier, at the age of just fifteen, she had married the dour, twenty-nine-year-old local boy Alex Gunn, and they have set up home in his humble hut. (It would have been grander digs but, having failed to make payment on the rent on his selection, he had just lost it and had to move down the road.) And yet still she likes to visit her family frequently, and on many such occasions helps her mother with the household chores as well as taking care of the young'uns.

On this day, she is sitting on a chair outside the Kelly hut, concentrating on some sewing, when she looks up to see a pig and fowl trader from the local Morses Creek Chinese camp, Ah Fook, staring down at her. His clothes are filthy, his face is dusty, and on the end of the bamboo pole he has over his shoulder is suspended a billycan. Immediately – at least the way the Kellys would tell this and subsequent details of the story ever afterwards – Annie feels uneasy, perhaps less because of Ah Fook himself than simply his race. From the time of the first Chinese immigrants to these parts, they had been a race apart and, for the most part, heavily distrusted by the white population.

'Can I have,' the Chinaman asks, in a thick accent, 'water, please?'

Oh. He is just thirsty. The billycan, which he is now proffering to her, is empty. Annie, a kindly soul, is quick to oblige and disappears to get some water. And yet no sooner has she returned with a filled cup and the Chinaman taken a sip of it than he angrily spits it out. Its gritty taste seemingly makes him think it is not rainwater from the tank but is creek water. (Or is it that, with this house's reputation as a sly grog shop, he was expecting and hoping for something much stronger?) Quite what he yells out at this point is not obvious to Annie, only that he is outraged and so loud about it that her fourteen-year-old brother, Ned, by now a bigger and more strapping lad than ever, comes bursting forth. With two other, older, men, Bill Gray – who is now employed by Ellen Kelly in return for £1 a week and his keep – and Bill Skillion, he has been grubbing out stumps from the paddocks and has now just returned to the homestead for lunch.

'He's insulting me!' says Annie.

'Clear out!' yells Ned. 'Clear out, you Chow!'[41]

When Ah Fook does no such thing, Ned is upon him and roughly pushes him away. The Chinaman, however, is enraged, and instantly starts wildly swinging his bamboo stick at Ned's head and shoulders, taking this descendant of the fighting Irish by surprise with the strength of his attack. Ah, say it, Ned, with your soft Irish brogue, for we know you must.

AH FOOK!

What happens now?

Ned will solemnly swear the Chinaman ran away. (No, really.)

Ah Fook's account, however, when he arrives at Benalla Police Station three hours later, is that he was then severely assaulted by the youngster and also robbed. The one solace he has is that, six weeks earlier, he had been equally held up and robbed by an Irishman with piercing blue eyes and a booming voice, and it was because of that bitter experience he had taken the precaution of hiding £25 in his boot, which this young ruffian had not found.

16 OCTOBER 1869, THE BENALLA COURTHOUSE WELCOMES ANOTHER KELLY

At last! At last, after Ah Fook makes a formal complaint, Sergeant James Whelan has a reason to go after Ned Kelly. No matter that Kelly is only fourteen, and the Chinaman gives the description of the robber as being 'about 20 years of age, five feet eight inches high, no beard or whiskers, brown hair, wore old moleskin trousers and a straw hat with a black band'.[42] Whelan knows from the first it has to be Ned.

Oh yes, the oddly patrician Whelan – all high forehead and rather sniffy airs, a former member of the Royal Irish Constabulary – knows Ned Kelly all right, just as he knows the whole scurvy Kelly family that had moved into the area a couple of years earlier. And he does not like them one bit, least of all Ned. Just three months earlier, Sergeant Whelan had crossed paths and very nearly swords with the burly brute when he'd been trying to convict the brother of Ned's brother-in-law Alex Gunn, Yeamann Gunn, for being in possession of stolen mutton and hides – only to have Ned testify, under oath, that on the same day, 'I sold him two sheep for 18 shillings. The sheep I sold were pets and were never branded.'[43]

The case had remained strong regardless, and the judge had found Gunn guilty, but for some unaccountable reason young Kelly had not been called to account for lying through his miserable teeth. It is an injustice which, rather than merely sticking in Sergeant Whelan's craw, had now consumed his whole being.

He had closely watched the activities of the family after that, and one of his fellow officers, Superintendent John Sadleir, would later say that he became 'a perfect encyclopaedia of all useful knowledge relating to the bushrangers, their habits, their associates and friends'.[44]

The next morning, a little before daylight, Sergeant Whelan, in the company of Ah Fook and Constable McInerny, go out to arrest Ned Kelly for Highway Robbery, thinking it will be a fairly routine matter. After all, how hard can it be to put handcuffs on a fellow who, at fourteen years old, is little more than a child?

Yes, well, the problem, Sergeant, is that young Kelly doesn't want to be arrested, and, as the trooper would have to subsequently explain, from that moment on things got rather out of hand.

As Beechworth's local paper, *The Ovens and Murray Advertiser*, goes on to report, 'On coming into view of the hut, Whelan noticed a woman suddenly enter, and immediately afterward a boy rushed out and took to the bush . . .'[45] For the young man had no sooner seen the trooper than – notwithstanding both troopers are dressed in civilian clothes to prevent exactly this happening – he had run into the bush at full speed.

Sergeant Whelan goes after him on horseback, only to be attacked by two of the Kelly dogs for his trouble. Finally, though, the young fellow is caught.

'Why did you run away?' Whelan asks.

'I don't know,' the young ruffian replies.

'You can't assign any reason for your flight?'

'No.'

A little while later, though, Ned does offer something. 'It was that bloody Chinaman who passed yesterday did this. He insulted the woman and I took a stick to him, but I never hit him. He hit me with a bamboo.'[46]

Of course, Sergeant Whelan arrests Ned and takes him back to where he had left Ah Fook. The latter immediately identifies him, and, with manacles on, Ned is forcibly removed to the lock-up at Benalla Police Station, where he is charged with Highway Robbery and thrown into a cell.

Despite there being a delay in court proceedings the following day, so that Sergeant Whelan has time to find an interpreter, Ned is denied bail and must remain in the cell. He does not like it.

19–26 OCTOBER 1869, BENALLA COURTHOUSE, NED GETS HIS DAY IN COURT

When Ned is brought back into the dock on 19 October, the interpreter has still not arrived from Beechworth. The police prosecutor apologises for the delay and applies for another remand, which is duly granted.

Though the law, of course, maintains that young Edward is innocent until proven guilty, *The Ovens and Murray Advertiser* does not wish to wait that long and describes Ned in its headline of that day as 'A Juvenile Bushranger', before detailing the case and concluding with a congratulatory note for Whelan. The Sergeant is undoubtedly 'worthy of recognition by the Police authorities'.[47]

Ned is thrice remanded and kept in lock-up for more than a week, when, at last, on 26 October, he again appears in court. This time, the interpreter has arrived and his case is heard.

Needless to say, the testimony of Ah Fook – who is sworn in 'by blowing out a match',[48] which is the Chinese version of swearing on the Bible (just as does 'the Hindoo by sipping a glass of water'[49]) – is exceedingly different from the account given by Ned. He recounts how, while travelling from Morses Creek to Benalla, he had passed the Kelly homestead, whereupon the accused – initially with three other men

– had approached him and, while holding 'a long stick', this young ruffian, wearing a straw hat with a black band around it, leering from atop his moleskins, had announced, 'I'm a bushranger; give up your money, or I'll beat you to death.'[50]

Ah Fook had rather eponymously remonstrated, albeit in his own language. But because the young man was so strong and armed with a big stick, he had had to go with him for half a mile, where, among a secluded clump of trees, the robbery had taken place.

'He put his hand into my pocket and took out the money,' the translator says carefully. 'The ten shillings taken from me I had in a purse in the right hand trousers' pocket. After taking the ten shillings he threw the purse away, and hit me with the stick on the arm and the leg . . .'[51]

He denies all of Ned Kelly's story as complete lies – he had never asked for water, never shaken his fist at the young woman – and none of his basic assertions of fact are shaken by cross-examination. The Chinaman's story, frankly, sounds credible.

And yet, with no fewer than three witnesses – Annie, Skillion and Gray – supporting Ned's alternative story, the judge is placed in a very difficult position. The only real supporting evidence for the Chinaman is the testimony of Sergeant Whelan of Benalla that the next day, upon examining Ah Fook, he had seen 'abrasions on his leg and arms',[52] but of course that could have happened any time before or after the alleged assault.

Magistrate Alfred Currie Wills has no choice. 'The three witnesses for the defence so confirm each other's evidence,' he says, almost regretfully, 'whereas the prosecutor's evidence is unsupported, that I have no option but to discharge the prisoner.'[53]

The case is closed, and, for the first time in a week, Ned breathes the fresh air of a free 'man'. As reported in the local paper, 'the young man left the dock inwardly rejoicing'.[54]

In response, Sergeant Whelan can barely breathe for fury. Perhaps his only solace is that, although Police Magistrate Wills has no choice but to acquit Kelly, he clearly indicates his basic disbelief of their story by noting just before he does so, 'You must have been a very quiet lot out there – three of you and to allow your friend to be beaten like that is most extraordinary.'[55] Quite.

To many who have followed the case, it does not seem as though either party is telling the whole truth. In the words of the reporter for Beechworth's *Ovens and Murray Advertiser*, 'It is impossible to avoid coming to any other conclusion than that the charge of robbery has been trumped up by the Chinaman to be revenged on Kelly, who had evidently assaulted him.'[56]

For its part, however, the *Benalla Ensign* seems convinced that it is the Chinaman who is telling the truth, telling its readers flatly, even if much later, that 'The cunning of [Ned Kelly] and his mates got him off.'[57]

Has Ned learned his lesson, however? Perhaps not, because it won't be long before he decides to return to at least some of his old ways.

16 MARCH 1870, KILFERA STATION RECEIVES VISITORS

While the Kelly property at Eleven Mile Creek is little more than a poxy pocket-handkerchief of 88 acres of dirt and wilderness, neighbouring Kilfera Station is an entire silken blanket of 44,000 acres of the finest fields, owned and run by the wealthiest, most powerful and, yes, likely the most respected squatter in the district, Robert McBean.

A canny Scot, McBean had come to these parts nine years before and, through great energy, enormous resources and judicious land management, built his holding up to the point that it now carries no fewer than 11,000 sheep. He is proud of what he has achieved, particularly as he has been up against a fair variety of natural enemies: floods, droughts, snakes, dingoes and selectors. Of those, the most dangerous in McBean's view are the selectors, who are continually picking at the edges of his land, making claims that in his view are not theirs to make. This most particularly includes the Kellys, who three years earlier had settled on land that used to be part of his run, land that he is eager to get back. Upon it, they have been as much a thorn in his side as they have been endless trouble to the local police.

On this day, just before noon, McBean is out and about, making sure that some fencing work on the eastern quarter of his property has been executed properly when, off in the distance, he spies two horsemen. This in itself is not unusual, as McBean has many workers and they frequently get around his run in pairs. No, the odd thing this time is that he does not instantly recognise either of them, nor their horses, which should be, after all, his horses. Are they neighbours, trespassers . . . *who?*

Riding after them, McBean is not long in seeing that it is a heavily bearded older man in a tweed jacket and moleskins, riding with a heavily built younger man. From a distance, he thinks the older man might be an Englishman by the name of Bill Frost, who had moved in with Ellen Kelly in recent times – in fact, impregnating her, for a baby is due in a few months' time – and who McBean knows has just got out of hospital. As to the young fellow, that might just possibly be Ellen's criminal kid, the one he'd seen in court in June the year before: Ned.

Still, this is no cause for alarm and, though the horsemen veer away as he approaches, McBean is a laird on his land and feels no fear of any man. Sure now that it is Frost, he hails him, 'Good day, Bill.'[58]

To his amazement, however, 'Bill' does not hail him in turn. Rather, the two stop and the younger man dismounts and turns his face away, as if he does not wish to be recognised. McBean has little time to focus on this, however, as the older man now whirls around and yells with rage, 'Confound your impertinence. I'll teach you how to speak to a gentleman. Fancy calling me "Bill!"'[59]

True, McBean is not inclined to do so again, for not only is it not Bill Frost but, whoever it is, he is now pointing a large revolver straight at his chest and telling him to dismount, take off his gold watch and tie it onto the bridle of his horse. Though reluctant to part with the family heirloom, McBean does as instructed.

'I don't suppose you have any money on you?' the gunman asks.[60]

McBean agrees this is the case and now musters the wherewithal to ask for the watch back.

Harry Power, for it is of course he, replies vaguely that, at 'a future time',[61] McBean could have the watch back, perhaps for £10. In a little more conversation, the squatter realises he is in the presence of the famous bushranger, but he still cannot identify the man's companion, who remains with his face turned away.

But enough chat . . .

After also taking McBean's fine mare and favourite saddle, Power turns to the squatter and says, 'Well, I suppose it is a matter of about two hours, and the police will be after me. Good day!'[62]

McBean is reduced to heading back to his homestead on shanks's pony – his own two legs – while the bushrangers ride off to the south in the direction of the Mansfield road with their newly acquired prize mare in tow.

After furiously tramping the three miles back to the homestead, and then getting a fresh steed to gallop into Benalla, McBean arrives in town at half past one, in such a towering rage that he can barely raise spit.

Infamy! Outrage! Him, a law-abiding subject of Her Majesty the Queen, a Justice of the Peace, accosted and held up by a bushranger, an escaped convict, *on his own property!*

And yet no sooner have the police at Benalla taken down McBean's statement, and sent off a couple of constables in hopeless pursuit, than another report comes in from a man with the unlikely name of Charles Dickens of Preston Station, who has been similarly bailed up, some 20 miles to the east, on the edge of the Wombat Ranges, by obviously the same man, riding a brown mare that is clearly McBean's.

Worse, for the old bushranger, Dickens recognises him, and he tells the police precisely who they are looking for: Harry Power, one and the same, who had escaped from Pentridge early the previous year.

A major manhunt is about to begin . . .

For the moment, however, Harry Power and young Ned, swallowed up by the thick Australian bush, are free to make camp high in the Strathbogie Ranges that night – swilling their smoky tea by a tiny campfire in such thick country that the fire is invisible at 50 yards distance – remaining blithely unaware of just what kind of bull-ants' nest they have now kicked.

For Harry Power and his new apprentice, Ned, could hardly have picked a worse man in the whole district to antagonise. Robert McBean is not just rich but also supremely well connected. He has been a member of the mighty Melbourne Club for the last six years, which is where he stays when in the colony's capital, and one of his closest friends is a fellow clubman, the mighty English-born Chief Commissioner of Police, Captain Frederick Charles Standish. Captain Standish is the most powerful policeman in all of Victoria – a former British military man, *suh*, hence his rank, now in charge of 1180 men – and within four days McBean has sought him out at the club.

Happily, Standish shares his outrage. It is inconceivable, and deeply embarrassing, that a criminal like Power should not only have thwarted his recapture for so long after escaping Pentridge but also is out and about robbing wealthy squatters like Robert McBean, a member of the Melbourne Club, no less, and his friend. The two, sunk deep into their leather armchairs, talk late into the dimly lit night as the muffled sounds of the city outside fade away, the waiters hover and the whiskey flows free, and it is McBean himself who comes up with the plan that Standish embraces. The government must lift its reward for information leading to the capture of Harry Power from its current £200 all the way up to £500.

This reward, of course, can be shared by the police and any informant who tells them where Power can be found. And McBean has a lead. During the robbery, Power had mentioned that if he wanted the gold watch heirloom back, it might be arranged in return for ten quid. McBean intends to put it about that he is very keen to make the exchange, and, hopefully, whoever the intermediary proves to be might lead them to where Power hides in the mountains. Excellent idea!

So seriously does Captain Standish take the affair that he soon approaches none other than 'the fittest and best man for the work',[63] his unofficial protégé, and some say pet, the South African-born

Superintendent Francis Hare, who is in charge of Melbourne's Richmond depot. He will play a role in the ruthless pursuit of Power and help him to wrap up this business once and for all.

A giant of a man with flowing locks and bounteous beard, Hare stands at nearly six foot three inches, 'tall, lank and ungainly'.[64] He is outgoing, confident, openly ambitious and, in Standish's admiring view, the right man – nay, the *only* man – to take over his own job as Commissioner come the time, many years hence, when he might choose to retire. (This notwithstanding the fact that, after arriving in Australia from his native South Africa in 1852, Hare had immediately gone to the goldfields, where his two key passions were looking for nuggets and dodging the troopers looking for those without mining licences, until 1854, when he became one of those troopers himself. Who is Standish to judge? The Police Commissioner had himself only come to Australia to flee bad gambling debts in England, and had first earned money by selling sly grog on those same goldfields.)

Hare, of course eager to please his patron, quickly sets about investigating the whole Power affair and, from his Richmond base, starts organising search parties.

LATE APRIL 1870, BENALLA, PEOPLE BEGIN TO TALK

Is Captain Standish up to the task? It is two weeks since the outrage on Robert McBean, and there are still no signs of an arrest. *The Ovens and Murray Advertiser* even quotes an ex-Minister of the Crown, Francis Longmore, who is nothing less than a 'tribune of the people', asserting that it is 'Captain Standish's love for metropolitan life'[65] that means he has no feeling for catching bushrangers. And, later, another of his senior police officers would be even more explicit, saying of Captain Standish, 'I doubt, however, whether he possessed as high a sense of duty. He was too much a man of pleasure to devote himself seriously to the work of his office, and his love of pleasure led him to form intimacies with some officers of like mind, and to think less of others who were much more worthy of regard.'[66]

To what do they refer? Well, there are stories. One of the most compelling yarns has it that one of Standish's great pleasures is to have private parties at the Melbourne Club for his closest male friends. Some specific women are invited, but the women must observe a very strict dress code: no dress at all.

Nude! They sit there naked – 'the whiteness of their forms contrasting with the black velvet of the chairs'[67] – while they all enjoy their meal and drink. Lots of drink . . .

In the meantime, the word that the young fellow with Harry Power was none other than Ned Kelly is starting to get out, with the *Benalla Ensign* reporting on 1 April that 'the effect of [Power's] example has already been to draw one young fellow into the open vortex of crime, and unless his career is speedily cut short young KELLY will blossom into a declared enemy of society'.[68]

Chapter Two

TROUBLED TIMES

There never was such a thing as Justice in the English laws but any amount of injustice to be had . . .
Ned Kelly

A great deal of the difficulty with these men would be got over if they felt they were treated with equal justice – that there was no 'down' upon them. They are much more tractable if they feel that they are treated with equal justice.
Inspector William B. Montfort

LATE APRIL 1870, KILFERA STATION, ROBERT MCBEAN GETS A BITE

Robert McBean has indeed passed the word, and now the word has come back: if he wishes to get his gold watch heirloom back, there is a local who will arrange the exchange. Ned Kelly's uncle, Jack Lloyd, the horse and cattle thief who had been in Pentridge with Harry Power, will be happy to help in return for some money for himself. The bushranger had even mentioned Lloyd in passing as he was holding up the squatter.

Excitedly, McBean writes to Captain Standish, informing him that:

> *I know of a man who will be likely to give valuable assistance to the police sent in pursuit of the . . . bushranger Power.*[1]

McBean now has an informant! Things begin to move . . .

APRIL 1870, NORTH-EASTERN VICTORIA, THE OLD'UN AND THE YOUNG'UN RIDE

Even Harry Power has to admit that young Ned Kelly has come a long way since their first time riding together. Though still only fifteen, Ned is a superb horseman who is none too particular about which side of the law he finds himself on, as strong as a bull, as durable as an old boot and as tough as any doing hard labour in Pentridge.

The two work well together, riding all over the country, committing robberies here and there – even though the lad never wields a gun, only holds the horses and always stays well back – and Ned is able to learn something of the ways of Harry Power the bushranger. The first thing is to make sure your base is in only the thickest, most impenetrable country, where any pursuer will have to be a superb bushman just to get there, let alone find you and fight you.

And there is no doubt that there's something about the sheer glorious beauty of the places where he and Harry make their home that grips Ned, just as it does the old bushranger. They often climb higher up the mountains than even birds would venture, where you can see for a hundred miles in any direction, feeling like a king in your all natural castle. In slightly lower parts, the bird life is stunning, with crested pigeons cooing, black-tailed native hens scurrying and grey currawongs making their *p'rink, cling, cling, ker-link* calls, ever and always mocked by the perpetually laughing kookaburras.

As Harry would later note: 'It's grand to be on the ranges, and to breathe the beautiful pure air, and to see Mount Feathertop far above ye, and down below, for miles and miles, the beautiful country. There's water all the year round, and it's always cool and pleasant. That's the place for a man to live . . .[2]'

Of all Power's abilities, his capacity to ride enormous distances is perhaps the key to evading capture. He insists on stealing only the best mounts and can cover as much as 70 miles in a day, meaning that while the police might be all over one area looking for him, he is more often than not in an entirely different region. Not only that, but when he does want to disappear, he has hiding places where he often keeps spare horses, and those hiding places are sustained by a network of trusted confederates and sympathisers who can keep him supplied when he needs it. Despite being a complete bushman and a brilliant horseman, able to live off the land barely leaving a trace – he frequently rides down creeks and across rock surfaces to thwart trackers, is careful to bury the ashes of whatever tiny fires he makes, and will not even break a twig off a tree if he can avoid it – he doesn't dress like a rough-as-guts bushranger but is careful in the way he presents himself, almost a bush dandy.

And nor does he actually shoot people, far preferring to achieve his ends by uttering dire threats that he never actually has to follow through on, because those he holds up are too terrified not to cooperate.

As his reputation grows, and his name resonates all the more, Harry becomes increasingly protective of his reputation as a kind of 'rogue gentleman', a man who has seen the worst that life has to throw but remains civil.

Alas, to young Ned personally, Harry proves to be something less than gentlemanly, and is so prone to losing his temper, 'swearing at him to such an extent, without his giving him any provocation'[3] that, by the first day of May, 1870, Ned has had enough and simply gallops away, heading home. In a manner that might make Harry proud, at last, he covers 180 miles in three days, to again walk through the door of the house at Eleven Mile Creek and into the arms of his waiting mother, who has his new infant sister at her breast. Young Ned's return, however, has been noted . . .

Quickly, quietly, in the silent watch of that very night, just gone four o'clock on the morning of Wednesday 4 May, four policemen, including Sergeant James Whelan, move into position outside the Kelly hut. The two horses outside are an indication that old Harry might be with young Ned, and it is Power, of course, who remains the main target.

And so it is, that, as the first full flush of dawn allows them to at least partially see what they are doing, the four policemen, with their guns drawn, throw open the hut door and burst inside to seize young Ned and . . . and . . . and no one else. For Harry is not there. Apart from Ned, there is just the angry Ellen and her terrified children.

But Ned is at least something, and the young delinquent – who appears 'much worn, jaded and altered from his former appearance and complains of being very sick'[4] – is quickly manacled and taken to the Benalla lock-up. News of his capture is well received by the *Benalla Ensign*, which faithfully reports that 'Power's cub has been taken'.[5]

Is young Ned intimidated by being in manacles, or crestfallen at what has befallen him? Not according to the same paper, which notes, 'The entrance of the escort into Benalla was quite imposing, the prisoner being surrounded by his captors, and every now and then a smile passed over his face as he recognised some one he knew.'[6]

Ah, but that is for public show. Back in the privacy of his own dim cell, an entirely different Ned is apparent. Here, he is 'very moody in his old quarters, not relishing them at all, and appeared quite exhausted with the life he had been leading. He is very pale and has learned to smoke while out at night with Power.'[7]

The next day, Ned appears in the Benalla Police Court, in front of a crowd of spectators, to face the charges of Robbery in Company of Robert McBean and Highway Robbery Under Arms of Joseph Balwoski near Seymour in early April.

'Kelly seemed quite indifferent to the danger of his position,' *The Ovens and Murray Advertiser* reports. 'While casting eyes among the crowd, he smiled complacently and assumed a jaunty air. Previous to his appearance in court, and while confined in the lock-up, he sang like a bird and seemed quite proud. The misguided youth evidently considers himself a character to be admired.'[8]

The police application for remand is granted and young Kelly is taken back to the lock-up for a week to await his trial.

EARLY MAY 1870, HARRY ON THE LAM

In the meantime, the search for Power goes on. With some enthusiasm!

For the government, desperate to find the renegade rogue and move on from the discredit that has been brought on the police force by his being so long at large, have indeed upped the reward for his apprehension from £300 to £500. Even the New South Wales Government has offered £200 if he is captured in their state. And here, as described in the reward notice, is what he looks like:

> Native of Liverpool, aged 48, 5 feet 6½ inches high, blue eyes, scar on the forehead, scar on the cheek, two scars on the right arm, scars on the left elbow, large scar on the left shin, left third finger deformed.[9]

Does Harry Power care? He does not. For, even without Ned, and even with his reward poster being pasted everywhere, a man has to follow his calling, and so Harry does: holding up people with a certain panache.

10 MAY 1870, LITTLE DO THEY KNOW, AS THEY MEET WITH YOUNG NED . . .

Superintendent Charles Hope Nicolson is an officer with twenty-five years' experience in the Victoria Police, of which fourteen have been spent in charge of the detective force. Alas, at the end of that long spell, his health had broken down and Captain Standish – who had never warmed to him in the first place – had sent him a year earlier to run the Kyneton district. This means Nicolson now finds himself in charge of the area where Power has been most active, which is propitious, as he had already dealt with the old scallywag many times and is familiar with his modus operandi.

And the strict Presbyterian police officer is keen, all right. Just this past week, he was supposed to be on leave and staying in Melbourne, but upon hearing of a reported appearance of Power near Lauriston, he had immediately gone straight back to his district, where, with his broad network of informers, he is soon closing in on the bushranger.

And then comes news from Standish of McBean's new informant. Nicolson returns to Melbourne to offer his services in following up this business, which Standish accepts, while also making a very odd suggestion. 'Nicolson,' he says, 'as you are not strong yet, I will send Hare to drive you up instead of allowing you to travel by coach, and he, perhaps, may be of use to you.'[10]

Yes, sir. If you say so, sir.

And so, on this morning, Nicolson must, with ill-disguised reluctance, accompany Superintendent Hare – a much younger officer of bragging bravado for whom he has little time – as they go to interview this young fellow Ned Kelly at the Benalla lock-up, to see what information they might be able to glean about the whereabouts of Power.

For his part, the athletic, raffish Hare feels much the same about Nicolson. Neither he nor Captain Standish has ever warmed to this cerebral sod – who looks a little like the Jack of Spades – and they rather disapprove of him in the same manner that the happily married and conservative Nicolson strongly disapproves of Standish's own excesses.

But to the meeting itself . . .

For the first time, both senior officers get a good look at this lad they have been hearing so much about, as the handcuffed fifteen-year-old is ushered into their presence. Hare is not impressed and would later describe Ned as 'a flash, ill-looking young blackguard'.[11]

Nicolson, however, is far more used to dealing with and questioning young criminals, and is better able to establish something of a rapport with young Ned, to the point that the youngster goes so far as to acknowledge that he had indeed been riding with Power.

But would he give him up, and tell these two officers where Power might be found now?

Yes . . . and . . . no.

That is, while young Ned does not offer specific information as to where the various hideaways of Power are situated, in the course of the general conversation Nicolson – a skilled questioner who manages to appear as if he is doing no more than having a general chat – does extract enough clues that the officers are able to give warning to police in various areas, including the small port of Eden, New South Wales, that Power might be heading their way.

That evening, the two police officers head off to Kilfera Station, where Robert McBean has arranged for them to meet Jack Lloyd, who wanders in at dusk.

And so now let's have a good look at you . . .

An old Irish labourer with a full beard, Lloyd stands five foot six inches and, so scarred and broken is his face, he looks rather like a man who has gone ten rounds with a sledgehammer, suffering several knockout blows in every round.

Just as had happened that morning with Ned, Superintendent Hare – who goes forward with Mr McBean to meet Lloyd, leaving Nicolson behind – is appalled from the first at having to deal with a man of such dubious character. Within ten minutes, Hare has returned to the others, reporting, 'the man knows nothing' and that he 'does not think the informer will do, as he is an old Pentridge man, who refuses to give any information, and in any case cannot be trusted'.[12]

And now it is McBean's turn to be 'very much disgusted' at Hare's summation. 'If that be the case,' he says plaintively, 'what risk do I run now, having trusted and arranged with this man to take the reward?'[13]

It is now that Nicolson's greater experience comes to the fore. Knowing that men of Lloyd's ilk like a bare minimum of witnesses at the best of times, he takes him to another room, where the other two cannot hear them. Fifteen minutes later, Nicolson returns alone – Lloyd has left by another door – and informs McBean and Hare that, once the old convict has found out where Power is concealed, he will 'contact them once more, within a month'.[14] McBean, in turn, promises to inform Captain Standish once that is done.

12 MAY 1870, BENALLA POLICE COURT, ELLEN KELLY IS SLY IN A GOOD WAY

Was it an omen? Three days earlier, Ned's mother, Ellen, had been acquitted in the Wangaratta Police Court on a charge of selling sly grog when the undercover policeman involved, William Thomas, had been unable to swear on the Bible that it was she who had actually served him the liquor in her shanty.

And on this day, Ned also escapes conviction, for much the same reason.

For not only can Robert McBean not positively identify him – perhaps as part of the deal struck with Ned's uncle – but on the second charge, of the robbing of Joseph Balwoski, there is the happy circumstance that the victim can now not be found to give testimony, so the charges are dropped . . .

But Ned is not free to go. A third charge is then brought up against him, that of having committed Robbery Under Arms against John Murray at Lauriston on 20 April, for which he is remanded in custody, first to Kyneton, and then to Melbourne for the weekend. It is there, as a very important prisoner, he is placed in the Richmond lock-up under Superintendent Hare's direct care, and on the Sunday morning even receives a visit from Captain Standish himself.

For its part, the *Benalla Ensign* is quick to communicate its observations and sentiments to its readers: 'The prisoner has greatly improved under the better and regular diet he has had since his incarceration and has become quite flash. We are told that his language is hideous, and if he recovers his liberty at Kyneton, and again joins Power – as he no doubt soon would – we are inclined to think he would be far more dangerous than heretofore. He has managed to get out of several ugly scrapes, and this success has not only emboldened but it has hardened him.'[15]

16 MAY 1870, NED AND NICOLSON HEAD DOWN THE SAME TRACK

All aboard! On the Monday-evening train leaving Spencer Street Station, Superintendent Nicolson escorts young Ned as they head back up to Kyneton. Ned is not handcuffed, as the police officer judges that he presents no risk of flight. Besides which, there is just something about this young Kelly that appeals to this twenty-five-year veteran of the Victoria Police Force. Yes, Ned is a young criminal, and yes, Nicolson has no doubt that those things he has been charged with are just the tip of the things that he has done. But, against that, there is an intelligence to him – perhaps even an integrity? – that suggests he is one who can be saved from the path he is heading down, and it is with that in mind that the dutiful Nicolson takes the time now to sit with Ned Kelly and level with him. The two talk, as the Victorian countryside falls back in the night, and the easy rhythm of the swaying train is somehow calming. Most particularly, the police officer talks to the troubled young man about the need to get away from the bad company he has been keeping, to move to New South Wales, to start afresh . . .

Why, Nicolson could even perhaps help him to get there, if Ned is interested?

Ned, sincerely, promises to think about it.

Upon arrival at the bluestone lock-up at Kyneton, Ned is pleasantly surprised to find that the Sergeant there, James Babington, is unlike most other police. He's warm, someone you can turn to – something Ned has not had since the death of his father, Red, whom he continues to miss terribly.

The two form an unlikely bond, and Ned seems almost lulled into a sense of security . . .

24 MAY 1870, CAPTAIN STANDISH CUTS THE HARE LOOSE

Summoning Hare, Standish tells him that McBean has sent word that Power's digs have been found. He then informs his underling of his decision to give him full command of the pursuit. Hare realises all too readily that this is the climactic moment in a long pursuit and a great opportunity. Yet, aware that blatant favouritism wins no friends among the rank and file, Hare feebly offers that his senior officers may be better suited to the task.

With a dismissive wave of the hand at such admittedly becoming modesty, Standish tells him that no less than the Chief Secretary of

Victoria, Sir James McCulloch, has identified *him*, Hare, as the man who can bring the bushranger to justice, and he is to begin to make his arrangements immediately. 'I will give you *carte blanche* to do as you please,' Captain Standish adds, 'and to take whom you please, and to spend what money you wish.'[16]

LATE MAY 1870, NICOLSON HOUNDS THE HARE, AND PURSUES THE POWER AND THE GLORY

There have been times in Charles Nicolson's long, solid career when he has been flabbergasted, but rarely more so than now. For, shortly after Jack Lloyd has indeed passed word to Captain Standish that he has found out where Harry Power is hiding, and just before departure of a party from Melbourne to capture the bushranger, Nicolson is none the wiser. The first Nicolson hears of all this is in a rather off the cuff note from Captain Standish:

> ***My dear Nicolson,***
> ***I cannot think of allowing you to go back to this duty in your present delicate state of health: Dr Ford says it would be injurious to you . . .***[17]

This is followed by another, even more infuriating note from Hare, beginning . . .

> *My dear fellow, I am so sorry to be off without you . . .*[18]

He's been phased out, and those two are playing innocent.

God help him, but what is Captain Standish thinking? For the life of him, Superintendent Nicolson cannot work it out. To have put such a junior officer as Superintendent Hare 'over the heads of at least eleven senior officers',[19] in charge of the pursuit of Power, is insulting to all of them and to none more so than himself.

Appalled, *outraged*, Nicolson journeys to Melbourne that evening and obtains a note from his medico, Dr Ford, to the effect that, if Nicolson feels equal to the fatigue, then such an expedition would do him no harm. Armed with that, Nicolson insists to Captain Standish that he must go.

Standish reluctantly concedes.

The major expedition to capture Power will depart with Nicolson at least nominally in charge and Hare, thank you very much, as his *second* in command – albeit with the patronage of the Commissioner.

29 MAY 1870, HARRY, I DREAMT YE WAS TOOK

Despite the antipathy that Superintendents Nicolson and Hare feel for each other, at least, at last, it has all come together to the point where, after two days' solid travel from Benalla, they arrive at Robert McBean's run, Kilfera Station, ready to set out in pursuit of Harry Power.

They are soon joined by Hare's offsider, Sergeant William B. Montfort, who, having spent some time stationed at Benalla and Wangaratta, is familiar with the search area. He is accompanied by a black-tracker by the name of Donald. Finally, an extremely reluctant Jack Lloyd arrives. Now, normally, old Jack – the one who had encouraged his sister-in-law Ellen Kelly to move up to Greta in the first place – is as rough as he is tough and gruff. But, on this day, there is something more, and it is not simply because he is again face to face with Sergeant Montfort, who arrested him for cattle stealing back in 1863, which had sent him to prison for five years. Clearly, Lloyd is a man who has slept little in recent days, who has worried himself sick over what he is doing, but in the end has not been able to resist the lure of £500.

Thirty pieces of silver? No, but after Superintendent Hare initials the banknotes first, for the purpose of evidence, McBean does give Jack Lloyd £15 for him to give to Power in exchange for the watch – an extra £5 included, to make sure the deal goes through – after which meeting it will be the old lag's job to come back and lead the small police posse to capture the bushranger.

Three days' hard riding ensues, setting off on a wet Wednesday morning, with all of the police dressed in plain clothes so as to not give any warning of their purpose. After pushing through terribly thick country, across rivers, up gullies, through towering ravines, they are close. (Not just to their destination but also starvation. Having taken insufficient provisions for the venture, they are reduced 'to digging up potatoes with their hands, without the owner's permission, for it was part of their plan to keep as far away from all habitations as possible'.[20])

In the meantime, on Friday morning, Ned Kelly is assuming his normal position, in the dock of the Kyneton courthouse, staring down his third charge. Once again, the police seem to take an amazingly soft approach, with Sergeant Babington requesting that the accused be discharged on the ground that Murray cannot now be located, and not bothering to present any other evidence. Ned is free to go, and does so, smiling.

'It seems strange,' the *Kyneton Observer* duly observes, 'that not a particle of evidence should have been produced against him but no doubt the police had good reasons for all that they did in the matter.'[21]

Ned does not return to Eleven Mile Creek immediately, but instead, at police expense, is invited to stay on at Murphy's Hotel in Kyneton for the next nine nights – to keep him well out of the way while they try to capture Power. Ned quickly agrees. A bed with sheets! A room with glass windows!

On the Saturday morning, in thick, teeming rain, Lloyd heads off to make contact with Power. Late that afternoon, after a wretched day waiting in the rain, just when the police are beginning to think they have been had, he returns.

'What luck have you had?' they cry out to him. Without a word, Lloyd dismounts, removes a handkerchief from his pocket, unties it and – the gloom of the wet afternoon notwithstanding – displays the squatter's gleaming watch and chain. Lloyd tells them the story. He had indeed made contact with the Quinns, who had reluctantly taken him to see Power's hiding place in the mountains, where the exchange had been made.

Late that evening, Harry Power stops off for a quick meal at the Quinns', and just as old Mrs Quinn is peeling 'pertaters' for supper, she bursts out, 'Harry, I dreamt as ye was took last night.' When Harry ignores it, she tries again. 'Harry, I dreamt as ye were taken; it might be tomorrow.'[22]

Harry ignores her and, after eating, soon moves up the hill to his 'mia-mia' – essentially a shelter made of bark and leaves, which he had learned to make from Aboriginal people.

The difficulty for the police is that Power's lair is in a singularly high and inaccessible spot, and the only way to get to it is on a track that goes past a house filled with a family of notorious convicted criminals, perhaps the original model for the 'den of thieves' of popular imagination. The house is guarded by dogs and has what is effectively a 'guard peacock' upon it – that is, a peacock upon the roof that cries out at the first sign of movement on the track, day or night.

It is Lloyd's suggestion that the police wait another day, allowing sufficient time between his visit to Power and Power's arrest to help to allay suspicion, but neither Hare nor Nicolson will hear of it. Power is close right now, and if suspicion falls upon Lloyd, then so be it – that is the price that Lloyd must pay for his £500 reward. The police insist on departing that evening, Lloyd's protests and the flooded rivers and creeks between them and Power notwithstanding.

'Lloyd,' Hare would record, 'was in a terribly frightened state, and would have given anything to have retracted his agreement, and bolted from us, but we were firm and severe, and threatened to shoot him if he attempted to escape.'[23]

In the meantime, there is a rather delicate matter that Nicolson wishes to discuss with Hare, and eventually he just comes out and says it. 'Mind you,' he tells his junior officer, 'I am senior officer of the party, I must run up and take the lead.'[24]

Really?

Really. It does seem a little odd to Hare, given that he had originally been the one commissioned by the Chief Secretary and Captain Standish to go after Power, but there remains no way to argue with the fact that Nicolson really is his senior in rank and, if that is the way he wants it, then that is the way it must be. 'All right,' Hare eventually agrees, and shortly thereafter the men are on their way.[25]

And yes, the rain does make things exceedingly difficult, most particularly when it comes to getting across flooded waterways in the dark, but on the other hand, after they get lost in the darkness many times, it does allow them to pass the Quinns' house at two o'clock on the Sunday morning without arousing either the dogs or the peacock, all of which must have their heads under cover away from the torrents.

Power's mia-mia, Lloyd has explained, lies up a track, about 200 or 300 yards from a hollow tree with a bed in it.

Impossible in the dark?

Very nearly. But, again, the skills of the black-tracker prove extraordinary. Despite the heavy rainfall, in the dimmest light of dawn, he is able to follow the tracks taken by Lloyd and his intermediary the day before.

'Remember,' Nicolson says one more time for good measure, 'I am in command of this party.'[26]

And, suddenly, the black-tracker has found the hollow tree they have been looking for.

Which direction from here?

Hare asks the black-tracker, 'Can you see any smoke?' on the reckoning that, by this time, Power may well have his fire alight.

'Smoke up along that hill there,' the black-tracker confirms, pointing up the mountain.[27]

They look and can see nothing, nothing at all, but hurry in that direction regardless, leaving behind the quivering and terrified Lloyd, as he does not want to be present for the denouement and immediately disappears. Running now, sensing they are extremely close – and just possibly racing each other – the two senior policemen and Sergeant Montfort keep pushing up the steep hill from the hollow tree, till they can see the source of the smoke themselves, and suddenly there, *there*! From beneath a rough shelter under some gum trees, they can see a pair of legs sticking out.

With an angry wave, Nicolson beckons Hare to go around the back. Unsure whether this is to prevent Power escaping out the back, or, more probably, to ensure that he will not have the honour and glory of personifying the strong hand of the law first placed on the notorious bushranger – not to mention having first claim on the reward – Hare hesitates but a moment.

For no sooner has Hare begun to obey the direct order than Nicolson starts to run towards the pair of feet. Not to be outdone, Hare sprints too, and they fall upon the bushranger simultaneously. (And that's one in the eye for *you*, Superintendent Nicolson.)

Somehow, in all the wild confusion, Harry Power – who has been 'banging' (bush parlance for sleeping deeply) but is instantly awake – manages to seize Superintendent Hare by the head and jam that head into a bag of flour, but the bushranger's resistance does not last long. Once Nicolson grabs hold of his wrist as he reaches for his pistol, Sergeant Montfort quickly seizes Power's other hand, and together they manage to heave the bushranger clear out of the shelter before he has time to grab his weapons. He is howling like a banshee, dragged forth into the mud with the gun of Superintendent Nicolson pointed at him, while Sergeant Montfort puts the handcuffs on.

As soon as Nicolson lifts the shawl from Power's eyes, the bushranger says, 'Hello, Nicolson, have you come from Melbourne?'

'Yes.'

'I have been betrayed . . .'

Nicolson doesn't wish to talk about it.

'Who is the man who rushed me?'

'Superintendent Hare . . .'[28]

And here he is now.

Superintendent Hare comes bursting forth, his coat torn at both shoulders, his face and hair covered in flour, giving him a comical look that his words do not match. For now, frantically brandishing both pistols, he says, 'Stand aside all, I will shoot him.'

'Shoot away, you coward,' Power replies.[29]

It is Nicolson who now re-establishes control, telling Hare to put his gun down, as Power is defenceless, and it would not do to shoot an unarmed man in handcuffs.

But the drama is not over. Suddenly contemplating the reality of heading back to Pentridge, Power spies the black-tracker Donald behind a tree, with his gun pointed, and so rushes at him, partly in the hope of being shot.

'Shoot him, Donald, shoot him, Donald!' Hare roars.[30]

Before anything can happen, however, Power trips and there is no need. Nicolson is quickly at his side and helps him to rise, and, with Montfort's assistance, he forces him down on a seat.

Things calm.

'So poor old Harry's taken!' the bushranger laments. 'But you had to come when I was asleep. If only I had seen you coming!' As to whose fault it is, Harry has no doubt. 'That bloody bird!'[31]

Power is soon told to pipe down, and – after his starving capturers are so rude as to sit down and gorge themselves on his supplies for a large breakfast – the whole party heads off on their long way back to Melbourne, via a night in Wangaratta. As they make their way, Power seems disposed to tell the policemen stories, many of them amusing, of his life as a bushranger, though he frequently interrupts himself when they cross paths with anyone else, to call out, 'They have got poor Power at last, but they caught him asleep.'[32]

Finally, that night at seven o'clock, the police have Power back at Wangaratta, securely under lock and key. Of course, they have no sooner arrived there than a telegram is sent to Melbourne announcing his capture. It is Superintendent Nicolson, naturally, who signs the telegram, and though Hare can barely stand it, he holds his tongue.

Who will get what proportion of the reward remains to be seen, but Hare would later put on the public record that, 'I considered myself organizer of the party. I reckoned that, in case of failure or mishap, the government would have held me responsible and no one else.'[33] (And that is another in the eye for you, Superintendent.)

As to Nicolson, he would be very happy to record of his rival that, after a day's hard ride of 50 miles through the bush to Wangaratta, it was 'Mr Hare the invalid this time, and I stronger than ever.'[34] As a matter of fact, the exuberant Nicolson was now in excellent health, and he would later tell one of his officers, Superintendent John Sadleir, that 'the excitement of [my] tramp after Power seemed to have acted as a cure'.[35]

As to the irrepressible Harry Power, all the way to Melbourne he can barely stop speaking of his adventures, to them, to the crowds that gather at every stop, to anyone who will listen!

Once Power really is back in Melbourne and under lock and key, awaiting Her Majesty's pleasure, Hare, for one, feels he has a feather in his cap to beat them all. Whatever Nicolson might claim, the truth is that Captain Standish had given Hare an important mission, and *he* had executed it. And, as a touchstone that will guide him ever afterwards, it has proved to him the virtues of expeditions into the bush to capture criminals, instead of merely waiting for them to emerge conveniently into the towns.

For his part, Nicolson has taken a different lesson from the exercise. It has confirmed in his own mind the worth of paid informers and spies when it comes to tracking down criminals. And he is particularly pleased to personally receive a warm commendation from Sir James McCulloch, who, as Nicolson would later recount, 'expressed himself very handsomely as Chief Secretary about my conduct in the arrest of Power'.[36]

The news of Ned's release, meanwhile, receives mixed reviews. 'Kelly was discharged by the Kyneton Bench on Friday last,' the *Benalla Ensign* reports on 10 June. 'The *Telegraph* of Wednesday hints that he was let off in consequence of giving information about Power. It is to be hoped that this young man will act with more prudence in future, and beware the fate of Power and . . .'[37]

And have you *heard*? The paper is reporting what many of us have suspected. It really was that Kelly kid, Ned, who snitched on ol' Harry Power. You know, Ned Kelly, the fifteen-year-old who rode with Power for a few months. He is the only one who really knew where Power's hideouts were, and as the kid was already in trouble with the law it had to be him who sold Power out, to get the reward, and to get out of trouble!

The rumours go all over Benalla, and all over Greta and surrounds, for weeks on end – so strong, so extensive, so believable, that for some time after he gets home Ned is practically afraid to show his face in public, even though he's totally innocent of the charge.

In the face of it, the only thing Ned can think to do is to write to Sergeant Babington, the trooper he had become close to while in Kyneton lock-up, and plead for help:

> James Babington 28th July [1870]
> I write you these lines hoping to find you and Mistr Nickilson in good health as I am myself at present I have arrived safe and I would like you would see what you and Mstr Nickelson could do for me I have done all circomstances would alow me which you now try what you con do answer letter as soon as posabel direct your letter to Daniel Kelly gretta post office that is my name no more at presant every one looks on me like a black snake send me an answer me as soon posable.
> Edward Kelly[38]

The good Sergeant does what he can to alleviate Ned's concerns, but the young man will be some time in living down the rumour. As to the offer by Superintendent Nicolson to get him work in New South Wales, Ned has not pursued it, in no small part because he does not feel right about leaving his beloved mother, Ellen.

4 AUGUST 1870, MELBOURNE GAOL WELCOMES ONE OF ITS OWN

Strange how, after a hanging, a combination of exhilaration and gloom lingers on, and so it is on this morning after prisoner Patrick Smith has gone to meet his maker before twenty-five witnesses, for having murdered his wife at Hotham the month before. Always, it takes an event of interest, of substance, to click the gaol out of it, and here it is now . . .

With his own long legal process complete – he had pleaded guilty to three counts of Robbery Under Arms at Beechworth Court two days earlier – it is a familiar figure who now arrives on a spring-cart, with Superintendent Francis Hare beside him, and the cart makes its way through the quickly shut gates of Melbourne Gaol. Yes, it is none other than Harry Power. And there to greet him is the gaol's newly installed Governor, transferred from the same role at Beechworth Gaol a couple of years earlier, John Castieau – a distinguished-looking man in his late forties, with a high intellectual forehead and enormous mutton-chop whiskers.

'How do you do, Mr Castieau?' Power asks pleasantly enough, albeit with a rather patronising nod of the head.

'Well, Power, you have had a long run this time,' Castieau laughs in return.

'I would have had,' replied Power, laughing, 'if they had only let me alone.'[39]

Indeed. Come on inside and rest a while before, this afternoon, we send you and your things back whence you came, over at Pentridge. At least for another fifteen years or so . . . hard labour.

(Yes. As reported in *The Argus*, 'Power had conducted himself with his usual braggadocio in court and told the judge to draw it mild, and he would be lenient with him should they meet each other in the bush when he was liberated . . .'[40] But it seems the judge had chosen not to 'draw it mild' regardless.)

30 OCTOBER 1870, ELEVEN MILE CREEK, THERE IS BALL TROUBLE

A mere creek? Right now, it is more like a raging torrent, as the rain has come tumbling down to the point that it is a wonder the heavens have any more to hold. So heavy is the rain, in fact, and so lasting, that before long all the tracks winding back around the Kelly place are impassable and, as Ned would later recount, 'the ground was that rotten it would bog a duck'.[41]

And not just ducks . . . On this day, Ben Gould, a one-time Nottingham pickpocket, Tasmanian convict and now travelling hawker, has his fine horses hauling his wagon laden with wares when it becomes so badly bogged that there is simply no way to get it moving again, and all he can do is to release the horses and walk onto the Kelly place, where he is invited to stop for a bit until dry weather returns. A couple by the name of Jeremiah and Catherine McCormick – themselves former Tasmanian convicts – are similarly afflicted and set up camp in nearby Greta. They, too, are hawkers, moving from outpost to outpost selling their wares, and are every bit as impatient as Gould to keep moving, most particularly as they are in competition with him.

On this particular morning, Gould is just pottering around outside the Kelly shack when he hears a bell. Looking up, he notes that it is McCormick's horse, sure enough with the bell that horses wear to identify their positions when they are grazing at night. The stallion has clearly got away – for, as a fellow traveller of these tracks, Gould knows both the McCormicks and the horse well – and he is quick to send eleven-year-old Jim Kelly out with a rope to return the horse to the hawkers. (The same Jim Kelly who, just a week earlier, had been arrested with his ten-year-old brother, Dan, for Horse Stealing – spending one night in the lock-up before being released.)

The lad does exactly that, and it is for this reason that Gould is amazed, later in the day, to be confronted by the outraged McCormicks, who, in the presence of both Mrs Kelly and her son Ned, accuse him of having organised to have stolen the horse.

'That's for your good nature!' Ned comments to Gould, far too sassily for Mrs McCormick's liking.

For now this enraged woman whirls on the youngster and accuses Ned of having been the one who had actually stolen the horse, at Gould's behest, to help to pull his wagon out of the bog.

Forget the horse; this time it is both Gould and Ned who are ropeable at the accusation, even if, in the presence of his beloved mother, Ned is careful to keep a civil tongue in his head. The fifteen-year-old forcefully pleads both his own and Mr Gould's innocence, as he has seen the whole thing and swears that Mr Gould had nothing but good intent from the beginning. In high dudgeon, not accepting a word that either young Kelly or the thieving Gould says, the McCormicks take their leave, heading back to Greta. Which is as well, because both the accused are feeling deeply aggrieved.

That afternoon, Ned and his uncle, Jack Lloyd – who, by the by, seems to have come into some money of late – are engaged in castrating some of their poddy calves as well as branding them. (True, branding doesn't totally stop thieves, but it helps.) It is a bitter, bloody business, cutting the testicles out of young sturdy beasts who are none too happy about it, but the ground is soon littered with their little fleshy globes. But, as it happens, it gives Ben Gould, who is watching, an idea. In short order, as a malicious joke, young Ned is dispatched with a pair of calf testicles and a note to give to the childless Mrs McCormick. The thrust of the note is that, given her husband's balls aren't working, he should take the testicles and '**tie them to his own cock [so] that he might shag her better the next time**'.[42]

When Ned arrives at the McCormicks' camp, the lady in question is not there, so – closely observed by Jeremiah McCormick – Ned merely leaves the note and the testicles with his own cousin, Tom Lloyd, with strict instructions to give them to her when she returns. Which Tom . . . nearly does.

For, in fact, he gives them to Mr McCormick instead, who is not long in expressing a rage almost as apoplectic as that of his wife, who now accompanies him as they walk to track down Ned once more, even threatening to call the police over the affair.

In response, Ned does not back down, no matter that he is only fifteen years old and that the man who is shouting at him is a strong and angry adult. 'Neither Gould nor I stole your horse,' he says, from atop his own horse as he glares down at his accuser.

'You are a liar!' McCormick roars back, at least by Ned's account. 'And I could welt you or any of your breed.'[43]

Now, in such a situation it may well be assumed that it would likely be six days' march in any direction before you'd find a fifteen-year-old willing to accept such a challenge, but this'un is a special case. For this'un is, yes, as game as Ned Kelly. He fancies his chances against this angry man and is just starting to dismount when – again, at least the way he would recount it afterwards, in a written explanation:

> Mrs McCormick struck my horse in the flank with a bullock's [shinbone] it jumped forward and my fist came in collision with McCormick's nose and caused him to loose his equillibrium and fall postrate . . .[44]

(Look – it happens.)

What now? Calmly, Ned ties up his horse, ready to resume the battle, but before he can get to it McCormick, with blood now pouring from his nose, has risen and, with his screaming wife beside him, immediately runs off. That night, he sits up at home clenching a loaded pistol, ready should Ned come again, and first thing the next morning goes to the newly opened Greta Police Station to make a formal complaint.

Consequently, just a couple of hours later, a furiously puffing Senior Constable Edward Hall – at sixteen stone, it is not his muscles that are bulging so much as his police uniform – arrives at the Kelly hut with the infuriated McCormicks in tow. Now it is the outraged constable, a notoriously violent and hot-tempered Protestant Irish bully himself, who has only recently faced charges for Assaulting a Prisoner and committing Perjury, who confronts young Ned.

What on earth is going on?

Ned replies in kind, telling the constable that the McCormicks had falsely accused him and Gould of stealing their horse and so . . .

'I hit him,' Ned says reasonably, in the manner of one who takes this as the natural course of things when one is accused of doing something one has not done. (And, in the case of Ned, irrespective of the fact that he has done the same thing dozens of times before, just not this time.) But Ned has not finished. After looking Constable Hall up and down, Ned decides to give him fair warning. 'And I will do the same to you if you challenge me,' says he, to this officer of the law.[45]

10 NOVEMBER 1870, WANGARATTA POLICE COURT DOES ITS BIT

These courtrooms are starting to look awfully familiar to young Kelly. For now, for the fifth time, and fourth time this year, Ned finds himself in the dock, accused of a crime that could send him to prison if he is found guilty. He had been arrested and charged with Violent Assault against Jeremiah McCormick and Indecent Behaviour just five days earlier.[46]

The solid granite building has a spacious interior with wooden benches for the gallery, wooden table and benches for the lawyers and wooden dock for defendants, all placed in deference before the elevated wooden and hooded bench where the judge presides.

This time, the atmosphere is tense as never before, as the case gets under way before Presiding Magistrate Alfred Currie Wills. The most damaging testimony comes from the McCormicks, a couple whom Ned detests for far more than their accusations. In the youngster's eyes, the only thing lower than a policeman is a convict who becomes a policeman, and that perfectly describes Jeremiah McCormick. Oh yes, Ben Gould had told Ned all about it, all right. Back in Tasmania, McCormick had turned his back on his fellow convicts to wield the whip on their backs, in return for easier treatment for himself. Actually, perhaps the one thing lower than that would be a woman who would marry a man such as that, and that woman is now glowering at Ned, as her husband tells the court of all the terrible things Ned has done, including the letter, the testicles and the assault on his good self.

'The prisoner came up to me on that day, about sunset,' McCormick tells the court, in the voice of one whose rage is still incandescent. 'He rode his horse past me, and then came back again. My wife and I were standing by the side of our covered cart. [The] prisoner rode past to talk to his uncle John Lloyd. When he rode back along with Lloyd he rode his horse about five yards from me. He then said, "I will ride my horse over you and kill you bloody wretches." He then jumped the horse upon me, and knocked me down . . . He then rode about 10 yards further away, and said "Come on, you old bastard, and fight me!" He held a stirrup iron and leather in his hand.'[47]

Ned, of course, denies it all. More upsetting still is when his uncle takes the stand. On his oath, Uncle Jack Lloyd swears that he saw 'Kelly try to ride over [Mr] McCormick' and how 'Mrs McCormick threw a stick at Kelly' when he was trying to 'ride over her husband'.[48]

In answer to the charge of Assault, Ned says, 'McCormick charged me with stealing his horse and cover, which vexed me, because I had not stolen anything.'[49] As to the testicles and abusive note, it is in vain for Ned to protest, truthfully, 'It wasn't me wrote 'em nor yet sent it,'[50] for the court seems to set little store by that, once a very pleased-looking jowly Senior Constable Hall claims that Ned had admitted to doing exactly that.

Finally, the judgment is delivered.

Though a complicated sentence, it boils down to the fact that first the family must come up with £60 surety that Ned will keep the peace, to avoid a preliminary twelve-month sentence. Beyond that, at the age of just fifteen, he is sentenced to three months' hard labour for Violent Assault on Mr McCormick and the choice of a £10 fine or a further three months' hard labour for Sending Indecent Letters and for Using Obscene Language to Mrs McCormick. It is a measure of the extreme poverty of the Kelly family and friends that, after just raising that £60, there is simply nothing left to cover the final £10.

Thus, all up, for engaging in a grubby adolescent lark and besting a fully grown adult in a fight after being accused of something he didn't do, Ned is taken off to begin – on 11 November 1870 – six months' hard labour behind the cold granite walls of towering Beechworth Gaol.

Carefully, late that afternoon, the Sergeant takes down the measurements of this broth of a boy standing naked before him. Standing all of *five feet ten inches* tall, he weighs an impressive *eleven stone four*, and the fact that he is happy to throw that weight about in lively fashion is indicated by no fewer than nine scars on his head and body, testament that this is a lad who has not so much engaged with life as crashed into it every bit as often as it has crashed into him. He has *hazel eyes, dark-brown hair* and a *sallow* complexion.

At least, he used to have dark-brown hair. For now, after Ned has been forced to take off all his clothes and have a long cold bath – is there any other kind? – the prison barber takes his shears to that hair and there is soon only stubble left. Ned is issued with the standard prison uniform, complete with moleskins that have buttons down the outsides of the trouser legs so they can be worn and removed without undoing the shackles, before he is escorted by a burly prison guard along the stone floors, past the cells of the other, much older, prisoners, glaring at him through their bars. So this is the young scoundrel who turned informer and put ol' Harry Power back in gaol.

Perhaps sniffing at the sudden stench of so many unwashed men in such a confined space, Ned meets their gaze and keeps walking, until arriving at his own cell – a tiny darkened rectangle of just five feet by ten feet, of which nearly half is taken up by a rough bunk. A small slit in the outside wall lets in air and the cold, while a bucket in the corner is there for his ablutions. This is to be his home until March of the following year, a young man who, more than most, has enjoyed the sheer exhilarating space of the bush and the valleys; has loved the clear air of the ranges; has gloried in the sweet songs of bellbirds in morning and the owls at night. *This?*

However low his emotions at this point, it is not as if others are not celebrating.

The Ovens and Murray Advertiser roundly applauds young Kelly's conviction and incarceration, only regretting that he isn't going to be beaten with a whip into the bargain. Beneath the headline of 'A PROMISING SCOUNDREL', the paper tells its readers the situation:

> The young man, Kelly, who, for a time acted as mate and bush telegraph of Power the bushranger, was brought up at the Wangaratta Police Court on Thursday, for a serious assault on a hawker named McCormick, and grossly indecent conduct towards McCormick's wife. Both cases were clearly proved against the young scoundrel, who received sentences equal to six months' imprisonment in Beechworth Gaol, at which place he arrived last night . . . Twenty-five or fifty lashes would be more efficacious in deterring such as Kelly from crime than a sentence of two or even four years imprisonment.[51]

As it is, even without being whipped, Ned's time in Beechworth is hard enough. For, beyond the loss of liberty, the terrible gruel, the endless boredom of it all, 'hard labour' proves to be just that, with most days starting by the prisoners donning their moleskin trousers, grey coats and large straw hats, throwing down some gruel and then being marched off in chains at dawn to the local quarry to carve out huge blocks of granite to be used in government buildings. Not that every day is like that, of course. Other days, the job is right there in the exercise yard, as they must take their hammers and chisels, from sunup to sundown, to shape granite boulders into building blocks, or break up other chunks of granite in the yard into small pebbles for use on the roads. The work goes five and a half days a week, with Saturday afternoon off for washing, and of course the Sabbath, when the prisoners spend the Lord's day confined to their cells. Young Ned, of course, at fifteen going on sixteen, is still growing, but few regimes could have hardened him as this one does, and he soon earns the respect of warders and even fellow prisoners for his capacity to work, his stamina and strength a wonder to behold . . .

Despite his efforts, however, time continues to crawl by. Day after day, on and on and on and on, each minute drags its weary way forward until enough of them are assembled for another hour to slowly drop away . . . whereupon another desultory, disinterested group of minutes begins to reluctantly gather. While the days pass slowly, the weeks positively crawl on all fours. Ned *aches* to get home.

19 MARCH 1871, SOMETHING HAPPENS TO THE MARE OF MANSFIELD

Like the railway lines they invariably accompany, the telegraph wires that snake across the wilderness – up hill, down dale, across gullies and creeks and up and over whole mountains – are not merely elongated pieces of metal. No, the telegraph wire, as everyone now knows, is the very thing that prevents thousands of tiny communities across the whole continent from being little more than specks of civilisation swirling in a vast wilderness. With the telegraph wire operational, these places are connected, able to send and receive news, capable of turning isolated outposts into outposts only.

The town of Mansfield, for example, just 40 miles south of Greta, is contactable instantly, at the end of the flying fingers of the deeply admired Mansfield telegraph master, the man always resplendent in his uniform of brightly coloured waistcoat, dapper white gloves and cane . . . George Wightman Newland. (Seriously, it is a wonder how fast he can send the Morse, and how quickly he can transcribe incoming messages. We just don't know how he does it.)

Without the telegraph, getting a message to Melbourne is three to four days' hard ride there and the same coming back. What used to take a week in terms of communications back and forth can now be done in mere minutes.

It is for this reason that Newland's position within the community is an important one, a respected one, and while 'Postmaster Newland', as he is known, is very proud to hold it, even then he is still more proud of his horse. A beautiful chestnut mare with a white face and severely docked tail, she has a large 'M' branded on her haunches, 'as plain as the hands on a town clock',[52] and Newland likes nothing better than to be seen riding her.

And that, in turn, is why Postmaster Newland is upset on this morning, when he goes to Maindample Park, about two miles from Mansfield, where his horse is on agistment, to find that she is gone. For the moment, he lives in hope that she has not been stolen and has either simply wandered away and might be somewhere in the nearby bush, or she has just been 'borrowed', as often happens in the area, and will soon be returned.

Either way, it's in the hope of both that over the next few days he ceaselessly searches for her, calls out for her, trudges the hill from dawn to dusk and asks everyone he knows to be on the lookout.

27 MARCH 1871, BEECHWORTH GAOL OPENS ITS GATES

At last, on this cold morning, the heavy wooden gates at Beechworth Gaol open to disgorge young Ned Kelly, with five weeks' remission off his sentence – though he is bound to 'keep the peace' – and he is able to make his way back to the Eleven Mile, to be once more in the bosom of his family. They have missed him terribly and treat him as the de facto patriarch of the family, even though he still is only sixteen years old.

Alas, he has returned to a house in mourning. For, on the day that Ned is released, the baby of his sister Annie and her husband, Alex Gunn, little Ellen, has died. The tiny body is buried in Greta cemetery, and Ned has arrived in time to share his sister's tears of grief. There is darkness in the air.

At least one who tries to alleviate it for the family is the constable on relief duty at Greta Police Station, Hugh Bracken, a thirty-year-old Irishman, now on his second long stint in uniform since arriving in the Great South Land a decade earlier.[53] Having just come from working at Beechworth Gaol, where he had come to know Ned a little, Constable Bracken makes a point of visiting the Kelly home – for he is a kindly soul – and, on this occasion, chats 'with the family in the hope that they would alter their way of living and become law-abiding citizens'.[54]

10 APRIL 1871, THE MANSFIELD POSTMASTER MAKES HIS MOVE

It is time to face facts. It is now three weeks since his mighty mare has disappeared and she is obviously not coming back. Thus, Newland feels he has no choice but to report her as stolen, and so on this day he reports the theft to the Mansfield Police. Where, oh where, can his beauty be?

14 APRIL 1871, ALEX GUNN RECEIVES A VISITOR ON THE WILD SIDE

On this day, there is a visitor at the Kelly selection on Eleven Mile Creek – a heavily bearded, tall man in a moleskin cloak, with the pitiless eyes of a dingo about to savage a sick rabbit. He has come to visit his friend Alex Gunn, but most of the Kelly family already know him well, as indeed do most people in the district, if only by reputation.

For, they don't call the strapping twenty-two-year-old 'Wild' Wright by that nickname for nothing. The only Christian thing about this farmer and horse-breaker from down Mansfield way is his formal Christian name, Isaiah, which is really only used by police and magistrates when they cite his full name and are not referring to him as 'the accused', 'the defendant' or, his most frequent one, 'the prisoner'.

Oh yes, they know Wild Wright all right, perpetually in trouble with the law and the community alike, and known locally as one who is as 'mad as a tiger snake that's been run over by a mob of sheep'.[55]

For relaxation, other men like to hunt or fish, chase women or drink, or all of the above, but not Wild, 'a great bony man with a great bony face',[56] a fair moustache and the fiercest pair of eyes you would ever see. No, his joy is to find a crowded hotel, any crowded hotel, and barge his way towards the bar, shoving the drinkers before him every which way, while growling, 'Men first, dogs come last!'[57]

This, of course, usually provokes a violent reaction, which is exactly what Wild wants. As he is a man capable of fighting like a whirling dervish blessed with ten fists, in an instant an otherwise peaceful scene can be transformed into a hurricane of haymakers, with Wild right in the middle of it and taking on all comers, all at once. As his head is simply a cone of bone, with seemingly little brain inside it to hurt, and his body all bristle and gristle, it doesn't seem to matter how hard they hit him; he does not fall. And he has so many fists flying it really does seem impossible to believe he had been born with only two of them. After all, birth abnormalities run in the family . . .

For Wild's brother, from whom he is rarely separated, is quietly – *very* quietly – known as Dummy, for the fact that he is a deaf mute, capable only of grunting loudly and, yes, fighting. Because of this latter ability, Dummy is treated with respect, even when alone. With Wild beside him, however, he is treated with elaborate respect, because the quickest way of being knocked cold in the whole area is to make fun of Dummy within sight or sound of Wild.

On this occasion, however, Wild is travelling alone, apart from the remarkably beautiful chestnut mare he is riding, which has a white face, a severely docked tail and a large 'M' branded on its haunches.

Having dropped by the Kelly shack to visit Alex Gunn, Wild has stayed on for the night, only to find in the morning that his prize mare, which had been tethered just outside the shack, has gone. Now, whether the mare has got free of her own accord or has been stolen is not clear, but if the latter it is something of a coincidence, because, unbeknownst to Ned – at least as he would ever after claim – the mare is, of course, one and the same horse that had been stolen from the

Mansfield telegraph master a month earlier. (Whether or not it takes a thief to catch a thief remains problematic, but to thieve a thief's thieved horse at least has a certain poetry about it.)

For now, all Wild Wright can do is to take young Ned with him as they search all day around the whole area, hoping for a sign of 'his' mare, but it is to no avail. And as Wright is in a hurry to get back to Mansfield – there is likely someone he has to bash – he borrows one of young Ned's other horses, asking the oldest Kelly lad to keep an eye out for the mare, and if 'you find her, keep her until I can bring yours back'.[58]

As luck would have it, however, only a couple of hours after Wild has departed the mare is found by Alex Gunn and a friend by the name of Brickey Williamson, and handed over to Ned to return, as promised.

Still, as Ned has never in all his born days had the care of such a beautiful horse as this, why do so immediately? He is a young man fresh out of a long stint in gaol, he has a fine horse, and it is a Saturday, so why not dress himself in whatever finery he can muster and head off to the big smoke of Wangaratta, just 18 miles away, to parade his steed to the locals, before handing it back to Wild Wright?

Why not indeed . . .

Ned proceeds to do exactly that, checking in to the Star Hotel, where he is notable over the next few days for riding around and even letting the publican's daughter have a go up on the saddle with him. There is, after all, no reason not to show her off, for she is a beauty.

And so is the horse . . .

Finally, however, after five days of such fun, it is time for Ned to go and find Wild Wright at his place just outside of Mansfield to give the horse back and retrieve his own mare, before getting back to work himself. So it is that, on the morning of Thursday 20 April, as Ned rides across the bridge into Greta on his fine steed, the young man sees Senior Constable Hall, the fat policeman with whom he had first clashed over his fight with the McCormicks, staring at him intently. What can it be?

Turns out, the senior constable informs him pleasantly enough, it is a matter over his bail bonds, which Ned had not properly signed off on at Beechworth Gaol before being released. Would Ned accompany him back to the police barracks to attend to them?

Reluctantly – for he does not like Hall, and is aware that the feeling is mutual – Ned agrees to do so. Yes, it was Hall's testimony that had done him the most damage in putting him into gaol in the first place, but this does sound like a simple matter, so why not go? And yes, too, Hall is also known to be hot-tempered, already in trouble with his own police force, but so what? This is apparently only a small matter of some paperwork, and Ned won't be with the constable for long.

And yet, just as Ned is alighting from his steed at the barracks, suddenly Hall grips him by the collar and attempts to throw him to the ground, as he roars, 'You are my prisoner for horse stealing!'[59]

Mistake. Big mistake. Nigh on eighteen months since his fight with Ah Fook – of which six months have been spent in jail – Ned is now strong enough to turn a block of granite into pebbles, and tussling with a fat constable is no challenge. At this point, it would have been but an easy matter for Kelly to put his foot on Hall's neck, grab his revolver and put *him* in the lock-up, but as his prize mare has suddenly galloped away Ned decides to pursue her instead – allowing the enraged Hall to get to his feet and draw his revolver, shouting a warning at him to 'Stop!'[60]

Ah, but it takes more than a fat policeman with a gun to stop Ned Kelly. For, though the young man does stop, he does not surrender. Instead, he turns and shouts back at Hall to 'Shoot and be damned!'[61]

And, in the end, the constable's colleagues don't call him 'Mad Hall'[62] for nothing. Hall does exactly that and, after aiming at Kelly's head, some 25 yards away, squeezes the trigger of his six-chambered .36 calibre Colt revolver, which is the standard Victoria Police issue. Mercifully, however, no bullet emerges. As often happens with the ageing Colt, it has misfired.

No matter, Constable Hall pulls the trigger twice more, for the same result, even as he walks closer to Kelly to make sure that, when the bullet does come, he will not miss.

'He had me covered,' Ned's likely self-serving account of the episode would run, 'and was shaking with fear and I knew he would pull the trigger before he would be game to put his hand on me.'[63]

In Kelly's view, there is only one thing he can do, and he now does it. When Hall is right upon him with his pistol, the younger man suddenly jumps out of the way, managing in the process to grab Hall by the collar.

Now, what he desperately wants to do is to give Edward Hall the thrashing he so richly deserves, but therein lies a problem. For Ned knows that to strike him just once will mean that those who have provided the bond money for his release will lose that money cold – and he will have to return to gaol. Instead, Ned contents himself by throwing the constable to the ground again and again, 'and let him take a mouth full of dust . . . as he was as helpless as a big goanna after [feasting on] a dead bullock or horse'.[64]

Continually, Ned picks the fat constable up before throwing him down into the dust, and, though the policeman yells in outrage all the while, he is powerless to do anything to stop the enraged Kelly.

Now, for a change, instead of letting him back up, the youngster compounds the constable's humiliation. 'I straddled him and rooted both spurs onto his thighs [and] he roared like a big calf attacked by dogs.'[65]

Now, Ned grabs the constable's hands and forces them to the back of his neck in an attempt to make him let the revolver go, 'but he stuck to it like grim death to a dead volunteer'.[66]

Of course, by this time, something of a crowd has gathered around the two men, and from his dusty mouth Hall now loudly croaks to them for help. No fewer than seven men – effectively the butcher, baker and candlestick maker, with extras from the workers building O'Brien's Victorian Hotel over yonder – answer the call, but still Ned Kelly is not intimidated.

'I dare not strike any of them as I was bound to keep the peace or I could have spread those curs like dung in a paddock . . .'[67]

As it is, once the men fall upon him, Ned is subdued just long enough for Constable Hall to hit him over the head five times with his gun, pistol-whipping him. To the policeman's horror and amazement, however, still this does not stop Kelly, or even seem to subdue him, and though his head is soon 'a mass of raw and bleeding flesh',[68] still the fight has not left him.

Finally, however, the sheer weight of numbers – seven men on one adolescent – means that they are able to drag him to the police cell, with Ned bleeding all the while.

So much so, in fact, that a few hours later, when Ellen Kelly and Wild Wright arrive, much of the story of what has happened is still plainly visible in the dust of the Greta main street, with splotches of blood spread not only across it but also 'spoiling the lustre of the paint on the gate-post of the Barracks'.[69]

While Constable Hall is relieved, in one sense of the word, to have Kelly under lock and key – and to have some extra evidence, in that when the young man was searched it was found he had a purse in which a piece of paper noted differing horse-brands – he soon wishes to be relieved in the other sense. For, always, the thing about the Kellys and their cohorts is that, if you have one of them under nominal control, you soon have to deal with all the rest and . . .

And what is that? It is shouting. Violent shouting. From many young men, just like Kelly. Hall looks out the window of the lock-up and pales as he sees 'a dozen of the prisoner's confederates . . . shouting about the place like wild savages saying they would take him out of the camp'.[70]

Whether or not Wild Wright is one of them is never proved, but it is likely.

Hall double-locks all the doors and dashes off a note to his immediate superior in Wangaratta – recently promoted, since the successful collaring of Harry Power – Sub-Inspector William Montfort:

> *I have arrested Young Kelly after a desperate row with him for horse stealing, I struck him on the head with the revolver in self defence while arresting him, he is now in the lock-up, please send a doctor and two constables I cannot open the lock-up until the latter come you will oblige me if*

> *you telegraph the occurrence to Supt Barclay.*
> *E Hall 569 S.C.*
> *Let the doctor come at once E. H.*[71]

Mercifully, once he receives the note from one of Hall's breathless underlings, Montfort is not long in sending one of his constables in support, while also telegraphing for a constable from Benalla to rush to Greta. As to the doctor, he, too, arrives from Wangaratta and proceeds to put nine stitches in Kelly's scalp, forehead and left eyebrow, succeeding finally, after two hours – by stitching off each little artery – in stopping the bleeding.

Dr James Hester would end up charging eight guineas for his services, occasioning a stiff note from Victoria's Chief Medical Officer, Dr McRea, to Captain Standish, asking that his men be less damaging to their prisoners, as it is becoming expensive:

> *If the Chief Commissioner concurs I shall feel obliged if he will caution Hall about recklessly causing medical expenditure the next time he breaks the head of an Irishman.*[72]

The following morning, it is with great care that Ned is handcuffed and, with his legs trussed together and linked to the cuffs by rope, then tied to the seat of a cart, he can be taken to Wangaratta for further legal processing. Even then, it is with grim satisfaction that Ned notes both that Hall is too scared to sit beside him and that the policeman who does, Constable James Arthur, laughs at his colleague for his cowardice.

While it goes against the grain for Ned to like any policeman of late, for Constable Arthur, Ned is almost happy to make an exception.

1 MAY 1871, WANGARATTA POLICE COURT, NED HAS HIS DAY IN COURT

In a courtroom once more, just one month after having been released from Beechworth Gaol, with His Honour Police Magistrate Alfred Currie Wills again presiding, Ned – who is now known around the traps as 'Young Kelly, a former mate of Power's'[73] – faces a committal hearing on the charges of Horse Stealing and Receiving.

It does not take long, as Constable Hall, Postmaster Newland and local labourer James Murdoch give their evidence. What is needed, of course, is for Wild Wright to appear and tell the truth: not only had Wright personally stolen the horse, but he had specifically not told Ned Kelly that it was stolen, meaning that the young man is not guilty on either count. After all, why would he, Ned Kelly, parade a recently stolen horse through both Greta and Wangaratta if he had known it was stolen? Ned knows what to do with stolen horses, as he has stolen dozens by this time: you secrete them, you sell them, but you do *not* parade them before the traps. Yes, he is guilty many times over of the crime with which he is charged, but he is nevertheless innocent of this particular crime.

But, to Ned's growing rage, of Wild Wright there is no sign, and he is still at large. The man whose testimony could have saved him has not stepped forward to tell the truth. Of course, Ned could have told the whole story and told the police it was Wild Wright who had stolen the horse, but, given his recent experience in being accused of having dobbed in Harry Power, this is not really an option. Ned would rather go to gaol first.

Which is as well . . .

For now, he is committed to stand trial at the next Court of General Sessions, to be held at Beechworth on 2 August, and he heads back to Beechworth Gaol.

The Ovens and Murray Advertiser, for one, strongly approves of both the decision and the manner in which the young ruffian has been brought to heel:

> A CANDIDATE FOR THE GALLOWS
> Edward Kelly, better known as Young Kelly, an accomplice of the bushranger

> Power, and who is generally credited with having given the information that led to the latter's arrest, was again brought up at Wangaratta Police Court on Monday, and committed for trial on the charge of having stolen a horse the property of Mr Newland . . . Kelly's arrest was very cleverly effected in the neighbourhood of Greta, by Senior Constable Hall, and it was not until that officer had tried conclusions between the handle of his revolver and the thickness of the young scoundrel's skull, that the latter agreed to surrender.[74]

2 AUGUST 1871, NED ON TRIAL FOR HIS FREEDOM

Ned's trial goes in much the same manner as his committal hearing had gone. Most interesting, however, is the testimony of Constable Hall, who swears on the Bible that, Your Honour, just an hour before arresting Kelly, he had, 'seen the *Police Gazette* containing an intimation that the horse was stolen'.[75]

This is more than surprising, given that Ned had been arrested on 20 April and the horse had not been gazetted as stolen until 25 April. In fact, it is perjury pure and simple, committed in an attempt to cover the fact that Hall had acted on suspicion only. If Ned Kelly was on a mount as fine as that, it must have been stolen.

As to the charge that Ned had personally stolen the horse, this, at least, is exposed as a lie when his legal counsel, Frederick Brown, calls 'Mr Thompson, governor of Beechworth Gaol, who deposed that the prisoner was confined in gaol and had not been released till March 27th'.[76]

Then another witness is called who testifies that he personally had seen Wild Wright take the mare from Maindample Park, saying, 'Hold on, old man, I want this,'[77] before putting his saddle and bridle on the horse and riding away.

As to testimony of Ned being seen riding the Mansfield Postmaster's horse, there is no lack of it, though one witness, ex-convict James Murdoch, gives a damaging account of a conversation with Ned, recalling how, when he asked Ned where he had got the mare he was riding, the young man had replied, 'I got her on the cheap . . . I bought her from the Plenty,'[78] referring to a well-known market for stolen horses. (Ned, in fact, had said no such thing, and that is not where he got the horse from. It will later be alleged that Murdoch was bribed £20 by Constable Hall to give such evidence. Murdoch will later be hanged for murder in Wagga Wagga.)

After Magistrate Henry Armstrong instructs the jury to retire to consider their verdict, it takes them only an hour. On their return, Ned is found guilty of feloniously receiving a horse. Shortly thereafter, in successive cases on the day, both Isaiah Wright and Alexander Gunn have their own trials. Wright had been nabbed in early May, shortly after an enormous pursuit on horseback in which Constable Hall and another trooper had fired a total four shots at him for no result. His trial goes better. After all, as Postmaster Newland himself acknowledges, in the thick Lancashire accent left over from his place of birth, 'borrowing' a horse is quite standard in the region and, 'It is not a very extraordinary thing about Mansfield to use a horse in the bush, without meaning to steal it.'[79] And so Wright is not found guilty of stealing but is found guilty of a lesser charge – while, for his part, Alex Gunn is found guilty of stealing another horse from a local by the name of William Adair.

The sentences of Ned Kelly, Wild Wright and Alex Gunn are read out together, as *The Ovens and Murray Advertiser* would report:

> Edward Kelly found guilty of feloniously receiving a horse, was sentenced to three years with hard labour in the Melbourne gaol.

> Alexander Gunn convicted of horse stealing, was also sentenced to three years imprisonment, with hard labour, in the Melbourne gaol.
>
> Isaiah Wright . . . was, for illegally using a horse, sentenced to 18 months imprisonment with hard labour.[80]

Somehow, even though Wright is found to have been Illegally Using[81] the horse, rather than receiving it as Ned had done, the older man is given a sentence half as heavy. (At least, however, Ned does not suffer the additional punishment, suggested by Beechworth's *Ovens and Murray Advertiser*, that he be lashed like the sodomite who had recently been convicted by the circuit court.)

Ned begins his sentence at Beechworth, only to be transferred to Pentridge several months later. This is more to do with what work needs to be done at their respective quarries than any issue of punishment, and, now eighteen years old, Ned – otherwise known as Prisoner 10926 – must settle down for the long haul. And there is no rest for the wicked – at least not comfortable rest. The closest the prisoners get to a bed is simply a coconut mat and a blanket, and even then they remain in chains. Strict rules govern all behaviour, and those who break them are given either a flogging, heavier irons to wear and bear, or solitary confinement on bread and water. Every three months, they are allowed one visit or one letter. At least, in a case of rare humanity from the gaol, the authorities also provide an hour a day's schooling and access to the gaol library – two activities of which Ned avails himself whenever able and not too exhausted from his work. The other, small blessing is that Ned is regularly visited by Father Charles O'Hea, the Irish priest who had christened him all those years ago, and together the two pray in the young man's cell, before the good father takes Ned's confession.

For prisoners like Ned, the key difference of being at Pentridge is that the work at Point Gellibrand quarry is hotter, harder and more hideous still than at Beechworth quarry, with the warders more severe.

WINTER 1873, LIKE FATHER, LIKE SON

So overcrowded is Pentridge with the burgeoning criminal class that Ned ends up spending most of the cruel winter of 1873 on hulks moored in Port Phillip Bay – ships not unlike the one that had brought his late father, Red, to Australia three decades earlier. In all that time, it seems that the Kelly family has not moved on far – like father, like son, in chains in the bowels of a ship.

After stone-cold Pentridge, there is something almost comforting about living in the whitewashed wooden cells of the hulk. Ned and his 116 fellow convicts are given square meals, a clay pipe and a daily ration of tobacco.

Each morning, the men are taken ashore and put to work in one of the artillery batteries that line the shore of Port Philip Bay. There, Ned is able to use and expand his skills in stonemasonry, as the prisoners are set to work in the quarries cutting bluestone, building the seawalls and further fortifying the batteries, which are positioned and manned to thwart any invasion plans the French might have from their base in New Caledonia, the Germans from Samoa and the Russians from *everywhere*.

It is gruelling work made harder by the biting gusts of wind that whip off the Southern Ocean and freeze the prisoners' grasping hands as they doggedly mould them around their heavy mallets.

Later, as spring blooms and the winds warm, Ned is rewarded for his good behaviour and transferred once more to live in one of the batteries onshore. He's now a member of the prisoner elite, as he receives a shilling a day and tea and sugar with his daily rations. The hard work continues, but Ned's endurance is unwavering, his discipline improving, and, thankfully in these finer conditions, the end of his sentence and freedom loom on the horizon.

2 FEBRUARY 1874, NED HEADS NORTH

In a now familiar scene, on this morning at Pentridge – known to its inmates as 'The Bluestone College' – Ned is about to graduate once more. After signing his discharge papers, he is given back the civilian clothes he had been arrested in three years before, and though they are now very tight on him, as he has grown so much, he is escorted to the massive front iron gates and allowed to leave as a free man who has done his time. Of course, he quickly heads for home, to the Eleven Mile.

How things have changed! When Ned had gone to gaol all the way back in 1871, he had been transported on the first part of the journey in a cart. Now that he is returning home, he is able to go all the way to Glenrowan, just four miles from home, on the train. The Melbourne to Wodonga line had been completed the year before – sadly passing by Greta, and leaving it as a backwater – but already plans are well underway for building a spur line from Wangaratta to Beechworth.

And, of course, it is not just in the building of the railways that things are transformed. When Ned comes through the door of his home at Eleven Mile Creek, to be smothered in the hugs and kisses of his family, it is a moot point as to which has changed more – him, or the situation at home.

For, as they are all quick to note, he is not the lad who left them, the bare-cheeked one still growing into himself. No, this'un returns to them as a man, a good inch and a bitty taller at a towering five foot eleven inches-plus, nearly a stone heavier, and with the beginnings of a full black beard that will soon stretch to his barrel chest – a beard that will never leave him ever after – bulging muscles and a certain hardness of approach that only prison life can bring.

As to everyone at home, nothing is as it was, most particularly not his sisters. Maggie is a beautiful young sixteen-year-old who married Bill Skillion the previous September and already has a four-month-old baby daughter, and, as to Kate, she is a very pretty ten-year-old and no longer the wee one she was when he had left for prison. And even young Grace is now eight.

But there is no Annie. Ned's beloved elder sister had died of complications while giving birth to her second child in November 1872, a child that herself had died from diphtheria just over a year later, in

December of 1873. Her body now lies next to her baby's, no more than 50 yards from the Kelly house, 'in a grave dug by her Uncle Bill, under the willows on the banks of the Eleven Mile Creek'.[82]

Ned misses his sister desperately and feels fury towards the man who had impregnated her in the absence of her husband, Alex Gunn, who had of course been in prison with Ned for horse theft. That man is Constable Ernest Flood, who – after the interregnum of another constable found to be hopeless – had succeeded Senior Constable Edward Hall at Greta when Hall had asked for a transfer after his episode with Ned. In fact, not only had Flood – good-looking, twenty-nine years old and married – seduced Ned's sister by buying her a new dress, among other things, but then, once she began to 'show', he had ceased all further association with her. That is, with the exception of coming to the house not long before Annie had died. But that had only been to arrest Ellen Kelly on a charge of 'receiving a saddle into [her] possession knowing it to have been stolen'.[83]

Ned's rage at Flood is all the greater for the fact that, when he goes to round up the horses he had owned before entering prison, they're all but gone! 'Of over thirty head of the very best horses the land could produce, I could only find one when I got my liberty,' he would later recall,[84] claiming that 'Constable Flood stole & sold the most of them to the navvies on the railway line. One bay cob he stole & sold four different times.'[85]

Worse, it is too late for restitution now. It is the nature of the railway work that, once the line had been completed, the navvies had scattered to the four winds, while Flood had judiciously had himself transferred to Oxley, some ten miles away.

One day, Ned vows, the account with Flood will be settled.

And Ned's next youngest brother, Jim? The family gives Ned the news they have deliberately kept from him all this time. A year earlier, Jim had been convicted of stealing and selling cattle and, at the age of just fourteen, 'and appearing before the court undefended by counsel',[86] had been sentenced to no less than five years in prison – one of the most severe sentences for one of that age in Victoria ever recorded.

Nor is Ned surprised to hear that James Dixon,[87] the man who had 'received' the stock, had not even been charged, likely because he was a squatter and the twice former Mayor of Wangaratta.

In passing sentence on Jim, the judge had even said he only regretted he could not give the second-eldest Kelly brother a flogging, too. If that is not persecution of his family, what is? Jim had entered Beechworth Gaol just two months after Ned had gone to Pentridge, and the older brother now understands why Jim had never come to visit him.

And, of course, it had been the way of the Kellys. When one male is in prison, it is the duty of the next oldest to take the weight, to chop the wood, cart the water, protect the house, look after the women. Just as Ned had done when Red Kelly had been taken to prison, and Jim had done when Ned had gone to prison, so too had their brother Dan carried the extra weight for their mother with Ned and Jim in prison. This is why Dan, now nigh on thirteen years old, suddenly looks all grown up. Though not as large or as strong as either of his brothers, he is wiry and tough, and has nearly as much rage as Ned at what the police continue to do to their family.

As to Ned's beloved mother, Ellen, forty-one years old, after she had become pregnant and given birth to a baby girl, named Ellen, towards the end of 1871, the fearfully fickle Bill Frost had abandoned her. Bereft, Mrs Kelly had successfully sued Frost for maintenance of their daughter, no doubt pushed to do so when she found out that he got married to another local woman within months of leaving her. Little Ellen had died in early 1872 of diarrhoea.

At the beginning of 1873, Mrs Kelly had taken up with another man, and already has a three-month-old baby girl to him. And her name? Ellen, of course. A tall, good-looking Californian with light brown whiskers, George King, at twenty-three, is just a few years older than Ned. Well, if it is Ellen's wish to be with this man, that is good enough for Ned, and only two weeks after being released from prison he stands with Bill Skillion as witness as Ellen marries George in the home of the Reverend William Gould of the Primitive Methodist Church in Benalla. The now forty-two-year-old Ellen indulged in the timeless and time less practice of fibbing about her age by recording herself as being thirty-six years old.

True, it is an odd thing to have a stepfather that close in age, but, on the other hand, King at least seems to be a regular kind of man – he likes stealing and fighting, and has spent some time in prison for having stolen horses. He is one of us.

AUTUMN–SPRING 1874, WORKING FOR THE MAN

Now, it is not every man released from Pentridge whose first thought is of honest work, but in the case of Ned Kelly he at least quickly finds such labour when he is employed as an axeman at a sawmill run by James Saunders and Richard Rule over Moyhu way, a stone's throw from Greta, just six miles to the east.

After all, Ned is as strong as a Mallee bull, has always been skilled with an axe in hand, and can work hard all day long. His principal job now is felling massive red gums and stringybarks, which the bullock teams then drag away to the mill. As ever, from sunup to sundown, Ned goes at it, his heart pounding, his breath coming steadily, his torso glistening as his body continues to strengthen through all of the work, the fresh air of liberty, and better tucker than wretched gaol gruel.

As it turns out, such a strong body, moulded to such resilience, is not simply an end in itself but very useful for another task that Ned has long had in mind: beating the bejeesus out of Wild Wright. (Even if Wright is now practically a member of the Kelly clan, as not long after he had emerged from prison – doing just six months, instead of the eighteen months he was sentenced to – he had married Tom Lloyd's oldest sister, Bridget.) For the truth of it is that Ned has done nearly three hard years in gaol for something he hadn't done, for something that Wild Wright had done. And yet Wild had never spoken up, never saved him from it.

It is another account that Ned has longed to settle, and, suddenly, here is his chance. On this particular Saturday afternoon of early August, Ned is just having a drink at one of the Beechworth area's sixty-one pubs – the mighty Imperial Hotel – when he sees Wright, drinking over there by the bar. That's him, the one with a twisted trail of angry men behind him, still not daring to protest too loudly.

'Men first, dogs come last!'[88]

Wild Wright!

Never one to hide his light under a bushel, Ned takes it upon himself to push forward and now tells Wild a few things that have long been on his mind. And the news, doctor, is not good. Wild does not take the diagnosis well – no one speaks to him like that – and the pub quietens. This is going to be interesting. If a fight does break out, it will be between the man said to be the toughest, meanest and most viciously violent bastard in all of North-Eastern Victoria, and probably beyond, and young Ned, who, though not thought to be particularly violent, at least to those who are not traps, is certainly already a young legend for his sheer strength.

But not here. That is not the way it is done in these parts. There is nothing wrong with a major fight, but not in here, thank you very much. Instead, the publican invites the two men, and whichever patrons would like to watch, to take their fight out the back, onto the small patch of grass right by the bubbling Spring Creek.

The nineteen-year-old Ned Kelly is six foot neat and twelve stone, without an ounce of fat on him. The twenty-five-year-old Wild Wright is six foot one inch in height for thirteen stone, and is equally all muscle and gristle. Wild definitely has it over Ned for reach, but Ned's strength and endurance are already the stuff of wonder.

In short order, the clientele of the hotel – for no one wants to miss it – file out the back, holding their nobblers and beers and licking their lips in anticipation. Now, as this kind of thing has happened many times before, the publican even has rough boxing uniforms ready, and, after stripping down in the back shed, both men emerge – can you believe it? – dressed in 'silk shorts over long underpants and undershirt with lightweight shoes'.[89]

Of course, they will be fighting bare-knuckle, the way real men do, whatever the recent and nonsensical Marquess of Queensberry code might have to say about it. Here in the bush, what rules they do have look to be rather more inspired by the Marquis de Sade.

First, the publican draws 'the scratch' – simply a line in the dirt – and now the two combatants must stand on opposite sides of it. Whatever happens, they must come back to the scratch, and the end of each round has nothing to do with time but is all to do with whether one man draws blood from the other or is knocked down. At this point, each man's 'picker-up' has thirty seconds to get his man back in shape ready for the next round, and the combatant has eight seconds to get back to the scratch before it begins again. All is in readiness . . .

As the crowd presses close, emitting a guttural roar that comes not just from them but from ages past, the two begin to shape up and the fists begin to fly. Wright is vicious, aiming blow after blow at Kelly's nose as, with his experience, he know this is the quickest way to not only demoralise a man, as the blood bursts forth, but also weaken him if the blood flows copiously enough. Yet Ned is fast, and nimble, swaying out of the way of most of Wild's furious flurries, before crashing in with his own body blows to Wright's ribs. Most amazingly, even when Wright does connect with him, Ned does not flinch but comes back with his own blows!

From both sides, blood is drawn, as are knockdowns, but, for round after round, as the sun begins to sink, neither man gives an inch, as the ground around the scratch – redrawn many times by the publican as their boots scuff it away – becomes sprinkled with red, and the odd tooth.

It is the best fight anyone has ever seen, and the ongoing roar of the crowd brings others from far and wide, as the crowd gets bigger still and so does the roar, meaning the crowd gets bigger still! When any particular blow sends one or other man reeling, of course he falls back into the pressing circle, who push him back, even as the other charges forward. Fifteen rounds in, the honours are fairly even, as both men have battered the other mercilessly, and it is a wonder to all that they can keep going.

But what is this? As subsequent rounds go on, it seems as though it is Ned who is getting on top, returning to the scratch quicker, inflicting more damage, while it is Wild Wright who is blowing steam like a train going up the long hill to Beechworth. It couldn't be, could it? It couldn't be that this nineteen-year-old is about to get on top of the most feared man in the land? For now it is Ned who is vicious, as he gets on top, smashing into Wright's face again and again, shattering his nose, bursting his lips, closing both his eyes to the point that he can barely see, and smashing into his ribs. It is only Wright's extraordinary strength and bountiful courage that keeps him standing at all.

Finally, the death knell . . . After a horrific twentieth round, more like a slaughter than a fight, Wright tries to come back to the scratch but just can't and instead waves a bloody hand of defeat.

Ned has bested him! Wild Wright has been beaten!

Cheers and beers. Acclaim for both men back in the hotel from all who have seen this fight for the ages.

If Wild is down on his defeat, he is also amazed, realising he has been taken down by a better man, who is only nineteen! 'He gave me the hiding of my life . . .' he would later say.[90]

And for that, as so often happens in the strange world of brutal men, Ned Kelly has also gained the respect, loyalty and even affection of the man he has bettered – a respect and loyalty that Ned returns in kind. Their battle has bound them. In fact, Wild will soon become nothing less than a *devotee* – even if he is about to go to gaol for three years for stealing a fine thoroughbred belonging to the Byrnes of Moyhu.

Their feud is over and they will proceed from here, as they once were – allies. But Ned, who is now well on his way to becoming a legend to his people, will always be the leader.

Chapter Three
WORKING FOR THE MAN

They seemed to have a very miserable way of living, and the general impression was that what they got they did not get by honesty.
Sergeant Ernest Flood on the Kelly clan

People who live in large towns have no idea of the tyrannical conduct of the police in country places far removed from court; they have no idea of the harsh and overbearing manner in which they execute their duty, or how they neglect their duty and abuse their powers.
Ned Kelly

1875, IN NORTH-EASTERN VICTORIA, THINGS TIGHTEN

Economic malaise is by its nature more drought than storm. There is no crash, no thunder, no flash of angry gods, and there are very few dramatic moments. Instead, it creeps, it worsens, it dries up and suffers, it tightens and slowly suffocates. Where once a man sauntered, he now gets gaunter, the lustre fades from both gold and hearts as shops start to empty, the banks foreclose and once merry eyes start to gaze with thousand-yard stares.

At this time, real drought begins to creep across Victoria. As the lack of rain affects both crop production and livestock raising, selectors struggle to make payments, squatters lay off workers and all of it is happening as the once-bountiful gold mines around Beechworth begin to run out.

The one industry that is able to sustain itself, at least temporarily, is the building of railroads financed by government money, and for Ned, who wants to escape his infamy around Beechworth after flogging Wild, it is a fortunate thing as he is able to find work with the sawmillers Heach and Dockendorff near Mount Killawarra – some ten miles to the north-west of Wangaratta. The mill provides sleepers of ironbark and planks of red gum to build the railway line and its attendant bridges from Wangaratta to Beechworth.

Those not able to find work locally must do what a lot of the young men of Greta do – including Ned's fourteen-year-old brother Dan and his cousin Tom Lloyd – and every spring take part in an exodus up Riverina way. On the runs around Jerilderie and beyond to the Darling River, they find work shearing, harvesting, fencing and labouring before making the return trek to Greta come winter, where they again scrape together whatever work, or other money-making activity, they can.

In the meantime, on the plains below Mount Killawarra, though not much of a mixer, Ned is pleasant enough and for the most part he is left alone, and stays out of trouble. He has, after all, made it known, 'I would rather face the gallows than go to gaol again.'[1]

Sometimes, however, trouble follows him.

One day at the Killawarra races, Ned is minding his own business when a man who recognises him as the conqueror of Wild Wright decides to try his luck and so picks a fight, as a circle of drunken revellers quickly gathers around them. It takes, however, more than a wild haymaker to fell Ned Kelly, who easily sways away bemused. So the fellow swings once more. Ned sways away again and, losing patience, tells the man that he must settle down, 'or else, I will make it a caution to you'.[2]

The fellow is not listening and swings once more. Ned's eyes flash crimson with rage and, a man possessed, he thrashes his attacker to within an inch of his life.

It is time to leave, to start again somewhere.

Ned has made one strong friend in his time at Killawarra, a fellow by the name of Walter Power. In late autumn, the two decide to head off on the 200-mile ride to Gippsland, where they find work fencing and in a sawmill.

However, missing home and family, in early spring of 1875, Ned decides to head back to Eleven Mile Creek, where he picks up whatever honest work he can, from the many skills he now has: fencer, farmer, splitter, axeman, quarryman, stonemason, builder, bullock-driver, sawmill worker and horse-breaker.

And he is impressive. One local youngster by the name of Joseph Ashmead, for whom 'Ned and Dan Kelly were the playmates of [his] early childhood',[3] would never forget when Ned was breaking a horse in for his father, and the horse got away . . .

'We chased [the horse] over hills and through swamps,' he would recall. 'I could not help thinking what a fearless fellow Ned Kelly was.'[4]

It is at sawmills, however, that the work is most consistent, and Ned finds work with James Saunders and Richard Rule at a newly opened mill at Burkes Holes, four miles north-east of Greta. The mill is thriving in its service of the second part of the Wangaratta to Beechworth railway line, which is now under construction. Ned is hired as nothing less than overseer of the whole mill, so highly do they regard both his work ethic and his leadership abilities. There, he again makes good friends with another worker, John McMonigle – a fair-haired, Irish-born lad with four kids at home, including newborn twins – and again he settles down reasonably well.

Not that it is easy, for all that.

For, try as he might to live a law-abiding life, Ned's past follows him. There is just something about Ned Kelly that makes people notice him, a strength, a self-sufficiency, a certain sadness even . . . but once they start talking about him, it is not long before his time in gaol comes up, his months spent as 'Harry Power's mate', and once that is known it means suspicion tends to attach itself to him whenever anything is awry. Frequently, he finds himself suspected of crimes he did not commit – and all of it is happening in an environment where crimes are being committed all around him, as the entire region and his own family is in turmoil. Just in the last five years, Ned's mother, Ellen, has been charged with Furious Riding in the Township of Benalla,[5] Stealing a Saddle,[6] being Drunk and Disorderly and Using Obscene Language, and Assaulting Mrs Clancy at the Star Hotel, Wangaratta,[7] while Dan's offences have ranged from Illegally Using a Horse to Stealing a Saddle, and Jim has been pursued for Illegally Using a Horse and Stealing Cattle.[8]

True, there are plenty of families in the district that are also often on the wrong side of the law, but they do not get close to the Kelly clan, who are always more trouble to the police than a wagonload of Kilkenny cats, and more prone to zebra suntans than anyone else in the entire district . . .

25 AUGUST 1875, CONSTABLE LONIGAN GOES TO THE DARK SIDE

Quite what makes Constable Thomas Lonigan do it is not clear, perhaps not even to the constable himself. But somehow, not long after local labourer William Johnson gets off the train from Melbourne at Violet Town, it is apparent that the working man is so drunk he must lie down . . . and it is Constable Lonigan who soon arrives to take him into custody. Once back in the darkened police yard, however, Lonigan delivers to the drunk 'a slap to the side of the head, and when he fell, kicked him', causing severe injury.[9] Constable Lonigan – soon also to be in trouble with his superiors for playing cards in a public house while in uniform – is charged with Assaulting a Prisoner and prosecuted by Superintendent Nicolson, fined two shillings and sixpence and temporarily transferred to another police station. Had a civilian done the same thing, it is almost certain the punishment would have been at least six months in gaol – or even longer if it was one of the Kelly clan.

SPRING 1876, FRANKSTON, NOT QUITE A MEETING OF MINDS

Some 50 miles down the shoreline of Port Phillip Bay, which runs south from Melbourne to the Mornington Peninsula, lies the small village of Frankston. Generally, it is a happy hamlet, and yet not so benign that there is not the occasional need for judges to visit and preside at Frankston Court, to sort out disputes, criminal activities and the like. Which is why Charles A. Smyth is here on this evening, at the Bayview Hotel, enjoying dinner before heading to bed upstairs, and holding court on the morrow. The forty-eight-year-old, Irish-born, English-educated lawyer works as a prosecutor who occasionally sits as a judge, a role he takes seriously.

Now, quite how Judge Smyth comes to meet young Alexander Fitzpatrick on this day is not documented, only that the two take an all but instant shine to each other. Fitzpatrick, just on twenty years old, works in the stables of the hotel, and it is likely they meet when he takes over care of the judge's horse.[10]

What is certain is that, on this occasion, Fitzpatrick confides to the well-connected Judge Smyth that what he really wants to do is to join the Victoria Police Force. He is fit, he is able, he is a superb horseman and he is in need of a steady income, from a job with a little more prestige to it than boundary riding and being a stablehand. Smyth – a notable Christian evangelical, aware of his duty to reach out with the hand of friendship to all – is impressed with the lad's enthusiasm, not to mention his charm. And, as a matter of fact, given that he knows Captain Standish, the Chief Commissioner of the Victoria Police, very well, he promises to put in a personal recommendation to him that young Alexander be so employed.[11] Fitzpatrick is filled with hope that at last his luck has changed. The two exchange details, and they continue to talk into the night.

3 OCTOBER 1876, OF WHIPS AND WELTS, HAMMER AND TONGS AT THE MELBOURNE CLUB

It is less a question of *in vino veritas* than *in vino inebriatas vulgaris*. For, on this evening, in the glorious ground-floor dining room of the mighty Melbourne Club, Captain Standish with two others happens to be at the table of Captain Robert Machell, formerly of the 62nd Regiment and now a fellow well known for his position as His Excellency Victorian

Governor George Ferguson Bowen's aide-de-camp. The wine has been flowing freely as these well-known citizens play cards, when, out of the blue, Captain Standish suddenly asks the forty-year-old Machell if he had been poaching up country, referring to the shooting trip that Machell had just returned from.

In response, Machell makes some light remarks, whereupon Captain Standish, after another long swig of wine, unaccountably glares and unleashes a verbal hammer blow, saying pointedly, 'At least my hand did not tremble as yours did, like an aspen-leaf, when shooting pigeons lately . . .'

Machell, who prides himself on his manly pursuits, is outraged, and promptly challenges the pompous policeman to 'ride cross country, shoot, and in fact, to compete with me in any manly exercise'.[12] For I will whip you, Captain, every time! (And he means it, actually, just see if he doesn't . . .)

The whole dining room falls quiet as the row escalates, and it is Standish who takes umbrage, calling Machell – who has, after all, only been elected to the club the year before and is therefore an upstart in these surrounds – 'a damned offensive beast'.[13]

Typical Standish, what? Known, according to *The Age*, as 'the "show" man of Melbourne, he is generally deemed bumptious, and sometimes insolent in his manners'.[14]

But this time he has gone too far. For when Machell demands an apology and does not receive one, he storms out, warning as he goes that if he does not have a written one by the following morning, a real whipping, a thrashing, in fact, will be in order.

And, sure enough. 'Is there a letter for me?' he asks the clerk upon his arrival at the club the following morning.[15]

There is not.

Striding to the Breakfast Room, where he knows he is sure to find Standish, he spies the cur having his kippers. Standing over Standish now, Machell thrice asks him for a written apology, and thrice is refused.

And so, as promised, taking up the horsewhip from behind his back

– the very one he has brought for the occasion – Machell does indeed give Standish the sound thrashing he so desperately deserves. First, he strikes him about the face and then about the body as uproar ensues. To defend himself, 'Captain Standish thereupon seized a large pair of tongs used for placing billets of wood upon the fire, and was preparing to defend himself when some friends interfered . . .'[16]

29 SEPTEMBER 1876, NED REACHES THE END OF THE LINE, AS MOB RULE TAKES OVER

It will be a great day for the entire region – the opening day of the railway line from Everton to Beechworth, described in the local paper as 'one of the most remarkable lines in the world . . . the iron road ascends nearly the whole of the distance between Everton and Beechworth, winding round and up hills, the end of an ordinary train being frequently out of sight of the engine'.[17]

Alas, with the end of the construction of the railway comes the end of the work at the Burkes Holes sawmill, and Ned must again look for work at a time when there is very little, most particularly at a time that he has a charge of Stealing a Horse once more hanging over his head. There is the possibility of more work with Saunders and Rule down Gippsland way to provide timber for the railway being constructed there, and Ned's great friend and leading hand at the sawmill, John McMonigle, even heads off early with a small advance team to get the sawmill machinery established, but, for the moment at least, Ned hangs back.

First, he must deal with the Horse Stealing charge. He presents himself to the Oxley Police Station on 19 July, the honest man that he now is, and his case is finally dismissed a couple of weeks later in early August, thanks to the testimony of several witnesses.[18] In the last week of August, his brother Jim is at last released from gaol, while his next youngest brother, Dan, risks going to gaol when he is charged, on the last day in September, with Stealing a Saddle. Dan is soon committed to stand trial for the charge in February the following year.

As the patriarch of the family, Ned feels strongly protective towards both brothers and decides to take them up to a place he knows in the Wombat Ranges. It is a hideaway that he first came across back in the days when he rode with Harry Power.

In those days with Harry, they had several times passed through a place called Bullock Creek, right by Stringybark Creek, high in the Wombat Ranges – those heavily timbered mountains that suddenly rise like a clenched fist of defiance just over ten miles south of Greta and continue for some 25 miles of thrusting ranges and plunging valleys all the way to just six miles north of Mansfield, all bordered by the King River on the eastern flank.

And deep within this area, unsettled and all but entirely unknown to the outside world, Ned leads his brothers to a small, flattish basin beside Bullock Creek with an abandoned prospector's hut upon it. So it is that the three Kelly brothers, accompanied by a couple of Ned's friends from the mill, get to work repairing the old shack, as well as making a beginning at putting in a dogleg fence to fashion a paddock for their horses and later, perhaps, whatever cattle they can muster . . . or steal. A pleasant summer is passed before they head back to Greta once more, in February of 1877.

At Greta, during their absence, both the ongoing drought and economic downturn have tightened their grip, and tensions between squatters and selectors flare to remind everyone that there is a land war still raging. The malaise of 1875 has crept into 1876 and spilled over to 1877, as gold yields continue to dwindle and government efforts to encourage farming and implement land reform splutter and choke at the hands of reluctant squatters, whose wealth is also crumbling in the sparse economic climate.

Ned, now with the mature eyes of one who has had plenty of time in prison to reflect on his situation, followed by three years travelling the country and working the land, which has shown him this war up close in many regions, understands it all better than he ever has, and is enraged by it.

Two particular tactics that the squatters use to keep the selectors down are 'dummying' – putting up their own people to select the land ahead of genuine selectors, before transferring it back to the squatters – and 'peacocking', also known as 'picking the eyes out of the country',[19] which is to say securing the best of the newly available land that lies along the rivers and creeks. Of course, the squatters are happy to leave the dregs of the dregs for those genuine selectors who want to make a new start, as such land offers precious little opportunity for successful cultivation. In the end, this land will most likely revert back to the squatters' original pastoral leases, so, in a cruel twist, it serves the Establishment well to leave the marginal land for the struggling selectors to do what they can to improve it, before the squatters get it back anyway. And, when disputes arise, who is it that sits in judgment? All too frequently, it is those same squatters, sitting on committees and as Justices of the Peace! (Oh yes, the squatters want to steal the land itself, but still squeal like stuck pigs if anyone takes one of their sheep or calves just to feed their families.)

Inevitably, more and more selectors had to do what Red Kelly had done a decade before – let the devil take the hindmost, while they take the hindquarters. Across the region, stock thefts are up, as is horse stealing, and the pressure on the police from the squatters to do something to stop it is overwhelming.

And into all of this rides Ned Kelly, the gaol bird, one-time Power's mate, and part of the infamous Kelly family with his two gaol-bird brothers. They are all obviously due for extra scrutiny, and whereas in places such as distant Gippsland and even up at Killawarra Ned had enjoyed relative anonymity, now, back in Greta after the stint at Bullock Creek, it is not long before he feels persecuted by the police, who seem to suspect him of every theft going. And not *all* of them are his . . .

Of course, it is not just Ned who is affected. For all over Greta there are young men similarly suffering the attention of the police and obliged to live on the other side of the law to live at all. Their alienation from the constabulary is compounded by the fact that just about none of these native-born lads joins a force that is almost exclusively born in

England or Ireland. In the eyes of the law, the natives are the problem only, and certainly not part of the solution.

Well, these young native Australians are forging a force of their own. There are so many of them, and they are so tightly bound to each other, they even start to go by the rough sobriquet of 'the Greta mob'. (Though not one of them knows it, the term 'mob' comes from the Latin term '*mobile vulgus*', or 'excitable peasants', and that describes them exactly.)

Oh, you can pick them all right, always moving as a pack and frequently found being loud and boisterous at race meetings, at bars and local dances – everywhere from Beechworth to Benalla and back again to Greta via Wangaratta and having plenty of fun all the way. See how they tend to wear bright sashes around their waist for no good reason? Then there are the long 'larrikin heels' on their riding boots. Those mark them as, whatever else, horsemen, and give them a distinctively peculiar gait, a flamboyant swagger.

'Yet it was the larrikin shirt,' one roughly contemporary account would run, 'which seemed to occasion most surprise. It was white; it was often clean. Unlike the impurity of life so often assigned him, the larrikin affected a shirt which would not conceal the length of use. Collarless as a rule, the front was held by a few "gee-gaw" studs . . . The jacket which the average larrikin wore gave him a jockey's look. Without a waistcoat, his coat hung freely about him, and his wobbling walk made his shirt sag out over his trouser's top in a rather untidy fashion.'[20]

In the case of the Greta mob specifically, the signature is their cabbage-tree hats tilted way down to partially obscure their faces from inquisitive police, and even the chin straps of those hats not going under the chin at all but under the nose. (From a distance, it often makes it look as if they have fabulously upturned moustaches.) That's the Greta mob – or at least that's the Greta mob you can see who aren't in gaol, for at any given time there are usually quite a few of those, and, in fact, many of the mob's strongest bonds are formed there.

One of the mob is the nineteen-year-old Tom Lloyd Jnr, Ned and

Dan's cousin, who has developed into a fine horseman and a good-looking fellow who loves nothing better than supporting his kin, even on the other side of the law. Another one is Dan Kelly's great friend Stephen Hart, who lives with his parents on a 53-acre selection on the outskirts of Wangaratta and another of 230 acres just a few miles away at the base of the Warby Ranges. Stephen has also been in his fair share of trouble with the law, most recently when Wangaratta's finest, Sergeant Arthur Steele – a well-built man with an enormous moustache that, from a distance, looks like a large, downturned mouth sandwiched 'tween a large nose and pointy chin – had arrested him for Illegally Using Horses.[21] As well as the time he and Dan have spent gambolling and rambling all over the countryside, the two have done time together inside, something that has forged a bond between them as solid as the iron bars on their gaol-cell window.

Rising seventeen years old, Hart is not a big lad, but he makes up for it with a certain ferocity, an eagerness to always prove himself to the others in the mob, most particularly in the realms of horsemanship, where he is superb – appearing as a jockey in races around Beechworth, Benalla and Wangaratta, even once winning the Benalla Handicap. Often, he is seen atop a mount hurdling the railway gates at Wangaratta as if those gates are just a foot high, as he makes his way to and from his home on the Three Mile.

And then there is the twenty-one-year-old Aaron Sherritt, who is also always in trouble with the law and has just been released from gaol – always a matter of increased prestige among the Greta mob. He hails from Sheep Station Creek, just up from the Woolshed Valley – the last a picturesque spot four miles north-west of Beechworth and named for the fact that its first gold deposit was found near an old woolshed. You can always pick out Sherritt by his swagger, his sway, his tight pants and tighter shirts, the fact that in his case his larrikin heels add a couple of inches to his already impressive six-foot height. Although he is from a relatively respectable family – his father even once having been in the Irish Police Force in the old country – there is just something about Aaron that lends itself to larceny. He is bored by normal life, does not want to earn an average wage, lead an average existence, kowtow to average people who think that is their due simply because they are richer than he is. *He* wants to be rich, too, and is always looking for the angle, the deal, the quick theft that can bring easy money.

With the exception of Dan Kelly, who simply does not like his air of superiority, or the fact that he is a Protestant, Sherritt is popular all around and right in the heart of the Greta mob. Soon enough, he brings another significant figure into its ranks. That is his great friend from childhood days onwards, Joe Byrne, a twenty-year-old who comes from an even more prosperous family than Aaron's, but who has also just been released from gaol for possessing meat for which he could not account. He and Aaron had been lucky to escape the more severe charge of Stealing Cattle as he had 'cut the brand from the hide of the beast', but it had been a close-run thing.[22] Like Ned and Dan Kelly, Joe's father is gone but, before dying in 1870, had established a quite well-to-do dairy farm at Sebastopol in the Woolshed, where he and his mother, the well-regarded Mrs Margret Byrne, live, together with many of his brothers and sisters.

Joe is good-looking, intelligent and better educated than most of the Greta mob, as he had always had an aptitude for reading and writing. He is also 'quietly spoken' and 'not flash'.[23] He, along with Sherritt, has grown up on the diggings in the Woolshed Valley and is an expert at sluicing for gold from creeks. Growing up in an area that is heavily populated by Chinese workers, Joe had not only picked up their passion for smoking opium but also speaks a rough kind of Cantonese. (Whether he is more eloquent after smoking opium is not obvious, but he certainly *thinks* he is.)

Joe so loves the Chinese ways, in fact, that among them he is called '*Ah Joe*', and it is even said he looks 'half-Chinese'. It is not quite that his eyes are distinctly elongated rather than round, but there is something about them, to the point that he is sometimes affectionately known as 'bullet eyes'.[24]

He stands five foot ten inches and is a solid fighter and great horseman, though his primary skill is as a marksman. Though of dubious veracity, it is even said he is capable of throwing coins into the air and shooting them out of the sky with his pistol. Where do such coins come from? Mostly horse and cattle thieving; Joe is not particular.

Perhaps Joe's primary recommendation for soon being right near the centre of the Greta mob is that the man at that centre – Ned Kelly – clicks with him from the first. Ned respects Joe's skills as a fighter, marksman and bushman, not to mention his obvious bravery and refusal to be cowed, but most deeply admires his more thoughtful approach . . . a rarity among the Greta mob. In some ways, Joe is a little like Ned too in that he is just that little bit apart, his own man, and Joe is one of the few in the mob who does not go in for the flashy dress of the others.

While Ned can be impulsive, Joe thinks things through and is not afraid to tell his friend that he has thought of a better way. Both have a gentle ease with women – for stepping out with each other's sisters is another feature of the mob, an area where Ned is a quiet success. They are both 'natives', born of the Australian soil and proud of that fact, while also honouring their Irish Catholic roots. They both smoke pipes, and, in long conversations going well into the night – on love, life and what it's all about – Ned develops the strong view that he can learn from this man, his friend Joe Byrne.

For his part, Joe feels exactly the same kind of deep admiration and affection for Ned, without ever presuming to challenge his leadership of the group. No one would.

For Ned, as they all know, has done serious time in prison, is the only man to have beaten Wild Wright in a bare-knuckle fight, is a superb horseman and, more importantly, horse stealer, a most skilled bushman, a dead-eye-dick marksman with any kind of firearm you could hand him – even when on horseback at full gallop – a great tracker and hunter, most charismatic with the ladies, and the toughest, roughest, strongest and most legendary confronter of the traps they have in their number. He rode with Harry Power!

If the Greta mob have natural enemies beyond whichever policeman happens to be closest, they are rich squatters such as James Whitty and Andrew Byrne – two of the largest landholders in the district, who have begun to band together with other squatters to give cash rewards and other gifts to constables who catch thieves. It is not simply that these men, and their brothers and other relatives, are wealthy and have vast tracts of land; it is that even that is not enough for them, and they use their weight and connections to crush the poor selectors down, which sticks in the craw of the locals. All that land, all that wealth, and still they screw the poor selectors to the wall with their peacocking and dummying – and their impounding of the selectors' animals when they wander on their often unfenced land.

As Ned himself would later recount, it is people like Whitty and Byrne who, 'not being satisfied with all the picked land on the Boggy Creek and King River and the run of their stock on the certificate ground free and no one interfering with them paid heavy rent to the banks for all the open ground so as a poor man could keep no stock, and impounded every beast they could get, even off government roads'.[25]

Those squatters, of course, see it differently and are becoming ever more angered by having to constantly deal with these unwashed hordes of selectors and labourers who are now causing so much trouble. For who are they, truly, most of them, but mere johnny-come-latelys, disaffected diggers and insolent youths who want land now that the easy pickings of the gold has run out and there is no easy work available? As men who created this wealth by first settling in these parts, they look no more kindly upon the diggers wanting parts of that land than they would a swarm of insects streaming over one of their wife's favourite roses.

It is with this in mind that, in mid-February 1877, Whitty and Byrne give formal notice, published in local newspapers, that henceforth they would:

> IMPOUND all cattle and other animals found trespassing thereon or SUE the owners thereof for trespass, on or after the 20th of February, Inst.[26]

Oh, and they mean it, too, soon enforcing that notice – something that incenses Ned still further. 'If a poor man happened to leave his horse or bit of a poddy calf outside his paddock,' he would later rage, 'they would be impounded. I have known over 60 head of horses impounded in one day by Whitty and Byrne all belonging to poor farmers they would have to leave their ploughing or harvest or other employment to go to Oxley. When they would get there perhaps not have money enough to release them & have to give a bill of sale or borrow money, which is no easy matter . . .'[27]

28 FEBRUARY 1877, THE TRIALS AND TRIBULATIONS OF THE GRETA MOB

It is not that the remarkably church-like confines of Beechworth Courthouse is a second home to the Greta mob, but certainly it is not that big a surprise that on this hot summer's morning – 'the oppressive heat of the weather . . . the day was sultry in the extreme'[28] – Dan Kelly is finally due to come up on his charge of Stealing a Saddle, just before Joe Byrne and Aaron Sherritt must answer charges of 'unlawfully wounding'[29] and severely injuring a Chinaman, Ah On, who had taken a grim view of them swimming in his dam.

Of course, Ned is there in support of them, and he gives sworn testimony in Dan's defence that in fact his brother had bought the saddle from a man named Roberts for £1 and Ned, personally, had made every effort to find this man, alas, to no avail. When three other witnesses swear the same, Judge Hackett, for one, seems impressed, and even says to the jury, 'I do not see why the prisoner is here at all.'[30]

Clearly, the jury agrees, for within ten minutes of retiring to consider their verdict they have come back with a firm 'not guilty', rendering Dan a free man once more, and he can head home. For Ned's part, given that Joe and Aaron's case has been postponed until the morrow, he decides to head off to the Moyhu Racing Club's annual meeting.

For . . . why not?

Racing might well be the 'sport of kings' in other countries, but not here in the colony of Victoria. Here, it is the sport of kings and paupers alike, of the rich man, poor man, beggar man and thief, all drawn together by a common passion for the horses. (And most of them can vote! On this day, *The Wangaratta Dispatch* would report, 'Mr Graves, who is one of the candidates for Delatite was on the ground, and might be seen actively pushing his fortunes with the farmers and others who were present.')[31]

On this day – as a fierce storm starts to brew overhead, the air pregnant with distant lightning and imminent rain – Ned Kelly is not surprised to see the wealthiest squatter of them all, James Whitty, moving among the heaving crowd. He is acting, along with his partners in peacocking, the Byrnes, as steward for the day's events. Ned Kelly glares at the rich squatter with more than his usual native malevolence, because of late he has heard that Whitty has been putting it about that he, Ned Kelly, had stolen his prize bull.

Now, the usual form for a poor man such as Ned – who is, after all, no less than a gaol bird – would be never to confront a man so high and mighty as James Whitty.[32] But Ned is not of this ilk. Whitty is a far richer man than he is, certainly, and no doubt a better educated man. But neither of those things makes him a better man. And, yes, Ned has stolen many horses and cattle in his time, but as it happens he hasn't stolen this *particular* bull, and so now walks up to Whitty and accosts him.

Momentarily, Whitty is disconcerted. For he has glanced up to see a heavily bearded, powerful-looking man with a spark in his eyes that broadcasts danger.

'Why,' Ned asks him, 'have you been saying that I stole your bull?'

Surprised, but perhaps impressed in spite of himself, Whitty replies. 'I have found my bull,' he says. 'I never blamed you, though my son-in-law Farrell told me that he heard that you had sold the bull to Carr.'

Ned is dissatisfied with the denial, for he knows that Whitty has been saying just that, but he is left with little to do but enjoy the last race.

As he rides back to Beechworth, the leaden clouds burst, and the rain comes down in a thick deluge as thoughts swirl in Ned's head, in rough tune with the tumultuous winds he battles through. On the upside, for the Greta mob at least, the next morning, back in Beechworth Court, Joe and Aaron are found not guilty of Assaulting the Chinaman.[33]

Over the coming weeks, Ned cannot seem to buck his gripe with Whitty and is all the more dissatisfied when, not long after this encounter, he hears that he is now being blamed for 'stealing a mob of calves from Whitty and Farrell which I knew nothing about'.[34]

As Ned would later recount, 'I began to think they wanted me to give them something to talk about.'[35] (After all, hadn't that been Ben Hall's famous line? 'May as well have the game as the blame.')[36]

12 MARCH 1877, NED PUTS THINGS TO RIGHTS

It is an irony of the human condition that, while it may take a thief to catch a thief, few men are more aggrieved than a thief who feels he has been thieved *from*. A case in point on this day is when Ned finds out that, as bad as their word, Whitty and Byrne had indeed impounded fifteen horses that had been found grazing on the roads going through their properties, and two of them were bay mares, with a filly each, owned by Ned and his cousin Tom Lloyd. According to the law of the land, the men now have until 7 April to pay the fine and the expenses or the horses would be sold at auction.

Unless there is another way?

There is!

For, on the next evening, the two cousins break the lock to get into the pound on the edge of the village of Oxley and take back what they view as rightfully theirs. They don't take any old stock, just theirs – with the bonus that Whitty and Byrne can't help but know who has taken the horses, even though they will never be able to prove it.

With this larrikin act, Ned abandons his 'bold attempt at reformation'[37] and starts to live up to his more notorious reputation, which had been moulded for him since his days as 'Power's cub'.

Though they know exactly who took the horses, Whitty and Byrne unofficially herald Ned's return to the life of a horse thief by publishing an official notice in *The Ovens and Murray Advertiser* of the horses' removal from the pound yards. Funnily enough, in the same issue appears a most intriguing interview with Harry Power in Pentridge that has been reprinted from *The Argus*. Power opens up to one of the colony's popular journalists of the day, the man known as The Vagabond, about his and Ned's exploits. And, of course, still believing it was Ned who sold him out, ol' Harry doesn't hold back, noting, 'Young Kelly . . . was no good . . .'[38]

Perhaps. But not a bad horse thief. The coincidence of the Power interview and the announcement of Ned's first crime in three years – well, his first known crime in three years – neatly heralds Ned's return to the life of horse stealing, and to showing aggressive indifference towards a system of justice that seems to him to be systematically *unjust*.

And isn't it fun, and lucrative . . .

The whole exercise pleases Ned and Tom so much that, one way or another, it is not long before they, with other key members of the Greta mob, enter into what Ned is pleased to call 'wholesale and retail horse and cattle dealing'.[39] Soon, George King, Ned, Joe and Aaron – together with Wild Wright and Brickey Williamson, among others – have developed a system whereby they manage to steal and sell horses practically on an industrial scale. After gathering as many as a dozen, they first set about rebranding them, in a manner taught to them by George King, who had learned it in California.

If, for example, a horse had the brand of *H* on its near shoulder, the boys would manage to turn the *H* into a *B*, 'by getting a pair of tweezers, pulling out the hair, to make a *B*, and then prick the skin with a needle dipped in iodine'.[40] As they had come to learn, the iodine burns the horse's skin in such a fashion that, for the next month – which is all the time they need – the B has the appearance of an old brand like the H. Now comes the next challenge: that is, to give their stolen horses some legitimate paperwork. Finding a squatter well removed from the area where they had stolen the horses, and in a region where they were unknown, they would ask permission to briefly put the horses into his stockyard, saying they had someone who was about to buy them – that someone being one of their own gang. Ned and Joe prove to be particularly good at pretending to be young, wealthy squatters – yet another common talent that forges the ever-stronger friendship between them.

While 'the squatter' watched, the 'sale' would take place at an agreed price, at which point the real squatter would be asked to be involved in the drawing up of a receipt on which all the (new) brands could be entered, and the squatter could witness the whole transaction, frequently affirming that fact on the squatter's own printed letterhead. Now, with re-branded horses, and 'proof' that the animals were legitimately bought, the mob would move on to the next region and sell them, before stealing some more horses while there, and so on.

For many months, as Aaron Sherritt later explained, they proceed on a rough circuit, making 'raids on horses from about Wagga to Albury, take them a back track to Melbourne, and on their return pick up a number of horses in Victoria and take them over to Wagga or Albury for sale'.[41] Sometimes, they even go as far out west as Jerilderie, in the New South Wales Riverina.

When staying closer to home, another method is to have the horses impounded before buying them back at cheap auction prices, together with the priceless clean certificate of title from the Poundkeeper.

APRIL 1877, AT GRETA, THE INSPECTING SUPERINTENDENT PAYS A ROUGH VISIT

Inspecting Superintendent of Police Charles Nicolson is now based in Melbourne as the second-ranked policeman in all of Victoria after Captain Standish – even though he is still not close to him. And Nicolson does not like untidiness, and still less slothfulness. 'In charge of the uniformed police,' as one writer would note, 'Nicolson was a strict disciplinarian, insisting on spick-and-span uniforms, rigid routine and military methods, including much drill and saluting of him by the lower ranks.'[42]

Something that he likes still less than slovenliness is constant criminal matters growing like weeds with nothing being done to arrest them – or the criminals involved. And he particularly dislikes report after report coming in from outraged squatters because their horses and cattle have been stolen. In North-Eastern Victoria, so lawless are the people, the rate of this theft is running at three times the rate of the rest of the colony.

Which is why Nicolson is in a towering rage on this day, as on this tour of the area, inspecting all the stations, he makes an unannounced visit to Greta Police Station. There is the dishevelled Constable Hugh Thom in a 'soiled dirty jumper, dirty breeches, and a crushed uniform hat, beard untrimmed',[43] with his horse getting fat through no exercise in patrolling the area. He is clearly doing nothing to stop the lawlessness all around him, a large part of which is obviously coming from the Kelly clan. Nicolson quickly takes a mental note to replace Thom.

Nicolson is also a man always more comfortable seeing things for himself than merely reading reports, so he heads out to Mrs Kelly's homestead on the road back to Benalla to have a look at the environment this troublesome family comes from. He finds an old wooden hut – little more than a shack – with a bark roof, on a piece of rough and only partly cultivated ground.

Knocking on the door, he is reluctantly admitted to the hut by a barely civil Mrs Kelly and is frankly appalled by the squalor and poverty on display. There are no internal walls – just five rough rooms, 'divided . . . by partitions of blanketing, rugs, &c'.[44] Neither inside the house nor on the land is there a man to be seen, and the oldest ones there after Mrs Kelly are two girls, said to be her daughters, both in their mid-teens.

'They all appeared to be existing in poverty and squalor,' Nicolson would report to Captain Standish of his visit. 'She said her sons were out at work, but did not indicate where, and that their relatives seldom came near them. However, their communications with each other are known to the police . . . Until the Gang referred to is rooted out of the neighbourhood one of the most experienced and successful mounted constables in the district will be required in charge of Greta. I do not think that the present arrangements are sufficient.'[45]

The present arrangements rely on the slovenly, unshaven and disorganised Constable Thom in Greta, plus the far more organised and energetic Sergeant Arthur Steele – a twenty-year veteran of the police – who took charge of the Wangaratta Police six months earlier and who, Nicolson knows, does his utmost to keep as strong an eye on the Kelly crowd as he can, despite not living in Greta and only having limited resources.

Nicolson finishes his visit convinced that something more is necessary, and it is with this in mind that he issues a directive. Choosing his words carefully, he tells the local troopers generally, and the officer in charge of the district specifically, that, 'without oppressing the people, or worrying them in any way . . . [you] should endeavour, whenever they commit any paltry crime, to bring them to justice, and send them to Pentridge even on a paltry sentence, the object being to take their prestige away from them, which has as good an effect as being sent into prison with very heavy sentences, because the prestige these men get up there from what is termed their flashness helped to keep them together, and that is a very good way of taking the flashness out of them.'[46]

Now, quite how the police are to 'send them to Pentridge even on a paltry sentence' without oppressing the Greta mob is not explained, but the upshot is the same. From now on – and notwithstanding that at the time no member of the Kelly family is facing charges – it is official police policy to look for an excuse to put the family and their cohorts behind bars, to take the flashness out of them, to give them a public lesson, to 'bring the Kellys in on any charge' and 'root the Kellys out of the district'.[47]

All the police need is the right opportunity.

In June, though not in Victoria, Jim Kelly is arrested for stealing a couple of horses in Wagga Wagga and – in the traditional Kelly manner – fiercely resisting arrest afterwards. Though giving his name as 'James Wilson' to hide his relationship with his infamous brother, Jim is shortly thereafter convicted and, after only ten months out of gaol since his last release, is sentenced to four years' hard labour, beginning in Berrima Gaol, before being transferred to Sydney's Darlinghurst Gaol.

Steve Hart is another to fall foul of the law at this time, arrested by Sergeant Steele in July on a combination of charges of Horse Stealing and Illegally Using. He is sent to Beechworth Gaol for twelve months.

20 AUGUST 1877, FLITTING THIEVES IN THE NIGHT

Grunts in the moonlight. Whinnying. Softly tramping feet. The sound of leather on horseflesh and small metallic clinking as bridles are thrown over eleven fine steeds. For it is, of course, Ned and his men, helping themselves to some of the most valuable horses in the land, on the fine property of Myrrhee, and quickly getting away.

Of the 280-odd horses that Ned Kelly steals in his time, it is not that these eleven horses stand out as the best, or most lucrative – though they are worth a small fortune of £170.[48] They do, however, give him the most satisfaction, because six of the beauties belong to James Whitty, while three are owned by his bastard son-in-law, John Farrell, and two by another squatter. In the months since their confrontation at Moyhu racecourse, Ned has continued to nurture his hatred of Whitty as the prime example of what is wrong with the ruling class.

It is this class of men, along with a complicit police force – taking extra money from the squatters – who drive the poor man to stealing, and vindicate, even sanctify, the mob's actions. Whitty and his lot had it coming when 'Farrell the Policeman stole a horse from George King. And had him in Whitty and Farrell's Paddocks until he left the force.'[49] Well now, Ned and his gang of the moment have Whitty's horses, and it is with great satisfaction that they are able to drive them north, first across the mighty Murray to a little, isolated settlement in New South Wales called Howlong. Here, they place them in a paddock on a German settler's property and set about altering their branding from the iconic W of Whitty's stock. Just two days later, after the gang have sold the best of the beasts, they drive the remaining six out of the paddock and back across the border, to a property at Barnawartha, just south of the Murray River, and sell them to two German settlers, William and Gustav Baumgarten, for the princely sum of £44.

17 SEPTEMBER 1877, BENALLA, NED CROSSES PATHS WITH THE WRONG CROWD

It is very strange, all things considered. For, in his entire long list of crimes and misdemeanours – caught and uncaught – never once had Ned been drunk and disorderly. As a matter of fact, he'd never been drunk. And yet, on this afternoon, he'd just been having a couple of drinks at a hotel in Benalla with Constable Alexander Fitzpatrick – a rough and ready fellow who, six months earlier, had been granted entry to the police force thanks to the patronage of Judge Charles Smyth, whom he'd met in the Frankston pub – when he can suddenly barely think straight. Ever after, Ned will be sure that his drink has been 'hocused', spiked. Next thing he knows, he is outside, trying to stay upright in his saddle, as his horse wanders over a footpath.

And who should be there to arrest him? *Nun udder dan Conshtable Fitshpatrick.* At least, he thinks it is. And, no matter that to this point Constable Fitzpatrick and Ned Kelly have been practically friends. For, like Ned, Fitzpatrick is in his early twenties, solidly built, a most accomplished horseman and something of a rogue, who could just as easily have been, like Ned, making money on the other side of the law.

Luckily, so publicly drunken is Ned, and so disapproving is the local police hierarchy of him and his family, that Fitzpatrick knows there will be great kudos in taking him in – and so he does. Fortunately for him, so out of it is Ned that it is a relatively easy matter to lead him into the police station and lock the cell door.

The following morning, however, when Ned has awoken like a bear with *two* sore heads, and is now convinced that his drink was tampered with, things are not so easy. He has a face like a thundercloud about to burst, and it is because of this that Sergeant Whelan, who had received Ah Fook's complaint about Ned nearly eight years before and had never given up on following the Kellys' moves, decides it might be as well to get some help in marching him to the local court house, 300 yards down the road.

Ned is let out of the cell, closely watched by Sergeant Whelan, Constable Lonigan, Constable Fitzpatrick and Constable Day. The trouble starts when Fitzpatrick suggests they put 'Darbies' on Ned, slang for the British firm Darby, which makes handcuffs.

But Ned is not interested.

'I'll go quietly,' he yells, 'but you won't put the Darbies on me without a fight!'[50]

And Ned is as serious as a bite from a brown snake. For, though he has four burly policemen surrounding him, still he fancies his chances of making a successful bid for freedom, and, after knocking over two of the troopers and pushing aside the other two, he makes a break for it. Though a big lump of a lad, he is extraordinarily fast, and before the police can gather themselves he is well away, and all the troopers can do is set off in hot pursuit, shouting as they go for others to bring the youth down.

Now, though it is a brave man who would put himself in the way of the rampaging Ned Kelly, some pedestrians at least manage to knock him sideways as he tears down the muddy street, allowing the troopers to catch up somewhat, and soon enough it is all Ned can do to duck into King's bootmaker shop, a weatherboard cottage just across the road from the courthouse. The shop has no rear door as he had been hoping, so Ned is suddenly trapped, allowing all four policemen to fall upon him, joined by the enraged shopkeeper. Still, the five men can't subdue the twenty-two-year-old. So strong does he prove to be, and so violent is his resistance, 'knocking them down like ninepins as fast as they came up',[51] that all six of them career all over the shop, as shoes, sheets of leather, lasts, awls, police helmets and punches are sent flying.

Ned is so strong and so angry it proves impossible to subdue him long enough to get the handcuffs on him, as he continues to thrash wildly. And it doesn't even stop when Ned's trousers are practically ripped off him. The falling of the trousers, however, does present another opportunity, and Constable Thomas Lonigan is not long in taking it. Driving his hand down to Ned's groin, the trooper grabs the young man by the part of the anatomy that defines him as exactly that, the part popularly known in the Australian vernacular as 'the family jewels', and exerts every ounce of force he has in him. Lonigan twists, he squeezes, he pulls so hard it is every bit as if he is a thief intent on ripping those jewels from their natural resting place.

Ned, of course, roars with fury and agony, and bucks like the totally out of control wild thing he is, throwing the other troopers off him like fleas off a raging dog – though still Lonigan holds on. Up and down Ned goes, and from side to side, twisting, threshing and lashing out with every limb, as men and now tables full of shoes are sent flying, but nothing the youngster does will make Lonigan – holding on like a man trying to break in a bucking bronco – let go. And, of course, the other troopers are quick to jump back on Ned, compounding the agony, though still he does not give in, causing the men in uniform to be ever more vicious in turn, as the whole bootmaker's shop continues to be turned upside down.

Fitzpatrick, arms outstretched and head way back out of the way of Ned's fists, clutches at Ned's right foot and finally latches onto the sole of his boot, holding on for dear life.

Perfect! For now Ned draws his foot into his haunches one more time, bringing the constable with it. In two moments of frozen horror, first Fitzpatrick feels the heel of the prisoner's boot rip clean off – damn, but boots are made ordinarily in these parts – and then Ned's spring-loaded leg draw back another inch, clearly about to go off like a one o'clock gun.

BOOM!

For, with one more mighty roar, Ned kicks out, lifting Fitzpatrick momentarily off the ground as he is sent 'sprawling against the wall'.[52] Enraged in turn, the other troopers fall upon Ned once more, though Lonigan has held onto Ned's nether regions throughout.

The whole battle becomes so vicious on the part of the troopers that, when the local Justice of the Peace and miller, William Maginness – a kindly man, held in high esteem in the community – is attracted by the commotion and comes into the shop, his first comment to the troopers is, 'You should be ashamed of yourselves!'[53]

They are likely the first kindly words that Ned has heard spoken on his behalf for some time – someone actually taking pity on him – and, amazingly, the words seem to act as some kind of balm to pacify him, where fists and boots have failed. In a couple of minutes of soothing talk, the miller is able to convince both the troopers to get off Ned and Lonigan, finally, to mercifully let go, while Ned – after uncurling himself from the foetal position of grasping his groin – allows Maginness to put the Darbies on him and escort him to court. And yet, while Ned is certainly calmer, the pain in his groin is not, and rightly or wrongly it would be the stuff of folklore long afterwards that, before going, he said to the brute who has caused this, 'Well, Lonigan, I never shot a man yet; but if ever I do, so help me God, you will be the first!'[54]

Once things have sufficiently calmed, and he is deposited once more in a cell, Ned risks a peek to examine the damage, and it is extensive.[55] Both his scrotum and his penis are swollen and purple, due to copious internal bleeding. It is so bad that he feels nauseated and can only walk with some difficulty. His abdomen aches, as if there are strings from his testicles to his stomach and they have been strained to breaking point. Through it all, the only salve is his fury at the 'cruel, cowardly, and disgusting . . . act of Lonigan, which cannot be described, [but] might have ruined me for life, if it did not actually kill me'.[56]

Ned Kelly is not the only one to nurse a grievance from the affair, however. All of the troopers are aggrieved at the trouble and pain that the twenty-two-year-old has put them through, none more than his former friend Alexander Fitzpatrick, who has been hurled into the wall by Kelly. That is an account that must be settled.

Nevertheless, when Ned is finally taken to court, the Bench takes a surprisingly benign view of his behaviour and, on the charge of being Drunk and Disorderly, to which he pleads guilty, he is fined 'one shilling or four hours imprisonment'. Assaulting Police in the Execution of their Duty? Guilty, Your Honour. Very well, then, that's one shilling or four hours in gaol for being drunk, £2 or one month's imprisonment for Assaulting Police, and an additional £2 or one month for resisting arrest. Ned also has to pay Constable Fitzpatrick five shillings for damaging his clothing. All put together, it comes to – dot three, carry one, subtract two – £4, 6 shillings, and once Ned hands over that exact amount he is allowed to walk free again, now a local legend to beat them all. For don't you know? Ned Kelly, the only man to have beaten Wild Wright in a bare-knuckle donnybrook, took on *four* troopers and the bootmaker, and he gave them the fight and fright of their lives!

After this and other outrages from the Greta mob, however, Beechworth's *Ovens and Murray Advertiser* is appalled, noting beneath a headline 'BUSHRANGING AND BURGLARY' that points right at the Greta mob:

> In the neighbourhood of Greta for many years there has lived a regular Gang of young ruffians, who from their infancy were brought up as rogues and vagabonds, and who have constantly been in trouble, and on Sunday we learnt that, though it is but a short time since some of them have been released from gaol, where they have been serving sentences for horse stealing, a little game of which they are thoroughly *au fait* . . .[57]

Bushrangers? *Bushrangers?* Them? Just like Ben Hall?

Well, it does have a certain seductive ring to it . . .

Chapter Four

A SIGNIFICANT VISIT

We were all living so happily at the old homestead . . .
We were not getting too rich, but were doing all right . . .
Before that . . . day when Fitzpatrick came we were so
happy. It was a lonely life, but we were all together, and we
all loved each other so dearly . . .
Ellen Kelly

Fitzpatrick will be the cause of greater slaughter to the
Union Jack than Saint Patrick was to the snakes and
toads in Ireland. The Queen of England was as guilty as
Baumgarten and Kennedy, Williamson and Skillion of
what they were convicted for.
Ned Kelly gives fair warning

10 NOVEMBER 1877, THE BAUMGARTEN BUSINESS IN BARNAWARTHA

All things considered, it is a very strange case. On this day, following a tip-off from a man from New South Wales who had been found in possession of two of the missing horses, Constable William Bell, disguised as a squatter's son from Hay, New South Wales, in company with his colleague, Constable John Stowe, turns up at the homestead of William Baumgarten, a well-to-do German emigrant who has settled along with his brother Gustav at Barnawartha, just on the Victorian side of the Murray River, on a large property. Bell meets Baumgarten on the road a short distance from his house and wonders if they might possibly have any horses for sale.

'No, I don't think so,' Baumgarten carefully replies.[1]

Bell persists, saying that 'a man called *Studders* has told me that you might have some horses for sale'.[2]

At the mention of the name, the German seems to relax. Yes, Baumgarten concedes. As a matter of fact, he has two beauties for sale . . . and he leads Bell and Stowe off to a paddock some quarter of a mile from his house. Once there, he points out a black mare and a filly in the paddock.

It takes Constable Bell only a moment to find what he is looking for – the original brand of James Whitty's Myrrhee run. Oh yes, the brands have been altered very well, all right, but the police are aware now of how easily that can be done. There, you see? On one of the horses, what had been a *W* has become a larger *KY*, while the others have become things like *AN*, *WB* and *AB*.

What is more, the horses match exactly the description of two of the horses that have been stolen from the Whitty property.

Going in for the kill now, Constable Bell makes an offer for the two horses, asking William Baumgarten, by the by, 'Do you know who you bought them from?'[3]

'A man named Thompson,' Baumgarten replies, adding that, although he didn't know him, he has receipts from the purchase.

In an instant, Baumgarten is arrested and, in handcuffs, taken by Constable Bell to the local lock-up and charged with Horse Stealing. And nor does it matter that Baumgarten and, shortly afterwards, Gustav, who is also arrested, quickly do produce what they swear are bona fide receipts for the horses that came from this man called Thompson.

None of that matters to the law. The Baumgartens are in possession of stolen horses and, at the Wangaratta Police Court of 6 December, they are committed for trial in March the following year. (For Constable Stowe, it is all the more useful, as, in the wake of the Whitty larceny and a subsequent similar theft, the 'North-Eastern Stock Protection

League', comprising twenty-seven squatters, is being formed under the presidency of James Whitty's close associate Andrew Byrne, for the purpose of 'taking the necessary steps to suppress Sheep, Cattle and Horse Stealing throughout the entire district'.[4] Most importantly, Whitty himself has already put up a £20 reward 'on conviction of the thief' of the horses,[5] which Stowe now intends to collect.)

Ned would later admit that the Baumgartens had 'paid me full value for the horses & could not have known they were stolen',[6] but, just as had been the case with Wild Wright not coming forward to save him after he had been charged with stealing the horse of the Mansfield Postmaster, Ned does not come forward to say the fault lies with him.

AS THE SUMMER OF 1877–78 BUILDS, SO DOES NED

Sometimes in a man's life, all his skills, all his energies and desires, all of his background come together as one to create something that will stand as a testament to what he has amounted to at this point, and this is such an occasion. In December of 1877 – not long after he and Joe Byrne had finished fencing Aaron Sherritt's new selection – Ned begins building a new house for his family, just on the other side of Eleven Mile Creek from where the current hut stands.

It brings together all Ned's skills in carpentry, stonemasonry, labouring and leadership. For most of the job, he commands a team that includes Brickey Williamson, Bill Skillion and – most particularly – the man who has become Ned's best friend, and such a soulmate that he has now effectively moved in with the Kelly family, Joe Byrne. All up, it is a pleasant job, which Ned enjoys, despite the fact that even at this point his testicles continue to ache, making him often think of Constable Lonigan . . . before getting back to work. The outside walls of the new house are carefully crafted slabs of ironbark that fit neatly together, with bark on the interior to give insulation. A verandah provides somewhere shady to sit, while the interior is divided into one large room for the kitchen and living room, boasting an expertly built enormous fireplace, and three bedrooms. Most impressive is that the hut has real interior walls. No more hessian partitions.

It may not be much in the wider scheme of things but, compared with the draughty hut the family has moved from, it is glorious.

'BLACK WEDNESDAY', 9 JANUARY 1878, PREMIER BERRY MAKES HIS MOVE

Graham Berry is now the most powerful elected official Victoria has seen. Since 1874, the colony has embraced the notion that the political head of government be anointed as 'Premier', which position he now fills since coming to power for the second time. His election manifesto, which proposed a punitive land tax designed to lessen the squatters' monopoly on the land, had won him the largest majority in the Assembly ever seen behind an elected Victorian leader in May of 1877. And yet he also retains the principally bureaucratic role of Chief Secretary with direct responsibility for many matters of government including the Aborigines, Agriculture, Education, Health, Mining and Goldfields Administration, Prisons and the Police.

No one has more power to crack the whip than him, and never has he cracked it more than now – making it clear to his liberal majority in the Assembly and his staunchly conservative opponents in the Legislative Council, who are elected on a limited, property-based franchise, that he is *not* a man to be thwarted.

As his future parliamentary colleague Alfred Deakin would recount, Berry had been born and raised tough. He had been 'obliged to leave school at eleven with the three R's, and to commence at once to earn his living. As youngest apprentice in a grocer's shop it was his lot to wait upon the others at lunch and satisfy himself with their leavings . . . As a child he had learned to secrete himself with his favourite books in a little closet or cellar under the stair where he could read while the door was ajar, holding it by a string which he drew whenever a footstep warned him of an approach to his cover . . .'[7]

Berry is a man who had been on one of the juries that had acquitted the Eureka Stockade rebels in 1855, so there is no doubt he has a sense of justice; and, as one who is well on his way to siring eighteen children, it would appear that he has a feel for what is best for the population of Victoria . . . but ultimately what drives him is the fourth 'R', which he had learned in adulthood: not religion but radicalism. He had been elected to parliament in 1861, becoming Premier for the first of three times in 1875 – and as a man of the people, not the aristocracy. Coming to the helm for his second time just the year before, he had been very proud of the first major move made by his Ministry. For, as promised, his Ministry – one of whom is Peter Lalor, the Eureka hero who acts as the Commissioner of Trade and Customs – had imposed a land tax, directly aimed at the great squatter runs, so as to get the government a fair return from those vast landholdings. Alas, it is a matter complicated by the fact that many of those squatters sat in the Legislative Council, which had to pass the legislation.

'In the Victoria of his visions,' it would be noted by Deakin, 'all honest, industrious men would prosper, no class would dominate and no economic or political theories should stand in his pragmatic way.'[8]

And yet, although the land-tax measure had such popular support that the Legislative Council had not dared to veto it, the members had not been long in taking their revenge. That is, when the Berry Ministry puts forward the *Appropriation Bill*, which includes the means to pay the salary of members of parliament, the Legislative Council rejects it! Victoria is plunged into deadlock, with the landed classes on one side, represented by the Legislative Council – and the great unwashed and effectively landless on the other side, represented by the Legislative Assembly and the Graham Berry Ministry.

With the *Appropriation Bill* unpassed, public servants cannot be paid for long, and the squatters in the Council, who have no 'apprehensions for themselves, chortling at the deprivation of salary to which they are subjecting their opponents',[9] are confident their contest must soon bring Berry, the scourge of 'Berryism' and his dreadful revolutionary rabble to heel. But they have underestimated Graham Berry's resolve.

Indeed, 'they had not calculated with Mr Berry or his Cabinet and their awakening to the fact that they had to deal with men who could not be trifled with was abrupt, utterly unexpected, and provocative of feelings of dismay'.[10]

For now comes the denouement. On a day that will ever after be known as 'Black Wednesday', Berry – this handsome man with a ready smile that could instantly turn to a snarl if he was thwarted, a man whose eyes are as blue as his beard is grey – dismisses from the public service no fewer than 200 police, magistrates and judges and other public servants. The most targeted are those who are judged to be in sympathy with the conservatives. This is all brutally announced via curt notices in the *Victorian Government Gazette*. It is a move calculated not only to save money – at a time when the budget is already severely strained as the Government prepares to host the Melbourne International Exhibition – but also to show the entire conservative class that it is the people who rule, not them, and that Graham Berry is quite capable of extreme measures himself.

Further, on the reckoning that the colony could be run solely with the militia – the volunteer defence force after the British troops had left – Berry also makes it known that the police force itself will be the next to be slashed.

How can the police save themselves? Therein lies a saga, with a most intriguing explanation later put forward by the senior Victoria Police officer Superintendent John Sadleir. 'A high ranking office of the State,' he would recount, 'a man notoriously of unclean life, was found late at night under ambiguous circumstances on the private premises of a gentleman residing in one of the suburbs.'[11] According to Sadleir, first thing the next morning this high official went straight to Captain Standish, who arranged for the whole matter to be hushed up. 'The high official recognised, of course, that it was the intervention of the head of the police service that saved the situation. It saved also the police department, for when the schedule for the disbanding of the service came before him he promptly vetoed it.'[12]

Was it then Sir George Ferguson Bowen, the man 'found late at night under ambiguous circumstances', who allowed the police department to survive in return for not being exposed? That would ever after be the speculation – as he was the only man capable of single-handedly vetoing anything – but, either way, the survival of the police has been a very close-run thing in this short term. In the long term, none of them can have any confidence that his job is secure.

LATE SUMMER/EARLY SPRING 1878, COMINGS AND GOINGS

Within the central dynamic of the Kelly family – an up for every down, a birth for every death, an in for every out – it is fairly typical. For it is in this period that, even as Dan is released in late January from Beechworth Gaol after serving three months for damaging property, a warrant is issued for the arrest of Ned on a charge of Horse Stealing.

It has taken some time, but finally the police are convinced – and believe they have proof – that the elusive **Thompson** marked on the Baumgarten receipt is none other than Edward Kelly. This will take the flashness out of him. For there it is, in black and white, in the *Victoria Police Gazette* of 20 March 1878:

> COMPLAINANTS John C. Farrell, James Whitty, James A. Whitty, and Robert Jeffrey – Edward Kelly is charged, on warrant from the Chiltern Bench with the offences hitherto referred to. He is about 22 or 23 years of age, 5 feet eleven inches or six feet high, stout, has dark complexion, hair, whiskers and beard, moustache of a lighter colour . . .[13]

Which is fine. For some time, the word that this would happen had been out on the 'bush telegraph' – for the Kellys, it is always a very worthy and powerful rival for the electric telegraph that the authorities have – and Ned had long gone, in the company of Joe, selling the last of the horses and rambling with him through Southern New South

Wales, well removed from pesky constables waving irritating pieces of paper. Which is as well, for now police parties, led by Sergeant Arthur Steele of Wangaratta and Senior Constable Anthony Strahan of Greta, go out looking for him, focusing first on the Kelly home and then in the hills around.

Sergeant Steele. (From an illustration by Thomas Carrington, *Australasian Sketcher,* 3 July 1880, courtesy State Library of Victoria)

5 APRIL 1878, MOVEMENT AT THE POLICE BARRACKS

Ah, but it soon gets more interesting still for the Kelly boys. For, on this day, in a case of the police working out that:

2
+
2 =
5,

the police come to the false conclusion that Dan Kelly and his cousin Jack Lloyd had also been involved in the Whitty larceny, and warrants for their arrest are immediately issued accordingly.

Curiously, despite this wave of warrants, Police Inspector Alexander Brooke Smith, who is in charge of the Wangaratta Police, chooses this time to send Senior Constable Strahan from the police station of Greta, regarded as 'the very focus of crime in the district',[14] in distant pursuit of yet another lead on Ned. To cover for Strahan's absence, on 12 April, Brooke Smith sends a cable to Sergeant James Whelan at Benalla Police Station, directing that 'Constable Fitzpatrick [must] be sent to Greta station to take charge there'.

Alas, typically for any police action involving Fitzpatrick, it does not go to plan. For, though on temporary duty 25 miles away at the small settlement of Cashel at the time, to Whelan's immense frustration, Fitzpatrick takes two days getting back to Benalla, not arriving until the 14th. Despite having received curt instruction from Sergeant Whelan to 'take charge of the station' at Greta and to remain with Mrs Strahan and her family until her husband's return,[15] Fitzpatrick does not begin the journey from Benalla to Greta until the next day.

15 APRIL 1878, MIGHTY MAYHEM ON THE ELEVEN MILE

Yes, there are two sides to a story, but what happens when there are two sides to each of those sides, and a few stray asides thrown in besides? And what about when there is so much fury and fog in equal measure generated by a particular event that it will not only deeply upset people at the time, and people will go to their graves because of it, but it will still be causing division and confusion well over a century later?

Such is the curious case of Constable Alexander Fitzpatrick and his actions, on this sunny day in April, as he makes his way on the 17-mile journey from Benalla to Greta. Time has shown that Constable Fitzpatrick is not much of a trooper – and his performance reflects badly on Judge Charles A. Smyth's judgement. He is neither dutiful nor diligent, neither honest nor humble, not courageous nor courteous. His key passions are pursuing the fairer sex and drinking, though usually in reverse order. On this particular day, he has troubles, real troubles. Since joining the police force in April of the previous year, his police record has been a litany of louche laxity, ill-disciplined drinking, slovenliness and being placed on official reports. And now he is in serious trouble with Sergeant Whelan for having turned up late from Cashel.

It is looking precarious as to whether Fitzpatrick can keep his job – the first real job he has had, or at least the first regular wage he has been able to draw. What he needs most of all right now is to show his superiors that he can be valuable, can make arrests, can do what regular troopers do.

The only thing he needs more?

A drink.

And this is exactly the right place to get one. While passing through the small settlement of Winton, a round dozen miles from Greta, he spies a rough drinking establishment known as 'Lindsay's shanty', where he can indulge the first of his passions with some discretion, knocking back several brandy and waters.

When he remounts his horse a couple of hours later, he is not drunk, per se, but certainly merry, which is his preferred state at the best of times and . . . and where was he? Arrests. Yes, he needs to make some arrests, valuable arrests. And he already has one in mind. Right now, the arrest of a Kelly is particularly valuable, he knows – for they are a family that still has not had the flashness taken out of them – and on the day that he had been in trouble with Sergeant Whelan he had noticed 'in the police gazette that there was a warrant issued by the Chiltern bench for the arrest of Dan Kelly and John Lloyd'.[16] The encouraging words of arrest warrants ring in his head: 'These are therefore to command you, in Her Majesty's name, forthwith to apprehend the said Daniel Kelly . . .'[17]

Yes, that's just what I'll do!

Like a sign from on high, Fitzpatrick's course to Greta takes him right by Eleven Mile Creek, and presently he spies the old Kelly hut on one side of the creek and the flash new one on the other, where the Kellys are now living.

Why not go to the Kelly house and arrest Daniel? (Apart from, that is, the strict policy instituted by Superintendent Nicolson that no visits are to be made to the Kellys unless at least two constables are present, and ideally more than that. No one, least of all Fitzpatrick, had forgotten that it had taken five men to subdue Ned Kelly back at Benalla six months earlier, and even then it had been a close-run thing. Ruefully, Fitzpatrick remembers being hurled into the wall by the sheer force of Ned's explosion.) A bonus for making such a visit would be that Fitzpatrick would very likely see the gorgeous Kate Kelly.

Very broadly, the Kelly version – most particularly Ned's version – of what happens from this point is clear. Fitzpatrick finds Dan Kelly not to be there. There is only Ellen Kelly, who is nursing her tiny baby, Alice, born just two days earlier, fourteen-year-old Kate and the gambolling younger children, twelve-year-old Grace and four-year-old Ellen. And there is no man of the house at all, as, apart from Dan and Ned not being there, baby Alice's father, George King, had abandoned his wife a few months earlier when things had begun to heat up after the Whitty larceny, and she is once more single.

Though disappointed Dan is not there, Fitzpatrick is more than happy to have a break from the track and settle down for a while in the hope that the horse thief might soon turn up and . . .

And what is that? It is the unmistakable sound – a curious combination of rhythm, violence and purpose – of wood being chopped, and Fitzpatrick is instantly on his feet. Though rarely enforced, there happens to be a law against chopping wood on Crown land unless one is licensed and, as the constable has come all this way, he is eager to do at least some law-enforcing while he is here. Besides, it might be Dan Kelly.

Alas, of Dan there is no sign, and it proves to be one of the Kelly neighbours, Brickey Williamson, now living in the old Kelly cottage, who is splitting fence rails and not breaking any law at all, and . . .

And now, suddenly, there is a new rhythmic sound to lightly disturb the rustic calm. Both Fitzpatrick and Williamson cock their ears towards it and instantly recognise the sound of two horses approaching. And there he is, coming through the trees at a gentle *clip-clop*. Why, it is Dan Kelly and another fellow – Bill Skillion, Fitzpatrick thinks – and they are heading straight to the Kelly shack.

Quickly priming his carbine, and scarcely daring to believe his luck, Constable Fitzpatrick moves swiftly in that direction himself. The constable now goes up to the younger Kelly and says, 'Dan, I want you to come into town with me.'

'No,' says Dan. 'I don't care to come into town. I have no business with you.'

'Oh,' says Fitzpatrick, 'there is a warrant against you for horse stealing.'

'Very well,' says Dan. 'If that is the case, I will go with you, but I have just come in from a long ride, so let me have something to eat before I go.'

Fitzpatrick, perhaps keenly aware of the fact that he is himself rather hungry, and assuming that he will be able to partake of the meal, agrees. With his gun carefully holstered, he takes his seat in the tiny, gloomy kitchen, while Ellen Kelly nurses her baby, and the other Kelly children sit up to eat.

At meal's end, however, when Dan says to his mother he is going into town with Fitzpatrick and Ellen Kelly asks what for, the constable interrupts.

'There is a warrant out against him,' he says casually.

'Well,' said Dan, 'you have said so much about a warrant. Show us your warrant.'

'I have no warrant, but a telegram came [from Chiltern] saying there was a warrant out for you.'

And that's when the trouble starts . . .

'Well,' says Ellen Kelly, as one who knows her way around the law, 'I do not see why any man should be taken on the mere word of a policeman, and Dan you need not go unless you like.'[18]

She now looks straight at the constable. 'And you, Fitzpatrick, have no business being on my premises without some authority besides your own word.'[19]

Suddenly, the air turns cold, despite the fact that at this moment Ellen Kelly is stoking the fire beneath the oven where she is baking bread.

'I will blow your brains out if you interfere,' Fitzpatrick snarls at her.

Does Ellen back down? She does not. She is a Kelly. 'You would not be so ready to show that popgun of yours if Ned were here,' Ellen Kelly replies.[20] 'He would ram that revolver down your throat!'[21]

And now Dan pipes up, looking out the window. 'There is Ned coming along by the side of the house . . .'[22]

The instant that Constable Fitzpatrick takes the bait and also looks out the window, Dan, in the now familiar Kelly fashion, knocks the trooper's revolver out of harm's way and wraps him in 'Heenan's Hug', a bear hug named after a famed professional wrestler.

By Dan Kelly's account, at this point he simply releases the constable unharmed on the strict proviso that he get on his horse, look neither left nor right and ride away.

Whatever the truth of what has just occurred, one thing is certain. Constable Fitzpatrick *needs a drink*. With this in mind, he goes back to the shanty house at Winton and drinks himself into a stupor, until the early hours of the morning. In fact, Fitzpatrick does not even make it back to Benalla Station under his own steam. Rather, he is taken there by the shanty owner, David Lindsay.

EARLY MORNING, 16 APRIL 1878, BENALLA POLICE STATION

There are three kinds of knocks on the door that come in the middle of the night. There is the apologetic 'I-am-hoping-against-hope-you-might-be-awake?' and the more insistent 'I-don't-want-to-be-waking-you-really-but-this-can't-wait.' And there is the kind that awakens Sergeant James Whelan in the wee hours of this morning. It is a *pounding*, an urgent banging on the door of his police barracks' married quarters, a summons to open the door quickly, because something so dire has happened that immediate action must be taken.

Whelan opens the door to be confronted by the perplexing vision of Constable Fitzpatrick. The trooper is dishevelled, has a bandage on his wrist, a dint in his helmet and an extraordinary, albeit garbled, story tumbling from his lips.

What Whelan does comprehend first up are the words 'shot at by Ned Kelly and wounded in the arm'.[23] After sending for Benalla's highly regarded, London-trained Dr John Nicholson to attend to his constable's wound, Whelan sits down and formally takes Fitzpatrick's statement, never mind that his words are slurred and the constable smells strongly of brandy.

His statement fills out with more detail in the coming days. As Fitzpatrick is to tell it and retell it for the rest of his life, he was indeed proceeding to Greta on duty, and stopped off to arrest Dan Kelly on the way.[24] When he got there, Dan was not there. He tells Sergeant Whelan, 'I saw Mrs Kelly and 3 children'[25] and, having stayed with them about an hour, heard chopping sounds coming from over the hill, behind the house.

He left the Kelly house and went up over the hill, where he met Brickey Williamson. Fitzpatrick asked him, 'Do you have a licence for splitting rails?' to which Brickey replied, 'No, I don't want one on selected land.'[26]

Satisfied, Fitzpatrick heads back down towards the Kelly house and soon sees two horsemen go 'through the slip panels by the old hut'.[27] When he goes to check them out, he sees Bill Skillion 'leading one horse by bridle and another horse by the mane'. He goes on . . . 'Bill Skillion was leading the horses away, and I asked him who had been riding; I said, "This is Dan Kelly's mare . . . where is he?" He replied, "Up at the house, I suppose."'[28]

Sure enough, by the constable's account, he had ridden up to the house and no sooner called out 'Dan!' than Dan Kelly had emerged, hatless and coatless, carrying a knife and fork. Fitzpatrick's recollection of what then happened is seemingly clear, with their conversation going like this:

'I am going to arrest you on a charge of horse stealing, Dan.'

'Very well, you will let me have something to eat before you take me?'

'All right.'

'I have been out riding all day.'[29]

They had then gone back into the hut, but as soon as Fitzpatrick had gone inside, Mrs Kelly had accosted him, saying he was 'a deceitful little bastard', and that she had always thought that. 'You will not take him out of this [hut] to-night,' she had said.

'Shut up, mother,' Dan had replied, 'that is all right.'[30]

And then?

It was just getting dark, but Fitzpatrick looked outside the door and could make out Bill Skillion passing right by the house leading a horse. 'Just afterwards,' the still shaken constable recounts, 'Ned Kelly came in at the door, and without a word fired at me with a revolver. I was about a yard and a half inside, rather behind the door with my back towards it; Mrs Kelly was standing with her back to the fire. The first shot did not strike me and he immediately fired again, the bullet lodging in my left arm, immediately above the wrist.'[31]

And still this murderous assault did not stop. Fitzpatrick goes on, the only other sound being Whelan's heavy breathing, and the scratch of his pen as he takes it all down, as all the others in the barracks stay fast asleep.

'Mrs Kelly at the same time rushed at me with a shovel, striking a heavy blow on my head, and making a large dent in the helmet I wore. I had raised my arm to guard from the shovel when he fired the second shot. I knocked the shovel down with my right hand, and then turned to draw my revolver, but it had been taken out of my belt. Dan Kelly had it in his hand. I then seized the revolver held in Ned's hand, saying, "You cowardly wretch, do you want to murder me?"

'We struggled for the pistol when it went off a third time, the bullet passing through the sleeve of my jumper.

'Skillion was by the side of Ned Kelly all the time, with a revolver in his hand, but he did not use it. Williamson came out of the bedroom just as the second shot was fired, he was also armed with a revolver or pistol. The pistols were all pointed at me.'[32]

In the face of such overwhelming numbers, Fitzpatrick ceases all resistance, and the fight stops.

'Ned turned to Skillion and said, "You bastard, why didn't you tell me who was here?" and then turning to me said, "If I had known it was you, Fitzpatrick, I would not have fired, but none of the other buggers would have left here alive."'[33]

By the drunken constable's account, Ned apologised for having shot him and then, 'took a rusty razor to cut [the bullet] out. I told him I wished to go home and get a medical man to remove it, but he refused. I then said I would operate myself and taking a sharp pen knife I cut it out. It was a small ball.'[34]

Ned had then taken the bullet from him, and Mrs Kelly had bandaged his wound. After accompanying him outside, as Fitzpatrick tells his superior, Ned then said to him, '"Now look here, I spared you and you must spare me. How will we manage to say that you were shot?"

'I said, "I won't mention who shot me."'[35]

At which point, by Fitzpatrick's account, Dan gave him detailed instructions on what he was to say happened, and even 'made me make an entry in my book at the time of the conversation'.[36]

Mrs Kelly added that, '"You had better tell him that if he does mention it, his life will be no good to him."'[37]

After giving Fitzpatrick back his gun and handcuffs, Ned and Dan escorted him away from the house around ten o'clock, shortly thereafter leaving him to go alone. About two and a half miles from the Kellys' place, Fitzpatrick noticed that Skillion and Williamson were in hot pursuit. So he 'spurred on'[38] until he had made it back to Lindsay's shanty at Winton, where, dismounting from his horse, he could hardly stand up. The shanty owners helped him inside, where the wound had been re-bandaged, and, after Fitzpatrick had had some food and brandy, David Lindsay had accompanied him to Benalla. Which is, broadly, the end of his account.

When Dr John Nicholson arrives to deal with the wound on Fitzpatrick's left wrist, he is surprised. For, whatever else, it is not a classic bullet wound. To begin with, a bullet fired from that close, which actually lodged in the wrist rather than merely winging it, would usually do a lot more damage. Instead, the two wounds are relatively minor. Whatever it is, he bandages it up, and all of them go to bed.

Whatever has happened, it has been a long night.

16 APRIL 1878, WANGARATTA POLICE STATION, SERGEANT STEELE GETS NEWS

Things move quickly. At nine in the morning, the cable comes through from Benalla, the same cable that has gone out to all police barracks in North-Eastern Victoria:

> Urgent Constable Fitzpatrick shot in attempting to arrest Dan Kelly at Greta yesterday for horse stealing was shot in the wrist by Ned Kelly when warding off a blow of a shovel made by Mrs Kelly other suspected offenders were there also armed.[39]

Arrest warrants have been issued for Ned Kelly for attempt to murder Constable Alexander Fitzpatrick the previous night, while there are also warrants to arrest Dan Kelly, Ellen Kelly, William Skillion and Brickey Williamson for 'aiding and abetting Edward Kelly when he did wound with intent to murder'.[40]

To many observers, such warrants, and Fitzpatrick's whole story, are preposterous. Ned Kelly had knocked out Wild Wright, but he needed a gun to take on Fitzpatrick? In a room filled with mainly little children, including his two-day-old sister, Ned had nevertheless fired that gun three times at a distance of never more than one and a half yards but, noted superb marksman that he is, had missed? And was Ellen Kelly actually aiding and abetting an attempt to murder Fitzpatrick when she hit him on the head with a shovel? And who believes that if the five accused really had collectively attempted to murder Fitzpatrick in the confined space of the hut, he would now be here among them?

No such questions seem to occur to Steele, however, who happens to receive notice of the warrant at a time when Inspecting Superintendent Nicolson is at the station on one of his frequent inspection tours. Steele is an Englishman with the instincts and sometimes aspect of a predator – born to move in for the kill – and he feels more than comfortable in such situations. His eyes sparkle, his lips glisten, and he has quickly gathered his men and they are on their way, his trademark tweed hat firmly perched atop his head.

Steele typifies the local rural policeman of the North-East. Rural police work is quite unpopular in the force, and too often the men stationed in these parts lack a certain finesse in their dealings with the population. As the local troopers have come to be a natural enemy of the selector, there is no better example of this than Steele, regarded by the struggling class as 'an unprincipled paltry policeman'.[41]

And, in turn, the Englishman Sergeant Steele does not like the selectors, and has a particular contempt for the next-generation natives. Having been in the force since 1857, and 'knocked a good deal about the district' since 1863,[42] he knows the Greta mob all too well. He was the one who arrested Steve Hart on a charge of Horse Stealing not long ago.

But it is the Kellys he really wants. In late March 1878, Steele had been ordered to set up a surveillance party over the Kelly residence, looking for evidence of criminality, only to come back with nothing at all except the news that the family had moved into their new home. He *knows* in his bones it is they who committed the Whitty larceny, and that Ned is the 'J. Thompson' fellow who signed the receipt. He just hasn't been able to prove it. Though he has already 'made several attempts to arrest Ned Kelly and Dan', he has always been unsuccessful.[43]

Until now, they have frustrated him at every turn, stealthily melting away into the bush the moment any information is laid on them. Steele is fed up with the apparent ease with which these louts parade around *his* district, flouting the law and ruining his reputation as an officer, an *enforcer* of that law, and the reputation of his station. The local papers, and even the Melbourne papers, constantly talk of his district as a lawless frontier, a land apart from the rest of the civilised colony, and it makes his blood boil. All because of these Kellys and their mob. Steele is determined that they will get their comeuppance . . . and now is his chance, with a charge of no less than Attempted Murder against the budding ringleader of this 'nice little Gang!'.[44]

And yet, as they approach the Kellys' place, Steele notices with some annoyance that local children run to warn the family. There is no point in approaching immediately, so instead he sets up a watch over the house from the hill opposite.

Having observed the dwelling for the better part of the afternoon and into the evening, Sergeant Steele, accompanied by Detective Joseph Brown and the just returned Senior Constable Strahan, now descend upon it.

True, of all the arrests that Sergeant Steele has made in his time, this one will not be a standout in terms of required courage – for Ellen Kelly is an unarmed forty-six-year-old woman, with none of her sons seemingly at home. Still, Sergeant Steele is taking no chances and, with Detective Brown and Strahan tightly behind, all with their guns drawn, bursts through the door of the Kelly hut . . . only to find Ellen Kelly there with her young children.

The Kelly matriarch does not seem particularly surprised to see them – lately, police charging into her house with their guns drawn is as much in the natural order of things as a train pulling into a station – but she professes ignorance of everything they are saying about Fitzpatrick.

'Fitzpatrick?' Ellen says, seemingly incredulous. 'It would be hard for me to see him when he was not at my place.'

'You mean to tell me,' Strahan replies, 'that Constable Fitzpatrick was not at your place on the night of 15 April?'

'I have not seen Constable Fitzpatrick since you and him was at my place, and that is over a month.' Then she adds, 'And as for seeing my son Ned, I have not seen him for the last four months.'[45]

A furious young Kate, her eyes flashing just like her oldest brother's, backs up her mother.

For the moment, Steele decides not to arrest Ellen Kelly, as he is confident that, with this many children and a three-day-old baby, she will not be going anywhere. Instead, he and his men first go to the selection next door, where they arrest Brickey Williamson and put handcuffs on him before searching the place for firearms, without any result. No matter that Brickey is now handcuffed; he is still covered with a police revolver as, in all the confusion, the two troopers and detective seem convinced that he himself might be one of the Kellys. In fact, Williamson would later claim that Sergeant Steele 'told me afterwards that he nearly shot me, as he intended to have one'.[46]

The police then proceed to the nearby hut of Bill Skillion, who proves to be absent for the moment.

Taking Williamson to the Greta lock-up, the police return first to Bill Skillion's place at one in the morning, and this time – despite the outraged protests of Skillion's wife and Ned's sister, Maggie – they do indeed arrest the completely stunned selector. For the truth of it is Skillion really had not been at the Kellys' place the previous evening at all. By the candlelight, and in the drunken confusion of it all, the man Constable Fitzpatrick had thought was Ned Kelly's brother-in-law was in fact Joe Byrne. How can Skillion prove that? It will be difficult, though he can but try.

After putting the Darbies on Skillion, Steele and his men take him along to pay one last visit to the Kelly house. As Sergeant Steele puts the handcuffs on Ellen, she asks what Fitzpatrick said she did.

'He accused you of wounding him with a shovel,' Steele replies.

Oh.

'I know I've a damn bad temper,' she acknowledges, almost ruefully. 'You would not like to see a son of yours ever taken away. If they got him into gaol there's no telling what those bloody wretches would swear against him . . .'[47]

You may do your talking before the judge, Mrs Kelly. For, with Bill Skillion, she is now taken to the Greta lock-up in the back of a dray – clutching her baby tightly in the freezing night air with her handcuffed hands – before being transferred to Benalla the next afternoon.

The Kelly brothers, when they hear of the whole episode, are incandescent with rage. Their mother and baby sister are in gaol? And their mother is charged with Aiding and Abetting an Attempt to Murder?

Attempt to Murder? Fitzpatrick? Why would you bother killing such a hopeless fool?

Though it is a close-run thing, it is Ned who is the most apoplectic. After all, the whole reason Fitzpatrick had been at the house in the first place was to arrest Dan for a crime that Ned had masterminded and executed but in which Dan had never been involved. And it had also been Ned who had insisted that the whole prosecution case would fall apart once it had been proven that Bill Skillion had never been there – and yet it hadn't worked out like that. Yes, Ned has already been convicted many times of various crimes, but never does he feel so guilty as now.

25 APRIL 1878, AT BENALLA RAILWAY STATION, A DETECTIVE'S NOUS COMES INTO PLAY

It is time for the government to get serious about bringing the Kellys to heel, specifically to find and arrest Ned and Dan Kelly. It is with this in mind that one of the Victoria Police Force's most accomplished detectives, Michael Ward, arrives at Benalla this afternoon. An Irish-born man of thirty-two years, who has been in the detective force since 1876, and around the district, at Wangaratta and Beechworth, since Harry Power's glory days, he is the man for the job. He knows the two Kelly lads well, as of course he knows their entire clan. For, although it's no claim to fame to have arrested Joe Byrne and Aaron Sherritt – many police in these parts have – Detective Ward was at least the first. Most importantly, he understands and has extensively dealt with the Greta mob over many years.

'During that time,' he would later recall, 'Ned and Dan Kelly, the Quinns, and all their relations were in the habit of being at the circuit courts; one of their friends was always before the circuit court at the general sessions . . . I do not think there was a year when some of their friends were not before the court for trial.'[48] Especially during his time as a trooper at Wangaratta, in 1874 and early '75, Ward had come to know Ned Kelly 'very well' as he 'had occasion to speak to him very often'.[49]

And now, a new mission. After the shooting of Fitzpatrick, Ward has received orders at his base at Beechworth, to 'proceed to Benalla, there to report . . . to the officer in charge of police, and to try and catch Edward Kelly and Dan Kelly'.[50] And here he is, ready to put his detective's wit and wily schemes to good use. He is something of a dandy, with a heavily waxed moustache that he likes to twirl when thinking hard . . . and he is soon twirling up a storm.

17 MAY 1878, BACK BEFORE BENALLA POLICE COURT

Whereas, on such a serious charge as Attempting to Aid and Abet an Attempted Murder, Ellen Kelly, Bill Skillion and Brickey Williamson might reasonably expect to have an experienced magistrate delicately weighing the scales of justice, there is no one available. Most of the local magistrates cannot be engaged, and in their place at this committal hearing are three 'honorary magistrates'.

Via their counsel, local solicitor William Zincke – a tiny man whose last remaining hairs grow in grey and wild profusion down low, to compensate for the shimmering desert on high – all three from the Kellys' place plead not guilty to the charge. Zincke reserves his defence, declining to put any of his clients on the stand and preferring to reveal what he has up his sleeve only at the trial proper. At the conclusion of the Crown case, all three accused are 'committed for trial at the Beechworth Assize Court on the 9th October next'.[51]

The frustrating five months' delay until the case can be heard is not unexpected, because of all the sacked magistrates. And yet, when Zincke applies for bail for Ellen Kelly, on the grounds that she has already been remanded in custody for four weeks and gaol is no place for a woman with a very young baby at nurse, the honorary justices give a rather cruel ruling, demanding an extraordinarily high price for even her temporary freedom, as 'bail was fixed at two sureties of £50 each'.[52]

Why so high? Perhaps one reason is that one of the honorary justices is none other than Ellen's neighbour, the squatter Robert McBean

– wearing his fine gold watch – who has long coveted the Kelly land to return to his run. Obviously, anything that will send Ellen Kelly to the financial wall is something that will increase the likelihood that she will be unable to make the regular rent payments, and so the land will return to the Crown.

As ever with the Kelly family, while it is one thing to have bail granted to any one of them charged with a serious offence, it is another for them to be able to raise it. Neither the family nor their friends can produce the money. Ellen and her baby are sent back to gaol.

At seven o'clock that evening, Detective Ward and Senior Constable Strahan, in the company of two other constables, start from Benalla for the Eleven Mile Creek. Ward is strongly of the view that, after the day's court proceedings, Ned Kelly will visit his sisters, Maggie and Kate, at the Kelly home to find out 'how his mother got on at the court',[53] and he is intent on nabbing him when he does.

But what a night it is! It is wild, wet and windy, and though they push on regardless, they do stop when about four miles from Maggie Skillion's place they find an abandoned dray, with two bags of flour but without a horse, right in the middle of the road. Scouting around, they soon find the owners – Maggie Skillion and Kate Kelly – sitting on a log! They are wet through, freezing and holding each other for warmth. On this dark night, in this weather, two women alone, they had decided they just could not go on. Ward is quick to offer the extremely fetching and single Kate a flask with some whiskey in it, and she sips it appreciatively.

Ward now has the two constables escort the women back to the Skillion selection, while he and Strahan push on to the homestead at Eleven Mile Creek, positioning themselves 'to see if any person came to the house during the night'.[54] But throughout the long, dreary night there is nothing and no one.

And so it starts, as this is among the first of many stake-outs that the police, and especially Michael Ward, are to conduct in the search for Ned Kelly.

As to Ellen Kelly, back in her cell, it is not that she is entirely without sympathy, as a small item that appears in *The Ovens and Murray Advertiser* three weeks later attests:

> MRS KELLY—A day or two since, Mr W. H. Foster attended at the Beechworth Gaol, and admitted to bail this woman, who had been committed for trial for aiding and abetting in an attempt to murder Constable Fitzpatrick, at Greta. It was an act of charity, as the poor woman, though not the most reputable of characters, had a babe in her arms, and in the cold gaol without a fire, it is a wonder the poor little child lived so long during this bitter wintry weather.[55]

With bail and a surety of £50 each paid by two kindly Greta farmers – William Dinning and his brother-in-law Robert Graham – at least Ellen Kelly and her baby are now safely at home until the trial takes place.

WINTER 1878, LOST IN THE WILDS? THEY CERTAINLY HOPE SO . . .

What to do when there are £100 reward posters up for you all over North-Eastern Victoria, proclaiming that you are wanted for 'Attempt to Murder at Greta'? The answer for Ned is do what ol' Harry Power taught him to do so well, all those years ago. Secrete yourself. Place yourself somewhere so remote that, in the highly unlikely event of the police ever finding you, they will be doing so on your turf. And Ned has just the place in mind – of course, the hut at Bullock Creek, which has already served them so well.

Bullock Creek hideout. (Courtesy Keith McMenomy)

In the words of one contemporary observer, the hideaway is in a place 'full of inextricable hills and valleys with the multiplicity of the minor water courses making it difficult to know whether you were on the fall of the Broken or the Ovens Rivers; the whole formed a hiding place in which an army corps might have searched for the offenders and being within a short distance of them still fail to find them'.[56]

And yet, Ned and Dan intend to do much more than merely hide. For the place also has the potential to deliver the key thing they want – money to finance the Kelly matriarch's legal defence.

No sooner have they arrived at Bullock Creek than Ned, Dan and Joe start to work, enhancing the improvements they had begun to make on their rough bolt-hole when they first stayed up here a couple of summers ago. They cut down the smaller trees, ring-bark the bigger ones and construct the roughest of a sapling, dogleg and brush fence going for half a mile around three sides of the 20 acres contained by the basin – with no fence necessary on the western side as it is a steep slope. The fence will keep in their horses, and also the cattle they manage to steal, to either sell or use for grub. They clear the land and plant two crops: mangel wurzels to feed the livestock; and barley, with a view to providing the raw material to make whiskey, which is where in the long term they hope to make a fortune.

Once those crops are established down on the creek in this once-busy gold area, they set up sluice boxes – wooden constructions with rippled bottoms that trap the heavier gold particles – and begin work, filled with confidence. After all, just over the next ridge are a couple of abandoned shepherd huts by a creek, as well as all the signs of old gold diggings. Joe Byrne can put to use his experience growing up on the Woolshed diggings and has no doubt that they can make the creek deliver gold. He is proved correct, as they are indeed soon able to make 'good wages as the creek is very rich'.[57] For the Kelly brothers, particularly, getting the gold is spiritually rewarding. After all, their dear departed father had once secured enough gold to provide their mother, Ellen, with a new freedom, as the family could buy its first plot of land, and now they are going after gold themselves, in her name, to provide a different sort of freedom.

The men settle down for this notably freezing winter, tending their crops and their animals, manning the sluice boxes and waiting to hear the results of the trial over the Fitzpatrick episode. Occasionally, they receive visits from those few intimate family and friends who know where they are, who bring them supplies, tools, news and newspapers – and to whom they can give some of the gold they have garnered to sell. Their most frequent visitor is Tom Lloyd, who tells them the trial is due to take place in early October. They are content to stay secreted till then. After all, Ned, for one, cannot believe that his mother will be found guilty, and he rests a great deal of hope on the fact that, once it is exposed that Bill Skillion had never been there in the first place, the rest of the case will fall apart.

But God help the judiciary and the police if they do find his mother guilty.

EARLY JULY 1878, MRS GRUNDY COMES TO TOWN

A fundamentally decent kind of fellow is Superintendent John Sadleir.

Softly spoken, and well educated, with grey hair and a standard-issue beard, the Irishman is as methodical as he is mild, as focused as he is fair. Back in the 1860s in Melbourne, he had had the difficult task of breaking down the sly grog and brothel trade, earning him the sobriquet of 'Mrs Grundy', as in a person of ever-priggish propriety.

But never – since leaving his previous position as head of the Mansfield Police to an Englishman by the name of Henry Pewtress – has he had a tougher task than this.

As the newly installed police chief of the just formed North-East Police District (after savage budget cuts following Black Wednesday, the Kilmore, Beechworth and Upper Goulburn districts have all been amalgamated, with Benalla as its headquarters), it will be Sadleir's task to get this whole troublesome area back under police control. In his view, ensuring law and order over 11,000 square miles of country with just forty-nine police stations and a hundred policemen is a nigh on impossible task, but he intends to try.

The most pressing problems are the continued stealing of stock and the fact that the Kelly brothers are still at large, despite enormous resources having been put towards their capture. It is Sadleir's strong preliminary view that the two things may not be unrelated. When he takes over at Benalla, the warrants for the arrest of the Kelly brothers are the two most outstanding ones in his area, and he feels it is his duty to have the wretches arrested. But where are they? In moving among the stations at his command, and making enquiries of all and sundry, Sadleir comes to a conclusion.

'It seems to be certain,' he writes to his old friend, Sergeant Michael Kennedy, in Mansfield, 'that "Ned Kelly" is in the neighbourhood of Greta, or from thence to Connolly's and the bogs near the Wombat. I am very anxious to make some special efforts to have the matter set at rest, and his apprehension effected, if possible . . . It has been proposed to collect, for the purposes of a thorough search, what constables are in the district who know Kelly personally, sending say two of them to Mansfield to act with [you] from that end, and the others to act with the Greta Police, and to search simultaneously up and down the King

River and neighbouring places. I shall be glad to receive any suggestions that [you] may have to offer on the subject . . .'[58]

One option that John Sadleir plans to pursue in the meantime is to convince Wild Wright, 'a young acquaintance of mine [of] the criminal class',[59] to first find the Kellys and then lead the police to them. Alas, approval of his plan does not come until after Detective Ward has been sent into the district undercover to do much the same job, so Sadleir never fully pursues it. And anyway, Wright is not remotely interested, and says from the first to anyone who asks after Ned that he would 'not betray Ned for all the money in Australia'.[60] He is also prone to warning the constabulary, saying to a local trooper on several occasions, 'Ned Kelly is mad and you will see it one of these days . . .'[61]

EARLY SEPTEMBER 1878, WORD COMES FROM THE WOMBAT

Of all the jobs in all the world, 'stumping' – pulling dead stumps and their root systems out of paddocks so that the grass can grow unfettered – is not only among the most difficult but also the most tedious. The digging, the crowbars, the heaving, the tying of ropes and chains and whipping of horses to take the strain . . . it is all so deadly dull.

Yet, for Steve Hart, just turned nineteen, it is at least a job, which he, after serving just under a year at Beechworth Gaol convicted on 'thirteen counts of illegally using horses'[62] finds really something. But on days like today, working hard on the family's selection just outside Wangaratta, when the blisters burst and the stump won't bloody move, it is almost enough to make him feel nostalgic for the cool and calm of his prison cell.

Yes, he can do it at least as well as his father and elder brother Richard all right – Steve is five foot seven inches and of notably wiry physique – for, apart from being one of North-Eastern Victoria's most renowned horsemen, he is as tough as teak and has great stamina. But this is just no way for a man to live, particularly on no more than £6 a month, when a good stolen horse could have earned him as much as £15 in one go. Certainly, the man who had put him inside in the first place, Sergeant Steele, had recently been to see him, and Hart had promised he was going to stick at his work, but a promise to a policeman doesn't count. And on this afternoon, something happens. Seemingly out of nowhere, a man rides up and asks if he can have a few words with Steve. Yes. He has a message for him. It is from his great friend Dan Kelly. Dan said to say he is in the Wombat Ranges with Ned, up near Bullock Creek, and they are waiting for him if he'd like to join them. Without another word, and certainly not waiting for an answer, the messenger departs.

For several minutes, Steve Hart sits on a log and turns it all over in his head. Just over a week earlier, his beloved sixteen-year-old brother Nicholas had died of pneumonia – a great kid and wonderful horseman with everything to live for, now dead. Life is fickle. And way too brief to waste time doing things you don't want to do.

His mind is made up. He stands up, walks over to his fiercely sweating father and brother straining at the stump with their crowbars and says to them simply, 'Here's to a short life but a merry one!'[63]

With which, he gathers his effects, throws his saddle on his faithful horse and, as the others silently stare after him, rides off.

Where to, though? Broadly in the direction of the Wombat Ranges, where Bullock Creek lies . . .[64]

9 OCTOBER 1878, BEECHWORTH COURTHOUSE

All rise.

In the dock at ten o'clock on this Wednesday morning stand the three accused, Ellen Kelly, Brickey Williamson and Bill Skillion. Presiding is Judge Redmond Barry, perhaps the most distinguished justice in the land, and – with his grey wig, red robes and baleful eyes, gazing out from on high – he certainly looks the part.

Looking up at the judge on this day, Ellen Kelly must inevitably remember the last time she had seen this imposing figure looking down on her, a little over ten years ago. It was after Red's bastard of a brother,

Tipperary Jim, had tried to wangle his way between her sheets, the whole saga ending with a gin bottle smashed over his head and the burning down of the hotel they called home. Barry had shown himself a tough judge on that occasion, handing Jim the sentence of death for Attempted Murder. Though the sentence had eventually been commuted to fifteen years' hard labour, Ellen is under no illusions that he is anything other than severe.

And so, how do the three – represented by barrister John Bowman, instructed by solicitor William Zincke, all paid for quietly by the proceeds of the gold sluicing – plead?

'Not guilty, Your Honour.'

Of course, once the jury is sworn in, the key witness for the Crown is Constable Fitzpatrick, and his testimony is nothing if not damaging, as he retells essentially the same story as he outlined at the Benalla Police Court back in May.

Under cross-examination, Fitzpatrick does allow he did not have a warrant for Dan Kelly's arrest with him, and also acknowledges drinking both before and after visiting the Kelly house, but vigorously denies being drunk. And, no, he most definitely had not caused the dent in his helmet himself, to make it appear he had been bashed over the head with a shovel, and nor had he made up the entries in his notebook to incriminate the Kellys – though, yes, he had written a few of the entries several days later.

Next in the witness box is Dr Nicholson of Benalla, who gives a careful account of what he observed of Fitzpatrick's wounds on the night, and the conclusions he drew. In the early hours of 16 April, he states, once called to the station by Sergeant Whelan, he had seen that Constable Fitzpatrick had two wounds, 'One a jagged one, and the other a clean incision.' He allows that the jagged one 'might have been produced by a bullet',[65] while the clean incision might have been caused by the knife to dig it out, but he sounds far from convinced.

At this point, two bullets are produced in evidence by Crown Prosecutor Arthur Chomley and presented to Dr Nicholson for his comment. Again, carefully, the good doctor grants that either one of them might have caused the wounds. 'They were about an inch and a half apart,' he relates. 'One was on the outside of the wrist, and the other near the centre. They might have been produced by a bullet, that is the outside wound, [but, really,] there could not have been much loss of blood . . . It was merely a skin wound.'[66]

In cross-examination by John Bowman – which lasts no longer than five minutes – Dr Nicholson agrees that, because he had not probed the wounds, he does not know if they might have been connected, and also that Fitzpatrick smelled of brandy.

This next witness, David Lindsay, the owner of the shanty, says he did not see Fitzpatrick come earlier in the day. He concedes that Fitzpatrick 'took some brandy and water', but insists that 'he was quite sober' when he headed off to Benalla late on the night in question. Lindsay testifies that Fitzpatrick told him that night that, 'Ned Kelly had shot him and that Williamson and Skillion were there.'[67]

After Sergeant Steele gives testimony as to the circumstances of the arrests, the prosecution rests.

It is the turn of barrister John Bowman to mount the case for the defence. It is his strong contention that, on such a serious charge as this – Aiding and Abetting a Murder – the twelve-man jury could not possibly accept the uncorroborated evidence of just one constable, particularly when his whole account is so preposterous: 'No credence can be placed on Fitzpatrick's story, which is exceedingly improbable.' He goes on to review the evidence and point out the discrepancies. 'Where did the men get their firearms? What did they get them for? There was no design against Fitzpatrick. Why did he go there without a warrant? Even Kelly, the principal, had no intention of hurting him. How could the prisoners be charged with complicity?'[68]

In fact, Mr Bowman says, he will provide two witnesses who will testify that Bill Skillion was not there on the night. It is further his strong contention that, if one part of the Crown's evidence were proved false, it would be impossible for the jury to believe the rest. He adds wryly that 'the constable knew nothing of the matter, being drunk'.[69]

Alas, in person, though both witnesses mount a credible case, they are torn apart by Chomley. He points out that the first witness, Francis Harty – who says Skillion was with him on the evening at his Winton property – is a very close neighbour and associate of the Kellys', and a friend of Ned's in particular. In fact, he'd once bought a mare from Ned Kelly. The implications of such a statement are not lost on the jury. (And, as Chomley knows, Harty had even once been heard to proclaim, within earshot of Constable Fitzpatrick – who has provided a sworn affidavit to this effect – 'Ned Kelly is the best bloody man that has been in Benalla. I would fight up to my knees in blood for him . . . I would take his word sooner than another man's oath.')[70]

As to the other witness, young farmer Joseph Ryan, his supporting testimony that he, too, had been with Skillion that afternoon and that, after his visit to Harty, the two had returned to the Kelly household to find 'the row was all over'[71] is fine as far as it goes. But when Ryan also acknowledges that he bought a horse from Ned on the 15th – establishing that Ned Kelly was in the area on the day – and is, ahem, the nephew of Ellen Kelly and the cousin to all her children, there is no doubt that his credibility is damaged somewhat.

Chomley concludes for the Crown, saying, 'the facts have been proved, and this alibi setup is worthless', going on to accuse Harty and Ryan of perjury.[72]

Staggeringly, neither Ellen Kelly nor any of her children in the hut at the time is called to the stand, and Ryan is the last witness for the 'defence'. In summing up to the jury, Judge Barry makes clear his own views, notwithstanding that Ellen's eldest son is not the one on trial. 'Well, gentlemen, you all know what this man Kelly is.'[73]

With this, the jury retires for no more than two hours to give their considered verdict.

'Guilty.'

All three are remanded for sentencing . . .

It is a verdict that does not sit well with many acquainted with the case – and all the more so when a story circulates that, afterwards, when Dr Nicholson runs into Fitzpatrick in the street, he tells him frankly that 'the wound in your wrist could not have been caused by a bullet'.[74]

12 OCTOBER 1878, BEECHWORTH, THE JUDGE PRONOUNCES

Sir Redmond Barry has had enough. Beyond being sick of it, he is out and out angry. Never, in all his time coming to this area, have the offences been so grave, and there is no doubt it is 'the heaviest calendar for years'.[75] It seems like all of North-Eastern Victoria is descending into lawlessness, and it is time for what law is left to make a stand. With this in mind, the eminent jurist is in a mood to hand out a lesson to those who continue to offend – to demonstrate to the entire community what happens to those who break the law – and, on this morning, he does not miss his mark.

First up is William Baumgarten. For his conviction of receiving horses, stolen by Ned Kelly, he is given – on Judge Barry's reckoning of the old proverb 'If there were no receivers there would be no thieves'[76] – four years. In handcuffs, Baumgarten is led away, as his wife, who is as shocked as she is infuriated, looks on.

And next are Brickey Williamson and Bill Skillion, followed by Ellen Kelly.

Judge Barry's view is firm: no mercy.

While Skillion and Williamson receive sentences of six years, Ellen Kelly, for the 'atrocious crime of aiding and abetting in the shooting of a police constable'[77] – read 'hitting a constable over the head with a shovel' – is sentenced to prison for three years.

Barry notes that his chief hope in passing this sentence is that it will 'lead to the disbanding of the Gang of lawless persons, who have for years banded themselves together in that neighbourhood against the police'.[78]

Oh, and one more thing. 'If your son Ned was standing by you in the dock,' Barry – at least as legend would have it – tells Ellen Kelly, in his remarkably high-pitched voice, 'I would give him 21 years.'[79] With which, the now convicted prisoners are taken away.[80]

If there is a nervousness among the troopers as they put the handcuffed Ellen Kelly and her baby in the cart to be taken off to Beechworth Gaol, it is because there is a strong word on the street that Ned Kelly himself had been spotted only a short distance outside of Beechworth, heavily armed and on horseback. There is no telling what he might do now.

Clearly, the one with most to fear is Constable Fitzpatrick, and, as he escorts Williamson and Skillion to the gaol, even he confesses himself to be stunned at the way it has turned out. 'Well, Billy,' he says tearfully to Williamson, dabbing his eyes with his handkerchief, 'I never thought you would get anything like that.'[81]

Fitzpatrick – who within days is transferred out of the district for his own safety – is not the only one amazed at the severity of the sentence. For his part, though not involved in the case, the Police Magistrate based at Benalla, Alfred Wyatt, who is familiar with the case and many of the people involved, is appalled. After forty years working in the legal field, his own view is that the sentence 'upon the old woman, Mrs Kelly, [is] a very severe one'.[82]

And that, of course, is the view of 'the old woman' herself, now Prisoner Number 3520. Beyond her rage at the unfairness of her own punishment, however, she is fearful of the overall consequences. For she knows her boys, and knows what the likely severity of their rage will be when they find out about not only her guilty verdict but also the fact that she and their sister have been placed in gaol for three years.

Upon first being taken to her cell, Ellen throws her baby, Alice, in the air and says, 'By God, they will get it for this.'[83] And she means it. A short time later, she is in the exercise yard and manages to speak to Brickey Williamson through the bars of his cell, predicting to him – as he would later recount to an inspector of the Victoria Police – 'They will play up, there will be murder now.'[84]

It is a widespread view. That very afternoon, when a man who knows the Kellys well comes across a Beechworth doctor he knows, he makes a bet of a bottle of champagne that, before four weeks have passed, the Kellys will have shot a policeman.

And Ned himself?

Well, there is anger, there is rage, there is fury . . . and then there is the intensity of white-hot emotion that Ned feels when told of the fate of his mother. Three years of hard labour, for a woman with a baby at her breast, simply for hitting a policeman with a shovel? And this they call an attempt to aid and abet a murder?

Fitzpatrick will pay for this, and Ned is not long in telling a friend that he 'would rush through a hundred bayonets to get at him',[85] but his rage is not confined to the constable alone. Every shred of his experience to this point has proved to him that the entire police force, guided by the government, is out to get him and his family, and, while a lesser man might have buckled before the overwhelming forces ranged against him, Ned does not. He is determined that there will be a reckoning of accounts. And yet . . . there might be one other way of getting his mother and sister released, as dire as the consequences might be for him and Dan personally.

MID-OCTOBER 1878, MAGISTRATE WYATT RECEIVES AN OFFER

And here, now, is an interesting proposal. It has come to Benalla Police Magistrate Alfred Wyatt via a circuitous route – nearly as circuitous as the one he follows from court to court around North-Eastern Victoria – but it is an offer, all right. It originates from Wild Wright and the uncle of the Kelly boys, Patrick Quinn, via the police involved in pursuing them. Twice, Quinn has appeared before Wyatt in the dock, as has Wild Wright countless times, and they both know the magistrate to be a fair man, hence the offer coming to him.

The proposition is that, 'if the Kellys' mother [is] liberated, some promise or some arrangement will be made by which the Kellys, Ned and Dan . . . would give themselves up'.[86] (Careful legal language for what the messenger for the two sons to the Judge actually says: 'They shall be brought in if the old woman is let out.')[87]

It is extraordinary and without precedent in Wyatt's forty-year-long experience of the law . . . but very difficult to pursue. While the Kellys are obviously great at horse thieving, the law is not well suited to engaging in this kind of 'horse-trading' on such a matter. Ellen Kelly had been found guilty and incarcerated, and the law could hardly suddenly find her not guilty because two even more prize plums presented themselves. Against that, Wyatt is disposed to at least try to pursue it.

And so Magistrate Wyatt – a rather eccentric Englishman, a gentleman prone to wearing velvet suits and travelling with an extra horse simply so his own horse would not be lonely – cannot resist making careful reply. 'I made answer thus,' Wyatt recounted later. 'That I could not make a shadow of a stipulation on behalf of the government, but if such efforts were made, and were successful, I would use my most strenuous endeavours to carry out the condition they wished to impose.'[88]

That is, he cannot make any promises but, yes, if the two Kelly rogues do present themselves to the mercy of the law, he would do everything possible to get Ellen Kelly out of Melbourne Gaol – where she has now been transferred, while Skillion and Williamson have gone to Pentridge – on remission or some such legal contrivance. But, and he is firm on this, one more time, so there can be no misunderstanding, there will be no guarantees.

Which, of course, is not good enough for Ned and Dan Kelly when the word is passed back to them at Bullock Creek, where Dan's great friend Steve Hart has recently joined them. Trust the law without an absolute cast-iron guarantee? Present themselves and be put in the same prison as their mother, so the Kellys could all rot together, as the law always wanted? Not them.

Ned is consumed with the desire to free his mother come what may, and, while the gold-sluicing operation up at Bullock Creek has been turning a fair profit, he is now convinced that he needs money a whole lot quicker than that to fund a legal challenge to his mother's conviction. It is with this in mind that he wishes to push forward on their distillation of whiskey – what the Americans call 'moonshine' or 'Mountain Dew'. After all, the crops they put in over the winter will soon be ready for harvesting, and they will have the raw material they need. They decide to put the still to make that whiskey in a hidden spot a little further down the creek, so that, if anyone informs on them, it won't be found.

They also busy themselves in continuing to strengthen their

defences, should the police come for them. Their shelter has become a hut specifically designed to withstand a siege. The logs that make up the walls are two-feet thick and singularly sturdy, laid one on top of the other. Yes, there are small holes between those logs, where they don't mesh quite right – allowing a certain amount of cold to come in – but, against that, such holes are ideal for firing a gun through, allowing the shooter to see perfectly what he is aiming at while remaining invisible. As to the windows, from outside they are tiny and high – so that even if bullets do go through them they will be above the height of a man's head, and on the inside of a thick slab door the men have even attached a piece of quarter-inch-thick bulletproof iron that has been taken from a ship's ballast tank. For a radius of 100 yards around the hut, all the trees have been cut down, meaning there is no cover for anyone trying to sneak up on it, and the men have enough food put by – flour, sugar, tea, salted beef – to last for months.

With what spare time they do have, these leading lights of the Greta mob practice their shooting skills, drawing charcoal targets on white gums at different distances and competing with each other as to who is the best shot – always Ned, at any distance, as it turns out, though he is perhaps at his best when showing himself capable of hitting a bullseye even at a distance of 200 yards.

As lead is in short supply, afterwards they take their knives and cut the bullets out, to be melted down and recast.

18 OCTOBER 1878, BENALLA POLICE STATION, ACTION STATION

For his part, Superintendent John Sadleir is determined that – now that Ellen Kelly and her associates have been sent to gaol – her sons will be sent there to join them. After informing the man who has replaced him at Mansfield, Henry Pewtress, that the 'whole matter must be dealt with by everyone concerned as strictly confidential',[89] in succeeding days Sadleir resuscitates the plan he had first formulated nearly ten weeks earlier and soon gives out specific instructions by cable:

> A party which will consist of Sergeant Kennedy, Constables McIntyre, Scanlan, and Lonigan, will start from Mansfield on Friday next commencing the search for offenders Kelly from the Wombat end . . . The other party start from this end on Friday morning; the men forming it are Sergeant Steele, Senior Constable Strahan, Constables Baird, Thom, and Ryan . . .[90]

22 OCTOBER 1878, A STRANGE OFFER IS MADE

On his farm just outside Greta on this sunny afternoon, Ned and Dan's uncle, Patrick Quinn, looks up from his plough to note that he has a visitor to his selection – one of the local troopers, Senior Constable Anthony Strahan. He does not like Strahan and Strahan does not like him, so little time is wasted on chatting.

For Strahan comes straight to the point. 'Will you show us,' he asks, 'where Ned Kelly is based?'

Patrick is considered in his reply. He suspects that his nephew Ned and his men will be caught anyway, likely at the hands of men with guns and serious intent, and so is prepared to bargain for their lives. 'If you get six men who are game, and will not shoot him,' he replies carefully, 'I will go with you at once. There are three men along with Kelly.'

'There's a £100 reward,' Strahan says by way of encouragement for Quinn not to put qualifications on it.

'I want no reward – let that go to the Wangaratta Hospital.'

'All right, but I would like to keep some of it. I'll tell the chief commissioner of your offer. I am going to the Omeo after two horses. I'll come back again in the course of three days.'

Just a moment. 'I will not show you where Kelly is,' Quinn repeats doggedly, 'if you are going to shoot him.'

In response, at least by Quinn's subsequent account, Strahan loses his temper, totally dismissive of any such bargaining over the life of a common criminal, a man who has tried to murder a fellow policeman. What, not shoot Kelly? 'I'll shoot him down like a dog,' he declares. 'I'll carry two revolvers, and one I'll place by his side, and swear that he had it on him when I shot him.'

'Well,' Quinn declares, 'I won't show you then where to find him.'[91]

And that is that.

The miffed Strahan huffs off.

LAST WEEK OF OCTOBER 1878, THE LADS RECEIVE VISITORS

On this afternoon, a trusted member of the Greta mob arrives to give word of something he has heard. A group of police will shortly be on their way from Greta to look for them, and it will be led by Ned's old nemesis, Sergeant Steele. Shortly thereafter, another informant comes, telling them a second party will also be coming from Mansfield, led by Senior Constable Strahan.

The news has been confirmed by the fact that the police horses have been observed hobbled in the police yards for the last few days, no doubt getting them ready for the hobbles – broadly, handcuffs for horses, so they cannot wander far at night – that they would soon be wearing in the bush.

In response, there is no panic from the four men at Bullock Creek, and certainly no move to flee. To begin with, there is nowhere better than right here to flee to – no more secure, secreted spot in the whole region – and secondly, fleeing is simply not in Ned's nature and he is their undisputed leader. As a small precaution, however, Ned does order that they take no more shots at target practice, or even in hunting game, as they do not wish the sound of their shots to roll to whatever patrols might be in their area. From now on, any shots fired will be from strangers, and not from them.

The only exception might be from them at strangers . . .

PART TWO

THE NOTORIOUS KELLY GANG

Chapter Five

STRINGYBARK CREEK

> I felt more keenly than I can express the unjust treatment meted out to my mother, who was arrested with a baby at her breast and convicted of a crime of which she was innocent . . .
>
> *Ned Kelly*

24 OCTOBER 1878, SOME CHANGES AFOOT

It is one of those things. No matter that Sergeant Arthur Steele has been looking forward to leading his party of four south from Greta the next day, a Friday; it turns out that he has been subpoenaed to give key testimony at the Equity Court, and so must stand down. In his stead, Senior Constable Edward Batten Shoebridge, stationed at Bright, steps up to join Constables Thom and Ryan in the party under the command of Senior Constable Strahan.

The Mansfield party, meanwhile, is just preparing for its own expedition when the regular gold shipment from Wood's Point to Melbourne with a police escort under the command of Senior Constable John Kelly – a man sometimes at pains to point out he is no relation to the Kelly brothers – passes through. That esteemed police officer is pleased to have a good stop here in Mansfield, as it gives him a chance to catch up with his old friend, Sergeant Michael Kennedy, who meets him at the coach as he pulls in, takes him aside and tells him in confidence they are going out after the Kellys.

The two talk as old friends do, catching up, among other things, with the news of each other's families. Kennedy has had a terrible bereavement the year before, as he and his faithful wife of ten years, Bridget, had to bury their infant son, John Thomas, but, apart from that, they and their five surviving children are thriving.

As to the exceedingly difficult task at hand, the softly spoken Kennedy is at least happy to be having his friend Constable Michael Scanlan going with them, and has in fact recommended him for the task. For, as he had said to Sadleir, 'No man could render more service in the proposed expedition than he could, as he knows every part of that country lying between here and the King River.'[1]

Kennedy does confess, however, that his one particular worry is that he feels that, even though his group has been issued with an unprecedented eighteen rounds of ammunition for their Webley Revolvers, still they are a little under-armed for the task at hand, and he would be much more comfortable if they could have the kind of weaponry that the gold escort boasts. 'Could we,' he wonders, 'have the rifle that Constable Horwood is going to take with him on the gold escort?'

'We only have one rifle between us,' Senior Constable Kelly replies, 'so it would be a very dangerous thing . . .'[2]

But, in the end, isn't that what friends are for? Upon consideration, John Kelly changes his mind. 'Get a second revolver and give it to Horwood,' he says. 'You can have the rifle.'[3]

With which, he hands over the Spencer Repeating Rifle – a magazine-fed, lever-action gun that can fire seven 0.52 calibre rounds before reloading, and with spare magazines is capable of pumping out twenty shots a minute. In return, Constable Horwood is given Senior Constable Kelly's rather more humble revolver.

Sergeant Kennedy is amazed to find that the seven rounds are loaded through the butt of the rifle, but he is delighted to have it. It can be a powerful twin to go with the double-barrelled shotgun they have borrowed from Samuel Sandiford, Mansfield's Church of England vicar. And he can also have the woollen ammunition belt that comes with the Spencer, made to hold twenty cartridges.

And now Senior Constable Kelly heads off to catch up with another old friend in the Kennedy party, Michael Scanlan of the Mooroopna Police Station. Fifteen years earlier, in the Western Districts town of Beaufort, Senior Constable Kelly had first encouraged Scanlan to join the police force at a time when he was managing the local general store, and they have remained close since. Scanlan, too, is in fair form. He has rarely regretted the exciting move to the police force, where he has prospered, and he takes the opportunity, one more time, of thanking John Kelly for his guidance.

Scanlan, too, has some trepidation about pursuing Ned and Dan Kelly – he has been nervous enough about this venture to have, before departure, told a friend at the Mooroopna Hospital, 'I may never come back, and, if so, you can take my dog . . .'[4] – but he is at least more confident for the fact that he has Sergeant Kennedy with him, as he has enormous regard for him. They have worked together for years and are also firm friends. (Over the years, the two have also made a great deal of money by catching stock thieves, including Wild Wright, and sharing the reward money – referred to colloquially as 'going whacks' – proffered by the Stock Protection Societies. Perhaps this will be another lucrative venture, as both Ned and Dan Kelly have £100 reward on them, after the Fitzpatrick episode.)

The third member of the party is Constable Thomas McIntyre, a thirty-two-year-old Irish bachelor with watery, wide-set eyes and a perpetually stern brow that stands in stark contrast to his generally friendly countenance. McIntyre had joined the police force in 1869, and, though broadly liked by his fellow troopers and seen as 'a very respectable . . . zealous, conscientious man',[5] his nous and bravery are yet to be 'put to the test'.[6] Soon after arriving at his post in Mansfield, he had been taken into the confidence of Sergeant Kennedy and the two had also 'gone whacks', bagging and sharing a handsome reward of £60 between them. He had spent his last six months going out on patrols under the charge of Kennedy, and was much impressed by his Sergeant's skills as a bushman, one of those rare police who 'seemed to have acquired that sixth sense which ages of civilization has robbed us'.[7]

Despite his inexperience, Kennedy likes and trusts McIntyre, and has requested that he come out on this particular search party, reckoning to his superior, 'I am of the opinion Constable Scanlan, Constable McIntyre, and myself would be quite sufficient to undertake the working of that country, without any more assistance.'[8] Also helping his selection is that Kennedy loves the tasty grub that McIntyre had become well known for knocking up, even in the bush.

The fourth and final member of the party is Constable Thomas Lonigan, of Violet Town, included at the insistence of Superintendent John Sadleir because it is his view that each party must have someone who can recognise the Kellys on sight, and of course Lonigan has a long history with them . . .

Of them all, it is Lonigan who is the quietest and most removed from the general discussion. Yes, he knows the Kellys well, and that is precisely why he is so uncomfortable now, for he knows what they are capable of. If it took five troopers to subdue Ned Kelly alone on police turf, how are just four of them going to go up against Ned and Dan and friends untold, when on Ned's turf? As a matter of fact, Lonigan had felt so uncomfortable about the whole thing that, when taking leave of his wife, Maria, and four young children two days earlier, he had only gone a short way before he turned back to say another tearful goodbye.

Once more, he had taken his leave, and . . . once more he had gone back to his family, for one more farewell. Only on the third attempt was he successful in departing, while still telling friends he met on his way out of Violet Town, 'I do not expect to come back alive, but am resolved to go where ever I am ordered . . .'[9]

And so he is here now, and he is going. To do his duty . . .

25 OCTOBER 1878, THE MEN FROM MANSFIELD MOVE NORTH

Time to move out. On this warm morning, the chase for the Kellys begins. The word is that they are somewhere in the forbidding terrain near the head of the King River in the Wombat Ranges, and the plan is for two parties to approach them from opposing directions, flush them out and, at least, arrest them. At much the same time as this group from Mansfield under Sergeant Kennedy gets ready to leave, a similarly constituted police patrol under the command of Senior Constable Anthony Strahan is setting out from Greta.

Just before the Mansfield group leave the police barracks, however, Sergeant Kennedy remembers the Spencer rifle and asks Constable Thomas McIntyre to retrieve it.

'Really?' McIntyre wonders out loud. It is unusual to take such a powerful weapon, which none of them is familiar with.

'I do not like the look of that fellow,' Kennedy replies, pointing to the likeness of Kelly that stares balefully back at them from a poster above the mantelpiece of the barrack room.[10] It is the last photograph of Ned Kelly that the police possess – taken in Pentridge Gaol four years earlier. Constable McIntyre, for one, is surprised when Kennedy tells him that Kelly is now just twenty-three years old, and this photo is therefore of a nineteen-year-old, for the closely shaven figure with the black eyes staring back at him has little of youth left about him.

He quickly goes to get the Spencer rifle.

Just before dawn, thus, at five o'clock, Sergeant Michael Kennedy and his mounted constables take their leave. They are equipped for the long haul, with a tent and provisions on a packhorse to last for no less than a fortnight, and these provisions include two long leather straps, specifically designed and made by the Mansfield saddler Charles Boles so that a pair of dead bodies could be easily suspended from them. And all the troopers are wearing plain clothes, pretending to be diggers going out to look for gold. For they don't want the Kellys to run at their sight, they want to get to grips with them, and the body straps are not mere accessories . . .

The key problem, of course, is first to locate the Kellys in such thick bushland, where they are as at home as dingoes in their lairs, and then work out a way to capture them. The best information the police have is, 'Kelly has secreted himself in some isolated part of that country, lying between the Wombat and King Rivers, in a similar way to which Power did . . .'[11] and so that is the broad direction they take.

Sadleir has cabled Kennedy that they are to search 'up and down the King River',[12] and Kennedy has replied, giving him their destination for the night:

> The distance from Mansfield to the King River is so great, and the country impenetrable, that a party of men from here would, in my opinion, require to establish a kind of depot at some distance beyond the Wombat – say Stringybark Creek, seven miles beyond Monk's [sawmill].[13]

And so off the policemen go, heading down the deserted and wonderfully wide streets of Mansfield – so built in order that bullock teams could do U-turns – with just one man, a stranger, to incuriously witness their departure. After going down the Benalla Road, they cross the Mill Paddock Lane into the Wombat road, thence across the Mount Battery run, choosing to ford the broken river at Carey's farm. Do the odd farmers they pass recognise them as troopers, despite their dress as prospectors? Perhaps, perhaps not – but one glance at the tracks left by the government-issue horseshoes of their fine mounts would put it beyond doubt.

'The night before had been frosty and the air of the early morning was keen and bracing,' Constable McIntyre would record, 'but as the sun rose it became warm and genial with a slight breeze barely perceptible, carrying with it a faint smell of blossoming nature, making one feel that it was good to be alive.'[14]

Gradually coming closer are the Wombat Ranges, which now rise before the police like a clenched fist – the contours of the distant ranges really are like bunched knuckles. As they enter those ranges, the track disappears, and such light as there is comes filtered through the heavy tree cover. They stop briefly for lunch not when the sun is high in the sky – for there is simply no way of seeing it through the trees – but when Kennedy's handsome gold watch says that it is noon. (It is a gold watch he and his family treasure not just for its value but also for the fact that it had been given to him by a Stock Protection Society, as a reward for capturing cattle thieves.)

They have not long resumed their journey on this languid afternoon when they pass through a welcome clearing and suddenly spy a lethal tiger snake soaking up some precious sun on some rocks.

Both McIntyre and Lonigan dismount, and a playful race ensues as to who can kill it first.

McIntyre wins, with one mighty blow that breaks the snake's back, and exults to his friend, 'First blood, Lonigan.'[15]

After passing the last outpost of civilisation, Monk's sawmill, the party pushes on, ever further into the thickening bush. It is eerie, and rather lonely, a world entirely apart from the cheery and familiar one they have left in Mansfield. Is it just them, or is there menace in the air? There is no more banter now between McIntyre and Lonigan. They push on, as their world gets darker.

Finally, after a journey of some 20 miles, Sergeant Kennedy and his men make camp near 'the ruins of two small huts, one of which was burnt down'[16] and the other an abandoned miner's hut, by some disused diggings in heavily timbered country at Stringybark Creek. Some rough, rusty mining equipment lies all around and, crucially, it is 'a cleared place . . . out of danger of any timber which might fall from the forest trees'.[17]

Sergeant Kennedy's plan at this point is to make camp here and use this spot as a preliminary base. And so, with the ease and familiarity of men who have done this kind of thing many times before, they get to work: tending the horses, unpacking such supplies as are necessary and putting up their tent.

Kennedy is quite satisfied with this choice of base. From here, his men can patrol the area all around and search for some signs of the Kellys. And then, a few days later, if unsuccessful, they can move the base closer to the head of the King River, some 15 miles away, and . . .

And the sound of the regular, rhythmic pounding of a kangaroo making its way through the bush is as unmistakably distinctive as that of the laugh of a kookaburra – *a-whump, a-whump, a-whump* – and

Sergeant Kennedy is not long in telling Thomas McIntyre to take his rifle and see if he can secure them some fresh meat for their supper.

A-whump, a-whump, a-whump . . .

McIntyre returns, however, having found nothing, without firing a shot.

In the evening, the men retire to rest early with no sentry posted, as they have, of course, 'no apprehension of an attack being made upon us'.[18] An uncomfortable night is spent, with little sleep, as they have nothing between them and the hard ground but oilcloth, and the frost falls by night. It is so cold that, several times, McIntyre rises to stoke the fire, just to try to warm the marrow of his bones, which he knows has turned to ice.

Under such circumstances, it is not surprising that, even before the crack of dawn, it is time to get cracking. First up is McIntyre, who, before the first bare wisp of light, puts the billy on to boil the water for the tea, and he is soon joined by the others, warming themselves before the now roaring fire as they have their breakfast of lightly charred damper just like mother used to make, washed down by the scalding-hot tea. The light thrown from the fluttering flames flickers over their faces, four troopers – each one of them born in Ireland – all alone in the Australian bush, and there is an easy air of companionship among them. Yes, Kennedy and Scanlan are Catholics, while Lonigan and McIntyre are Protestants, but somehow things like that matter less in the Australian bush.

With breakfast over, though, it is time to get to grips, and Sergeant Kennedy tells McIntyre and Lonigan that he and Scanlan are going on patrol, to look for, with luck, the Kellys and, failing that, at least some signs of them. 'Mac,' Sergeant Kennedy says as he mounts his horse, 'don't be uneasy if we are not home tonight.'[19] For there is no telling how far they will go, and what they might find. They hope to be back before sundown, but there is no certainty. With storm clouds gathering, it may be easier to make their own camp, instead of pushing back in a storm.

And then the two of them are off, heading nearly due north right down Stringybark Creek. As they go, of course, they are scanning the heavy bush to the for'ard and left and right to see if there is any sign of the bushranger brutes.

In the meantime, Lonigan and McIntyre busy themselves – at least, McIntyre does, as he is a little more disposed to work than the other – getting their camp better established. To make the tent more comfortable, McIntyre cuts down many ferns and much long grass to provide some padding beneath their sleeping swags, and – after cutting a large sheet of bark off a white gum, out of which he improvises a table and a baking board – gets busy baking some bread from the flour they have brought with them.

Lonigan, meanwhile, at least looks after the three horses that remain with them, allowing the animals to graze on distant bits of grass in the clearing before rounding them up again, and filling in the rest of the time by reading the *Vagabond Papers*.[20] For the work of the colony's most mysterious journalist, 'The Vagabond', has become so popular that *The Argus* had printed his fascinating series of articles about the inside workings of many Melbourne institutions and sold them as separate pamphlets. McIntyre had bought the pamphlet 'The Vagabond's Visit to the Pentridge Prison' some months ago and had lent it to Lonigan just the night before their departure. The pamphlet, of course, includes that most in-depth interview with Harry Power, and the old bushranger's reminiscences now engross Lonigan. His interest particularly quickens when he comes to the part about their quarry, the very lad they're now after: 'I always was stuck for want of a mate . . . There's young Kelly was with me for a time, but he was no good, and helped to sell me at last. They say that he or one of the Quinns was dressed up as a black-tracker to deceive me. God will judge them for taking blood-money.'[21]

Around noon, after they hear a strange noise down by the creek, Lonigan tells McIntyre to take the light shotgun lent to them by the Mansfield vicar to investigate. McIntyre, hoping it might be a kangaroo or wombat that would provide fresh meat for supper, heads off and pushes his way through the wattle and sassafras scrub that clothes the banks of the creek. Alas, finding nothing of the edible kind, he is heading back when he spies a pair of Lory parrots – coloured bright red with blue flecks – that look a lot like supper if he can just shoot them.

Twice he fires, with the cracks of his shotgun rolling on through the thick bush . . . all the way . . . *all the way* . . . all the way to the Kelly camp, where, just outside the log hut, Ned suddenly stops with a start, cocks his ear and then turns in the clear direction of the shot.[22] He is not alarmed. The shot has come from way too far away to be an attack on their encampment, but it is certainly something to be investigated, and Ned heads off with his younger brother to do exactly that.

For his part, McIntyre simply heads back to camp. It is not surprising that his two shots have missed. Strangely, in the three years in the Irish Constabulary, and just shy of nine years with the Victoria Police, this is the first time he has ever actually fired a weapon of any description. Constable McIntyre does not really like guns, and in any case the Victorian Government – while very keen that he and other police be well drilled with their brightly polished swords for public parades – has never provided him or other troopers with the means or munitions to practice their marksmanship, as it is very expensive.

No more than half an hour later, Dan and Ned are back, reporting that, only a bit over a mile away from their hut, armed troopers have set up camp by the 'old shingle hut', as they know it.

Obviously, the brutes do not know that the Kellys are as close as they are, for the troopers have no sentries posted and they had had little trouble getting close enough to observe them. Oh, they are dressed in plain clothes, but they are troopers all right. They have seen someone they mistakenly think is Senior Constable Anthony Strahan, the man who boasts that he'll shoot Ned 'like a dog'.[23] As for the other fellow, they mistake him to be the great enemy of the Kellys, Constable Ernest Flood, who had seduced their sister Annie six years earlier and sent her to an early grave with his abandonment. *And* he had come to the house to arrest their mother not only days before Annie died but again for a separate charge on the very day that Annie was buried. All these years on, Ned still nurtures hate for him, a man he would describe as 'the greatest horse stealer with the exception of myself and George King I know of'.[24]

And they are part of a troupe of troopers in plain clothes, come to their area, obviously to kill them, exactly as their informant had told them would happen.

'We saw [the troopers],' Ned would later explain, 'carried long firearms and we knew our doom was sealed if we could not beat those before the others would come, as I knew the other party of Police would soon join them, and if they came on us at our camp they would shoot us down like dogs at our work as we only had two guns.'[25]

What to do then?

'We thought it best to try and bail those up, take their firearms and ammunition and horses and we could stand a chance with the rest.'[26]

Still, on the reckoning that the troopers do not pose any immediate danger to his camp, Ned decides to do nothing for the moment but starts to form a plan. To Ned, the broad brushstrokes of that plan seem obvious. While, in the face of police pursuit, other men might flee deeper into the bush to get away, that is simply not Ned's way. Besides which, while he knows this country like the back of his clenched fist, the police are little more than babes in the woods. *His* woods. So why flee? Why not go after them? Why not make the point that all who pursue the Kellys do so at the risk of their lives, that in these parts it is Ned Kelly who rules and *not* the police?

And no matter that the police are likely to be heavily armed, while the only workable weapons they have are a pocket revolver, a sawn-off carbine bound up with waxed string and a shotgun between them, for Ned knows that if he and his men do it right they can overwhelm the police and get their guns. If it all goes well, the police will surrender immediately, hand over their much-needed guns, ammunition and horses, and be sent on their way.

Ned tells the others of his plan, which they agree to, and, as the already wet day begins to darken further, they make final preparations.

Quickly, but carefully, their guns have the shot replaced by the bullets the bushrangers have manufactured themselves, the heavier slugs better suited for hitting a man even at a distance. Shot is for those who can't shoot and so must scatter their fire. Ned *can* shoot and is proud of it. On the reckoning that the guns must be distributed to the man where they will be most effective, Dan takes the shotgun and fills his pockets with ammunition while Ned takes the favoured carbine in his right hand and slips the revolver in the waistband at the back of his pants. As always, Ned will be at the front of the attack, with Dan covering whoever might be in the tent, and Steve and Joe will follow tightly behind, ready to lend assistance as required. All have their hats on, with the string under the nose in classic Greta mob manner. To a man, they are native-born sons of Irishmen heading off to take on the troopers.

Soon enough, the four of them smell the smoke of a roaring fire – in fact, a bonfire that McIntyre and Lonigan have just lit at the junction of two huge logs to give Kennedy and Scanlan help in locating the police camp in the thick bushland, as they are shortly due to return from their day-long reconnaissance, if indeed they have not camped further up the ranges.

Carefully now, oh so carefully, the bushrangers begin their stealthy approach. In a semi-crouch, fiercely concentrating on where they put their feet so as not to snap twigs or loosen stones that might roll, the four outlaw men start to close in. Ned is in the lead, with Dan just behind and the other two just after him. As a storm has passed overhead just thirty minutes before, the air is filled with the unique sound of the Australian bush after recent rain, the crickets wetly chirping their joy, the singular smell of eucalyptus trees dripping from on high, the kookaburras coming back from shelter unknown for a light laugh, the growing gurgle of Stringybark Creek itself, which is now rushing pleasantly as water pours in from the surrounding ranges. The closer the Kellys get to the police camp, the more the delicious scent of the bonfire fills the air, and they can also hear the irregular snort of horses just up ahead. Before long, through the blades of the heavy spear grass that gives them plenty of cover as they approach, the men get their first glimpse of the police encampment. There is the calico tent strung between two saplings, the roaring flames from the fire, which is situated some 20 yards from the tent, and, just to the right, a couple of horses tethered to a log.

Slowly now, and with great care, Ned goes just a little ahead of the others and . . .

And there are the two police now that they had spotted earlier.

One policeman is sitting on a log by the fire; the other tending his horse. Ned remains certain that he is looking at constables Strahan and Flood. The oldest Kelly brother looks forward to dealing with both of them again, so much so that, even after observing them closely, he fails to recognise his mistaken identification.

Ned has little doubt that, with the element of surprise, his men can easily take the two police in view – and whatever other police might be around – but still he is cautious. Long experience has taught him the virtues of observation before action, of becoming fully aware of all the dangers before making a move.

One of the police now gets up and goes to the tent, returning with a billy full of water, which he puts on the fire in preparation for making tea. In this kind of thick bush, the scene could not have been more domestic or unthreatening, but still Ned keeps watching, just to be sure, even as the billy boils and the tea is made and served.

Finally, however, as the shadows in this thick forest start to deepen further, Ned is satisfied, and he signals to the others that he is about to begin the attack. With a nod, the others indicate they are with him and, with Dan to the fore, his gun forward, they follow Ned in as he first breaks cover and heads towards the policemen.

'Bail up! Hold up your hands!' Ned Kelly roars at them.[27]

Hearing the shout, McIntyre thinks it must be 'Kennedy and Scanlan who, coming from an unexpected quarter, were jesting' but on turning around sees it is not them at all.[28]

Strangely, for both the attackers and the attacked, the whole episode happens so quickly that it almost seems like a cruelly stuttering dream – something unreal that is nevertheless punctuated by shock after shock – and all of it happening too quickly to be comprehended on the instant. Though Ned doesn't yet recognise them, the policeman sitting on the log, who Ned thinks is Strahan, and who now looks back at him with complete bewilderment, is in fact Constable Thomas

Lonigan, while the other, 'Flood', over by the horses and returning to get the billy tea off the fire, is Constable Thomas McIntyre.

Still, Ned keeps coming at them, still roaring at them to throw down their weapons and put their hands in the air, and Constable McIntyre would be ever after grateful that he does exactly as he is told by the bushranger on the far right, Ned, whose gun is pointed right at his chest. He drops the only weapon he has, which is the fork he is using to stir his tea. McIntyre's revolver and shotgun are both back in the tent, and he couldn't have resisted even if he had wanted to.

Not so the other trooper, Lonigan, who had been on the log. Immediately leaping to his feet and drawing his gun, he runs a little to his right, where he can take cover behind another, bigger log and prepare to fight back. And yet, no sooner has he lifted his head above that log and thrust his revolver forward to fire at the leading bushranger than, from 14 yards away, Ned has lined him up and fired a single shot from his carbine.

'I shot him that instant,' Ned would later explain, 'or he would have shot me.'[29]

The bullet hits the policeman in his right eye. There is a small scream, before Lonigan leaps to his feet, his hands raised in surrender, and, bloodily staggers some distance before crying out, 'Oh, Christ! I'm shot!'[30] Then he suddenly collapses and, within seconds, after some convulsing, is still, with nary a twitch coming from him and only a few drops of blood coming from the ghastly wound that had been his right eye. Nevertheless, he is still alive, just, as they can all hear his long, laborious, gurgling breaths.

'Keep your hands up!' the gunman calls to McIntyre, while closing quickly, with a revolver in his right hand and his carbine in the other.

The shocked constable, who to this point has had his hands straight out in front of him, now practically stands on tiptoes as he puts his hands up as high as they can possibly go. The other three bushrangers are fanned out behind the gunman, with three yards between them all.

Seeing that there will be no resistance from him, the gunman softens marginally. 'Have you got any firearms?' Ned Kelly asks him.[31]

'I have not,' the terrified McIntyre replies.

'Where is your revolver?'

'In the tent.'

Upon which Dan Kelly spins around and calls into the tent, 'Come out here you bastards.'[32]

'They're *out* . . .' McIntyre replies, trying to calm him.

'Keep him covered, lads,' Ned says, as he conducts a full body search of the constable, including under his coat and in his boots.

Satisfied that McIntyre is indeed unarmed, and getting the nod from the others that the tent is indeed empty, Ned asks where the other two troopers are. Told that they had gone out looking for the Kellys at dawn, and should be back before dusk, Ned relaxes a little.[33]

Dan Kelly, however, remains wary of the trooper and, after finishing the tea he has already helped himself to, makes towards McIntyre with a set of handcuffs he has found in the tent. 'We will put these upon the bugger,' he says.

'What is the use of putting these on me?' McIntyre remonstrates. 'How can I get away while you are all armed as you are?'

Ned agrees. Tapping his rifle, he makes the point to his brother, 'There's something better than handcuffs here.'[34]

Dan desists accordingly, but Ned still gives the constable fair warning. 'Don't attempt to go away. If you do I shall track you to Mansfield and shoot you at the police station.'[35]

McIntyre nods, and it is only Dan Kelly who remains unhappy. 'The bastards would soon put the handcuffs on us if they had us,' he says, not unreasonably.[36]

As they keep talking, Lonigan's laboured breathing stops, and he is obviously dead. While Dan keeps his gun trained upon McIntyre, Ned jumps the log to have a quick look at the man he has just shot, retrieves his revolver and comes back.

'Dear a'dear!' he says to McIntyre. 'What a pity. What made that fellow run?'[37] He had not wanted it to come to this. 'Who's that?' Ned goes on, nodding towards the corpse.

'It's Tom Lonigan.'

'No, no,' Ned replies, confused. 'I know Lonigan well.'

But then, after going and having another look at him, and indeed making out facial features in the ghastly and bloody shattered mess of what had been the constable's head, the bushranger comes back and concurs. 'I'm glad for that,' Ned says to the others, within earshot of McIntyre, 'for the fellow once gave me a hiding at Benalla.'[38]

'He will lock no more of us poor buggers up,' Dan Kelly offers, drawing a wan smile from the older brother.[39]

Not that Dan Kelly is not admiring of the dead man for all that, adding, 'He was a plucky fellow. Did you see how he caught at his revolver?'[40]

Plucky, yes. But once upon a time he had been vicious, too. Briefly, Ned then tells McIntyre and his own men the story of Lonigan having grabbed him by the privates and how it had caused him such agony. And then he realises a very odd thing – for the first time since that had happened, his balls don't hurt.

A dedicated policeman, McIntyre tries to ignore the horror of his situation and focus on the appearances of his four captors, the first close-up look by a policeman at the 'notorious Kelly Gang', as they will soon become known. Ned, he thinks, stands at an impressive six foot tall, looks a lot older than twenty-three and has a 'sallow complexion, dark-brown hair, full beard and moustache of a dirty dark red colour, moustache cut square across the mouth, hazel eyes with a greenish tint; wore dark tweed clothes, red silk sash, dark low hat'.[41] His gun is a very old, battered one, with fractured stock bound with wire, while 'the stock and barrel were bound together by similar means'.[42]

The seventeen-year-old Dan Kelly, who brandishes a single-barrelled shotgun, is a lot smaller, about '5 feet 5 or 6 inches high, very dark hair and complexion, small dark piercing eyes, beard not grown', and, in classic little brother pose, is dressed in clothes obviously too big for him. And while Ned and the other two are relatively calm and certainly in control, Dan is 'nervously excited and . . . laughing with a short laugh, almost hysterical. There is . . . something grotesque about his appearance.'[43]

As to the other two men, McIntyre knows only that they are of the Greta mob, without knowing their names, but notes that the smaller man, who looks a little like a jockey, is '19 or 20 years of age, 5 feet 8 inches high, fairish complexion, rather stout, straggling hairs over face, hooked nose, cruel expression', and recalls him carrying a double-barrelled shotgun, while the bigger one is remarkable for the fact that he does not have 'the villainous expression of the others'.[44] The bigger figure looks to be '21 years of age, 5 feet 9 inches high, very fair complexion, fair moustache and long beard on chin, very fine, like first growth, respectable looking'.[45] According to McIntyre, he had an old-fashioned gun with a very large bore. It seems odd to McIntyre that such a softly spoken, seemingly refined man as this has fallen among thieves.

Who worry him most, though, are Dan Kelly and the smaller one, Steve Hart, 'two bush larrikins, having all the vices of that genus homo, and not being possessed of the steadying influence of mature years they were two exceedingly dangerous men but only so when the power lay upon their side'.[46]

Now, with the other two troopers due to return at any time, the most important thing is to determine what kind of weapons and ammunition the gang might be able to secure, and they are not long in finding them. For there, inside the tent, is stored a rifle, a shotgun with thirty-six shells, breech-loading shotguns and so much ammunition it is dizzying.

Ned is pleased with the haul, glad that this array is not *against* them – and gives McIntyre's shotgun to Byrne – while being realistic about why the weapons are so plentiful. 'You buggers came to shoot me, I suppose,' he says simply to McIntyre.

'No,' replies McIntyre, 'we came to *apprehend* you.'[47]

Ned is not persuaded and is strongly of the view – as witness the enormous cache of weapons and ammunition in the tent – that the police, just as they had done to Ben Hall, 'meant not only to shoot me, but to riddle me'.[48]

Personally, shooting Ned Kelly or any of his men now appears to be the last thing on McIntyre's mind. For all the fight has clearly gone out of the trooper – he is even quick to accede to Joe Byrne's request that he make some more tea and provide some food for them.

But wait . . .

Before the other three begin to have their tea, and Joe Byrne even fills a pannikin with tea and hands it to McIntyre, Ned asks, 'Is there any poison about here?'

'No,' McIntyre replies, genuinely mystified, 'why should we have poison?'[49]

It is a fair point – the police party was unlikely to be carrying poison against the possibility that four bushrangers might drop by for tea. Again, Ned relaxes a little, and though he does not take the tea at least he wolfs down with the others the cooked ham with the bread that McIntyre had baked that morning.

'They all expressed so much approval of my bread,' McIntyre would record, 'that I believe I could have got a testimonial from them as a first class baker.'[50]

But back to the business at hand . . .

For now, Ned takes the cartridges out of the police shotgun, picks out the ends and, after throwing away the shot, places a ball in each cartridge before reloading it. Referring to his own curious rifle, bound together with wire – the one with which he has shot Lonigan – Kelly invites conversation with McIntyre, saying, 'That is a curious old gun for a man to carry about the country with him . . .'

'Yes,' McIntyre replies carefully, 'perhaps it is better than it looks.'

'I will back it against any rifle in the country,' Ned says proudly. 'I can shoot a kangaroo at 100 yards every shot with it.'[51]

McIntyre continues to watch, as Ned keeps extracting the shot from the cartridges and replacing it with balls, of which he has a plentiful supply.

'Here,' Ned says to Joe Byrne, handing him the shotgun, 'you take this gun and give me yours.' The two exchange weapons, and, as Ned brandishes his two guns, he says to McIntyre, 'There is one of these for you if you don't obey me.'

Yes, boss.

'Do you smoke, mate?' Byrne asks the constable.

'Yes.'

'Light your pipe, and have a smoke with me.'[52]

And so they do, sitting companionably on one of the logs and lightly chatting while Lonigan lies dead, just 15 yards away, where the flies have already started to buzz around his bloody eye socket, despite the wet conditions.

And yet, at least by his later account, McIntyre actually does have some fight left in him, and as Ned keeps looking down Stringybark Creek in the direction from which the other troopers are due to return, the constable focuses on the two guns he has resting against the log in front of him. Might it be possible, he wonders, 'to get one of the guns?'.[53] Again, by his account, he even goes so far as to take a short step to that effect, only to hear Steve Hart call from the tent, 'Look out, Ned, or that bastard will be on top of you.'[54]

Almost amused, Ned offers some kindly advice to his prisoner. 'You had better not, mate, because if you do you will soon find your match, for you know there are not three men in the force a match for me.'[55] Which raises his next point: 'Are there any others out?'[56]

McIntyre confirms that there is another police party from Greta looking for them, under the command of Sergeant Steele, but that is all he knows.

Softening a little, Ned then turns the conversation back to the other two men out on patrol. McIntyre tries to sound casual, saying he actually wasn't expecting them back this night. Eager to do all he can to protect their lives, he points out they are both Irish Catholics, just like Ned, thinking to himself, 'He might be possessed of some of that patriotic-religious feeling which is such a bond of sympathy among the Irish people.'[57]

Strangely, however, this seems to have little effect, because, 'like a great many young bushmen he prided himself more upon his Australian birth than he did his extraction from any particular race. A favourite expression of his was "I will let them see what one native can do".'[58]

Then, finding some pluck from deep within, McIntyre asks, 'What are you going to do with them, because if you are going to shoot them down in cold blood I would rather be shot myself a thousand times than tell you anything about them.'

'Well,' Ned nods. 'I like to see a brave man.' Then he simply adds, 'You can depend on me . . . I will not shoot any man who will hold his hands up and surrender.'[59]

'Are you going to shoot me?' Constable McIntyre persists.

'No, what am I going to shoot you for?' Ned replies, mystified. 'I could have shot you half an hour ago if I wanted to . . . At first I thought you were Flood and . . . if you had been I'd have roasted you upon that fire!'[60] He adds, 'There are four men in the police and if ever I lay hands upon them I will roast them alive; they are Flood, Steele, Strahan and Fitzpatrick.'[61]

McIntyre falls silent.

'But,' Ned says, his focus coming back to McIntyre, 'if I let you go you will have to leave the Police for it is a shame to see big strapping fellows in a lazy loafing billet like the police force.'[62] In Ned's world, a man who chooses to join the Victoria Police Force is no man at all.

Done!

'I will do so. My health is bad, and I have been thinking of going some time.'[63]

Ned doesn't believe a word of McIntyre's story but is happy to play along. 'If you attempt to let them know we are here you will be shot at once. If you get them to surrender I will allow you all to go in the morning, but you will have to go on foot, for we want your horses. We will handcuff you at night, as we want to sleep.'[64]

'Do you promise faithfully not to shoot them if they surrender,' McIntyre asks, 'nor let your mates fire?'[65]

'I won't shoot them,' Ned replies, again with his wan grin, 'but the rest can please themselves.'[66]

Then Ned asks the names and stations of the missing troopers, and, upon McIntyre's reply, he says, 'I have never heard of Kennedy but I believe Scanlan is a flash fellow.'[67]

He then grills McIntyre on their firearms, asking particularly if they have any 'long firearms'. The constable hesitates and Ned instantly flies into a rage, threatening him yet again. So McIntyre quickly acquiesces, admitting that they had a rifle with them.

Ned's rage boils. 'Well that looks as if you had come out to shoot me, you have no right to carry anything but revolvers.'[68]

Ned demands McIntyre's name and station, and the constable quickly tells him and begins to turn the conversation around by talking about a wanted man from Sydney.

Ned asks, 'What became of the Sydney man?'

McIntyre retorts, 'The Police shot him.'

Having regained a more composed air, Ned says, 'Well if the Police shot him they shot the wrong man and I suppose some of you fellows will shoot me some day, but I will make some of you suffer first, for you know I am no coward . . .'[69] In any case, Ned says, 'Fitzpatrick is the cause of all this.'

'But you cannot blame us,' McIntyre replies carefully, 'for what Fitzpatrick has done to you.'[70]

But now Ned suddenly stops . . . and cocks his ear.

Yes, he can hear it – the unmistakable sound of approaching horses.

'[Listen,] lads,' Ned calls out softly to the others, 'I hear them coming.'[71]

Following Ned's hand signals, the freshly armed Steve Hart secretes himself in the tent, gazing at the approaching horsemen through the slit, while Dan Kelly and Joe Byrne take cover behind some clumps of spear grass that go as high as five feet, giving the bushrangers plenty of easy cover. As to Ned, he kneels down behind the butt of the large log near the fire, not far from the dead Lonigan, with just his eyes peeking over, so he can carefully watch the troopers approach.

They are about 50 yards away in the gathering gloom, with Kennedy a dozen yards in the lead of Scanlan, riding their horses at walking pace. Ned quickly determines where the dangers lie: the Spencer rifle, strapped across Scanlan's back in the classic fashion of a trooper expecting no trouble, and the revolver securely latched in Kennedy's holster.

Turning to McIntyre, and pointing to a fallen tree ten yards away, Ned whispers, 'Mind you, give no alarm or I'll put a hole in you.'[72]

McIntyre does as instructed as the horsemen come closer and gets to his feet, walking towards them, just as he would had everything been normal. The two horsemen, still unaware that anything is amiss, come into the clearing, lightly chatting about the barrenness of their day – absolutely no sign of the Kellys – when they are hailed by McIntyre.

'Oh, Sergeant,' the constable calls out, rather nervously, 'I think you had better dismount and surrender, for you are surrounded.'[73]

In response, Kennedy first smiles, as this is obviously a jest, and even self-mockingly puts his hand to his revolver, as if he is about to draw it and fire. The smile, however, does not last long.

For the moment Kennedy's hand touches his revolver, Ned Kelly fires a warning shot and, suddenly, all four of the heavily armed bushrangers charge out from their hiding places, yelling as Ned had done before, 'You wretches! Throw up your hands!'[74]

No matter that, by firing the warning shot and rushing the troopers, instead of simply shooting them dead immediately as the Kellys so easily could have done, they demonstrated that their intent is to capture, not kill, the reaction of the troopers is not what the bushrangers expect. For lesser men and wiser men would have immediately surrendered. But Kennedy and Scanlan are made of sterner, if not quite as sage, stuff – and they react as instinctively as they do immediately.

Using his horse as a shield, Kennedy instantaneously throws the bulk of his body to the beast's left side, away from the muzzles of the guns, and then jumps off as three more shots are fired at him. For his part, Scanlan at first tries to wheel away to the right, but his frightened beast refuses to go and instead bounds forward, towards the danger. All the constable can think to do is swing his rifle around to his front, and, still without unslinging it, he manages to fire off a shot in the rough direction of Ned Kelly. It misses.

Kelly immediately fires back, this time hitting Scanlan. At first, the trooper falls forward onto his horse's neck, but, as his horse bucks, the trooper falls heavily to the ground . . .

Kennedy, too, now joins the fray. He dismounts with one massive leap and gets a shot off from above the rump of the bucking beast at Dan Kelly, just grazing the bushranger on the shoulder.

As Scanlan tries to stand, his horse bolts away, leaving him entirely exposed. He collapses once more onto his hands and knees, and it is while he is like this, on all fours, almost like a wounded animal, that Joe Byrne uses one of the captured police revolvers and fires at the trooper from just ten yards away. The lead ball hits Scanlan just under the right arm, and, as McIntyre sees blood spurt out, the trooper falls face and body flat to the ground.

Amid the shouting, shooting and sheer confusion of it all, suddenly McIntyre sees Kennedy's horse before him. In an instant, the previously meek trooper who Ned insisted had not needed to be placed in handcuffs has leaped upon the horse, only for it to rear up! McIntyre loses a stirrup in the process, and, as the only way to retain his seat and regain his stirrup is to lean forward on the horse's neck, the constable does exactly that. The horse, with its four feet back on the ground, bolts, and it is all McIntyre can do to grab its reins and drive his boots into its sides, exhorting it to gallop for its life . . . and his. The horse charges away as though the Melbourne Cup has just started in the bush, as behind him McIntyre hears Dan Kelly roar, 'Shoot that bugger! Shoot that bugger!'[75]

And indeed shots do ring out – though not from Ned Kelly.

'I could have shot him if I chose,' Ned would later recount, 'as he was right against me, but rather than break my word I let him go.'[76]

Nevertheless, when the horse momentarily stumbles, meaning that McIntyre very nearly falls off and must hug the horse's neck even tighter, there is a cheer from the bushrangers as they think he must have been hit, but he quickly rights himself and manages to keep going north, down Stringybark Creek – not daring to look back for fear of being knocked off the horse by a low-lying branch.

The bushrangers are not particularly concerned, as the fleeing trooper is relatively unimportant. He presents no immediate danger to them, as he is unarmed, whereas Kennedy – ***CRACK! CRACK!*** – is now firing at them from behind a tree.

The Kelly men frame their attack on Kennedy, coming at him from different angles and firing their guns with great rapidity to keep him pinned down. Aghast, appalled and terrified, McIntyre continues to gallop away, meaning that Kennedy is on his own, behind a tree, armed only with a revolver and his sense of duty – against four bushrangers with rifles, carbines and revolvers.

There have been sicker dogs that have got well . . . but very few.

Realising that the best he can hope for in such a situation is to escape with his life, Kennedy decides to attempt exactly that. He suddenly bolts from his position behind the stringybark tree and runs off into the scrub, taking the direction that McIntyre has gone on his horse.

Resolutely, Ned Kelly takes the police's double-barrelled shotgun and sets off alone in pursuit. It is not hard to work out where Kennedy is, so much noise does the trooper make, crashing and bashing his way furiously forward, first across the creek and then up and over a low ridge, that Ned, a natural bushman for whom this kind of scrub is akin to his mother's womb, manages to practically glide after him, a bearded angel of death.

Desperate, frightened and panicky, Kennedy turns and fires at his pursuer when he can, sometimes trying to take shelter behind trees but always trying to keep moving, to get away . . . away . . . *away*.

One of Kennedy's bullets passes close enough to sear Ned's whiskers, while another plucks at his sleeve. Two shots go wild, but Ned of course counts them and knows that Kennedy has used up four bullets from a six-bullet chamber. He can't have any more than two left. Ned pushes on, implacable, merciless. Kennedy knows he must make the last two bullets in his revolver count, before he will have to pause to reload with his final six bullets. Exhausted, terrified, he takes shelter behind a tree, waiting for Kelly to come on to him.

He can just hear Kelly's footsteps approaching, padding softly through the thick undergrowth, while, by comparison, Kennedy's breaths now sound to his own ears like the angry belches of a steam train. How can Kelly not hear him? Kennedy thinks of his wife. He thinks of his five children. He knows if these shots miss, he is unlikely to ever see them again.

Waiting . . . waiting . . . waiting . . . breathing . . . breathing . . . breathing . . . waiting . . . *NOW!*

In one movement, Kennedy springs from behind the tree, to see Kelly just 20 yards away and closing fast. With the trooper's revolver already out before him, he only has to swivel a little and pull the trigger.

The revolver roars, the muzzle flashes, the bullet . . . grazes the bushranger's ribs.

In response, however, Ned Kelly, in one practised movement as swift as it is smooth, lifts the shotgun and fires at Kennedy, causing a loud crack, a thick puff of white smoke and . . . a small lead ball hurtling forth. The ball hits Kennedy under his right armpit and yet, though the trooper lurches sickeningly, he does not fall. Instead, he tries to keep going, to get away, away, *away* . . .

Calmly, quietly, Ned Kelly follows tightly, his shotgun foremost as dusk descends, but still wary as he knows Kennedy has one shot left.

'The Murderous Attack on Victoria Police, Breaking from Ambush'.

(From a rough sketch by Constable McIntyre, *Sydney Mail,* 16 November 1878, courtesy Queensland State Library)

The light is ebbing. The darkness deepening. Only just able to remain upright, Kennedy finally realises he has no chance of escape and all he can do is surrender.

He stops. He drops his revolver. He turns. The best he can, he starts to raise his arms in the air.

Only a few yards away by now, Ned Kelly – at least the way he would recount it – finds himself confronted in the fading light by a man raising his right arm exactly the way a man who intended to shoot him would. Unable to see that Kennedy has dropped his revolver, Ned jumps to his right, away from the bullet he is certain is coming, and manages to fire his shotgun . . .

—

He is flying now. Galloping. Thundering hooves. Branches tearing at his clothes, whipping him in the face, scratching his horse's flanks. Constable McIntyre doesn't care. All he knows is that behind him lies *murder, bloody murder*, and his only hope of salvation lies ahead. He *must* get away from the murderers. Always, he has the fear that the bushrangers are behind him, and at one point, as he looks over his shoulder, he fails to spot the oncoming branch that knocks him to the ground.

Must get away . . . MUST get away . . .

And bless that horse. Instead of making good her own escape, the faithful mare has stopped and he is just able to remount.

Finally, however, whatever McIntyre's desperation to keep going, his horse proves to be simply incapable of it, and, after slowing to a canter and then a walk . . . no matter how much he continues to try to drive her on . . . she finally lurches to a dead stop, no more than two miles from Stringybark Creek. McIntyre concludes she has likely been wounded. After dismounting, he removes the poor beast's bridle and saddle, which he hides in the undergrowth, and shoos her away in the hope she might somehow survive. He staggers forward for another mile or so, taking his boots off as he crosses a stream so as not to leave boot-prints on the other side. Finally, he knows he must stop in order to secrete himself somewhere, on the chance that the Kellys are following him hard. All he can find in the first instance is a muddy wombat hole, but it will have to do, so he carefully squeezes himself into it, feet first. Before settling down, however, McIntyre is careful to make a quick entry in his notebook:

> *Ned Kelly, Dan, and two others stuck us up while we were unarmed. Lonigan and Scanlan are shot. I am hiding in a Wombat hole until dark. The Lord have mercy on me. Scanlan tried to get his gun out.*[77]

Trying not to breathe, not to make the slightest noise, he settles down, his ears straining for the tiniest sound that might indicate they are coming. Finally, mercifully, mother night wraps her black arms around him and, for the first time in hours, the terrified trooper starts to calm just a little. As soon as it is properly dark, he intends to start moving again.

—

Ned Kelly fires.

Sergeant Michael Kennedy falls.

The ball has hit him square on the right side of his chest, the force of it hurling him backward and down.

As Ned walks towards the now unmoving Kennedy, he is appalled to see the trooper's revolver on the ground and realises he has just shot an unarmed man, who had likely been trying to surrender.

Ned, deeply upset by the turn of events, now stands over the fallen trooper, whose breaths are coming in large, rasping gulps as his life ebbs from him, his three wounds bleeding copiously. He is still conscious, but only just.

Kennedy at least can talk, and he starts to speak of his beloved wife, his five surviving children and his eleven-month-old son, John Thomas Kennedy, whom they had buried eighteen months before, and whom he now suspects he will soon be joining in heaven. If Ned Kelly had felt badly before, he now feels positively wretched, even going so far as to say, 'Well, Kennedy, I am sorry that I shot you. Here, take my gun and shoot me.'

'No,' Kennedy replies, 'I forgive you, and may God forgive you too.'[78] But let Kelly allow him just this . . .

With faltering and bloody hand, Sergeant Kennedy now takes a notebook from a pocket, and a pencil, and then writes a note to his wife, before tearing the pages out, giving them to Ned and begging the bushranger to give his last loving words to her. Kelly promises to do exactly that, but then is distressed to see the Sergeant begin to writhe in agony as he clearly moves into his death throes. Ned feels he has no choice. It is more merciful to end it.

Taking his shotgun thus, he brings the muzzle down to just above the trooper's breast.

'I . . . have to go,' Ned tells him, 'and, as I don't want to leave you in a dying state, I will have to shoot you.'[79]

Stricken, Kennedy opens his eyes, and he looks into the eyes of Ned Kelly – at least the best he can, for his vision is now blurry. 'Let me alone to live, if I can,' he pleads weakly, 'for the sake of my poor wife and family. Surely you have shed blood enough.'[80]

Ned shakes his head that, no, he must do this.

Do Kennedy's previous words still echo?

'God forgive you . . .'[81]

God forgive you . . .

Ned Kelly grits his teeth and squeezes the trigger, and, in an instant, the quiet of the dusk is shattered by the shotgun's roar, rolling across the quiet glade, into the thick bush and away.

Quickly now, the dead Kennedy's pockets are searched by Ned, and the Sergeant's valuable gold watch is retrieved, together with – *hulloa!* – two photos of Ned himself, together with a little money. And then, in a gesture of admiration for the courage with which the trooper has died – 'The bravest man [I] ever heard of . . .' would be Ned's summation[82] – he lays out Kennedy's corpse as neatly as possible, even returning briefly to the camp to retrieve the dead trooper's police cloak, which he now opens over the corpse to give it some protection against animals.

It has been a brutal, bloody business, and three men now lie dead, but Ned still does not feel himself to be a cold-blooded killer. 'This cannot be called wilful murder for,' he would claim, 'I was compelled to shoot them or lie down like a cur and die.'[83]

And though he has regret for what has happened, still it is not without qualification. 'I could not be more sorry for them, with the exception of Lonigan,' he would recount. 'I did not begrudge him what bit of lead he got as he was the flashest and meanest man that I had any account against.'[84]

Back at the camp once more, it is time to get to work. Most importantly, Ned and his men round up the police horses and whatever provisions and ammunition the troopers had, before – in an effort to destroy evidence – Ned growls the order to set the police tent and remaining supplies alight. It is by the flickering light of the subsequent flames that, in a rather ghoulish exercise, Joe Byrne takes the distinctive dress rings off the fingers of Thomas Lonigan and Michael Scanlan, and puts them on the ring fingers of, respectively, his left and right hands. Explosions from the burning tent indicate that they had not recovered all the ammunition before setting the shelter alight.

Quickly and quietly now, with no talking – as the enormity of what has happened hits them anew – the four bushrangers head back to their digs at Bullock Creek, where they intend to snatch a few hours' sleep before getting away to the north . . .

They arrive back at their hut just before Tom Lloyd turns up bearing supplies as well as cash, courtesy of the gold he had sold on their behalf. After a meal of police rations – as grim and cold as the three corpses in the near distance – the four bushrangers try to sleep, while the wide-awake Tom stands guard against the chance that Constable McIntyre has already been able to raise the alarm. The thoughts of Steve Hart and Joe Byrne as they toss and turn on this restless night go unrecorded, but surely there are some wild eyes in the darkness, their pupils flitting like fireflies in a tiny bottle. What is to be their fate *now*? Joining up for a short time with Ned and Dan in their hut on the Wombat had been one thing, a larrikin lark on the wrong side of the law. But now, with three policemen dead, they will all be hunted – and seriously hunted by whatever forces of the law that the authorities can throw at them – as *murderers*. And all because they just happened to be there at the time, for it might just as easily have been Wild Wright or Tom Lloyd with the Kelly brothers when the police arrived. If caught, there will be no mercy. The likelihood is that a bullet in the battle would take them, and, if they survived that, the gallows thereafter.

It is a cold night with a rustling wind that makes the door of the hut rattle and the roof creak. There is no snoring. Who does sleep, does not sleep profoundly. Such is the price when three men less than a mile away have just begun the sleep of all eternity, at their hands.

—

The night does not sleep. Deep in the wombat hole, Constable McIntyre stirs. It all comes back to him. The horror, the *horror*!

And perhaps the bushrangers are still stalking him now?

Taking no chances, once he has wriggled his way out of his hole, he scrapes as much of the clinging mud as he can off himself, removes his boots, ties their laces together and drapes them around his neck. Until he is completely sure that the Kellys are not in pursuit, he wants to walk as quietly as possible.

For the next hour, he staggers barefoot through the dark bush as he tries to get back to Mansfield to raise the alarm.[85] After resting for a short time, he puts his boots back on and, the best he can, keeps stumbling onwards, almost like a blind man groping in the dark, but after another hour he drops from exhaustion.

Several hours later, when he can again rouse himself, at least the moon has come up, and, feeling a little stronger, he begins again. Though he initially had fled north from the bushrangers, as that was the easiest way, going down Stringybark Creek, he has since headed west, knowing he must eventually come to the telegraph line between

Benalla and Mansfield, which he intends to follow to Mansfield.

Soon, by virtue of the evening star, which of course always sets in the west, he is able to get his bearings. Whenever that disappears behind a ridge, he is able to rely on a small compass – illuminated by the occasional lighted wax match – to keep moving in the right direction the best he can. Still he is not sure that the gang are not just behind him, and so yanks off his boots once more.

—

Before dawn, the gang are up and moving. After packing, they attempt to burn their hut in much the same manner, and for the same reasons, as they had torched everything at the police camp the night before. Alas, in the heavy rain, the small building will not blaze and they have to leave anyway.

They are on their way then – riding their own best mounts and driving the four fresh police horses, and two spares, ahead of them in the pouring rain – and Tom again goes on ahead as a scout, looking for whatever trouble might be in their way.

Though they do stop in Greta at about eleven o'clock at the Lloyds' and then the Tanners' – Ned is very close to William Tanner, whose wife, Mary, is Tom Lloyd's sister – where they are able to eat some hot food and change into dry clothes, from that point on they keep to thick bush as they push cross-country in a looping passage towards Beechworth, some 50 miles south of the Murray River. But it is hard going all right, as the rain continues to tumble down, their horses become ever more exhausted and the swollen rivers and creeks become all the more difficult to traverse.

27 OCTOBER 1878, A RAGGED TROOPER ARRIVES AT THE MCCOLL RUN WITH UPSETTING NEWS

Constable McIntyre has now been walking for most of the last 20 hours, always through difficult country, for even with the coming of daylight he had stayed away from open ground, where pursuers might see him, and stuck close to the bushy fringes.

Finally, however, near three o'clock in the afternoon, his journey is at an end as he approaches the McColl run, just a couple of miles from Mansfield.

Murder! *Bloody murder!* he cries.

The shattered and fever-stricken constable who stumbles into John McColl's run on this waterlogged afternoon, with tattered clothes, and scratches and bruises all over him, ragged and hatless, with one boot on and the other under his arm, is almost insensible from exhaustion. The several ladies present immediately rise in surprise, but McIntyre's first words change this to alarm.

For, turning to Mr McColl, he says, 'Have you got any firearms?'

'No,' McColl replies, glancing at the ladies.

McIntyre tries to explain that he is a policeman, so it is all right . . .

'I know you are a trooper,' says McColl, 'but we have got no gun.'[86]

And so McIntyre's story bursts forth, that there have been some killings by the . . . did he say '*Kellys*'? . . . yes, by the KELLYS! One trooper definitely dead; others likely. What is urgent is that McIntyre get to Mansfield to raise the alarm.

'The ladies, recognizing I was not mad . . .' McIntyre later recounted, 'quickly supplied me with a cup of tea and some refreshments. My blessings on them.'[87]

He gulps down the tea, and a neighbour's buggy is quickly commandeered. The trooper is taken back to Mansfield Police Station – from where he had started two days earlier – arriving just after four o'clock.

Constable Thomas Meehan looks up from his desk, completely stunned at the shattered vision before him.

'This is *hell*,' McIntyre bursts forth.[88]

'What is up, McIntyre?' Meehan asks.

'Poor Scanlan is shot, Lonigan is shot, and I believe Sergeant Kennedy is shot.'

Stunned, Meehan wishes to take McIntyre to their superior officer, Sub-Inspector Henry Pewtress, to report what has happened, but before he can get away McIntyre begs him for his pistol.

Why?

Because, the distressed trooper tells him, 'Dan Kelly swore at the Wombat that he would come in and roast [me] in Mansfield.'[89]

More than a little shaken himself, Meehan quickly takes McIntyre to see Pewtress – a veteran of the London Metropolitan Police before he came to Victoria in 1852 – who this afternoon is to be found in his residence.

'Good God, McIntyre,' the shocked Pewtress says upon the shattered McIntyre's very sight, 'what has *happened?*'

'They are all killed, sir,' McIntyre bursts out. 'Everyone shot by the Kellys except myself. The Kellys have murdered them all.'[90]

Pewtress is shocked to hear of the deaths and shattered, too, to hear news of the likely fate of Kennedy. The two had been working together closely in recent times, and he had come to know and like him well. Most devastatingly, he knows Kennedy to be the father and husband of a tight-knit family, who will now be without a bread-winner.

But to grips. Because it is a Sunday, the town's telegraph office is closed, so Meehan will have to take his horse to Benalla to get the news out to Melbourne, while Pewtress will have to get to Stringybark Creek as quickly as possible with as many men as he can muster. One thing that must be done first, however, is McIntyre's formal statement, and it goes over nine pages in the constable's spidery hand. He is exhausted, but he nevertheless rushes to get it down, as Inspector Pewtress is waiting . . .

> *Yesterday afternoon, about 5 p.m. I being cook for the day was in the act of making some tea, Const. Lonigan standing beside me, suddenly and without us being aware of their approach four men with rifles presented at us called upon us to 'bail up hold up your hands'. I being disarmed at the time did so. Constable Lonigan made a motion to draw his revolver which he was carrying. Immediately he did so he was shot by Edward Kelly . . .*[91]

No more than two hours after McIntyre has arrived with the tragic news, Pewtress has gathered in horses, supplies and eight men from the town, including the medical man Dr Samuel Reynolds. Their number includes McIntyre, despite his being so violently ill that he can keep neither food nor drink down. Together, the party sets off, pausing only to bodily haul poor McIntyre into his saddle. This is not a posse, as between the lot of them they have only a rifle and a revolver, which is all the weaponry they can gather from the police station. Rather, it is a party specifically devoted to retrieving a dead body and searching for the two men who are still missing (one of whom has definitely been shot), hoping against hope to find them both still alive.

Just after the search party leaves, the redoubtable Mansfield Postmaster, George Newland, is found, the telegraph office opened and news of the atrocity is sent to the outside world, via a series of cables. One of them is from the Mansfield correspondent for *The Argus*, and his report is soon flying down the wires:

> MANSFIELD, SUNDAY, 6 P.M.
> News has just reached Mansfield that Constables Lonigan and Scanlan have been shot dead by four bushrangers at Stringybark Creek, about 20 miles from here. Constable McIntyre, who escaped, has just arrived with the intelligence. His horse was shot from under him. Sergeant Kennedy is also missing. Sub-Inspector Pewtress, Dr Reynolds, Collopy, and others left now on horseback to scour the country, and bring home dead bodies. The bushrangers are supposed to be the notorious Kelly's party, for whom the constables were in search.[92]

Grunts and curses in the night. Dogs barking at intruders, somewhere out there.

Just over three hours since leaving Mansfield, in the pitch black of a wretchedly wet night, as the rain falls down upon them in torrents, the search party led by Sub-Inspector Pewtress at last manages to reach the home of a settler, where they stop to ask for refreshments and directions. Alas, the man, as McIntyre later recounts, 'point-blank refused to have anything to do with us'.[93] The old man tells the police that he once before helped troopers, when they had been pursuing Mad Dan Morgan, and had afterwards received threats from the bushranger for his trouble. Not this time. Goodbye.

Aghast, exhausted, they push on until they arrive at another habitation in the area of Stringybark Creek, a sawmill owned by one Ted Monk. A hard-working man in his mid-thirties, a selector right on the fringe of the Wombat Ranges, Monk has 'the last place where any kind of vehicle could reach on the way to Stringybark Creek',[94] meaning he does receive occasional visitors, but never at this time of night. It is in the wee hours of half past nine!

Monk has been lying in bed beside his heavily pregnant wife, Anne, but rises to find out why the dogs are barking so. Mercifully, he opens his front door to find Sub-Inspector Henry Pewtress and his troop of men there. After Pewtress explains the tragic situation to him – that two police have been shot and Sergeant Kennedy is missing – that good man of course agrees to help. He had known both Scanlan and Kennedy well, liked them a great deal, and now has no hesitation in lending the police one of his packhorses. Most importantly, he agrees to act as their guide for the last haul to Stringybark Creek, which is still seven miles away through difficult country, and he even wakes two of his employees in nearby huts and has them come too.

Off the group heads into the mournful night, travelling in single file, each man barely willing to believe it has actually come to this. No one speaks. Heads down, they follow the Monk. Occasionally, the sound of a disturbed wallaby can be heard, a-whumping away in the receding distance.

They push on. Trudging. Trudging. Trudging.

Riding, riding, riding. The most important thing now for the Kelly Gang is to put as much distance as possible between themselves and the dead troopers. And, as that means riding through the night, crossing swollen creeks, on their way to crossing the Ovens River proper, that is what they do.

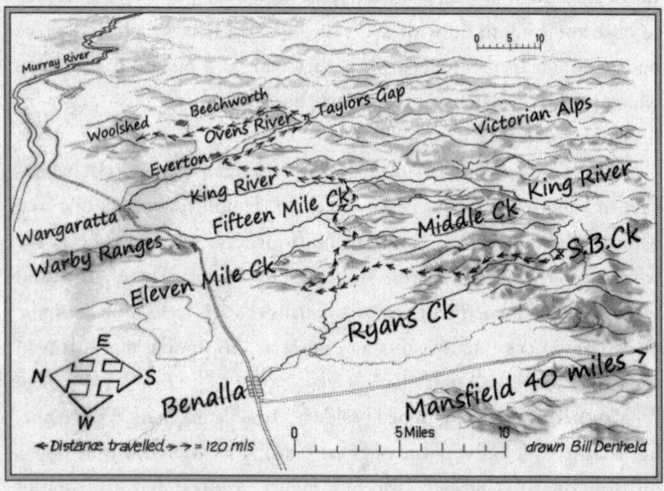

View looking east over rugged country showing the Kelly Gang's flight from Stringybark Creek to Aaron Sherritt's house in the Woolshed Valley. (Map by Bill Denheld)

Then, finding that the river has flooded its banks – now of all times – all they can do is to keep pushing up to the right along the edge of the flood waters, looking for a place to ford, eventually finding a spot at Taylor Gap, some ten miles south of Beechworth. Drenched, exhausted, freezing, they push on.

28 OCTOBER 1878, THE GRUESOME DISCOVERY IS MADE

For the exhausted, shattered troop, it is no easy thing to find the camp at Stringybark Creek in the middle of a wet night, but, at half past two in the morning, after a journey of 20 miles total, lasting over eight hours from Mansfield, they are finally getting near. For the last mile, Monk and his two men, Dr Reynolds, Pewtress, Constable James Allwood and McIntyre go ahead on foot and at last they are there.

'Here is where you had your fire,' Monk suddenly tells McIntyre.

'We had no fire in the open,' McIntyre replies, confused, referring to the fact that their bonfire of the previous afternoon had been at the junction of two logs, not here, in the open.

Oh.

'This must have been your tent,' Monk says. 'It is all burned, here is a number of papers.'[95]

With the position of the tent affirmed, McIntyre quickly has his bearings and, sure enough, by lighting matches under their coats in the still-pouring rain, they find the bodies of both dead troopers – Scanlan where he fell, and Lonigan six yards from where he fell. Most appalling is Lonigan's head with the shot through the eyeball, which has caused what is now a cavernous hole through what were once his remarkably fine features. Scanlan's corpse is at least cleaner, as his principal wounds remain covered by his uniform, and yet, so agonised is the expression on his face – he has clearly died hard – that it is somehow even more moving. All the men reel in horror from these sodden corpses, and a couple of them gag, but they have come to do a job, and it must be done.

As to the rest of the encampment, it is unrecognisable to McIntyre from what it had been on the Saturday evening when this all happened – incredibly, less than thirty-six hours earlier. There is now nothing left but a blackened smudge on the ground where the tent used to be, and a blackened tin plate that has been left behind. 'Our eight days supplies of provisions, arms and ammunition taken away, the tent and bed clothing were burnt, the horses were gone . . .'[96]

As dawn breaks, Dr Reynolds wraps bandages around the heads of the two dead troopers, to prepare their corpses for transportation, while the others search for the missing Sergeant Kennedy, branching out in different directions, examining the scrub in a half-mile radius, looking for even a trace of the missing lawman. They even risk one *coo-ee*, trying to achieve just the right amount of volume that will attract the attention of the missing Sergeant without alerting bushrangers at up to ten miles away that they are here, defenceless and just waiting to be killed. Ted Monk follows the tracks of the Kellys – the broken twigs and overturned stones make it more of a path than a track – but does not go far before returning. He is not *that* foolish, or brave.

The body of Constable Lonigan transported from Stringybark Creek.

(Courtesy Matt Shore)

With still no sign of Sergeant Kennedy, the search party has no choice. The bodies are strapped to the side of the deeply unsettled packhorses – do they sense their catastrophic cargo? – and the party begins the long journey back to Mansfield.

It is to be a difficult journey, and not for misery alone. It is more because, sometimes, these mourning men of Mansfield feel alone in that misery. As they pass by the home of a selector by the name of Perkins, his daughter comes out and one of the troopers says that two constables have been shot.

'Yes,' she says, as, over her shoulder, the man sees her father grin as the dead bodies are carried past.

And here, now, is Mrs Perkins. 'Excuse a woman's curiosity,' she asks without the barest hint of sorrow, 'but how many were shot?'[97]

28 OCTOBER 1878, AROUND THE RUGGED ROCKS, THE RAGGEDY RASCALS RAN, UNTIL . . .

When dawn breaks over the Kelly Gang – exhausted, cold, wet and hungry – they all know what they most need is help, succour and someone they can trust with their lives, and Joe Byrne knows just who to turn to. It is with this in mind that they ride into the Woolshed Valley just west of Beechworth, the place in which he grew up, and steal to within coo-ee of the cottage of Joe's oldest friend, Aaron Sherritt.

Once they have secreted themselves, eight gunshots skywards soon enough rouses Sherritt to come to the usual cave, and, of course, he quickly agrees to help, taking the bushrangers to another nearby cave he knows of, where they can rest, light a fire, have a meal and get themselves dry. Now it is Sherritt who stands guard while they sleep.

After the bushrangers are properly rested on the Monday morning, they push on once more, right into the teeth of a thunderstorm for the ages, pelting rain so heavy it is all they can do to keep moving through it, let alone across the many creeks and rivers they must cross as they continue to push north to the Murray, which they hope to get across in just a day. Sherritt helps out again by going on ahead as their scout for the first leg of the journey.

Chapter Six

AFTER STRINGYBARK

The father (a man of ill-repute) died some years ago, leaving the widow (now in Pentridge), the two sons Edward and Daniel, and four girls. The house of the family has been the rendezvous of thieves and criminals for years past, and indeed has been the centre of a system of crime that almost surpasses belief. They lived on the Eleven Mile Creek between Winton and Greta, and there can be no doubt made a living by horse stealing and theft generally. They were surrounded by neighbours of the same bad reputation, and it was notorious that to obtain evidence, or arrest the accused, owing to the network of confederates for miles around, was almost impossible.

The Argus informs its readers where the Kelly brothers hail from[1]

All things considered, the man at the head of a department so threatened needed to be a very strong man and one possessed of a true sense of duty to enter upon any far-sighted policy. Captain Standish, the Chief Commissioner of Police, was not such a one . . .

Superintendent John Sadleir

These outrages would never have happened if it had not been for the shooting of Constable Fitzpatrick, and the consequent anger and indignation of the Kellys at their mother having received that severe sentence . . .

Captain Standish, looking back

MORNING, 28 OCTOBER 1878, THE NEWS SPREADS

As ever, *The Argus* tells the terrible tale, and on this Monday it is a tale that everyone in Melbourne is talking about, just as people soon will be all over the continent:

> BUSHRANGING IN VICTORIA
> TWO CONSTABLES SHOT AND A SERGEANT MISSING
> A terrible encounter, almost without parallel in Victoria, has taken place near Mansfield, between the police and four bushrangers. The particulars to hand are but meagre, owing to the intelligence having only been received at Mansfield yesterday evening, but they are of such a character as to show that four most unscrupulous ruffians are at large in the colony, and that no effort must be spared to secure them immediately . . . Two constables have been murdered, a third has had his horse shot under him, while the fate of Sergeant Kennedy is dubious . . .[2]

In the face of the outcry, the government must move quickly, and so it does. The first meeting of the morning for Premier and Chief Secretary Graham Berry in his lavishly appointed offices at the Premier Building on Collins Street is with Captain Standish, and they quickly agree that extreme circumstances call for extreme measures. On this same morning, Superintendent Charles Nicolson – the man who had first put forward the policy that the way to control the Kellys was to take the 'flashness' out of them – will be given instructions to proceed and base himself in Benalla, to command a special force of police solely devoted to capturing or killing the Kelly Gang. The troopers for the force will come from all over Victoria and will work in tandem with the local force, commanded by Superintendent John Sadleir in Benalla.

As to how, precisely, Nicolson will go about his task, that will be left largely up to him, but, as detailed by Captain Standish, he is to have the 'authority to take any steps you think proper, and to incur any expenditure you think necessary'.[3]

The government also quickly ensures that Nicolson – who leaves Spencer Street Station on the train north at three o'clock, in the company of three troopers – will lack neither manpower nor firepower. For, as *The Argus* reports, the following day:

> Captain Standish, chief commissioner of police, yesterday afternoon ordered all the available troopers in Richmond police depot to proceed with their horses by 'special train' – a train commissioned for exclusive police use only – to Benalla. The men are all picked troopers, and others are being collected from different parts of the colony to follow.[4]

That special train, when it leaves, has on board the first of the seventy-nine police reinforcements that are to be sent into the district in the coming weeks, mercifully without anyone being injured, while a police order is made to the most famous gunsmith shop in Melbourne, Rosier's in Elizabeth Street, for no fewer than twenty-four double-barrelled shotguns and ample ammunition to also be sent north.

For his part, Premier Berry is quick to announce by mid-afternoon that, in regards to the four men responsible for the Mansfield murders:

> **A Reward of Two hundred Pounds will be paid by the Government for such information as will lead to the apprehension of each offender.**[5]

And Premier Berry also has one other step in mind, which he does not announce for the moment . . .

LATE AFTERNOON, 28 OCTOBER 1878, MANSFIELD SHUDDERS AND WEEPS

A pall of grief hangs low and dark over the town. As reported in *The Argus*:

> The sorrow felt for the death of Scanlan is universal throughout the district. He seems to have been a brave, cool, amiable, excellent man. Kennedy was an efficient bushman and a resolute officer. He has a wife and five children, and, fortunately for them, should he be killed, his circumstances are good. Scanlan was unmarried, and his station was Benalla. Lonigan was from Violet Town. He has left a widow and four children, badly off.[6]

Ah, but there is an exception to this misery. For, on the Monday evening, none other than Wild Wright and his brother Dummy arrive in Mansfield from Benalla and quickly set up camp in the local bar – 'Men first, dogs come last!' – where Wild begins to bray to all and sundry that a couple of the locals in particular would do better 'to stay in the township to-day unless they want to get shot'.[7]

Worse, far from Wild expressing any sympathy for the slain men and missing man, he says, with Dummy grinning evilly beside him, that it is his view that Ned Kelly would torture Kennedy.

Going on with it, and enjoying themselves hugely, the two brothers are soon found standing outside the local church, where Wild is continuing to shout at passers-by, 'Dogs! Curs! Cowards! Follow me if you want to catch the Kellys. I'm going to join the Gang! Come out a little way and I'll shoot the lot of you.'[8] Dummy, of course, cannot shout out in the same manner, but by his hand gestures he indicates that he agrees with everything his brother says, only double.

Of course, it does not take long for the police to hear of such braying, and they move swiftly. It is not just the offensiveness of the statements but also that the brothers have their well-provisioned horses outside the bar and there is a fear that they might ride to join the Kellys, and give them information of what is happening in town. It is better to move now, and so they do.

Several troopers fall upon the brothers, and a general melee – just what the brothers love – ensues. In the end, the only way that Wild can be subdued is by pointing a gun at his head, with the threat that the troopers are quite happy to start to even the score a little if he does not stop. Wild reluctantly does so, and the brothers are dragged to the lock-up, charged with 'using threatening language towards members of the search party'.[9]

One of the policemen who has arrested them is none other than the exhausted Constable McIntyre, and, seeing him, Wild is quick to give out a threat.

'You have escaped once,' he mutters darkly, 'but you won't next time.'[10]

EVENING, 28 OCTOBER 1878, A GATHERING AT MONK'S SAWMILL HEARS BOASTS

Given the events of the night before, it is not surprising that Ted Monk is exhausted, nor that there are no fewer than twenty friends and neighbours crowded into his small home as, through the thick cloud of pipe smoke, his wife labours hard to keep the hot tea up to them. This is the most extraordinary thing to have happened in this region, ever, and as Monk is the man of the moment, the one local who has been involved, of course everyone wants to hear about it from the man himself. And of course Monk doesn't mind telling the events of the previous night, of how he had been knocked up late in the evening and had then headed out into the night with the police and *personally* guided them to Stringybark Creek, where they had retrieved the bodies and briefly looked for Sergeant Kennedy before returning.

'I tracked the Kellys and their horses from the camp,' Monk says in passing, 'and could track them to where they've gone.'[11]

MORNING, 29 OCTOBER 1878, MOVING OUT AT MANSFIELD

Outside the courthouse, the search party for Sergeant Kennedy prepares to head out again. Yes, they are all exhausted, but they know they owe it to Kennedy and his weeping wife, Bridget – a local lass from a well-respected family – to make every effort possible to find him.

For there does remain at least a vague hope that Kennedy can still be found alive. It is thought he might have 'been taken by Kelly and his band to the King River',[12] and it is with this in mind that, under the command of the worthy if already exhausted Sub-Inspector Pewtress, the seven mounted troopers of the search party are joined by seven townspeople, with provisions for four days.

'The search parties . . . include storekeepers, clerks, clergymen, wardsmen, contractors, labourers, and bushmen,' the *Gippsland Times* would report, 'headed by the president of the shire. Business is entirely suspended at Mansfield.'[13]

Yes, there had been a suggestion the evening before that the police and good citizens go unarmed, so that, on the off-chance they do come across the Kellys, their lack of weaponry will be 'proof of their inoffensive purpose'.[14] But that idea has not survived the silent and sleepless watch of the night, and has been so abandoned by dawn that the men are now positively *weighed down* with weapons and ammunition. The troopers are sharing five rifles – 'two of them excellent weapons, sent by a private individual'[15] – and all of them have revolvers, though that is less significant. For it has been the specific advice of McIntyre that, 'for an expedition against men like the Kellys, revolvers are comparatively useless, and the police ought to have breech-loaders'.[16] That is, if the search party does come across the Kellys, having revolvers accurate only to 20 yards will be rather beside the point, when rifles capable of killing a man at 100 yards will be rather more valuable.

MORNING, 29 OCTOBER 1878, JOHN SADLEIR HEARS THE NEWS

After several days out on patrol, Superintendent Sadleir, the officer in charge of the district, arrives in the tiny settlement of Dookie, 25 miles north-west of Benalla, and for the first time hears of the confirmed death of two of his troopers and the likely death of his dear friend and long-time colleague Sergeant Kennedy, with whom he has worked for the last ten years. Shocked and outraged in equal measure, he turns his horse's head in the direction of Benalla and digs his spurs in.

Arriving at Benalla just before noon, he quickly consults Superintendent Nicolson, who happens to share the prevailing view among the constabulary that the Kellys are likely still in the area of the murders. Sadleir, however, is of the belief that 'men new to crime of this character would get away from the scene as far and speedily as possible'. He urges that 'police parties should be despatched to watch the crossings on the River Murray'.[17] As the river is in high flood, the number of places to cross will be limited, making it all the easier to catch the bushrangers.

Superintendent Nicolson, however, will not hear of it. What police they have, he says – and they are now arriving from all parts – must focus their attention on the immediate area in which the murders have occurred, with the particular aim of finding a possibly wounded Sergeant Kennedy. The public would expect nothing less. He intends to keep doing what he has been doing all morning, sending out police patrols in the immediate area, understood, Sadleir?

Yes, sir.

For his part, Sadleir now heads straight for Mansfield, 40 miles away, and his ride there is instructive. For, as he gallops along, as fast as his fresh horse can take him, he sees dozens of travellers pulled over by the side of the track, 'fearing lest they should run up against the Kellys; and each man I met was astonished that I should ride through the country without an escort, some of them imploring me to turn back. My answer to them was – "The Kellys are a hundred miles away by this time".'[18]

AFTERNOON, 29 OCTOBER 1878, APPROACHING STRINGYBARK CREEK

This time, Sub-Inspector Pewtress's expedition proceeds a little more quickly and comfortably than the one on Sunday night, but, because they get lost, they arrive at Stringybark Creek at half past three, with only four hours of daylight left. Swiftly, therefore, the party spread out and carefully examine all the area immediately surrounding the ruined police camp – the eyes of some of the men frequently darting to where poor Lonigan and Scanlan had been found – as well as up and down Stringybark Creek, including several miles in the direction of the King River. Nothing is found. It is really impossible country to search, so steep are the slopes, so deep the gullies, so thick the scrub, but the men do their best until it begins to grow dark.

Of Kennedy, not the slightest trace is found, though the searchers are able to follow the tracks of four horses a short distance before losing them. The one interesting thing is that those tracks cross the tracks left by McIntyre, so the searchers are at least able to surmise that he had not been pursued. As darkness falls, it is decided to head back to shelter. No one wants to camp in this eerie spot, and it is known that Ted Monk is happy to accommodate them at his cheery quarters at the sawmill, so this is considered the best option. With reinforcements, a few of them will try looking for Kennedy again the following morning, while the rest will return to town.

LATE EVENING, 29 OCTOBER 1878, SADLEIR ARRIVES

Arriving in Mansfield at ten o'clock that night, Superintendent Sadleir finds the tiny town caught between grief and sheer panic. Two of the three troopers lost are family men, which makes the grief so much worse.

The panic arises because the townspeople are, as Sadleir recounted, 'possessed by the fear that the Gang would raid their town, and apart from this there was the danger of their being ambushed by the Gang as the unfortunate police had been'.[19]

Sadleir does what he can to calm such fears, repeating his firm view that the Kelly Gang are a long, long way away. 'They're sure to clear out across the Murray,' he tells all and sundry.[20]

For Sadleir, the hardest part of all comes on the following morning. He heads off to visit the wife – and, he strongly suspects, widow – of Sergeant Kennedy to offer what comfort he can in the dreadful circumstances. 'Her grief,' he would soberly record, 'was piteous to witness, and one dared not venture to buoy her up with the hope of her husband's safety.'[21]

Thereafter, he heads straight to the Mansfield lock-up and immediately goes to see Wild Wright, for he wishes to do a deal. The way it works, Wild, see, is that you can either cooperate with us or you can spend a long time in gaol. What Sadleir wants, he explains, is for Wild to, in the first place, 'go amongst the friends of the Kellys, so as to ascertain if possible the fate of the missing sergeant'.[22] Sadleir even promises Wild £30 if he succeeds in 'finding the body of Kennedy, or brings him in alive'.[23]

While Wright broadly agrees to this – at least, he says he does, and notes that he will begin by asking Ned Kelly's sister for information – he will not agree to do more. When Sadleir asks him to also go out with the troopers to help to look for the Kellys in their old haunts, he gets a flat-out refusal. As Sadleir later recounted the conversation, '[Wright] knew the fierceness of [Kelly's] disposition so well, he assured me, that he would be risking his life in going near him.'[24]

Turn on Ned Kelly? Not on your Nelly.

When, shortly afterward, Wild and Dummy Wright appear in court, charged with Using Threatening Language Towards Members of the Search Party, Wild is remanded for seven days with bail refused, while Dummy, reasonably, is found innocent on the grounds that, as a deaf mute, he could not have verbally threatened anyone!

AFTERNOON, 30 OCTOBER 1878, THE VICTORIAN PARLIAMENT GETS TO GRIPS

Not surprisingly, the Legislative Assembly is in great agitation on this day, with the Honourable Members on both sides of the chamber seeking assurances from Graham Berry that 'everything possible is being done to apprehend the murderers who are still at large, and to rescue the unfortunate missing Sergeant Kennedy'.[25]

In response, Premier Berry tells the Assembly that, after consultation with the Chief Commissioner of Police, it had been 'resolved to increase the reward offered for the arrest of the offenders from £200 to £500 per man',[26] and also to introduce the *Felons Apprehension Act*, similar to the Act introduced by the New South Wales Government in 1865 to bring down Ben Hall.

It is Sir Bryan O'Loghlen, the baronet of high Irish birth, who, as the Attorney General of Victoria, has the honour to move that the Bill be introduced into the Legislative Assembly, describing it as 'An Act to facilitate the taking or apprehending of persons charged with certain felonies and the punishment of those by whom they are harboured . . .'[27]

Under its provisions, if a judge agrees that a 'person at large will probably resist all attempts by the ordinary legal means to apprehend him', the judge may issue a warrant for the apprehension of the person so charged, and, 'if the person so charged shall not surrender himself for trial pursuant to such summons' and if 'such outlaw shall afterwards be found at large armed or there being reasonable ground to believe that he is armed it shall be lawful for any of Her Majesty's subjects whether a constable or not to . . . take such outlaw alive or dead'.

Furthermore, by virtue of that same Act, be it heretofore known that if 'any person shall voluntarily and knowingly harbour, conceal or receive or give any aid, shelter or sustenance to such outlaw or provide him with fire-arms or any other weapon or with ammunition or any horse, equipment or other assistance or directly or indirectly . . . or shall withhold information or give false information concerning such outlaw . . . the person so offending shall be guilty of felony and being thereof convicted shall be liable to imprisonment with or without hard labour for such period not exceeding fifteen years . . . This Act shall continue in force until the end of the next Session of Parliament.'

The central idea of the legislation, just like it had been for Ben Hall, is to enable both police *and* civilians to go after Ned and Dan Kelly and the two other unidentified men, with far fewer restrictions. What it means is that anyone knowingly dealing with this gang will likely be committing a criminal act – while anyone who shoots them down will be fully within the law, no questions asked. (And will also likely get the lion's share of the reward.) Once the law is passed, both the gang and their sympathisers essentially have the presumption of being innocent until proven guilty reversed . . .

All those in favour say 'Aye'.

Aye. Aye. Aye.

The *Felons Apprehension Act 1878* is hereby passed in the Legislative Assembly, requiring only the agreement of the Legislative Council and the governor to be the law of the land until the end of the next Session of Parliament.

That afternoon, fresh reward posters begin to appear around Melbourne and shortly thereafter in regional Victoria, including both the increase in the reward to £500 and the latest information that has been garnered about the identity of the four bushrangers being sought:

DESCRIPTION OF THE OFFENDERS

Two of the four murderers are supposed to be Edward and Daniel Kelly. Of the other two the following description has been furnished by Constable McIntyre:

First Man – Name unknown, about 21 years of

age, 5 feet high, slight build, very fair complexion, whiskers, beard, and moustache, thin, mild expression of features.

Second man – Name unknown, about 19 years of age, stout build, only a few straggling hairs on face, sinister expression.[28]

30 OCTOBER 1878, WITH THE KELLY GANG

There are rainy days, wet days, teeming wet days, days when it pours cats and dogs like never before and then . . . there are days like today. Perhaps the heavens are weeping at what God's children have done, and are doing, to each other. In fact, so heavily does the rain fall that it necessitates the altering of Ned's plans, as the men are forced to navigate their way around rising flood waters as they keep pressing north.

One roughly contemporary writer would describe it particularly well: 'The Murray, which is at times a mere brown thread, is liable to floods, and when they come the low lying banks on either side become one vast lagoon, with islands peeping out here and there. The men . . . ventured deep into the lagoons in the hope of reaching the main stream, but were forced to abandon the attempt, for the river was higher than it had been for many years . . .'[29]

Within just a couple of hours, further progress north is clearly impossible and they know they must look for a place of shelter to rest up.

MORNING, 31 OCTOBER 1878, AT STRINGYBARK CREEK, A DISCOVERY

Despite it all, Bridget Kennedy, a warm, maternal woman of stoical disposition, continues to hold out hope that her husband is somehow still alive. He must be! He must have got away! After all, two searches have failed to reveal him, so perhaps he escaped from the murderers, perhaps he is now simply lost in the bush somewhere and will soon emerge . . .

As astutely observed by the *Australasian Sketcher*, 'Many conjectures had been made as to the probable fate of the missing sergeant, but while a general impression appeared to gain ground amongst the people in the locality that Edward Kelly and his band of marauders had taken Kennedy with them to the King River, scarcely anybody ventured to do more than hope that the gallant officer, who appears to have been ruthlessly shot, had not been murdered.'[30]

Sub-Inspector Pewtress holds out no such hopes and is convinced that Kennedy has been killed like the other two troopers. Either way, dead or alive, Kennedy must be found. It is with this in mind that Pewtress puts together the largest search party so far, of sixteen volunteers and five constables, and on this Thursday morning – after spending the night at Monk's hut and leaving at the crack of dawn – he and the party arrive on site at the police camp at half past seven and renew the search in a methodical manner.

This time, fanning out, they broadly search the area in which McIntyre had retreated. Within thirty minutes, the normal buzz and crackle of the bush is interrupted by a strong loud *coo-ee*, and a voice cries out in the bush, 'Here is something, here it is!'[31]

The voice belongs to Henry Sparrow, an overseer at the Mount Battery Station. In the middle of a small clearing about eight yards across, as the others rush towards him, he is found resolutely gazing down at something.

As they all quickly gather, it is obvious what it is. It is the body of a man, lying on his back, covered by a cloak, with his upturned legs and feet showing out clearly from beneath it. A tree within two yards of the body, near the body's head, bears the mark of a bullet.

When they are all there, slowly, carefully, Sub-Inspector Pewtress pulls back the cloak and, as one, they reel back in horror, with again some men gagging at both the sight *and* now stench of rotting death.

Of course, it is the body of Sergeant Kennedy. One bullet has hit him in the back of the head, and as the Sub-Inspector later describes it in a cable to the Commissioner, the bullet had continued on, 'carrying away part of the face'.[32] What is left of the blackened face is severely decomposed. Maggots have hatched and are furiously at work in what used to be the eye socket and have already eaten half the nose.

Several other shots have clearly hit Kennedy, the most upsetting of which is the large hole in the breast, with the uniform around the terrible wound blackened and burned. For the more experienced of the police, it is obvious that such a wound can only have happened if a gun had been held right against the chest and fired – a murderous, merciless, cold-blooded execution. It even appears that Kennedy's right ear has been cut off with a knife, together with some of the fingertips.

What kind of *monsters* are these men of the Kelly Gang?

(In fact, the parts of Kennedy that are missing have been nibbled off by animals, not members of the Kelly Gang, but that is lost in the moment.)

An examination of the area immediately around the corpse reveals bullet marks on the trees near the path taken by the Sergeant, indicating he had been hunted down like a dog, likely by several of the bushrangers . . .

It is, thus, with a strange mix of white-hot fury, black misery and a kind of yellow, gagging nausea that the search party gathers up the earthly remains of Sergeant Michael Kennedy, places them in two new cornsacks brought for the purpose – lashed together with saddle-straps – and delicately straps them on the back of a horse ready for the long, mournful journey back to Mansfield. Meanwhile, one constable goes out ahead of the main party so that a cart can be sent back to meet them.

This is done, allowing a more dignified entry for the slain policeman, and the horrified town turns out in force at three o'clock in the afternoon, to stand silent sentinel as the tragic train of police and volunteers arrives at the head of the cart. The body is quickly taken to the morgue, where a post-mortem examination and inquiry can be held on the morning of the morrow.

The return party reports that, while returning, they happened upon the other party of police, from Greta, that had also gone in search of the Kelly Gang. It is their report that, only hours earlier, they had come across the tracks of the Kelly Gang after 'discovering a native bear recently shot by a rifle ball'.[33] The group is now engaged in following up the tracks. They are sure the Kellys are heading north but feel themselves entirely under-equipped – they are armed only with breech-loaders against the myriad guns the Kellys have stolen from Sergeant Kennedy's group – and undermanned for the task at hand. As a matter of urgency, every available policeman in the area must be alerted. Those citizens who can help them to pursue the Kellys must. Those between the Kellys and where they are heading must try to stop them.

With the exception of Kennedy's family, no one is more affected by the confirmation of Kennedy's death than Constable McIntyre. It confirms his worst fears that, of the four policemen who had gone to Stringybark Creek, there has been only one survivor: him. And why has he survived? Clearly, because he had taken his opportunity to escape, by jumping on Kennedy's horse and galloping away, even while Kennedy was fighting for his life.

Personally, McIntyre has no doubt that he had done the right thing. He had taken the only opportunity that beckoned to survive and so tell the world what had happened and who was responsible, but he has also become aware that there are others who take a different view. No, no one has yet said anything to him directly, but certainly it is a point of quiet discussion and sometimes averted eyes, and he is acutely aware of it. He is also lashing himself over the fact that he had needlessly divulged that he had hidden in a wombat hole, something that has clearly caused enormous comment and even amusement.

'I could very easily have said that I concealed myself,' he would later note, 'without mentioning in what particular manner I had done so, it would have injured no person and saved me from many humiliating and vexatious remarks.'[34]

Mercifully, Superintendent Sadleir is not of the view that the constable has done anything wrong at all, and makes a point of seeking out McIntyre to 'shake him warmly by the hand', as he 'endeavoured to set him at ease'.[35] Of course, the two talk over what happened, and

McIntyre is clear on the circumstances of Lonigan's death, telling his superior that he 'was sitting on a log, and on hearing the call to throw up his hands, he put his hands to his revolver, at the same time slipping down for cover behind the log on which he had been sitting. Lonigan had his head above the level of the log and was about to use his revolver when he was shot through the head.'[36]

This is McIntyre's third confirmation that Lonigan had been about to shoot when Ned had shot him first. Indeed, his second confirmation had come two days earlier at the inquest, when McIntyre gave a more detailed and considered account: 'Lonigan endeavoured to get behind a tree, three or four yards off, at the same time placing his hand upon his revolver. Before he could get his revolver out he was shot and fell.'[37]

Another upsetting rumour that circulates is that Kennedy and Scanlan had actually gone off on their own, intent on killing or capturing the Kellys, purely to claim the reward.

31 OCTOBER 1878, A LAW FOR OUTLAWS

Never in anyone's memory has the Hon. Henry Cuthbert been so impassioned, as he implores, yes, *implores,* his fellow Honourable Members of the Legislative Council to pass the *Felons Apprehension Act* that the Legislative Assembly had passed the day before, so it can become law.

'The Bill is framed,' he thunders, 'for the purpose of enabling the ends of justice to be carried into effect against a Gang of ruffians that have committed grave and serious outrages during the last few days . . . Sometimes occasions arise – and the outrages lately committed form one – in which we may fairly assume from the facts revealed that the accused is guilty and we may come to that conclusion even before conviction . . . Now this Bill is to enable every well-disposed subject of Her Majesty, whether a police officer or civilian, to take and apprehend these men – to take them alive or dead.'[38]

Of course, such is the mood that the Bill passes 'through all its stages with applause',[39] and, after it receives the governor's assent, notices are quickly printed and put up all over Victoria, calling on Ned

Kelly, Dan Kelly and 'Two Men Whose Names are Unknown' to surrender at Mansfield Court House before five o'clock in the evening, 12 November, or face the consequences.

31 OCTOBER 1878, MINE EYES HAVE SEEN THE HORROR

The Anglican Bishop of Melbourne, James Moorhouse, educated at St John's College, Oxford, has experienced many things in his travels before migrating to Australia. He has witnessed terrible scenes in his pastoral rounds, been right in the middle of terrible tragedies and called in to provide spiritual solace on countless occasions. But rarely, if ever, has he seen anything quite as appalling as this . . .

After travelling up from Melbourne to give comfort to those most devastated by the murders, he is there when the body of Sergeant Kennedy, 'a fine and upright man of about forty years of age', as he would write of him, 'the terror of criminals and the pride of the troopers',[40] is brought back to the township.

Moorhouse has made it is his business in the hours since he has arrived to seek out the Lonigan widow, and presumed widow in Mrs Kennedy – for her husband's death had not been confirmed when he met her – and he hurries to visit Bridget Kennedy again now that the worst has happened. Though nearly insensible with grief, that good woman nevertheless expresses a determination to see the corpse of her beloved husband, and it is all Bishop Moorhouse can do to hold her back. After some discussion, they come to an agreement. He will go into the Mansfield morgue to see if 'the sight [is] fit for her'[41] and advise her afterwards.

And so there it is.

On the table in front of him, Bishop Moorhouse gazes down upon the rotting corpse of a once fine man. Yes, the good Sergeant has been cleaned up from how he was found in the bush, but still the Bishop can only just stop himself from gagging at the sight and stench. Moorhouse has no hesitation. Closing the door firmly behind him, he gently seeks out the widow Kennedy and implores her not to see her husband. 'In your state of health,' he says gently, 'it would be wicked for you to subject yourself to such a shock, and to imprint such a fearful spectacle on your mind.'[42]

Finally, Mrs Kennedy agrees, and she goes quietly home to be with her children, leaving her husband, the father of those children, to the care of his fellow policemen, who are now coming by to pay their respects to one of their own, murdered by vicious criminals.

EVENING, 31 OCTOBER 1878, BEECHWORTH, A LETTER IS WRITTEN

To hell with the Kellys . . .

Yes, Hugh Bracken had known them well in two stints working as a constable, and dealt with them many times. He not only knows what kind of men they are, but also the damage they had long done with their thieving. For, after his first stint, Bracken had tried his hand as a selector but been devastated to have his horse and cattle stolen by wretched rustlers, and so had returned to the police for a time before taking up his current job as a guard at the Beechworth Lunatic Asylum.

But now this? Now the Kellys are going out murdering policemen who are just doing their duty? Policemen, in fact, who were friends of his, and with whom he had worked many times. Eight years earlier, he and Michael Kennedy had even been sworn in as bailiffs of Crown lands on the same day. And now Kennedy is *dead*, to go with the confirmed deaths of the other two fine policemen.

It is not right. And so now Bracken takes pen in hand and writes a letter to Captain Standish . . .

Lunatic Asylum
Beechworth
Oct 31st 1878
Sir
I most respectfully beg to volunteer my services as an auxiliary in the force now engaged in the pursuit of the notorious Gang

of Bushrangers Kellys and others. My reasons for proffering this request is that I am intimately acquainted with every inch of the fastness of these ranges where the outrage was committed. Having often traversed this district when stationed as Mounted Constable at Buckland for over three years. Also at [the head of the] King river for about three years – and because I know personally the Kellys, Wrights, Lloyds and others. I am also ambitious to share in the encounter. I am well mounted and only require [some] ammunition . . .
I have the honour to be your obedient servant,
Hugh Bracken
Attendant[43]

As it turns out, Hugh Bracken is one of eleven ex-policemen who apply to rejoin the force at this point, to take part in the Kelly Hunt, many of them motivated by the massive reward posted on the gang's heads.

AFTERNOON, 1 NOVEMBER 1878, MANSFIELD BURIES ONE OF ITS FINEST

The procession going into Mansfield Cemetery on this sunny afternoon is as big as the tiny town has ever seen, with all but the entire population turning out – for every business in town has closed – as well as many people from other towns, over 200 persons in all. At the procession's head comes no less than the Bishop of Melbourne, James Moorhouse, flanked by the local priest, Father Scanlan, and the Church of England pastor, the Reverend Mr Sandiford, who had previously lent his double-barrelled shotgun to the man now lying in the coffin.

Now come the grim-faced police, led by Superintendent Sadleir and a clearly exhausted Sub-Inspector Pewtress. Right behind is the hearse, bearing the coffin of poor Kennedy, which at least is covered in an enormous wreath made by the wife of Bishop Moorhouse.

In the wagonette just behind, ahead of the long line of people, is the black-clad widow Bridget Kennedy, with four crying and confused children holding tightly to her dress as she alights, while she holds her baby in her arms. Sobbing lightly, trying to stay calm for her children but failing, she follows her husband's coffin, borne by six policemen, as it makes its way to its final resting place alongside the fresh graves of Thomas Lonigan and Michael Scanlan, buried three days earlier on the Tuesday afternoon, the three men set to lie together for eternity.

'I am the Resurrection and the Life . . .' Father Scanlan, who is no relation to the dead constable, begins his service as the gathering tightens around him. More prayers follow as Sergeant Kennedy's coffin is lowered into the grave, his children leaning over the gaping maw for a last glimpse at the box containing their fine father, and Father Scanlan raises his voice to the heavens.

'Grant this mercy, O Lord, we beseech Thee, to Thy servant departed, that he may not receive in punishment the requital of his deeds, who in desire did keep Thy will, and as the true faith here united him to the company of the faithful, so may Thy mercy unite him above to the choirs of angels. Through Jesus Christ, our Lord. Amen . . .

'May his soul and the souls of all the faithful departed through the mercy of God rest in peace.'[44]

At funeral's end, the many journalists covering it head to the Postmaster's office to send their accounts to their newspapers, only to find, very strangely, that the telegraph wires near Mansfield have been cut by villains unknown.

But many can guess . . .

Hopefully, these villains will be dealt with soon, as, before the telegraph was cut, a telegram had arrived informing the police that a large lot of 'repeating rifles and ammunition'[45] was on its way to Mansfield. It is the earnest hope of all decent people that the criminals who have killed these fine men will soon be made to pay heavily for these murders, a view strongly expressed by Bishop Moorhouse to all and sundry.

'Poor wretches!' he is recorded thundering. 'One cannot help pitying them, crouching among the trees like wild beasts – afraid to sleep, afraid to speak, and only awaiting their execution. But bushranging is so horrible, so ruthless, so utterly abominable a thing, that it must be stamped out at any cost.'[46]

1–5 NOVEMBER 1878, THE KELLYS ON THE RUN

Poor wretches. One cannot help pitying them, crouching among the trees like wild beasts.

For it is a measure of how desperate the Kelly Gang now are that, blocked at every turn by the endlessly rising flood waters, the only place Ned can think to find shelter is at the home of William Baumgarten.

For, as he is about to find out, the saying that hell hath no fury like a woman scorned is not correct. For that fury is as *nothing* on that felt by a woman whose innocent husband – and that is the way she sees it – has been sent to gaol in disgrace for dealing with the *very* man who now stands *before her*, wanting her HELP!

For Margaret Baumgarten has no sooner opened her door to see a drenched Ned Kelly requesting shelter than she begins shouting abuse, hurling accusations and epithets with equal bitter abandon. She does not give a *damn* if he is Ned Kelly, known to have killed three policemen, he can GET OFF her property now! Of course, Ned and his men – exhausted, drenched, starving, fighting for their lives – could have forced their way in regardless, to simply take the food and shelter they so desperately need, but they don't. Yes, they have killed three policemen just a little under a week ago, but force their way into a defenceless woman's home when she has said no? That wouldn't be right.

Dejectedly, thus, they simply move off to a paddock 'some 200 yards away',[47] and set up a rough camp within sight of the homestead, perhaps even hoping the lady of the house might change her mind. But not her. Glaring at them through the window, she watches closely as, just before sunset, they strike camp and head off again across one of the Murray's flood channels, with water swirling and roaring around them. Which is as well for them, for within only minutes one of the many police patrols now searching all over Victoria gallops up to the homestead, and the Kellys – on their way back from an impassable channel – can actually see Mrs Baumgarten on her front porch, gesturing in their direction.

The Kellys! Left here only minutes ago! And they went, she says – pointing due east to where a tributary of the Murray River lies just near the homestead – thataway. Immediately, Detective Douglas Kennedy and Sergeant Harkin, with their one black-tracker and half-dozen troopers, set out in strong pursuit. It seems the Kelly Gang must have forded the tributary right near the homestead, but when the troopers try to do the same it proves impassable, so they head further downstream looking for an easier spot that Harkin happens to know of. As they go, of course, they look eagerly for tracks to see if the Kellys are just ahead of them, but fail to make sense of a ground that is redrawn every second by the deluge, as rivulets and rivers spring up all around them. They push on regardless.

Just behind them, standing on their tiptoes in the reeds, with the water rising around them, and their weapons completely immersed and useless, Ned Kelly, Joe Byrne, Steve Hart and Dan Kelly have their heads tilted way back and just their nostrils out of the water. Freezing, and only just managing to hold on – with Dan, the smallest, particularly struggling as the rushing water threatens to sweep him away – never have they been so vulnerable.

As soon as the police round the corner of the river, the gang are immediately out of the water and shaking themselves off like mangy dogs that have fallen into a dam, before quickly gathering in their horses, which they have left tied up in the scrub, and riding off in the exact opposite direction.

As dusk falls, and the darkness and cold close in, they at last feel safe enough to stop. Soon, they are poor, freezing wretches.

Things are so desperate that they decide to take a chance and light a fire deep in the sodden bush – the bushman's trick is to get tiny wet twigs to burn, then use the burning twigs to dry and burn sticks, which are used to dry and burn larger sticks, and so on. Whatever the risk, at least their guns can be dry once more, and they can get some precious warmth back in their bones before facing the long, wet night ahead.

As they do so, Ned is furiously thinking. It is now obvious that continuing to move north in an effort to get across the Murray is hopeless.

And it is equally impossible to stay where they are. So it is that, just as a dingo to his den and an eagle to his eyrie, Ned decides to steer the Kelly Gang back to their home turf, into bush so impenetrably thick it is only such as they who can manoeuvre around within it, and pursuing police will once more be like sick rabbits within coo-ee of a dingo's den . . .

They head towards a familiar haven: Joe Byrne's neck of the woods on the tablelands just west of Beechworth, the Woolshed Valley. Once Ned's men are saddled up again and moving off, it is to the south they head, as the rain continues to pour down. They ride through the night, driving their horses and minding they stay discreet.

Exhausted and beginning to teeter in their saturated saddles, they arrive back at Aaron Sherritt's shack on Sheep Station Creek atop the luscious Woolshed Valley. Relieved to see a familiar friend, they dismount to the ground to take some rest, only to be told the disturbing news. With a cocktail of fear and excitement in his voice, Aaron tells the boys that a *Felons Apprehension Act* has been passed, meaning they can now be shot on sight, by anyone, police or public, and the reward on their collective heads has risen to a staggering £2000, no less than £500 for each man.

Christ.

Utterly worn down by their close shave with the police the night before, the arduous ride and their days of flight, their tired minds swirl like the Murray, with thoughts of how they are going to stay a nose ahead of the traps. With that level of temptation, how long could it possibly be before someone sold them out, perhaps even someone close to them? It is sobering news and, more than ever, they know that they must keep moving, on the reckoning that a moving target will be so much harder to hit, let alone capture. After taking their leave of Aaron Sherritt just before dusk, they head off into the still-teeming weather and wilds, unaware that they have been spotted by a local bark-stripper, who recognises them.

What to do? After consideration, the man decides to head to Beechworth, to report his sighting to the police. But . . . what if the Kellys find out it is him who is reporting them? Would they kill him?

Murder his family? They've already killed three police, so what would killing the likes of him be to them? He feels he needs a drink, and so stops off at a hotel to have one, and then several more. And then several more again. Perhaps his intent is to give himself some Dutch courage, or perhaps simply to dull the agonising debate going on in his head about whether to report this sighting to the police or not, but either way the drinking feels so good he just keeps going.

Meanwhile, at the Victoria Hotel and Dining Rooms in Everton late on this Saturday night, Mary Vandenberg is just getting ready for bed – alone, because her husband, the publican, is away – when she hears 'the rattle of a whip on the door'.

Strange. Who could think the hotel would be open this late? Still, a trusting soul, she wraps her dressing gown around her to make herself decent, takes the bedside lantern and pulls back the bolt on the door, allowing in a gust of cold air, the sound of pouring rain and the vision of a very tall man with a beard, a stockwhip in his hand and a rifle over his shoulder. Just behind him are three similarly drenched, similarly armed men.

Very politely, the tall man touches the brim of his hat and says gently, 'My men are in rags and must be fed.'

Of course, it is Ned Kelly and his gang, and Mary knows it from the first. The request is unrefusable and, without a word, she steps back to allow them in – with Ned, strangely, staying back.

'What of you?' she says.

'I'll keep watch,' he replies, taking up a seat on the verandah.

Mary takes the other three to the dining room and, after encouraging them to take off their wet things, lights the fire and then wakes the young Irish girl who has recently joined the establishment as a maid. 'Get a bucket of potatoes and get them peeled.'

'I'll not do it,' the shaken girl weeps.

'You'll do it, or where will you go!'[48]

It is a fair point and so, crying all the while and shaking with either fear or cold, or both, she gets to work. Within half an hour, Mary is able to provide for the three bushrangers at her table and the one on the verandah steaming-hot plates of stew with potatoes.

'Thank you,' Ned replies, before apologising for the fact that they have no money to pay for it.

Shortly thereafter, they are all gone. When her husband returns the following day, she does not mention the visit to him for fear of worrying him unduly, and gives the Irish maid strict instructions to do the same. Of course, she will remember them ever afterwards, later reminiscing, 'Of all the sorrowful sights I saw, it was those poor men.' As to Ned, he was 'a gentleman, nicely spoken, not bold'.[49]

Between them and where they want to go, the gang face two great barriers, which are – in a curious symmetry of the man-made and the natural – the rivers and railway lines. Both have only very limited crossings and it is sure that the police have all such crossings heavily patrolled. Steve, however, has an idea and, as the man most familiar with this part of the world, says there is a little-known crossing of the Ovens River at Wangaratta, and they can use that. So it is to Wangaratta they now ride . . .

Early the next morning in Wangaratta, some 15 miles away, at a time when just the first grey streaks of dawn have penetrated the miserable wetness of it all, a woman on the outskirts of town, Catherine Delaney, awakes to the sound of galloping horses. Where are they? And who would be up at this hour? Looking out her window, she sees them, 'four young men riding four horses, two pack-horses in front with two heavy packs on each horse . . . and four others running bare-back in front of them. The horses seemed exhausted and the men were forcing the horses from the township before daylight as well as they could.'[50] Strange that they should be galloping, in the town, and so early in the morning.

She wakes her two sons, and they also look. They recognise one of the horsemen as Steve Hart, a local. It is obviously the Kelly Gang, coming through Wangaratta at this time because it is the only place within 30 miles they can be sure of crossing the raging river.

The Delaney family are not long in spreading the news among their tight family and friends, and it is only a short time before word of what the Delaneys have seen comes to the ears of Stationmaster

Henry Laing. 'This morning, at 4 o'clock,' one of the railway workers tells him, 'the outlaws, instead of going through the railway gate . . . crossed by the back of the hospital, behind Delaney's house . . . [the boys] recognized the outlaws, and they were armed.'[51]

Stunned, excited, Laing immediately reports the sighting to Wangaratta's Senior Constable Patrick Walsh, who instantly tells his superior, Police Inspector Brooke Smith, who in turn . . . *does nothing.* The forty-four-year-old police veteran of dubious character – he had once spent a few days in prison himself for failure to pay a gambling debt – neither telegraphs the news to Sadleir at Benalla nor sends his men out looking for tracks.

Instead, he dismisses the sighting as not credible and, to prove it, goes out that day with a rudimentary search party, in the gushing rain, only to find nothing – as he had predicted all along. He quickly returns to the safety of his warm quarters, where the Kellys are unlikely to get him, for Inspector Brooke Smith – one of the few men who could hold his own on the other end of a see-saw with fat Constable Hall – likes excursions no more than the poor horse that must bear him.

Meanwhile, back at Wangaratta Station, Stationmaster Laing is amazed to receive a cable from Benalla:

> A special train of constables is to leave tonight for Beechworth.[52]

Beechworth? Why Beechworth, when the Kellys have just been here, this very morning, in Wangaratta? Clearly, Benalla has not yet been told, so Laing sends through the Delaneys' story . . .

As it happens, both Superintendent Sadleir and Sergeant Arthur Steele are over in Benalla, and they are standing right beside the telegraph master as the news comes through. A recent, credible sighting of the Kelly Gang! Do Sadleir and Steele then react instantly, and set out in hot pursuit? Not particularly. They had been planning to take their special train to Beechworth with their large party of men to follow another, earlier lead, that the gang had been spotted in the ranges near a place known as Rats' Castle, and they are reluctant to change plans. Still, Sadleir tells Steele he must 'go on to Wangaratta', adding that 'the train is at your disposal, you can delay it for half an hour or an hour if you consider it necessary . . . see if there is anything in this rumour'.[53]

Steele arrives at Wangaratta at one o'clock the following morning to be met on the platform by Constable Michael Twomey and Stationmaster Henry Laing. Immediately, Steele asks if the rumours are true.

'I have just been down at the back of the hospital to the One Mile bridge,' Constable Twomey replies, 'and there were the tracks of the horses right enough there.' He adds that the 'horses were shod, some of them, and with very large feet'.[54]

'When you heard about it,' Steele asks, 'what was done?'

'Nothing has been done so far,' the constable replies.[55]

Though Steele agrees, from the description, that it must be the Kellys, he is one more who makes no move to do anything. Rather, he tells the constable that it is his firm view that 'the outlaws must be making for the Warby ranges', and that he must 'go up at once and report the matter to Mr [Brooke] Smith'.

Personally, Steele – his tweed hat firmly atop his pate, as ever – then pushes on with his men and special train to Beechworth, to follow up on the previous lead at Rats' Castle. It is every bit as if he does not actually *want* to come to grips with men capable of killing three policemen in cold blood, least of all in their own lair. The upshot, as Stationmaster Laing would later recall, is that 'away went the special at all events, and the Kellys were down the other way'.[56]

Meanwhile, as instructed, Constable Twomey diligently goes to find Police Inspector Brooke Smith, who is both in charge of twenty-two policemen in Wangaratta specifically detailed for pursuit of the Kellys and . . . now fast asleep in his quarters at Ketts' Royal Hotel. Groggily, over the roar of the rain on the corrugated-iron roof, the inspector tells Twomey to get another constable and go down to the Delaney house and find out exactly what they saw. The constable returns an hour later with news that the Delaneys are suddenly not so sure who the men in the grey morning were, but they can say that 'they were headed in the direction of the Warby Ranges'.[57] Inspector Brooke Smith, petrified by the spectre of the Kelly Gang at every turn, again feigns disbelief and does nothing but send his constables out yet again to get more information from the reticent locals, while he remains inside, safe, sound and dry.

So passes the fourth day of November, and the fifth, with no action out of Wangaratta. A great opportunity is missed, as the gang, it will soon be discovered, became exhausted and doubled back on their tracks that Sunday before going to stay at Timothy Ryan's at Lake Rowan. They could very well have been captured with little resistance, if only the police had moved promptly towards the Warby Ranges . . .

6–7 NOVEMBER 1878, AT BEECHWORTH AND SEBASTOPOL, HERE COMES THE CAVALRY

Is it a breakthrough or a breakout? On this wonderfully bright, moonlit evening after so much rain, the man in charge of all normal policing in the district, Superintendent John Sadleir, is heading into Beechworth from an afternoon's patrol at Taylor Gap with Senior Constable Frank James when, arriving at half past ten, they are momentarily stunned to see the whole police encampment – which Sadleir knows has just two policemen on duty – 'overrun with armed men!'.[58]

'Look out,' Sadleir calls in a low voice to his colleague, even as he reaches for his gun.[59]

Mercifully, however, as soon as they get close, they recognise the armed mob as consisting of respectable townsfolk. As it turns out, one of the policemen on duty at the station, Constable Robert Vincent Keating, had received information from a bark-stripper who on the Monday morning had been near Aaron Sherritt's shack, spotted the Kelly Gang, and been drinking and 'blowing' – boasting about it – ever since. He'd finally arrived in Beechworth that afternoon, still drunk, and once the constable had heard of his claims he confronted him, determined they were credible and, commendably and quickly, called together this group of volunteers to go out after the Kellys. For the bark-stripper is sure he knows where they now are!

Sadleir quickly takes the matter in hand. First of all, he talks to the informer in question, which is easy enough as he has been placed in the lock-up for his own safety. *Despite* still being drunk, the man makes a most credible case that it was the Kellys – his description matches perfectly what McIntyre has stated – and is very particular that, if they are not found where he has seen them, he knows of another place they would likely be, up 'in the rocks where it would take fifty men to get them out!'.[60]

All up, Sadleir is satisfied that it is indeed the Kellys and quickly sends a telegram to Beechworth:

> Very positive information that Kellys are concealed in range near here. My informant is not quite sober, and has been talking rather openly, but I am convinced his information is genuine . . .[61]

He ends it by requesting more police to be immediately sent up overnight.

While Sadleir approves of the initiative of Keating, he is nevertheless of the view that he wants to go after the Kellys with professionals, not amateurs. Gathering the volunteers around, he thanks them for their willingness to help but advises that, for the moment, they must return to their homes until further notice.

Before dawn the following morning, a large body of troopers and officers from nearby barracks has formed up, together with Captain Standish himself, accompanied by Superintendent Nicolson, as they have come by special train from Benalla overnight. Also on that train had been two local press reporters who had heard of what is about to happen and . . . and . . . and is that a particularly strange-looking black-tracker with them?

No, it is the informant, the bark-stripper, who has taken boot black to his face in an effort to preserve his anonymity both from this posse of police and press, and the Kellys, should the police find them. Four other men stand out for the grim and weather-worn expressions on their faces. They are Senior Constable Strahan, Senior Constable Shoebridge and their two fellow troopers, the other party that had been searching for the Kellys around Greta. They had only been able to rest in Benalla for a few hours on returning before they had been called out again, and – haunted by how easily it could have been them instead of Kennedy and his men in their graves – they are deeply committed to the cause of tracking down the murderers and settling accounts.

But will they? Nicolson for one is far from convinced. With now thirty troopers and extras travelling across very rough country, up and over great ranges of granite, 'the rumbling noise that the party made was simply just like thunder,'[62] and they must certainly be heard at least a mile away.

And yet, with Superintendent Sadleir and Captain Standish constantly seeming to want to talk separately from him, Nicolson – not for the first time when around Standish – feels quite excluded. Captain Standish, as the Commissioner of Police, is of course in charge of the whole thing, and there is nothing Nicolson can do. It might have been easier to bear had Nicolson not also known that Captain Standish could have arrived in the region earlier but had wanted first to see the running of the Melbourne Cup, the day before last. (In the Captain's defence, he is *the* man who may be credited with inventing the Melbourne Cup. A great racing enthusiast, and, more importantly, a great gambling man, he had been a leading member of the Victoria Turf Club from the moment he stepped into Melbourne town, and pushed from the first 'for an annual feature betting race'.[63] On Saturday 2 November 1861, the first Melbourne Cup had come to pass, and, pushing two decades later, there is no way Captain Standish is giving up his favourite day out, *his* day out, for some criminals in the North-East.)

At last, the mass of troopers arrive before the said hut where the Sherritt family live on their modest selection. It is, frankly, not much to look at, a veritable house that Jack built – rough-cut hardwood slabs of timber supporting a shingled roof. All troopers now check the staggering array of weaponry they have been issued with.

Superintendent Nicolson selects three troopers, saying, 'Come along with me'[64] and gallops away. (In fact, one of them is not quite *yet* a trooper. Hugh Bracken's offer to rejoin the force five days earlier has been so quickly accepted that there has been no time to put all the paperwork through, and for the moment he is here as an armed volunteer.)

As Captain Standish drops back to command a reserve of a dozen men, Nicolson and Sadleir, with separate groups of mounted troopers, position themselves on opposite sides of the house, some 100 yards away from its front and back door.

And . . . NOW!

On Nicolson's signal, the two groups charge at the house in a full-on gallop, gripping their bridles tightly with one hand and their weapons even more tightly with the other. 'Logs that would have been looked at twice before leaping on another occasion were taken recklessly,' *The Argus* reported, 'rotten ground was plunged through . . .'[65]

It is Nicolson's group that arrives first, and it is the brave Nicolson himself, and the redoubtable Hugh Bracken, who jump off their horses and, in much the same movement – and in Nicolson's case with every bit as much enthusiasm as he had once rushed at Harry Power – charge at the front door with their shoulders forward.

As it happens, Bracken is so eager to get there that he gets marginally in front of Nicolson, who, as a matter of protocol, roughly shoves the volunteer aside, resulting in Bracken's shotgun suddenly blasting by accident, the roar deafening to all those around him. For a split second, there is a pause to see if, perchance, someone has fallen down, bleeding from the chest or head, but as there is no one – and Nicolson does not seem to particularly remark upon it – they keep charging forward. In an instant, the front door gives way. As one, the troopers rush in to find themselves 'inside a rambling sort of building without windows, and so dark within that nothing could be seen for the first few moments'.[66]

From the back, Sadleir – who has been slightly delayed as his horse would not jump a fence and he had to knock it over first – finds himself in a room lined with double bunks, 'the top row of bunks so high that one could not see whether they were occupied without climbing up'.[67] Quickly, Sadleir takes off his hat, places it on the end of his rifle and pushes it above the level of the bunk, expecting it might be shot off by a bushranger with a pistol.

But there is nothing. Stone-cold, motherless nothing, at least in terms of bushrangers. All there is in the front rooms are the members of the Sherritt family – outraged at this extraordinarily violent intrusion into their lives. Mr Sherritt Snr had been a policeman in Ireland and cannot believe that anyone would think he would harbour the Kelly Gang!

The bitter truth is the troopers are too late. Even if the old man is lying, and the Kellys had been here, they are obviously long gone. Unless, perhaps, they are at his son Aaron's 107-acre selection, a mile away?[68] So the troopers storm it, only to find, as *Argus* journalist Joe Melvin reports, a 'squalid den . . . the sole furniture of which consisted of a large bunk, a rough table, and stool . . . [and] it was evident that neither the proprietor nor any of his acquaintances had been there that night'.[69] Anyone else's place to charge? What about the house owned by the widow Margret Byrne, the mother of a known friend of Ned Kelly's, who lives just down the way? As described by the worthy Melvin, the cavalcade is soon descending 'a precipitous and dangerous gorge about 800ft. [It] came upon a green valley known as Sebastopol, having a creek running through it, and overshadowed on either side by the high ranges known as the Woolshed Ranges. A sharp turn to the left brought us in front of a slab hut situated in a nicely-cleared piece of land. This was the hut of Mrs Byrne . . .'[70]

It is stormed too, with their only reward being a scattered shotgun of searing verbal epithets from that formidable woman, who, like the Sherritts, is infuriated that the police feel free to charge into her home on mere suspicion that the bushrangers might be there.

Humiliated, exhausted, the police retreat to a nearby grassy spot to have their rough breakfast, when they notice 'a slip of a lad . . . a native of the same class of youth as [one] supposed the Kellys to be'[71] approaching. 'Here,' says Senior Constable Strahan to Superintendent Sadleir, 'is a man that knows the Kellys well, and will be of use to you; he knows all that is going on.'[72]

It is Aaron Sherritt himself. After sleeping in Mrs Byrne's house the night before – for he is sweet on her daughter, Catherine, and gets on well with her younger brothers, Patrick and Denny – he was chopping wood for her nearby when he heard all the excitement, and has come to investigate. Strahan knows him well and is quick to introduce him to both Nicolson and Sadleir, but in this environment the only one Sherritt really wants to speak to is the Police Commissioner.

This is soon arranged, and Sherritt – after laughing out loud at the vision of the bark-stripper with the black-face on, as he recognises him immediately – is soon engaged in deep conversation with Standish. Somehow, they seem strangely intimate after only a few minutes together, as Standish makes clear that they desire Sherritt to become an informer for them, to feed them information on where the Kellys might be found, where they have been sighted and where they are said to be heading. On the spot, Sherritt agrees, with just the one condition. He will endeavour to give the police the information they require if the police in turn 'save Joe Byrne, and guarantee his life'.[73] (This is already a breakthrough as, by so doing, Sherritt has tacitly confirmed that Joe Byrne is one of the gang members.)

Captain Standish agrees in turn, at least in his own manner. 'No doubt,' he says carefully, 'the government will set upon your recommendation in the matter.'[74] Broadly, an agreement is made that if Sherritt will henceforth pass information to the police about the Kellys, Captain Standish will guarantee 'that Joe Byrne's life should be saved, not his liberty, and that he should be tempted through Aaron Sherritt to lead the police on to the other three'.[75]

The two men shake hands, and their agreement is forged.

Again, Nicolson is disapproving of the manner in which the whole thing is done. Shortly afterwards, he remonstrates strongly with

Captain Standish, 'for making such proposals to a man like that in the hearing of others, of any person whatever.'[76]

After getting Aaron Sherritt onside, and finding out that one of the unknown murderers is Joe Byrne, Standish, Nicolson and Sadleir decide to put a bit of pressure on the indignant Mrs Byrne and visit her once more. Alas, the redoubtable woman is not impressed with the police officers' attempt to 'make arrangements'[77] with her and their assertions that, 'her son had gone got his neck into a halter, and that she could save him if she liked'. For her answer seems far from the protective, maternal one they had been hoping for . . .

'He has made his own bed,' she says flatly, 'let him lie on it.'[78]

And yet, although unsuccessful in recruiting the widow, they have at least got her to corroborate Aaron's story that Joe is in the gang, and that is really something – though too little to please the press.

The Sydney Morning Herald, for one, is far from impressed at the way the hunt for the bushrangers is being carried out, and its Melbourne correspondent is scathing. 'What, however, is still more humiliating to us,' it opines, 'is the disgraceful inadequacy of our police to grapple with the evil . . . We have been apt to boast that our police were superior to all other police and that, in respect of organization, courage, and equipment, they distanced all others. The result shows that they are wretchedly furnished with arms, that their boasted military discipline is imaginary, and that even their personal courage is only exceptional.'[79]

8 NOVEMBER 1878, UP AT LAKE ROWAN, QUESTIONS ARE ASKED

Within the police force, more and more troopers quietly – and even not so quietly – question how keen their commanders are to actually get to grips with the murderous Kellys.

Senior Constable Charles Johnston – a very good if notoriously impetuous bushman, tracker and trooper of fifteen years' experience – is one of twenty-two troopers who, under the command of Inspector Brooke Smith, had finally left Wangaratta in pursuit of the Kellys, three days after their confirmed sighting going through the town on the Sunday morning. The party had split up, with thirteen men going west, skirting the northern edge of the Warby Ranges towards Lake Rowan, while the inspector and his remaining men had headed north, far away from the Warby to Yarrawonga on the Murray, where they stopped for the night. The next day, they slowly circled back down south to Lake Rowan, where they stayed another night before planning to head back to Wangaratta the next day.

But, on this morning, Senior Constable Johnston discovers promising tracks no more than a couple of days old, both in Mr Ryan's stockyard and then some quarter of a mile away from the house. When he brings it to Brooke Smith's attention, the inspector concurs with him but seems keen to push on. But Johnston is insistent and when he and a local volunteer follow the tracks anyway for a short while and find white hairs on a brush fence it becomes even more promising, as the trooper remembers that one of the police horses had white legs. It *must* be them.

Extremely reluctantly, Brooke Smith cedes, and they follow the fresh tracks till dusk approaches, whereupon the inspector announces that he 'deems it desirable' they return to Wangaratta as they have no provisions. Once they ride into town, the inspector goes off to meet Superintendent Nicolson, who has arrived that day, while the boys put up their horses at the Ketts Hotel. Coming back to his men, Brooke Smith announces they will start off again at four in the morning, as he has 'received instructions from Mr Nicolson to pick up the tracks and follow them'.[80]

In the morning, Johnston is indeed ready with seven men and the horses by four o'clock, but there is no sign of the inspector. Johnston goes to wake him twice, once at four and once at five, and both times he is told that he would 'get up immediately'.[81] When Brooke Smith finally arises at seven, he tells Johnston to go on ahead with the men to their position the previous day, at Morgans Gap, and he will be right behind them. When he still has not appeared by one o'clock, Johnston and his men follow the tracks anyway, and find the outlaws' camp at the foot of the Warby Ranges. Searching about to find the direction they moved off in, they find a horse. From the description and brand, *B87*, they soon realise it is the horse of their dead colleague Constable Michael Scanlan. They are close, very close.

As dusk is falling, Johnston's intention is to camp here for the night and continue on the morrow, but now, at last, Inspector Brooke Smith arrives.

'Halt; form up!' he calls, every bit as if they are back on the police parade ground.

Stunned, the troopers do so form up.

'Any applications or complaints?'[82]

No, sir. But we found Constable Scanlan's horse.

'Right,' replies their fearless leader. 'Proceed to Wangaratta.'[83]

A small parenthesis here. Not for nothing would Ned later pen his views of this police officer: 'I would like to know who put that article that reminds me of a poodle dog half clipped in the lion fashion, called Brooke. E. Smith Superintendent of Police he knows as much about commanding Police as Captain Standish does about mustering mosquitoes and boiling them down for their fat on the back blocks of the Lachlan for he has a head like a turnip . . . He gets as much pay as a dozen good troopers, [and yet] he cannot look behind him without turning his whole frame [for] it takes three or four police to keep sentry while he sleeps in Wangaratta, for fear of body snatchers.'[84] Close parenthesis.

After secreting the horse in a stable and having their dinner, Johnston and the inspector go to meet Nicolson at ten o'clock that night. They are given much the same instruction, 'to proceed in the morning the first thing, and follow the tracks on'.[85]

On the morning of the 10th, taking no chances, Johnston is up at a quarter to four, has the horses fed, and the men all out and breakfasted. Again, no Brooke Smith. Again, he personally wakes Brooke Smith at four, and, when he does not appear, once more a couple of hours later. Johnston refuses to wait for him, taking the men towards their position of the previous evening. Brooke Smith comes down at half past eight, after a rousing order from Nicolson, who has walked into Brooke Smith's room and ordered him to head out. Alas, again, Brooke Smith thwarts Johnston, for after he has caught up with the party just two miles out of town he insists on their starting point being ten miles prior to where the horse was found and goes with them until – surprise, surprise – by mid-afternoon they get to exactly where they had found the horse.

They camp that night on the side of the range, and Johnston is buoyed to find, right there, what appears to be fresh orange peel. The bushrangers must have taken some oranges from the orchard behind the Ryan place at Lake Rowan . . . The troopers can't be too far behind. Just so long as they stick to these tracks, they are sure to catch them!

That night, the Kelly Gang – nearly as exhausted as their horses and aware that the police are very close – barely sleep in their bush hideaway and keep their horses saddled, ready to go at a moment's notice.

By the next day, as the troopers follow the tracks, it is clear that the Kellys are heading in the direction of Glenrowan, and likely onwards from there to Greta. They cannot be far away, *right now!*

In fact, when the police reach Glenrowan, they are told that 'on the previous Friday night . . . three men had been seen near the railway station when the train came in'.[86] The police and black-trackers find the spot where the men were seen, follow their tracks and find themselves 'going up on to the ranges again in the direction of a place called Hell's Hole back on to the Warby Ranges . . .'[87]

As night comes on, Inspector Brooke Smith again orders the men back to Wangaratta, much to their frustration. It is quite plain to Nicolson, as he would later describe it, that 'the men who had been out with Mr Smith were very much dissatisfied, and that he was quite unfit for that work, as he had abandoned the pursuit while on what he believed to be a genuine track'.[88]

Indeed, his intuition proves right, as a highly frustrated Constable Johnston, still mulling over the bungled affair some weeks later, takes his grievance to his superior officers, Superintendents Hare and Sadleir, and makes clear that, 'If I am baulked again in the same way I will take the responsibility on myself, and go . . .'[89]

In the end, Nicolson decides that on the morrow – if only to appease the men rather than with any great hope of actually finding the Kellys, whom he reckons to be '100 miles away at the time'[90] – they will all go out on a search party together. Brooke Smith's party is to join with Sergeant Steele's party at Glenrowan, together with Superintendent Sadleir and his two Aboriginal trackers. Sure enough, by dawn of the next day, they are on their way, and soon enough they are following the tracks that lead from near Glenrowan past Morgans Lookout and then along the edge of the Warby Ranges.

But what's this?

For now the tracks – and very fresh they are too – are leading into thick scrub; the perfect place for an ambush. At these points, the black-trackers, likely recognising the danger – as do the troopers – appear to suddenly lead them away from the direction of the tracks and straight towards a swamp frequented by thirsty cattle, where, even if the gang's tracks had gone there, it would have been impossible to follow.

What to do?

To the amazement of the troopers, and the particular frustration of Johnston, it is decided they will have lunch on the spot and then return to barracks.

'But, sir,' Johnston dares to tell Brooke Smith, 'the men are all very anxious to go on . . .'[91]

That is as may be, Senior Constable Johnston, but we are not doing that. We are stopping for lunch.

For the moment, all the seething Johnston can do is sit down with the others, as the whole troop of them sit by a spring and eat their lunch. No more than 400 yards away, in the scrub, Ned Kelly and his men – scarcely breathing – are watching them closely, their guns primed, ready for a fight if it comes to it.

But it does not. Wandering off, Sergeant Steele and a small group of men go ahead and get separated from the main party. They continue to search in desultory fashion, while the rest of the troopers head back to Wangaratta.

For Ned and his men, the danger has substantially passed, but not the fury. For, watching closely through the light scrub and thick brush wire grass, as the day heats up and the Australian bush comes to life with the sound of buzzing insects, Ned has noticed that among the Steele party is Constable Fitzpatrick. And so, far from fleeing, the Kelly Gang now track the trackers, monitoring their every move.

For Ned, having the cur who had arrested his mother, Steele, and that lying fool Fitzpatrick – who started all this – in the one group at the one time is an opportunity to . . . to . . . well, Ned is not sure, but apart from everything else it is simply too good a chance to miss to demonstrate their mastery over these bastard babes in the woods. In any case, it does not take long, as Steele clearly has no heart for the chase either, and their tracks soon head straight back to the safety of Wangaratta.

Still boiling with rage at what he sees as craven cowardice from his officers, Constable Johnston puts in for a transfer to Benalla the following day, which is accepted. He cannot stand to be around such incompetent weakness; nor can the three other men who leave with him.

For his part, Hare is not sorry to see him go. Yes, the Superintendent would concede, Johnston really was 'a magnificent rider, but he required some restraint, being both wild and reckless, and inclined to lose his head'.[92]

9 NOVEMBER 1878, MANSFIELD, MR MONK RECEIVES A SURPRISE

Calling in at the Mansfield Post Office on this afternoon, the sawmiller Ted Monk sees that there are two letters for him. Just the first one, however, is enough:

> To E. Monk,
> You think you have done a grate thing by searching for the traps but you have made

> a grate mistake for your friend Kennedy is gone although you made him confess many things and many littel things you have told him in confidence and we heard you say you could track us and our horses but we will track you to Hell . . . we will make your place a government camp when we come and give them some more bodies to pack. What a fine thing it is to cut their ears off but we will poke your eyes out. Yours until we meet. E & D Kelly[93]

Feeling his life is in danger, Monk rides with great haste straight to the police, continually looking around, feeling that a shot might ring out at any moment. After handing the letter over to Sub-Inspector Pewtress, he pours out his anxiety. He is convinced the Kellys are still on the Wombat, and that they intend to kill him. Sub-Inspector Pewtress – no doubt feeling a long way from his native England – does his best to calm the sawmiller and then provides him with an escort of two troopers to get him home, as Monk is desperate to get back to his wife and children, who are all alone.

Mercifully, after arriving, the two troopers stay on guard through the night, even though that leaves only Sub-Inspector Pewtress and two regular troopers back in Mansfield.

Nevertheless, that night, with every creak in the night sounding like murderers approaching, the Monks' hearts beat in rhythm to the clattering branches on the roof – wildly, on the whistle of the wind. Ted Monk just *knows* the Kellys are out there!

12 NOVEMBER 1878, MANSFIELD COURTHOUSE IS OPEN FOR BUSINESS

Look, it is not as if they are really expecting the Kelly Gang to turn up en masse and give themselves up, as the *Felons Apprehension Act* has demanded. But, against that, it is not only important that justice be done, it is important that it be seen to be done, and it is with this in mind that on this Tuesday Sub-Inspector Pewtress and a rather nervous constable stay on duty at the courthouse ready to receive the Kellys on the one in a thousand chance that they appear. There is, frankly, more chance of Christ's second coming than this happening, and yet there is no choice. At least Pewtress is able to pass the time a little by visiting in the cells, just down the way, one Walter Lynch, a local who had just been arrested and charged with writing the threatening letter to Ted Monk. He had been in Monk's house on the Monday night, heard the sawmiller's boast that he could track the Kellys anywhere and had written the threatening letter to scare him out of it. A stupid man, he had not bothered to disguise his writing, and it had matched exactly a letter among the correspondence at the shire office signed Walter Lynch.

Pewtress is happy to inform him that, under the new legislation, the penalty for aiding or abetting the Kellys in this manner is likely to be fifteen years.

Both policemen are relieved when seven o'clock comes around and they can finally close the courthouse doors for the night, spared from having to wait for the most murderous gang in the country to turn up.

Three days later, it becomes official.

After formal application is made by the Crown Solicitor, Henry Field Gurner, to the Chief Justice, Sir William Foster Stawell, KCMG, 'for an order adjudging the Kellys and the two unknown men to be outlaws for not having surrendered at Mansfield on the 12th inst. as required by a former order'[94] and an affidavit is tendered by Captain Standish to that effect, a positive ruling is made.

All of the Kelly Gang are now 'outlaws' – the first in the history of Victoria – and can be legally shot on sight by *anyone.*

MID-NOVEMBER 1878, AT GRETA, MAGGIE MAKES MOVES

It remains the way of the Kellys. When one family member is sent to gaol, it is for the next one to step up and take over. Now that Maggie's mother is behind bars, as is her husband, Bill, and brother Jim, while two brothers are on the run, it is Maggie who comes to the fore.

Taking her younger siblings into her house – which lies about five miles south of Glenrowan and three-quarters of a mile west of her mother's place at Eleven Mile Creek, with just one selection between them – Maggie, with the notable help of her younger sister, Kate, runs both her selection and her mother's and looks after all the children. This will soon include her baby sister, Alice, whom she will retrieve from her mother, Ellen, at Melbourne Gaol and bring back to this more normal existence.

And she does one other thing. As witnessed by the carefully secreted police, just about every night Maggie emerges from the house carrying a large basket and, after gathering in her horse, Whitefoot, she rides off. Oh, they try to follow, of course, but it is simply not possible. A fine horsewoman, who knows where she is going even in darkness, she is quickly able to evade all pursuers and is then seen to return just after sunup. Even if the police had been able to follow her, she doubtless is only leaving the food at an agreed spot anyway, rather than delivering directly into the hands of her brothers. But it is deeply frustrating.

MID-NOVEMBER 1878, ANOTHER VISIT FOR PATRICK QUINN

This month sees another visit for Ellen Kelly's brother-in-law, Patrick Quinn, from Senior Constable Strahan and Detective Ward. They talk about the obvious: the killings at Stringybark Creek. Strahan is, understandably, furious at what has taken place and tells Quinn that he was not far away when it happened. And what he wants now is to bring the Kelly Gang to justice. He has a message for Quinn and is insistent that the grizzled farmer quickly makes a visit to Superintendent Nicolson to talk over the situation.

Before the sun has gone down, Quinn is standing before Charles Nicolson in the Benalla Police Station. Nicolson is seated behind his large desk, with Sergeant Arthur Steele standing behind him over his right shoulder.

'Will you assist the police?' Nicolson asks him bluntly.

'Yes,' Quinn replies, with little choice but to answer in this exact manner, 'but I don't suppose, after what has happened, they will let me know of their movements.'[95]

It is a fair point.

Patrick Quinn puts in his own two cents to Nicolson, warning him, 'If you do not mind, those men will have a long reign, because they are good bushmen and good horsemen, and they do not care about grog, and it will be very hard to entrap them into any place.'[96]

There's something about this man that alerts Nicolson's honed senses; he's not a man to be relied upon. For the moment, however, both Patrick Quinn and the police agree to keep in touch and see how events unfold.

MID-NOVEMBER 1878, THE KELLYS HAVE DISAPPEARED

And so where are the Kelly Gang, actually?

Exactly. Occasionally, there really are confirmed sightings of them, usually from several days before. Though patrols are always sent out after them, and the accompanying black-trackers do try to follow their tracks, those tracks ever and always lead along a road to nowhere. Either the trackers are incapable of following the tracks, or they simply don't want to – after all, following the trail of a murderous gang into the heart of their own lair is not necessarily for everyone.

And when it comes to retreating into the ranges they have made their home, the gang are well equipped. As would later be noted by Superintendent Hare, as 'the Kelly family lived near Greta, the Hart family near Wangaratta, with the Warby ranges behind them, and Joe Byrne's family resided at Woolshed',[97] it mattered little where they were . . . they had both intimate knowledge of hiding places impenetrable to those from the outside world and a sure network of family and friends who could provide support when they needed it.

And the police up against them? Most are city police with no bush skills, who have never fired a gun and are riding inferior horses, as the best horses have been kept in Melbourne for use in parades.

Through it all, however, the police are acutely aware that the Kellys are still out there, watching their movements closely. Sergeant Arthur Steele, for one, is unnerved to receive a message from a sympathiser, directly to him from Ned: 'Tell that bastard Steele that if he is in this country another month I'll shoot him, make him into soup and make his bloody pals . . . drink it! Tell him he can't escape and that I'll get him if I have to come and pull him out of his hiding place with my bare hands! I'll serve him worse than Kennedy!'[98]

For his part, Joe Byrne nurtures an abiding hatred of Detective Michael Ward and makes it known that, 'I would swing easy, if I could shoot Ward and put his body in a hollow log and burn it to ashes . . .'[99]

13 NOVEMBER 1878, IN THE VICTORIAN PARLIAMENT, THE HONOURABLE MEMBER FOR WEST BOURKE SPEAKS OUT

Order! Order!

The member for West Bourke, Don Cameron, has the floor. Mr Speaker, he wishes to speak about the Kelly Gang. No, not about their evil, for that has been well covered by many members many times before. What he truly wishes to talk about is the ineptitude of the police, who, despite using expensive resources, have still not caught the bushrangers. It is his strong view that the public is not satisfied with the steps taken by the police in the matter.[100] The situation is so bad, the eloquent bachelor and former journalist calls upon Premier Berry to instigate an inquiry.

'Will you, Chief Secretary,' he thunders, 'cause a searching inquiry to be made into the origin of the Kelly outbreak, and the action of the police authorities in taking the preliminary steps for the arrest of the criminals? It appears that statements have been made in the Benalla district, which seem to point to the conduct of certain members of the police force as having led up to the Mansfield murders.'[101]

Of course, there is an outcry at the suggestion that the three policemen might in any way have been responsible for their own demise. But Cameron is in full cry. He brushes away the interjections like so many pesky mosquitoes and charges on. 'There ought to be a searching inquiry into whether these statements are true or not,' he says. 'The public will not be satisfied unless this inquiry is instituted. I am sure that every honourable member who reads of the proceedings of the police for the first few days must have been astonished. Two parties of eleven men were sent out with only two rifles between them. That is nothing less than sending out men to be butchered.'[102]

Uproar! Outcry!

Of all the dissenting voices, the loudest comes from the member for Ararat, David Gaunson, who interjects that 'the rumours referred to by the honourable member for West Bourke are of a disgraceful character, and are known to be thoroughly untrue'.[103]

Yes, you can always count on Gaunson to make a scene, and a later parliamentary colleague, Alfred Deakin, would say of him, 'Endowed with a musical voice, good presence, fine flow of language, great quickness of mind, readiness of retort and a good deal of industry, ability and humour, he was only disqualified from marked successes by his utter instability, egregious egotism, want of consistency and violence of temper.'[104]

For his part, Graham Berry assures the member for West Bourke that, if reliable information comes to hand regarding his concerns, he would indeed order an inquiry.

An account of Cameron's speech is reported in the press, where it is read far and wide, including high up in the Strathbogie Ranges . . .

Whatever else, it is an improvement on the suggestion put forth by the rich squatter, magistrate and fellow member of the Legislative Assembly, James Howlin Graves, that the water from which the Kellys draw should be poisoned, and that the grass should be burned.

LATE NOVEMBER 1878, EVERTON HOTEL GETS ANOTHER VISITOR

Another wet, windy and wild night. Another knock on the door of the pub, which has just closed. The young Irish maid stops with a start and starts shivering. This time, it is the publican, Henry, who goes to open the door, while both Mary and the maid exchange looks. What is it going to be?

Just a minute later, Henry returns, completely baffled. He is holding eight shillings, which he says was given to him by the tall, bearded bushman who was standing there, to give to Mary. If that wasn't curious enough, just as the man had turned to go the wind had blown back his coat, showing that he was carrying a serious revolver. What on *earth* is going on?

'It's Ned Kelly . . .' Mary says.

'Damn Ned Kelly!' Henry roars. 'What's he doing here?'[105]

Mary has some explaining to do.

But as for Ned, he is gone in the night.

EARLY DECEMBER 1878, THE PLAN IS FINISHED

All is now in near readiness. For the last month, even as they are being pursued through the ranges, Ned and Joe have been working on a plan. Yes, they have done well to escape the clutches of the law since Stringybark Creek, but now their resources, and those of their sympathisers, are running low. Being on the run, they can no longer pan for gold as they did at Bullock Creek. All of the gang supporters are stony broke, and what they most need is money, the kind of money that can only be found in a bank. With that, they can buy their way out of some trouble, reward the sympathisers who have been most good to them and hopefully allow themselves the space they need to regroup.

And here is the plan to do it. Written in Joe's surprisingly elegant hand – 'for a bushman, rather clever with his pen'[106] – the plan is highly detailed, with specific roles for each of them, together with the timings, the clothes they will wear, the place they will position their horses, where they will go after the robbery is completed, and all the rest.

Again and again, they go over it, so that each totally understands his role, making refinements here and there, all carefully written down by Joe. Occasionally, Steve Hart and Dan Kelly have input, but they are followers not leaders, and the operation they are about to embark upon remains fundamentally the work of Joe and Ned.

6 DECEMBER 1878, SUPERINTENDENT SADLEIR RECEIVES A TIP

Some mail for you, Superintendent.

As tip-offs go, it is a fascinating one. On this morning in his Benalla bureau, the worthy police officer receives an anonymously penned letter that has come to him via Constable Ernest Flood – who is so friendly with the local Postmaster it is even said that on 'occasion [he] took charge of the Post Office'.[107]

The tip-off is seemingly credible. The Superintendent should know:

> *Arrangements are being made by the editor of one of the small newspapers on the New South Wales border, to provide a boat and fresh horses, to enable the Kellys to make their way across the Murray into New South Wales.*[108]

There is even a rough map on the letter, indicating the exact place of crossing, and, while a date is not given, it is obvious from the tone of the rest of the letter that it will be soon. What gives the letter authenticity is 'that the newspaper man referred to was well known to be one of the few cranks who had taken up the cause of the Kellys'.[109]

This may be the breakthrough they have been looking for. Quickly now, Sadleir makes arrangements to go to Albury so he can consult with the police there and make sure that they have troopers on both sides of the river at all the major, and even minor, crossings to intercept and capture the Kellys when they come . . .

Chapter Seven

EUROA

In many respects, Joe Byrne, the fourth member of the party, was physically the finest, and morally the least objectionable, member of the Gang, and he carried the brains of the entire party. Tall, straight, good-looking, fairly well educated, and certainly clever, he might have had an honourable and successful career but for the bias towards crime, or the fascination of adventure that led him into partnership with the Kellys.

William Henry Fitchett, series in the Euroa Advertiser

The Queen must surely be proud of such heroic men as the police . . . it takes eight or eleven of the biggest mud-crushers in Melbourne to take one poor little half-starved larrikin to a watch-house . . .
[They are] big & ugly enough to lift Mount Macedon out of a crab hole more like the species of a baboon or Guerilla than a man.

Ned Kelly

While an outlaw reigns [the police] pocket swells – 'Tis double pay and country girls.

Ned Kelly

8 DECEMBER 1878, EUROA RECEIVES VISITORS

Out on the western edges of Victoria's North-Eastern district, on the road from Melbourne to Benalla, Euroa is a bucolic burgh of just 300 souls, a 'sleepy hollow'[1] that lies on the North-Eastern Line of railway, a little more than 100 miles north-east of Melbourne. It is the western gateway into North-Eastern Victoria, and it lives off the agriculture of the fertile fields that nearly encircle it, bar the mighty and impenetrable, heavily timbered, Strathbogie Ranges, which butt up against the small town's south-eastern flank and go for 40 miles of heavily timbered country to Benalla in the north-east, Mansfield to the south-east and Seymour in the south-west.

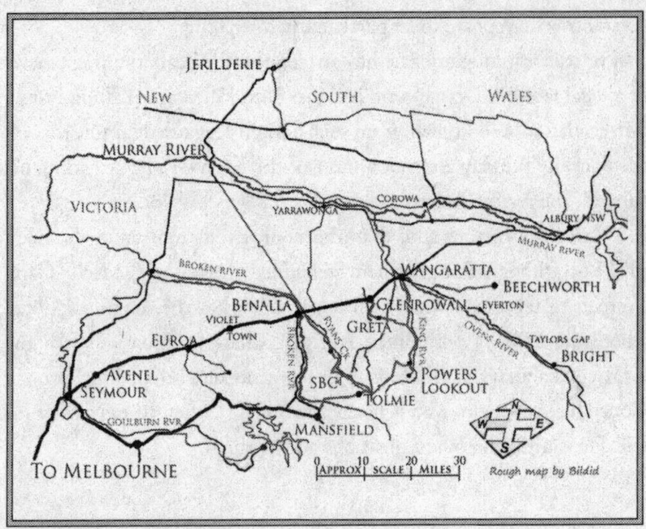

Map of North-Eastern Victoria, including the location of Stringybark Creek. (Map by Bill Denheld)

Euroa boasts a police station, where just one mounted trooper is stationed, a couple of hotels, a railway station and . . . one bank.

—

Early on this brightly shining afternoon, when the lassitude of the long hot summer to come is just starting to settle in, a stranger rides into the town. Good-looking and well-built, he has the air about him of a man who has travelled widely and perhaps, yes, has seen some things that those in Euroa haven't. It is not that he swaggers as he gets off his horse, for – far from it – he is nothing if not self-contained and discreet as he makes his way into De Boos' Hotel. But there is no mistaking his confidence, his air of happy assuredness.

In fact, if Joe Byrne is feeling upbeat on this day, it is for the reason that it is a rare pleasure, after so long in the bush, to be able to walk into a pub, sit down, order a drink and a meal, and have a precious couple of hours as a normal man, even striking up conversations with the locals, several of whom prove to be particularly interesting.

For it is not long after he has arrived that he hears the tragic news of a local lad, Bill Gouge, who had just been killed after falling from a horse, a lad so well known, from such a highly regarded family, that on the coming Tuesday afternoon most of the town will be attending his funeral. Interesting indeed . . .

With little further ado, that afternoon Byrne returns to the nook in the Strathbogie Ranges where he had left the rest of the Kelly Gang camped to report on what he has learned, what the town looks like, where the bank is positioned, and just what the situation with the local constabulary is. There is only one trooper stationed at Euroa, a Constable Anderson, who is not renowned for either his bravery or his wit. He is unlikely to be a great obstacle to them.

9–10 DECEMBER 1878, FAITHFULL'S CREEK STATION, IN THE LEE OF THE STRATHBOGIE RANGES, RECEIVES A VISITOR

Pass the salt, please.

At noon, on this sunny and cloudless day at the gracious Faithfull's Creek homestead – situated in a grove of willow trees amid towering gums just 150 yards east of the Melbourne–Wodonga railway line, some four miles north of Euroa – senior station hand William Fitzgerald is just having lunch with the station's groom, an ex-policeman by the name of George Stephens, when a stranger, a big, bearded bushman, pokes his head in the door, looking for the manager.

'Is Mr Macauley about?' the stranger asks, taking his pipe out of his mouth as he does so.

'No, but he will be back towards evening,' Fitzgerald replies. 'Is it anything in particular? Perhaps I will do as well?'[2]

'No, never mind,' the fellow replies, 'it is of no consequence.'

It is a bit odd, but no more than that. In any case, Fitzgerald has been so crook of late, having just come back from hospital, that he 'did not take particular notice of anything so long as [he] was left alone'.[3]

This 11,000-acre station, stocking no fewer than 5000 sheep, is part of one of the richest conglomerate runs in Victoria – just over 500,000 acres under the control of Isaac Younghusband and the Honourable Andrew Lyall, member of the Legislative Assembly – and there is a constant stream of visitors to it, most particularly right now, when it is wheat-harvesting time.

While Stephens simply goes back to work at the stables, Fitzgerald continues eating his lunch, though he can't help but notice that the bushman has gone outside and is beckoning to someone in the distance.[4] A few minutes later, two very rough-looking bushmen turn up, leading four extremely impressive horses, three bays and a grey. Leaving one man behind with the horses, two of the men wander up to the homestead, where it is the turn of Fitzgerald's wife – 'old Mrs Fitzgerald', as she is known – the homestead's housekeeper, to be surprised.

Who are these rough-looking men who have suddenly barged into her kitchen, sniffing appreciatively and deeply the wafts of her wholesome home-cooked fare? And who is the big man with the beard now smiling at her?

Allow him to introduce himself . . .

'I am Ned Kelly,' this most imposing fellow says, 'but you have nothing to fear from us, we shall do you no harm; but you will have to give us some refreshment, and also food for our horses. That is all we want.'

In response, Mrs Fitzgerald remains calm but calls for her husband to come quickly from the hut.

'There is Mr *Kelly*,' she says and nods towards Ned. She is speaking in a stiff manner immediately recognisable to her husband. 'He wants some refreshments, and food for his horses.'[5]

The fact that, by this time, Ned Kelly has drawn his revolver is testament to the fact that he is *the* Ned Kelly and that he and his men are quite serious. They won't be getting any argument from the Fitzgeralds.

'Well, if the gentlemen want any refreshment,' Mr Fitzgerald says, 'they must have it.'[6]

George Stephens has been back in the stables for just a few minutes, working with another fellow, when he looks up to see the stranger once more, this time in the company of William Fitzgerald.

'These are the other two men,' says Fitzgerald, pointing to the two of them.

'All right,' says the stranger, addressing the two workers. 'I suppose you don't know who I am.'

'Perhaps you are Ned Kelly?' Stephens replies, jocularly, barely looking at him.

'You are a damned good guesser.'

There is just something in the way the stranger says it.

Suddenly a'fearful, Stephens whirls around to see that the stranger is pointing a revolver at him.

'I beg your pardon,' the groom babbles, 'I thought you were joking, and not Ned Kelly.'

'All right,' Kelly says, 'I like to see you take it in good part. Which is the groom?'

'I am.'

'I want some feed for my horses.'

'All right,' Stephens answers, 'there is plenty here.'[7]

Which is as well, for no sooner are the oats secured than Ned Kelly lifts an arm and the third man comes over, leading four magnificent horses, far superior to any horses Stephens has seen in these parts before.

Stephens immediately gets to work, caring for the horses – feeding and watering them, before attending to their manes and shoes – with his focus aided by the fact that a gun is trained on him the whole time.

Fitzgerald and his wife, meanwhile, notice a fourth man standing at the gates to the station, 'evidently keeping watch'.[8]

As the horses are fed, Ned orders Fitzgerald into the wooden slab storehouse with one door and one window, just 20 yards down from the homestead, where, just before turning the lock on the station hand, he assures him one more time that 'no harm is intended to anybody'.[9] Never one to incarcerate a lady, Ned allows Mrs Fitzgerald to go back up to the house, while he returns to the stables and Stephens.

It is not that Ned Kelly is unfriendly for all that. After having put the horses into the stalls, Stephens feels so un-threatened that, as they stand in an empty stall together, he dares to ask Kelly an extremely sensitive question.

'How about the police murders?'

'We were behind a log,' Ned replies quite calmly. 'I told Dan to cover Lonigan, and I would cover the other man. I then called out "Throw up your hands". McIntyre did so, and Lonigan made off for the logs, trying to draw his revolver as he did so, and he got down behind a log, rested his revolver on the top of it. I then took my rifle . . . and fired at Lonigan, and the ball grazed him along the temple. Lonigan then disappeared behind a log. He gradually then rose his hands up above the log, and when his head appeared again I fired again, and shot him through the head.'[10]

(This, though Ned does not know it, matches exactly with McIntyre's first account of how Lonigan was shot – that the constable had drawn his gun and was about to shoot when Ned shot him.)

As to the other two who were shot, Ned is equally forthright, acknowledging that he had shot at Scanlan and personally killed Kennedy. Quietly, Stephens is amazed that the bushranger does not seem to dissemble at all. Kelly has no shame at what has happened and even makes it sound half-reasonable.

As the sun sears its lazy arc across the sky, the hungry station hands come up to the homestead to get their dinner. They are 'very quietly ordered to bail up, and are unresistingly marched into the store-house and locked up with Fitzgerald, no violence being offered them'.[11]

Ned offers each of them the assurance that they have nothing to fear, as all he and his men want is shelter and food for themselves, and food for their horses. The several women of the station, meanwhile, are treated with elaborate courtesy, each assured that no harm will come to her or the couple of small children with them if they cooperate. (Yes, at one point later, Dan Kelly is heard to say he'd like to have a 'a lark' with some of the women,[12] but a single growl from his brother and that is the end of it.)

Just as the light starts to show a red tinge with the coming sundown, the manager of the station, William Macauley, at last returns. Riding up, he is amazed at how quiet everything seems, without the usual flurry of activity that brings daytime to a close around the homestead, and he notices the fine horses in the stables where he leaves his own steed. Still he continues, until he happens upon an enormous bearded man, who says to him, 'Good day. It is warm . . .'

'Tell me who you are,' says Macauley.

Ah, a familiar question. Ned has become used to introducing himself in a way that captivates, even paralyses his prey. 'If you want to know, I am Ned Kelly,' he says matter-of-factly. 'You have the reputation of being a good athlete, and a good shot, and if you attempt to take me or get away, you will be shot, as I have plenty of men outside. If you do get away I will burn the homestead and shoot the horses. You need not be alarmed that I will try to take you, as I do not want blood money. I do not want to take anything or molest you.'[13]

Charmed, he is sure. Still, Mr Macauley feels bound to argue the point. 'What is the good of your sticking up the station?' he remonstrates. 'We have got no better horses than those you have.'

'We are not going to take anything,' Ned replies. 'We only want some food, and rest for our horses, and sleep for ourselves.'[14]

Because he is the manager, William Macauley is not immediately treated like a common prisoner and is allowed to remain outside the storehouse prison, pottering uncomfortably, though he is closely watched. Still reeling at what has happened, he cannot quite bring himself to believe that it really *is* the Kelly Gang until he sees Dan Kelly coming out of the main house and immediately recognises the 'ugly face'[15] he has seen on reward posters and in the newspapers. So, it really is happening!

'Well, as we are to remain here,' Macauley says resignedly, 'we may as well make ourselves as comfortable as possible, and have our tea.'[16]

And now, at around seven o'clock, there are yet more new arrivals. It is a hawker by the name of James Gloster – a draper from Seymour – who arrives at Faithfull's Creek Station in the company of his friend Frank Becroft.

As ever, they unhitch the two horses from the cart, in preparation for making camp for the night, before Gloster heads to the station kitchen to fill his billy with boiling water. Strangely, however, when he enters the back door, instead of the usual cheery welcome one of the station hands immediately says to him very tensely, 'The Kellys are here . . .'

'I wish they were,' Gloster replies glibly. 'It would be £2000 in my pocket.'[17]

But then he looks around to see a large, heavily bearded man sitting at the table, looking up at him, a man who looks remarkably like . . .

'What is that you say?' Ned asks him, mildly.

The seemingly shocked Gloster does not wait for a reply but suddenly turns on his heel and races towards his cart, just outside, where he has left his revolver.

Apparently bemused, Ned, closely accompanied by Joe Byrne, follows up tightly and calls out for Gloster to come back. The hawker ignores this instruction as he quickly climbs up onto the cart and looks for his gun. Suddenly, however, the two men are upon him and, from opposite sides of the vehicle, are pointing the muzzles of their revolvers at his head.

'Get down,' the heavily bearded one instructs him, a hint of amusement lingering in his voice.

Whatever is about to happen, it is obvious that the most dangerous thing Gloster could do right now would be to have a revolver in his hands, and so he stops searching entirely, puts his hands by his side and climbs down.

'I had a good mind to put a bullet through you for not obeying,' the leader says.

'Who and what are you? What business have you in interfering with me?' Gloster asks.

'I am Ned Kelly, son of Red Kelly,' the bushranger boldly replies, 'and a better man never stepped in two shoes.'[18]

'If you are, I suppose there is no use resisting,' Gloster replies miserably, though he at least protests fiercely at Kelly's outrageous actions. But such remonstrations do not last long.

'If you keep a civil tongue in your head you will receive no harm,' Ned says, brandishing his revolver, 'but you were nearer being shot than any other man here.' Then, changing the subject, Ned bangs firmly on the side of the wagon and asks, 'Have you any firearms in your wagon?'

'I don't carry firearms for sale.'

'I know you have a pistol, and if you don't give it to me at once I will burn the wagon down.'[19]

Gloster gives it up at once. To some observers, it is amazing that he has not been shot. And it also seems very odd that the hawker, not particularly known as a courageous man, seems happy to speak back to Ned Kelly without fearing for his life.

The two late arrivals are then invited to have their supper, while Ned holds a revolver on them, before they are taken to the kitchen, where they see two other armed men who are obviously members of the Kelly Gang. Then, like all the rest of the men on the station – after being closely searched to ensure they have no hidden weaponry – they are locked in the wooden storehouse. By the time the sun has gone down, there are no fewer than fourteen men in there. With no ventilation, and too many people in too tight a space, the atmosphere is very close, but they simply must make the best of it.

On a visit to the storehouse, Ned, with a pistol in one hand and a rifle in the other, tells the prisoners to make themselves comfortable for the night. In such situations, Ned just can't resist, and he uses the opportunity to talk to his prisoners, to make his case as to why he has done what he has done, and to answer any questions they might have. He seems particularly keen to take full responsibility for what happened at Stringybark Creek.

'I did all the shooting in the ranges,' he tells them, by the flickering light of a lantern, 'and none of the others shot the police. The people and the papers call me a murderer, but I never murdered anybody in my life.'

'How about Sergeant Kennedy?' Gloster replies, reasonably.[20]

'I killed him in a fair stand up fight,' Ned says. 'A man killing his enemy, is not murder. The police are my natural enemies.'[21]

As to why he had turned to crime in the first place, their captor says it is all the fault of the police. Yes, he had stolen around 280 horses in his time, and if the police had only pursued him for that, then he would have nothing to grumble about. But when the police first have it against you and pursue you for everything, including things you didn't do, that's when it becomes infuriating.

What has completely obsessed him in recent times, however – and on this subject he is at his most vehement – is the sentencing of his beloved mother, with a baby at her breast, to three years' imprisonment, 'on the perjured statements of Constable Fitzpatrick'. He had been 200 miles away at the time of the attack, and yet Fitzpatrick had sworn it was Ned who had shot him. And did anyone really think that Ellen Kelly had actually attempted to murder Fitzpatrick when she hit him with the shovel?

Always, Ned Kelly brings it back to his mother and the injustice that has been visited upon her. For then comes the part of the conversation that Gloster will ever after quote. 'If my mother is not released,' Ned Kelly says blackly, 'I will overturn a railway train.'[22]

While the prisoners pass a reasonably uncomfortable night, Ned and Joe Byrne get busy on another project they have going, writing a letter to the only person in public life who appears to have criticised the government for its conduct over the Kelly outbreak. For, if he has done so once, perhaps he might be convinced to do so again if he knew what truly happened? Ned is convinced that that is the case, at least, and so dictates the letter while Joe faithfully records his views by the flickering light of a lamp – in the red ink he has brought especially for the occasion – adding his own twist and turn of phrase here and there. Broadly, Ned warms to the theme that he has been passionately discussing all evening with his captive audience: the outrageous treatment meted out to him and his family by the Victoria Police.

> I wish to give timely warning that if my people do not get justice and those innocents released from prison and the Police wear their uniforms I shall be forced to seek revenge of everything of the human race for the future. I will not take innocent life if justice is given but as it is the Police are afraid or ashamed to wear their uniform therefore every mans life is in danger as I was outlawed without any cause and cannot be no worse and have but once to die and if the Public do not see justice done I will seek revenge for the name and character which has been given to me and my relations while God gives me strength to pull a trigger.

As Joe keeps writing it down, Ned, with a burning sense of injustice, makes the case as to why he and his men have been provoked into doing what they have done, why they had no choice but to escape into the wild and why the killing of the three policemen at Stringybark Creek was tragic but provoked by the authorities themselves:

> In April last an information was (which must have come under your notice) sworn against

me for shooting trooper Fitzpatrick which was false and my mother with an infant baby and Brother was taken for aiding and abetting and attempting to murder him a charge of sir they are as purely innocent as the child unborn . . .

This sort of cruelty and disgraceful conduct to my brothers and sisters who had no protection coupled with the conviction of my Mother and those innocent men certainly made my blood boil as I don't think there is a man born could have the patience to suffer what I did.[23]

For it is the lies put about by Fitzpatrick that have brought them all to this point. If this falsehood is not exposed, Ned gives fair warning:

. . . horrible disaster shall follow. Fitzpatrick shall be the cause of greater slaughter to the rising generation than St Patrick was to the snakes and toads in Ireland. For had I robbed plundered ravished and murdered everything I met my character could not be painted blacker than it is at present but thank God my conscience is as clear as the snow in Peru . . .[24]

It is well after midnight when they finish writing this draft. As is Joe Byrne's wont, he will redo the whole thing the following morning, including a neater copy to be given to Superintendent Sadleir. And yet the thrust will remain the same: the Kelly Gang are not mere bushrangers, they are warriors for justice for their people, and they are giving fair warning to the authorities that the penalties for not granting that justice will be severe.

Dawn promises a classically warm day of summer, just like mother used to make. The gang are up with the sparrows and immediately continue their preparations. At two o'clock, after a leisurely lunch, they hear the sound of laughter coming from down beyond the station gates. There is a party approaching. Ned mounts his horse and circles around so that he can get behind the party, while Joe walks down towards the gates on foot.

Just arrived at Younghusband's station, fresh from a hunting expedition in the thick scrub of the Strathbogie Ranges, the approaching party are surprised at the sudden arrival of a man on horseback, presenting a revolver at them.

As Ned rides up from behind them, he cries out, 'Turn your horse round, the station is stuck up.'[25]

One of the party, an aged gentleman by the name of Henry Dudley, is particularly affronted. 'What authority have you got for sticking us up?'

Authority? *Authority?*

Amused, Ned decides to present his authority, something far better even than an authority signed by Queen Victoria. Holding his revolver to the head of Dudley, he says, 'I'll shoot you dead on the spot if you give me any cheek.'[26]

The leader of the party, Robert MacDougall, fearing that exactly this will come to pass, asks Dudley to surrender quietly and, turning to Kelly, says, 'You would not shoot an old man!'

'I won't harm the old man if he surrenders quietly,' Ned says.

Now, softening a little, the bushranger says to another member of the party, David Casement, 'Where did you steal this cart?'

'We did not steal this spring-cart,' the still affronted Mr Dudley replies, thinking this fellow must be a policeman, 'we are honest men.'

This impression now firms as the fellow produces a pair of handcuffs and says, 'Look here, I'll put these on you if you're not quiet.'

The hide of this policeman. 'Look here, I'll report you to your superior officer,' Mr Dudley threatens.[27]

Ned Kelly bursts into laughter. Not that the merriment lasts long.

For, in a sudden flash of fury, Ned grabs Dudley by the collar, puts his revolver to the old man's temple and says he will blow his brains out if he does not keep quiet. 'It's hard enough to be an outlaw without taking cheek from a thing like you,' Ned adds morosely.[28]

Similar treatment is needed for another of the party, by the name of Tennant, a proud Scot who refuses to cooperate with these ruffians, no matter what they might threaten.

Oh, really?

Roughly grabbing him, Ned forces him to open his mouth and then jams the muzzle of his revolver between his teeth. How about some cooperation *now?*

'Eh! Mon,' comes the muffled, and indeed muzzled, reply. 'I smell that pooder noo.'[29]

It is an answer that makes the bushranger laugh and restores him somewhat to good humour.

It takes a little doing, but finally – now joined by Joe Byrne, who has arrived on foot – Ned persuades the hunters to come over to the homestead. They are approaching it when George Stephens appears and Ned, with a renewed twinkle in his eye, says to him, 'These gentlemen don't seem to understand or comprehend who I am . . .'[30]

Stephens rises to the occasion. 'Gentlemen,' George Stephens says with a flourish, 'allow me to introduce Mr Edward Kelly and his party.'[31]

Total cooperation is instant from this point on, and the hunting party are taken up towards the storehouse. As they are ushered along, MacDougall smells smoke and looks over to see old clothes burning in a heap by one of the station buildings. A glance at the obviously new clothes of his captors – with not a single patch upon them – tells him where the garments have come from. For, as it happens, the gang have helped themselves to the plentiful supply of clothing they found in Gloster the hawker's cart. There are enough clothes for each of them to have a new outfit, right down to the boots. (Amazingly, all of the hawker's clothes seem to fit them perfectly, as do the boots – and he even has hats with Greta mob chinstraps! – almost as if he had been expecting this very thing to happen.)

In their more refined clothes, they had appeared to be police to the hunting party, and in Euroa they will look far more the part of well-to-do townies or well-dressed station hands – with Ned particularly fetching in his blue sack coat with white handkerchief, grey-striped flannel shirt, brown tweed trousers, matching vest and one streak of colour in a magenta tie – than the men of the bush they truly are. For good measure, they even splash on liberal amounts of scent from Mr Gloster's bottles. From bush dandies to city dandies in thirty minutes . . .

After the four newly made prisoners are firmly locked away with the fourteen men already in the stiflingly hot and close storehouse, it is coming time to begin the main event.

But first things first . . .

Dan Kelly is left to watch over their captives, and the other bushrangers walk over to the five telegraph wires strung alongside the railway, one of which is for exclusive railway use, while, on the other side of the line, the other four are for the government. First, the men take their tomahawks to bring down the poles bearing the wires, and then, with equal vigour, they start chopping the fallen wires to pieces, as well as using nippers, taken from the station, to cut huge sections off them so that anyone who comes to repair the lines will be unable to simply splice them together again.

Leaving nothing to chance, the men smash every earthenware insulator they can see and put some energy into tying knots with what wire remains. One way or another, it will be at least forty-eight hours before Euroa is in touch with the outside world again, and it will take a well-equipped work crew to make the repairs.

As they work, four fettlers labouring on a part of the line nearby come up to see what they are doing. Immediately, they too are taken captive, showing no resistance upon learning that their captors are the Kelly Gang. They too are herded into the now even more crowded storehouse.

—

Though generally busy on other matters, on several occasions throughout the day Ned visits those in the storehouse and at one point strikes up a brief conversation with the old man, Henry Dudley, and the hunter, Robert MacDougall. Almost like a circus hypnotist, Kelly takes from his pocket a golden timepiece.

'This is a nice watch, ain't it?' he asks the two rhetorically, as he shows it to them.

'Yes,' allows Dudley.

'That was poor Kennedy's watch,' the bushranger says. 'Wasn't it better for me that I shot the police than have them carrying my body into Mansfield as a mangled corpse?'[32]

—

Joe Byrne, meanwhile, who will be staying behind to guard the prisoners, asks Mrs Fitzgerald for a stamp to put on the envelope in which he has just enclosed the letter he and Ned have been working on. Obscuring the address with a piece of paper as she puts the stamp on, he weighs it up in his hands and asks her to put another stamp on, just to be sure, after which he puts it inside his jacket pocket. Standing in the kitchen, he and Mrs Fitzgerald begin to chat as she busies herself cooking, and he is even relaxed enough to play her a couple of tunes on a concertina he finds. One thing of particular interest is the 23 November 1878 issue of the *Australasian Sketcher*, which he finds lying on the table, detailing the Stringybark Creek murders and the aftermath, and he reads it all avidly. It details the murders of Lonigan, Scanlan and Kennedy, the horrors of finding their bodies, the devastation wrought on their families, the debacle of the 'Rats' Castle Fiasco', as it has become known, the fact that 'certain burned saddles which had been found in the bush were those which belonged to the horses stolen from the police'[33] and . . .

And Joe Byrne is appalled. They had done no such thing, he hotly tells Mrs Fitzgerald. They had *not* burned saddles and would never do such a thing.

—

All is now nearly ready. Before heading off, the three bushrangers who are leaving bid Mrs Fitzgerald to give them water, a comb and a hairbrush, and they all complete their toilet carefully. All ready, they then shake hands with their prisoners, give silver coins to the children who have been with the women, and, as the time nears three o'clock on this stiflingly hot day of the early summer, they prepare to move out.

'I'll make Scott wink through his spectacles today,' Ned says to Mr Macauley, referring to the manager of the National Bank of Euroa.[34] Macauley is not surprised that Ned knows Robert Scott's name and that he wears glasses, realising by now that the bushrangers appear to have discovered all about the personnel of the bank, and its workings. Almost apologetically now, Ned ushers Macauley to join the others in the lock-up for the first time.

Leaving Joe Byrne behind to guard the couple of dozen prisoners – armed 'with two revolvers in his belt, a double-barrelled gun in his hand, and two rifles placed within easy reach'[35] – the Kelly brothers and Steve Hart take their leave.

For now is the time for the main event . . .

Their vehicle of choice to get into town is the humble hawker's cart owned by Gloster and well known in Euroa, but driven by Gloster's offsider, Frank Becroft, a local lad whom many would come to believe they had secretly engaged for the occasion. With the newly stylish Ned Kelly sitting right beside him – with the hood pulled up over the cart – Becroft flicks his reins to get the horses moving, while Steve rides behind on a station horse followed by Dan Kelly in the shooting party's spring-cart.

Inside his jacket, Ned has a cheque for £1 4s, with Mr Macauley's signature on it, drawn on the *Oriental Bank of Melbourne*. Now, no matter that they reach the bank well after its three o'clock closing time.

Not only are there no customers in the National Bank on Binney Street – which conveniently lies on the Faithfull's Creek Station side of Euroa, and just 50 yards from the railway track – but the nearby thoroughfares are only thin with pedestrians, as most of the townspeople have gone home to clean up and dress for the funeral of the young lad who had died after falling from his horse. As instructed, Becroft takes the cart to the bank's rear entrance, and is closely followed by Dan Kelly and Steve Hart, while Ned lithely leaps down to knock on the front door.

Kelly is confident, precisely following the plan that he and Joe have worked out so carefully, all of it courtesy of information provided by Benjamin Gould, the former convict and travelling hawker Ned had come to know so well after Gould had suggested he send the calf's testicles with the note to the wife of Jeremiah McCormick all those years ago. For weeks now, Gould has been staying in the town, at a place right opposite the bank, studying the rhythms of its daily life. Gould had handed all the information over to the Kelly Gang several days earlier and will be well rewarded for his trouble.

—

And who can that be?

At the end of a long, slow day, just as this particular bank specialises in, the young clerk Edward Bradley is doing his final accounts when he hears a knock on the front door.

'I have a cheque of Mr Macauley's to change,' a voice rings out. 'Will you please cash it?'[36]

Bradley is peeved. Don't people know that the bank is not only closed at three o'clock on this day, but three o'clock every day? It's been closed for an hour! How can they be so obtuse? 'The office is closed for the day,' he calls back, 'and we cannot open the door now.'[37]

Still the knocking and pleading persists. Bradley ignores it but finally can stand it no more and gets up to answer it. This is a damned impertinence. 'The office is closed for the da –' he says, opening the door, but he never gets to finish the sentence.[38] For the instant he has unlocked the barricade, Ned Kelly has put his shoulder to it and sent him reeling backward, a shove that says the bank is open after all. In an instant, the bushranger is inside with the door closed behind him.

And, speaking of business, Bradley now has that end of Ned's gun pointing at him.

'I am Kelly,' says Ned, by way of introduction.[39]

Not so pleased to meet you.

Though Bradley is not a tall man, his hands now reach seemingly high enough to almost touch the ceiling as, with the bushranger's gun in the small of his back, at the larger man's behest he proceeds into the bank proper, where a teller by the name of Edward Booth is just finishing up. He, too, is taken prisoner, even as next door, at the back of the bank manager's residence, Steve Hart is heading through the kitchen door, only to encounter something unexpected . . .

Yes, running into old school friends many years later when in entirely different situations can be difficult at the best of times, but on this occasion Hart shows no embarrassment at coming across Miss Fanny Shaw. In her role as the maid for the Scott family, of whom the father is Robert Scott, the manager of the bank, she is doing some ironing – ensuring that all the family can be looking spick and span for the tragic funeral they are about to head off to. Hearing the door open, she turns, and instantly recognises Hart.

'Hello, Steve Hart,' she says happily, 'what are you doing here?'

'Oh! Nothing much, Miss Shaw,' Steve replies casually. 'I had a little business to do with the boss.'[40]

The two chat for a minute or so, exchanging news of family, when Steve says, 'I think your missus wants you inside.'

'Oh no, she does not,' says Fanny. 'I have just come out of the dining room.'

'I am sure she does, you go in and see.'[41]

Quizzically, Fanny goes in to see, only to have the mystified Mrs Scott reply that no, she had not called for her.

What is going on? It suddenly gets very strange for both women when Fanny tries to leave the dining room. The door has closed on her, and she can't open it. On the other side, Steve Hart is standing against it.

—

Meanwhile, Ned has first knocked and then entered the office of the bank manager.

The balding and bespectacled Robert Scott does not even look up from his small, neat desk, thinking it must be one of his clerks, and he is eager to finish the last of his work before heading off to the funeral.

Ah, but now he looks up.

'I am Ned Kelly,' the bushranger roars, as he advances to one end of the bank manager's desk, 'bail up!'[42]

Before Mr Scott can even think to do anything, Kelly has grabbed the revolver Scott keeps on his desk, and he asks him to put his hands in the air.

'There is no hurry, I suppose?' Scott replies, still with his hands by his sides, proving he is a man of mettle.[43]

With one flick of Ned's wrist, indicating with the muzzle of his revolver the direction in which he wants the bank manager's hands to go, he manages to convey that there actually *is* a bit of a hurry; and this time Scott obeys instantly, raising his hands. The fact that Steve Hart has also just burst in, holding a revolver in each hand, rather emphasises the wisdom of Scott's cooperation.

Quickly, while Hart keeps his guns trained on Scott, Ned manages to gather up around £300 or £400 in cash from the tellers' tables and drawers and stuff it all into the gunny bag they have brought for the occasion. As impressive a haul as it is, however, Ned knows that there is a whole lot more money to be had if they can just get the key to the bank's strongroom.

As the sound of a train roaring by outside lightly reverberates, Robert Scott steadfastly refuses to give the key to them. 'You have come here to take what you want,' he says, 'not have it given to you, and I will not give to anyone what has been entrusted to my care.'[44]

Ned is sure that Scott will think again once his wife and seven children are involved, and he announces he will go and get them from the house next door.

Bravery, however, is not just found in the bearded and bold but also sometimes in the bald and bespectacled . . . 'Kelly,' Scott declares, 'if you go in there I'll strike you, whatever the consequences may be.'[45]

On the other hand . . . there is bravery and there is suicide. When Steve Hart cocks both of his revolvers and points them at Scott's temples, the bank manager decides that sometimes virtue may be found in cooperation, even with a ruffian, and he does not move to strike the bushranger.

'It's no use objecting,' says Ned, perhaps softening a little, 'for I am going but I promise you I will not do any harm.'[46]

And he is as good as his word.

The response of the manager's wife, the handsome and well-groomed Susy Scott, however, when confronted with Ned Kelly holding a gun, could not have been more different from what her husband might have been expecting. Far from alarmed, Mrs Scott is charmed, even saying to Ned as an opener, 'Oh, nonsense, you are not that bloodthirsty villain you have been represented to be.'[47]

As a matter of fact, she seems to have 'almost enjoyed the excitement of it, and she even chaffed Ned Kelly about his personal appearance, telling him that he was a much more handsome and well-dressed man than she had expected, and by no means the ferocious ruffian she imagined him to be'.[48]

Susy Scott's mother, on the other hand, who is at her son-in-law's house on a visit, has not quite the sangfroid of her daughter and blanches at the bushranger's sudden appearance. ('Goodbye,' she had said to a friend, before departing from her home in Loddon for this visit, 'the next thing you will hear of me will be that I am in the hands of the Kellys . . .'[49] And now here she is – her worst nightmare.)

But there Ned goes again, proving his charm, at least in the eyes of Susy Scott. 'Don't be frightened,' Ned tells the old lady softly, 'nothing will happen to you. I have a mother of my own.'[50]

Truly? He doesn't really come across as a desperate ruffian at all. And, while her husband continues to maintain he does not know where the keys to the strongroom are, Susy Scott has no stomach for the ruse. Their conversation on the matter is brief.

'Those keys must be found,' Ned says to her. 'Have you got them?'

'No,' she replies but announces she is happy to go and look for them.[51]

Putting the safety of her children above all else, she conducts a thorough search and is not long in finding where the key is hidden, in the drawer of her husband's desk. She hands it over to Ned Kelly without a word.

In an instant, the vault is opened, and the Kelly Gang help themselves.

Now, *now*, they have a real haul, and when added to their previous booty they now have stuffed into their bag about £1500 in crisp pound notes, about £90 worth of silver, £300 in sovereigns and 31 ounces of gold. Ned is also careful to take 'a number of deeds and mortgages which they placed in a bag', hopeful that it will help the dirt-poor farmers in their perpetual struggle against the evil banks.[52]

—

Back in the sweltering and stinking storehouse at Faithfull's Creek Station, with Joe Byrne on guard outside, thoughts of possible escape are brewing. George Stephens, after all, is an ex-constable and feels it is his duty to escape. Noticing that Joe Byrne frequently stands with his back to the small window of their prison, Stephens looks at the possibility of smashing the window with the right harvesting implement and simultaneously hitting Byrne in the head . . . but reluctantly concludes that 'the window opening was too narrow to allow an effective blow'.[53]

Perhaps just an axe might do the trick then, to attack Byrne with next time he entered? But the other prisoners will have none of it, and they crowd around Stephens, threatening to 'hand him over to the Kellys' if he continues any such nonsense.[54]

Robert MacDougall is another who looks into ways of escaping. Noting the sixteen axes that are hanging up in the storehouse, he suggests to the others, 'If each of us takes one, and commences chopping our way out, we can easily manage it.'[55] Which is true enough. Just what Byrne would have to say about it, however, would be another matter – for the noise from the axes would likely be almost as immediate and fearful as the bushrangers' subsequent shotgun blasts. And that is the immediate focus of the many naysayers, one of whom points out that 'some of us must be shot in the attempt'.[56]

And there is another factor. By a later newspaper account, 'Among those who might otherwise have been in favour of some bold step there was also a knowledge that the store-room contained strong sympathisers with the Kellys as well as bona fide prisoners, and it was also suspected that other of the outlaws' friends were lurking near the station.'[57]

In the end, nothing is done.

—

All up in the National Bank, the bushrangers have made an impressive haul worth around £2260.

With their principal task thus accomplished, it is time to make good their escape, but leaving the Scott family there to sound the alarm by riding to tell neighbours is out of the question. Though it won't be an easy matter moving a household consisting of Mr and Mrs Scott, her mother, seven children and Miss Fanny the maid, it has to be done. 'You have such a large household,' Ned Kelly says rather peremptorily to Robert Scott, 'I must have your buggy. Go and put your horse in it.'[58]

Scott rises up like a frill-necked lizard defending its turf against an aggressive goanna. He will be *damned* if he will do any such thing. His groom is out, he says, and if Kelly wants it done he had better do it himself.

Admiring the man's pluck, amused at his impudence, Kelly tells him straight, 'Well, I *will* do it myself.'[59] As to a driver for it, though, Ned has another idea. 'You drive, I believe?' he says to Mrs Scott.

'Yes . . .'

'I am going to take you all away with me.'

'What, take me away?' she gasps, a little fluttery. 'Where to?'

'I can't tell you where to but you have to come . . . I will likely be away all night.'

'If you insist on us going of course we must obey, but will you not leave my mother, the old nurse, and the young children behind? They are not fit to travel the roads where I expect you will take us, the fatigue would be too much for them.'

'I am very sorry, Mrs Scott, but you must all come for my own safety, you can drive your own buggy and take your mother, nurse and the young children. I'll manage the rest.'[60]

With which, Mrs Scott goes off to change from her linen morning gown into something more appropriate, while also ensuring that her offspring are ready for the journey. Quickly, children, you must put on your hats and coats, as we are about to go for a drive.

The most nervous in this regard is still young George, who, at the first appearance of Ned Kelly, had burst into tears and asked, 'Are we to be all shot?'

'Don't be silly, George, we are alright,' his mother had told him then.[61] And it will be all right, George. But now we must all get ready.

As they take some time doing this, and Ned Kelly has the buggy harnessed long before Mrs Scott is ready, her husband softens somewhat and offers the bushrangers some of his whiskey. They agree – it has been a rather long day, after all – with Ned Kelly only insisting that the banker drink some of his glass first, before they even go so far as to toast each other's health. (For he would be damned if he would allow himself to be 'hocused' once more, as that bastard Fitzpatrick had done to him at Benalla.)

And now Mrs Scott arrives back, a ship of the realm, in full sail, with billowing bosom and all flags flying otherwise. A vision splendid, she is wearing the gorgeous French dress she had purchased a short time before from Robertson & Moffats, all set off with lace and ribbons, a gloriously large hat all covered with tulle and flowers, and of course not forgetting the pair of long white gloves. She had insisted that Dan Kelly close the door to her bedroom while she prepared, and prepare she has.

So excited does Mrs Scott appear to be at the whole adventure, so unintimidated by the fact that she is with bushrangers, dammit, that Ned feels obliged to tell her, in a friendly fashion, even as he helps her into the driving seat, that she must calm down. Already in the buggy are her mother, the nurse, the baby and her younger children.

Ned says to Mr Scott, 'Will you get in.'

'No, I won't,' Scott replies, 'it is too heavily loaded already.'

Too bad. 'Now, none of your larks,' Ned insists. 'You will, then, have to go with me.'

Becroft drives the hawker's cart, with the clerks, the older Scott children and Miss Fanny the maid, while Dan Kelly puts himself in the back of the cart by virtue of cutting a hole in the canvas and is therefore able to keep a gun trained on Mrs Scott driving the buggy behind. Then comes Ned Kelly in the spring-cart with Mr Scott beside him, and Steve Hart alone brings up the rear on horseback.

Seeing them go, through her window, the Stationmaster's wife would later gaily remark to her husband that, 'I saw the bank people with a lot of friends going off for a picnic.'[62]

Another who notes them is the deeply grieving Ann Gouge, the mother of the lad who is then and there being buried in Euroa Cemetery. While heading out on Sydney Road, the Kelly party rushes past the tragic graveside gathering. For the life of her, Mrs Gouge cannot fathom why Mrs Scott 'would drive past at such a pace when the poor boy was being laid in his grave'.[63] And, of course, Mrs Scott does try to slow down, only to see Dan in the hawker's cart pointing his revolver and insisting she get a wriggle on.

As they proceed, with the worst of the day's heat dissipating and the relative cool of the evening beckoning, Ned Kelly and Robert Scott chat. Lightly, Ned tells Scott that while he had been told that the bank manager would be difficult, he had found him 'the most obstinate fellow I have ever met with'.[64]

Scott is, frankly, more than a little proud to hear it. But where will the bushrangers go, Scott idly wonders, once they have left these parts?

'Oh,' says Ned, expansively, 'the country belongs to us. We can go anywhere we like.'[65] Though Kelly acknowledges that the police have got so close to him and his gang that 'I have seen the police often, and have heard them often', it simply doesn't bother him.[66]

'He did not seem a bit afraid of the police,' Scott would later recount, 'but on the contrary, laughed at them and at their efforts to capture him and his mates. The other ruffians appeared to have as little dread of their pursuers.'[67]

In fact, so little fear does he have of being captured that Ned remains extraordinarily open about his past crimes and misdemeanours. When, for example, Scott asks him about the Stringybark Creek murders and, specifically, who shot Lonigan, Ned could not have been more forthright.

'Oh,' he says nonchalantly, 'I shot Lonigan.'[68]

And what, Scott wonders, would Steve Hart have done if I'd gone ahead and hit you in the bank, as I threatened to do?

'He would,' Ned replies simply, 'have shot you dead on the spot.'[69]

Of course. What staggers Robert Scott regardless is how such an extraordinary conversation can take place amid the ordinary and familiar sounds of his horses' clopping hooves and the cart's rattling wheels. Scott has travelled over this track countless times, and looked to the slowly fading colours of the Strathbogie Ranges as the summer sun fades more times than he can remember. But now he is doing it in the not unpleasant company of Ned Kelly, confessed murderer.

And so their convoy jangles on . . .

A mile from Faithfull's Creek Station, Steve Hart doubles back to make sure no one is following while the rest continue on their way, arriving back at the station at half past five. As arranged, Ned can see by the green blanket Joe Byrne has left on the garden fence that everything is okay, and he goes to the lock-up to find that Joe has just taken yet another prisoner.

While the bank party had been away, a fellow by the name of Watt, a telegraph-line repairer, had got a lift on a train heading south to Melbourne and been dropped off at the spot where the line had come down. The unfortunate man had no sooner seen the obviously calculated damage and wandered over to the homestead to see what they knew than he had been greeted by Joe Byrne with a gun. After being searched for firearms, he, too, had been placed in the stifling storehouse. (Watt later reported that Byrne had been so nervous and shaking he could only just get the key in the lock.) Now, all the older males who have come back with the Kelly Gang are placed in that same packed storehouse, while the females and children are permitted to join the other ladies in the homestead.

—

And yet, before alighting from the train, Watt had told Police Magistrate Alfred Wyatt, who was on the same train, to pass a message to the Euroa Stationmaster that he would be needing 'Six telegraph posts, thirty-six insulators, and a corresponding quantity of line wire'[70] to be sent out on the next train heading north.

Wyatt had continued on into Euroa and passed the message on to the Stationmaster, before heading off to the courthouse. After presiding over the brief licensing hearing, though, Police Magistrate Wyatt keeps thinking about it. There had been no storms that afternoon, and there were no trees or branches near to the fallen wires in any case.

The other thing that seems odd is that, despite the train slowing to let the line repairer off, there had been no one around, no one wandering over from the homestead as was usual, and Wyatt hadn't seen anyone anywhere. The whole thing looks somehow suspicious – though he can't quite put his finger on it – and after due reflection, and after finishing his judicial business earlier than expected that afternoon, he decides to head back out in a borrowed buggy to where he saw the wires down, so he can have a closer look himself.[71]

Once he gets close to Faithfull's Creek Station, however, the wheels on his buggy lock and he is about to get down to look at them when a very brusque young fellow arrives on horseback. 'Is this the way to Faithfull's Creek Station?' the seeming ruffian asks.[72]

'Cannot tell you . . .' Magistrate Wyatt replies, barely looking up, as he has been lost himself and is concentrating on his wheels.

'Go to hell!' the young fellow yells.[73]

Magistrate Wyatt is shocked, and though he does not recognise Steve Hart, or know his name, there is such an air of menace about this fellow, such an implied warning to get away from this road, that Wyatt decides to do exactly that and turns back towards Euroa, on foot, leaving behind the valuable buggy and horse.

The more he walks, the more convinced he becomes that something is going on.

He arrives at Euroa at a quarter to seven in the evening to find that Watt has still not returned, and the penny drops. This *must* be the work of the Kelly Gang. Quickly, Wyatt convinces Stationmaster Gorman to allow him to ride on the next engine going back to Benalla and allow it to stop briefly at Faithfull's Creek Station, so he can have a quick look to confirm his suspicions, at which point he could head on to Benalla to raise the alarm.

—

Back at Faithfull's Creek, there is something of a festive atmosphere.

The Kelly Gang have achieved an extraordinary haul and seem to have got away without anyone the wiser. They can see that the telegraph wires are still down, so there is no chance that a major force of police will be arriving any time soon.

For the now thirty-seven prisoners – who are soon all let out to stretch their legs and even have some refreshments – there is no escaping two conclusions. The first is that, despite reports, the Kelly Gang appear to threaten very little violence towards them so long as they don't try anything stupid. This is surprising from a gang with such a fearsome reputation. And the second is that, in their exceedingly dull little town, where nothing newsworthy occurs from one oh-so-dreary-oh-so-weary month to the next, something . . . has . . . actually . . . *happened!*

And not just something anything, but something *important*. There is no more notorious gang in the entire continent than the Kelly Gang, and they are not only in Euroa but right here, right now, in this room with the prisoners having dinner. And the big, bearded fellow is Ned Kelly himself. Most amazing of all? The gang had no sooner returned than Ned had handed over to Mrs Fitzgerald a large bag of coins, for distribution among them, a kind of compensation for their trouble. Their pockets are fairly jingling with those coins now, though Mrs Fitzgerald's new bag seems to have retained the lion's share as it sways heavily in her hand.

For most of the prisoners, it is the most exciting thing that has ever happened to them, and the strange truth is that they are in no hurry to be set free, just as the Kelly Gang – having a rare moment of home comfort – seem to be in no particular hurry to get going. From the beginning, the plan of Ned and Joe Byrne has been to make their escape when the sun goes down and the moon comes up, so they actually have time to enjoy themselves.

And then they hear the sound of a train coming. Everybody out of sight! And now the train is, yes . . . slowing down!

Instantly, the gang are on the alert, with Ned Kelly calling out to all and sundry, 'Here comes a special train with Bobbies, but we are ready for them, we don't care how many there are, we can fight them.'[74]

Mercifully, however, no police emerge. For, in fact, the driver is only looking for the line repairer Watt, who he had been told should be there, ready for a lift after being dropped off an hour before. When there is no sign of Watt, the driver builds up steam and heads off for Benalla.

To men such as Bill Macauley, the lack of concern shown by the gang when it comes to confronting the police is nothing short of extraordinary. When he says as much to Ned, adding that the police may very well be on their way, the jovial bushranger replies, 'I wish they would, for there is plenty of cover here.'[75]

It really does appear as if what Ned Kelly truly wants most is a full-on clash with the constabulary: winners take all, losers die.

In the meantime, it is soon time for tea, and the surprisingly jovial Mrs Scott and some of the other ladies ensure, firstly, that the children are properly fed. As to tea for the rest, it is another jovial affair – for there is a certain sense of community, even between captors and prisoners – where the Kelly Gang effectively hold court as the steaks are eaten, the whiskey is drunk and the stories are told. Of them all, it is Ned who is the most garrulous, happy to talk to all and sundry, as well as asking pointed questions about the movements of the police and making particular enquiries of the telegraph repairer – asking him to fully explain how long it takes to repair a wire, how they will try to do it, and so forth. It is obvious to all that it is Ned who is totally in charge.

When tea is over, the males are let out once more, only to be hustled back inside the slab storehouse when, one more time, the sound of a train approaching is heard and . . . yes . . . it too is stopping.

Is this the police, now come in force to arrest the gang for robbing the National Bank? Their guns drawn, the Kelly Gang watch very closely, half-expecting a dozen troopers to burst forth from the train once it has stopped. But, no, just one old man descends. No matter his age, his movements are quick, furtive and very much as if he is aware that he is likely being watched, perhaps even with the sights of a rifle bearing upon him.

Quickly now, Police Magistrate Wyatt simply gathers up some broken insulators and pieces of broken wire and climbs back on the train, which quickly choofs off. Wyatt is stunned. All the lines have been cut, and clearly with very powerful nippers. The magistrate has all the evidence he needs that something has happened at Faithfull's Creek Station – and he is sure it is the doing of the Kelly Gang.

But careful now. As he gets back on the train, of course the passengers ask, 'What is the matter?'

'The line is down, and it looks like a whirlwind,' Wyatt replies, not wanting to panic anyone.[76] Though he confides the truth to the engine driver and guard, he instructs them to say not a word.

—

With the train gone, all the prisoners are yet again let out, and before the gang leave there is time to do just one more thing. That is a rather dashing display of trick riding – performing feats on horses at full gallop that an ordinary rider could barely conceive, let alone execute.

Ned, in particular, gallops about, 'lying or sitting upon his saddle in all kinds of apparently impossible positions'.[77] No one is more impressed than the old man, Henry Dudley, who would later recount of Ned's performance, 'He maintains his seat in the middle in any position, sometimes resting his legs at full length along the horse's neck, and at others extending his whole body till his toes rested on its tail, dashing along at full speed in view of the prisoners, with the evident desire of impressing them with his skill.'[78]

—

It is eight o'clock in the evening when the train from Euroa pulls into Benalla Station, and it has no sooner pulled to a stop than Police Magistrate Wyatt bursts from it.

And there they are!

By some kind of miracle, there on the platform are Superintendent Nicolson and Superintendent Sadleir, pursuing the tip-off from Constable Flood that the Kelly Gang are then and there on their way to crossing the Murray River. As Nicolson is far and away the highest ranking man, Wyatt immediately rushes him into a private room to brief him and tell him he is all but certain that Euroa has been stuck up by the Kellys, and right now he thinks they are probably at Faithfull's Creek Station.[79] Quickly, *quickly*, they must act!

Strangely, Nicolson barely seems to react, saying only that he and Sadleir are pursuing another lead, that the Kellys will soon be crossing the Murray, and they are about to catch this same train to Albury. He is not particularly fussed by this other tip. Incredulous, Magistrate Wyatt repeats, 'Nicolson, the line is cut, all five wires; four of the government wires and one of the railway lines are cut, not broken. The Kellys are about. Now you know as much as I know, and what you know yourself, will it alter your plans?'[80]

'We know what it means, Mr Wyatt,' Nicolson says, after a few moments' reflection. 'It will not influence our plans.'[81]

To Wyatt's stunned amazement, despite everything he has said – *the Kellys have struck just south of here only hours ago!* – he is left standing on the platform as the two most senior police in the area board a train heading in *exactly* the opposite direction.

All Wyatt can think to do is to first go to the Benalla Police Station to report his suspicions to Sergeant James Whelan, in the hope the troopers there can send a special train. Whelan is receptive but declines to order a train, saying he does not have the authority. It is only after a great deal of thought and endless pacing – not wishing to go over the head of the two senior police officers who have taken an alternative decision, but feeling he has no choice – that Wyatt finally sends a cable to Captain Standish in Melbourne, reporting his suspicions and begging for action.

—

It is just gone half past eight on this pleasantly warm evening. Finally, as darkness falls, it is time to leave Faithfull's Creek Station. Quickly now, the loot from the bank is divided up among the gang, as are the weapons. Though they will leave broadly together, following the plan worked out by Ned and Joe, they will then separate and meet at a series of rendezvous points to confound the trackers. The divvying-up accomplished, there remains just one more thing to do.

Before departure, just after the sun goes down, Ned goes to the storehouse and gives all of the thirty-seven prisoners fair warning that they are to give the gang a good start before anyone tries to raise the alarm. 'If one of you leaves this spot within three hours,' Ned says, 'I will shoot that man dead. You cannot any of you escape me in this country, I can track you anywhere, and I can assure you I will keep my word.'

Now, turning to the most senior-ranking man from the station there, Mr Macauley – as he is known to all – and asking him to come to the front, Ned says to him, 'I will hold you responsible for the escape of any of these prisoners until the period I have named has expired. Mind! If you let one of them go, I will meet you some time or other, and then you may consider yourself a dead man.'[82]

And one more thing.

Ned happens to notice that one of the more troublesome prisoners, Robert MacDougall, has a valuable watch, and asks for it. Reluctantly, and with high dudgeon, MacDougall hands it over, though he says he treasures it, as it was given to him by his late mother.

Instantly, Kelly hands it back. 'No, I will never take that from you,' he says.[83]

God forbid.

Instead, he takes Macauley's watch, while Joe Byrne helps himself to Robert Scott's timepiece.

The Kelly Gang saddle up. Their mood is one of excitement. They have pulled off an amazing hold-up, which has enriched them and their supporters and will humiliate the police force. They have hurt no one, have had fun and demonstrated that they are a gang like no other in the colony's history. And now, on this perfectly moonlit night – just as Ned and Joe had planned so they could profit from it for this escape – they drive their spurs into the sides of their magnificent horses and gallop away towards the moonlit Strathbogie Ranges, which loom to the south-east.

Watching them from every available vantage point inside the homestead, the female prisoners are speechless. A'riding, a'riding, a'riding . . . they keep watching as the four horsemen keep . . . a'riding away . . . and disappear into the night.

The moment that the sounds of their thundering hooves stop, however, there is immediate discussion among the prisoners as to what to do next: raise the alarm or keep to the three hours set by Ned Kelly? On the reckoning that one of the party might have remained behind, and is then and there preparing to shoot the first person who tries to leave the station, the answer is 'not sure'. Some of the prisoners, after all, still have watches and will be able to tell when three hours are up.

Nevertheless, after only a few minutes, Mr Macauley has had enough and breaks free of the storeroom, the other prisoners slowly, wearily trickling out behind and making their cautious way up to the homestead. Some of the prisoners now race to Euroa on whatever horses they can muster to raise the alarm.

For those who remain in the homestead, the atmosphere becomes festive . . . as they enjoy a late supper, with plenty to eat and drink, and exult over what has happened. They talk of what Ned Kelly had said, what he was like, how impressive it was, the way he rode his horse during the trick show and so on. When the subject of the stolen watches comes up, Watt the line repairer gleefully takes from his boot the beautiful gold watch he had secreted there. He has got away with it!

For his part, Gloster's assistant, Frank Becroft, has been given £2 for his services, along with Constable Lonigan's watch, which, in a pang of conscience, Dan Kelly has given to him with the request that it be forwarded to Lonigan's widow.

—

Far to their north, the train to Albury, via Wangaratta, keeps roaring along.

Why, specifically, are Superintendents Nicolson and Sadleir heading north, at the very time that they have a credible report that the Kellys have struck to the south of them at Euroa? Upon reflection, as the northern Victorian countryside falls backward in the night, John Sadleir, for one, would never be quite sure. 'There was no pressing reason why Nicolson and I should both proceed to Albury,' he would later write, 'but there was little time for reflection, and there was no possibility of returning, once the train had started.'[84]

The thing is . . . they were already on their way to Albury to intercept the Kellys before the bushrangers crossed the Murray, and the intervention of Police Magistrate Wyatt had seemed to confirm that that was indeed the gang's destination. And it was Nicolson's call to make, not Sadleir's. So the police officers had kept going . . .

—

Finally, back at Faithfull's Creek Station at half past ten, the Scotts decide enough is enough. They are exhausted, the Kelly Gang are clearly long gone and they have at least given them two hours' start. Just as they are leaving the homestead, however, they hear a *coo-ee* in the night, and freeze. Is it *them*, back again?

No, it proves to be a brave country schoolmaster from Euroa, who heard what had happened when the first of the prisoners made it back there. He had immediately called for volunteers to go out there to see what could be done to help, only to find not a single hand raised in the town. So he has come by himself, and finding everyone unharmed he now accompanies the Scott party as they head home.

To the party's amazement, they are just about to cross the bridge that leads into town when they are met by practically its entire population, who have been safely waiting for them, and now treat them as conquering heroes, cheering them three times through and wildly pumping their hands in congratulation. The most amazing thing! Held up by the Kellys, taken prisoner, and they live to tell the tale!

'Of course,' one account ran, 'the excitement was great, the people were all at fever heights by this time.'[85]

MIDNIGHT, 10 DECEMBER 1878, AT ALBURY STATION, TWO TICKETS FOR THE EMBARRASSMENT EXPRESS, PLEASE

It is while Nicolson and Sadleir are conferring with a New South Wales Police officer on the platform at Albury Station that they are approached by the Stationmaster, bearing a cable he has just received from Captain Standish to pass on to them.

The National Bank at Euroa has indeed been stuck up by the Kelly Gang. Nicolson and Sadleir must return to Euroa immediately. The Stationmaster promises to make provision for a special train.

Try as he might, Sadleir would record, 'the New South Wales officer could not conceal his satisfaction that the exploit had occurred in Victoria, and not in his own territory. Not that he boasted of any superiority; he simply rejoiced at his own good luck, and attempted to offer us such sympathy as decency required.'[86]

In the meantime, other police, summoned by Sergeant Whelan, are converging on Euroa with black-trackers, ready to pursue the Kelly Gang from first light. The obvious thing to do, of course, is to track the fugitives, but therein lies a problem. When a start is made at Faithfull's Creek Station on that very project from the first flush of dawn, there are tracks going *everywhere*.

It seems that not all those who had been confined the night before had gone straight home as the Scotts had done. Instead, some sympathisers – perhaps joined by scouts for the Kelly Gang who had been watching from the near distance – had taken their horses and ridden right around and around the station in every direction, before taking offshoots and doubling back. Just which of the tracks belonged to them and which to the Kellys is anyone's guess. And it is not so simple a matter as following the tracks of four horsemen, for the Kellys now had established a new modus operandi, whereby they would split up and go by different routes to a series of meeting points. At this time, in this environment, four horsemen are always going to be extremely suspicious, so the gang had simply adapted.

For his part, Superintendent Nicolson does his best, of course, and by half-eight in the morning is on the ground at Faithfull's Creek with Senior Constable Johnston – who has returned to the fray, like a racehorse after too long a spell in the holding paddock – in the company of Detective Ward and five troopers. Then, realising that they are well behind, without yet a clue as to which direction the robbers have taken, they have little choice but to race off madly in all directions.

In fact, they gallop off to the north, nominally on the trail of the gang, though, somehow, by dusk they have completed something very close to a circle. By dinnertime, they are back in Euroa, where they snatch a quick meal before racing off into the night once more, roaring after every wild goose that comes their way. By dawn, they are back at Euroa again, exhausted beyond redemption. Senior Constable

Johnston, described by Nicolson as 'the strongest and hardiest man of the party, a most energetic man', is so shattered that he falls asleep on the sofa and, even when the old man who owns the hotel – thinking Johnston must be suffering from sunstroke – pours a bucket of water on him, he proves to be 'so dead asleep that he was not awaked'.[87]

The other police parties have done no better.

The black-trackers? Well, in the words of one policeman, they are, 'Victorian blacks, whose sense of sight and sagacity had been destroyed by drink. All day long search was made, but no trace of the outlaws could be obtained. The police were sent in every direction, trying to find out some tidings of the outlaws, but without effect.'[88]

The Kelly Gang really have disappeared . . .

Chapter Eight

AFTER EUROA

The amazing coolness and daring which characterized this remarkable exploit would have done credit to the heroes of a three-penny novel . . .

The Age reacts to the 'Euroa outrage'

Come, all my hearties,
We'll roam the mountains high,
Together we will plunder,
Together we will die.
We'll wander over valleys,
And gallop over plains,
And we'll scorn to live in slavery,
Bound down with iron chains.

Chorus of 'The Wild Colonial Boy', a popular song in the time of Ned Kelly

The hunt for them was like trying to discover, say, four ants in a thousand acres of wheat.

William Henry Fitchett's series in the Euroa Advertiser

LATE EVENING, 10 DECEMBER 1878, FOR CAPTAIN STANDISH, MANY MARAUDING SUBJECTS MAKE LATE-NIGHT NEWS

Long day. But an even longer night, which is just the way Captain Standish likes it. After returning from a public dinner at Melbourne Town Hall, he arrives at the Melbourne Club and is on his way to his room when one of the white-coated staff hurriedly approaches him and gives him the sheaf of cables that have been piling up in his absence. Oh dear. A Kelly outbreak at Euroa! Immediately, Standish rushes to the telegraph office to try to marshal his forces in North-Eastern Victoria, an activity he continues late into the night and spends most of the next day doing too. The day is mixed with more meetings with the Chief Secretary Graham Berry, who tells him he has '*carte blanche* in the matter, and . . . no effort ought to be spared to avert the disgrace which the impunity of the bushrangers brings upon the colony at large'.[1]

The whole thing is just so *outrageous*, and humiliating! And Captain Standish and Chief Secretary Berry are far from the only ones who think so . . . For the subsequent headlines declare the primary emotion generated by the Euroa story, above stories that fill fully one-third of the editorial space in the major Victorian papers on the day the news breaks:

> OUTRAGE BY THE KELLYS. A Bank Bailed Up[2]
> Re-Appearance of the Bushrangers: The Outrage at Euroa
> Further Outrages by the Kellys[3]
> THE KELLY OUTRAGES[4]
> KELLY GANG AGAIN: Bank Stuck Up in Broad Daylight[5]

Yes, despite the seventy-nine members of the police force who had been sent into the North-East to hunt the gang since the murders at Stringybark Creek, 'the outlaws coolly disported themselves at Euroa and insulted the whole country through the utter contempt they displayed for the law'.[6]

And where on earth *was* the law?

The Melbourne *Herald* takes a dim view, beneath a headline blaring:

> THE POLICE INCOMPETENCY
> The incompetency of the Police to trace or capture the Kelly Gang fully proves what has long been suspected and hinted at in the press . . . [the force] was essentially weak in efficient constables for bush work. What is required is a change in the police system. Bush troopers should be used . . . men to whom the bush has been a nursery. We do not for a moment believe that our policemen, foot or mounted, are deficient in courage, but they are certainly disheartened, and to all appearances over-officered. There is too much of going out under orders and returning. Any bushman will smile at such a notion of catching the cutest bushrangers who have ever turned out in Victoria.[7]

Beyond, however, the anger of the newspapers at the Kellys' actions, there is another story spreading among the people. That is the extraordinary gentility of the Kelly Gang. Yes, the press had made them out to be murderous cut-throats, but person after person who had been a part of the siege and the hold-up attests that the bushrangers had not been like that at all.

The Euroa bank manager, Robert Scott, sounds almost more enamoured of Kelly than even his wife had been – which is saying something. Scott gushes to the *Australasian Sketcher* that 'Ned Kelly is a good looking man'[8] and even goes a little further still to tell *The Herald* that Kelly is 'a splendid specimen of the human kind, tall, active, rather handsome, with a reddish beard and hair . . .'[9]

Ah, but of course this positive response is mainly among the common people, from whom the Kelly Gang have sprung. Among the higher echelons of society, the ruling classes – the ones who are most humiliated by what has happened, the ones to whom the challenge has been thrown down – the fury at the Kellys is widespread, the demand that the gang be brought to heel compelling.

And it is in response to such an outcry that – upon the insistence of Graham Berry – Captain Standish rather grandiosely announces he personally is so eager to capture the Kellys that he will move his base from Melbourne to Wangaratta forthwith. Perhaps that will calm the press down.

So it is that, on the morning of 12 December, the second day after the robbery, Standish takes the early train out of Melbourne and is on the ground in Euroa by ten.

From the first, it is obvious that Superintendent Charles Nicolson is 'very much knocked up in appearance, and his eyes bad'.[10] Obviously, new leadership is required.

On the spot, Captain Standish instructs the exhausted Nicolson to return to Melbourne to take charge of the police department, while he stays up in the country for a short while. Standish then sends a telegraph down the newly repaired lines to his favourite underling . . .

Superintendent Francis Hare is in the absent Standish's office when a clerk hands him a telegram directing him to report with horse and his accoutrements to Euroa that very *evening*. He is on his way ere two hours have passed – even allowing for packing his shotgun and white sun helmet, and organising his greyhound to come with him – stunned at the way events have turned out. For he knows the Kellys all right, from the Harry Power episode and his subsequent service in the district. Ned he remembers from those days as a 'flash, ill-looking young blackguard',[11] while the youngest Kelly brother is a lesser mirror image of the oldest, 'a cunning low little sneak'.[12]

One thing Hare does not lack from the moment he arrives on site that early evening is reported sightings. For, as had happened after the Mansfield murders at Stringybark Creek, the bushrangers are indeed spied on all spots of the map, from Benalla to Beechworth, from Echuca to back in Euroa.

Yes, there has been one breakthrough in that at least the fourth member of the gang has now been positively identified by Fanny Shaw as Steve Hart. But what particularly frustrates the police is that, as it had been reported in the papers that the gang had left Euroa on three bay horses and a grey, all over the countryside sympathisers have got together in bands of four, riding three bay horses and a grey . . . meaning that sightings simply *pour* in, and there is nothing the police can do to stop them.

And, of course, all such reports, even the most absurd, must be followed up. A constable is dispatched to check on whether, indeed, the Kelly Gang have been seen shooting parrots near a squatter's garden in Benalla. Notwithstanding that quick enquiry proves the shooters in question are a local survey party, the squatter – thinking no one had been sent to capture the Kellys when he had told the police exactly where they were, tries to bring a charge against the officer in charge of the local district for wilfully ignoring his duty. In Melbourne on the Sunday morning, the Chief Justice of the Supreme Court receives a telegram informing him that 'the Gang had been in Mrs Rowe's garden cutting cabbages, near Euroa',[13] and that, too, has to be investigated. Those reports at least are the relatively easy ones to follow up. Far more difficult is when more credible reports come in that the outlaws can be found living in wild country at the heads of rivers, or in wild cattle country 150 miles from Benalla. Of course, those reports, too, must be investigated, and the call on manpower is excessive.

At least, however, the government has recognised that the police force in all of North-Eastern Victoria has been totally inadequate to this point, and another fifty-eight men, most selected by Hare, are sent from stations all over Victoria in the first weeks after the raid, spread through the major townships of Wangaratta, Mansfield, Benalla and Beechworth, together with such tiny dots as Greta and Glenrowan. The North-East's police strength come the end of December has grown to 217 men, nearly three times what it had been before the police murders.

Meanwhile, no fewer than seventy non-commissioned officers and soldiers of the Garrison Corps, whose usual job is to man the forts defending Victoria's coastline from invasion, as well as guard the government's most important institutional buildings, such as Government House and the Treasury, are suddenly given a new assignment. In squads of seven, with the first group leaving Melbourne on 15 December, they are rushed up to North-Eastern Victoria, an area that, as *The Herald* helpfully points out, 'may now be called the "Kelly Country"'.[14] (It is a phrase that instantly sticks, as opposed to the suggestion of another reporter that it be called 'Kellyfornia'.)[15]

The job of the squads is to defend individual banks, especially at 'those townships along the line of railways',[16] allowing local police to pursue the Kellys.

Such a criminal outrage must not be allowed to happen again, and if it needs that many police, that many soldiers and that large a reward to stop four ruffians, then so be it. (Not that it always works out. Up at Euroa, the soldiers sent for the town's salvation become notable for always 'making love to the maids'[17] of the Scotts, including, of course, Miss Fanny Shaw.)

Also helping to concentrate the minds of the populace is that, on the day after his arrival at Euroa, Captain Standish writes to Graham Berry, 'I have the honour to recommend that the reward of £500 for the apprehension of Edward Kelly be increased to £1000 as he appears to be the leader of the Gang of bushrangers now at large . . .'[18] Graham Berry quickly agrees.

As tempting as that might be, however, it is shortly noticed that many of those known to be closest to the Kelly Gang, including most particularly Ned and Dan's sisters, are already in the money. That young lady over there, in the Benalla saddle store? That is the thirteen-year-old Grace Kelly, and you will note that she is paying for a top-class side-saddle and bridle in bright, shiny shilling pieces – while not far away, and not long afterwards, her elder sisters Maggie and Kate are equally liberal in opening their purses to buy supplies, clothing, hats and even children's toys. From being so poor that the families couldn't afford to walk into a shop, let alone saunter in casually with cash to burn, Kate suddenly becomes notable for going into a Benalla store 'and taking a bundle of £10 notes from her blouse to pay [the storekeeper] from it',[19] while Joe Byrne's mother is herself suddenly so flush with cash she is able to slap down £65 to settle a long-standing account with a shopkeeper.

Captain Standish's grim countenance?

There are many causes. One particular reason is that he has just been advised that, down in Melbourne, through the patronage of the powerful politician and seven-time Lord Mayor, John Thomas Smith, Superintendent Nicolson has just had conferred upon him the honorary title of Assistant Commissioner. All without reference to the Commissioner himself – and not least because John Thomas Smith is Nicolson's *father-in-law*. Captain Standish is outraged and appalled in equal measure.

(And nor will he forgive John Thomas Smith. When that gentleman dies, just weeks after conferring the new title on Nicolson, Captain Standish is quick to comment to an underling with ill-disguised glee, 'Now Nicolson's [position] as Assistant Commissioner will soon be done away with, as the Hon. John Thomas Smith got it for him; the [position] is a farce, and it will be all up with him now, as he has no other friend left.')[20]

MID-DECEMBER 1878, TOCUMWAL, ON THE MURRAY RIVER, A SHOT IN THE DARK

There is madness abroad, sheer madness. Seemingly all of the police in North-Eastern Victoria and a good portion of those in Southern New South Wales are scouring the landscape for signs of the Kellys, and, as ever, reports continue to come in from everywhere of confirmed sightings – so many that there would have to be a hundred Kelly Gangs for the reports all to be true. But, against that, who wants to take chances? One of them is obviously the real Kelly Gang, and it is on that reckoning that extreme tension reigns supreme, with outright panic riding shotgun, ready to fire in even the general *direction* where the bushrangers might be.

On one particular evening just before Christmas, up on the Murray River, New South Wales Police Constable Henry Richards is on patrol with a fellow trooper when suddenly they see them: four men in a punt, trying to cross the river into New South Wales. The punters are big, bearded and burly, just the way bushrangers look, and despite his racing heart and the fact that he, personally, is of rather more diminutive stature – and they are only two troopers against four ruffians – Constable Richards is immediate in his challenge. 'If you don't respond, I will shoot you!'[21]

There is no response – or at least no intelligible response, so he repeats it. 'Stop, or I will shoot!'

Still no answer of acquiescence.

Constable Richards feels he has no choice and squeezes the trigger.

In the soft and silent darkness, there is an instantaneous roar, a flash from his muzzle, and out on the Murray River four troopers of the Victoria Police Force throw themselves to the bottom of their punt – a long, narrow, flat-bottomed boat propelled with a long pole. Mercifully, none of them is hit, and they soon return fire – in turn convinced that they are under fire from the Kellys. They have been out on patrol for the gang, have heard someone shouting something unintelligible from the shore, and the next thing they know they are being shot at. Well . . . take this!

It takes some time to sort it all out, and for Constable Richards to apologise to his colleagues for having nearly killed them, but at least they don't forbear from pointing out certain flaws they have found in his character and parentage. Perhaps, in hindsight, it has not been the wisest idea for all of these police patrols to be travelling in bushman's clothes themselves, in the hope of being able to get close enough to the gang to shoot them.

And yet, at least Richards is not the only one. Down Corowa way, also on the Murray, it is thought that the trigger-happy nature of the police, all issued with new shotguns, had been to blame for a remarkably similar near-tragedy.

False alarms aside, *The Argus* is quick to report, 'The impression prevails that the Kellys have crossed the Murray . . .'[22]

Which is as may be. For now, more than 200 troopers continue to search Victoria. It is a particularly expensive exercise because, to compensate for the dangers they are facing when out on search parties, and because many of them are working well away from their home districts and their families, most of the policemen are being paid an extra five shillings a day in travelling allowances.[23] In the later words of Ned Kelly, 'while an outlaw reigns their pocket swells – 'Tis double pay and country girls'.[24]

And what is Captain Standish doing in all this? As ever, as little as he can, yet all the while feeling himself the mastermind of the hunt, manning the office and sifting through information that is coming in. A later official verdict would be that he is 'rusticating peacefully'.[25] Indeed, so self-assuredly peaceful is the Commissioner's rusticating frame of mind that, when Mr D. T. Seymour, the Queensland Commissioner of Police, writes to him offering to place a number of skilled native trackers at the service of the Victorian Government, Captain Standish promptly turns the offer down.[26]

The only times he does get animated – it seems to some of his underlings – is when he is around Superintendent Hare. For, as John Sadleir would record, 'I have spoken of evil friendships, but his devotion to Frank Hare was of another kind – it was like the love of Jonathan for David. It was almost pathetic to see, during the months Captain Standish spent at Benalla . . . how restless and uneasy he became were Hare out of his company. I have seen Standish on the top rail of a fence watching anxiously for Hare's return from a short ride of a mile or two. He said to me that he was in constant fear lest some accident should happen to him . . .'[27]

For his part, the always energetic Hare continues to put his newly bolstered force to work, to 'scour the country with large parties of men',[28] even in the absence of information. It is the strong opinion of one of Hare's constables that, though it is highly unlikely that this strategy could get them close to the outlaws, 'the principal object was to harass [the outlaws], and keep them in the back country'.[29]

17 DECEMBER 1878, IN THE VICTORIAN PARLIAMENT, AN OLIVE BRANCH FOR DON CAMERON

It is his daily routine when the Legislative Assembly is not in session. After a morning attending to matters concerning his electorate, and then a spot of lunch, the newly installed member for West Bourke, Donald Cameron, returns to his chambers to open his mail, most of which is requests for help from his constituents. One particularly rough and bulky-looking letter he leaves aside on his desk, only opening it when he returns to his chambers later in the afternoon, tearing up the envelope as he does so and throwing it into the bin.

Just the opening passage of the letter, however, gives him pause . . .

14 December
Dear Sir,
Take no offence if I take the opportunity of writing a few lines to you wherein I wish to state a few remarks concerning the case of Trooper Fitzpatrick against Mrs Kelly, W. Skillion & W. Williamson and to state the facts of the case to you. It seems impossible for me to get any justice without I make a statement to some one that will take notice of it as it is no use in me complaining about anything that the Police may choose to say or swear against me and the public in their ignorance and blindness will undoubtedly back them up to their utmost . . .[30]

It couldn't be, could it?

Hurriedly, Cameron turns to the last page of the letter to look at the signature.

Edward Kelly, a forced outlaw[31]

It is!

Written 'by a clever illiterate person in red ink',[32] the letter goes for some twenty-two pages, and Cameron quickly reads the rest of it, as Kelly makes the case that he is an innocent man maligned, that he has been 'wronged and persecuted', and 'cannot be blamed'.[33]

Ned Kelly makes terrible accusations of police brutality, how the police, in his absence, would repeatedly rush into the Kelly house:

> revolver in hand upset milk dishes empty the flour out on the ground break tins of eggs and even throw the meat out of the cask on to the floor and dirty & destroy all the provisions which can be proved and shove the girls in front of them into the rooms like dogs & abuse and insult them. Detective Ward & Constable Hayes took out their revolvers and threatened to shoot the girls and children whilst Mrs Skillion was absent, the oldest being with her. The greatest murderers and ruffians would not be guilty of such an action.[34]

Kelly admits to shooting Lonigan, and notes the circumstances, once more asserting he had shot him in self-defence:

> Lonigan ran to a battery of logs and put his head up to take aim at me when I shot him, or he would have shot me . . .[35]

Most worryingly of all, to Cameron, Ned Kelly makes a very clear threat:

> I will not take innocent life if justice is given . . . but if the Public do not see justice

> done I will seek revenge for the name and character which has been given to me and my relations while god gives me strength to pull a trigger . . .
>
> By concluding as I have no more paper unless I rob for it, if I get justice I will cry a go. For I need no lead or powder to revenge my cause, and if words be louder I will oppose your laws. With no offence (remember your railroads) and a sweet goodbye from
>
> Edward Kelly, a forced outlaw[36]

Once finished, Cameron quickly retrieves the pieces of the envelope from the bin and notes they bear the Glenrowan postmark, marked with the date of 14 December. Exactly what Kelly wants Cameron to do is not clear, though it is obvious that the bushranger has taken Cameron's criticism of the government's conduct as support of the Kelly Gang, which is simply not the case.

And so what else could a law-abiding loyal subject like the politician do, when in possession of admissions of guilt from the most noted criminal in the land, together with threats to commit slaughter, including, seemingly, blowing up a railway? The next day, he hands the letter over to Premier and Chief Secretary Berry, who immediately passes it on to the Crown Law Department.

As Captain Standish has already been given the copy received by John Sadleir in the same day's mail, it is he who gets to Berry first, insisting that the letter 'contains a tissue of falsehoods' and should not be published, on the grounds that it is 'inadvisable that publicity should be given to such a production'.[37]

Some small excerpts nevertheless do make it via leaks into the press, most particularly the Melbourne *Herald*, which publishes Ned's key claim that Lonigan had tried to fire at him first. The paper even strikes an almost sympathetic tone in reporting:

> Kelly declares that neither himself nor his comrades intended to commit murder. He says that they had heard that the whole of the district was 'woven' with police, who were out after them, and as they had only two not very good guns, and but a few rounds of ammunition, they held a council of war, and decided to surprise the police, secure their arms, ammunition, and horses, and make their way out of the colony.
>
> The writer does not ask for mercy for himself, and admits that he knows he is outside the pale of mercy. He, however, asks that the grievous wrongs inflicted on his sisters may be righted, and that justice may be done to his mother . . . Altogether, the document is a remarkable one, and exhibits both ability and manliness in its construction and tone.[38]

Beyond that, however, if Ned is waiting for Cameron to take up his cause in the public domain and help to make Victoria see that he is an innocent man, he is to be sorely disappointed.

One government department that takes the Cameron letter most seriously is the railways, who are alarmed at Kelly's threat. Henceforth, detectives are placed at important stations where it is thought the risk of attacks might be greatest, and many employees are issued with arms.

28 DECEMBER 1878, GRAHAM BERRY SEEKS HELP FROM OVER THE SEAS

The Kelly outbreak is certainly not the only concern of the parliament of the day, as the liberal Assembly remains in deadlock with the conservative Legislative Council. The hard move by Graham Berry on 'Black Wednesday' has not yielded the long-term change he had hoped for, and the squatters' grip on the land is still every bit as strong as their hold on the Legislative Council. (Unlike the sixty members of the Assembly, the thirty Council members have to be landowners themselves, and only huge landowners at that.)[39]

With the two houses in an enduring stalemate, unemployment levels rising and drought setting in . . . the colony's economy is twisting in the wind, suffering from what the conservative Opposition delights in calling the 'Berry Blight'.

Yes, the *Appropriations Bill* to pay members had finally passed, but all of Graham Berry's efforts to introduce a bill that reduces the power of the Council have come to nothing, which . . . hardens his resolve and ramps up his now near-revolutionary rhetoric. For he is clear that it is specifically the *land* issue that can break the Victorian Legislative Council's 'absolute and perpetual veto' and 'supreme power'.[40] At a recent public meeting in the bustling Western Victorian town of Hamilton, the Premier had gone so far as to proclaim that 'certain persons owning large estates in this colony must be dispossessed of them by violence, by a civil war, and after a bloody struggle'.[41]

His Minister of Lands, Francis Longmore, had supported the leader's view, thundering at another meeting, 'In most cases where the lands of a country have been monopolised by a class, blood has had to be shed in the recovery. Victoria is no exception to the rule.'[42]

Of course, hopefully, the issue can be resolved *peacefully*, without bloodshed, and it is with this specific idea in mind that on this day Premier Berry prepares to leave the city and head to RMSS *Assam* at Williamstown in Port Phillip Bay, bound for London, where he will 'ask the Imperial Government to give the people of this colony what they only gave to a section of the colony . . . and to let the *lands* of the colony come into the hands of the vast majority of the people'.[43]

And, yes, he has opposition, but let them be warned. For he is forthright in saying he will 'decapitate the [Legislative] Council and stick its head on a pole'.[44] One man he is sure to talk closely with is his Attorney General Sir Bryan O'Loghlen – an 'Irish barrister, most amiable and upright', who views their 'opponents as Saxon oppressors due to suffer for their past sins against his country'[45] – to whom he is entrusting the role of Acting Premier and Chief Secretary.

After half an hour spent bidding his extensive party farewell, the colony's Premier can be seen waving from the deck as RMSS *Assam* leaves its moorings, full steam ahead to London. The crowd send out loud cheers in his wake, as the women wave their handkerchiefs enthusiastically.

Hooray! And bon voyage.[46]

1–4 JANUARY 1879, THE POLICE POUNCE

With now three weeks gone since the outrage at Euroa, and still no one captured, Captain Standish is insistent that it is time to make a move against those who have been so blatantly supporting the murderous Kelly Gang. After all, in those three weeks, only one man has been locked up – on 14 December, Benjamin Gould, the hawker, had been arrested by Detective Michael Ward under the *Felons Apprehension Act* thanks to his loose lips, as he had boasted to all and sundry that he had been a plant at Euroa and been there to help the Kelly Gang all along.

Captain Standish, a rather domineering man, is used to having his every word hung upon, and his instructions in the Benalla Police barracks to this gathering of the responsible sub-officers of the police stations of the region are crisp and clear. What he wants each of them to do, he says, *right now*, is to provide a list of the key sympathisers in their area, those who are known to provide sustenance and warnings to the Kelly Gang – so they can be charged under the auspices of the *Felons Apprehension Act*. After all, to this point, the new law seems to have had no effect, with the gang receiving plentiful support, despite that Act decreeing that anyone who helps them risks fifteen years' imprisonment. Most of the sympathisers are from families just like the Kellys – small selectors in North-Eastern Victoria struggling to survive – and the estimate of *The Ovens and Murray Advertiser* is that there are no fewer than 800 of them.

This move is against the wishes of Superintendent Sadleir, who has strongly counselled against this 'unwise step',[47] which to him seems well outside the law. It is one thing to brand people as sympathisers, but what evidence do they have?

Captain Standish does not care. The courts can sort that out. What he wants now is the list drawn up, and then to organise it so that all those on the list can be rounded up and arrested, all on the one day, or as simultaneously as possible – otherwise, forewarned, many of them might head bush too. Each officer present then submits his piece of paper.

On Thursday 2 January, the compiled list of names is put before a judge, and warrants are issued for arrests. All is now in readiness, bar moving the police into position.

Up Broken River way on Friday morning, four men – Wild Wright, Robert Miller, Henry Perkins and John Hart – are all simply going about their business on their farms and allotments, getting in the crops, etc., when suddenly they find themselves surrounded by troopers on horseback. After quickly being arrested and handcuffed, they are marched into Mansfield. Soon after, Jack Lloyd and Daniel Delaney are brought in and put in the next cell.

And what, the outraged farmers want to know, are they to be charged with?

'[You are to be] charged under the 5th section of the *Felons Apprehension Act* with having at different times aided and abetted the Kelly Gang of outlaws.'[48]

And what is the evidence for that?

We will get to that. You will be advised.

Wild Wright is at least reminded that on New Year's Day, at the sports day held at Dry Creek, he had been telling all and sundry that he had 'seen the Kellys that morning, that they were not two miles from the place, and that he would see them shortly on his road home'.[49]

The six men are kept in the Mansfield Police Camp overnight and taken before a magistrate early on Saturday morning. Upon application of the authorities, all six are remanded for one week. Then, with two troopers assigned for every two prisoners, they are handcuffed in pairs and put on a coach to Benalla.

Hope the handcuffs are not too tight?

Especially stunned and horrified among this lot is hard-working farmer Robert Miller, who, though once married to one of Ellen Kelly's sisters – who had died several years before – has never had any association with the Kellys whatsoever, even if his daughter is said to be an admirer of them. On that morning, he, like the others, had been out in his fields, with his scythe, beginning to harvest his small crop of wheat, when suddenly confronted by four armed troopers on horseback and promptly arrested. So upset is Mr Miller that, on his way into Benalla, when asked by a kindly trooper if he would like a cup of tea, he burst into tears and said, 'I want nothing while in handcuffs.'[50]

Near Benalla, the Kellys' uncle Thomas Lloyd Snr is taken, together with four others, to spend the night in the Benalla police lock-up. The next morning, they appear before Mr Robertson JP with none other than Superintendent John Sadleir prosecuting on behalf of the authorities. But what's this? For Sadleir at once intimates that he does not intend to proceed with the charges against the prisoners and asks for a remand for a week, so as to allow time for the police to bring forward their evidence. The prisoners are 'remanded to Beechworth Gaol till the 11th instant',[51] despite the protest of the accused sympathisers for the case to be heard immediately.

One of the most surprised – and outraged – is John McMonigle in Benalla, who had worked closely with Ned as his leading hand at the Burkes Holes sawmill. Yes, he had indeed been very friendly with Ned and, no mistake about it, had liked him well. Nevertheless, once he had heard what had happened at Stringybark Creek, he had been so disgusted and outraged by the murders that he 'had sent word to the family that he wanted nothing further to do with them'.[52]

When the time comes to take a group of the prisoners from Benalla to Beechworth, they are paraded around on the platform of Benalla Station, handcuffed to each other like common criminals, merely on the suspicion that they might have been aiding the Kelly Gang. For many of the common folk, it is too much. They know some of these men to be good men, who have nothing to do with the Kellys, and to see them humiliated like this is beyond the pale. The police deserve to be heckled for it, and, right there and then on the station, so they are.

For shame! For *shame*!

The Ovens and Murray Advertiser, nevertheless, warmly approves the move and editorialises on the whole issue of the myriad Kelly sympathisers . . . and the trouble they have caused throughout the land:

> It is difficult, adequately, to estimate the evil that is being wrought amongst the youth of the country . . . On all sides boys and young men who have never known much about restraint, read the accounts of the murderers' doings and come to regard them as heroes, and it is mournful to think that in this they are actually encouraged rather than discouraged by men who should know better.[53]

None of which appears to convince the people in Kelly Country. For, across the whole region, stories spread of the hardships now visited on the families of these innocent men, who have done nothing – *nothing* – but are being rounded up and thrown into gaol. The outrage grows, and, as *The Argus* notes, 'a very unhealthy sympathy prevails throughout the district with the Kellys'.[54] Selectors who had dilly-dallied on the fence when it came to the Kellys now choose to sit squarely in their camp.

And yet even being locked up for allegedly helping the Kelly Gang can't curb the pluck of many of those sympathisers. For one, the effrontery of the Kelly brothers' uncle, Tom Lloyd, only shines brighter once behind bars. Old Tom had been busy getting in his crop when a trooper had arrived to take him in, and it had been no matter that the aged farmer had quite rightly protested his perfect innocence, avowing that, 'If I am taken away from this farm at the present time, I am a ruined man.' For the only reply received had been, 'Come along old man,'[55] and come along he had had to, leaving his wife and youngest two children to get in the crop the best they could.

Deftly playing the old-man card, feigning a great need to send directives back to his family on the farm at Greta, he manages to convince his gaoler to allow him one telegram:

> Turn the four bullocks out of the paddock.[56]

The police penny doesn't drop until a few weeks later. As Hare comes to admit, 'Undoubtedly it meant, turn the four outlaws out of the paddock in which they were in.'[57]

Having been tipped off by Uncle Tom, the Kelly Gang are greatly concerned for their friends under lock and key, now facing charges with no legal counsel. And so, via an intermediary, they send money for their legal defence.

Throughout much of January, the gang are spotted all over the North-East. On 5 January alone, they are supposedly seen at Wodonga, Broken River and on the Chiltern Road. The next day, they are spotted just 'three miles from Kilfera to Greta',[58] and at Stony Creek near Violet Town. And people can hear the Kellys too! One particular story that makes the people laugh concerns a Police Magistrate who heard his cook drop a saucepan in the middle of the night and, convinced that it is the Kellys coming for him as he always knew they would, runs out of the house and climbs a tree, staying there 'till he saw the woman come out to get water for the kettle in the morning'.[59]

Wherever the Kelly Gang really are, whichever of these alleged sightings, and *hearings!* are true, the gang have definitely not gone too far from home.

As ever, *The Ovens and Murray Advertiser* puts it rather well: 'As usual all sorts of rumours are flying about with reference to the whereabouts of these celebrated desperadoes, and if all are to be believed, they must be ubiquitous . . .'[60]

11 JANUARY 1879, FOR FEAR OF THE KELLY GANG

Of course, it is not just Victorian newspapers that are following the Kelly affair closely. The New South Wales press are also particularly interested, what with constant rumours swirling around the state that the Kelly Gang either have made it across the Murray or will soon. Albury, Wagga Wagga, Goulburn and many other towns in the lower half of New South Wales are convinced that the Kellys will attack soon. And, in fact, it is not just the big towns, either.

To the amusement of many, on this day Samuel Gill, the editor of the *Jerilderie Gazette* – the bugle for that tiny town, lost in the red dusty wilds of the Southern Riverina district of Southern New South Wales – writes a thunderous editorial, pointing out to the populace that their town, too, is a vulnerable target. For is it not true that we are now totally exposed? Yes! Gill complains that Jerilderie is currently 'entirely without police protection – one of the constables being away on duty, the other sent on a wild goose chase after the Kellys to watch the Murray at Tocumwal, to see that they did not cross the river at that town and enter New South Wales'.

This is not right!

'We also hear it stated that notwithstanding all the police stationed at Tocumwal, the Kellys could cross unperceived 200 yards below the township, and enter New South Wales under the very nose of the police and march straight across to the Murrumbidgee, without the police knowing they had crossed the border . . . If the Kellys get to know, and they appear to be well acquainted with the movements of the police, what is to prevent them paying a visit . . . and stop them carrying off what booty they think proper?'[61]

Well, Jerilderie, never!

It is such a pointed editorial, so strong and scathing against the Kelly Gang, and so topical, that of course the whole town talks about it, and Samuel Gill becomes quite the focus of attention. 'Watch out,' many people in the town jokingly tell him, 'if the Kellys do happen to come to Jerilderie, you will be one of the first men they come after!'[62]

10–11 JANUARY 1879, BEECHWORTH GAOL, ANOTHER REMAND CASE

Something's up. Beechworth residents note the arrival of Chief Commissioner Standish and Superintendent Sadleir into their town on the Friday evening before the sympathisers' remand hearing. At the request of his chief, the reluctant Sadleir is to appear for the police in court the following afternoon.

And so it proves as, come the hearing, the dutiful Sadleir asks Presiding Magistrate W. H. Foster for a remand for a week, as the police are still not prepared to give evidence for a committal.

Only one prisoner, John McMonigle, has legal counsel, in the form of William Zincke – well known to the Kellys for having unsuccessfully defended them on many occasions. In this instance, Zincke is outspoken right to the point of contempt of court that these constant remands are 'in direct violation of law, as my client has been already twice remanded, and no evidence [has] on either occasion been brought forward to show why he should be deprived of his liberty'.[63]

In response, Superintendent Sadleir reports that, while he is not yet ready to present evidence, he can 'assure the Bench that the prisoner is a most active confederate of the outlaws'.[64]

This is an outrage! Zincke asserts that neither the police nor the courts are 'justified in tampering with the liberty of the subject as granted by Magna Carta unless the *Habeas Corpus Act* were suspended!'.[65]

Magistrate Foster listens to both sides of the argument but in the end clearly feels he has no choice but to back the police in this extreme situation, and so grants remand for another week.

18 JANUARY 1879, LONG DAZE IN COURT

Somehow, despite being everywhere and nowhere all at once, the Kelly Gang have rustled up enough funds to pay for the defence of their comrades. First up, they have procured the local man William Zincke, impressed by how zealously he had defended McMonigle the week before, and also Albert Reade, a solicitor of some repute in the City

Court in Melbourne. Both men of the law are only too happy to have a well-publicised soapbox from which to decry the government's blatant disregard for the most basic tenets of the rule of law and the rights of man.

And so, twenty Kelly sympathisers are again brought before Magistrate W. H. Foster at the Beechworth Courthouse charged under the *Felons Apprehension Act*. First things first, Reade demands that each man should be tried separately.

Granted.

Thomas Lloyd is brought up, the old man with his snow-white hair, sending withering glares at the prosecution counsel, not to forget the Bench for good measure. On behalf of the police, Bowman immediately applies for a remand for this prisoner.

As the exchange warms up, Zincke weighs in, pointing out that Sadleir had said last week that he would be ready to provide evidence this week 'to show an overt act on the part of the prisoner. I challenge him to show this overt act with which the prisoner is charged.'[66]

There is no response, and so Zincke adds with calculated righteousness, from the towering heights of his own very high dudgeon, 'Was it the intention of this act to lock these men up for a fortnight without any reasonable cause assigned?'[67]

'The Act itself,' Mr Bowman retorts, 'is a reasonable cause.'

'We are here to talk *law*,' Reade breaks in, 'not nonsense.'[68]

In the end, the Police Magistrate sides with Bowman's argument, agreeing that this exceptional case calls for exceptional measures, and Uncle Tom is remanded, for the third time, for eight days.

Mr Bowman then drops charges against six of the prisoners, including the sad-faced Robert Miller, but all the remaining men, despite having counsel to defend them, are equally remanded for eight more days in front of a swelling crowd in the courthouse.

One small victory is nevertheless won for Reade and Zincke on this day, as Bowman at least guarantees 'either to withdraw the charges, or else prosecute to an issue at the end of the week . . .'[69]

22 JANUARY 1879, CROWN PROSECUTOR BOWMAN JUGGLES FOR JUSTICE

A man of his word, especially if uttered in a courthouse, Crown Prosecutor Bowman is much perturbed when, by Wednesday, he has still not received news of police evidence against the prisoners on remand.

Unwilling to again try to feebly deflect the barrage of legal truths that would be hurled at him this Saturday if he is to appear with no evidence against the accused, he writes a double-edged telegram to the man who had proposed the *Felons Apprehension Act* in the first place, the Acting Chief Secretary and Attorney General Sir Bryan O'Loghlen:

> Am I to prosecute prisoners held on remand re Kelly on Saturday? If evidence to be taken have received no information from Police since Saturday last.[70]

O'Loghlen immediately hands the note on to Standish, making it clear to the Chief Commissioner that the matter is 'entirely in your hands'.[71]

Indeed, it is in his hands, and all Standish can do is wash his hands entirely of the pesky Bowman. He sends word that, 'It is not my intention to retain the services of Mr Bowman, and I command him to be so informed.'[72]

He adds that, of course, his favourite police officer, Superintendent Hare, 'will proceed to Beechworth to conduct the case on Saturday.'[73]

Meanwhile, the discharged Bowman finds himself in the odd position of being offered a place on the opposing side of the courtroom, to act as counsel for the defendants. He accepts with enthusiasm. A strange twist indeed, as it is said that Ned Kelly is to pay his fees.

LATE JANUARY 1879, THE LEGAL FARCE GOES ON AT BEECHWORTH

Week after wretched week, it is the same thing. With heavy heart, Superintendent Hare must head to Beechworth every Friday and go through the whole charade of earnestly beseeching the Bench for a further remand, all, as he would bitterly note, 'without being able to adduce a tittle of evidence against them'.[74]

'This move was a very unfortunate one,' Hare would record. 'It did no good, and evoked sympathy for the men in custody. The police, I found out, had no evidence against these persons beyond the fact that they were known to be associates, relatives, and friends of the outlaws.'[75]

However, at the time, as a loyal policeman, he has no choice but to do his duty as he sees it, and at Captain Standish's intense insistence the legal farce goes on, as the outrage at this abuse of the legal process continues.

Whatever has been accomplished by the government in terms of putting these particular sympathisers in gaol, a lot more has been lost by the government's demonstration of its own venality. Almost as one, the entire region of North-Eastern Victoria rises against the authorities and, instead of having fewer sympathisers, the Kelly Gang now have many.

Even in Melbourne, a *Herald* editorial, 'The Liberty of the Subject', presents a scarifying attack on the sympathiser debacle, pointing out that while ordinary criminals were brought into court by policemen armed with batons, 'those suspected men now lying in the Beechworth Gaol, however, are brought up between rows of soldiers and police, with loaded guns and bayonets fixed. Was ever so sorry a farce enacted?'[76]

Likely not. And so great is the outrage of the people that, as a precaution, the heavy wooden gates on Beechworth Gaol are replaced with iron ones, less for fear of a breakout than a break-*in*, to release the sympathisers.

25 JANUARY 1879, NED WRITES ANOTHER LETTER

Ned Kelly again does his best to bring to the attention of the authorities the essential innocence of the Kelly Gang and the uselessness of locking up their supporters. A new letter is addressed to Acting Chief Secretary Sir Bryan O'Loghlen:

Sir,
I take the liberty of addressing you with respect to the matter of myself, my brother and my two friends, Hart and Byrne. I take this opportunity to declare most positively that we did not kill the policemen in cold blood, as has been stated by that rascal McIntyre. We only fired on them to save ourselves, and we are not the cold-blooded murderers which people presume us to be. Circumstances have forced us to become what we are – outcasts and outlaws, and, bad as we are, we are not as bad as we are supposed to be.

But my chief reason for writing this is to tell you that you are committing a manifest injustice in imprisoning so many innocent people just because they are supposed to be friendly to us. There is not the least foundation for the charge of aiding and abetting us against any of them, and you may know this is correct, or we would not be obtaining our food as usual since they have been arrested.

Your policemen are cowards – every one of them. I have been with one party two hours while riding in the ranges, and they did not know me. I will show you that we are determined men, and I warn you that within a week we will leave your colony, but we will not leave it until we have made the country ring with the name Kelly and taken terrible revenge for the injustice and oppression we have been subjected to.

Beware, for we are now desperate men.

Edward Kelly[77]

LATE JANUARY 1879, OF NEEDLES AND HAYSTACKS

In the meantime, another line of police enquiry, using Patrick Quinn to take a party to the head of the King River, has come to nothing.

Though, as agreed, Quinn has taken them out that way, a recent bushfire has destroyed all vegetation, meaning that – at least as far as Quinn tells the police – the major landmarks have gone and the group soon gets hopelessly lost.

The person most upset by this is Senior Constable Anthony Strahan, who, like many people in the community, is still not convinced that this dirt-poor farmer who comes of the criminal class is genuinely trying to help them. And he doesn't mind telling the cur. 'We'll never catch the Kellys until we arrest you,' Strahan says to Quinn bluntly.

But Quinn is not even momentarily intimidated. 'All you want,' he sneers in reply, 'is to get the reward raised and promotion, and to put the country to trouble and expense, all of which might have been saved but for your blundering, and threatening to shoot the Kellys.'[78]

EARLY FEBRUARY 1879, HARE MEETS HIS MATCH

Superintendent Hare, meanwhile, between court appearances, is in the thick of expedition after expedition, looking for the Kellys, seemingly in every valley, up every hill, down every dale, in every cave in Kelly Country. What is sure is that he does not spare himself at all in the pursuit and asks nothing of his troopers that he does not do himself.

Quietly and privately, Sadleir is of the view that these endless search parties are in operation because they are the only idea Hare has in his head, and that he is doing so 'on the mere hope of their coming across the Kellys',[79] but he still has some grudging admiration for the energy Hare puts into it.

One thing that is obvious is that most of the police now patrolling the region are not bushmen. Yes, yes, they are 'a fine body of courageous men . . . in discipline they were splendid',[80] . . . but courage alone does not make a bushman. One officer, thoroughly aware of Hare's style and the workings of his men, reflected on the police's lack of success in bringing the Kellys to heel: 'the first principal point I always considered was the want of knowledge on the part of the police of the bush, they did not know the country. In conversation which I had with a gentleman up there, a thorough bushman, he pointed this out. He said to me, "Men in the police here, what they want to do in this country districts is to learn the bush. These men never go off the main road."'[81]

And yet it is not as if there are a lot of other plans in play. '[Hare] certainly did not spare himself,' Superintendent Sadleir would record, 'and he shared with his men all the discomforts of camping out, but his fault, as I have always thought, was in confining his efforts to this one line and dispensing with the use of secret agents.'[82]

There is, however, one notable exception: Aaron Sherritt.

One night in early February, when Sherritt comes looking for Captain Standish at the Benalla Police Station – on a rare occasion when Hare happens to be there between his bush bashes – they meet. Hare, of course, knows the young man to be a 'friend and bush telegraph of the Gang',[83] and is very pleased to meet Sherritt, recording as his first impression that Sherritt is 'a splendid man, tall, strong, hardy'.[84] Sherritt's impression of Hare goes unrecorded, but it is certain that the Superintendent is impressed enough for *both* of them, as he would still be gushing many years later of the younger man, 'If he walked down Collins Street, everybody would have stared at him – his walk, his appearance, and everything else was remarkable . . .'[85] (Indeed, in a curious parallel, Francis Hare is smitten from the first with Aaron Sherritt in much the same manner as Captain Standish is smitten with Francis Hare.) But to the business at hand . . .

'What do you want to see Captain Standish about?' Superintendent Hare asks him.

'I have some important information to give him, and I wish to speak to him privately . . .'[86]

Well, Captain Standish won't be back tonight, Hare explains, and the two begin a long conversation, over a drink in Hare's office. Now, despite the fact that Sherritt has not given any information to the police since he was first engaged by Captain Standish at Sebastopol, and seems to have a natural wariness of troopers, Hare, at least in his own view, is able to skilfully – nay, masterfully – overcome that wariness and gain the young man's trust. Really, in Hare's view, it is quite remarkable how expertly he plays the young man.

And there is no doubt that Aaron Sherritt's credentials in speaking about the Kellys are impeccable. Not only does he know both Kellys well but he is also best friends with Joe Byrne, with whom he has gone to school, grown up and committed crimes. He is currently engaged to Joe Byrne's sister, Catherine, who is living with her mother in the family hut at the Woolshed, a place where he is a constant visitor. Oh, certainly, Hare can see that the young fellow doesn't necessarily want to tell him all these things, but so skilfully does he talk to Sherritt that, after only an hour, he can see that 'my influence over him was very great'.[87]

So much so, in fact, that one hour and a few drinks later it is Sherritt who comes out with it. 'I think I can trust you with my information . . .' he says almost playfully to Hare, before telling all.[88]

Just the previous afternoon, Sherritt says, at about two o'clock, Joe Byrne and Dan Kelly had come to his selection, midway between his mother's and Joe's mother's houses. He'd been working away when he'd looked up to see Joe and Dan on horseback. Joe had jumped off, come and sat down beside him and they had begun to talk. (Not Dan, though – Dan had never trusted Aaron, and had no real presumption of friendship with him. He just stayed on his horse, glaring down at him.)

Hare, beside himself with excitement at the news – *two of the Kelly Gang, up at the Woolshed, just yesterday!* – presses the young man to go on.

'Well,' Sherritt says, 'Dan asked me to join them, as they are going across the Murray, and intended going to Goulburn, in New South Wales, where the Kellys have a cousin. They wanted me to act as a scout.'[89]

Sherritt recounts how they had pressed him hard, but he had declined. Finally, Joe had said to him after thirty minutes or so, with Dan Kelly still glaring down all the while, 'Well, Aaron, you are perfectly right; why should you get yourself into this trouble and mix yourself up with us?'[90] And then they had gone, 'Joe Byrne . . . riding a magnificent grey horse, and the other a bay . . .'[91]

It is, of course, stunning information, if it indeed proves true, and after another hour of gleaning everything about the two members of the Kelly Gang – what they were wearing, how they were armed, how they looked – Superintendent Hare gives the young man £2 for his trouble and now makes an offer. If Sherritt gives information that will directly lead to the capture of the Kelly Gang, he will get all of the £4000 reward. In the meantime, if what he has said so far proves true, then the government could perhaps put him on a stipend of seven shillings a day or so, to keep him informing for them. With such endearing terms, the tacit agreement that Sherritt had made with Standish back in early November, when the police cavalcade had rolled through the Woolshed, is now nailed down. He will do it, he tells Hare.

And nor does he think there will be much trouble at all in catching the Kelly Gang, as he personally is always well apprised of their movements, often well beforehand. And if the gang are going to Goulburn to rob a bank, they will be sure to drop in on Mrs Byrne's place on their return to leave her some of the money, and, when they do, Aaron intends to be there. 'You have a most difficult and dangerous job before you,' he says to the Superintendent, 'but I will do all I can to assist you.'[92]

As to where that danger most lies, Sherritt is specific: Ned Kelly himself – the hardest, toughest, most skilled bushman there ever was, with not another man like him in the entire colony. 'He is about the only man I ever was afraid of in my life,' Sherritt says, 'and I certainly give him best in everything.'

But can they, together, bring him to justice and capture the Kelly Gang? The answer is a definite yes. 'If you really want to take them,' the young man promises the now beaming police officer, 'I will lay you on them.'[93]

What a breakthrough!

'Be careful, now you are in Benalla, that you are not seen here,'

Hare says. 'Do not go into town, but get some hotel near the railway station.'[94]

The two arrange to meet each other again shortly, and Hare is thrilled at what seems to be a major breakthrough. Others at the station, however, do not share the Superintendent's joy. When he describes the arrangement to Detective Ward, who is the policeman best acquainted with young Sherritt and who had sent him into Benalla looking for Standish in the first place, Ward urgently exhorts his superior, 'He is only deceiving you, sir, please don't trust him. He would not sell his friend Joe Byrne for all the money in the world.'[95] (Yes, Ward agrees, Aaron may be useful, but not as a trustworthy informant – only in the hope that he could be used as bait to bring the Kellys out of cover.)

Hare begs to differ. He trusts his instinct on men and feels sure that his opinion of Sherritt is correct and that he 'means to work for us honestly'.[96]

Still others, though, such as Superintendent Sadleir, have their misgivings. While he is glad to see Hare going down a different path to endless expeditions, he is of the view that Hare has 'none of the skill and patience of Nicolson in handling [informants] of this sort'.[97]

But what would they know? When more enquiries quickly reveal that Joe Byrne and Dan Kelly had indeed been spotted heading north in recent days, even calling 'for supplies at a shanty where Byrne was well known',[98] Hare is more convinced than ever that the young man is trustworthy. 'I at once informed Mr Sadleir,' he later recounted, 'and we set to work sending information . . . by telegraph, to all border police on both sides of the river.'[99]

The word is passed to the New South Wales Police, with the pointer that the banks at Goulburn should be particularly alert.

EARLY FEBRUARY 1879, ELEVEN MILE CREEK, ONE MORE SIDE TO THE STORY

All up, it is a very strange episode. A party of gentlemen on their way from Sydney to Melbourne, and therefore passing within coo-ee of

Eleven Mile Creek, decide to stop off for some refreshments in the most talked about hut in the land: the home of Ned Kelly. The door is answered by fifteen-year-old Kate Kelly, and though she is 'at first very reserved and uncommunicative, and indeed appeared to be rather suspicious of her visitors', little by little she warms up and even starts to chat liberally. The men find her to be 'a fine, apparently spirited and rather prepossessing young woman, with a considerable resemblance to her brother Ned, although her features are better than his'.

'Are you not lonely here, and afraid to remain here without male protection?' one of them asks.

'Not the least lonely or afraid,' she replies lightly, 'as I am well guarded, and will be until the affair is over.'

Guarded? What on earth does she mean by this?

And then it clicks. She explains that her every movement, as are those of her sister, is closely watched by the police, who are hiding in yonder bush, and on yonder hill, in yonder caves, and who are continually around her place: 'They come at all times, day and night, in all disguises, and on any pretence, and even when I don't see them, I still know I am being watched. At night I can hear stealthy footsteps around the house, and am conscious of whispering and prying through chinks in the bark walls of the hut. At other times they come boldly up, push open the door, and walk in demanding Ned Kelly. At night when the doors are locked they knock, and I have to get up and let them in.'

Strangely, the striking young woman seems more amused by it than anything else and even recounts one manner of revenge: 'Sometimes when they barge in, I tell them that my brothers are in the bedroom and I dare them to go in for them.' This results, she says, in four or five stalwart troopers, with cocked revolvers in hand, stealthily approaching the bedroom she has designated, only to find that there is no one there.

Oh, the police are watching all right.

'The police are sure to be here presently,' she remarks, and sure enough, within minutes a trooper turns up on horseback – dressed in plain clothes – who asks the men their business and is presumptuous enough to search their trap and even their luggage, against the possibility that the bushrangers might be hiding within.

They are not, and soon enough the trooper is on his way. Having seen up close the harassment this engaging young woman is subject to, there is a complicity, an empathy between Kate and her guests, and now one of them dares ask about the rumours abroad that the problems between Fitzpatrick and the family had begun when the trooper had attempted an outrage on her . . .

Kate, by their subsequent account, acknowledges it to be so: 'I was in the house alone when he came,' she tells them candidly, 'and he commenced in a violent manner to behave improperly towards me. Just then my brother Ned came to the door, and caught Fitzpatrick in the act of attempting an outrage, whereupon he, with the natural instinct of a brother under such circumstances, rushed for his revolver . . . fired, and this was how it came that Fitzpatrick was shot in the wrist.'

A fine man, her brother, and she obviously adores him. Taking up a prayer-book from the mantelpiece, she withdraws from it a photo – it is Ned.

With great emotion and 'in a most affecting manner, she caressingly kissed the portrait'.

In further talk, it is obvious she is frustrated that because of the police vigilance she has been unable to see her family, and it further seems to be her assumption that one way or another her brothers will not be long for this world. 'Yes,' she says pitifully, 'when poor Ned and poor Dan are gone, I shall be the last of the Kellys.'

Ah, but there is also an upside that seems to brighten her up no end. 'But they'll never be taken alive,' says she, 'and I can tell you that they will astonish Melbourne yet . . .'[100]

What does she mean by that?

The Melbourne *Herald*, which goes on to publish the travellers' account of the visit, says the remark is 'taken to mean that the outlaws contemplated some daring escapade'.[101]

But come, come. If the assertion that Fitzpatrick had made salacious moves against Kate be true, why had that not come out in the court case? Kate had not said at the time, but it will later be asserted that it is because Ned has insisted to his family that Kate was *not* to have her dignity offended by any public discussion of such a thing.

FIRST WEEK OF FEBRUARY 1879, THE KELLY GANG HEAD TO THE OTHER SIDE

Careful now. Very, very careful . . .

Acting on Sherritt's solid tip-off, for several days the Victoria Police have been discreetly examining every group of men crossing the Murray, particularly in the vicinity of Corryong, the most obvious place to cross for anyone heading from Kelly Country to Goulburn. Superintendent Hare has put great credence in what Sherritt has said, and it is apparently certain that the gang should be crossing sometime this week, on their way to Goulburn. Which is one thing. The next thing to decide, though, is what the police should do if they spot the outlaws. The Kelly Gang are established killers, with three noble policemen in their graves to prove it, and if they are spotted it is obviously going to be no simple thing to subdue them without bloodshed – hopefully not the police's.

So vigilant are the police that each fresh group of men crossing the river in this area acts as a fresh alarm that this must finally be the gang . . . but always it is merely a group of farmers, or labourers, or townsfolk, simply going about their business.

Often, it proves to be a group of troopers in plain clothes . . . 'Tocumwal targets', if you will.

Where, oh where, can the Kelly Gang be?

Chapter Nine

JERILDERIE

Of [Francis Hare's] courage, brute strength and endurance there was no doubt, but he was vain and tactless.
Frank Clune, The Kelly Hunters

The present state of Victoria is indeed deplorable. Credit is at a discount; money is scarce, and what there is of it is locked up; mobocracy reigns supreme; a terrorism exists, whose baneful effects are making themselves everywhere apparent, and what with a Communist Government and a Gang of outlawed ruffians at large, the outlook is indeed, a gloomy one . . .
The Ovens and Murray Advertiser, 14 January 1879

8 FEBRUARY 1879, THERE ARE STRANGERS IN THE HOUSE, UP JERILDERIE WAY

Slowly but surely on this late summer's evening, two strangers on horseback amble up to Mrs Davidson's busy Woolpack Inn on the south bank of the bubbling Billabong Creek, some two miles east of the anonymous small town of Jerilderie, and on the main road between Wagga Wagga and Deniliquin. By the look of these strangers, they have come a long way, and likely have even further to go, for they have the air of hard travelling men – a big, bearded one, and a smaller version of the larger one, though without a beard. They might be brothers.

It is the large one who is the most talkative, telling the barmaid they've come from up the way of the Lachlan River and are heading south. Of course, the conversation inevitably turns to the same subject that everyone at least touches on these days, the Kelly Gang, and on this topic the older one seems more than usually interested.

'What do the people of Jerilderie have to say about them?' he asks.

'They think they're brave,' the barmaid replies, and the big, bearded man beams.[1]

Encouraged, the barmaid, known to everyone far and wide as Mary the Larrikin, even sings a few lines of a newly popular song, 'The Kellys have made another escape.'[2]

The two strangers are amused and perhaps even seem oddly heartened that the lass knows the words. A few drinks later, and after having learned the names of the police officers in town and other information about its residents from their obliging hostess, the two decide to head on their way. Before leaving, they don't fail to very generously tip the cheeky and buxom barmaid – just the way Joe Byrne likes 'em, for it is of course him with Ned – a florin.

Up and out, the two mount their horses and head west. There is no one there to notice, but once away from the lights of the hotel they are soon joined by Dan Kelly and Steve Hart, who have been waiting for them.

LATE SATURDAY NIGHT, 8 FEBRUARY 1879, JERILDERIE WAKES UP

Sure, Jerilderie, from the Aboriginal, meaning 'reedy place'[3] – a good 100 miles west of Wagga Wagga and 60 miles north of the Murray River – is a small settlement of just 400 souls, which might have been the original model of the 'one-horse town' of popular imagination. But at least it has two policemen, and very occasionally they even have something to do. This afternoon, for example, Senior Constable George Devine and Probationary Constable Henry Richards put in their log lock-up – known to the local folk as 'the Logs' – an unruly elderly drunk, for his own safety. And that will be enough work for one day. It is, after all, the end of the week, and in this flat town surrounded by billabongs that has just a bank, a telegraph office, five hotels, a courthouse that doubles as a church, a newspaper, the usual assortment of butchers, bakers, blacksmiths and the like – together with a police barracks and lock-up out on the eastern edge of town – it is really only the hotels that remain open. Nothing much to worry about here . . .

It is for this reason that, nearing midnight on this steamy night, both George Devine and his heavily pregnant wife, Mary, are surprised, but not alarmed, to be roused by the sound of loud shouting and snorting horses outside their residence. In this town, shouting is unlikely to be a harbinger of serious danger, for the simple reason that what danger there is in the region is rarely man-made. (Not surprisingly, such shouting arouses no one else, as the police barracks is a good quarter of a mile from most of the town's main buildings, and set 60 yards back from the road in the police paddock.) Still, what is it that the intense distant voice is shouting?

'Police! Police! Get up, there is a great row at Davidson's Hotel.'[4]

It is something about Davidson's Hotel, which is a couple of miles out of town, and how the police must come. What is it saying now?

'For **God's** sake get **up**,' the voice roars again, but this time closer and louder, 'there's a row going on up at Davidson's and they're fighting. If they are not stopped there will be murder before the morning. Get up at once and come and bring Richards with you.'[5]

A *murder?*

Stunned, Devine is instantly wide awake and fumbling to light the bedside oil lantern, even as he scrambles to get his trousers and socks on, together with his boots. Such are the travails of being a lawman, that, though late at night, one can be called from one's bed to keep the peace – necessarily giving up your own peace to do so.

Devine emerges onto the verandah to be immediately confronted by a large man with a beard that appears as black as the fine horse on which he sits, yelling in the eerily bright moonlight that the fight is serious, that they're killing each other!

'*Who* is fighting?' Devine demands.

'A lot of drunken fellows. Where's Richards?'[6]

The equally dishevelled and hurriedly dressed trooper Richards now appears on cue, coming from his own quarters and saying, 'I'm here. What's up?'

The horseman expostulates, 'Are there not more than two of you to come and stop the row? The men are mad with drink.'[7]

Once advised, however, that that is the case, and that there are no more than two policemen in all of Jerilderie, an extraordinary thing happens. On the instant, the bearded stranger who has been asking for help suddenly pulls out a revolver from beneath his coat, points it at them and growls menacingly, 'Throw up your hands. I'm Ned Kelly.'[8]

For a split second, it seems that resistance might be possible – after all, they are two policemen, and he is one bushranger – but it lasts no longer than that. For, seeing their way of thinking, Kelly adds, 'Don't move, for you are also covered by my men from both ends of the verandah, and on the slightest movement on the part of either of you, you will be shot by them.'[9]

On the instant, coming from the darkness, three other armed men suddenly appear on their flanks. Though never formally introduced, the two now terrified policemen soon learn that they are Dan Kelly, Joe Byrne and Steve Hart.

It is all so shocking. One minute, the two men had been asleep in their respective and respectable beds, and now they have the entire Kelly Gang pointing their guns at them, calling on them to surrender! Who would ever have thought these outlaws would strike this far from their home base in North-Eastern Victoria? (Apart from Samuel Gill, that is.) Certainly not the Jerilderie Police, and certainly not their superiors, who had given their men no warning that this was even a possibility.

Of course, both policemen do immediately surrender, and carefully . . . slowly . . . slowly . . . so as not to alarm anyone with sudden movements of any kind . . . they put their hands in the air. All police resistance to the Kelly Gang in Jerilderie ceases from this moment.

At least physical resistance . . .

For, despite his surrender, Senior Constable Devine cannot resist saying what he feels. 'My police career will be ruined by this.'

'You should resign anyway,' Ned snaps back without an ounce of sympathy, 'and look for an honest job.'[10]

After Ned dismounts, the two troopers are marched back into the dining room of the barracks at gunpoint, just as Senior Constable Devine's wife, Mary, bursts through the dining-room door in her nightdress, puts down the candle she is holding, wraps her arms around her husband and begs Ned Kelly not to shoot her beloved and the father of her three children on the ground and one in her belly.

They are safe, the elder Kelly man assures her, while glaring balefully at Devine and Richards, so long as there are no 'signs of hanky panky work'. If there is, Ned says, tapping his revolver with menace, 'I'll shoot them without a moment's hesitation.'[11]

What the gang want now, he tells her, is – right after she shows them where the police and arms and ammunition are kept – some supper, if she would be so kind?

She does so show them and she would be so kind indeed. A minute later, the two constables suffer the indignity of being locked in with the same elderly drunk they had arrested earlier in the day, a man who, from between the log slabs of the lock-up walls, has watched slack-mouthed the whole affair unfold under the bright moonlight.

One thing before you go, however, Mr Kelly.

For Ned is just taking his leave when George Devine begs him, 'Please don't interfere with my wife.'[12]

Ned is mortified at the very suggestion. 'No female,' he says, 'could say otherwise than that my mates and I have always treated women with the greatest respect and courtesy . . . Which is a lot more than can be said about many of the Victorian Police whose cowardly conduct towards defenceless women is well known.'

Ned guarantees the policeman, 'Mrs Devine and her children will have every respect shown them.'[13]

The entire Kelly Gang treat Mrs Devine with elaborate respect as she rustles up some grub. They have now taken over the whole police station, including the stables, where they have secured, fed and watered their horses. Their supper finished, Mrs Devine is allowed to retire to her bedroom, where her three children are sleeping soundly, as only growing bodies can . . . There they will stay, under the guard of Steve Hart, and they are told that the life of the father of the family now depends on them remaining quiet and not attempting to raise an alarm.

When dawn comes, again Mrs Devine is asked to do the honours, and get them breakfast. Led from their lock-up to join the gang, George Devine must suffer the indignity of seeing Ned Kelly sitting in *his* chair, at the head of *his* table, wearing *his* police uniform, while *his* wife makes the *criminal* breakfast!

But it is about to get worse still. For, shortly thereafter, the bush-rangers are handling *his* guns – cleaning and loading them to get them ready for the job ahead. What on earth are they planning?

As this is a Sunday, his wife tells the outlaws that she must go to 'church' – in fact, it is the town's courthouse, used for the Sunday service, which lies 100 yards distant from the barracks – to prepare the altar as she does every Sunday, arrange the flowers and the like, otherwise people would realise that something was amiss. It is a reasonable point, and Ned Kelly agrees, so long as his brother can, in his police uniform, accompany her for the entire time.

Tensely, the two set off – the lady and the brigand – Mrs Devine's eyes set rigidly forward in the manner of someone who does not wish to speak to anyone she meets, which is most definitely the case. Acutely aware that the man beside her is armed and dangerous, she wishes only to fulfil her duties at the chapel as quickly as possible and then get back to her husband and children. Under the keen eye of Dan Kelly, who even lends a helping hand, she arranges the flowers, dusts the altar, the tables and window sills, sweeps between the pews, puts out the hymn books and candlesticks, and generally tidies up, ensuring that all is in order.

And yet . . . wait just a moment before we head back, Mrs Devine.

After she is done, Dan Kelly quickly checks under each vase and every hymn book and Bible that she has been near, to ensure that no note has been left behind for the priest to find, no warning given. Once he is assured – and it does not take long, as Dan has watched her closely throughout and has little fear that she would risk the lives of her family in that manner – the two head stiffly back to the police barracks.

As soon as they are inside again, the men move about the house as if going about normal duties. A few members of the congregation who pass the barracks on the way to church notice the visiting policemen and simply conclude that they are a party 'going to the border in quest of the Kelly gang'.[14] As they have been used to such parties coming through town over the past few months, it does not occasion comment. The only visitor is the butcher, who knocks on the door to deliver the meat for the Sunday roast, and, as Ned hovers closely, Mrs Devine answers the door and hurriedly takes delivery.

Later in the afternoon, Joe Byrne and Steve Hart take Probationary Constable Richards with them for a look around the town, on the reckoning that it is Richards who is the more docile of the two policemen and 'would "go quietly" rather than take risks'.[15] For his part, Richards – at least relieved to be out of the lock-up, even for this reason – must explain that the two surly-looking policemen in ill-fitting uniforms who are with him are new postings to the area. Though the curious trio do walk from one end of the tiny town to the other (it does not take long), they do linger longer outside the Bank of New South Wales, which is part of the same iron-roofed building as the Royal Mail Hotel, no doubt ensuring that it is secure against any robbers or bushrangers such as the ones who have been running wild south of the Murray, the Kelly Gang. The local newspaper editor, Samuel Gill, has been going on about that a bit lately, so it is good to see more men in uniforms about the town.

The curious trio also seem to take a quick look at the post and telegraph office, which stands at the other end of town, a full half-mile from the police barracks, down by Billabong Creek.

Back inside the Devine family residence at the police barracks, all remains as it had been in the morning. The Devine family are still under the tight guard of the Kelly brothers when the others get back, at which point Ned and Joe get together to further refine their already carefully worked-out plans for what is to happen on the morrow, while the other two keep a close watch on their prisoners. At one point in the afternoon, the bushrangers get their horses out to give them some grooming and exercise in the police paddock.

Ned is in a more garrulous mood come the evening. As a matter of fact, there is something on his mind that he wishes to share with Mrs Devine – parts of a fifty-six-page letter he had been dictating to Joe over previous days, explaining his side of what has only been the one-sided story of the Kelly Gang so far. After the failure of his letter to Don Cameron to get any traction or make it into the papers, this time Ned wants to *see* it personally published by Samuel Gill – laid out on the page before his eyes – so that the public, at least, can know why Kelly has been pushed to do what he has done, and also know that he has not done all that he has been accused of. What drives him most, he makes clear to Mrs Devine, is the injustice done to his mother, by the bastards who both gave false testimony against her and put her in prison, for something *his mother didn't do*.

Whatever else, Ned's anger at what has happened pours from the page:[16] 'The police got great credit and praise in the papers for arresting the mother of 12 children, one an infant on her breast and those two quiet hard working innocent men who would not know the difference between a revolver and a saucepan handle and kept them six months awaiting trial and then convicted them on the evidence of the meanest article that ever the sun shone on . . . For to a keen observer [Fitzpatrick] has the wrong appearance or a manly heart the deceit and cowardice is too plain to be seen in the puny cabbage hearted looking face.'[17]

One thing he wishes to make clear, however: 'Remember there is not one drop of murderous blood in my veins.'[18]

But, push him like they have? They know what they'll get. 'If I hear any more of it I will not exactly show them what cold blooded murder is but wholesale and retail slaughter something different to shooting three troopers in self defence and robbing a bank.'[19]

Well, be warned of the fate that awaits those who assist the police: 'pegged on an ant-bed with their bellies opened their fat taken out rendered and poured down their throat boiling hot will be fool to what pleasure I will give some of them and any person aiding or harbouring or assisting the Police in any way whatever or employing any person whom they know to be a detective or cad or those who would be so deprived as to take blood money will be outlawed and declared unfit to be allowed human burial their property either consumed or confiscated and them theirs and all belonging to them exterminated off the face of the earth, the enemy I cannot catch myself I shall give a payable reward for . . .'[20]

Key, however, is the notion that he is not simply a murderer but has been severely pushed to do what he has done, and only done it because he is a man, standing up for his people, after so many others had wilted before the tyranny of the Victoria Police, before men such as those he had been forced to kill at Stringybark Creek.

'Certainly their wives and children are to be pitied, but they must remember those men came into the bush with the intention of scattering pieces of me and my brother all over the bush, and yet they know and acknowledge I have been wronged . . . And is my mother and brothers and sisters not to be pitied also? Who has no alternative, only to put up with the brutal and cowardly conduct of the parcel of big, ugly, fat necked, wombat headed, big bellied, magpie legged, narrow hipped, splay-footed sons of Irish bailiffs, or English landlords which is better known as the Victoria Police?'[21]

Friends, Victorians, this letter is very close to a declaration that the old way is no more, that the Victorian Government is not to be obeyed, that Ned Kelly is the new power in the land, and it is his rule that counts. To wit, 'I wish those men who joined the Stock Protection Society to withdraw their money and give it and as much more to the widows and orphans and poor of Greta district . . . as it only aids the police to procure false witnesses and go whacks with men to steal horses and lag innocent men . . .'

He goes on, 'I give fair warning to all those who has reason to fear me to sell out and give £10 out of every hundred towards the widow and orphan fund and do not attempt to reside in Victoria but as short a time as possible after reading this notice, neglect this and abide by the consequences, which shall be worse than the rust in the wheat in Victoria or the druth of a dry season to the grasshoppers in New South Wales.'[22]

Oh, he's serious all right. 'It will pay government to give those people who are suffering innocence justice and liberty if not I will be compelled to show some colonial stratagem which will open the eyes of not only the Victorian Police and inhabitants but also the whole British army.'[23]

And make no mistake as to who is in full command here. 'I do not wish to give the order full force without giving timely warning, but I am a widow's son outlawed and my orders *must be obeyed*.'[24]

Of course, there is no record of just which of these passages are read to Mrs Devine, but it makes little difference. For to Ned's likely enormous disappointment, this good lady – faithful partner of a policeman, devout Catholic, pregnant mother – having sat quietly throughout, simply waits till he has finished and shortly thereafter readies herself for bed. It seems like a lot longer than just twenty-four hours since the Kelly Gang arrived.

MORNING, 10 FEBRUARY 1879, THE BAIL-UP BECKONS

Time to move. Today is the day. Obviously, every hour the gang spend in this town brings ever greater risk, but now that the town is once again open for business the gang can do what they have come to do. First, however, Joe and Dan have a quick task, and – again dressed in the police uniforms of the men they still have cooped up in the Logs – they take two horses to the local blacksmith in Powell Street to be shod before returning. After Ned tells Mrs Devine that, if she or her children, let alone her husband, even set foot outside their home after they leave, he will return to burn the whole place down with them inside it, the gang are ready.

Just on eleven o'clock, the front door of the barracks opens and the Kelly Gang emerge, with Ned and Dan now in police uniforms, Joe and Steve in normal attire and all of them accompanied by Constable Richards – who has a revolver in his holster, albeit emptied of bullets by the bushrangers. Joe and Ned stick on either side of the terrified trooper, while Steve and Dan are some distance back on their freshly shod horses.

'Who is your best and most reliable man in the gang?' Richards asks Ned, as they walk. 'Your brother?'

'No,' says Ned firmly, before pointing to Joe. 'No, that's the fellow. He's as cool and firm as steel.'[25]

Their first port of call is the most august building in town, the Royal Mail Hotel – a low-slung brick building with a corrugated-iron roof, just like Grandpa used to make – where the grizzly landlord, Charlie Cox, has no sooner looked up with pleasure at these early customers than he is confronted by an enormous man with a beard, pointing a gun straight at his chest.

'Cox,' says Constable Richards, 'this is Ned Kelly.'

And it has been ever thus. While violence oft begets violence, at least as often the mere threat of violence begets politeness. For Cox is quick with his reply, and a model of decorum about it. 'How do you do, Ned?'

'All right, Cox,' the bushranger replies equally politely, before getting down to the business at hand. 'I'll tell you what I want. I want a room in the hotel for a few hours, to put the people in as they come along, for I have come here to stick up and rob the bank today. I intend to do it quietly if possible, but if not there will be bloodshed over it.'

Now pointing to the bar parlour, he says, 'That room will do.'[26]

Yes, Mr Kelly. If you say so, Mr Kelly. Delighted, Mr Kelly. (*Ned Kelly! Here, in Jerilderie!*)

Dan Kelly and Steve Hart, meanwhile, have followed their part of the plan and taken the horses to the back of the hotel, where they instruct the groom to put their steeds in the stables, but *not* to feed them. (On the chance that the gang will need to leave Jerilderie at full gallop, they don't want their horses to have full bellies.) The pair then muster up all the hotel employees and line them up in the yard. After

Ned is done explaining the situation to the still stunned Charlie Cox, and instructing him to find a 'big strong bag to carry away the money we are about to take from the bank',[27] he sticks his head out the back door and calls on Dan and Hart to bring the captives into the bar parlour.

That task accomplished, Dan places himself just inside the front entrance of the hotel to take in all fresh arrivals, while still keeping an eye on the thirty or so prisoners from one end. Steve Hart, meantime, covers the parlour's back door that leads out to the back verandah. In the gang's now renowned spirit of fearsome benevolence, each of the prisoners is allowed, if they please, to order drinks from the bar while under the watchful glare of Dan and Hart's revolvers.

All is now in place . . .

Joe Byrne heads to the rear entrance of the bank.

Alone in the bank at this time – it is just ten past twelve on this Monday afternoon – the accountant Edward Living is sitting at his desk when he hears footsteps on the back deck, approaching the back door. Thinking it must be the bank manager, John Tarleton, at last returning from a long trip away on business with a distant squatter, Living only just registers it when some sixth sense makes him turn on his stool, and he is immediately alarmed.

For this is not the bank manager; it is someone else entirely.

Is it a drunk? Perhaps . . .

For, on the reckoning that it is better to look like a drunk than a bushranger, particularly next door to a bar where drunks are as common as flies in a stockyard in summer, Byrne feigns exactly that. (It is not much of a stretch of his thespian abilities.) And yet as he opens the bank's back door and pushes through, he is suddenly confronted by Living – a surprisingly athletic-looking fellow for a bank man, an expert cricketer and horseman – who instantly remonstrates with the drunk that he has no right to be there, and he must use the front doo . . .

Oh yes, Joe does have a right. A saying in America in this epoch has it that 'A Smith & Wesson beats four aces every time', and the same dynamic applies to the Colt revolver that Byrne now has in his hand

– the gun he had taken from Senior Constable Devine on Saturday night – which says that whatever the accountant's protestations as to the law, the bushranger has every right to be there and will not brook any argument.

'I am Kelly,' the bushranger adds by way of emphasis,[28] aware that this will have far more impact than saying the rather more modest and far less intimidating, 'I am Byrne.'

And so it does.

At the very utterance of the Kelly name, not to mention the gun pointing at his chest, Living turns pale, and instantly decides that Byrne *does* have the right to enter by the back entrance after all. Handing over his guns, however, as Byrne asks him, is more problematic.

'I have none,' Living tells him, before the attention of the two men is turned to the front door, where the third employee of the bank, a clerk by the name of James Mackie, enters. For his part, the young clerk had been out the front when he had heard the voices inside and come to investigate, only to find Joe Byrne pointing two guns at him.

'Come in to Cox's,' Joe says by way of welcome. 'We have all the police stuck-up.'[29]

At Joe's behest, thus, and at the points of his guns, they all head off to the hotel next door . . .

The three of them have only just left when John Tarleton arrives at the bank by the back door, entirely uninterrupted.

Yes, it is a tad odd that the whole place seems unaccustomedly quiet, but after a gruelling journey of 40 miles in the hot sun to deal with a recalcitrant creditor, Tarleton does not mind that. What he really most wants to do right now – however peculiar it might seem later to investigators – is to run himself a bath in one of the back rooms.

John Tarleton really likes baths.

—

In the parlour of the hotel, the two bank employees are presented to a very powerful-looking bearded man whom they instantly know to be

Ned Kelly, and whose primary concern is just where the bank manager, Tarleton, can be found.

'In his room in the bank,' Living replies, assuming that Tarleton will have arrived by this time.[30] The oldest Kelly tells Joe Byrne to take the two men back to find him and is annoyed when, shortly afterwards, they return without him. The employees are very sorry, Mr Kelly, but Mr Tarleton had simply not been in his office where they had expected to find him.

Well, search harder.

For now, Kelly looks hard at Living and says with some menace, 'Then where is he? You have to find him quickly.'[31]

Living, in the company of Ned Kelly and Steve Hart, tries to do exactly that, returning to the bank once more . . . only to find that the bank manager is still not in his office. *Where can he be?* Personally, Living reluctantly comes to the depressing conclusion that Tarleton must have got wind of the arrival of bushrangers and escaped, leaving Living as the only living thing between the bushrangers and a live bank robbery.

And then Living remembers. Sometimes, when not in his office, the manager likes to have a bath in the back room, so perhaps he is there . . .

—

And so it is that, at about half past twelve, John Tarleton is just luxuriating in his bath, scrubbing his back, when suddenly the door opens and there is his accountant, Living. The bank manager, 'usually a man of cool, quiet temperament',[32] is about to furiously protest this damned impertinent intrusion when Living tells him bluntly, 'We are stuck up at last; there is no use resisting.'[33]

Now, Tarleton is really furious that Living would play such a joke at his expense. 'Oh, rubbish,' he says dismissively. 'What do you mean by this damned nonsense?'[34]

'There is no nonsense about it,' Steve Hart says, as, with Ned Kelly tightly behind him, he barges past Living and proves the point by pointing his revolver at the man in the bath. 'It is true enough and we want your keys to the safe.'[35]

Resistance when fully clothed and with a gun in your hand is one thing. But it is quite another when you are as naked as the day you are born, without a single weapon to hand, and never in his life has Tarleton felt so vulnerable.

'There is no use resisting,' Living adds. 'The police are locked up, and they have got about twenty people bailed up in the Royal.'[36]

'Oh, well, all right,' Tarleton replies, curious cove that he is. 'Soon as I have done my bath I will come in.'[37]

Nay, John Tarleton *loves* baths.

Even with Ned Kelly pointing a gun at him, finishing his bath is more important than any other consideration.

And, for his part, Steve Hart, who is now left guarding the bathing bank manager, is polite enough. True, the bushranger does steal Tarleton's watch, which he spies in the vest hanging on the back of the door, but at least he allows his host to finish his *bath* before taking him back to the others, and that is the main thing. The only time Hart shows any aggression is when Tarleton starts to question him, from the bath, about the gang's past movements and future intentions.

'Come,' the young bushranger replies irritably, 'no more of those questions. I will not have any more.'[38]

—

For the Kelly Gang, it is time to do what they have come to this town to do – rob the bank – and Ned Kelly now takes Living back there for the purpose.

'How much money is here?' Kelly asks the accountant.

'There is between £600 and £700,' Living replies,[39] and then hands over to him all the cash from the teller's safe, which adds up to – *dot three, carry one, subtract two* – £691.

No more money in the locked treasury drawer of the safe?

'No,' replies Living with perhaps the slightest quaver in his voice.

Ned Kelly does not believe him and says, 'You must have at least £10,000 in the bank.'[40]

Which is as maybe, but though Living has one key, Tarleton has the other. Deciding against Joe Byrne's suggestion that they break the whole thing open with a sledgehammer, Ned now departs to get the bank manager and his key, and . . .

And suddenly the bank has a customer, the portly local schoolmaster William Elliott, who is on his lunchbreak. He has dropped in to make a deposit from the collection he had taken the previous day at Reverend Gribble's Sunday service, and proceeds to do just that – the key difference being that, instead of going into his account, his money actually comes to be deposited . . . in the top pocket of Joe Byrne's jacket.

But say, while he's here, would Elliott mind helping with the robbery?

'Jump over the counter,' Byrne orders him.

'Can I not walk round just as well?' replies Elliott, plaintively.

'No, you don't,' Byrne growls. 'Jump over!'[41]

Elliott is initially not sure if it can be done, but, strangely, with Byrne pointing two revolvers at him it is like magic! On the instant, Elliott is suddenly able to place one hand on the counter and vault across like a sixteen-year-old boy in the springtime with a pretty girl watching.

Which is as well, for there is work to be done.

Here now is Ned, returned with Tarleton, dressed in a pale set of trousers, a smoking cap and his favourite silk coat – freshly bathed, and as clean and pure as a newborn lamb, though it will not be long before he is sweating profusely – and, once his second key is put in the safe's second lock, it opens.

Inside, there is no less than £1450. Now, as Elliott and Joe hold open the sugar sack brought for the occasion, it is Tarleton who is obliged to stuff the rolls of notes and heavy chamois-leather bags of coins into it. So much money, it's a good thing that Cox has given them a big sugar sack, to hold the sizeable loot. Oh, the *indignity*.

Put together with their previous teller's haul, the gang now have over £2000 for their trouble. Also noticing a deed-box, Ned makes to open it, too, only to be told by Tarleton that there are just a few documents in there, which will be of no use to him. That's as may be, but, on principle, Ned is disposed to burn the documents anyway, and all the books in the office for that matter. For what are banks if not the enemy of the common poor people, keeping them in penury and making them beholden for life?

Nevertheless, because Edward Living has been cooperative, Ned does grant the accountant's teary and desperate request that an insurance policy that happens to be – please! – his own, not be burned.

'You come along,' he says to Living. 'I want to see about the bank's books.'[42]

As good as his word, Ned not only sees those books, he grabs some of them and orders his three unwilling accomplices to walk before him down the passage, out onto the back verandah and back into the parlour of the Royal Hotel. Joe Byrne follows them, carrying the two bags of riches. Seeing that the three men are safely under the guard of Steve Hart's revolver after entering the parlour, Ned continues along the verandah and goes directly into the bar, where he leaves the loot with Dan.

Now, Ned marches Living, Elliott and Tarleton to the bar and, putting down a florin, invites the three to have some drinks, which are ever so quickly supplied by Mrs Cox.

Ned then takes two prisoners out the back of the premises and burns four of those bank books, noting beforehand that 'banks, as a rule, are crushing the life's blood out of the poor struggling man'.[43]

It is, as Superintendent Francis Hare would later note, archetypal Ned Kelly, as the bushranger always positions himself 'as a friend of the working man, and all they wanted was bank money, and not that of private individuals . . . In this manner he was looked upon as a great hero, and gained a number of sympathizers, so in burning the books of the bank he thought he was protecting the poor man, as against the bank.'[44]

Something that also helps Ned at this time in gaining the rough affection of those who are his prisoners is that he continually shouts the bar, and pays the publican Cox for every drink.

—

Call it the instincts of an old newspaperman.

It is not that the editor of the *Jerilderie Gazette*, Samuel Gill, knows anything, specifically, of what is occurring. But he does know that there is a strange buzz about the town, that in this sleepy burgh over 100 miles north of nowhere, 50 miles south of the Black Stump, easily east of the back of beyond, and well west of Woop Woop . . . something strange is going on.

The first lead to pursue is the four new constables who have been seen in town – perhaps in response to his thundering editorial – and so, with notebook in hand, Gill decides to address himself to the police barracks to see what George Devine will tell him. He arrives at the door to find it closed, and the shutters down, but, good newspaperman that he is, he is undeterred and proceeds to knock. Still nothing. But he can hear a crying child, and someone trying to hush it. Going around the side, where he knows there is a broken pane on a window, he puts his hand through to push aside the curtain, and sees a haggard and obviously upset Mrs Devine, sitting on a couch, trying to quieten her youngest child.

'What is the matter?' Gill asks softly.

'I cannot tell you anything,' she replies tearfully, her voice strained to breaking point. 'Run, for your life is in danger.'[45]

Shocked, Gill would love nothing better than to do exactly that, but instead he quickly takes his leave and heads back into town, where he tells the local mainstay storekeeper, James Rankin, the news – something terrible has happened. But what?

For his part, Rankin – a short, stout man, who is nevertheless of great stature as a Justice of the Peace – is not long in taking a stab at it, having noted that he had seen four strange policemen that morning, passing with Constable Richards. 'Perhaps they may be the Kellys,' he says. 'We will go along and see what Mr Tarleton thinks of it.'[46]

The Kellys! Samuel Gill can barely believe it, but he agrees they should warn the bank manager. On the way, they decide to tell a neighbouring storekeeper, Hugh Harkin, who is also a Justice of the Peace.

And so it is that all three now descend on the bank just one more door along, eager to do what they can to preserve that very peace. Strangely, however, although they arrive to find the bank door unlocked and go inside, the whole place is oddly quiet, and there seem to be a whole lot of papers unaccustomedly strewn about.

It is open, but there is no one to be seen . . .

The senior man, Rankin, knocks rather impatiently on the counter, calling out, 'Are you in, Mr Tarleton?' whereupon a voice emerges from the back room, sounding surprisingly young. 'Just a minute . . .'[47]

Strange. Very strange. Say . . . you don't suppose . . .?

Of an instant, the thought occurs to them all at once. Is it possible that they have walked in on a hold-up?

It is not worth waiting around to find out, so all three suddenly charge for the exit doors. But their timing is out. For, in the Tarleton quarters, Ned had tired of being dressed as a fake policeman and instead had been donning the manager's fine Bedford cord pants and riding boots, which fit him like a glove. When he had heard the men in the bank, he had instantly jumped up on the bed to look over the partition at his new guests. There were two standing at the counter and one out on the porch peering in through the window, and so he had called, 'Just a minute . . .' to give them a moment's delay.

He emerges just in time to see the scramble for the exits. After first calling 'Stand!' for no result, Ned quickly charges after them. Gill's sheer terror seems to give his legs wings, and he gets away – even vaulting over the extraordinarily corpulent Rankin, who, older, fatter and slower than the other men, finds himself trampled in the doorway.

In response, Ned, after himself vaulting the counter like a kangaroo stung on the bottom by a bee, has no trouble in capturing Rankin by the collar, and he corrals him with the other thirty prisoners in the parlour of the Royal Mail, yelling, 'Why did you run away?'[48] And yet, before Rankin even has a chance to answer, he pushes him up against the wall, levels his revolver at him and gives him fair warning: 'I'm going to shoot you!'

Amazingly, Rankin, who has now gathered his wits, appears to rise to the occasion, something that does not necessarily come easily to this 22 stone man. For now, lifting up his chin to Ned Kelly, this most feared man in the land, the very man who has just announced a sentence of death upon him, Rankin asks the bushranger, for all the world as if he would really like to know, 'What are you going to shoot me *for*?'

'You and those other two went into the bank to try and cop us.'

'We did no such thing! We did not know you were in the bank at the time. We went in to see the manager on business.'

What is this, a *debate*? Steve Hart, for one, is tired of it, and now shouts at Ned, 'Put the bugger on his knees and I'll put a bullet into him.'[49]

But Ned has no interest in such talk, while also waving away the many pleas to spare the man's life. Now moderating his tone, he merely asks Rankin who the other two were. Alas, when Ned receives the news that one of the men who got away was the very publisher, Gill, whom he had wanted to publish his letter, he is *ropeable*. Even so, Ned decides not to shoot Rankin after all, and puts his revolver away. For the point he had wanted to make has been made: never cross a cross bushranger.

Still, to ensure that everyone *stays* intimidated, he calls to Hart by his sometime gang nickname of 'Revenge,'[50] and orders him, 'Shoot the first man who shows any signs of resistance.'

Taking Rankin in tow, together with Constable Richards and Edward Living, Ned starts to search the town and surrounds for Gill, leaving Hart and his brother Dan behind.

Behind him, the prisoners gaze at the singularly hard Hart nervously. Whatever else, Ned Kelly had seemed to be in control of himself. But not Hart, who paces angrily, looking for someone to be doing something wrong. As one prisoner would note, Hart 'seemed to be most particularly anxious to shoot somebody',[51] and he continues to threaten to do so for a variety of offences. At least Hugh Harkin is soon found, and brought back to be with the other prisoners. Of Gill, however, there is no sign. Where has the bugger got to?

—

How alarmed does a man have to be to run seven miles without stopping, all to sound a warning? At least as alarmed as Samuel Gill, who – now convinced that Kelly wants to kill him because of all the terrible things that the editor has written about him in the *Gazette* – suddenly bursts through the distant doors of Carrah Homestead. Mercifully, he'd had a lucky break as he hightailed it out of the bank and into the middle of the road, where he had turned left back past the Royal Mail Hotel. For there out the front had been parked a brewer's wagon, packed with brew and drawn by six horses. The wagon and horses had shielded him as he ran madly down the whole street, and all the way out of town, to get the word out that the Kellys were here. Of course, many later joked that Gill was more worried about getting *himself* out of town than the word!

Now, to the stunned people in the homestead's dining room, he cries out that the town has been *taken*, that the Kelly Gang are *here*, that they have held up the *bank*, that he has personally seen *Ned Kelly*, that prisoners have been *taken*, that *the Kelly Gang are here, I tell you!*

In response, the owner of the Carrah run, Samuel Wilson, quickly sends one of his lads to catch a horse and gallop over to Coree Homestead, in order that a messenger can immediately ride to Deniliquin to alert the police.

—

With still no sign of Gill around town, Ned now takes Living and Constable Richards with him to the home of the newspaperman, to see if he might be hiding there somewhere and, failing that, to look into getting the letter printed even without the newspaperman himself.

'Mrs Gill,' Richards addresses her when she opens the door to their knock, before giving an unlikely form of introduction. 'Don't be afraid, this is Kelly.'

'I am not afraid,' Mrs Gill replies, doing rather better than her husband under the circumstances.

'I won't hurt you nor your husband,' Ned assures her. 'He should not have run away.'

'You gave him such a fright I expect he is lying dead somewhere.'

'All I wanted him for is to print this letter, the history of my life, and wanted to see him to explain it to him.'[52]

But will Mrs Gill take it? Perhaps even have it printed herself?

She will not. Not, *not*, NOT!

Mrs Gill continues to insist that not only has she no idea where her husband is, she doesn't know how to get the letter printed. After all, typesetting a letter of over 7000 words would be a matter as exhausting as it would be exacting for even so experienced a professional as Gill – at least two days' solid work – let alone for his wife, who has never attempted such a thing. It is out of the question for her to do it while he waits!

When the bushranger starts to blow like a storm of fury, saying it must be done, Living can stand it no more. 'For God's sake, Kelly,' the otherwise mild-mannered accountant says. 'Give me the papers, and I will give them to Gill.'[53]

Very reluctantly, Ned finally hands the letter over to Living. 'Get it printed,' he tells Living, 'it is a bit of my life. I have not had time to finish it. I will finish it some other time.'[54] And yet, also be told, 'Mind you get it printed.'[55]

'I promise,' says Living.

'All right; I will leave it to you to get it done.'[56]

—

And now there's a story, though it will be disputed by some. One lad later said to be around at this time is the son of the Jerilderie storekeeper Louis Monash. Young John, all of fourteen years old, has spent this last day of the Christmas holidays getting ready to head back to his famous school of Scotch College Melbourne, where he is a boarder, only to have it all interrupted by the bushrangers.

'He beckoned me over,' the lad would later recount, as a mature adult, 'asked me my name, and so forth, and then gave me a short lecture. A Sunday school superintendent couldn't have given me better advice as to human conduct.'[57]

For Ned Kelly, it is a matter of no particular moment to speak to such a lad. After all, it's only ten years earlier that Ned had been fourteen himself, and even though by that age he already knew what the inside of a gaol cell looked like – while young Monash knows only the gracious towers of Scotch College – the bushranger is not without empathy for young fellas.

(Nigh on four decades from this date, John Monash would be acclaimed as the finest general in the Allied cause in the First World War – an officer who had so covered himself in glory at Gallipoli and on the Western Front that he was made commander of the entire Australian Corps, and been knighted during the war by King George V – but he would still say that never in his life had he been in such awe as when meeting Ned Kelly. When asked by a journalist his proudest moments, he was quick with his reply, 'One was when I called a council of war just before we broke the Hindenburg line, the other was when I had a yarn with Ned Kelly.')[58]

—

Joe Byrne, meanwhile, has been busy. Still disguised as a constable, he has bailed up the telegraph office to accomplish an extremely important task. That is, by carefully presenting the supreme and incontrovertible logic represented by his pointed revolver, he convinces the Postmaster that it would be an *excellent* idea to destroy his Morse key, and so scatter the parts that it cannot be easily repaired. Oh, and one more thing. Show Joe all the cables that have gone out that morning, by way of confirming that word of the gang's presence has not got out yet.

This done, and their secrecy so far confirmed, the Postmaster, Henry

B. Jefferson, is just thinking that his day could get no worse when . . . Ned Kelly arrives, and begins the visit by taking the butt of his revolver and smashing all the insulators.

'Stand away!' Ned cries as he does so. 'This might go off!'[59]

They stand away.

Now that the danger of word getting out of town has been averted, there is far less reason for the gang to be discreet about their actions. To make absolutely sure that the telegraph wires cannot easily be repaired, Ned Kelly orders Steve Hart to take the Postmaster and his assistant back to the hotel to join the other prisoners and there secure the services of a couple of big men from among their captives to come out and cut no fewer than eight telegraph poles down, before equally cutting the wires they carry into so many small pieces.

And be warned, Ned tells the Postmaster and his assistant before they go, 'I'll have those telegraph poles cut down for some distance out, and anyone who touches those wires before half past nine tomorrow morning I'll shoot him down like a bloody dog. We are coming back to stick up the Deniliquin mail coach when it reaches here tonight, and we will go on up with it and stick up the Urana bank tomorrow.'[60]

As Jefferson and his assistant are being led out, Ned gives them fair warning. 'If anything happens to you, it will be your own fault.'[61]

Of course, Jefferson agrees to go, asking only that he be allowed to lock up first – there may be robbers about – something that Ned readily agrees to.

—

At Deniliquin Post Office at this time, Postmaster Peter Dunne suddenly takes pause, completely mystified. For the line to Sydney has gone dead. And the problem seems to be something to do with the Jerilderie connection. Though there are two wires from Deniliquin to Sydney, passing within a mile of Jerilderie, a loop-line does go to Jerilderie Post Office with two wires in and two wires out. Dunne finds that, by shutting down that loop, he can get through to Sydney, but for the life of him he can get no response from Jerilderie, no matter how many times he tries. With flying fingers, he taps out the news to Sydney:

> There must be something seriously wrong there, as Mr Jefferson (the postmaster) is never known to be out of call.[62]

Dunne keeps trying to reach Jerilderie regardless.

Still disappointed at his failure to have his letter published as he had long planned, Ned decides to do something that had never failed to cheer him up in the past: steal a horse. As it happens, there has rarely been a better opportunity to do so, as one of their informants in the town has told him that quartered at the Albion Travellers Rest Hotel is a famous black mare by the name of Minnie, who has seen service as a racehorse. With Living and Richards still in tow, thus, Ned heads round to Thomas McDougall's hotel and asks the bossman if he does indeed have a racing mare of that name.

'Yes,' the publican replies, uncertainly.

'I want her,' Ned says simply, before ordering McDougall's groom to bring her from the stable. 'What do you value the mare at?'

'Fifty pounds,' says McDougall.

'If I take the mare away I will give you that amount for her.'[63]

Brought out of the stable with naught but a bridle upon her, there is no doubt that Minnie is a beauty. As Ned is almost as comfortable bareback as in the saddle, he is instantly astride her and in all but total command, even if she does baulk at jumping a fence. It is an impressive thing to see a man as big as Ned Kelly astride such a beast, exuding such confidence, and not for nothing would Constable Richards say afterwards of him that Ned was 'the gamest man I ever saw'.[64]

—

And now it is coming time to leave.

While Joe, with their ill-gotten gains, heads back to the police barracks to gather their effects and ensure that Devine is still under lock and key, and that Mrs Devine has not run off to sound the alarm, Ned takes Richards back to the Royal Mail Hotel. Ned wants to hold court with the prisoners one last time, even as the beer and whiskey continue to flow at his expense – he is suddenly flush with cash, after all. Never a man to waste an audience, Ned gathers the people, *his* people, to him one more time.

'Boys,' he says to those gathered, 'I'll tell you how I'm an outlaw, and how I've been treated by the police in Victoria. When I was accused by Fitzpatrick of shooting him, I swear I was 400 miles away from home. When I heard of the way he treated my sister, I hurried home, and found that I was accused of shooting Fitzpatrick and that a reward of £100 had been placed on my head. I don't like to present a revolver at any man, as it naturally makes him tremble, unless I am compelled to do so. And what must have been the feelings of my sister – a mere child – when she had a revolver put to her head demanding her to submit her virtue or be shot by the villain Fitzpatrick?[65] I don't deny having stolen 250 horses, and sold them, but of shooting Fitzpatrick I was entirely innocent . . .'

As if he were on a horse galloping down a mountain, there is no stopping him. 'Supposing you came home and heard that two or three detectives had been to the house and presented revolvers at the heads of your mother and sisters, saying, "Where is this Ned Kelly? If you don't tell us where he is we will shoot you." Why, no man could stand such a fright as that, much less a woman. Was not that enough to make me turn outlaw and shoot those bloody police? When we came upon the police they were fully armed. All I had was an old crooked musket, in which, if you held it up to your shoulder, you could see the curves, with a barrel shaking about. I shot Lonigan with that bloody musket; it could shoot round a corner.'

His captives continue to listen closely, soaking up every word.

'There's Lonigan's revolver,' Ned goes on, displaying the police weapon he now pulls from his very belt. 'Enough of this, you will find it all in the paper I have left to be printed . . .'[66]

Ah, but boys, one more thing, though. Yes, the police had been killed, but it had been a fair fight. 'Had the police shot us,' he points out, 'they would have been praised by the people and the papers for their courage, but as it turned out they were shot, we were denounced as murderers and blood-thirsty ruffians. And yet, where is the difference? We all had to risk our lives in the encounter.'[67]

But to the task at hand. 'I have come here,' he suddenly announces, 'not so much to stick up the bank, but to shoot these two policemen. They are worse than any black-trackers, especially that man Richards.'[68]

For there really is one other thing he needs to do before leaving, and he is quite specific in announcing it. 'Now,' he says, 'I'm going to shoot Constable Richards before I leave.'[69]

It is now Tarleton who steps forward, protesting. 'Well, if he has followed you up closely, it has been in the execution of his duty, and what he is paid for doing. You should not find fault with him for that.'[70]

But Ned has long before thought his way through this very question. 'Suppose you had your revolver ready when I came in,' he replies to the bank manager, 'would you not have shot me?'

'Yes.'

'Well,' Kelly replies, reasonably, 'that's just what I am going to do with Richards – shoot him before he shoots me.'[71]

All eyes turn to the hangdog young constable now being obliged to come forward, the fellow who, for the last two days, proud trooper that he is, has been reduced to being little more than the gang's servant. And now he is going to be shot?

Yes, it would seem so. After all, Ned – a keen reader of all newspaper reports about the Kellys – explains that Richards had been one of the party that had fired on four men at Tocumwal whom they had thought were the Kelly Gang.

'You were one of those who fired?' Ned confirms.

'Yes, I fired across the river at them.'

'You did your best to bring us down?'

'Yes, I did my best.'

'You did not know me, and yet you tried to kill a man you never saw before, or who never did you any harm?'

'I was doing my duty; you were outlawed at the time.'

'You would have taken my life if you could, so you now cannot blame me for shooting you?'

'Yes, I can,' replies Richards fiercely, neither wavering nor quavering. 'We were both armed then and had an equal chance in a fight. If you shoot me now, you shoot an unarmed man who has no chance of his life . . . give me a loaded revolver and I'll fight you now, and if you shoot me, it will be a fair fight.'

It has been a thing of wonder to see how Richards has risen to the occasion, and all of his hangdog expression has now gone. For Ned, the job has now been done. 'You can go now, for I'm damned if I don't like your pluck,' the bushranger says magnanimously, once again seen to spare a man's life. 'But if we ever meet again, I'll shoot you.'

'That's all right,' says Richards, the new hero of the town, for Ned Kelly *himself* has applauded his pluck, 'so long as the two of us are armed; it will be you and me for it.'[72]

And yet, obviously, one so plucky as Richards cannot be allowed his freedom while the Kelly Gang make good their escape. It is for this reason that Ned now prepares to leave, taking Richards with him, to be first put back in the lock-up with Devine. All the prisoners, he now announces, are free to go on condition they do not try to free constables Devine and Richards.

Oh, and one *last* thing. 'None of us in the Gang are afraid of being shot, for if one of us falls the lives of every person in the town will be taken as revenge.'[73]

And now Ned takes Constable Richards, together with Postmaster Jefferson and his young assistant, *and* James Rankin back to the police barracks, where they are to be placed safely under lock and key with Devine, who has been there all that time.

Dan Kelly and Steve Hart go too, but whereas Ned is quiet, they are noisy, galloping up the street, 'shouting and gesticulating, Dan Kelly flourishing his revolver round his head in the most approved braggadocio fashion. Dan Kelly also carried a rifle slung over his shoulder.'[74]

They arrive to find that, sure enough, Devine remains in the cell where they had left him, together with the drunk from Saturday. That drunk, now more sober than he has ever been, *ever*, is set free so as to make room for Richards, Rankin and the men from the telegraph office.

—

Somehow, though in captivity in the Royal Hotel, John Tarleton manages to see off a messenger to ride thirty miles across country to the nearby township of Urana to warn the bank manager of a possible hold-up. When the Kellys have left the hotel, Tarleton sends the junior clerk, James Mackie, to retrieve his horse from the parson's paddock, so he can catch up with Edward Living, who has already departed, heading off to Deniliquin, some 60 miles away. From there, the two bank men intend to get a train to Melbourne to report everything that has happened to head office.

So, at a quarter to four in the afternoon, Tarleton strikes out.

—

In the meantime, the local Methodist minister, Reverend Gribble is amazed to see as he walks on into town that, like autumnal leaves still blowing around after a major storm has passed, the streets of Jerilderie are loosely scattered with the Kelly Gang's one-time prisoners, 'laughing and talking over their amusing adventures'.

Asked what they were going to do, they reply, 'Do? Do nothing of course. Why should we interfere with the men, unless they interfere with [us]? They came to stick up the bank and they have stuck it up, and that is all they want to do. Having got the bank money, they will not trouble us any more. They will soon make themselves scarce.'

Appalling!

Well, Gribble is not a coward and, with the Lord on his side, decides to set off after the bushrangers, in the direction they were last seen heading, towards the police barracks. Among other things, the pastor has heard that Ned Kelly has stolen Minnie, the black racehorse, which he knows is owned and treasured by the daughter of McDougall, the publican of the Albion Travellers Rest Hotel. Perhaps – *Thou shalt not steal* – he could persuade Kelly to give it back?

—

Before taking his leave of the police barracks, Ned, curiously, gives Mrs Devine the key to the lock-up, with strict instruction not to open the cells until seven in the evening, when the gang will be well gone. This is not on pain of her death, mind, but on her husband's death. For, as Ned makes clear, if Devine comes after them, the bushrangers will be sure to kill him, so she is well advised to keep the whole lot of prisoners locked up, and so ensure that her husband will live. Are we *clear*, Mrs Devine?

Mrs Devine nods solemnly. She understands. She faithfully promises that she won't release anyone before that time, and she means it, too. Strangely, despite it all, Mrs Devine will later say of Ned Kelly that he was 'the kindest man I ever met'.[75]

—

Striding forth, the Reverend Gribble is not far from the barracks when he looks up to see four men on horseback just leaving the building. One of them looks a lot like . . . a lot like . . . *Ned Kelly!*

While two of the horsemen ride off in one direction, and one notably surly one gallops past the pastor without looking, Ned Kelly comes straight towards him, with his eyes right upon him every moment. Certainly, Gribble knows this man – wearing a leather belt from which hang a number of revolvers, just as another revolver hangs from his right hand – to have killed three policemen. And yet still he takes the opportunity to introduce himself to the towering figure above him, saying he would like to talk to him about the horse.

'Kelly, I want to speak to you about this matter as to a reasonable man,' he says. 'Do you think, now, that it is right or gentlemanly of you to take a young lady's horse?'

'Well, sir,' says Ned, even as he deferentially dismounts, 'I must say it isn't.'

'Will you do one thing for me, then?'

'What's that?'

Gribble explains that Minnie's owner is distraught. 'The poor young girl,' he says meaningfully, 'is inconsolable over the loss of her mare. Don't take her away with you, Mr Kelly, but give her back to her owner.'

'Certainly,' Ned replies, 'I will, Mr Gribble.'[76]

'Ride to the Travellers Rest Hotel and see McDougall about it,' Gribble further requests.

'Yes, I will, sir,' replies Ned,[77] before vaulting back into the saddle with the ease of a grasshopper and heading into town for one last visit to the Albion Travellers Rest Hotel, while Gribble makes his own way back to the tiny township, sure enough, on Shanks's pony.

In town, Ned catches up with Steve Hart, the notably surly man who had ignored the pastor, and tells him to return Minnie to young Miss McDougall. In its stead, he allows Steve to take Devine's iron-grey horse. Ned then enters the Albion Hotel, where he shouts the bar and holds court one last time.

Steve, putting his new stolen saddle on his new stolen horse, mounts and bids Jerilderie a fond farewell. He is off to join Dan and Joe, who have themselves taken separate paths to the rendezvous point. Joe Byrne, at this point, atop his own fine mount, is heading south in the rough direction of the Murray River, leading one of the police pack-horses, loaded down with all that they have taken from the bank.

This leaves Ned all alone in Jerilderie, at the Albion Travellers Rest Hotel, having one more drink for the road. Theatrically placing his revolver by his glass of beer, he says for all to hear, 'There's my revolver. Anyone here may take it and shoot me dead, but if I'm shot, Jerilderie shall swim in its own blood.'[78]

A cheer goes up. Such bravado!

Ned drinks up, and no one takes him up on his challenge. A long journey awaits, and it is likely to be some time before he will again have the luxury of being in a bar and being able to order a drink.

But before long, he, too, prepares to take his leave, and the crowd comes out to farewell him.

Make no mistake, he tells them before mounting, 'I will never be taken alive.'[79]

Brandishing a small revolver that he takes from his breast pocket, he shows the crowd just how he will shoot himself, if it comes to it. And now he swings up on his horse and, with a final wave, gallops away down the Deniliquin Road. And what is that he is shouting as he goes? Yes, I heard it too! He is singing out, 'Hurrah for the good old times of Morgan and Ben Hall!'[80]

It is an indication of the support that the bushrangers enjoy, despite everything, that from within several establishments along the main street cheers are heard to this sentiment.

Ned keeps going, before changing direction once out of sight to join up with his gang, just as the twilight of dusk is deepening and the darkness of the sweet night is readying to swallow them whole.

—

In short order, there are shouts heard from the police barracks as Devine and Richards, together with Postmaster Jefferson and his offsider, are liberated from their cells by Mrs Devine on the dot of seven o'clock.

George Devine immediately expresses his loud desire to pursue the gang, and Henry Richards agrees to accompany him, as do two armed civilians, but a problem immediately poses itself. Their horses have been taken by the Kelly Gang, as has their weaponry. Perhaps, then, they can take the next regular coach service?

Eventually, after much discussion, George Devine has an even better idea. He decides to go to bed instead, where – at his wife's insistence – he remains for several days.

—

In the meantime, Postmaster Jefferson takes matters into his own hands and, with the aid of his assistant, starts splicing together every piece of wire they can get their hands on, finding some spare insulators, and then – in the absence of telegraph poles – rigging the whole thing up against the railway fence.[81]

At nine o'clock, Jefferson manages to send his first cable out, to his masters in Melbourne:

> The Kelly Gang stuck up the office here today at 2 o'clock, cut the office connections and cut down seven poles. My assistant and I were covered by revolvers, and were marched to the lock-up, which the Gang had stuck up. We were there locked up together with two constables. We were released at 7 p.m. and told not to touch the wire till morning, but I have done so and fixed a wire along the fence. They stuck up the Bank of New South Wales.[82]

At Deniliquin shortly afterwards, Postmaster Peter Dunne is just preparing for bed when his brother, who is one of his staff, bursts through the door and, in a state of great excitement, says, 'The Kellys have stuck up Jerilderie and cut the lines, and you have to start out and repair them in the morning!'[83]

Just half an hour later, Superintendent Hare is at his desk at Benalla, 100 miles away, when he receives a wire from Deniliquin telling him what has happened at Jerilderie. Hare moves quickly, immediately sending out cables instructing all those police stations who are by the crossings of the Murray to set up a guard, to ensure that if the Kelly Gang try to slip back into Victoria – as he strongly suspects – they will be nabbed.

Over Jerilderie and the surrounding region, heavy clouds now gather, almost as if – just as happened at Stringybark Creek – the weather is forming in sympathy with the outrage that will soon be abroad in the land, and furious rain falls upon the four outlaws. Far from being unhappy with it, however, the Kelly Gang bless every drop, as the more rain that falls, the more it will cover their tracks against whichever black-trackers are sent out after them. Even better, after the rain has accomplished that, after a few hours the moon peeks through the black clouds, which soon dissipate, and, just as Ned had always planned, the full moon shines their way south to the mighty Murray, which they manage to cross before dawn, to be heading back to their own territory, to Kelly Country. Together, they are a group of four men atop four mighty steeds, leading two packhorses.

It has been an extraordinary day in the life and growing legend of the Kelly Gang . . .

Chapter Ten

AFTER JERILDERIE

The Gang never behaved badly to, or assaulted, a woman . . . They seldom, if ever, made a victim of a poor man. And thus they weaved a certain halo of romance and rough chivalry around themselves . . .

Superintendent Francis Hare

Heavy men and large of stature, reckless how they bore their guns, or how they sate their horses, with leathern jerkins, and long boots, and iron plates on breast and head, plunder heaped behind their saddles, and flagons slung in front of them; I counted more than thirty pass, like clouds upon red sunset.

Lorna Doone, Richard Doddridge Blackmore, 1869.
This was said to be Ned's favourite story, and possibly his inspiration for making his own iron plates

FEBRUARY 1879, NEW SOUTH WALES AND VICTORIA, TRUTH IS STRANGER THAN FICTION

Melbourne is stupefied, Sydney outraged, and all across the countryside of both New South Wales and Victoria there is only one topic of conversation: the Kelly Gang! How on earth do they *do* it? Somehow, despite reward posters being put up all over the land, despite policemen in two states scouring the countryside for them for weeks and months on end, they have been able to strike twice in locations hundreds of miles apart, before suddenly disappearing again. And the police seem powerless to stop them.

It is a major embarrassment to the men in uniform and to the governments of the day, charged with keeping law and order but demonstrably incapable of the task. In the words of *The Ovens and Murray Advertiser*, 'The Kellys have proved that truth is stranger than fiction, and their exploits read more like some Eastern romance than a plain narration of what has happened in Australia in the nineteenth century . . . Here we have the whole police force of Victoria, which we had fondly regarded as one of the most efficient and best organised in the world, completely baffled, and defied by four youths, who exercised a terrorism which exceeds even that of the bandits of Italy, and the [pirates] of Spain . . .'[1]

And yet, while the press is free to fire its ire at the police, many of the police in turn are infuriated by the lack of reaction from the townspeople of Jerilderie. For the Kelly Gang did *what?* Rounded up a whole town like sheep, held the inhabitants prisoner as they robbed the bank, and then got away, all without a single arm being either raised or fired against them – just as had happened at Euroa?

It is inconceivable. Few are more appalled than Superintendent John Sadleir. 'The fact is,' he would later record in disgust, 'that one bold man, armed with say a double gun, could have picked them off one by one. Jerilderie had not that one man within its bounds that day!'[2]

Perhaps not. But beneath the press outcry, just as happened after the siege of Euroa, there is an alternative truth among the common people. For have you heard about the Kellys at Jerilderie? It wasn't just a straight hold-up, you see. No, they also burned some of the debt documents of the farmers to relieve their load; they treated the women and children well and didn't fire a single shot in anger. They hurt no one.

All up, the legend of the Kelly Gang continues to grow, helped along by the growing collection of poems being penned and even songs written that gain great currency. Altogether sing:

The Bold Kelly Gang
Oh, there's not a dodge worth knowing
Or showing, that's going,
But you'll learn (this isn't blowing)
From the Bold Kelly Gang.

We have mates where e'er we go
That somehow let us know
The approach of every foe
To the Bold Kelly Gang.

There's not a peeler riding
Wombat ranges, hill or siding
But would rather be for hiding
Though he'd like to see us hang.

We thin their ranks, we rob their banks
And say no thanks for what we do—
Oh the terror of the Camp
Is the Bold Kelly Gang.

Then if you want a spree
Come with me and you'll see
How grand it is to be
In the Bold Kelly Gang.[3]

The Kelly Gang are thrilled with the public acclaim, the humiliation of the traps and governments of two colonies, and their own growing notoriety, recorded in every paper they get their hands on. *Them!* More famous now than Ben Hall and Mad Dan Morgan . . .

Meanwhile, perhaps what is most troubling for the authorities is to ponder just where the gang will strike next. For it is not as if the Kellys have entirely disappeared. In fact, it is the reverse – they are *everywhere.* Yes, every time any four strangers arrive in a far-flung town, the instant suspicion is that they must be the Kelly Gang; any sound of thundering hooves in the distance on the moonlit night *a'riding, a'riding, a'riding awayyyyy* . . . and many are morally certain that it is Ned and his men heading to their new hideout. And indeed, all across the land, travellers on lonely tracks are keenly aware that within every shadowy nook, atop every bushy hill, the bushrangers may very well be there, watching, waiting to bail them up.

Strangely, the fact that it always proves to be a false alarm does nothing to dissipate the tension. For the longer it goes that there is no confirmed sighting – even though, by God, I am just about certain it was them – the sooner it must be that they will re-emerge.

In the meantime, security on banks all over Victoria, and now New South Wales, is strengthened further still – even if, up Tocumwal way, the troopers are reluctant to fire on anyone until it is absolutely confirmed they are not fellow police.

14 FEBRUARY 1879, SYDNEY, TWO COLONIES UNITE AGAINST THE KELLYS

In the wake of the Jerilderie outrage, the Premier of New South Wales, Sir Henry Parkes, has decided that the time for action is nigh. In his elegant hand, he writes to the Acting Chief Secretary of Victoria, Sir Bryan O'Loghlen, and informs him that the New South Wales Government, with the help of the border banks, would like to put £4000 towards capturing the Kelly Gang:

> *If a like sum was raised in Melbourne, the joint reward would amount to £8000, or £2000 for each of the four outlaws.*[4]

After consulting with his Cabinet, Sir Bryan is quick in his response: Yes!

Never in the history of any colony in Australia has there been such a prize offered for turning in criminals. Eight thousand pounds. At a time when the average workingman's annual wage is a mere £40–£50, it is a staggering figure – 200 times your annual wage, just for pointing to the Kelly Gang!

The Ovens and Murray Advertiser, for one, is impressed, noting it as 'a sum far larger than was ever offered for the apprehension of any criminals in the history of the world'.[5]

15 FEBRUARY 1879, IN BEECHWORTH, WILD WRIGHT GETS MORE WILD

As time passes, the interest in the fate of the sympathisers is growing, even as the dynamics of drama in the courtroom change with new characters. In the remand hearing the previous week, the talkative and opinionated Magistrate Alfred Wyatt – who had narrowly missed the gang at Euroa – had replaced Magistrate Foster. Of particular interest had been the interaction between Wyatt and Wild Wright.

'Wright,' the Magistrate had said to the glowering man before him, 'you and I have met before.'[6]

Wild Wright ignored the Magistrate's comment – you know one Magistrate, you know them all – and launched into making his own case for his release. 'There is no fear of the Kellys killing me if I was out,' he told the Magistrate. 'You will not get the Kellys until Parliament meets, and Mrs Kelly is let go, and Fitzpatrick lagged in her place. I could not have done much, as for four months before I was arrested, the police had their eyes on me . . .'[7]

Which is as may be. Reluctantly, Magistrate Wyatt had remanded Wild Wright in custody for *another* seven days, along with the other prisoners. As he had done so, however, he had felt obliged to quietly apologise to Wright, saying to him, 'I would give you fair play if I could . . .'[8] Wright huffed and was led away.

On this morning, Wild Wright is appearing once more before Magistrate Wyatt and can no longer hold himself in. First turning to the very uncomfortable looking Superintendent Hare, he says, 'No wonder you blush; you ought to be ashamed of yourself.'[9]

When Hare refuses to meet his eye, Wright turns to Magistrate Wyatt. 'Your Worship said you would give me fair play,' he roars, 'but you are not giving me fair play now. I don't know how some of these men stand it!'[10]

Nor, frankly, do Hare and Wyatt, as both are keenly aware of this abuse of process that they are engaged in, but both feel it is not their call to stop it.

Nevertheless, just ten days after being denied justice again, John McElroy and five others, including John McMonigle, are indeed released. As to Wild Wright, of course, he is left to rot in gaol.

15 FEBRUARY 1879, A MEETING OF MINDS IN BEECHWORTH

To round out yet another Saturday at Beechworth Court, Superintendent Hare has asked Detective Ward to arrange a meeting with Aaron Sherritt, just after eleven o'clock on Saturday night. Hare will ever after remember his informer's first words.

'Did I not tell you,' the young man says pointedly, 'they would stick up a bank in New South Wales?'

'Yes, but you told me they were going to Goulburn.'[11]

These things happen. Sherritt – at least the way he tells it – maintains he had thought that was their plan, but perhaps that had changed. The point is, Superintendent, I predicted an imminent Kelly breakout in New South Wales and that is precisely what happened!

Sherritt quickly goes on, however, to tell Hare his most important news. Just three days earlier, 'Dan Kelly had called at Mrs Byrne's house, and had his breakfast there . . . He told Mrs Byrne that, "After the bank robbery we all divided [up] and agreed to meet at a certain place . . . I kept my appointment, and I have come to see if anything is wrong with the other men, as they did not keep theirs . . ."'[12]

Hare is stunned to hear it – they are so close!

Encouraged with the reaction, young Sherritt is quick to make a suggestion. 'Now you had better come tomorrow night. I have good reason to believe they will be at Mrs Byrne's house – the other three men – you have better come and watch the place.'[13]

Done! The two arrange to meet at eight, at the spot designated, despite Hare's men serving him yet another warning. 'You will come to grief with that man some day, he will "sell" you to the Kellys.'

But Hare still will not hear of it.

At eight o'clock on Sunday evening, Superintendent Hare and Detective Ward indeed meet Sherritt at the designated spot, with the only frustration being that the posse of police that Hare has also arranged to meet them there are late.

By nine o'clock, Sherritt can contain himself no more. 'Mr Hare, if we do not go at once, you will lose the chance of getting the Gang.'[14]

And so they go alone.

With great difficulty – travelling through such thick, scrubby, stony territory that Hare would say of it, 'I had never been through country like that before'[15] – they arrive at a spot where Sherritt stops them. The darkness presses.

'Mr Hare, do you see anything?' Sherritt says.

'No, I do not see anything,' the mystified Hare replies.

'Do you not see a fire ahead there?'

Yes, Hare can just see a small glow in the gloom.

'Those are the bushrangers, they have made a fire to-night, and they are camping there, and it is a thing I never knew them do before; they must have some drink in them, otherwise they would not make the fire so foolishly. This is the bushranger's country, and no one but them would be out in this country.'[16]

Excitedly dismounting, the two discuss the position, and it is agreed that Sherritt should go on ahead and confirm it. The young man does exactly that, and for ten minutes Hare and Ward – beside themselves with impatience – wait, until they suddenly see Sherritt appearing once more out of the darkness.

'By God, we are sold,' Ward whispers at his first vision.

'What is the matter, Aaron?' the Superintendent asks.

'Mr Hare, how far do you think the fire is from us?'

'About 150 yards, I thought.'

'It is nothing of the kind, it is three miles away.'

'Nonsense, Aaron, you have sold me; you have gone and warned those fellows to be off.'

'No, come, get on your horses.'

Reluctantly, Hare and Ward do so, accompanying Sherritt for a great distance until they arrive at the edge of a precipice, and they can see that indeed the fire is on the other side of the gully, high up from the Woolshed diggings.

'You are right,' Hare says, 'what is to be done?'

'Hurry along as quick as you can, and come away from this mistake we have made, and come on towards Byrne's house.'[17]

After an even more difficult trek, at around half past ten they arrive within sight of an extremely humble cottage from which Hare can see the odd spark swirling up from the chimney. It rather puts him in mind of the house that had stood between him and Harry Power nearly a decade earlier, so loudly do the dogs now bark at their unseen presence. Leaving their horses behind, the three men slowly move forward, and as it turns out the dogs present no problem.

For in Aaron, the police have nothing less than Mrs Byrne's prospective son-in-law, and he now strides out confidently, knowing that even if discovered he has every reason to be there. Hare and Ward simply must wait, listening carefully for the sound of approaching horsemen, for they are sure that the Kelly Gang can't be far away.

At last, after five or six minutes, Sherritt suddenly materialises out of the darkness.

'They expect them tonight,' he says, confidently. 'You see, they have left the candle burning, and some supper ready on the table. Let us go up to a clump of trees at the back of the house, where they generally tie up their horses.'[18]

Sherritt swears that, often, after supper, the bushrangers lie down and have a sleep in this very clump. Of them, there is no sign, though Hare can at least see that the bark has been eaten off the trees in this spot, indicating that horses are frequently tethered there. Entirely unperturbed, Sherritt, who has taken command of the situation, gives instructions. 'We must now wait in this stockyard, which leads up to the clump. If they come they will come through here.'[19]

By now it is two o'clock in the morning, and everyone is exhausted, but, still following Sherritt's lead, they wait until daylight confirms there will be no sign of the Kelly Gang here, before upping sticks.

Sherritt is unapologetic. 'Those men will be here,' he assures them. 'They have disappointed me tonight, but they will come within a day or two. Now, if you want the outlaws, you must watch this place.'

'All right, Aaron, we will watch it.'[20]

With which, exhausted, they all return to Beechworth, reflecting heavily. All up, they have spent an entire night more devoted to chasing wild geese than bushrangers, all on the say so of the quick-talking Aaron Sherritt, but Hare has not remotely lost faith in him. Far from it, the Superintendent remains convinced that, even though the bushrangers weren't there last night, they surely soon will be at some point, and it is against that prospect that he quickly gives the orders for a party of seven troopers to set up a secret post outside Mrs Byrne's place so they can pounce as soon as the bushrangers do arrive. And, always one wanting to be there for the kill, he commits himself to joining his men on the stake-out.

MID-FEBRUARY 1879, THE KELLYS WAIT FOR A LETTER THAT NEVER COMES

Every day, even in the wilderness of the Warby Ranges, Ned waits for word that the letter he and Joe penned for the Jerilderie siege has been published. For, ideally, this is the document that will change everything, the one that explains their side of things – a letter that will make the public, the press and the politicians know that they are *not* the bloodthirsty murderers they have been made out to be. They have achieved that with the people they captured at Euroa and at Jerilderie, and the letter will hopefully let the wider world know it too: all they had done was to fight bravely against injustices.

And every day, Ned is disappointed, and progressively more

frustrated. What can have happened to the letter? Edward Living had promised that he would see it published, it is obviously newsworthy, so how can this plan have been thwarted?

In fact, the papers are keen to publish the letter, and both *The Argus* and *The Age* send emissaries to Jerilderie, looking to give Living £10 and ten guineas, respectively, but as no less than the New South Wales Attorney General has sent a cable to Living commanding him 'not to allow it to be published on any account',[21] they are unsuccessful. Edward Living at least shares its contents with the police – who pass it on to the government – and his friends, providing a copy to local publican John Hanlon, as well as giving a thorough synopsis to his editor friend for whom the letter was intended, Samuel Gill. And yet, Living remains careful for the moment never to let this most contentious manuscript stray too far into the public eye.

Both Captain Standish and Sir Bryan O'Loghlen examine the letter closely, as do their leading officials. It makes for horrifying reading as Ned gives actual *orders* for the Stock Protection Societies to be disbanded; for those who have most reason to fear him to 'give 10 pounds out of every hundred towards the widow and orphan fund and do not attempt to reside in Victoria'. Anyone who neglects his commands must 'abide by the consequences':

> I do not wish to give the order full force without giving timely warning, but I am a widow's son outlawed, and my orders must be obeyed.
> Edward Kelly.[22]

There is no doubt the hubris of the statement is shocking. It is almost as if Kelly is framing himself as the king of Kelly Country, bestowing favour on his loyal subjects, while threatening cruel punishment to those who do not honour him. There is even a rumour circulating that the bushranger is going to declare Kelly Country an independent republic!

In the meantime, what can be done to heighten the chances of catching the gang in the trackless wilderness in which they have disappeared? One obvious way is to have the best black-trackers on the continent go out after them. Though Standish had point-blank rejected Queensland's offer to send black-trackers after Euroa, the outbreak at Jerilderie has changed everything.

For once Superintendent Hare hears that the new Victorian Governor, the Marquess of Normanby, had spoken highly of the native troopers in Queensland, where His Excellency had just completed a stint of governorship, he begins to urge that an effort be made to see if Victoria can secure the services of a few of them. After all, it had been a black-tracker, Donald, who had been hugely significant in capturing Harry Power a decade earlier.

Captain Standish argues vociferously against the idea, asserting that the trackers 'would be very little use in a district where there is a large traffic on all the roads, and where the movements of the outlaws was known to be wonderfully rapid . . . it is a well-known fact that they often used to ride 50, 60, and 70 miles between night and morning'.[23]

But, in the end, when the Governor argues for it, backed by the press – for they also begin agitating on the matter – and with even his own underlings now pressing him to take action, Captain Standish reluctantly does so, sending a cable to his Queensland counterpart:

> Can you send me down a party of Black-Trackers say eight with someone accustomed to manage them . . . The country where the Outlaws hide is very mountainous in places covered with dense scrub, very rocky with deep gullies. Quite inaccessible to horsemen . . . .[24]

The answer is not long in coming back:

> `The Colonial Secretary approves of my sending trackers provided they volunteer for the service, receive extra pay and are assured of a fair share of reward offered provided their efforts lead to capture of Gang.`[25]

Captain Standish assures his counterpart by return cable that this will be done, that the black-trackers would be paid `any sum per day you may fix` and . . . `they will receive a fair proportion of the Government reward should they succeed in leading to capture or death of the outlaws . . .`[26] and the agreement is forged.

18 FEBRUARY 1879, THE STAKE-OUT BEGINS

And so it starts. At Aaron Sherritt's suggestion on this evening, at a time when the darkness renders them practically invisible, Sherritt, with Superintendent Francis Hare and seven troopers, carrying blankets and provisions a'plenty, pick their careful way along the gully that lies at the bottom of the Woolshed Valley, and then slowly climb to the spot that, from the distance of half a mile, overlooks the back of Mrs Margret Byrne's house.

High on the side of a very deep, rough gully, in a position surrounded by such high hills that horsemen could come at them from neither in front nor behind, the party make the first of two camps. At the bottom of the gully is a track that the Kelly Gang would likely use on approach to Mrs Byrne's house, and on the other side of the gully, about half a mile away, is that house, in full view.

'This spot,' Aaron says, almost in the manner of mine host, 'is unknown to any one except the bushrangers, and the only danger of you being discovered is by them.'[27]

All Hare and the troopers have to do is stay here and, in shifts, watch the house by day before moving down to the stockyard by night, and they are bound to get the Kelly Gang some time over the next few weeks. While three of the troopers stay with Hare, another four go another half a mile up in the ranges, to the 'wonderfully formed camp of the outlaws',[28] ready to ambush the bushrangers should they decide to stop there before visiting Mrs Byrne.

Among the party, there is a feeling of near certainty that the bushrangers will soon come. For, while it is known that Ned Kelly is very close to his mother, it is assumed that Joe is close to his own and will likely find a way to visit her.

All good. The mood of Hare and his men is upbeat, and remains that way even through the unending monotony of the coming days. They are going to catch the Kellys.

Every evening at dusk, Superintendent Hare leads his men off, and as, one by one, they make their way to their assigned positions behind Mrs Byrne's, settling themselves just far enough away that the dogs don't bark, but close enough that they will be able to pounce once the Kellys show up. Each trooper is positioned behind trees about fifteen yards from the next one along, as they wait in the bitter, penetrating cold that goes right to the marrow of their bones.

And wait. And wait. And wait.

Most nights, Aaron is inside Mrs Bryne's house in complete comfort, with his young woman and Mrs Byrne, eating, drinking, and talking to them. Usually, he leaves at midnight or even one o'clock in the morning, whereupon, by circuitous route, he makes his way to where he knows the troopers are lying and takes up his position with them, always right by Superintendent Hare.

One thing that stuns Hare is that, while he and all the troopers are heavily rugged up, Sherritt is able to endure the cold and lack of sleep with neither coat nor complaint. 'I do not care about coats,' he says simply.

'Can the outlaws endure as you are doing?' Hare asks him with wonder.

'Ned Kelly would beat me into fits,' Sherritt replies. 'I can beat all the others; I am a better man than Joe Byrne, and I am a better man

Ellen Kelly and her family outside the Kelly homestead, 1881. (*Left to right*): Alice Kelly (King); Kate Kelly (seated); Grace Kelly with Faith, the Kellys' cattle dog; Mrs Ellen Kelly (seated); Jack Kelly (King); Ellen Kelly (King), feeding a lamb from a bottle; Reverend William Gould, who married Ellen and George King in 1874. (Photo: State Library of Victoria)

'Boxing Ned', 1874. Ned Kelly, aged nineteen, after his victory over Wild Wright in a twenty-round bare-knuckle fight at Beechworth. (Photo courtesy Matt Shore)

Portrait of Ned, 1874. Pentridge Gaol photographer Charles Nettleton likely took this photo in late January 1874, prior to Ned's release on 2 February. (Photo: State Library of Victoria)

The Bushranger 'Mad' Dan Morgan, from the *Illustrated Melbourne Post*, 25 January 1865. Mad Dan was active around Victoria's north-east when Ned Kelly was growing up. Many of his notorious antics, such as holding up entire stations, were later mimicked by the Kelly Gang.

Harry Power, 1870. Photo taken at Pentridge Gaol by Charles Nettleton after Power was recaptured and sentenced to fifteen years. (Photo: State Library of Victoria)

The capture of Harry Power, 1870. Superintendents Nicolson and Hare and Sergeant Montfort capture Harry Power while he is sleeping in his mia-mia, high up in the Wombat Ranges. (Image courtesy Matt Shore)

Constable Alexander Fitzpatrick, the 'perjurer and drunkard' trooper who Ned Kelly said was the 'cause' of the Kelly outbreak. (Photo courtesy Matt Shore)

Isaiah 'Wild' Wright, a true larrikin of the north-east and friend of the Kelly Gang. (Photo courtesy Matt Shore)

Aaron Sherritt, childhood friend of Joe Byrne and double agent. He was to play a key role in the Kelly Gang's strategy to lure a special train full of police to their deaths at Glenrowan. (PHOTO: BURKE MUSEUM, BEECHWORTH)

Tom Lloyd, cousin of Ned and Dan. Tom was a friend and active supporter of the Gang, and later married Ned's sister Maggie. (PHOTO COURTESY MATT SHORE)

Steve Hart, circa 1878. A Wangaratta lad and friend of Dan Kelly's whose presence at Stringybark Creek in 1878 led to his ill-fated membership of the outlawed Kelly Gang. (Photo: State Library of Victoria)

Dan Kelly, 1877. The youngest of the Kelly brothers and active member of the 'Greta Mob', Dan was outlawed at the age of seventeen. (Photo: Victoria Police Museum)

The Kelly Gang, circa 1879. The three men on horseback are said to be (*from left*) Wild Wright (scouting for the Gang), Ned Kelly and Steve Hart. Though their identities are unverified, this image persists as an important piece of Kellyana. (Photo: State Library of Victoria)

Sergeant Arthur Steele. The grandly moustachioed, energetic police officer was a central figure at Glenrowan. He was both censured and praised for his role in the Kelly pursuit. (Photo: State Library of Victoria)

Senior Constable John Kelly (*third from the right*) and the six troopers who were the first to arrive on the scene at Glenrowan. (PHOTO: STATE LIBRARY OF VICTORIA)

The site of the police camp at Stringybark Creek. Photograph taken by F. C. Burman in October 1878. (PHOTO: VICTORIAN POLICE MUSEUM)

Constable Michael Scanlan, 1878, killed at Stringybark Creek. Heading out on his last assignment, Scanlan told a friend, 'I may never come back, and, if so, you can take my dog.'

Constable Thomas McIntyre was the only police survivor of the Stringybark Creek murders in 1878. He was the key witness for the prosecution in the trial against Ned Kelly in 1880.

Constable Thomas Lonigan, 1878, the policeman responsible for brutalising Ned's 'crown jewels'. Lonigan was killed at Stringybark Creek, true to Ned's threat: 'Well, Lonigan, I never shot a man yet; but if ever I do, so help me God, you will be the first.'

Sergeant Michael Kennedy, 1878, a well-respected member of Victoria Police, murdered at Stringybark Creek. His memory was revered, even by Ned Kelly himself, who said that Kennedy was 'the bravest man [I] ever heard of'. (All photos courtesy Matt Shore)

Looking south-west over the police camp at Stringybark Creek on 26 October 1878. The scene shows the initial encounter between the Kelly Gang and the encamped police. Constable McIntyre holds his hands up while Constable Lonigan, taking cover with his revolver, is shot dead by Ned Kelly as he rises to get off a shot of his own. Dan Kelly and his mates take aim at McIntyre, who had attended to the horses now startled by gun shots. (Illustration by Bill Denheld after photo by Burman and description by McIntyre)

Looking north-west over the police camp at Stringybark Creek on 26 October 1878. The two returning police are met by the bailed-up Constable McIntyre telling them to surrender – they are surrounded. Joe Byrne and Dan Kelly are crouched in the bush at bottom left. Steve Hart takes aim beside the tent while Ned Kelly fires at Sergeant Kennedy with Constable Scanlan at the rear, where he will be shot dead by the Gang. The murdered Constable Lonigan is hidden from the officers' view behind the log. (Illustration by Bill Denheld after photo by Burman and description by McIntyre)

Queensland Aboriginal trackers with police command: (*from left*) Senior Constable King, Stanhope O'Connor (seated), Superintendent Sadleir and Chief Commissioner Standish. Native trackers were brought into the Kelly pursuit as many of the Victorian police lacked bush skills. (Photo courtesy Matt Shore)

Superintendent Hare and his police cave party, 1879. Hare and his men camped out in a cave while watching Mrs Byrne's place for a sign of the Gang. (Photo: Victoria Police Museum)

Superintendent Francis Hare was placed in command of the Kelly pursuit following the Gang's escapades at Euroa. After quitting due to exhaustion, he reassumed control of the hunt for the Gang prior to Glenrowan. Hare received the largest share of the Kelly reward. (Photo courtesy Victoria Police Museum)

'Interior of the press carriage in the special train' by Thomas Carrington of the *Australasian Sketcher*. The only artist on board the police special, Carrington later witnessed Ned's Last Stand from near the railway station. (Image courtesy Matt Shore)

Ann Jones's Glenrowan Inn became 'a house of sports' on Sunday, 27 June 1880. The Kelly Gang and their prisoners played music and danced to pass the time. (Image: State Library of Victoria)

Tom Curnow, Glenrowan's crippled schoolteacher. Curnow played a crucial role in the events at Glenrowan – winning him both friends and enemies. (Photo: State Library of New South Wales)

Examination and remand of Ned Kelly in Melbourne Gaol. On Saturday, 31 July 1880, an impromptu remand hearing was heard in the kitchen attached to the Melbourne Gaol hospital. (IMAGE COURTESY MATT SHORE)

Kelly in the dock at Beechworth, August 1880. (IMAGE COURTESY MATT SHORE)

Ned Kelly's armour, from a sketch by Mr T. Carrington. (Image: State Library of Victoria)

Sidney Nolan's depiction of Ned Kelly sitting atop a horse is one of twenty-seven paintings in his iconic Ned Kelly series, a testament to the bushranger's enduring legacy. (Sidney Nolan, Kelly and horse, 1946, enamel on composition board, Nolan Collection, managed by Canberra Museum and Gallery on behalf of the Australian Government)

than Dan Kelly, and I am a better man than Steve Hart. I can lick those two youngsters to fits; I have always beaten Joe, but I look upon Ned Kelly as an extraordinary man; there is no man in the world like him, he is superhuman.'[29]

Sherritt also leaves Hare in no doubt as to just what kind of bushman he is up against when it comes to Ned Kelly. On one occasion, as the police officer is talking to Sherritt, the older man happens to absent-mindedly break a twig off a tree and start tearing off its leaves. Sherritt immediately stops him and says, 'You would never do for a bushranger.'

'Why not?'

'If Ned Kelly saw any of his men break a twig off a tree when he was camped, he would have an awful row with them.'[30]

And so it goes. Night after night, the men wait, and night after night there is nothing. But not to lose hope . . .

For equally each night, in an excited whisper, Sherritt gives Hare all the exciting news of the Kellys he has learned on the day and into the evening, and it is always pretty good. The Kellys are *close*, I tell you! If they don't come tonight, it must be tomorrow night at the outside. Inevitably, the subject of Joe Byrne comes up, and Aaron never fails to plead that should Joe turn up at the stockyard the next night, as he expects, then the Superintendent must 'give Joe a chance of his life'[31] and not simply shoot him stone-dead on the spot.

'Of course,' Sherritt would sometimes add, 'if he fights and shoots at you, you must do the same to him.'[32]

—

Clearly, Mrs Byrne is extraordinarily active for such an old woman. Ever and always, she seems to be on her guard once she comes out of the house, looking around suspiciously, cocking her ear to the wind, walking around her property looking for any sign of tracks. One day, about two weeks after the police have begun their stake-out, she is spotted walking along the bank of the creek in the gully when she suddenly stops and examines something on the ground. It is the spot of the creek where the four troopers at the higher stake-out go to get their water. That evening, she tells Aaron what she has found. Shaved bits of stick. Someone has been 'whittling' there and, to judge by the boot-prints that go with it, she is just about sure it has come from police that must be camped close by. And near the whittling point was what looked to be a piece of small soap, as if someone had been washing in the creek.

'Aaron,' she tells him, 'you must have a good look in the ranges tomorrow, to see if you can find them.'[33]

Aaron promises to do exactly that, and shortly afterwards excuses himself to report this troubling conversation to Superintendent Hare, waiting in the stockyard. Among other things, Hare is stunned to know that he is dealing with people where even the little old ladies – yes, only forty-five years old, but remarkably withered from a hard life – can find the boot-prints left by a trooper on the side of a creek.

As agreed, the next day Aaron makes a great show of taking his horse and heading off to do exactly as she has asked, and that evening he tells Mrs Byrne her fears are ungrounded, because there is neither hide nor hair or even Hare of any police patrols. Mrs Byrne is certain he is wrong regardless. She knows what she saw, what those boot-prints looked like, and is sure the police are out there.

20 FEBRUARY 1879, MELBOURNE, HOW FAR CAN A WRIT RUN?

It is no small thing to be in the Chambers of Judge Redmond Barry, the formidable legal force of nature who the year before had put Ellen Kelly and her baby in gaol for three years. On this day, the issue before him is the ongoing incarceration of the thirty-one-year-old sympathiser John McElroy – who happens to be married to Ned and Dan's cousin, Mary Lloyd – and it is not simply to be a matter of remanding him for another week, as has happened to all the other sympathisers.

No, this time McElroy has serious legal representation in the form of a barrister by the name of McFarland, and the strong rumour is that his legal fees have been paid by none other than Ned Kelly.

To the proceedings proper . . .

McFarland seeks nothing less than a writ of habeas corpus on behalf of his client, 'now prisoner in the gaol at Beechworth . . . directing Mr C. G. Thomson, the governor of the gaol, to bring before the Court the body of John McElroy, and show by what authority he was detained in custody'.[34] Since 3 January, McElroy has been placed on remand, still with no evidence presented against him.

It is a compelling point.

Still, His Honour does his best in this case by denying the application on a small legal technicality: McElroy's affidavit does not have the signatures of two witnesses, as required by law.

Nevertheless, when advised by counsel that the error would be attended to, and another application made the following week, it becomes obvious to all that now the prisoners have some serious legal representation, the ability of the government to hold the sympathisers indefinitely is diminishing, and it can only be a matter of time before everyone is free again.

In the wider community, the outrage at the treatment of the sympathisers continues to grow, to the point that Superintendents Hare and Sadleir start to receive tip-offs 'that the outlaws intend to blow up a train with dynamite'.[35] Both are shocked, scarcely believing that the Kelly Gang could take things that far . . . but, on reflection, it really *might* be possible.

EARLY MARCH 1879, THE BLACK-TRACKERS START OUT ON THE TRACK WINDING BACK

The six native black-trackers from Queensland, led by Sub-Inspector Stanhope O'Connor – the quietly spoken, well-connected nephew of the Governor of New South Wales, who boasts one of the best moustaches in the Queensland Police Force – are on their way. Corporal Sambo and troopers Hero, Johnny, Jimmy, Barney and Jack are aged between eighteen and twenty-five, recruited from up Mackay way, and all are dressed smartly in blue uniforms with Snider rifles and revolvers, but still these are not their main weapon. No, that would be their capacity to track a magpie that headed south a week ago, into a gale, across a blank rock face. Their powers of tracking, honed since birth and passed down from countless generations, are legendary, and if anyone can track the Kelly Gang it is them.

As a matter of fact, just before they had been called to Victoria, O'Connor and his men had been involved in an exercise that had received great commendation from the Queensland Government. On 20 February 1879 at Cape Bedford,[36] north of Cooktown, O'Connor and his men had cornered in a narrow gorge twenty-eight men and thirteen women of the Guugu-Yimidhirr tribe, who had been trouble to the settlers of late. Twenty-four of the men had been subsequently shot on the beach, while the other four swam out to sea and were never seen again.[37] (On a previous occasion, when Sub-Inspector O'Connor had tried to negotiate with the Aboriginal people, he had been severely criticised by the pastoralists, who had just wanted them all killed, and this time he and his native troopers had just got on with it.)

The killing completed, they had gone back to the camp and, as the newspaper would report, having found 'a meerschaum pipe and tomahawk in their possession belonging to [settler] Mr. Hartley, the inspector was satisfied that he had not killed innocent people. This was explained to the lubras, and they were then permitted to go away.'[38]

This exercise in Victoria, however, will likely be more difficult, as the Kelly Gang will have real weapons to fight back with, but still O'Connor has confidence it can be done. True, getting on this coal-fuelled ocean steamer bound for Sydney and heading out into the mighty swell of the Pacific Ocean does not sit easily with the trackers, as they all quickly become terribly, terribly seasick, and Corporal Sambo even develops a bad case of congested lungs, but they will just have to put up with it. The bossman, Stanhope O'Connor ('Marmie' they call him – the old Queensland black word for 'Mister') has said this is very important, that the bad fella Ned Kelly and the bad fellas in his gang have made many problems and they must track them down.

After the five-day journey to Sydney, they know, they will have to catch a train to Albury and then Benalla and start tracking the Kelly Gang from there. Generally, they are happy, as they are going to be paid £3 a month while away. True, this is only one-tenth of what O'Connor will be paid, but in the first place the trackers don't know that and in the second place it is the view of the Queensland Government that that amount is more than enough for a native anyway.

In response to the news, the Melbourne *Herald* confirms that the trackers are 'a fine body of fellows', of whom 'nearly all . . . are splendid shots', while also noting – with typical nonsense – that their superior officer 'denies them the prerequisite of eating the vanquished bushrangers, although most of the natives of Northern Queensland, to which these men belong, are cannibals to the extent of eating enemies slain in battle'.[39]

9 MARCH 1879, THE STAKE-OUT GOES ON

For no fewer than nineteen gruelling days and freezing nights – they cannot light a fire, for obvious reasons – Superintendent Hare's group have remained, carefully watching Mrs Byrne's place. The experience has been every bit as monotonous as their meals – bread and sardines washed down by water, with the occasional can of preserved beef. As the days go by, and the winter looms, they start to get bottles of porter, ale and whiskey among their provisions, thankfully. (At least they have plenty of provisions, with Beechworth store owner Paddy Allen, a friend of Detective Ward's, who sold them supplies, later commenting that the police, 'lived fat and cut it thick. They had plenty of liquor.')[40]

On this particular morning, after another long night of nothing but watching for no result, the men, including Aaron, who this time has been with them all night long, come back to their camp and have their breakfast, and then lie in their various shady spots to have some blessed sleep. As befitting his rank, Hare is highest up the hill, where he can look down on all the others, and not far from him is the spot where the sentry must stand guard. The man furthest down the hill, in a hollow by a large rock, is Aaron, and he is sleeping. Like all bar the sentry, Superintendent Hare nods off to sleep, only to be woken by an urgent hiss from the sentry, who alerts him, *'The old woman is in the camp!'*[41]

Hare immediately sits up and, sure enough, looks down aghast to see old Mrs Byrne just coming up the hill and into their camp. 'She stood for a moment,' Hare would later recount, 'saw articles lying about the camp, then came a few steps further on, looked down in the direction of where one of the men was lying, then halted for a moment, and retreated.'[42]

His heart in his mouth, Hare waits till the woman has gone and then goes down to see who, exactly, it was that she had been staring at. To his complete horror, he finds it to be . . . Aaron.

Their only hope is that she has not recognised him, as he had been lying partially on his side, and part of his form obscured by a police hat and overcoat. And when Hare wakes Aaron to tell him – 'Good heavens! You are discovered; the old woman has seen you'[43] – the young man is under no illusions as to the likely ramifications. For immediately that he is informed of just who has had a close look at him, Sherritt turns deadly pale, even as huge drops of perspiration break out on his face. Gasping for air, scarcely able to speak, his first words are, 'Now I am a dead man.'[44]

Hare and Aaron decide that the best thing is for him to quickly establish an alibi by rousing a friend who lives nearby, so if there's a dispute that friend can confirm that Aaron was with him – and therefore Mrs Byrne must be mistaken – and for the rest of it act as if nothing has happened.

That evening, as Sherritt visits the Byrne household, taking a flute with him to break the ice, the old lady is not long in challenging him after a fashion, once the two are momentarily alone. 'A nice trick you have been playing on me,' she says.

'What do you mean?'

'Who could have put the police into that camp in the mountains but you?'

'I don't know what you mean.'[45]

She tells him of her adventure of the morning, of how she had spotted the glint of sunlight off a sardine tin and followed it up the hill to discover the camp, how there are thirty troopers there, and how she is certain that Aaron knows all about it. 'If only I can find out the number of men in the camp,' she says, 'I can get Joe to shoot any number under fifteen or twenty.'[46]

While immensely relieved that she is not saying she saw him there that morning, still Sherritt professes total ignorance of the police camp, to which Mrs Byrne asks a very pertinent question. 'How is it that an old woman like me can become aware of such a camp, and a young cove like you cannot?'[47]

Aaron has no answer, which only confirms her suspicions more. After leaving the Byrne house, Sherritt comes back to Hare 'in a mortal funk for fear the old woman had seen him'. Aaron reports, 'She has lost her faith in me, but she did not recognise me.'[48]

The very next morning, Mrs Byrne is seen heading back up the slope towards them once again, deciding to confront them after all. Quickly, Aaron, you must hide. Sherritt does exactly that, while Hare says to Senior Constable Mills, 'Go up and give the old woman a fright.'[49] In a flash, Mills positions himself behind a rock and then jumps out at her, roaring like a bear with a sore tooth.

For a moment, the old woman goes on the defensive, saying, 'What, what? I am only looking for cattle . . .' but she is not long in climbing back upon her high dudgeon, to yell, 'I will get my son to shoot the whole bloody lot of you!'[50]

The last straw, the clincher that Aaron's game is up in the eyes of old Mrs Byrne, is when she turns up at his selection just three days later and asks how it is that there are police horses grazing in his paddock – and again he has no answer. It is the end. After a bitter row between the two, his engagement to Catherine Byrne is off, and he is not long in becoming, effectively, a sworn enemy of the entire Byrne family.

8 MARCH 1879 AND ONWARDS, BENALLA BURIES A VISITOR

At first glance, Benalla is impressed with the Queensland black-trackers when they arrive on this day, just as it is impressed with their commanding officer, who is found to be 'a fine, smart, dashing-looking young man' with 'the appearance of one who would care very little whether he met one or a half-dozen Kellys. He carried a belt around his waist in which are about a dozen sockets, which are filled with rifle and revolver cartridges.'[51]

As to his trackers, they are notable from the first, not simply for the comparative novelty of seeing black faces in uniforms, but because, even in town, they walk around together in single file. Though the townspeople don't understand it, it is a practice ingrained since their youth, where they learned never to needlessly disturb the tracks that could be the difference between a big meal and a breezy hunger. They can read those tracks as if all the information is scratched deeply into the ground.

'If the tracks are those of a mammal,' it would later be noted, '[the tracker] can probably tell you, from the size and "weight" or depth of the tracks, its gender and approximate age.'[52]

If the tracks, however, are those of a human, it is all so much easier: 'Every person's footprints . . . are unique, and most people are familiar with all the barefoot prints of all the people in their neighbourhood, and of almost every one of their acquaintances . . . not only the pattern on the underside of the footwear gives away its owner, but the size, the angle of the feet as they walk, and the characteristic way the shoe is worn . . . All these idiosyncrasies are recognised by the person who studies tracks . . .'[53]

Nevertheless, Captain Standish, who remains uncomfortable at the idea of 'the ornamental Queensland sub-inspector'[54] and 'his niggers',[55] as he refers to them, coming to Victoria to do the work of Victorians, is not surprised that the first foray of the black-trackers does not go well. For his opinion has not changed: 'No doubt trackers can be utilized in following the traces of men on foot, but for this kind of work they are really perfectly useless, because their movements are so slow.'[56]

And yet it is not their lack of speed that is the key problem. For no sooner do they arrive in Benalla than O'Connor takes them on a trek through the Wombat Ranges, where his men – born and bred in sunny Queensland, where their family trees have roots into the Dreamtime – suffer terribly in the wet and cold they are suddenly exposed to in the high altitude of Kelly Country. Worst hit is the twenty-five-year-old Corporal Sambo, who has not recovered from the sea voyage and, after coughing till he can cough no more – and despite being closely attended by Doctors Nicholson and Henry – dies from pneumonia on the night of 19 March, two days after arriving back in Benalla. All of the tracking troop are devastated, but none more than Sambo's brother Barney, another of the trackers. The following day, it is Barney and Sub-Inspector O'Connor alone who follow the corpse of Sambo to Benalla Cemetery, where Barney's cries of grief are so strong the kookaburras in nearby gum trees can laugh no more and simply fly away.

By the time they return to the barracks, one of the Victorian trackers, Moses, has claimed Sambo's uniform, saying 'to allow it to lie in the barracks to rot would be a shame'.[57]

From this point on, the Queensland trackers always carry extra blankets when going out on patrol. When in Benalla, they sleep at the police barracks, while O'Connor moves into the Craven's Commercial Hotel, to share a sitting room with Captain Standish and Superintendent Hare. '[We] lived together like brothers,' Hare would later recall.[58]

LATE MARCH 1879, SANDRIDGE, PORT PHILLIP BAY, HAS THEIR SHIP COME IN?

A couple of young ladies here to see you, Cap'n . . .

Do tell? It is not the usual thing for Captain Hamilton Oliver of the mighty three-masted iron sailing ship *Victoria Cross* to receive visitors in this manner, but he is an amiable old sea dog, so he doesn't mind, particularly today, when they are two young and beautiful ladies. Still, what strange young women they prove to be.

For despite their youthful beauty, they are of grim countenance, and seemingly from up the country somewhere. As the newspapers would subsequently report it, they have come, they explain in rather strained tones, to make enquiries about whether the captain would be happy to take 'four or five gentlemen friends'[59] across the Pacific Ocean to California and, if so, how much would he charge?

This is even odder. The way one enquires about arranging passage across the oceans is not like this, furtively, but openly at one of the shipping offices that proliferate around the docks. The way these women are speaking, it is almost as if – though they are not saying it – almost as if they wish the captain to *smuggle* these men out of the country. This impression is heightened when the older of the two women says that the men 'would not come on board at Sandridge, but probably at Queenscliff'.[60]

In response, the captain is non-committal, saying only that he will wait to hear from them. With no satisfaction on the matter, and little information, Kate Kelly and Maggie Skillion, Ned's sisters, take their leave.

A few days later, however, a strange man in a slouch hat, of 'somewhat suspicious appearance',[61] turns up and asks the captain whether he is agreeable to proceed on the terms discussed by the young ladies. Cap'n Oliver, suspecting that he is either talking to one of the Kelly Gang, or at least to someone associated with them, makes an appointment with him to meet at the General Post Office in a couple of days' time. Once the stranger has departed, Oliver quickly gets word to his dear friend, Constable Thomas McIntyre.

Come the time, the GPO is crawling with detectives and plain-clothes constables, hoping to make a major arrest – perhaps of Ned Kelly himself – but, alas, of the man, there is now no sign. A strange episode, but fascinating for the newspaper folk while it lasts, whatever the truth or otherwise of it.

EARLY APRIL 1879, BENALLA, THE IDEAS FLOW

Whatever else, it is not as if ideas about how to capture the Kelly Gang are in short supply. In fact, they have been coming from everywhere for months, including from the office of the especially impatient Minister for Railways, John Woods. Some of his advisers had come up with a plan that is 'expected to make short work of the Kelly pursuit',[62] and it is passed on to Superintendent John Sadleir.

'The plan,' as Sadleir would later recount, 'was simplicity itself. Each mountain in the ranges could be successively surrounded by a cordon of several hundred police and military, who would then march to its summit, where – it was assumed – the Gang would be waiting capture.'[63]

Meanwhile, of course, the real work of pursuing the Kellys goes on. And active, exhausting work it is too. For, at the conclusion of the 'cave party' – as Superintendent Hare would ever after refer to their fruitless stint watching Mrs Byrne's house – Hare has returned to Benalla and thrown himself back into organising and leading expeditions into the ranges. 'I was constantly on the move,' he would later report. 'My object was to harass the outlaws as much as possible. I had parties of men out in every direction, going all day, and watching for fires at night.'[64]

Two places that remain under full surveillance are the Kelly hut on Eleven Mile Creek and Maggie Skillion's place nearby. Hare feels sure that, 'sooner or later, one of the different parties who were out in search of them would drop across them, as the outlaws had always to be on the alert, never knowing when a party would be on them'.[65]

As to the black-trackers, Hare – perhaps in deference to Captain Standish's continuing opposition to their presence – does not rely on them and, in the words of Sadleir, 'showed no interest in their work and failed altogether to appreciate their useful qualities'.[66] As a rule, it would be noted, 'He looked forward to the Kellys being captured by the white police alone.'[67]

Other troopers, however, are not so reticent about using the black-trackers and are staggered to note how they can follow a trail across rock, simply by following the tiniest of fresh scratches caused by horse-shoes, or put together the smallest of sweat marks on a loose rail from the trace of a man's hand, or associate a tiny indent by a creek with the mark of a spur strap to show where a man had dismounted to have a drink of water.

Of course, thanks to the papers and their bush telegraph, the Kelly Gang know all about the black-trackers' arrival. As Ned himself would later note of the 'black devils . . . what told on us most was the perpetual dread of surprise', and the fact that they 'robbed us even of sleep'.[68]

Inevitably, the gang have little choice but to spend more time in remote, isolated and defensible camps, where the only tracks they leave are around their caves or campsites. At nights, they put on a sentry, just in case, and for any long journeys they do have to make they rely on the support of the Greta mob and their other sympathisers.

To communicate with their supporters, the gang are able to develop various signals. Stones placed in particular positions at a designated spot on a track might indicate in which direction the gang can be found, and 'one of the Gang would ride in a circle near a sympathiser's hut, and then jump a fence, and again ride circuitously, and finally strike off in the direction where the outlaws were hid. The sympathiser, on seeing this track, would carry provisions in the direction indicated.'[69]

Never, but never, do the gang leave visible signs of where they have made camp. Each morning, after rising, not only is their exceedingly small campfire extinguished, but its ashes are scattered and then fresh earth lightly spread over the spot where the fire had been. Yes, those devils of black-trackers might still be able to determine their campsite, but there will be no question of judging the warmth of the ashes to determine how long since anyone has been there.

Overall, reports of Kelly Gang sightings begin to diminish, and it seems they have gone to ground.

19 MARCH 1879, ASSISTANT COMMISSIONER NICOLSON HAS IDEAS TOO

Even though he is stuck working in Melbourne, Assistant Commissioner Nicolson – who has kept his title despite Standish's vow to do him down, once his father-in-law has died – has an idea that he thinks might help to drain the Kelly Gang of support, something that will paralyse their network of sympathisers the way perpetually remanding them in gaol has not. For where else to attack the criminal selector class than where it truly hurts them most? Take their land! It is with this in mind that on this day he writes to the Secretary for Lands, suggesting that:

> *It might be desirable that the government should take all the legal means in its power to eject from the land all selectors of bad character who have not yet acquired a title to the ground they occupy. Wherever the police can show on good grounds that a selector is of bad or of doubtful character, and he gives the Government an opportunity of dispossessing him, the Minister might at once take the necessary to do so . . .*[70]

The answer comes promptly from the Secretary for Lands, who is more than happy to oblige his request and makes a suggestion of how their cooperation may be most fruitful: 'Be good enough to state whether a list of selectors suspected by the Police of sympathising with, or aiding the outlaws, can be furnished. If so, it might be of service to both Departments.'[71]

Delighted with this cooperation, Nicolson informs Sadleir, who begins to put together a 'List of Persons (Belonging to the Criminal Classes) holding Selections in Secluded Parts of the North-Eastern District'.[72]

23 APRIL 1879, BEECHWORTH, REMAND COMMANDS

Another week, another wretched remand session . . .

As the prisoners are ushered from their tiny holding cells and out through the front courtyard of the sandstone gaol, as ever they blink in the harsh light – dirty moles emerging from their holes. The locals of the town have mostly lost interest in this weekly parade of the prisoners in this affair that seems to merely drag on, though at least a few stare as if they care when the captives walk by, and that is at least something, as dismal as their situation remains.

And yet, on this morning, there is something different. For finally, after 107 days of being continually remanded in custody, there is a breakthrough as the final seven sympathisers brought before Magistrate Foster are discharged.

'I feel it my duty,' Foster says to the first man, 'to act independently, and to do that which, to my conscience, seems just and legal, and I do not feel justified in granting a further remand. I therefore discharge the accused . . .'

When Wild Wright, the final prisoner, enters the dock, Foster chooses his words carefully. 'Wright,' he says, 'your fellow prisoners have been discharged, and I propose to discharge you also. It is several weeks since you, when in that dock, were foolish enough and cowardly enough to threaten me. Foolish, because what you said could but prejudice your position; as a coward, because you attempted to intimidate me when simply doing my duty, and that a very unpleasant one. My acts were official ones, and done in the interest of society, and it was a cowardly thing to make them the subject of personal enmity. It has been the subject of serious reflection with me whether I ought not to place you under substantial bonds to keep the peace; but this would probably cause your return to gaol, where you have so long been, and trusting that the words were uttered in the heat of the moment, and that there is no ulterior intention of wrong, I discharge you.'[73]

Stunned, Wright simply says, 'Thank you,' and leaves the court with some speed.

Captain Standish, when he hears of the prisoners' release, is appalled, as he had wanted all the sympathisers to remain incarcerated indefinitely. He breaks the news to Acting Chief Secretary Sir Bryan O'Loghlen by cable:

> As soon as prisoners were discharged they ran away as fast as they could in every

direction and in less than five minutes had left Beechworth.[74]

MAY 1879, THE LAW MOVES IN MYSTERIOUS WAYS

For once, Captain Standish likes Nicolson's ideas to do down the sympathisers, the 'poor but semi-criminal class . . .'[75] It is with Captain Standish's approval, thus, that Sadleir provides a list of eighty-six names to Assistant Commissioner Nicolson, who is happy to forward it to the Secretary for Lands on 7 May.

This 'Black List', as it becomes known, is nothing less than 'A list of suspected persons and criminals in possession of holdings of lands in the North-Eastern district . . . Besides the men referred to, there are many young men, members of those same families and others, who are coming to the age at which they may select land and whom it would be most desirable to prevent settling in such places . . .'[76]

The list is then sent to local Land Boards with the request that any on that list who desire to increase their holdings be denied. Most particularly . . . Ellen Kelly, even though she is currently in gaol. For it is Assistant Commissioner Nicolson himself who impresses upon the Secretary for Lands that:

> *this woman and her family have, since coming to the North-Eastern District, lived by immorality and dishonesty . . . the forfeiture of Mrs Kelly's selection would of course prevent the family from returning to the old house but as it is desirable that there should be a complete clearance of the family from that locality, I would recommend the forfeiture of Williamson's selection also.*[77]

It is not long before the effects of these background moves are felt. In June, Kelly friend William Tanner has his application for 44 acres at Myrrhee refused, and when he furiously enquires for the reason, he is informed by the secretary for the local land board, Mr Blundell, 'I have the honour to inform you that the land in question was refused on the recommendation of the police department.'[78]

Yes, it has come to this. Lack of land has always been the key grievance of the whole Kelly class. Now the ruling class has upped the ante and is using it as a blunt instrument against them, to beat them down. *Again.*

MAY 1879, SUPERINTENDENT HARE AND AARON SHERRITT TALK

Many of the police continue their distrust of Sherritt, but never Hare. The senior policeman and the ruffian have formed a tight friendship by this point, whereby Sherritt affirms that no one has ever had such an influence on him as Hare has, and the older man confesses himself thrilled to hear it. But is Aaron Sherritt totally trustworthy?

One night after Hare has returned from a patrol, he and Sherritt are sitting together, talking as they do many evenings, when Hare puts forth an interesting proposition. 'Well, Aaron, I feel sure you will get the reward offered for the Kellys,' Hare says, referring to the £8000 sum currently on offer. 'Supposing you do get it, what will you do with it?'

'I should like to have a few mares . . . and a nice farm.'

Goodo. Hare says that if Aaron does get such riches, he should 'get a respectable girl, marry her, leave all [your] old associates, and begin life again amongst new people'.

Sherritt agrees, with one qualification, as he simply knows himself too well. 'Mr Hare,' he says, 'do you think, if you got me the best mares you could buy, and got me the best entire horse you could purchase, that I could withstand the temptation of taking my neighbour's horses and selling them? No, I could not, no more than fly.'[79]

The two keep talking in the almost paternal/filial fashion to which they have become accustomed, and Sherritt now asks Hare for advice on taking up with another young woman, and even becoming engaged to her.

Kate Kelly.

There is no doubt the near sixteen-year-old is a beauty, with a happy nature, at least around her family – 'always bright and cheerful', her mother would later describe her, 'just like a sunbeam about the house'.[80] In the wider world, as described in the *Benalla Standard*, 'Kate is a girl of medium height and nice lithe form, she is good-looking, with wild, dark eyes, with which she seems to speak more than with her tongue, for she uses the latter organ but little . . .'[81]

For Hare, the benefits of having Aaron inside the Kelly household are enormous, and so he certainly does not dissuade him, though it proves to be a very difficult exercise from the moment that Maggie Skillion takes a set against him. Likely sensing Aaron for what he is, and perhaps having talked to Mrs Byrne, Maggie does not want him about the place at Eleven Mile Creek, even if the delectable Kate does seem to take a shine to him. One night, when Maggie leaves him and Kate alone in the house while she goes to see a friend, she comes back to find that Aaron has induced Kate to go for a walk, so Maggie goes to see the Oxley Police, to complain about him.

The police, in turn, take it seriously enough that a constable is dispatched to talk to Aaron, who bolts at the very sight of him, pursued by the constable, who even draws his revolver and fires a couple of shots in an effort to bring him down. After all, if he is running, he must be guilty of something, surely? By the following day, a shaken Sherritt is in Beechworth with Detective Ward and begging him to send a wire to Hare, to ask him to come to Beechworth immediately, as he is, 'afraid of being arrested by the police'.[82]

Hare sorts it out, as he always does, and Sherritt appears grateful, as he always is.

It is not just Aaron that Maggie has a set against, however, and typically, she – ably assisted by Kate – continues to do everything possible to make life as difficult as possible for the constables watching them. Oh, they know the constables are there all right, and every night before bed the sisters come out of the house, gather in the dogs and go on a large circuit of the house to work out just exactly where the policemen are. It is a frequent occurrence for the dogs to find the constables, whereupon they bark, bare their fangs and generally put the fear of God into them until such time as the women leisurely come up to call them off.

'It appeared,' Francis Hare would note, 'as if the dogs knew the police were their natural enemies.'[83]

To try to counter this, Hare has his men carry poisoned baits, which they drop at spots around Maggie Skillion's house – a small slab hut, with pitched roof lined with stringybark, dirt floor and stone-lined fireplace on a selection just off the Greta Road – but the sisters quickly solve that problem too, as the dogs almost as quickly show up with muzzles on.

And, of course, it is not just the Kelly sisters who need watching. For Steve Hart also has a sister and a brother constantly on the move, particularly older brother Dick, who is a leading figure in the Greta mob, while Joe Byrne has a couple of brothers and three sisters who are constantly sighted on horseback, heading to parts unknown, though the police keep track of them the best they can. It is *exhausting*.

—

High up in the Buffalo Ranges, some 50 miles east of Mansfield, the Kelly Gang are settling in for the winter, at a spot well above the snow-line. As a matter of fact, they are so high, and the winter is so cold, that, as Ned would later explain, sometimes he and his Gang 'had to clear several feet of snow off a hut we lived in to prevent it falling in'.[84]

Tired of continually dodging patrols, and extremely wary of the unworldly powers of the black-trackers, Ned and Joe – who are effectively the commander and deputy commander of the gang – have decided the best thing is to withdraw for a time. Since the Jerilderie breakout, they have moved from hideout to hideout in the ranges, places whose very names give some clue as to their calibre and inaccessibility: Rats' Castle, Hurdle Creek and Gum Flat, to name a few. Now, however, they have decided to withdraw still further. After all, the gang have plenty of money, and they are almost as comfortable in the bush as in a hut, so why not? True, it is a little hard to be away from their friends and family, but, for the moment, better than that being hunted like wild dogs.

SECOND WEEK OF JUNE 1879, ODD GOINGS-ON KEEP GOING ON

Strange. Very strange. Now one of Hare's men reports on the strange trip taken to Melbourne by Maggie Skillion, Tom Lloyd and one of their young associates in his early twenties, described as 'beardless excepting a very small fair goatee, fresh complexion and wide awake'.[85]

Leaving Glenrowan Station on Friday 13 June,[86] they are closely followed all the way to Melbourne, where that night they are seen to check into the rather swish Robert Burns Hotel in Lonsdale Street, before splitting up the next morning. On the Saturday, Maggie and Tom do nothing much in particular – though they are noted to spend some time examining the monument to the lost explorers Burke and Wills – but the young man goes to the most famous gunsmith shop in Melbourne, Rosier's in Elizabeth Street.

Here, he tries to buy every Spencer-revolving-rifle cartridge in the shop – obviously perfect for the Spencer rifle taken from Sergeant Kennedy's party – as well as 200 Webley revolver cartridges and 200 Martini-Henry rifle cartridges. This seems to be a lot of ammunition, Rosier idly notes. (For while he is the chief supplier of guns and ammo to the Victoria Police Force, he rarely sells as much as this to individuals.) Yes, the fellow replies. He and his brother are shortly going over to New Zealand to do a spot of hunting for red deer. Well, Rosier tells the young man, he can only sell him six Spencer cartridges for the moment, 'as there has been a run on them since the Kelly murders'.

Indeed.

'This observation,' the police report would detail, 'seemed to disturb the nerves of the purchaser.'[87]

Nevertheless, the fellow takes the ammunition he has purchased and promises to come back on the Monday, when new supplies will be in. In the interim, of course, Rosier immediately reports the details of the conversation to the police, and so all is soon in readiness. And yet, though detectives are there on the Monday, waiting for the young man's return, he does not show and seems to have disappeared.

As to Tom Lloyd and Maggie Skillion, when they alight at Glenrowan Station on their return trip on the Monday, Sadleir's men – armed with warrants under the *Felons Apprehension Act* – pounce and quickly search their bags, together with the bags of another noted sympathiser who is also on the train. But there is nothing, and so they cannot be arrested. The ammunition has been purchased but it is has somehow disappeared. No doubt, it will make its way to the Kellys. What could they possibly be needing such firepower for? That is, apart from the obvious. Are the Kellys about to execute another outbreak?

17 JUNE 1879, PREMIER BERRY'S SHIP COMES IN

No sooner has the mail steamer RMS *Tanjoro* sailed into Port Phillip Bay just after seven o'clock on this cold Melbourne morning than it is met by the government steamer *Victoria*, carrying Sir Bryan O'Loghlen and other Ministry colleagues. Berry climbs on board the smaller vessel, greeting his colleagues jovially, as they are taken to the moorings at Queenscliff. Of course, Berry and O'Loghlen are soon in close consultation, exchanging news and views.

There is no hiding from O'Loghlen, at least, that Berry has returned essentially empty-handed from England – with not the slightest concession from the Imperial Government in terms of changing Victoria's constitution, so that the Legislative Council can be forced to release the lands from the hold of the squatters – but they will just have to make the best of it. And nor should the returning Premier be under any illusions as to just how hostile the anti-Berry press has been, most particularly as his return has loomed.

The Argus, for one, is horrified at Berry's sustained revolutionary stance and a fortnight earlier had recalled his reckless rhetoric at the meeting in Hamilton, where he had threatened bloodshed, the paper thundering that the inevitable effect of such talk might even be 'the "exact" parallel of that terrible conflict by which "the [Yankee] North killed slavery in the South"'.[88]

And yet, it is not as if Berry is without support from the people. When he lands at Queenscliff and then leaves by special train to Geelong, crowds greet him in both places, just as they do at Williamstown Junction and Footscray as he makes his triumphal return to Melbourne proper. He emerges at Spencer Street Station into the chilly evening air to be met by no fewer than six brass and drum and fife bands, and a throng of loud supporters heralding his return. After wading through the crowds, which stretch all the way up Collins Street – estimated at 20,000 strong – Berry hops into an open carriage with his colleagues. His is the first in a line of carriages that are, within minutes, 'starting off at a walking pace up Collins Street'[89] – regularly stopping as the crowd presses in close – surrounded by 'a torchlight procession and accompanied by rolling volleys of cheers'.[90]

After the slightly ailing but no less imposing Graham Berry has pushed his way through the crowd and up the steps of the Treasury, the torchbearers dutifully take up their position on either side of him as he turns around to address the crowd. Alas, the crowd presses in *so* strongly that the only way Berry can address them safely is to go upstairs and speak from the balcony of the Chief Secretary's Office, where his appearance is again met by booming applause.

'I feel deeply the compliment you have paid me tonight,' the Premier begins, 'as the representative of the colony of Victoria.' No, the Imperial Government has not agreed to anything yet, but Berry remains confident that, because of his submissions, 'a measure of reform will be assented to which will be satisfactory to the colony'. In the meantime, 'I again thank you for this mark of esteem and confidence, and I ask you not to rest until the battle we are engaged in has been won beyond a doubt.'[91] *(Cheers)*

Standing on the next balcony, watching his leader for the first time at such close range, the young Alfred Deakin – a Liberal who had taken up the largely rural seat of West Bourke during the leader's absence

– could not help but be impressed. 'It was a great homecoming, a real demonstration,' he was to recall. 'It marked the zenith of his career. His power was at that moment and for some time before and after actually despotic.'[92]

The Argus, of course, is happy to underplay the whole affair, sniffing in its columns the next day, 'As a spectacle the "procession" was infinitely inferior to the torchlight display given in honour of the Australian cricketers, and insignificant as compared with the annual fire brigades' demonstration.'[93] That paper will even sponsor massive torchlit processions of those associated with the landed elite through the streets of Melbourne, protesting against his rule. At least these are countered by equally large torchlit, pro-Berry, workingman processions sponsored by *The Age,* but there is no hiding the fact that Berry has become an enormously polarising figure. While the government is in a political war with the most powerful constituency in the land, because *of* the land, the people, the press and the police are all out of step with each other.

And yet, while Premier Berry is popular with most selectors for his stance on the issue, it is the very man his government is pursuing, Ned Kelly, who is the true hero of many battling selectors, most particularly in North-Eastern Victoria. For Ned is *out there,* don't you know! Humiliating the squatters' police, a better horseman than any of the troopers, a better bushman, a better shot, a leader of his people, demonstrating that the selectors don't have to just accept their lot – always a tiny one – but can actually take up arms and make a rise.

Oh, and don't the police know it. For if ever they have rows with any of the sympathisers, and there are said to be some 2000 in North-Eastern Victoria alone, they are quick with their response.

'I will tell Ned about you,' the selectors would threaten them to their face. 'He will make it hot for you some day . . .'[94]

It is never any of the other gang members who are referred to in this manner, just Ned, and most of the folk songs and poems that are written at this time have him as their focus.

Soon enough, the kids in the North-East 'congregate occasionally at street corners and elsewhere to sing ballads – hymns of triumph, as it were – in their praise',[95] and some are even reciting nursery rhymes about Ned!

Kelly is a bushranger,
Kelly is a thief;
Kelly came to our town,
His stay was very brief.
The police went to Kelly's place,
Kelly them had sold;
Kelly came to our Bank,
And stole a sack of gold.[96]

LATE JUNE 1879, BENALLA AND SURROUNDS, THE TORTOISE CATCHES THE HARE

On one late evening, Hare is with his men as they approach the small township of Glenrowan, which is little more than a railway station and crossing supported by a couple of hotels, a blacksmith's shop, a general store and a dozen modest dwellings, together with a small collection of tents for contract labourers at the nearby quarry. It is perched in the low hills that lie on the edge of the Warby Ranges, and its most prominent feature is Morgans Lookout, which stands imperiously above it – probably as close to imperious as Glenrowan will ever come.

At such places, Hare has found, getting across the railway gates is frequently a problem for the police, as many of the gatekeepers are in cahoots with the friends of the Kelly Gang. As it happens, this time, too, it takes a lot of calling before the keeper, Stationmaster John Stanistreet, does get up to open the gates – though there is no question but that this man is on their side. A formal, proper cove, exceedingly proud of being *the* Stationmaster, he is one of the old school. The police are soon on their way once more, striking out across the bush on their way to a spot in the Warby Ranges where they have been assured the Kellys are bound to be. As ever, however, they must be careful to be quiet near farmhouses for fear of signalling their presence, as, in the words of Hare, 'we looked upon every one as a sympathiser of the outlaws'.[97]

After four hours of hard travel, and now in the later of the wee hours of the morning, the constable who is guiding them tells them they are close, and so they dismount and walk the rest of the way, to get themselves in position outside the house just half an hour before daybreak.

Quietly, oh so quietly, Hare gives his instructions. While he remains at the front of the house with his three troopers, his sergeant is to take the other three around the back and await his signal – the Superintendent's hat waved on a rifle – upon daylight before they all make their approach. Quickly, quietly, the sergeant and his small group head off.

At last it is time, and Hare waves his hat, at which point all eight men from both sides rush to the house like dogs let off a leash.

When they arrive, it is Hare who knocks.

'Who's there?' a voice comes back.

'Police. Open the door.'

There is a small stirring, and shortly afterwards the door is indeed opened by a rough-looking character of middle years.

'Have you any strangers in your house?'

'I have,' the voice from inside says tremulously.

With this, all the troopers burst into the house uninvited, searching through every room, expecting to find the Kelly Gang, but . . . alas. There is one man who is known to be a Kelly sympathiser, but that is it. Just as has happened so many times before, the police search the haystack, the outbuildings and every other place they can think of, but there is no one. One more time, just as has happened so many times before, and doubtless will many times again, they are too late, or too early, or in the wrong place, or have simply followed a bad lead or a false trail set for them. It is dispiriting and worse.

On their way back to their camp, Hare and his men make an early start to get to a particular place belonging to a Kelly sympathiser, when, late in the morning, they come to a high fence, with the only way across being to jump it. All his men sail over with no problem and wait on the other side for Hare to do the same.

This, men, is how it is done.

Racing towards it, at the last second the horse suddenly refuses and Hare is lucky not to come off. No matter, Hare brings his horse around once more and charges at the fence so fast that the horse has no choice but to leap, and so it does, magnificently, sailing over with a tremendous spring.

Alas, as horse and rider come back to earth once more, 'something gave way in my back, just above my right hip, and the agony I went through that day was beyond anything I ever experienced'.[98]

It is so bad that, before long, Hare must send the men on without him, and the following day he returns to Euroa, and then back to Benalla, still in agony.

Upon arriving back at his base, he is quick to tell Captain Standish straight, 'The hardships I have gone through have affected my constitution. I am not fit to go out with the search party again, and I wish you to relieve me.'[99]

With enormous reluctance, Captain Standish realises it is time to call in 'Assistant Commissioner' *(cough)* Nicolson, the only man of sufficient rank he has on call to take over.

PART THREE

GLENROWAN

Chapter Eleven

NICOLSON TAKES OVER

At that time we could get little or no assistance from the inhabitants, and the people were all through the country in such a state of terror. Civility was shown us in every town in the district, but no information given. The people seemed to be more afraid of the Gang than confident in the police.

Assistant Commissioner Charles Hope Nicolson

3 JULY 1879, NICOLSON ASSERTS HIMSELF

The arrival of the Assistant Commissioner is a welcome one.

Superintendent Sadleir knows he will get along with Nicolson from the moment the one-time chief officer of the Detective Police walks through the door and Sadleir dares say to him, 'I hope to heaven you are not going to continue this fooling any longer with the search parties,' and Nicolson quickly replies, 'I have had enough of it.'[1]

Hooray!

In the words of Sadleir, Nicolson was 'by no means as brilliant in some respect as Hare, but he was an expert in dealing with criminals, an art that Hare knew nothing of; and he possessed a higher sense of duty without the element of self-seeking. The part he had now to play had become more difficult than before, for a considerable number of police had been withdrawn from the district against his judgment and mine.'[2]

This is not just the eighteen troopers who had left with Hare . . .[3]

For reasons of economy, in the endeavour to severely limit the budget put to the pursuit of the Kelly Gang, it has also been decided to withdraw the men of the Garrison Artillery from the banks. And even Captain Standish has returned to Melbourne, after finding that 'all the business in my office was being frightfully muddled, and that things were going wrong both in Melbourne and the country districts'.[4]

From the beginning, thus, Nicolson, who does not have '*carte blanche* for expenditure as Captain Standish had',[5] knows he must try a new approach, for it is obvious to him that not only are the troopers who remain under his command completely exhausted by endless days and nights roaming the wild bushlands, as well as staking out homes of relatives and sympathisers, but also that . . . all that effort has delivered not the slightest bit of success. Not *one* arrest! Not *one* confirmed sighting of the gang. In fact, for all that effort and extra expense, at the time Nicolson takes over, as he will be quick to note, Hare did 'not know if the Kellys were in Victoria'.[6]

He later put his view on the uselessness of the Hare approach in a strong letter to Captain Standish:

My own experience of active search in the ranges here, without something like precise information of the whereabouts of the Gang, is that it is worse than useless, and I am supported in this opinion by the experience of every officer whom I have spoken to on the subject. It is most costly and most harassing to men and horses, and, owing to the bush skill and wariness of the outlaws, and to the security afforded them by the nature of the country, and by the character of a large number of

> the inhabitants, it is the most unlikely mode to be attended with success.
>
> I believe it may be positively asserted of all the numerous search parties that were sent out at so much trouble and cost, no one connected with them went out or returned with a 'correct' notion of in what point of the compass the Kellys were secreted, or, in fact, whether they were in Victoria at all. Knowing this, it would have been folly on my part to have continued such a system.[7]

No, what is needed, in Nicolson's view, is pursuit of the model that he knows has already worked. For, as he later notes, 'How was Power arrested after being out two years, and costing the country £30,000, but by informers; and most of the notorious criminals have been arrested in this way.'[8]

From the beginning, this man whose whole background is as a detective undertakes to cultivate yet more informers throughout all of Kelly Country – paid for their trouble – who can keep their eyes peeled, their ears to the ground, and hopefully provide the crucial bit of information that will see the Kelly Gang captured. His basic idea is to use the resources that he has 'to secure places from outrage where there was treasure, so that the outlaws would be baffled in any attempt to replenish their coffers',[9] and make his troopers as well organised and as mobile as possible to react quickly to a breakout, but for the rest to rely on his spy network.

It is Nicolson's reckoning that by stopping the search parties and ramping up the agents he will be able to give the Kelly Gang the feeling that the police must think they have gone to Queensland, so encouraging them to emerge once more, at which point . . . his agents will pounce.

3 JULY 1879, THE LAST STRAW COMES WITH A STAMP UPON IT

Oh dear. On this day, the proprietor of the *Jerilderie Gazette* receives a letter, postmarked at Wangaratta:

> Mr Gill,
> You would oblige me very much if you sent me the statement of Ned Kelly. He is my brother, and I would like to see what he has to say of his life. I would be very thankful to you if you would send me the letter of Ned Kelly . . .
> Maggie Skillion[10]

When will this ever end? Since the time of the infernal visit of the Kelly Gang, the whole damned business of the letter has never ceased. Everywhere he goes, everywhere and always, all anyone ever wants to talk about is the whole Kelly affair, and what Ned Kelly had written. All when Gill doesn't even *have* the letter. And now this has come at a time when everyone has noted that Kelly's friend and now near relative Wild Wright – a brute of a man if ever he saw one – has been hanging around town. And worse . . .

As *The Ovens and Murray Advertiser* has already detailed, on receiving a cable from Jerilderie:

> Isaiah ('Wild') Wright . . . has been in . . . town since Monday, and is still there. During that time he has been locked up and fined 5s for being drunk and disorderly. On Thursday he was indulging in a heavy drinking bout, and behaving in a most disgraceful manner, calling out in the street, when there were no

> police within hearing, 'Hurrah for the Kellys!' He is accompanied by a similar character to himself.[11]

Something is clearly up, and Samuel Gill is taking no chances. He informs the authorities, and by Saturday 'a large reinforcement of police arrive . . . in anticipation of an attack by the Kelly Gang. Great uneasiness prevails.'[12]

MID-JULY 1879, LOVE BLOOMS IN BENALLA

Another who is very pleased with the arrival of Nicolson on the scene is Sub-Inspector Stanhope O'Connor. It is not that the Queenslander and Superintendent Hare have not got on, but certainly Hare has never embraced the use of the black-trackers the way O'Connor thought he should have.

As to Nicolson, he is at least far easier to warm to and, far more importantly, his wife's sister, Louisa Smith, is the most attractive woman O'Connor has ever met, something the dashing police officer is not long in expressing. And Louisa returns his ardour in kind. In fact, it is such a case of 'love at first sight',[13] and so powerfully do they both feel it, that within days of meeting they are quietly wed in Benalla. Not sure how the rest of the world might regard such a whirlwind romance culminating in a marriage, the O'Connors decide to keep their wedding secret for the moment and have a large, public one in February of the following year,[14] meantime living apart as Mr O'Connor and Miss Smith.

Captain Standish, for his part – and despite his own ill-disguised indiscretions – is appalled when he finds out about the subterfuge, and takes an even firmer set against O'Connor because of it.

The captain's antipathy, however, changes nothing. O'Connor and Nicolson are now married to daughters of the late Lord Mayor of Melbourne, John Thomas Smith, and their alliance is solid. The fact that a third sister is married to one of Melbourne's leading lawyers

– Thomas Prout Webb, of the exceedingly powerful and well-connected Prout Webb family – confirms that these two police officers have a voice within the Melbourne Establishment, and an alternative voice it is to the one long provided by the Captain Standish–Superintendent Hare axis.

16 SEPTEMBER 1879, BEECHWORTH, THINGS ARE QUIET . . . MAYBE A LITTLE TOO QUIET?

That, at least, seems to be the view of *The Ovens and Murray Advertiser* on this day, as it notes that by now most people seem to believe that the Kelly Gang have left the colony. After all, 'there is nothing apparent in Benalla, save the presence of Assistant Commissioner Nicolson, Inspector O'Connor and the black-trackers, to show that the pursuit of the Kelly Gang of outlaws has not been given up. We no longer have the marching and counter-marching of armed men, which at one time gave the town the appearance of a garrison settlement in a war country, and matters have settled down into a very humdrum condition . . . The murders of the police took place on the 26 October of last year, so that close upon twelve months have elapsed. During that time it is not pretended that the Gang have ever been seen by the police, and now that the pursuit has slackened, it does not appear that they will ever be.'[15]

END OF 1879, NICOLSON AND WARD SPY WITH THEIR LITTLE SPIES

It does not take long for Nicolson, with the zealous help of Detective Ward, to rally up no fewer than thirty-two agents, providing a constant flow of rumours, purported sightings, tips and general gossip, as well as news of the movements and activities of Kelly sympathisers. All the agents are given a regular stipend of a few shillings a day, with extra money given for valuable tips, and all have code names.

One, for example, a local Greta schoolteacher by the name of Daniel

Kennedy, goes by the sobriquet of both 'Denny' and the 'Diseased Stock Agent'. As a man dealing with dozens of the families of the pupils in his school, Kennedy is well connected throughout his district and is able to pass a constant stream of information: 'the talk and family gossip of the place came to him without seeking; he moved about without suspicion even amongst persons who favoured the Kellys'.[16] Further adding to his value is that he is the brother-in-law of the local Greta Victorian Hotel publican, Bridget O'Brien, and since the death of her husband, Laurence, he has been helping to run this very establishment, where many of the sympathisers congregate and talk of Kelly affairs.

As to the latter of his curious code names, it originates from the fact that he chooses to call the Kelly Gang 'Diseased Stock', and in his reports refers to just where the diseased stock might be likely to be found, what he has heard about their activities, and so on.

Another to whom Detective Michael Ward speaks shows promise. In the absence of her husband, who has gone to work on the distant railways in Gippsland, Ann Jones has run the Glenrowan Inn on her own for the last year and seems sympathetic to the cause of the police, most particularly when Ward points out that the three police killed had been his intimate friends. But would the plump, buxom and garrulous Mrs Jones – a mature barmaid of the old school – help to find the information they needed to locate the gang?

'You can have the money,' Ward entices, twirling his waxed moustache all the while, 'and I would have the credit for capturing them.'[17]

In response, Ann Jones waxes cooperation. She says that, though she has no knowledge of where the gang are, and it is unlikely they will come to her inn, she will certainly keep her eyes and ears open, and let Ward know if she can find out anything as to their whereabouts.

Sometimes, as in the case of George Stephens – the former policeman who had been among those taken prisoner at Faithfull's Creek Station, Euroa – the informants come to the authorities. Stephens travels to Benalla, seeks an appointment with Assistant Commissioner Nicolson and soon does a deal, under the supervision of Detective Ward, whereby he is to 'go out and try to come across the Kellys'.[18] He is to be paid six shillings a day, plus whatever expenses he incurs.

As to Aaron Sherritt, whose code name is 'Moses', Detective Ward regularly meets him in the evening at around eight o'clock, at a rocky gorge into which a waterfall pours, about two miles from Sherritt's shack. Always before talking, the two descend to the bottom of the gorge and sit by the cascade so that whatever they say to each other can only be heard by leaning in close. As ever, Aaron is insistent on one particular thing: whatever happens, the life of his friend Joe Byrne must be spared. Detective Ward promises to do that, and equally listens to what Aaron has to say about the gang's movements. But . . . truthfully? Ward has not changed his view from the first: he believes Aaron's tips are worthless. But what he might be useful for, however, is as *bait*. Let the Kelly Gang think he is a real threat, and they just might emerge from cover to deal with him. Keep talking, Aaron, just keep talking . . .

Yet another informant is Ned and Dan's uncle, Patrick Quinn, who, despite his dubious past, once again agrees to pass on whatever he hears, and his code name is Foote.

And yet, while the police are indeed developing their network of spies, so too are they suffering casualties among their own numbers, none more notable than Inspector Brooke Smith. In the words of Assistant Commissioner Nicolson to Captain Standish in mid-November, begging for the senior Wangaratta Police officer to be relieved of duty, 'his appearance is wretched, and his memory apparently much gone. He seems to go about muttering and speaking incoherently about the Kellys, &c. He evidently has broken down in mind . . . It appears to me that the Kelly business has preyed upon Brooke Smith's mind, and that he requires a change and medical attention and relief from duty for some time.'[19]

It is done quickly, and few are sorry to see him go.

EARLY DECEMBER 1879, NICOLSON THROWS ANOTHER CAVE PARTY

With the buzz of cicadas drifting through the air, heralding the beautiful summer months of the North-East, Nicolson and Ward continue to nurture their blossoming network. Aaron Sherritt insists upon rumours of the 'appearance of one of the outlaws . . . sometimes singly and sometimes in couples' around the district, and even that Byrne still occasionally visits his mother. Having learned of Hare's cave party the previous summer, Nicolson reckons that, with the district in a lull, and the gang at ease, the same tactic might actually work this time.

So it is that, on the first day of summer, he sends four men to move into a cave 'thoroughly secret . . . away in the centre of rocks and stones'[20] above Mrs Byrne's house. Just as it had been with the first cave party, from this daytime hideaway the men are instructed to come down the hill each night before midnight and meet up with Sherritt, 'and take up positions apart from each other, to surprise the outlaws if they should attempt to visit that house'.[21] And then they would head back to their cave before daylight, with one man put on watch while the others gobble and gulp down the provisions provided by Paddy Allen (it seems there is a lot more whiskey on the order these days!) and then sleep. The result?

Nothing.

24 DECEMBER 1879, ONCE AN OUTLAW, ALWAYS AN OUTLAW

Look, the *Supplement to the Victoria Government Gazette* is not really a hold-the-front-page type of publication. But this morning it does carry an item of some significance, concerning the *Expiring Laws Continuance Act 1879*, which affirms that, 'The Acts mentioned in column one of the Schedule to this Act shall be and the same are hereby continued in full force and effect until the end of the next session of Parliament . . .'[22]

And right there in column one, sitting on the last rung, right under the *Diseases in Vines Act 1877*, is Act No. 612, the *Felons Apprehension Act*.[23] Enshrined in law, it means that the Kelly Gang, whom nobody thought would remain at large for so long, are still outlaws, ripe for the wild hunt . . . at least until the next Session of Parliament ends.

BOXING DAY 1879, AARON SHERRITT SHOWS THEM ALL

Life after the departure of Superintendent Hare has been more difficult for Aaron Sherritt.

Most troublesome has been the fact that his friendship with both the Byrne family and the Kellys has completely collapsed. Yes, he had tried his luck with the gorgeous Kate Kelly, and she had shown some interest, but things had become terribly complicated when Aaron's enthusiasm for dealing in stolen horses had seen him sell one to Maggie Skillion, only for her to find that it had been stolen from . . . Aaron's former fiancée, Catherine Byrne. There had been hell to pay, of course, and Mrs Byrne had threatened to have him put in prison for five years. In court, she had even given testimony, 'We had a falling out about his giving the police assistance . . . I . . . thought that Sherritt was giving assistance to the police in the pursuit of the bushrangers.'[24]

Yes, Kate Kelly had even turned up at his court case – meaning she must have had some feeling for him, right? – but, though with the help of his friends in the police Sherritt was finally discharged, he has rarely seen her since, and has taken up with the daughter of a well-respected farmer from the Woolshed: fifteen-year-old Ellen Barry (nicknamed Belle), daughter of Edmund and Ellen Barry. Typically of this young man, he had moved fast. So fast that just two spare months after stepping out with Belle, on this very day, Father Tierney presides as Aaron marries his already pregnant bride in Beechworth. Given that Belle is Catholic, and Aaron is Protestant, their marriage is celebrated '"behind the altar", in the austere parlour of Father Tierney's presbytery, beside St Joseph's Church'.[25] After moving in with her parents for a short time, in early March they move into an abandoned miner's hut in Aaron's old stomping ground, between the Woolshed and Sebastopol. It is not much, just a weatherboard place of two rooms beneath a shingle roof, but it will do.

The best thing? Aaron doesn't have to work too hard, as he is still on the pay of seven shillings a day as a police informant, allowing him to live in a manner that in part justifies his naturally arrogant manner. And in fact his relationship with the police is still so tight that for the first eight weeks or so of 1880, four troopers move first into some caves where they can watch the Sherritt hut by day and by night, and then they move into the back bedroom of the hut itself. Still the Kelly Gang do not come near him, however.

28 FEBRUARY 1880, VICTORIAN MEN VOTE TO REMOVE THE BERRY BLIGHT

It is all but over and Graham Berry knows it. He has done what he can since returning from London in June the previous year, but by now his majority has slowly crumbled along with his popularity on the streets. After a third and final push in December to pass a bill to amend the Constitution, he had missed out by one vote to gain the necessary two-thirds in an Assembly that had once staunchly been in his favour. His visions of a fine Victoria for the workingman have not been realised, and now even those workingmen are turning against him. As the male population of Victoria go to the polls in the General Election on this fine Saturday morning, there is little doubt the conservatives will form the next government.

5 MARCH 1880, A MERRY DAY AT THE MOYHU RACES

I tell you, it is as if the Lord Himself has smiled upon us.

For despite the fact that on this most important day of the year on the local calendar, the day of the mighty Moyhu Races – renowned as the best annual racing meeting in the whole of North-Eastern Victoria – the rain has fallen so heavily from dawn that it has looked like the meeting might have to be postponed, at mid-morning the teeming rain suddenly turns to pitter-patter petering out.

And then, as would be described by the correspondent for *The Ovens and Murray Advertiser*, 'The rain clouds vanished, and sunshine flooded the scene; and all went merrily as the sounds of marriage-bells ushering in a bridal day . . .'[26]

Among those coming from far and wide are many of the women

from the Kelly family, and in the fourth race of the day, in early afternoon, the Ladies' Hack Race, these women come to the fore. For who should come first, second and third? Why, none other than Miss Bridget Lloyd – the fiancée of one Wild Wright – Mrs Maggie Skillion and Miss Kate Lloyd. Of course, none of them is riding the way ladies are meant to ride, side-saddle, and there has been some ill comment seeing women with their legs straddling their beasts the way men do it, but that is forgotten at the sight of their extraordinary skill.

'The ladies are to be praised highly for their judicious riding,' *The Ovens and Murray Advertiser* correspondent reports. 'They sat with graceful and firm seats low in their saddles, and handled their respective nags better than many paid jocks that we have seen, riding all over their horses. The fair winner and her competitors were loudly cheered on the finish of the race.'[27]

And yet, this is still far from the most noteworthy thing about the day when it comes to the Kellys. For what attracts most comment is that there, watching the crowd, are most of the Kelly clan, including, as the writer for *The Ovens and Murray Advertiser* notes, a particularly familiar face.

There he is. Right beside his sister Kate Kelly is 'Mr Dan Kelly, splendidly mounted on a bay thoroughbred horse, [who had] gaily escorted his sisters and cousins to the course . . . and is keeping a good look-out that none of the police, or others likely to betray her brother's presence, got a chance of coming near him. He remained near a thickly timbered corner of the course, where his female relatives joined him, and whence he could enjoy the races without danger of being surrounded by those who would desire his capture. I have also been informed that others of the outlaws were in close vicinity to the course. The faithfulness of men and women to those men is something wonderful. £8000 reward fails to induce those who are in the secret to reveal their concealed rendezvous.'[28]

The report of this correspondent does not go unremarked. For, as the Melbourne correspondent of the *Bendigo Advertiser* reports, 'So little interest seems to be taken in the Kellys now that an account of the proceedings of some of the family which appeared in a recent number of *The Ovens and Murray Advertiser*, and which a year ago would have been flashed to every township in the colony, seems to have passed almost entirely without notice.'[29]

And it is true that a lot of the sting seems to have gone out of the hunt, even at the highest of levels. A frequent complaint of John Sadleir to Stanhope O'Connor is that, 'I can never get two minutes' conversation with Captain Standish upon Kelly business. The moment I begin to talk upon the subject, Captain Standish takes up a novel and commences to read.'[30]

At least part of the problem is identified by *The Argus*, in its edition of 5 March 1880, the day of the Moyhu Races: 'It is well-known that owing to the bungling – if not worse – of the late Ministry, the finances of the country are in the utmost confusion. The muddle, according to the scanty information that has oozed out from time to time, must be something extraordinary.'[31]

And nobody is more aware of the state of public finances than the newly elected Premier of Victoria. For even as the Moyhu Races are in full swing, Graham Berry officially retires after 1020 days in office, to make way for the weak Conservative Ministry under Premier James Service. Unlike Berry, Service chooses not to take on the additional role of Chief Secretary. Instead, he appoints to the position thirty-eight-year-old Robert Ramsay, a conservative University of Melbourne Law graduate who has represented East Bourke in the Legislative Assembly since 1870. As Chief Secretary, of course, Ramsay is in charge of Victoria's Police. So now Captain Standish has a new boss, and the efficient and pragmatic Ramsay takes the immediate lead in trying to cut costs and bring the Kelly matter to an end.

Ramsay's first step is to begin consultations with Captain Standish as to how hunting the Kellys might be better done. For his part, Standish is in no doubt where the problem lies and is quick to point it out: Nicolson. The so-called Assistant Commissioner is simply not up to it, he says, and his whole network of informers is a farce.

As Captain Standish would later recount, 'Mr Nicolson used to say to me on every possible occasion, "I have the outlaws surrounded by my spies, and have my hands upon them. It is not a chase of months or weeks, but of days and hours." That was his favourite utterance . . .'[32]

One thing the two agree to do is to give notice that the £8000 reward for the capture of the Kelly Gang will soon be withdrawn. This, it is hoped, might encourage those who do have information to come forward immediately or lose their chances at fabulous riches.

MID-MARCH 1880, THE KELLY GANG COME UP WITH A PLAN

For all the rare days of joy like the one at the Moyhu Races, the truth remains for the Kelly Gang that, in other parts of their lives on the run, living in the Warby Ranges and other hideaways throughout Kelly Country, things are beginning to tighten. The continued presence of the Queensland black-trackers means the gang must remain circumspect in their movements, and they are aware, of course, of the network of informers out there, watching for them. The other sobering reality is that their money from the raids on the Euroa and Jerilderie banks is now all but gone, meaning that they can no longer help to finance the most important of their sympathisers. All put together, it means they must take action, and, typically, Ned and Joe have been working on a plan, which they now start to refine. It is a plan shocking in its daring, for its innovation, for the fact that nothing remotely like it has ever been attempted, but both men remain confident that if anyone can pull it off, they can . . .

22 MARCH 1880, ON A FARM JUST OUTSIDE GRETA, SOMETHING IS MISSING

Now there is an odd thing. On this morning, an old Greta farmer by the name of Sinclair has just finished his bacon and eggs for breakfast and gone out to get ready to plough the bottom paddock, the one still filled with the wretched roots, when he notices it: the iron mouldboard of his plough has, strangely, gone missing in the night.

Strange, very strange. Farmer Sinclair has had robberies before, and has lost everything from horses to tools, and suffered straight-out theft of money, but no one has ever come and taken the mouldboard off his plough before.

Stranger still, it soon turns out that Sinclair is not the only one to find something amiss. For Sinclair's report to the police is soon followed by similar reports from another four farmers in the rough bush triangle carved by the Glenrowan, Greta and Oxley area. Always the same: in the night, someone has come and taken either one or several mouldboards from their plough.

What the blazes is going on?

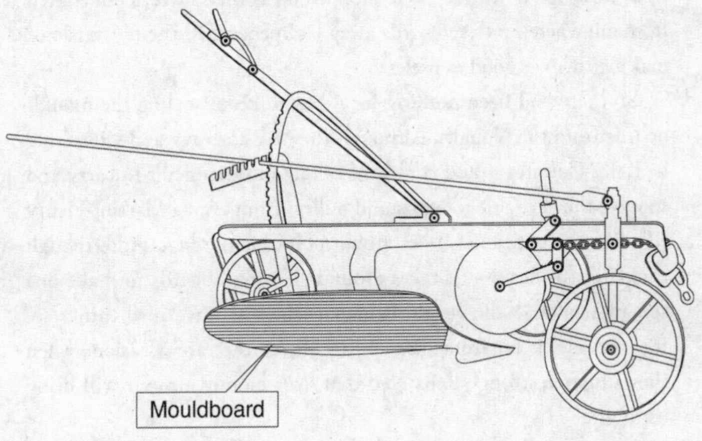

—

The blaze from the bush forge is a wonder to behold. Built beside a creek and fired by wood rather than coal, it throws out such a roaring, throbbing heat there is not butterfly nor even sparrow within at least 50 yards in any direction. Carefully now, using long, iron tongs, the purloined plough mouldboards are buried among the burning coals until they become red-hot themselves, at which point they are quickly removed and placed across freshly felled heavy green logs above the bubbling creek which helps muffle the sound for what comes next. Now, the logs must serve as anvils, as the mouldboards begin to be beaten into the shape of a man's torso and, eventually, riveted together.

Slowly, slowly, after significant experimentation, the first part of Ned's plan literally starts to take shape before their eyes, and by their own hands – even though there had been problems at first.

For the first version of the armour, thick boiler-plate, had been found far too heavy to wear, and so other, lighter materials – such as India-rubber, circular saws and chain mail – had been tested, but there had always been a key problem. They could not withstand bullets fired from close up. When they were propped up against a tree, a bullet fired from anywhere up to ten yards away had penetrated the test versions, making them as good as useless.

So there had been nothing for it but to keep stealing the mouldboards from the ploughs. Although they are as heavy as a wintry fog in Kelly Country – and commensurately more difficult to carry and shape – they are able to withstand bullets from even a Martini-Henry rifle like the police use, from all but point-blank range. And, though they are still heavy – it takes around six mouldboards to make one suit of armour – the weight is manageable. At least, Ned thinks so. Joe, for one, is far from sure and in one of the rare occasions when they disagree strongly tells Ned that 'this bloody armour will bring us to grief'.[33]

But Ned insists, and that is the end of it.

So it is that, deep in the bush, for days, nights and weeks on end, the bush furnace roars, and the mouldboards take shape, all with the swinging hammers of several sympathiser smithies and the bushrangers themselves. Matching helmets are formed similarly, albeit over and then around a much smaller log, which can then be cut to free the helmet.

It is long, painstaking work – perspiration from the furrowed brow of the man with the hammer cascades onto the metal, only to instantly *ssssst* into oblivion – but there is no complaint. It is all too likely a matter of life and death, their own, that the bushrangers get it right, and so the work goes on, including stealing more mouldboards, though some are supplied by sympathisers. Each piece of armour is made to measure for each member of the gang – from Ned, the largest at nigh on six foot for thirteen and a half stone, to the smallest, Steve, at five foot seven and ten stone – and consists fundamentally of a large breastplate to cover the front part of the torso, curving round to meet a back plate. A lappet hanging from the breastplate protects the groin and goes down to the knees, while a helmet protects the head. The suit made for Ned also has two narrow plates that protect his upper-arms down to his elbows. Also made is a back lappet hanging from his back plate to protect his hindquarters – to thwart those who would shoot his arse off – but this is abandoned as too heavy even for Ned, and impossible to use when riding a horse.

APRIL 1880, SOMETHING STRANGE IS GOING ON IN KELLY COUNTRY

Senior Constable John Kelly from Benalla is stumped. For the life of him, he cannot work out what is behind the theft of all these mouldboards, and it is not as if he has not put considerable effort into it. This has included taking out a couple of the Queensland black-trackers to try to follow the tracks of the thieves.

Though this has not proved successful, as the tracks always lead to a creek or river where the trail is soon lost – whoever it is having likely re-emerged miles up or downstream on a rocky surface – the one bit of information that does come back that intrigues this Kelly is that one of the thieves has a remarkably small boot print for a grown man, one with what is known as a 'larrikin heel', the long, sharp protuberance on their boots that always makes a deep imprint.

The remarkably small feet matches one of the things known about Ned Kelly, while both Ned and his gang are also said to have a streak of flashiness about them, displaying their ill-gotten gains by wearing boots boasting exactly that kind of heel. And so, put together with the fact that there have been reports of them in the area, it likely really *is* the Kelly Gang! But as to what they would be using the mouldboards for, Senior Constable Kelly does not pretend to have the first clue. And nor, frankly, do he and other police feel they'll be able to find out very easily, as always in Kelly Country they feel like 'foreign troops in a hostile country'.[34]

Meanwhile, other troubling reports are coming in to Assistant Commissioner Nicolson. Something is going on up Glenrowan way, where known Kelly sympathisers are said to be congregating like fleas on a mangy dog, in and about Ann Jones's Glenrowan Inn. The first report had been tendered by one of Detective Ward's informers, a railway porter at Glenrowan, who had passed a message saying, 'Ettie Hart, sister of the outlaw, at Mrs Jones's Hotel, visited by sympathisers, but no sign of outlaws.'[35]

And it has gone on from there. Something is stirring up that way, where more and more of the Greta mob are showing up and hanging around the Glenrowan Inn, which seems strange, as the usual sympathiser centre in that town is McDonnell's Hotel, across the other side of the line. And they're not hiding their lights under a bushel, either. Soon, there is no need for spy reports, as even the local Benalla paper reports there is 'riotous conduct' going on at the hotel.[36]

It is not that those sympathisers are doing anything illegal, per se, beyond spending money like drunken sailors; it is just that when whole platoons of people on the side of the Kellys are gathering in the one place at the one time it is simply troubling. And this gathering of Kelly sympathisers seems to get stronger every day, as if, somehow, this inn has become a magnet for every Kelly sympathiser in all of Kelly Country.

Even Dick Hart, Steve Hart's older brother, has been seen there. One informer has it that, on the night of 14 April, Dick Hart had been seen to leave the Glenrowan Inn for two hours and head off into the darkness for a rendezvous unknown, before returning. The next night, he had gone out, cracked his stockwhip loudly three times, as if sending a signal, and then gone back inside . . . Three days later, a report comes in from an agent by the code name of 'Renwick' that Steve Hart's eighteen-year-old sister, Ettie, is particularly notable at Glenrowan and has been there for several weeks. This is intriguing. A beautiful young woman, she is said to be Ned's sweetheart – there is even one dubious report that they have become married. And yet another report has it that 'the McAuliffes, Lloyd and other sympathisers at Mrs Jones are rowdy, especially to strangers'.[37]

Meanwhile, in recent times, Sergeant Whelan had been distressed to report to his superiors that one of his contacts had been in Benalla's general store, 'when Mrs Skillion and her sister Kate purchased about seven pounds worth of goods, consisting of groceries, potted fish, and four bottles of grog. He states that he has no doubt but the sisters and the McAuliffes are supplying the Gang with all their provisions.'[38]

It is in response to such reports that Nicolson makes a key move. Though the Greta Police Station had been closed six months earlier, as it had been judged too dangerous to maintain such an isolated outpost surrounded by selections of Kelly sympathisers, Nicolson had organised the previous November for a station to open at Glenrowan, in the police barracks that he has established in a large building next to the post office.[39] It was much better positioned, in any case, than the Greta station, as it was right by the telegraph and the railway lines. What is more, in the wake of all the activity of late in that town, Nicolson has already organised for one of his best men, Constable Hugh Bracken, to take over from 13 May and be in charge of four troopers. Bracken, with his pregnant wife, Amelia, and two-year-old son, can live in separate quarters in the same barracks. It will be for these police at Glenrowan to take over all the tasks previously conducted by those at Greta, including providing a watch at night over Maggie Skillion's place, four miles away, just down from the Kelly hut.

Now there is a strong sense that, if so many of the sympathisers are at Glenrowan, then surely the Kelly Gang themselves can't be too far away – but where? There has been so little sign of them around Mrs Byrne's place that the four troopers who had been placed in the cave above the Woolshed Valley four months before are withdrawn from

1 April. As to Glenrowan, it is surrounded by such thick and impenetrable bush that it is anyone's guess just where the gang are, and, even if you could know, who actually wants to go in and get them? The murders at Stringybark Creek stand as a stark warning as to what happens to those who try to take on the Kellys on their turf.

For the moment, that is where it is left, as a period of uneasy calm settles over the whole matter of the Kelly Gang. While the police of both New South Wales and Victoria have proved themselves incapable of finding the Kellys in the wild and mountainous bushland they have made their home, so, too, have the gang been stymied from continuing their spate of robberies in distant outposts, as now all banks have taken precautions against such as them, and security has been strengthened.

And yet, such is the nature of this and all impasses that it cannot last . . .

21 APRIL 1880, A BLACK MOURNING IN MANSFIELD

It has taken nigh on eighteen months, but now, at last, the monument in memory of the three murdered policemen is paid for by public subscription, built in the middle of town, standing in the centre of the junction of High and Highett Streets, and now ready to be unveiled.

And, yes, though it seems the heavens themselves have been weeping for days now, on this, the morning of the ceremony, the rain miraculously stops, as a visibly moved Captain Standish steps forward before the gathering of 200 people, which includes the Chief Secretary of Victoria, Robert Ramsay. As Standish pulls aside the cloth that envelops the base, for the first time all can get a look at the whole monument, which sombrely bears the inscription:

To the Memory
of the
THREE BRAVE MEN

WHO LOST THEIR LIVES WHILE ENDEAVOURING TO CAPTURE A BAND OF ARMED CRIMINALS *IN THE WOMBAT RANGES.*
NEAR MANSFIELD, 26TH OCTOBER, 1878.
IN MEMORIAM OF MICHAEL KENNEDY, BORN AT WESTMEATH, IRELAND, AGED 36 YEARS; THOMAS LONIGAN, BORN AT SLIGO, IRELAND, AGED 34 YEARS; MICHAEL SCANLAN, BORN AT KERRY, IRELAND, AGED 35 YEARS.[40]

LATE APRIL 1880, STANDISH MAKES A STAND

Chief Secretary Ramsay is more than usually unhappy on this crisp Melbourne morning – which for a frequently sick, strictly Presbyterian and strongly conservative Scotsman is saying something. When he had taken up his present position nearly two months earlier, he had made it known that his major priority was to capture the Kellys. And here we are, two months later and they are *still* on the loose. So free and easy, they are even turning up at country race meetings!

Here and now, in the office of the Chief Secretary, Captain Standish once again identifies the problem for him: Nicolson. 'Nothing is being done now,' Standish tells him, 'and beyond employing unreliable spies, I do not see what good Mr Nicolson will ever effect.'[41] Standish feels it is time to make a replacement for Nicolson, and the Chief Secretary agrees.

LATE APRIL 1880, LANCEFIELD, AND SO THE END FOR THE CROOKED CONSTABLE

There is just no escaping it. On this day, Constable Alexander Wilson Fitzpatrick becomes simply Alex Fitzpatrick, as he is dismissed from the Victoria Police Force for being, in the words of Superintendent Chomley, 'a liar and larrikin'.[42] More, he is a 'perjurer and drunkard' who has 'associated with the lowest persons [in Lancefield], and could not be trusted out of sight and never did his duty'.[43]

Not even Captain Standish – who had pulled strings to get him into the force, on the advice of his friend Charles A. Smyth – tries to defend Fitzpatrick, officially recording his view that 'the Ex Constable's conduct during the time he was a member of the Force was generally bad and discreditable to the Force. I cannot hold out any hope of his ever being reinstated to the position of Constable in the Victoria Police.'[44]

And that is the end. The man on whose sole testimony Ellen Kelly had been gaoled – the very episode that lies at the base of the whole terrible saga – is now entirely discredited as a liar and perjurer without redemption.

LATE APRIL 1880, AT THE WOOLSHED, MRS BYRNE HAS WORDS

The more that Mrs Margret Byrne has thought about it, the more she has become convinced that Aaron Sherritt is a paid police informer, and has been all along – taking the filthy coin of the police in return for betraying his one-time best friend, her son Joe.

She feels it so strongly that, as she passes him on the track between their homes this morning, she cannot help herself. Glaring at him, she stops, leans forward and hisses, *'What would Joe think of you now?'*

Stung, stunned, Sherritt gathers himself and roars back, 'I'll shoot Joe Byrne and I'll f— him before his body gets cold!'[45]

30 APRIL 1880, MELBOURNE, THE DEAL IS DONE

Without preamble on this morning, Captain Standish tells his protégé, Superintendent Hare, that the Chief Secretary, Mr Ramsay, has taken the decision that he is to relieve Nicolson up in Benalla and resume his former post, in charge of the police pursuing the Kelly Gang.

In response, Francis Hare is underwhelmed. 'I have already tried my hand and failed,' he says, frankly.[46] 'There are officers senior to me, none of whom have been called upon to undertake the hardship and the responsibility that I had during my seven months there . . .!

The responsibility should fall on the senior officers.'[47]

And there is one other matter, which he raises delicately. He wants no repeat of the events surrounding the capture of Power a decade before. 'On the previous occasion I had been selected to undertake the duty that others had failed in, that my *senior* had failed in,' he says, 'I reaped no profit . . . Mr Nicolson and Mr Montfort had reaped the benefit of the capture, and I, who was directed to organize the whole affair, am still in the same position as I was then, notwithstanding the promises made . . .'[48] All these years on, he still only holds the rank of Superintendent, which he held then.

But Standish is adamant. 'It is no use saying anything about it, you will have to go.'[49]

Still not taking yes for an answer, Hare seeks a meeting with the Chief Secretary, and, when this is granted, he again puts his case. But the mind of the Chief Secretary is made up. 'Mr Hare,' he says, 'this Kelly business has been fully discussed by the Cabinet, and it is their unanimous decision that you should be sent up to take charge of affairs. I give you *carte blanche* to do whatever you think proper, and I leave you entirely untrammelled.'[50]

Hare cannot help feeling flattered in the confidence reposed in him and cedes. 'Very well, Mr Ramsay, if that is your decision, I suppose I must go.'[51]

3 MAY 1880, MELBOURNE, MATTERS START TO SORT THEMSELVES OUT

Assistant Commissioner Nicolson has not taken the news of his demotion well. His first response to Captain Standish had set the tone: 'What! Be relieved by that underling?'[52]

It is simply not right, and it is with this in mind that he has travelled from Benalla to personally express to Chief Secretary Ramsay, in the presence of Captain Standish, the reason for his view that he should be allowed to stay on. After all, after ten months of his labours, they are *just about* to capture the Kelly Gang.

In the face of the devastated Nicolson, Ramsay tries to explain that it is 'just a change, like in a game of cricket – a change of bowlers'.[53]

No, it is not, Nicolson responds. With great passion, he respectfully puts his view that this is a very wrong-headed approach, that there 'is very little analogy between the Kelly business and the game of cricket', and, what is more, this kind of change is nothing less than 'dangerous'.[54]

Nicolson begs to have leave to pursue the Kelly Gang for another month, swearing that, in that time, he can nab the bushrangers. For forty-five minutes, he continues to argue his case, though Captain Standish, for one, is not impressed, characterising it later as 'the most incoherent nonsense I ever heard in my life'.[55]

And yet, so passionate is Nicolson, so sure is he that the capture of the Kellys is just days away, that the Chief Secretary feels he has no choice but to allow him a month's grace. But Ramsay equally makes it clear that he will not be disposed to grant more. Nicolson must find the Kellys or move on.

Yes, sir, thank you, sir.

Though relieved, Nicolson leaves the meeting also quietly outraged. Once more, he is sure, his two great enemies, Captain Standish and Superintendent Hare, are moving in on him, standing in the wings to replace him just in time for the final triumph. This whole thing, he would later recount, was 'simply a second attempt . . . to deprive me of the credit of the work'.[56]

20 MAY 1880, ASSISTANT COMMISSIONER NICOLSON RECEIVES A LETTER THAT IS MORE THAN PASSING STRANGE

One of the Superintendent's informers, the cleverly named Diseased Stock Agent, appears to have come good. And yet what strange claims Daniel Kennedy is making:

> *Dear Sir –*
> *Nothing definite on the diseased stock of this*

locality. I have made careful inspection, but did find exact source of disease . . .

All others I have not been able to see. Missing portions of cultivators described as jackets are now being worked, and fit splendidly. Tested previous to using, and proof at 10 yards. I shall be in Wangaratta on Monday, before when I may learn how to treat the disease. I am perfectly satisfied that it is where last indicated, but in what region I can't discover. A break-out may be anticipated, as feed is getting very scarce. Five are now bad . . . Other animals are, I fear, diseased.[57]

Denny

For Nicolson, it does not take long to decipher the schoolteacher's basic code language. The 'disease' in question is the Kelly Gang; the fact that feed is low means he has heard that they are running out of money, and therefore might soon emerge to make another heist. And he also has the fear that more and more locals are getting involved in supporting the bushrangers.

Most intriguing, though, is his statement that, 'Missing portions of cultivators described as jackets are now being worked, and fit splendidly. Tested previous to using, and proof at 10 yards.' What is this? It would appear that Kennedy is making the claim that the gang are making for themselves some kind of metal jackets from the mouldboards of ploughs, and that they work against bullets fired from even as close as 10 yards. Could that possibly be?

Assistant Commissioner Nicolson doesn't quite dismiss it out of hand, but, as it happens, he is so busy trying to hold onto his job that within a couple of days he is on his way to Melbourne to plead for still *more* time from the Chief Secretary, and one way or another the lead is not pursued vigorously. For, in fact, under the circumstances, his whole energy for the exercise is dissipating. As he later recounts,

'I found it was no use my continuing going on with the prospect of being withdrawn at the end of the month . . .'[58]

What he does manage to do, however, when he arrives in Melbourne – despite Captain Standish's best efforts to stop it – is to have a meeting alone with the Chief Secretary in his private office in the early afternoon of 26 May.

'Captain Standish,' he tells Ramsay earnestly, 'is no authority on any matters of the kind that he has no practical experience in. At any rate, I cannot get him to attend to me ten minutes at a time – to sit down and talk over the Kelly business . . . It is a great pity, Chief Secretary, that before you decided to move me on, you did not consult me. Though I am Captain Standish's subordinate . . . I have been up there a considerable time, and I am an experienced officer, and I am a better authority on the matter than Captain Standish possibly could be.'[59]

Though he had not shown the 'diseased stock' letter to Captain Standish, he does show it to the Chief Secretary, who makes no comment worthy of note. What Robert Ramsay does say, however, is to the point: 'Mr Nicolson, supposing you were head of a department, and one of your subordinate officers came to me and abused you behind your back, what would you think?'[60] As to moving him on from his position, Ramsay does his best to explain. 'Well, you see, Mr Nicolson, having made all these arrangements with the head of the department, it is very difficult to alter them.'

Nicolson takes his leave, and, after a quick meeting with Sir James McCulloch, the former Victorian Premier with whom he'd worked in the Power hunt – asking him to put in a word with Ramsay on his behalf – he makes his way back to Spencer Street Railway Station, preparing to buy a ticket and head back to Benalla. Just as he is boarding at half past two, he is suddenly confronted by Captain Standish, who is blowing more steam than the locomotive. Standish hands him a telegram that has just come for him from Benalla, before opening up on him . . .

'I hear you have had an interview with Mr Ramsay,' he snarls, 'and you have been abusing me. I consider your conduct very disloyal.'

Nicolson smiles at the suggestion that *he* is the disloyal one, allowing Captain Standish to assert that Nicolson had conducted himself 'so violently in the meeting that Mr Ramsay had to check you'.[61]

'Never,' Nicolson replies, while jumping on the now departing train without a ticket.

'I believe Mr Ramsay!' Standish calls after him, as the train pulls away, effectively calling Nicolson a liar.

All up, it has not been a very fruitful trip, and Nicolson has little hope that he will continue to be allowed to pursue the Kellys. As Melbourne falls behind, however, he opens the telegram that has come from Superintendent John Sadleir. It contains stunning news, of something that had occurred that morning, at Mrs Sherritt's place.

MORNING, 26 MAY 1880, MRS SHERRITT RECEIVES A VISIT

Of course, Mrs Anne Sherritt loves all of her three sons and seven daughters, but there is no doubt which one is the most trouble to her: Aaron, her second boy. If only he could be like his elder brother, John, who is as solid as the day is long. Aaron . . . is not like that, and even beyond all the police trouble his sudden marriage to that young Catholic girl has troubled her more than somewhat.

But to the events at hand. The evening before, John, who had returned home to do some ploughing, had gone into Beechworth, and very early this morning the first thing Mrs Sherritt does is gently knock on his door, before poking her head into his room to see if he had returned. But, no, his bed is just as she had made it the previous morning.

Heading outside to check that all is as it should be – and following the sound of the bells she has put on the horses for this very purpose – she is just walking along the fence of a distant paddock when she suddenly sees a man with a bridle over his arm, who seems to be 'waiting to see who would come over for the horses'.[62] Instantly, she recognises him. It is Joe Byrne, the once-great friend of Aaron's.

No matter that Joe is an outlaw, hunted all over the country, with a reward of £2000 on his head. As soon as he sees Mrs Sherritt, he walks towards her, as friendly as you please, and the two chat, briefly, about news from the neighbourhood.

But then they get to the point.

'What are you doing here, Joe?' Mrs Sherritt asks.

'Looking for Aaron, to shoot him,' Joe Byrne replies casually.[63] And he also wants to shoot Detective Ward, while he's at it. He makes it clear that he knows that Aaron has been informing on the Kelly Gang, that he is in cahoots with Detective Ward, and that very soon a price will have to be paid for this treachery.

'We could go anywhere were it not for your sanguinary son there,' says Joe.[64] 'Because of him and Ward we have been near starved to death . . . Ward goes about the hills like a black-tracker. Once we have them two out of the way . . . we can go where we like once more.'[65]

'He has no harm,' Mrs Sherritt implores, 'he would not hurt you.'

But Joe will not be swayed. 'You need not try to impress that on my mind, because I tell you now that there was Ward and him and Hare very nearly twice catching us, and that tells you whether they will hurt me or not.'[66]

Mrs Sherritt begs, she pleads, but none of it impresses Joe Byrne. He is firm that that is what he intends to do, and shortly thereafter he takes his leave.

Teary and panicky, Mrs Sherritt soon presents herself at the Beechworth Police Station to report the whole episode to Detective Ward.

Joe Byrne? In this area just *a couple of hours ago*?

Ward quickly sends a cable to Superintendent Sadleir in Benalla, and later that very evening a very shaken Aaron Sherritt is meeting with Assistant Commissioner Nicolson, whose train has just arrived from Melbourne – accompanied by Superintendent Sadleir and Sub-Inspector O'Connor. Aaron begs the police not to go out after Joe Byrne for the moment as, firstly, he has already tried to follow the tracks himself, and tells them that the heavy rain has washed them away. More importantly, if the police pursue Byrne now, the outlaws would immediately know who had told the police, and they would 'come and murder me and my connections'.[67]

And yet, for some reason, Byrne has given warning of his next move. It is with this in mind that, in the coming days, Assistant Commissioner Nicolson instructs Detective Ward to gather three men and head up Woolshed way where Aaron Sherritt lives, to command a view of Mrs Byrne's house, and to 'keep a look out in that neighbourhood'.[68]

Nicolson then heads back to Benalla, where he keeps the telegraph open all day Sunday and has all his informers on high alert. Indeed, after word spreads of Joe Byrne being spotted shortly thereafter in a long gully at the back of his mother's house, Sadleir, O'Connor and Nicolson decide to head out for one final hoorah. The result? As ever – no result.

When Nicolson returns home from this last search party, it is time to go back to Melbourne.

—

For his part, much of Sherritt's braggadocio is simply gone. For, by now, Detective Ward's plan that the brash selector be known as a paid informer has worked so well it is all but universally known.

So much so that, a few days later, when Sherritt has to go to Benalla to give evidence on a case of Horse Stealing, he tells his wife before departure that, 'You will certainly not see me again alive . . . If you hear of me being shot by the Gang, all I desire is that you come down to Benalla and bury my remains quietly.'[69]

31 MAY 1880, ASSISTANT COMMISSIONER NICOLSON GETS THE WORD

And so it has come to this. After eleven months pursuing Ned Kelly, there is no escaping the point that, despite all the promises, Nicolson has *not* caught the bushranger, or his gang. It is to Nicolson's great chagrin and no little humiliation that he receives the order he has been expecting from Captain Standish:

> Mr Nicolson being aware that the Government has decided that he should be relieved from the special duty in connection with the outlaws, on which he has been engaged since July last, I beg to inform him that Mr Hare will proceed to Benalla on Wednesday the 2nd prox., to take charge . . .
> (Signed)
> F. C. STANDISH,
> Chief Commissioner of Police[70]

Of course, the news soon spreads to other police officers, including Superintendent John Sadleir, who is appalled but not surprised. As he would later note, when it came to Hare, Captain Standish's 'regard for him had become an infatuation, a mild form of insanity'.[71] Sadleir feels so strongly about it at the time, he writes to Hare, urging him not to take up the post. It makes no difference. Though disappointed at receiving Sadleir's letter, Hare undertakes to work closely with him regardless when he arrives at Benalla Police Station on 2 June.

One thing Hare makes clear from the first is that he wishes to get rid of the native black-trackers. He does not believe they are good for the pursuit, as the gang have hardly been spotted since they arrived, thinks them an affront to the Victoria Police and wishes them gone back to their native state. As he explains to Chief Secretary Ramsay, 'as long as they are in the district the outlaws will not show out',[72] whereas Hare wants the gang to do something so he may capture them. With this in mind, Hare arranges with Captain Standish for the trackers to leave as soon as their travel arrangements can be organised.

Privately, it is Sadleir's view that, 'as a rule, Hare looked forward to the Kellys being captured by the white police alone'.[73]

So be it. O'Connor, a shrewd operator, understands that that is the way it is going to be, and soon applies to the Queensland Government for permission to bring his trackers home – which will allow him, in the process, to take his gorgeous new bride home to Brisbane too.

The local press is less enthusiastic. When the move had first been mooted a fortnight earlier, at the behest of Captain Standish, the *Benalla Ensign* had strongly expressed its view:

> It is generally recognised that the fear of the tracking power of the Queensland 'boys' has been a strong deterrent of further crimes by the Gang – indeed the officers of police know as much. Once they are removed and on the sea journeying homeward, there is little doubt the Gang of outlaws will consider the coast clear and commit a fresh outrage, possibly with loss of life . . .[74]

Meanwhile, Hare quickly introduces many of his old stratagems, just as he renews his previous alliances, starting with his favourite, Aaron Sherritt. He finds Sherritt living in his two-roomed slab and bark hut near Sebastopol, right by the road from Eldorado, about six miles from Beechworth. In the time since the two have last seen each other, Aaron has married a very young woman, and quietly tells Hare there is some friction as his wife is a Catholic, while he is a Protestant, and their two families do not get on.

But the main thing is he is delighted at Superintendent Hare's return, as he simply did not get on as well with the 'crankie Scotchman'[75] as he does with Hare.[76] (Not surprising. Nicolson was never a believer in Sherritt, and would later say, 'What did Aaron ever do for the police? Nothing.')[77]

As to the Kelly Gang, well, now, that's interesting, Superintendent. For, just a fortnight earlier, they had been 'at my mother's house looking for my brother Jack, whom they wanted to join them',[78] and it had been on that basis that Assistant Commissioner Nicolson, at the behest of Detective Ward, had sent four constables to this very house in the hope the Kellys might appear, but those constables had disappeared with Assistant Commissioner Nicolson. If he may say, Superintendent, it would be as well to send them back?

Hare – as he so often does with Aaron – entirely agrees. In fact, his first order after visiting his favourite informer is to get four constables to go back to the Sherritts', with strict instructions that they should 'stay indoors all day and watch Mrs Byrne's house by night'.[79] Mrs Byrne, after all, lives just three-quarters of a mile away, and by having the police so based, they could cover two possible points of interest for the Kelly Gang at the one time.

(Madness in Sadleir's view. Keeping four troopers secreted in a two-room hut for weeks on end without anyone noticing? Nonsense. Sadleir argues strenuously against it but is overruled by the insistent Hare.)

In a similar fashion, Hare orders the Harts' house at Three Mile Creek to be watched by constables from Wangaratta and, most particularly, the house of Ned's sister, Maggie Skillion, to be watched by the constables from Glenrowan, who are now under the command of Constable Hugh Bracken in their newly established police station in that tiny town.

Hare's orders to all the troopers in these stations is uniform: 'After dark every night you are to leave your abode singly, and walk away to the watching place, so that if any of you should be met, no notice will be taken of a man walking alone. You are to take up your positions within view of the houses, but not near enough for the inmates to discover your whereabouts.'[80]

The one thing that Hare feels certain of as he renews his command is that the Kellys and their sympathisers are about. Everywhere he goes, he hears word that the sympathisers are on the move, and that something is about to happen, about to break. Horses are being reported as stolen all over the region, and more often than not the rumour mill points to the Kelly Gang as being responsible. So obvious is their presence that even Ann Jones, the quirky and rather capricious publican of the Glenrowan Inn, is wont to discuss the gang as if she is often in their company, expressing her fondness for them quite openly.

One evening, the newly arrived Constable Hugh Bracken is sitting in her establishment, rubbing shoulders with the landlady herself and with Julia Hart, Steve's sister. In the course of their conversation, which so often turns to the gang, Bracken remarks casually that it is 'a bad job that the bushrangers . . . shot the police. Were it not for so doing they would have the good wishes of the people more than they have'.[81]

Mrs Jones, even though she's an admirer of Sergeant Kennedy, gives a most unusual reply. 'If they were after shooting my own son,' she says, 'I could not help but like them.' She adds that, 'Joe Byrne is the nicest man that I've ever seen.'[82]

Having been in the district a while, Bracken is not surprised by this strong show of feeling for the gang, as they have for some time held a popular, nearly mystical sway among the loyal locals. It is not an easy force to tie down. But tie it down they must, as the feeling continues to grow that there will soon be another Kelly breakout.

One of Hare's acquaintances, who has been in touch with Mrs Byrne, even quietly passes on to Hare that the old woman has boasted that the outlaws are 'about to commence some outrages which [will] not only astonish Australia, but the whole world'.[83]

What on earth does *that* mean?

Hare has no idea, and he does not pursue it.

EARLY JUNE 1880, IN THE BUSH NEAR GRETA, FIRST AUSTRALIAN IRONMEN

It is all continuing to take shape. What had been merely a collection of plough mouldboards is now forming up into a collection of rounded suits of armour, a quarter of an inch thick, with the long breastplates internally joined by leather straps to the back guards. Ned's particular suit even has shoulder plates. Topping it all off, of course, are the pill-box helmets, which come complete with a long slit for the eyes.

There is some mirth when the bushrangers first try on the suits – for the effect is quite other-worldly – but there is something far more important than their look. For when they put Ned's armour – the first suit complete – up against a tree and fire at it from various ranges, it is to their great satisfaction they find that there is no penetration. Their riveted armour is bulletproof.

That is to the good. What is more difficult, however, is the sheer *weight* of the armour. Once fully fitted out, the normally thirteen-and-a-half-stone Ned suddenly weighs nigh on another seven stone. In an effort to make the massive weight a little more comfortable, Ned is careful to place padding sewn by his sisters Maggie and Kate inside the armour, so that its rougher inner points do not cut into his flesh. As to his helmet, he finds that, by wearing a skullcap with heavy padding inside, he is more easily able to take the strain. One thing is for sure: no man wearing one of these would be inclined to try to run away. For running is, of course, out of the question. No, this is armour uniquely designed for those who intend to make a *stand*, and maybe even a last stand at that.

Undoubtedly the best of the helmets is the one that has been made for Joe Byrne. In a clever design twist, a curve at the top of his visor reaches down almost to the bottom, covering the exposure of his nose and leaving his two piercing blue eyes staring out, rather like a bemused koala.

There remain significant problems, however, beside the sheer weight of the armour. The eye-slit in the helmet is so narrow, both vertically and laterally, that it is difficult to see anything that – or anyone *who* – is not straight in front of you. And then, even when you do see something, so cumbersome is the whole metal casing that one cannot easily bring a gun to bear on a target. Pulling up a rifle and looking down the barrel is all but impossible with one of these helmets on, and so revolvers become the preferred option – though, even then, the men find they can only shoot with any accuracy by holding the revolvers straight out in front and turning their bodies to the side.

As to the armour not covering all the body, further protection against those who will be trying to find the vulnerable points is provided by the men wearing bulky overcoats over the metal suits, so that just which parts are metal and which are not will be concealed. Besides, the gang decide, there is no doubt that with the coats on they look all the larger and more terrifying.

As well as organising the armour, again and again and again the gang go over the new plan they are forming. If they can pull this off

– and Ned and Joe have no doubt that they can – they are going to astonish not just the colony but the world!

EARLY JUNE 1880, AARON SHERRITT RECEIVES VISITORS, WELCOME AND UNWELCOME

Good evening, Constables Armstrong, Alexander and McCall, soon to be joined by Constable Magor. They have come at the behest of Superintendent Hare, and under the direct instructions of Detective Ward, to both protect Sherritt and his family and continue surveillance of Mrs Byrne's house. Ward has even 'bought calico for the door and blinds for the window, in order to have them not seen'.[84]

Every evening, after it has gone dark, the men finish the meal provided by young Mrs Sherritt and take their leave. Heading out the back door, they go down into the lowlands below Sherritt's shack, down to the bottom of the valley, to cross the freezing creek that marks the valley floor, before climbing up the other side to pick their way through the thick bush and along the range, until they come to the same clump of trees that Superintendent Hare and his men had positioned themselves in eighteen months before, where they can watch Mrs Byrne's house through the night, looking out for signs of the Kelly Gang. Sometimes, they are forced back from that position by her dogs, sometimes by her infernal quacking and aggressive geese, which are every bit as bad. Either way, after a long, sleepless night, the troopers make their way back the way they have come, returning to the Sherritt shack just before daybreak, their pants always sopping wet, to rest up before doing the same thing the next night. It is wretched work, and after a fortnight the sickly Constables Magor and McCall are replaced by Constables William Duross and Thomas Dowling.

23 JUNE 1880, BENALLA, A PROBLEM WITH THE GLENROWAN QUARTER

The newly re-installed Superintendent Francis Hare thinks little enough about it at the time. It is more an administrative thing than anything else. But, on this day, he receives a cable from Constable Bracken, in charge of the Glenrowan Police Barracks, informing him that, because his men have been out night after night watching Maggie Skillion's place in the highlands, in the middle of a notably wet Victorian winter, they are all completely knocked up. It is his respectful request that they be allowed to return to Benalla for a few days' rest while, as he is crook himself – he has been going out two nights a week with another constable to relieve his men – he will stay with his family in the Glenrowan Barracks.

Hare reluctantly consents, notwithstanding that he has no other men to replace them. They will just have to make do.

25 JUNE 1880, BENALLA, TIME TO MOVE OUT

The black-trackers under the command of Sub-Inspector Stanhope O'Connor are excited. After over a year away from tropical Queensland, pursuing the Kellys in alpine Victoria, at last they are going home – Hero, Johnny, Jimmy, Barney and Jack – all except poor Corporal Sambo, whom they have had to leave behind in Benalla Cemetery. On this Friday morning, they load their pitifully small swags on the train at Benalla and head off to Melbourne, where – once their replacements are in place – they will be able to catch the ship to take them north. And, no, finally, they have not been successful in tracking the Kelly Gang down, but there is little doubt they have troubled the bushrangers hugely, and since they started tracking them in March of the previous year there have been no further Kelly outbreaks.

Personally, John Sadleir is sorry to see them go, as he had always believed that, if they had been used properly, they really could have led the Victoria Police Force to the Kelly Gang.

25 JUNE 1880, HARE MEETS SPY

But, back to the task at hand . . .

Hare, with Nicolson's spy network dropped in his lap, has little choice but to acquaint himself with the ways of the Nicolson system and try to make some kind of new arrangement with the police informants. Even if he doesn't believe in its worth.

With the help of Sadleir, he does just that, and begins to arrange meetings with the secret agents. One of particular interest is the Diseased Stock Agent, whom he knows from his previous time in the district. Hare writes to the man in early June and asks him to come to Benalla to see him.

The Stock Agent comes in on this very afternoon and is taken first to John Sadleir's office, where, in person, he tells the policeman that he has further vital information to add to his letter. Taken then to see the Superintendent, Denny does not back off from his extraordinary claim, despite Hare's strongly stated scepticism from the outset. But Denny now says he knows even more about it than when he wrote the letter. He says, 'There is no doubt that they are going to make a raid very shortly on some bank.'

'How do you know?' Hare asks.

'I know it for various reasons.'

Mr Sadleir chimes in, 'But have you not been telling us this for the last six or seven months?'

'Yes, I have. I thought they would have stuck up a bank long ago.'

Then Hare asks, 'I hear they are going to appear in armour?'

'Yes, no doubt of it.'

'How is it to be used?'

'They will wear it when they are robbing the bank.'

'Is it bulletproof?'

Denny says gravely, 'Yes, at ten yards.'

'I do not believe that any armour ever made that man could carry would stand a Martini-Henry bullet at ten yards,' says Hare.

'Well,' Denny replies, 'this is proof.'[85]

Not only do the gang have armour, he continues, 'part of their plan is to effect something that would cause the ears of the Australian world to tingle'.[86]

When?

Soon. 'The Kellys,' Denny says, 'are now entirely out of funds and their "friends", who had been sharing in the loot from Euroa and Jerilderie, are putting pressure on them, and a fresh exploit is to be expected immediately.'[87]

With a withering wave of his hand that only a man long in command of many men could muster, Hare tells Denny that what he has reported is 'nonsense' and 'an impossibility', and then dismisses him from all further service.

Good day to you, sir, *I said good day.*

Even as the schoolteacher is taking his hat, his coat, his umbrage and finally his leave in high dudgeon, Hare turns to the aghast Sadleir and says, witheringly, 'If this is the sort of person Nicolson and you have been depending on, it is no wonder you have not caught the Kellys.'[88]

Hare simply does not believe that the Kelly Gang will be appearing any time soon. Sadleir, on the other hand, tends to think they just might, while still keeping Hare onside by conceding that Denny had been giving them 'similar information for many months past'.[89] He adds for nervous good measure, 'He is the most sanguine and tantalizing man I ever saw.'[90]

24 JUNE 1880, RUSTLINGS IN THE BUSH NEAR GRETA

One more time, Ned and Joe go over the finer points of the plan with Steve and Dan. Firstly, and most importantly, they are going to need a serious diversion, something that will announce to the world that the Kelly Gang have re-emerged, something guaranteed to lure every policeman and black-tracker in the area to a given spot – at which point they will have a major trap set a small distance away to take all those policemen to their deserved deaths.

With those police and black-trackers out of the way, the rich banks of Benalla would be left unprotected and the gang could rob them at their leisure.

First up, however, they must create that diversion, execute the act that will have the police racing towards them. And Ned and Joe have just the thing, too, a long overdue settling of accounts with an outstanding piece of human bait, guaranteed to bring the police quickly.

Chapter Twelve

A PLAN INTERRUPTED

For nearly two years they had been hunted through scrub and forest like rats, and something of the destructive fury of rats burned in their blood.

William Henry Fitchett

25 JUNE 1880, A SETTLING OF ACCOUNTS IN THE WOOLSHED

The two men slowly riding into the valley of Woolshed are not strangers to these parts.

For Joe Byrne – who has Dan Kelly riding beside him – it is a homecoming. He knows every tree, every blade of grass on every bit of open ground, every nook and cranny in every gully, every cave in yonder hills – and every person who lives both here and within half a dozen horizons. Including, of course, Aaron Sherritt . . .

Aaron's small farm is just half a mile from Joe's childhood home and the place his mother still lives, on the Eldorado road. As darkness falls, Joe and Dan secrete themselves in some nearby bush and intently watch the Sherritts' modest slab shack, from which cheery smoke is billowing, the sparks arcing up into the night sky. They both know the property's layout well, both internally and externally. Inside the shack, there are two rough rooms – one is the kitchen and the other is the bedroom – while at the rear there are some stables. Between the shack and the main Eldorado road, there are several large trees, but from Joe and Dan's patch of bush they are still able to watch the place closely, trying to understand its rhythm, the routine of the place, the holes in the whole where they might penetrate. The most evident resident is Aaron's missus, young Belle Sherritt, the overworked lass – just fifteen years old and now heavily pregnant – doing her chores. And there, too, is the red-headed mother, Mrs Ellen Barry, who is a frequent visitor to her daughter and new son-in-law.

But of Aaron there is no sign, any more than there is sign of the four policemen the bush telegraph tells them are holed up in there with them, but . . .

But wait!

As the duo of bushrangers watch closely, an old, shambolic, German man whom Joe recognises as Anton Wicks,[1] a some-time miner and meantime market gardener on the next block, is now approaching to knock on the door. And now, there is the silhouette of Aaron himself, answering the door alone.

Well, well. So the traitorous bastard *is* there after all. And he is even answering the door to a familiar voice, and relaxing when he sees a familiar face. Excellent. The two watchers have seen enough. Just minutes later, the gentle *clip-clop* of horses' hooves is heard in the night as Joe Byrne and Dan Kelly make their way back to their camp in the bush just a little up into the ranges. It has been time well spent.[2]

MORNING, 26 JUNE 1880, VICTORIA, OUTLAWS NO MORE

If a coward dies a thousand deaths . . . a man breathes his last . . . and a dog dies in a ditch with a faint whimper . . . what happens when legislation expires and four outlaws liable to be shot on sight *legally* become just ordinary criminals?

Nothing at all – at least not that you can see. There is no last hurrah, no flash of light, no clash of cymbals, not even the stentorian tones of a judge making a ruling. The law simply ceases to take effect, ceases to empower those whose duty in life it is to enforce it and frees those at whom it was originally aimed.

And so it proves on this morning when, with the governor's signature, the Parliament of Victoria is prorogued and, as had been written into the *Felons Apprehension Act*, that legislation simply ceases to be. There is no flash of lightning above Joe Byrne and Dan Kelly in their camp near the Woolshed, no siren sounding near Steve Hart and Ned Kelly in their own camp to the west, back across the Oxley Flats . . . no nothing.

So, the legal status of the Kelly Gang has now changed. Although Ned and Dan still have arrest warrants outstanding for the Attempted Murder of Fitzpatrick two years earlier, they are no longer presumed guilty until found innocent and, as the bench warrants for the murders at Stringybark Creek have now expired, technically, Steve and Joe are free men.

(As for the prorogued parliament, it seems that, once again, the Government of Victoria looks set to change. James Service's weak Conservative government has lasted less than four months, and, failing to get anywhere on the issue of reform, just like his predecessors, the tumultuous parliament seems set for dissolution.)

EVENING, 26 JUNE 1880, AT THE WOOLSHED, A SHOT IN THE DARK

On this pleasant evening, just after six o'clock, Anton Wicks is returning from an attempted visit to his neighbour, ol' Weiner – the old fellow is not there – when in the dusk he suddenly sees two men on horseback coming towards him, with one of them leading a packhorse.

'*Gut effenning*,' says Wicks, in his thick accent – a salutation that is completely ignored until one of the men, some five yards on, turns back.

'What is your name?' the horseman asks pleasantly enough.[3]

'Wicks, from *ze* Woolshed,' the German man says tentatively, as he looks up at the stranger, sensing danger.

The stranger brings his horse forward a couple of yards, brings his head down low and looks straight into the German's eyes. 'Do you know me?'

'No, I don't.'

'Well, I'm Joe Byrne.'[4]

Anton Wicks gives a start. He has distantly known Joe Byrne since he was a child, and in more recent times, back in 1873, even reported him to the police for stealing his horse. (Amazingly, local solicitor William Zincke had got Byrne off with a fine.) But could this be that young man? This fellow seems so weathered, so hardened, it is hard to fathom. 'I don't believe it,' Wicks says.

Amused, Joe Byrne draws his revolver, points it at the German's head and says, 'Perhaps you will believe it now.' Then, pointing to the man behind him, Byrne says, 'That is Mr Kelly.'

The German, glancing at the surly and glowering ruffian indicated, *definitely* believes it now.

'Put the handcuffs on him,' Byrne instructs Dan, who dismounts and does exactly that.

'Don't be frightened,' Byrne tells the now shaking German. 'I won't hurt you. You summoned me [to Beechworth Court] once for a horse, but I forgive you that. You have to go with us to Sherritt's shack, and you must do what we want, and we will do you no harm.'[5]

And so, with the market gardener now handcuffed, and walking between the two mounted bushrangers, the trio proceed along the road to Aaron Sherritt's shack.

Arriving in the bushes nearby, they secure the horses, including the packhorse, from which the two bushrangers now purposefully take their guns. Byrne chooses the double-barrelled shotgun that the Mansfield vicar had originally lent to Sergeant Kennedy before his party departed for Stringybark Creek – and which Ned used to kill Kennedy.

Again, it is Byrne who takes matters in hand in dealing with Wicks. 'You have nothing to do but what I tell you,' Byrne tells him. 'Me and you go to the door and knock at it.'[6]

Slowly, carefully, the German approaches Sherritt's back door – which, unlike the front door, has no windows on either side of it – excruciatingly aware that the barrels of Joe Byrne's shotgun are pointed at his back from the darkness, just a yard behind him. Just let him make one wrong move, try to sound one warning, and he will be dead.

If he wishes to live, he has no choice but to follow the ruffians' orders, and he knows it. To the right of the back door is the chimney, radiating a little pleasant heat on this freezing night in the lofty North-East, and, as Wicks stops a yard before the door, Byrne moves to the right to take cover behind it.

'Knock,' Byrne hisses at the German,[7] who slowly now – oh so slowly, like a man shambling and ambling towards a noose as it sways before him – takes tiny steps to the door. He can hear laughter from inside.

Around the Sherritt table, Constable William Duross is having his tea with Sherritt and his wife and mother-in-law. And it is funny the way it works – for while Duross is dressed, as all the constables are, in a blue jacket, 'like a butchers smock', known as 'bush dress', so they won't necessarily look like policemen if discovered, Aaron is decked out from head to toe in the clothes of his now seemingly close friend Detective Ward. The others – Constables Robert Alexander, Thomas Dowling and Harry Armstrong[8] – are still in their beds in the back bedroom, resting and sleeping, readying for the gruelling and freezing night ahead. As ever, when it falls fully dark, they will have to go and watch Mrs Byrne's house. This day, however, has been upsetting, with Sherritt having told Armstrong bluntly that morning, 'You are discovered. Denny Byrne passed in the rear of the hut, and looked in twice. They can set fire to this hut, and shoot you one by one as you run out.'

'We will have to chance that,' Armstrong had replied. 'They can shoot us, too, any night on the way to Byrne's. However, I will go in tonight and tell Ward, and he can tell Mr Hare if he likes.'[9]

But at least now all is warm and good, as Duross tucks into his tucker while Sherritt tells yet another story about his great friend Joe Byrne. Despite everything that has occurred, Sherritt clearly still has an enormous affection for Byrne, and his theme on this night has been how hotheaded Joe could get. Once, he recounts, the two of them assaulted a Chinaman and hurt him so badly he had to be fed with a silver tube. Typically, Joe had headed bush to get away from the police, while Sherritt had been arrested and taken to the Beechworth lock-up.

'One night,' Aaron recounts, 'I heard someone knocking on the bars of my cell window, and when I asked who it was, Joe replied, "It is me; I am going to help you to escape." I told him, "The Chinaman is getting better, so you had better give yourself up, and do not be a fool." Joe took my advice, surrendered, secured legal assistance and was acquitted!'[10]

Laughter all round, suddenly interrupted by a knock on the back door . . .

—

No sooner has Wicks gently rapped his knuckles than all laughter and talk stops, and suddenly he can hear muted voices and rushed, alarmed movement. Someone seems to have just knocked over a chair in all the haste. In these parts, under these circumstances, knocks on the back door after dark are rare, and it is the more alarming here because, without windows to peek out of, there is no way for the people inside the shack to tell who it is. (Eager to keep the police presence a secret, Duross quickly pushes aside the hanging calico screen that must pass for a door to the bedroom, to whisper the other three police awake. *Something is happening! There is someone at the door!* Sherritt, his wife, Belle, and mother-in-law, Ellen, stay seated at the table, as if frozen in time, looking to the door.)

'Call Aaron . . .' Byrne hisses once more. 'Call *loud*.'[11]

Tentatively, the German does so. 'Aaron . . . *Aaron* . . .' he calls a little more urgently.[12]

And now a voice comes from inside, the familiar voice of Aaron Sherritt. 'Who is there?'[13]

Belle Sherritt, however, already knows. 'Mr Wicks, I know his voice,' she whispers.[14]

Nudged by Joe Byrne, the German man replies. '*Vicks* . . .' he calls back in his thick German accent. 'Sherritt, I *haff* lost my *vay*.'[15]

The tension drains from Sherritt as if from an open tap. Belle is right – it is only their neighbour, Anton. 'You must be drunk, Anton,' Sherritt calls back merrily to his neighbour, who is notorious for frequently being just that.

'You had better get to the door,' Constable Duross whispers.[16]

Pausing only to motion Duross to go back into the bedroom, Sherritt, with his mother-in-law Ellen tightly behind him, opens the door with a tired smile on his face. 'Do you see that sapling over there, at the back of the door?' he begins, laughingly giving directions, only for Belle to add, 'Go out and show him the way.'[17]

When Joe Byrne hears the door open, he first steps a yard further to his right behind the chimney to get more cover, and then, the instant Sherritt takes a step outside, he skips back to a position over Wicks's right shoulder . . .

Sherritt has just enough time to sense a second presence and say, with sudden alarm, 'Who is there?'[18] before Byrne makes his final move.

Aiming directly at the man who was once his best friend, Byrne pulls the trigger.

In an instant, the air is filled with a deafening roar, as, at a range of less than five yards, the huge slug hits Sherritt in the left side of the throat, severing his jugular vein and spinning him backward into the house, where he narrowly misses Ellen Barry before, somehow, righting himself. Now, to finish the job, Byrne steps forward, and, aiming broadly where Aaron's heart would have been – had he been a loyal friend – he fires once more. This shot hits Sherritt in his full torso, two and a half inches below the left nipple, and goes on to shatter two ribs.

This time, Sherritt falls at the feet of his mother-in-law, his head cruelly hitting a box right by the kitchen table.

Momentary silence after the roar of a gunshot has a tragically poignant quality all its own, and it is this silence that Joe Byrne fills now. 'You will not blow now what you do with us any more,' he says over the prone body.[19]

'I went and stooped down, and knelt down just by his head,' Mrs Ellen Barry would later recount, 'and I could see he was dying.'[20]

—

In the darkened back bedroom, Constable Harry Armstrong – as awake as he has ever been in his life – moves quickly. 'Take your arms, boys,' he says grimly, 'the Kellys are here.'[21]

As one, the shocked and frightened constables scrabble for their double-barrelled guns and revolvers, trying to make sure they are fully loaded – a difficult exercise in the darkened room. Armstrong is ready first and positions himself kneeling on the bed, looking for an opportunity to fire out the window that is on the front side of the hut.

—

Now, Sherritt's wife rushes forward, screaming, 'Oh, Joe, Joe! What have you done? What did you shoot poor Aaron for?'[22]

'If I had not shot him, he would have shot me if he could get the chance,' Byrne replies simply,[23] and without an ounce of sympathy, even if his eyes are drawn back to the vision of his once best friend, dead on the floor, by his hand. 'The bastard will never put me away again.'[24]

However, Joe Byrne and Dan Kelly – who is now standing guard just outside the very front door that Byrne has instructed Mrs Barry to open – are still far from done. For it is now time to deal with the police who must be hiding in the bedroom.

Dan Kelly takes a shot through the wall of the bedroom, the bullet passing close to the head of Constable Armstrong – who is still on the bed – before rolling, spent, onto the floor. Outside, the sound of Aaron's dog whimpering pitifully can be heard. Though it is tethered to a tree and has not yet seen its master, it surely knows that Aaron is no more.

—

As the back door had opened, Byrne had seen the flitting figure of a man stealing through the scant calico curtain into the bedroom and now asks young Belle, 'Who is that man?'

'It is . . . a man,' she sobs, 'who . . . was going to stay with us tonight . . . a man looking for work.'

'Bring that man out!' barks Joe as, with his gun trained on the calico partition, he eases himself back out the back door.[25]

While the weeping Belle goes inside the bedroom to talk to the troopers, Ellen Barry, with the permission of Joe Byrne, goes outside to stand by the chimney with Anton Wicks. Inside, as the sound of rifles being cocked emerges from the bedroom, Joe Byrne calls out to Dan with positive glee, 'Hark! Look out! Do you hear that? They are cocking their guns.'[26]

In the bedroom, the four policemen are indeed doing exactly that – getting ready to blast the first man who appears over their sights, coming from the kitchen. But go out into the kitchen themselves? They are not stupid. It is obvious that any such move would result in their own deaths. Constable Armstrong, at this point, slowly moves off the bed, making sure not to raise his head above the window's ledge, and carefully positions himself next to the doorway. Thanks to gentle gusts that blow the calico partition back into the room, he has a good view of the back door, which is lit up by the strong glow coming from the log fire in the kitchen. On the other side of the doorway is Constable Alexander, with the tip of his gun peeking shyly out from behind the calico, aimed at the front door. Beyond the doors, and out into the darkness where the bushrangers are hidden, however, they can see nothing.

Still, they generate enough noise with their movements that Joe Byrne hears it outside. After firing a shot through the wall, he turns to Ellen Barry. 'How many is in that room?' he asks.

'Two.'

'No more?'

Ellen Barry shakes her head.

'What are their names?'

'I do not know.'

'How green you are. And if you be telling me lies, I will murder both of you . . .'[27] With which he fires another shot into the hut.

'Come out of that, you bloody dogs, and surrender!' the bushrangers call.

'We'll die before surrendering!' the police call back.[28]

Byrne now turns to the returned and weeping Belle Sherritt. 'Why don't you bring that man out of the room?'

'He won't come out with me.'[29]

Again hearing sounds from the police, and frustrated that his orders are being disobeyed, Byrne sends her inside once more, saying that if she does not bring the troopers out, then he will shoot both her and her mother.

The young woman then goes back inside once more to tell the troopers just that, but not only do they still refuse to come out, they also refuse to let her rejoin her mother, for fear she will be shot. They order the heavily pregnant young widow to lie under one of the beds. She is hesitant to do so, but Constable Dowling pulls her down and, with the help of Armstrong, the two of them shove the young woman under the bed and pinion her there with their feet.[30] Mrs Barry is on her own.

The murder of Aaron Sherritt. (From the front page of *The Illustrated Australian News*, 3 July 1880, courtesy Matt Shore)

It is, thus, something of a stalemate.

All that Joe Byrne can do for the moment is to call on Aaron's widow to 'Come outside here'[31] before taking two shots at the wooden slab walls from outside. The bullet hits right opposite where Constable Dowling is standing. As the inside walls are lined with paper bags and plaster, the impact of the bullet dislodges some of the plaster, which falls down Dowling's neck and back, so frightening him that he jumps forward onto a bag of flour, just before another shot rings out.

Byrne fires into the bedroom again and says to the terrified Wicks, 'I want those men out, or I'll burn the place down.'[32]

'Come out and surrender, or we'll roast you,' Byrne calls to the police.

'We'll die first!' the collective response comes again.[33]

When the firing has stopped, Mrs Barry, with extraordinary calm, engages Joe Byrne in conversation as they stand outside by the chimney.

'I am satisfied now. I wanted that fellow,' Joe Byrne says to her, of the dead Aaron.

'Well, Joe,' she replies, 'I never heard Aaron say anything against you.'

'He would do me harm if he could,' Joe says flatly. 'He did his best.'[34]

Throughout, Joe is always careful to keep his own body shielded by Wicks and Mrs Barry, so that there is no chance of anyone inside firing through the doorway and hitting him.

After Byrne then goes to fire into the bedroom once more, he asks Mrs Barry to go inside to see if the bullet has penetrated or not. Of course, once she goes inside, the troopers try to keep her there for her own safety, but she reassures them. 'I knew Joe Byrne when he was a boy,' she says. 'He had slept between me and his mother when he was little, and I am confident he will not shoot women.'[35]

With which she goes back outside and reports to Joe Byrne that the bullet has not penetrated the shack. Then they continue to chat, with Byrne walking her a little away from the house so he can catch up on news in the neighbourhood without worrying about shots coming from inside.

'How long since you've seen my mother?' he asks her.

'Not since [the] funeral . . .' Ellen Barry replies, referring to a woman who had died some weeks previously.[36]

They continue to talk, until Joe Byrne, like a gentleman, takes her by the arm and walks her back to the house.

—

In the back room, Constable Armstrong is trying to rally his men, seeing if it might be possible to break some 'portholes' in the walls so that they can fire out at the bushrangers. When this does not prove possible, Armstrong speaks again. 'Men, have you got any suggestions to make; our conduct will be severely commented upon in this matter if we don't make a bold fight.'

No suggestions emerge, so Armstrong tentatively makes one of his own. 'We'll rush them, are you game to follow?'

Each man is asked separately, and each one gravely replies, 'Yes.'

And then?

And then, as Armstrong later recounts, 'We . . . decided to wait for a better chance, thinking they might try to rush us . . .'[37] After all, with the fire and the candle still burning in the main room throwing a bright light, they would be easy targets for the bushrangers in the darkness outside. Better to stay safe, just for the moment . . .

For one thing, with Ellen Barry and Anton Wicks outside, there is always the danger of hitting one of them if they start firing randomly. In short, despite their avowed best intent, the four policemen make no aggressive move to the two bushrangers outside laying siege on them.

Dan Kelly, meantime, is gathering up bushes to help to set fire to the house, and he now starts stacking kindling up at its side. He strikes a match, only for the light breeze to blow it out.

Mrs Barry has been tracking his every move and, finally understanding his intentions, now walks over to him and offers, 'If you set fire to the house, and the girl gets shot or burned, you can just kill me along with them.'[38]

Dan, who clearly has no compunction about burning a house in which troopers are trapped, with a young, innocent woman beside them, ignores this warning and simply asks Mrs Barry pleasantly, 'Do you have any kerosene in the house?'[39]

'No,' Mrs Barry replies coldly.

'What is burning on the table, then?'

'A candle.'

Even without the kerosene, Dan keeps amassing the kindling beside the house.

'We will burn the place,' Joe says, entirely unnecessarily.[40]

'Do not burn down the house,' Mrs Barry pleads. 'I know, Byrne, you have got a soft heart.'

'I have a heart as hard as stone,' Joe Byrne insists. 'I will shoot the whole lot of them like dogs.'[41]

'Don't, for God's sake,' Mrs Barry continues to plead, 'or the girl will be burnt too.'

'You go in and bring her out.'

'If I go in I shan't be let out again perhaps.'

'We will see about that.'

'Well, don't burn the house whatever you do.'[42]

While Joe Byrne takes the handcuffs off Anton Wicks, Ellen Barry goes inside, where Aaron's body lies, and the four policemen remain in the bedroom, with Belle still under the bed with them. As Mrs Barry enters the bedroom, with her heavy step, Armstrong calls out, 'Oh, my God! Mrs Barry, I was near shooting you. If you go out again you will be shot.'[43]

Once she has affirmed that her daughter is still okay, Dowling adds, 'Stop inside, and if they set fire to the place, we will let the both of you out.'[44]

It is the troopers' view that, with two women inside, even the bush-rangers would not set fire to the place. As to Belle Sherritt, profoundly shocked by the events of the last twenty minutes, and having taken something of a turn, she remains under the bed, despite her mother exhorting her to come out.

With the two women now secure inside the bedroom, and the bushrangers sounding distracted, Constable Armstrong carefully crawls into the main room to close both the front and back doors. After shifting the body of Aaron Sherritt a little, he is able to use his rifle to nudge the back door closed, followed by the front door, before rolling the logs off the fire, dousing the red-hot coals with cold tea and snuffing out the candle.

Realising that the old woman is not coming back out of the house, Byrne calls out to Dan Kelly, who has given up on lighting his fire for the moment. 'Shall I send Wicks in too?'

'No, don't send him in,' Kelly replies.[45]

With this, Byrne turns to the shaking German and asks, 'Is your horse at home?'

'No, I turned him out.'

'Mind you, give no information.'[46]

Yes, Byrne seems to be intimating that the German can go, so long as he never breathes a word about what he has seen, but as Wicks has not been specifically told he is free to go, for forty-five minutes he remains where he is, straining his ears for further sounds of the bushrangers, who seem to have suddenly vanished. Then, summoning up his pluck, he goes straight back to his house, arriving there at half past nine – relieved to be still alive – and does not venture out thereafter.

—

Inside the hut – unaware that the mooted fire has simply refused to take – the nostrils of the policemen and the two women are constantly sniffing, fearful that the little building is about to be engulfed in flames.

At the first smell of smoke, or at least a sense that the shack is on fire, of course they will have to do something. The two women will flee and the policemen will fight their way out. For the moment, mercifully, there is nothing – just the sound of the dogs barking. It is not clear to the waiting group whether Joe Byrne and Dan Kelly – and probably Ned Kelly and Steve Hart too – are still there outside, or have fled, but the policemen are taking no chances and do not dare leave the house.

LATE AT NIGHT, 26 JUNE 1880, GLENROWAN AHEAD

Each man is on his committed course, the long night awaits, and they must keep moving through it, on the tasks that Ned has set them. For Joe Byrne and Dan Kelly are pushing on hard. After quietly leaving the Sherritts' shack, they had passed by Margret Byrne's hut – Joe's childhood home – pushed through the break in the hills, crossed the railway line at Everton, right by the Victoria Hotel where they had got the stew and potatoes that night, and by midnight are at the mighty bridge crossing the King River. From there, in the wee hours of the night, they push on through Oxley, where 'some of the people in the township heard the horses go by'.[47] Then on through Greta, on their way to Glenrowan. Sometimes, they stick to the main track. Sometimes, they head cross-country to save time, 'often being up to the saddle-girths in water',[48] but always they keep moving fast, knowing they must get to Glenrowan as quickly as possible.

Crossing creek after creek, pushing through pass after pass, it is hard travelling, and Joe, particularly, is quick to tighten his coat against a gust of shivery cold – either the falling temperature of the freezing night or the remembered horror of having shot his best friend just hours before.

EVENING, 26 JUNE 1880, THE TIME IS NIGH FOR NED KELLY

Just after ten o'clock, Ned Kelly and Steve Hart, with another small band of supporters from the Greta mob, ride quietly down the main street of the curiously constructed town of Glenrowan, just four miles from Greta. Though entirely sustained by the lifeblood of the railway, the settlement really has no heart. Instead, the elongated township consists of a school, police station and post office on the west side of the line, a mile south of the Glenrowan Railway Station, which stands as the focal point of a couple of hotels positioned on either side of the tracks.

In the wake of Ned and Steve, linked by a rope, come a trail of four packhorses rather in the image of their masters: sturdy, hardy, grim and . . . burdened. All of them are here on serious business, as witness the fact that the particular burden of the packhorses is not just four sets of the new armour but also an enormous drum of blasting powder with attendant fuses, huge amounts of ammunition and a couple of signal rockets. If there are any townsfolk there to witness the gang's arrival, none of them announces it. The dusty path, on either side of which the town's buildings are loosely scattered, is deserted, the two hotels – the slightly genteel Glenrowan Inn on the right side of the tracks, the rough-as-guts McDonnell's Hotel on the wrong side – all closed up and dark as Morgans Lookout looks out balefully upon them.

Quietly, Ned leads his men to the back of McDonnell's Hotel, where the horses are secured, and, after some hurried, fond farewells, all but Ned and Steve Hart disappear into the night. Most of the Greta mob do not go far, but what is to be done now on the wrong side of the law will be done by only the two bushrangers initially. Somewhere in the distance, someone can be heard playing a concertina, the melody rising and falling on the light gusts of wind.

The two men silently head back to the railway tracks and, quietly passing the Stationmaster's house and the station, head north along the tracks to the spot they have already intimately reconnoitred. Just half a mile north of the station, they arrive. The first curve out of Glenrowan going north lies above a cruel culvert at the bottom of a hill, with a vicious fall on one side of 20 feet and the other of 30 feet. If the two men can pull up the rails here, any train coming along would tumble into that gully, and any passengers on that train not killed outright by the crash would be easy kills for the men with guns who would be waiting. And therein lies the beauty of the scheme worked out by Ned Kelly and Joe Byrne.

For, if the police follow form, once they hear that Aaron Sherritt has been killed and that there is a Kelly Gang breakout, a special train will soon be on its way, filled with the two entities that the bushrangers hate most, and fear most: troopers and black-trackers.

Their timing for the whole exercise has been carefully calculated. For this is Saturday night. The last train to belch its way past Glenrowan in any direction has been the nine o'clock one from Benalla to Wangaratta. Tomorrow is Sunday. Effectively, the whole railway system in these parts shuts down on the Sabbath. Unless it is a special train . . .

And so to their execution of the plan. Ned and Steve retrieve the shovels and crowbars from the backs of their packhorses and get to work.

The Victorian night is soon filled with the sound of two men straining, with every ounce of their being, to remove the fish plates that join the rails together and the steel chocks that hold them down. But no matter how they strain, how they curse, how they both put all their weight and strength on just the one tool to lift the one plate, it does not budge and in fact barely even squeaks in protest. It is as if the rails are horizontal Excaliburs, which simply refuse to be moved.

These tracks have been put there by professionals, and Ned is not long in concluding that he is going to need a lot of help, with serious workers using specialist tools way beyond mere crowbars and shovels, to undo their handiwork. Fortunately, Ned happens to know that a group of hardy workers from the nearby Glenrowan quarry is quartered in four tents that lie in a glade of light timber just up from the railway line, on a patch of rough ground 75 yards from the Glenrowan Inn, so positioned in order to use that inn's kitchen to cook. They'll do . . .

Bird's-eye view of Glenrowan. (From *The Illustrated Australian News*, 17 July 1880, courtesy Matt Shore)

—

Now, when it comes to sex, it is perhaps the great Lord Chesterfield who said it best: 'The pleasure is momentary, the position ridiculous, and the expense *damnable* . . .'[49] Ah yes, but at least he was never interrupted, in flagrante, by a bushranger firing a gun at his head to get him to stop.

Quarry worker Alphonse Piazzi could not say the same. For in his tent – composed of canvas on timber frames with bunks inside – his own train is just about to reach its destination, with a certain young local woman of his very recent acquaintance, when suddenly there is a lot of shouting to the high heavens.[50]

Alas, it is coming from outside . . .

No sooner have Ned Kelly and Steve Hart arrived at the glade of gum trees than – first claiming to be the police – they have gone from tent to tent calling on the 'stonemen', as they are often known, to get up. All of the workers comply, until the bushrangers get to their foreman, Alphonse 'Louis' Piazzi. For not only does Piazzi refuse to come out when called on by a workmate to do so – those bastards have been joyously ragging him for far too long about having a woman with him – but he also goes so far as to threaten to shoot anyone who comes into his tent. (Enough is enough! Is nothing sacred? Can a workingman on the job not finish the job any more?)

Impatient with such nonsense, Ned simply steps forward and kicks the tent door open, before stepping inside – to be confronted by Piazzi pointing a pistol at him, back over his own bare buttocks.

'You bastard,' Ned roars, 'You lift a gun to me.'[51] With which, he brings his own rifle to bear and fires off a shot. Luckily for Piazzi, he is able to knock the barrel aside just in time, and the bullet does no damage – even though, after the shot, the night air is filled with a penetrating female scream.

Not that the woman's terror lasts long, however. For when Ned asks her and Piazzi if they know who he is, she drunkenly replies, even as she gets up and tries to kiss him, 'I know you, Ned Kelly.'[52]

Ned pushes her away.

Worse, when the bushranger explains to the foreman what he wants them to do, the shaken Piazzi, still tucking his shirt back into his trousers, replies that they can't help, for they are labourers at the local quarry, not railway workers, and they have neither the tools nor the know-how to lift the rails.

Oh. This problem will have to be resolved in another fashion, but in the meantime all of the workers are to come with the bushrangers.

Quickly.

For, if everything has gone to plan, the special train should be coming through Glenrowan very shortly, and there is no time to lose. At gunpoint now, the whole group is taken just up the slope to the Glenrowan Inn, which, surprisingly, seems to be untroubled by the recent gunshot – at least, no lanterns or activity are visible within.

Well, they will wake up now.

Striding up to the front door, Ned raps on it and calls out, 'Jump up and open the door!'[53]

After a momentary pause where nothing is heard but a vague stirring, from somewhere deep within the building a voice comes back asking him to wait a moment. It is the voice of Ann Jones, the plump publican, rising forty and only just recovering from a nervous breakdown. Her husband is absent due to the fact he had gone bankrupt and is away working in the South Gippsland town of Bunyip as a railway-line repairer.

As a bushranger who waits for no man, let alone a woman, Ned quickly walks around to the back door of the inn – it is an exceedingly small stringybark, weatherboard construction, 30 feet across by 27 feet deep, lined with hessian and paper, a ceiling of calico and roof of corrugated iron – and fiercely pounds again, demanding the door be opened.

'Who is it?'[54]

'Never mind,' Ned replies, by way of indicating that he wants the door opened anyway.

'If you are a policeman, go to the men's tents to look for whom you want.'

'If I was one, you would like me better.'[55]

Another long pause. Perhaps the door should be answered after all. But it couldn't be, could it?

Ann's fourteen-year-old daughter, Jane, is sent to open the door.

It is.

Ned Kelly in the moonlight!

Quickly, Ann Jones is told that she and her family must dress and come with him. A bushranger, but still a gentleman, Ned waits outside in the passageway while Mrs Jones and Jane get properly dressed – in the case of Ann Jones, into her best red dress, almost as if she is about to appear at a grand occasion. Ned then takes them to the building at the rear of the inn to confirm that Jones's other children – her young sons John, Owen, Jeremiah and Heddington – are still all asleep, and, that confirmed, he leaves them there, as the Jones women, with the quarry workers, are now taken by Ned across the Railway Reserve and towards the Stationmaster's house.

—

In Melbourne, where Captain Standish is fast asleep, entirely unaware that his worst nightmare is then and there coming to fruition, the clock towers have just struck one o'clock.

In Glenrowan, shortly afterwards, a heavy knock comes on the door of the Stationmaster's house, situated some 100 yards south of the station, right by the line. John Stanistreet is fast asleep, but he wakes quickly, sure it must be someone wanting to get through the railway gates in a hurry. There has been a lot of this lately – rough people wanting the gates opened in the middle of the night, threatening violence if he doesn't do so – and he has already complained to the police about it, but of course nothing has been done. And now, here they are again! Furious, thus, Stanistreet puts on just enough clothes for decency and hurries to the door. And yet, even before he can get to that door, it bursts open and he is confronted, and affronted, by an enormous bearded man in a heavy oilskin overcoat.

'Who are you?' Stanistreet asks. 'What is this for?'

The answer would curdle steel, let alone the soul of a gentle Stationmaster. 'I am Ned Kelly.'[56]

Good Lord above, it is. As the keeper of a public place, Stanistreet recognises the face on the reward poster he had personally pinned on the wall at the station.

But how can this be happening in a town that in the last few weeks has had four troopers stationed here, in a barracks opened just eight months earlier to prevent exactly this kind of thing occurring? One answer, Stanistreet guesses, is that three of those troopers had become so ill through constantly watching the house of Maggie Skillion in cold weather that they had been withdrawn just the previous day, for fear they 'would have to go to hospital',[57] while the man remaining, Constable Hugh Bracken, has been confined to bed in recent days with a severe case of gastric flu. He has nowhere to withdraw to, really, as this place is now his home.

'You have to come with me and take up the rails,' Kelly growls at the Stationmaster.

'Wait until I dress,' Stanistreet replies.[58]

With his revolver foremost, the bushranger turns the railway official around and marches him back to his bedroom, where the fearful and tearful Mrs Stanistreet and their two little girls and one infant lie. The good woman is warned not to try to raise any alarm while they are away, or it is her husband who will face the consequences.

With which her husband is once more marched forward, this time out of the house to receive a slap in the face from the bitter night cold, and over to the railway gate, where he finds a group of eight men or so, one appearing strangely dissatisfied, looking over the railway line.

'Now,' says Ned, 'you direct those men how to raise some of the rails, as we expect a special train very soon.'

'I know nothing about lifting rails off the line,' Stanistreet genuinely protests. 'The only persons that understand it are the repairers, and they live outside and along the line.'[59]

Armed with this information, Ned moves quickly. Ann and Jane Jones are to go back to the Stationmaster's house, so they can stay warm with Stanistreet's family. Meanwhile, the stonemen can stay here at the inn under the guard of Steve Hart, while Ned personally goes, as directed, a quarter of a mile down the line to the houses of Dennis Sullivan and James Reardon – men whose job in life it is to lay the rails in such a precise, secure manner that they cannot be easily interfered with by anyone, such as passing bushrangers with crowbars.

In the meantime, Steve Hart prods Stanistreet with his gun towards the chest in the toolshed and says, 'You get the tools out that are necessary to raise those rails.'

'I have not the key of the chest,' Stanistreet protests, determined to do as little as possible to help these men in their murderous plan.

'Break the lock,' Hart replies, untroubled, and it is quickly done.[60]

—

It goes as before.

On this night, the Reardon family – James and Margaret, with their eighteen-year-old son Michael and seven other children, including baby Bridget – are fast asleep when, at twenty past two, both parents awake to the sound of the family dog barking furiously. How on earth has the dog got out of the stable? Margaret Reardon replies she has no idea, but she has just heard a horseman jump the fence. And now her husband, James, can also hear the sound of a horse whinnying down by the railway line, no doubt the horse of a friend that has got loose.

Putting on his slippers and dressing gown, Reardon goes outside and is not long in finding what the problem is. For there in the moonlight is his fellow platelayer Dennis Sullivan, who, amazingly, announces that he has been 'arrested'.

'What trouble have you fallen into?' Reardon asks.[61]

This kind of trouble . . .

For now, out of the darkness steps a huge, bearded man, bringing the muzzle of his revolver right up to Reardon's cheek.

'I am Ned Kelly,' he says, uttering perhaps the most terrifying four words of introduction then possible on the continent. 'What is your name?'

'Reardon.'[62]

'I want you to come up and break the line . . .' Ned says. 'I expect a train from Benalla with a lot of police and black fellows, and I am going to kill all the bloody traps.'[63]

Is it the light of the lantern flickering, or does Reardon turn an even paler shade of pale? 'For God's sake, don't take me,' the forty-six-year-old says. 'I have a large family to look after.'

But Ned explains he has no choice. 'I have got several others up, but they are no use to me.'

'They can do it without me.'

Enough. 'You must do it,' the burly bushranger says, 'or I will shoot you.'[64]

Right, then.

The whole family – Reardon, Margaret and their eight children, still only half-dressed – are obliged to accompany Ned. A house-guest, labourer John Larkins, is also rounded up from a back room.

And hail fellow well met, for as they all arrive back at the Stationmaster's house it is to find that Dan and Joe have arrived, after a long night's journey. Quickly, quietly, they exchange news. The railway tracks have not yet been lifted, but, yes, Aaron Sherritt is dead. And when they left his shack, the troopers had been inside in the bedroom, but they would surely be well out by now and would have likely raised the alarm. It makes the lifting of the railway line all the more urgent now.

When Reardon continues to say he does not have the necessary tools, because they are in the locked shed, he is interrupted by Steve Hart, who tells him the lock has been broken and the tools are now easily accessible.

. . .

Oh.

. . .

At gunpoint, Reardon gets the tools he needs: two spanners and a hammer.

Turning to Ann Jones, Ned Kelly exults, 'I'll show you a sight now! I'll kill all your traps!'[65]

And then, after Margaret Reardon and the children are left at the Stationmaster's house, the small party, which now includes the captured quarry workers, head down the line to where Steve and Ned had previously tried to lift the rails, just half a mile north of Glenrowan Station. Initially, this time, they are led by Steve, accompanied by the young woman who has caught his eye, Jane Jones. When they arrive at the spot, the bushranger is quick to lie down with his head on Jane's knee, saying he is sick, and it is not until Ned arrives that things become serious.

For, having arrived at the spot, Reardon and Sullivan have realised for the first time just how devastating the consequences would be for any train derailed at this point, if they do as Kelly has asked.

Reardon, shocked, remonstrates strongly with Ned when he arrives. 'I beg to be excused,' he tells the Kelly Gang leader, 'owing to my position on the railway, and on account of my wife and family, whom I will not be able to support if I lost my position.'

'If you refuse,' Ned replies, evenly, 'you are a dead man.'[66]

With no choice thus in the matter, Reardon still asks that the other men do the work, while he directs them – that way, at least he would not be directly responsible. With Ned's agreement, the platelayer then kneels in the moonlight and demonstrates how to unscrew the bolts, how to remove the spikes and lift the said plates, which will in turn release the rails.

And though he sets to, Kelly is soon at him once more. 'Old man, you are a long time breaking up this road.'

'I cannot do it quicker,' Reardon protests.

'If you don't look sharp, I will tickle you up with this revolver.'

'I cannot do it quicker, do what you will.'

'Give me no cheek.'[67]

Reardon gives him no cheek. He does, however, try to give the oncoming train the tiniest chance. When Kelly says he wants no fewer than four lengths of the railway line destroyed, the platelayer tries to dissuade him. 'One will do as well as twenty.'

'Do you think so?'

'I am certain.'[68]

Despite all the threats, Reardon still manages to thwart the gang's desires after a fashion. Normally, to do this kind of work, with this many workers, he and Sullivan would have the skills to lift the two sets of 22-foot rails in as little as five minutes. But it is precisely because he is so skilled that he manages to make it take ninety minutes – having 'forgotten' to apply some of the necessary tools – while being busy the whole time and giving a constant stream of sometimes contradictory instructions.

Nevertheless, by half past three in the morning, the job is indeed done, and what had been a secure railway line is now nothing less than a death trap for the next train that comes along it.

Ned Kelly surveys it all with grim satisfaction.

The Victoria Police, who so unjustly imprisoned his mother, harassed his family's whole existence and pursued his gang, declared *war* on him. Very well, he has declared war on them. In war, there must be deaths, and he is now intent, without the slightest hint of mercy, on ensuring the collective death of a couple of dozen of his enemies at the one time. He is not a criminal planning the murder of innocents; he is a general planning the destruction of his enemies.

—

After cutting down some saplings in the bush, and putting them over the line to disguise the break, the men walk back to the Stationmaster's house. There is complete silence as they contemplate what would happen to the next train that comes along. It will be death and destruction for all those on board.

Re-entering the house, Ned takes Stanistreet aside and asks how the signalling on the line works.

Stanistreet repeats the famous railway-man mantra: *'White is right and red is wrong, and green generally "come along".'*

'There is a special train coming, and you will give no signal,' Ned orders him.[69]

After the Stationmaster nods his reluctant acquiescence, Ned turns to Hart and gives another, even more pertinent order, gesturing at Stanistreet, 'Watch his countenance, and if he gives any signal, shoot him.'[70] With which Stanistreet is left with the rest of his family, under the guard of the scowling Hart.

As to Ann Jones – who has been waiting all this time at the Stationmaster's house – she, to James Reardon's ears, suddenly seems surprisingly friendly to Ned Kelly. 'Come on, old man, and have some breakfast and a wash,' the innkeeper says to Ned Kelly, 'it will do you good.'[71]

Strange. Reardon, for one, has never had any sense of Ann Jones as a sympathiser, and as far as he had known she had always kept a decent, respectable place.

After displaying some reluctance, Kelly soon enough agrees, and he and all the men under guard head to the Glenrowan Inn, where, as dawn begins to break, they in turn get ready to break bread in the tiny weatherboard building, barely big enough to change your mind in, let alone stay for the night. It consists of just five rooms.

While the gang and the prisoners sit around the dining room – which opens onto the large verandah – the breakfast is prepared in the kitchen, which, down a passage that passes by the bar and two back bedrooms, lies across a six-foot breezeway in the small slab outhouse building where Ann's younger children have been sleeping. Dan Kelly has said that he will pay for it. Together with whatever crusts they can put on the table, Ann Jones and her family serve up a breakfast of ham and eggs washed down with many cups of scalding-hot tea. Ned's only condition is that someone test his food and drink first, as he is wary of being 'hocused'.

With the breakfast over, the prisoners are free to spread themselves throughout the inn, with the exception of the two back bedrooms, which the gang have claimed for themselves along with some curiously bulky, and obviously heavy, sacks that they have carried in there.

With the luggage all in, Dan Kelly tries, and fails, to lock the door. Ann Jones helps. 'That is not the key, Dan,' she says. 'I will get you the key.'

Retrieving it, she hands it to the bushranger and says, 'You take this key, Dan, and give me the one you have, as it is the key of the bar.'[72]

With which, it is the hotelkeeper herself who locks the door that prevents the prisoners from escaping.

—

Inside the shattered home of the deceased Aaron Sherritt – still lying where he fell – very little has happened since his murder the night before. Though his weeping wife has closed his glazed eyes before collapsing in the arms of her mother, while Armstrong has laid a blanket over his grisly form, to spare poor Belle the horrific vision, still the four terrified policemen have not made a move. Obviously, it is a matter of urgency to get the word of the murder out and raise the alarm that the Kellys are on the loose, but how?

Leave the relative safety of the bedroom and venture through the front door, where the murderous Joe Byrne and Dan Kelly likely await? Men who already have three murders of policemen at Stringybark Creek on their record, even beyond the murder of Aaron Sherritt?

Not me, mate. You go.

But no one does. Not even when they realise that the dog has gone to sleep, an all but sure sign that the strangers have gone.

—

As the sun continues to rise at Glenrowan, ever more prisoners are herded towards Ann Jones's establishment. And yet in many cases this is just for the sake of appearances. There is no doubt that Paddy McDonnell and his family, for example – who run Glenrowan's other pub – are sympathisers with the Kellys, and even close friends, but because it wouldn't do to leave them out while others are herded in, they, with other sympathisers such as the McAuliffe brothers, join all the rest.

Through it all, every member of the Kelly Gang has his ears pricked, straining for the sound of the special train they are expecting. But, of course, there is nothing – as, with the exception of the quivering Anton Wicks, news of the murder has not yet moved beyond the Sherritt shack. By nine o'clock in the morning, Dan Kelly is concerned enough to express his doubts. Perhaps the police train is not coming after all? Perhaps the plan to kill a whole lot of troopers at once won't work? Perhaps the gang would be better to take their chances now to get away to the thick bush before the police do arrive?

It is Ned who refuses any such notion. There is to be no more running, he says. He, for one, is sick of it. No, this time, he repeats, they will stand and fight, come what may. Glenrowan will be either their first major victory against the mass of the police force or their last stand. But it will *not* be a place they flee from.

As the morning wears on, inevitably the number of prisoners increases, as the gang take in hand all fresh arrivals in town, to be secured either at the Stationmaster's house or Jones's hotel. As had happened at Faithfull's Creek, some of them are secretly sympathisers, and Ned is satisfied that they now have a good number of their own informants, sprinkled among the others, who can tell him if anything untoward is planned.

One prisoner who is not a sympathiser is one of the town's original settlers and most-liked characters – 'an Irishman of the good old school . . . a merry old soul'[73] – fifty-eight-year-old Martin Cherry, who, living just outside the town on the Benalla Road, had been excited to hear of the town's famous visitors, apparently now at the Glenrowan Inn.

'I don't believe it. I will go and see,' he had said,[74] only to find a pistol pointed at his chest shortly afterwards, before he is escorted up to the inn. Well, he never. Not that he protests too vigorously for all that. A gentle man and a gentleman, that is not his way. The old fellow merely does as instructed and is soon in the inn's dining room with all the rest, reflecting on the morning's extraordinary events.

—

Back at Sherritt's shack, even when the sun comes up and relative safety returns, those inside still find they have a reluctance to set foot outside.

Finally, though, Constable Alexander exits the shack and does a quick circuit to make a preliminary conclusion that the bushrangers have indeed gone. Armstrong then goes out and checks the bush around the place. Still, however, none of them volunteers to do what needs to be done: to rush to the police at Beechworth and raise the alarm. Who knows if, perhaps, the murderers are waiting for them over the next hill, expecting them to do exactly that?

Maybe, then, someone can be convinced to do it for them? And so they decide to send all the messengers they can find. Armstrong pens three letters addressed to the Beechworth Police.

And here comes the first messenger. A passing Chinaman is hailed by Constable Armstrong and prevailed upon to take one of the notes to Beechworth Police Station seven miles away – with five shillings promised now and five more when he comes back – but he soon returns, telling them he has decided that he has too much work to do. When Armstrong himself proposes going, he is talked out of it by the others, on the grounds 'it was not considered advisable to separate, as another attack might be made'.[75]

And so they get the Chinaman to go over to the local schoolteacher, Cornelius O'Donoghue, who comes promptly. O'Donoghue – who had in fact once taught both Joe Byrne and Aaron Sherritt – agrees to go to Beechworth, exclaiming bravely, '*I'm* not afraid of Joe Byrne.'[76] Alas, he *is* afraid of his own wife, and he also soon returns, telling them that that good woman has forbidden him to do any such thing, him being a family man and all.

Then, another neighbour, Mr Duckett, is asked and indeed nominally agrees, but he seems so diffident about it that not one of the constables has confidence that he actually will go.

Finally, Constable Armstrong, who is the man in command of the four-trooper party, decides that there is only one choice. He will go, and let the devil take the hindmost. He leaves for Beechworth at nine o'clock. So eager is he now to get there, realising how bad their long delay is going to look, that – in the absence of the troopers having horses of their own – he even bails up a man by the name of Considine and takes his horse from him by force, and is soon galloping away to raise the alarm.[77]

—

And now, here are some more arrivals in Glenrowan.

On this bright, shining Sunday morning at eleven o'clock, Thomas Curnow, the English-born twenty-five-year-old who has been teaching at the Glenrowan School for the last four years, decides it is the perfect day to take his wife, Isobel, and their eleven-month-old child for a drive along the road from Glenrowan to Greta Swamp to go duck shooting. They are accompanied by Thomas's sister Cathy, who is visiting from Ballarat and rides in the gig with Isobel and her brother, David Mortimer.

With that in mind, all but David, who rides alongside, climb into the buggy and they gaily proceed. But what is this?

Just as they are coming into Glenrowan proper and within sight of Mrs Jones's hotel, they notice a number of people standing out the front. 'Mrs Jones must be dead,' Curnow says to the others. 'She has been very ill.'[78]

But no, as they get near the hotel, it is obvious that this is not a morning mourning crowd at all. Far from it. For, as Curnow takes his buggy past the Glenrowan Inn and its attendant crowd, he spies the Stationmaster, Mr Stanistreet, and asks, 'What's the matter?'

'The Kellys are here,' that good man replies. 'You can't go through.'[79]

Thinking he must be joking, Curnow makes to proceed regardless, when just up ahead he sees an enormous bearded man on horseback, talking to a young man by the name of John Delaney, who stands before him, and between them they are blocking the passage across the railway.

Suddenly, the bearded man wheels his horse around to confront him. 'Who are you?'[80]

It is only now that Curnow sees the two revolvers in his belt and realises it is true – this is Ned Kelly, right before him. Glenrowan is being held up, just as Euroa and Jerilderie had been. Still, Curnow has no choice but to introduce himself.

'Oh!' says Ned. 'You are the schoolmaster here, are you? And who are those?'

Nervously, Curnow introduces his wife, sister and brother-in-law.

'Where are you going?'

'Out for a drive.'

'I am sorry, but I must detain you.'[81]

There will be no argument from Thomas Curnow or any of his family. Following directions, they get out of the buggy, while David Mortimer dismounts from his horse. The women and the baby are quickly ushered to the Stationmaster's house, where they join the other relatively benign prisoners who can be guarded by Steve Hart. As to Curnow and his brother-in-law, they are marked to go to the Glenrowan Inn, where most of the men are and those who may prove to be trouble can be properly watched by the three other members of the Kelly Gang.

First, though, Curnow has a quick conversation with John Stanistreet, where he hears the terrible news. 'Glenrowan,' the Stationmaster tells him, 'has been stuck up since 3 o'clock this morning, and . . . the Gang has forced Reardon and others to tear up part of the railway line beyond the station, for the purpose of wrecking a special train of police and black-trackers, which the outlaws said would pass through Glenrowan.'[82]

Curnow is horrified, and all the more so when he hears an unconfirmed rumour that some of the Gang had been in Beechworth the previous night and had shot several policemen. And now they want to kill a couple of dozen more police by derailing the special train?

Meanwhile, Ned Kelly has been continuing to upbraid young John Delaney, all of eighteen years old, who had been out walking with his younger brothers and their friend Tom Cameron – all of them hoping to go hunting with the eldest Reardon boy, the eighteen-year-old Michael[83] – when they had all been made Ned Kelly's prisoners. In the case of John, Ned has a real problem. For it has come to his ears that not only had John Delaney's father, the Greta blacksmith, sold a horse to the Victoria Police Force, but young John himself had recently done a favour for a policeman and, infinitely worse, even tried to *join* the Victoria Police.

Well, in Ned's book, this is a crime punishable by death, and he is just the man to do it. Pointing his revolver at the terrified young man, who has tears running down his cheeks and onto his shirt, Ned says to all who are listening that he would, personally, 'have the life of anyone who aided the police in any way, or who even showed a friendly feeling for them'.[84]

'I can and will find you out,' he goes on. 'Just as they have passed a law making it a crime for anyone to help us, I have made it a crime for anyone to aid the police against the Kelly Gang.'[85]

And yet, is he being too harsh? Ned theatrically appears to consider that possibility for a moment and then softens his approach. 'But I'm a fair man,' he says,[86] and he takes his pistol from his belt and holds it out to Delaney, daring him to take it, telling him he could even take the first shot!

Of course, the still sobbing, now shaking young man refuses to take it.

As Ned continues his haranguing, alternately pointing the revolver at the weeping young man's head and then putting it down again, many of the women in the crowd plead with the bushranger to spare his life. Just what is about to happen now, no one is sure, but, finally, after young Delaney faithfully promises that he will never again try to join the police force, Ned's play at being a cold-blooded murderer comes to an end. He has made his point. 'I forgive you this time,' he says, 'but, mind you, be careful for the future.'[87]

With this now resolved, Joe Byrne produces a bottle of brandy and a tumbler and offers a swig to all adults who would like some. None take it more gratefully than young Delaney, who knocks back two-thirds of a tumbler with a couple of gulps.

Not Ned, though. Refusing even a sip – he wants to remain entirely clear-headed for the task ahead – he instructs some of the young lads who are among his prisoners to take the Curnow horse and buggy into Mrs Jones's yard and unhitch the horse. As to young Delaney, he and his young brothers are added to the prisoners, who have the run of the inn, still excepting the back room where the outlaws have left their bulky baggage and for which they keep a key. The prisoners can even stretch their legs outside under supervision, though mostly they keep to the largish dining room, the smaller bar and the tiny parlour.

It is getting to be late on Sunday morning and, at the Beechworth Police Station, Detective Michael Ward is getting through some paperwork when told that there is a man outside who wishes to see him.

Very well, show him in.

Good God! It proves to be Harry Armstrong, last seen before he was sent to the Sherritt household, and usually as neat as a new pin, as confident as a kookaburra. This time, however, Armstrong is clearly exhausted, dishevelled and shivering, while also greatly excited. The story bursts out of him. The knock on the door. The blast from the gun. Aaron falling dead! Joe Byrne and Dan Kelly mocking them, threatening *to roast them all alive.* The fact that after staying inside all night, he had only finally got away at nine o'clock that morning.

At this part of the account, the stunned Detective Ward, furiously twirling his waxed moustache, bursts forth, 'Good god! What were you doing?'

Miserably, Constable Armstrong offers a confused explanation that Ward finds unacceptable.

'This happened *last night*! Why didn't you let us know before? You just sat there over the body, and never went for help?'[88]

Ward has heard enough. Immediately, he sends Armstrong back to the Sherritt shack with other troopers to organise the retrieval of the body for the inquest, while he busies himself organising other police to pursue the Kellys, and, most importantly, composing the cable that he intends to send to police headquarters in Benalla, but . . .

But isn't that always the way?

Just when he most urgently needs the telegraph to work, the wretched thing goes on the blink. As furiously as the telegraph operator taps, for no result, Ward matches him in fury as the message refuses to go through to Benalla.

The detective is beside himself.

—

Of all those taken prisoner, it is Thomas Curnow who is most alarmed at the situation – not particularly for his own safety but for what is going to happen to the police on the special train. He can't quite believe that not everyone is talking about it, not everyone is alarmed.

Least concerned is Dan Kelly himself, who, when Curnow enters the bar, asks him to have a drink with him. Up close, Dan is surprising. Yes, a mighty and notorious bushranger by reputation, but, up close to talk to, he is little more than a nineteen-year-old only just out of boyhood, clearly in the thrall of his oldest brother.

Is it true, the schoolteacher asks shortly after the clock on the mantelpiece has struck midday, that the gang have been at Beechworth during the previous night and shot several police?

Dan replies carefully that they had been near Beechworth last night and had done 'some shooting', and burned the 'bastards out',[89] alluding to police, but goes no further, as Joe Byrne enters the bar and stares at Dan drinking.

'Be careful, old man,' he says, gently.

'All right,' Dan replies, before pouring water into his brandy.[90]

Curnow then strikes up a conversation with the two of them and expresses surprise at them sticking up Glenrowan, of all places. They are upfront in reply, confirming his worst fears. They have come to Glenrowan, they say, 'in order to wreck a special train of inspectors, police, and black-trackers, which would pass through Glenrowan for Beechworth, to take up their trail from there'. To get there, they acknowledge, they have 'ridden hard across country . . . and had the line torn up at a dangerous part, and are going to send the train and its occupants to hell'.[91]

For Thomas Curnow, it is a stunning turn of events. In the blink of an eye, he has gone from being on a pleasant Sunday-morning drive with his nearest and dearest, to suddenly being the prisoner of the most notoriously murderous gang on the entire continent. And his wife and baby are in the same predicament. The conversation ends, Curnow more shocked than ever at what the gang are planning, and their callous approach to so many innocent deaths in prospect, though he of course tries not to show it.

To others, beyond the alarm of what is planned, there is also enormous worry about just who is on whose side. At one point, as the brother of the Postmaster, Edward Reynolds, is walking at the back of the inn, he notes Ann Jones and Ned Kelly talking in the breezeway, and is struck by the intimate nature of their stances, with the portly innkeeper even resting a languid arm on the big man's shoulder. There is nothing about them of bushranger and prisoner, but rather that of old friends and even closer.

It gets worse, for when Reynolds gets to the stables on his small walk, Jones turns and says to the bearded one, 'Look out, Ned, he is going to escape.'[92] Reynolds is trying to do no such thing and walks back to the inn, his ears ringing with what seems to be a staggering betrayal. Just who are the real prisoners in this whole scenario? It is very difficult to tell.

At last, at last, at Beechworth, the telegraph operator gives Detective Ward a grim but relieved nod. The cable has gone through. Well, it has gone through to Melbourne, at least, informing them:

> Watch party stuck up by the Kelly Gang at 6 o'clock Saturday night. Aaron Sherritt shot dead in the hut he occupied by Joe Byrne. Fired seven shots into the hut, the bullets passing besides the constables' heads . . . They remained outside until about half past 6 a.m., and it was only at half past 11 one of

> the constables was able to get to Beechworth.
> M. E. WARD, Detective[93]

This is followed up with another cable from Ward:

> We cannot get the Benalla office to inform Mr Hare we have instructed Wangaratta to send man on horseback to Benalla.
> M. E. Ward
> Detective[94]

The Melbourne office is not long in getting the news through to the telegraph master at Benalla.

Outside the Glenrowan Inn, Thomas Curnow is standing in the yard, wrestling with his emotions. On the one hand, he is worried for his family. On the other hand, he is appalled and outraged at the intentions of the gang to derail the special train. He cannot help but feel it is his duty to do whatever he can to prevent it. Yes, to do something would entail a risk to both himself and his family, but how could he *not* do something? A couple of dozen men to tumble to their deaths, creating a couple of dozen widows, while he sat idly by? He could never live with himself if he did nothing. But what?

He is not yet sure. Only that he must look for an opportunity.

And there is Dan Kelly now, come out in the yard, asking him inside to have a dance, for Curnow, despite being born with a hip disability and having an obvious limp, is reputed to be one of the best dancers in the district.

'I cannot dance in the boots which I have on,' Curnow replies.

The remark is overheard by Ned Kelly, who has also just come out for some air. 'Come on,' he says. 'Never mind your boots.'[95]

Sensing that this might be the very chance he has been looking for, Curnow replies that while it is awkward for him to dance in these particular boots, as he is lame, he would dance with pleasure if Ned would just accompany him to his home by the school, just by the road to Benalla, where he keeps his dancing boots. (For if Ned can accompany him, their normal route would take them in front of the Glenrowan Police Barracks, where Constable Hugh Bracken is stationed, and he might see them.) Bracken had been stationed at Greta for three years in one of his first two stints as constable and would surely recognise Ned Kelly.

And Ned would have gone, too, bar the fact that first Dan intervenes, saying it would be better for him or Joe to accompany Curnow. And then, to Curnow's consternation, one of the prisoners, surely a sympathiser, warns the bushranger that he would have to pass by the police barracks to get the shoes. Can this be true, Ned asks Curnow, suspiciously.

'Yes, we shall have to pass the barracks. I had forgotten that.'[96]

Ned looks at him curiously but, a trusting man by nature, lets it pass. Under the circumstances, Curnow suddenly decides that he can and should dance with Dan Kelly after all, and goes back into the inn to do exactly that.

Once the dancing is over, Ned Kelly announces that he will personally go down to the police barracks to bring Constable Bracken back to the inn, whereupon Curnow is careful to laugh lightly and wax lyrical at the prospect. 'I would rather than a hundred pounds that you would,' he says. 'Could I be allowed to accompany you when you go, and take home my wife, sister, and child?'[97]

Kelly gives no reply, which at least means he does not say no. More than ever, Curnow is convinced he must 'do something to baffle the murderous designs of the Gang', and he 'resolved to do my utmost to gain the confidence of the outlaws, and to make them believe me to be a sympathiser with them. I saw clearly that unless I succeeded in doing this, I should not be able to get their permission to go home with my wife, child, and sister, and consequently should not be able to do anything to prevent the destruction of the special train and its occupants.'[98] His broad plan is to be allowed to go home, at which point he would retrieve his horse and buggy from behind the inn and race as quickly as possible to the police in Benalla, 14 miles away.

—

At this time, at about half past two in the afternoon, Superintendent Hare is enjoying lunch at the Commercial Hotel in Benalla when a breathless messenger arrives to tell him there is an extremely important cable for him at the Benalla Railway Station Telegraph Office, and he must come right away.

The news, which he soon shares with the equally summoned John Sadleir, is not good. Aaron Sherritt had been shot at his own house at nine o'clock the previous night by the Kelly Gang.

In short, everything the Diseased Stock Agent had told them just three days earlier had been proven correct, just as Sadleir had thought it would be. Sadleir does not like to say 'I told you so', under the serious circumstances, but that notion is certainly in the air as the men discuss what must be done.

Now, at this point, it has been Ned's expectation that Superintendent Hare would simply issue immediate orders for every available policeman, together with the two local trackers he has on call, to get into the special police train and immediately head north. But, on an issue as important as this, the deeply shocked and almost grieving Hare – poor, poor *Aaron*! – is nevertheless eager to have every move he makes signed off by his superiors.

And so, after reading the telegraph from Beechworth, he immediately sends his own telegraph to Police Commissioner Standish in Melbourne, informing him that the murder of Aaron Sherritt means that there is a fresh Kelly outbreak. At the insistence of Superintendent Sadleir, he makes a specific request:

> Would it not be as well to ask Mr
> O'Connor to come up by special train to
> Beechworth with his trackers he is at
> John Thomas Smith's place at Flemington
> please reply at once
> Francis Hare[99]

Alas, the telegram arrives at the Melbourne Club, where Captain Standish lives, just minutes after Victoria's principal policeman has headed out for the afternoon.

With this frustrating lack of reply, and no instruction, Superintendent Hare's first instinct is to set off with troopers immediately from Benalla, but he is persuaded against this by Superintendent Sadleir, who insists it would be better to see if they can find the black-trackers so recently departed and have them come too.

While they wait, the two remain all afternoon at the telegraph office, sending cables to the police scattered over North-Eastern Victoria, informing them of what has occurred and organising them to be ready for the next move by the authorities, with special reference to the special train that would surely soon be on its way, with the trackers. Where cables cannot reach the intended recipients – because on this sleepy Sunday afternoon many of the cable offices are unattended – men are sent on horseback. The word goes out.

As Sadleir would later recount, 'messengers were despatched in accordance with an arrangement of some months standing in anticipation of an outbreak of this sort . . . Police in different localities were, on the report of an outbreak, to send other constables and assistants to different crossings, townships, bridges, and points where the Kellys would be likely to pass in case of a pursuit, either by the ordinary police or the trackers . . .'[100]

On the chance that Melbourne does not send a special train, Hare issues instructions via his subordinates for a special train of his own. It is to take a group of a dozen troopers with their horses – plus two of his own black-trackers, Moses and Spider – to be ready to go to Beechworth on this night. They must have provisions for several days, in order to chase the Kellys into the mountains. But be quick about it!

The important thing is that they be ready to leave by midnight, so they can be at Sherritt's shack by dawn at the latest, so the black-trackers can do their work.

And, no, he certainly does not want to agree to Sadleir's suggestion that, because Hare is suffering from a cold, Sadleir go in his place on the special train. 'As always,' Sadleir would recount, '[Hare was] too eager for the fray to consent.'[101]

Chapter Thirteen

GLENROWAN DANCES

Am not I an honest man?
Ned Kelly

You are looked upon as great a hero as
General Roberts of Kabul . . .
Constable Hugh Bracken to Ned Kelly

EARLY AFTERNOON, 27 JUNE 1880, GLENROWAN SHIMMIES, SHAKES AND JUMPS

It is some time since Glenrowan has had this much fun, if ever. The heavy furniture has been shifted out of the dining room onto the verandah, 'neath the eaves of the corrugated-iron roof, a fiddle has been found, as has a player for little Jack Jones's concertina, and the dance takes place.

For, as it happens, David Mortimer is as accomplished a player as Tom Curnow is a dancer – their talents have meshed many times since Tom married his sister – and as Dave works the concertina like a blacksmith on his bellows, Tom and Dan Kelly lead off all the others, doing their jigs and quadrilles.

They all dance and sing along to the favourite folk song of all, 'The Wild Colonial Boy', telling the story of the bushranger Jack Doolan, who is known to *'roam the mountains high . . . gallop o'er plains, And we'll scorn to live in slavery, Bound down with iron chains.'* Now, altogether sing:

One day as [Jack] was riding
The mountain-side along,
A-listening to the little birds,
Their pleasant laughing song,
Three mounted troopers rode along,
Kelly, Davis and FitzRoy
They thought that they would capture him,
The wild Colonial boy.

'Surrender now, Jack Doolan,
You see there's three to one.
Surrender now, Jack Doolan,
You daring highwayman.'
[Jack] drew a pistol from his belt,
And shook the little toy.
'I'll fight, but not surrender,'
Said the wild Colonial boy.[1]

Ned and Joe sing it with the best of them, and also dance from time to time, and even drink, sparingly, while remaining alert and watchful.

THAT AFTERNOON AT BENALLA, NO NEWS IS BAD NEWS

Well over two hours after they sent the cable to Melbourne, there is still no reply from Captain Standish. It is frustrating, though at least things are beginning to move elsewhere, in terms of getting their special train prepared to leave from Benalla that night and organising police from other stations to be on the lookout for the Kellys.

As to the police at Benalla, Hare's first move had been to send for Senior Constable John Kelly with the message that he must 'bring down a horse with you to the telegraph office'.[2] Upon his arrival, Hare meets him at the door of the office, holding the telegraph and bluntly telling him, 'Aaron Sherritt is shot.'[3] Hare tells the senior constable to go over to Mr Stevens, the Stationmaster, and ask if he can get a special train.

Within twenty minutes, Kelly is back, advising that Mr Stevens has quickly agreed to do exactly that, and Hare gives his under-officer further instructions to 'get some provisions and get ready',[4] also providing a list of the men he wants to catch the special train when it is ready: Constables Barry, Canny, Gascoigne, Kirkham, Arthur and Phillips.

Just 25 miles away, up in Wangaratta, Sergeant Arthur Steele – who had been one of the first to receive a cable from Detective Ward, and the one responsible for sending the messenger to Hare – does all he can to ensure that, if the Kelly Gang pass through his region, they will be caught. Following 'instructions previously supplied by Assistant Commissioner Nicolson . . . to watch all the crossings and fords and so forth about the bridges',[5] Steele positions posts on all the major crossing places of the Ovens River, as well as placing other posts looking for them along the obvious roads. He sticks close to the telegraph office, awaiting further instructions, while keeping in touch the best he can with his patrols and posts. With just one fresh sighting of the Kellys, the police can all move.

Up at Milawa, meantime, Constable James Arthur opens his copy of sealed instructions that Superintendent Sadleir had composed the year before and begins to read:

> Benalla, 24th September 1879. Strictly confidential. Memo.—On receipt of instructions to carry these arrangements into effect, Constable Arthur will first have the township of Milawa patrolled by a constable, for the purpose of watching for the appearance of the outlaws; and should they pass through, it will be the duty of the constable simply to note carefully the direction by which they leave, preserve the tracks, and report without delay to Constable Arthur, who will immediately pass on the information to Sergeant Steele . . .[6]

Across North-Eastern Victoria, armed men start to move into position, waiting for the next sighting of the Kelly Gang, so their net can tighten.

MID-AFTERNOON, GLENROWAN, LET THE GAMES BEGIN

With the dancing now done, at least for the moment, Ned and Dan do the obvious. They take the prisoners out into the yard of the inn and lead them in a competition of quoits, and then 'hop, step and jump', just the way the brothers had done when they were kids.

When Ned loses to one of the more athletic of the prisoners – probably because, at least the way he tells it, he has been handicapped by the heavy weight of a revolver in each hand and one in his belt – he suggests a standing long jump instead, determining how far you could leap from a line drawn in the dirt.

Sadly, *N. Kelly* records another narrow loss. Perhaps, this time, it is his extraordinary boots with their larrikin heels that is the problem! That, at least, is the way Ned tells it to all who will listen, which is everyone.

And so it all goes on, amid much merriment, so many contests that Ann Jones will later describe her inn on this occasion as 'a house of sports during the day'.[7] All the while, the beer flows free, paid for down to the last penny by the Kelly Gang. And, soon enough, it is time for a sporting display that Ned simply can't lose. As the shadows begin to lengthen, the three members of the Kelly Gang – for Steve Hart is still down at the Stationmaster's house, guarding the women – put on a display of horse-riding for the ages. They gallop, they wheel, they jump, they ride with gay abandon, sometimes with no saddles and sometimes with no hands, all as the prisoners warmly applaud. Say what you will about the Kelly Gang, but they can *ride*. And none more so than Ned, on his mighty mare, Music, to which the bushranger seems so joined it is not obvious whether the horse is a natural extension of him or vice versa . . .

In the atmosphere of goodwill that immediately follows, Thomas Curnow asks the beaming Ned for permission to shortly go to the

Stationmaster's house to visit his wife, child and sister . . .

Of course, no problem.

LATE AFTERNOON, 27 JUNE 1880, THE MELBOURNE CLUB RECEIVES NEWS

A famously genteel place is the Melbourne Club on Collins Street. With its silverware and brass as polished as the collars of its staff and attitudes of its members are starched, its ceilings as high as its windows are large, it is old world for the old school. On this sunny Sunday afternoon, there are few people around. Most of those who have come to the club for lunch in the ground-floor dining room have now finished not only their meal but also their cigars and brandy, and have gone home, while those coming for dinner have not yet arrived.

The defining feature, thus, for those here on this late afternoon is that the Melbourne Club practically *is* home, and that describes Captain Standish more than anyone, for he lives in one of the thirty rooms set aside for members on the second floor and has done since 1872. As ever, he feels contented just to enter through the portals once more as he returns at half past four, but this time the contentment does not last long. For there, waiting for him, is a swag of ever more upsetting cables, informing him firstly of the Kelly breakout and secondly of the steps that have been taken since.

Quickly, the Englishman sets himself to responding to the most urgent cables, though that doesn't cut them down by much, including the suggestion from Hare that O'Connor be prevailed upon immediately to bring his black-trackers up by special train. Standish notes Sub-Inspector O'Connor's address in Flemington – where else but *(sniff)* at his late father-in-law's place? – and has a messenger in a hansom cab take a message to him:

Melbourne Club, 27 June 1880
My Dear Sir,
I have just received telegraphic information that the

outlaws stuck up the police party that was watching Mrs Byrne's house and shot Aaron Sherritt dead . . .

In the urgent position of affairs, could you return to Beechworth with your trackers by the early train to-morrow, or by a special train, if that can be arranged. If you can oblige us in this way, could you manage to come in at once to see me at the Club by the hansom which I send out with this?

Yours Faithfully,
F. C. Standish[8]

The letter dispatched, Standish then dashes off a note to Chief Secretary Robert Ramsay, informing him of the situation before receiving an urgent message asking him to come to the telegraph office at once as Hare wishes to communicate with him. And yet, when Standish informs Hare that he has written to O'Connor and, if the Queenslander agrees, will send him up by train the next morning, Hare is unaccountably terse in reply:

Time recd: 5:25
From: Benalla
Dated: 27.6.80
Telegram for: Capt Standish C. C. Police
You had better go out and see O'Connor and ask him to come up at once by special train so that he may be on the ground at daylight tomorrow morning. I am waiting here until I know whether O'Connor is coming if so I will join him at Benalla . . .

It will be no use the trackers coming up by tomorrow morning train because they could not get to work before Tuesday morning.

```
Francis Hare
Supt
Time lodged at the Sending Station: 5:20[9]
```

This from his underling, the one he has favoured above all others over the last decade?

As Thomas Curnow's family comes out from the Stationmaster's house to embrace and kiss the just-arrived teacher, the relief on all sides is overwhelming. Despite the shock of what has happened, they are all still okay. And yet, for Thomas Curnow, even in this state of high emotion, holding his pregnant wife Isobel's hand tightly as he insists she go back inside to sit down and rest, he can't help but notice the red llama scarf wrapped around his sister's neck. It is an extraordinary thing, under the circumstances, that the gentle angel of inspiration still manages to alight on his shoulders and whisper, 'What a splendid danger signal that would make.'[10] If a train was coming in the dark, and he could get some form of light behind that scarf, then it would glow red and be a clear warning to the driver that he must stop the train.

Now entering the Stationmaster's house, the first thing Curnow comes across is the slight, youthful figure of Steve Hart lying on the couch with three loaded guns by his side, moaning about how swollen and painful his feet are after having had his boots on for several days and nights without relief. There is the smell of brandy about the bushranger, as, even though he has sobered up in the last couple of hours, he had spent much of the day drinking.

Taking the opportunity to ingratiate himself, Curnow quickly advises Hart to bathe his feet in hot water, and then organises one of the women to get some for him, which the bushranger appreciates. Curnow's plan is forming. A short time later, the teacher is chatting in the yard of the Stationmaster's house to Mr Stanistreet himself, the only resident of Glenrowan that Curnow feels he can trust, as they are both in the employ of the government, when Mrs Stanistreet comes out to join them.

'Would it be wrong,' the schoolteacher poses the question, 'to break a promise given to the outlaws?'

The couple both say it would not be wrong, and Curnow takes some comfort in that.

Does Mr Stanistreet still have his revolver with him?

Yes, Mr Stanistreet allows, he does.

Curnow's plan forms further . . .

'Let us go back inside,' he says to the couple, 'as it is better they don't see us and think we might be plotting something.'[11]

Which is as well, for, as it happens, Curnow has just separated from the couple when Dan Kelly arrives, as scowling and suspicious looking as ever. Again, as ingratiatingly as he can, Curnow asks Dan if he might be able to have a quick word with his older brother on a matter of some importance.

A short time later, up at the inn, Dan ushers Curnow into Ned's presence as he stands outside the kitchen door of the inn. Curnow babbles out his message. He feels that Mr Kelly should know that it has come to his attention that, yes, the Stationmaster, Mr Stanistreet, has a loaded revolver in his office, and he really feels that for the safety of the Kelly Gang, and indeed them all, the revolver should be retrieved. Quickly, the teacher adds that it is not Mr Stanistreet who is the danger, for that good man would never use it, but he cannot vouch for others who may know of it. Ned looks at him quizzically, thanks him for passing on such valuable information and is soon on the way to the Stationmaster's house himself, where the revolver is quickly secured.

Ned also now announces that all bar Stationmaster Stanistreet and his family, and the Curnow family, who will remain guarded by Steve Hart, must come back to the Glenrowan Inn with him so that all the prisoners can be looked after together. No fewer than twenty-one people, nevertheless, are allowed to return to their homes, including Hanorah McDonnell and her kids, together with other sympathisers Ned knows he can trust.

One more thing, though, before you go, Mr Kelly . . .

John Stanistreet wishes to inform the bushranger that the first

Monday-morning passenger train, the Wodonga–Benalla, will be coming through just after nine o'clock, and he must 'allow the rails torn up to be replaced', otherwise 'the sacrifice of innocent lives which would ensue' would be on his head.[12]

Could Mr Kelly organise that to happen, please?

No.

Ned Kelly outright refuses to do so. He happens to think there will be another, more important train arriving before then.

Speaking of which, however, where is it? To this point, the whole plan has been predicated on a train filled with policemen and black-trackers arriving, and yet of that there is no sign. As the day has worn on, and the evening has approached, the absence of the train has begun to wear on Ned. Where can it be? How long can it take to get a police force organised? Don't they know that the Kelly Gang have been loose in the Woolshed, that they have murdered a police informant, that they must be *stopped*? Why aren't they rushing to the scene?

Where is the special train? He has special plans for it . . .

—

Things are beginning to move at the Melbourne Club. After conferring with Hare via several cables back and forth down at the telegraph office, Captain Standish returns to the club to find that Chief Secretary Ramsay has arrived in response to the urgent note he had sent to him, and as Ramsay speaks, Standish – as unaccustomed as he is – listens.

Ramsay is insistent they will indeed need a special train, *tonight*, and the two quickly put the steps in motion with the Victorian Railways to have it ready for O'Connor and his men, if they do prove to be available. Standish returns to the club just before O'Connor does indeed turn up.

The Queenslander had been staying with his wife at her sister's place – Katherine is married to one of Melbourne's leading lawyers, Thomas Prout Webb, who has a grand residence in Flemington, The Ferns.

Captain Standish immediately comes to the point. 'Mr O'Connor, in the urgent state of the case, can you manage to accede to my request?'

'It has always been my wish,' O'Connor replies crisply, 'to have the chance of getting those fellows.'[13]

So of course the Queenslander agrees, invoking only one condition: as he is under orders to proceed to Brisbane, he would be obliged if Chief Secretary Ramsay could negotiate with his Queensland counterpart to ensure that O'Connor would be held blameless with his government for not having followed orders.

Done!

'How long will you be before you are ready to start?' Captain Standish asks a little anxiously.

O'Connor looks at his watch, does some quick calculations and replies, 'I will be ready at ten tonight.'[14]

There is, ahem, however, one other thing, cap'n. Before coming to the Melbourne Club, O'Connor had explained the situation to his wife and she and her sister had decided that they would like to come with him to Beechworth, as in all probability he would be out tracking for several days, if not a week, and she would like to be near where the work was going on. 'Therefore,' O'Connor says, 'I would like there to be a first-class carriage on the special train for her convenience.'[15]

Does Captain Standish blanch at this upstart whom he had wanted banished back to Queensland with his black-trackers, now saying he will only return to the work he was banished from if a first-class carriage is laid on for his wife, a marriage and romance Standish had heartily disapproved of from the first? He does not. He accedes to the request.

Exit, Sub-Inspector O'Connor. He has much to do, including getting his black-trackers from where they are staying in their digs at Essendon.

—

Shortly thereafter in Benalla, Superintendent Hare is greatly relieved to receive a cable from Standish informing him that O'Connor and his black-trackers should be at Benalla Station at around one o'clock in the morning.

Nevertheless, Hare decides to ask Standish that he be allowed to keep fired up the other special train he has had on standby at Benalla, and – at John Sadleir's earnest suggestion – use it as a 'pilot' to the train from Melbourne. That is, send the two trains in a convoy, with the first special train at Benalla going on just a little ahead, as protection for the next train with all the troopers. For who knows what the Kellys may have in store for the special train?

By now, the Diseased Stock Agent's warning of several days before is coming true before their very eyes, meaning that other ignored warnings – such as that the Kellys are planning something that should astonish not only the people of Victoria but of the world, and Kelly's own warning in his letter of the previous February that they might blow up a train – also might need another look. Within the bounds of urgency, it is well to use some caution in all things, and, happily, the Police Commissioner agrees.

'A good idea,' Standish replies, 'there is no knowing what desperate deed the outlaws may now be guilty of – have a pilot.'[16]

Hare hopes to get to Beechworth at around four o'clock in the morning with their special-train convoy, at which point they would be able to unload their horses and go straight to Sherritt's shack. From there, at first light, with the trackers, they would be able to start off pursuing the Kelly Gang, on a still relatively fresh trail.

—

Not long afterwards, just on dusk, Thomas Curnow is standing outside, near the back of the inn, when he overhears Ned Kelly telling Ann Jones that he is 'going down soon to the police barracks to capture Bracken',[17] and, as a matter of fact, Ned wants to take Ann's daughter Jane with him, to call the constable outside. While Jones is supportive of the general idea, she does not want her daughter to be a part of it.

Calm, madam, calm.

Ned assures her that he does not intend to shoot Bracken, and affirms that he needs her daughter to lure Bracken from his lair (in much the same manner as Sherritt had successfully been lured the night before).

Again, Curnow seizes his chance. Why not, he dares suggest, take his brother-in-law, Dave Mortimer, down, as Bracken knows his voice well, and by hearing it would suspect nothing. It is the obvious solution, and again, Ned, after a pause, agrees he will do so, before traipsing off towards the stables.

Now?

Now.

Following closely, Curnow hails the bushranger and carefully asks him would it be all right if he took his whole family home, as they went down for Bracken? 'I assure you,' he says, 'that you have no cause for fearing me, as I am with you heart and soul.'

'I know that,' Kelly says, 'and can see it.'[18]

He agrees to the request, adding only that they must all wait till he is ready to go and retrieve Bracken. But, yes, in the meantime Curnow can at least go down to the Stationmaster's house to retrieve his wife, child and sister, and bring them back to the inn, so they can be ready when Ned gives the word.

By the time the small family return to the inn, a log fire has been started on the north side of the hotel yard, around which many prisoners are cheerfully enough standing in the freshly fallen dusk, warming themselves in the suddenly freezing temperatures, while others are dancing inside. It is an extraordinarily happy scene for people who are now being held at gunpoint. After all, there is a rumour that beyond the murders at Stringybark Creek the Kellys have just killed another man, and they know there are plans in place to murder a couple of dozen others, while no fewer than forty people are being held prisoner . . . and yet the mood is far from desolate. As a matter of fact, it might be just a little too free and easy.

'Boys,' Ned Kelly says, after suddenly appearing beside those standing at the bonfire, 'you had all better come in now, as I cannot mind you out here, and I believe half of you are gone already.'[19]

Soon, most of the prisoners sit down in the dining room, parlour and bar to eat the hearty dinner provided by Ann Jones and her family – boosted by bread the stonemen have retrieved from their tents – while Dan and Joe play a little cards on a corner table in the bar. Oddly, it is noted that while they play it is none other than Jane Jones who keeps guard on the women and children, many of whom have only recently arrived from the quite different atmosphere of the Stationmaster's house. Young Jones holds Dan's revolver and is constantly counting heads with small up and down movements with the gun to make sure that all are present and accounted for. (And, yes, Jane had been reluctant to do so, having previously said to Dan, 'I would rather not do it.' But he had given her an order, 'Take this revolver and do it at once,'[20] and she had done so.)

In the meantime, Dan is overheard telling his older brother that he is worried at the continued non-arrival of the special train, by the number of prisoners they have to guard, by the way the whole thing is turning and it might be better if they get on their horses and ride out of Glenrowan while they still can.

But, one more time, he is overruled by Ned. 'I'm tired of running,' he says simply. 'We'll stand and fight.'[21]

And that is that. Ned has spoken.

It is time to get dressed. To venture as far as they intend to, to get Bracken, it is as well to be protected. So it is that Ned heads to the back room where the armour has been left and emerges ten minutes later, wearing his heavy overcoat.

—

Farewell, farewell! Outside The Ferns in Flemington, Stanhope O'Connor's wife, Louisa, and her sister, Katherine, are bundled into a buggy, with a driver, and sent on their way to Essendon Station, where they will meet Stanhope and his black-trackers to catch the special train to Beechworth. Such an adventure!

—

At last, at last, just before nine o'clock in the evening, Ned Kelly gives the word. Coming into the kitchen, he tells Thomas Curnow it is time to retrieve Bracken and he must go to the stables to put his horse onto the buggy. Yes, boss.

Bringing that buggy around to the front of the inn, Curnow puts his wife and sister into it, as well as young Alec Reynolds, the seven-year-old son of the Glenrowan Postmaster, who, Ned has ordered, is going to come too.

And so what does one do while waiting for a bushranger? One *waits* for the bushranger. Patiently. Even for an hour, one waits. One doesn't complain, stamp one's foot, look at one's watch, betray any frustration whatsoever. Not even when one is aware that a train is likely by now on its way, rushing to its doom, unless one can warn its driver in time. One waits.

—

All aboard!

Just a few minutes before ten o'clock, the special train, Engine No. 107 – which had been stone cold just a couple of hours earlier but has now at last built up a satisfactory head of steam – pulls out of Spencer Street Station. After much work, all of it difficult on a Sunday, when most crews have the day off, Victorian Railways has managed to get a crew together, with driver John Bowman being backed by guard Frank Bell and fireman Herbert Hollows. All are a bit nervous because, as Bell would subsequently recount, 'no notice had been given along the line, and it being a very dark night there was a great risk of running through some of the gates'.[22]

Behind the engine is the first-class carriage O'Connor has demanded, and it is already bearing four reporters from the Melbourne papers – the *Australasian Sketcher*'s Thomas Carrington, *The Age*'s John McWhirter, *The Daily Telegraph*'s George Allen, and Joe Melvin of *The Argus*, who has secreted within his several layers of clothing a small pistol, on the off-chance he might come within shooting distance of Kelly himself. What a story that would be!

As to Sub-Inspector Stanhope O'Connor and his five black-trackers, they are picked up at Essendon Station at a quarter past ten, with, sure enough, O'Connor's wife and her sister in tow. It has all happened so quickly that both handsome women are still wearing the evening gowns they were wearing when the hansom-cab driver bearing the message from Captain Standish had interrupted their formal dinner.

As the train makes its way, without stopping, through such stations as Strathmore, Broadmeadows and Craigieburn – *crack!* – and Melbourne proper falls backward through the night, the police instinctively and repeatedly check their guns and their ammunition to ensure all is in order, as there is a strong sense they will be needing them.

All is dark now, as the train continues to roar north, its *CLICKETY-CLACK-CLICKETY-CLACK* and occasional steam-whistle rolling out over the fields and homesteads and causing many people to cock their heads curiously towards it.

It is Sunday night. Trains don't run on Sunday night. Something must be going on . . .

—

At last, just after ten o'clock, Ned on horseback appears beside the waiting buggy and tells Curnow he may proceed to the police barracks so they can capture Constable Bracken.

Giddy-up.

Out on the track that leads to the barracks, Curnow soon realises that, as well as Ned Kelly, they are to be accompanied by Joe Byrne and his own brother-in-law David Mortimer, all of them on horseback, together with two prisoners walking in front of them, Edward Reynolds, who lodges with his brother, Hillmorton Reynolds – Bracken's neighbour on one side – and Robert Gibbons, who lives on the other side.

For light conversation on their way to the police barracks, along the bumpy, dusty and well-worn track, Ned mentions that he intends to soon 'fill the ruts around with the fat carcases of the police'.[23] Looking at him closely now, Thomas Curnow notices how extraordinarily bulky the bushranger looks as he sits on his panting horse in his heavy overcoat, holding his rifle. Something is going on, but the schoolteacher does not quite know what. Ned also has a massive bundle of something resting on his lap.

Twenty yards from the front door of the barracks, Ned calls a halt. He orders David Mortimer to go to the door and knock, which he does, while Ned secretes himself behind a wall and levels his rifle – all to the consternation of Thomas Curnow, who feels that a murder is about to be committed.

'Constable Bracken? Constable Bracken?' Mortimer keeps calling while knocking, with no result.

'Keep going!' Ned keeps commanding in a whisper.

'Constable Bracken? Constable Bracken!'[24]

There is no reply, and Ned decides on another tack. Taking the seven-year-old Alec Reynolds around the back with his uncle, he starts again. After instruction from Ned, the child does as asked.

'Constable Bracken? Constable Bracken!' his piping voice soon fills the night air.

And now his uncle joins in too, going around to where he knows the bedroom window is.

'Bracken! Bracken!'

—

In his bed at the back of the barracks near to where the lad is calling out, Hugh Bracken is fiercely struggling with gastric flu, which has seen him suffer from vomiting, diarrhoea, stomach cramps, headaches, fever and shivers all at once. It has all been so ghastly that, while for the first day he was afraid he was going to die, for the last twelve hours he has been afraid he is not going to die. Right now, he is lost in the depths of a mercifully deep sleep, only obtainable to those so sick that much of their body has effectively shut down.

'Bracken! Bracken!'

Constable Bracken stirs. Focuses a little. Looks to the clock on the wall.

It is nearly half past ten. Who could be wanting him at this time of night?

'Bracken!'

Oh, it is Edward Reynolds, who lives right next door. Now the last thing Bracken wants to do is get up, but he knows it is his duty to do so, and this constable is nothing if not dutiful. Get up, he must.

Struggling first to stand, he then shambles his way to the door with his service revolver and shotgun in hand and just manages to open it before, before . . . *a-man-in-an-iron-mask-is-through-the-door-holding-a-revolver-above-his-head!* From somewhere within that unworldly metallic cylinder – which Ned has just retrieved from the sack he is carrying – a disembodied voice tells Bracken, 'I am Ned Kelly, bail up, or you are a dead man.'[25]

Shocked, Bracken nevertheless makes strong reply, even though the revolver has now been lowered and is in line with his chest from just four feet away. 'You be blowed,' he says, bravely, 'you are not Ned Kelly, you are some of the police trying my mettle.'[26]

Exasperated, Ned will have none of it. 'Throw up your arms, or you are a *dead* man.'

In response, the still plucky Bracken puts one languid hand up, only to be told by the bushranger, 'Put the other up; we want no nonsense.'[27]

Bracken puts his two arms down – the shotgun against the wall and the revolver at his feet – and both hands up, after which Kelly quickly searches him for his ammunition.

'I believe you have a very fast horse,' says Ned, a whole lot more pleasantly now.[28]

Instantly, Bracken knows the bushranger is referring to his favourite horse, Sir Solomon, which, alas, of late, has been crippled. He tells Ned of this fact, but allows he does have another good horse in the stable.

Good.

Constable Bracken is to immediately dress himself and get his horse, at which point Ned would be pleased if he would accompany him down to the station . . . Beforehand, however, Ned accompanies Bracken inside to his sitting room, where he strikes a match and lights a candle, before taking possession of his firearms. 'Where is your ammunition?'

'I have none except what is in the gun,' the constable lies. 'I have used it all shooting hares as there is no butcher here.'

'Where are your handcuffs?'

'I have none.'

'How is that?'

'Well, you can look the place over and you will find that there is none.'

'You seem to have nothing here.'

'There is not a thing here except a few sheets of foolscap paper. I was only sent here temporarily to satisfy the Press.'

'Be damned, you were sent here as a smart man to catch me.'

'Well, Ned, you have caught me.'[29]

As Bracken starts to get dressed with the clothes he has retrieved from the bedroom, the constable tries to talk the bushranger out of whatever it is he has in mind. 'What ever fetched you here,' he says, 'there is no money nor banks to be had here.'

'I have an object in it,' Ned replies. 'I have blown the head off one bloody traitor already at Sheep Station Creek and ridden down the streets of Beechworth. I have done enough to make all the bloody police in the colony be here before now.'[30]

Once Bracken is dressed, Ned asks him, 'What do the people make of us chaps?'

'You are looked upon as great a hero as General Roberts of Kabul but it was a pity that you shot Sergeant Kennedy as he was a bit of a favourite amongst the people.'

'I had to shoot him or he would have shot me,' Ned replies with feeling. 'The bugger was a rich man and he had no business to come after me for a lousy hundred pounds. I was a poor man without money and arms and poor horses and we wanted the police horses and arms to make a rise.'[31]

The two then go into the Brackens' bedroom, where Hugh carefully wakes his wife – who is just two weeks away from her confinement and heavily asleep after a long day – as well as their two-year-old lad. Solemnly shaking hands with the wide-eyed little boy, Ned says, 'I may be worth £2,000 to you yet, my child.'[32]

Both mother and son are allowed to remain in the barracks, but on condition. 'Now, Mrs Bracken,' Ned says gently, 'don't you move from here until Bracken comes back or you will be shot.'[33]

Charmed, she is sure. She watches, terrified, as the bushranger takes her husband off into the night.

Outside, getting on his horse, Bracken is both ill and angry, saying to the bushranger that, 'Had I not been ill in bed all day you would not have taken me so easily.'[34] Ned Kelly ignores him, so the redoubtable Bracken adds, 'If this horse was as strong as it used to be, it would take more than Ned Kelly to keep me a prisoner.'[35]

Neither Ned Kelly nor Joe Byrne seem particularly fussed either way. The fact is that Bracken now is their prisoner, and that is all that counts. Giving Byrne the reins of the constable's troop horse, Ned says to his great friend, 'Look out for Bracken, he is pretty slippery and can cross country as well as you can.'[36]

Before heading back to the Glenrowan Inn, Ned keeps his promise to the Curnows, who have been waiting all this time. Satisfied that the gang's main danger in the town is now under their control, Ned says to the schoolteacher, who has been stamping his feet to try to keep warm, that he may take his family home. 'Go quietly to bed,' he says, 'and don't dream too loud.'[37]

Otherwise, he makes clear, they will be shot. Oh, and one more thing. One of the gang will come down during the night, he says, to see that they are all present and accounted for.

Quickly now, Curnow heads his family for home, acutely aware that the train might be coming any time. Once they are out of hearing of the outlaws and their prisoners, who are heading back to the inn, Curnow announces to his wife Isobel and sister Cathy his intention to go to Benalla to raise the alarm and have the train stopped.

Both women, and particularly his wife, raise tearful objections to this. Does Thomas want to have them all *killed*? Hasn't Ned Kelly himself specifically told him that he will be sending someone to check on them shortly? And what does Tom think will happen once that person comes to find that Tom is not there? Does he really think the gang would have let them go if they didn't have someone watching the house in the first place? Is he mad?

For, if Tom does do this, everyone is placed at risk. He, to begin with, would be shot on the road by spies, and even if he did succeed in warning those on the train, once the Kellys found out what he had done, back here at the house they would 'be hunted out and shot'.[38]

Curnow remains resolute regardless. He acknowledges there is risk to his family, but he simply cannot, in good conscience, do nothing at all when dozens of fathers and husbands from other families – innocent men all, doing their brave duty – are murdered.

Nothing he says, however, is sufficient to calm his wife, and, already ill, she becomes ever more hysterical as they arrive inside their home. There, her loud wailing is less of an issue.

—

What to do when it is well past midnight and you have forty prisoners?

The obvious. Ned decides they will have a concert and another dance.

For the concert, one prisoner makes a fair effort at a couple of ballads, and then, at the burly bushranger's behest, Ann Jones's thirteen-year-old boy, Jack, continues the evening's entertainment by giving a rendition of 'The Kelly Song', a recently penned folk song that has become Ned's favourite. Tentatively at first, and then with confidence rising and beaming slowly like the rising sun, the young lad gives it his all, as they gather around, and some softly sing along . . .

Farewell to my home in Greta,
My loved ones fare thee well,
It grieves my heart to leave you
But here I must not dwell.

They placed a price upon my head
My hands are stained with gore,
And I must roam the forest wild
Within the Australian shore.

But if they cross my cherished path,
By all I hold on earth
I'll give them cause to rue the day
Their mothers gave them birth.

I'll shoot them down like carrion crows
That roam our country wide,
And leave their bodies bleaching
Along some woodland side . . .

See yonder ride four troopers,
One kiss before we part,
Now haste and join your comrades – Dan,
Joe Byrne and Stevey Hart.[39]

More! More! Next comes 'The Wild Colonial Boy' and 'The Pretty Girl Milking the Cow'. Jack is a small, frail kid, with a small, frail voice, but he is rewarded with warm applause, none clapping more vigorously than Ned – though it is perhaps the sixpence from his mother that the lad treasures most. But now to the main event, after all the furniture is cleared out of the parlour once more and onto the verandah, so the dancing can begin . . .

For, as a prisoner, it matters little how tired or upset you might feel. When a big, bearded man with a gun feels like dancing, *everyone* dances, and Dan Kelly is the one leading the charge, just as he had been that afternoon. It was such a success then, why not do it again?

Again, Dave Mortimer does the honours, as he squeezes his concertina with expert enthusiasm and blows tune after tune for quadrilles as four couples stand in a square and perform the intricate manoeuvres. Ned dances with young Jane, and Dan with Mrs Jones, while Joe Byrne dances with a sympathiser by the name of Kershaw, and two other prisoners make up the fourth pair. And yet, whatever Ned's ability on a horse, where he can do anything, when it comes to dancing he looks like he has three left feet, something that clearly amuses him as much as the other prisoners, as he is seen to be laughing heartily.

As is Ann Jones, enjoying herself hugely. After all these years of struggle, here she is in her finest red dress, dancing with the most important man in the room. 'Ned was a darling man,' she will later say of him.[40]

This, she is heard to confide later to one of the prisoners, will show some of the locals, who for years have treated her 'like a blackfellow'. Yes, she would tell him, 'Revenge is sweet.'[41]

And like mother, like daughter. For sixteen-year-old Tom Cameron notes that his classmate, young Jane – a buxom lass, despite her tender years – is altogether too involved with the bushrangers, 'making very free with them, getting on their knees and dancing with them and kissing them'. It is disgraceful, that is what it is – and it is Tom's strong view that 'six months gaol would do her no harm'.[42]

Hugh Bracken, for one, is stunned at the whole scene. He had not quite known what to expect, but certainly not this. For just what is going on here? Do these prisoners not know that the Kelly Gang are murderous thugs who have already killed three policemen and likely will not hesitate to kill again?

Perhaps they do, but, on the other hand, it seems obvious to Bracken after some quick observation – for of course he declines to dance himself – that not all of them really are prisoners. As a policeman with experience in the area as wide as it is deep, he knows better than most just how prevalent Kelly sympathisers are, and it is obvious that among this crowd there will be more than a sprinkling, there to help keep an eye on the bulk of the prisoners and ready to report to the Kellys the first sign of any serious resistance being formed. Of the five men he doesn't recognise, Bracken, while still feeling like death warmed up, is sure to go to all of them to ask their names.

—

In the Curnow house, the hysteria goes on, most particularly as Thomas makes it clear that his primary concern is to go out again, and as quickly as possible. For the discussion between him and his wife and sister has become ever more animated, not that it puts him off. Even while the ladies continue to voice their objections as they prepare some late supper, Curnow manages to quietly prepare everything he feels he needs, including the red llama scarf, candle and matches. He explains to the women that he will head to Benalla not on the main road but rather as close to the railway line as he can, on the grassy verge that generally runs alongside it. Should the special train appear, he will be able to jump on the line and light a warning to them.

With this explanation, his sister, at last, understands and agrees that he should do it, but not the pregnant Isobel. Working herself into an excited and hysterical state such as her husband has never seen before, she screams, 'If you go, I will stay here, and I, the baby, and your sister will be murdered!'[43]

To try to calm her, Curnow offers to take her to her mother's place, a third of a mile away, to which she consents. As a visit is expected from a gang member at any minute, Curnow leaves a note on the table, explaining where they are and why they are going: to get medicine for Curnow's sister, who has taken ill. At Curnow's request, Cathy wears her red llama scarf.

The moon has just risen over the Great Dividing Range.

—

What is that?

Somehow, over the squeal of the concertina, some of the dancers are sure they hear something different. Is that . . . in the far distance, a whistle? Perhaps the whistle of a train?

The dance stops and Dan Kelly goes outside to investigate, while inside the inn the tension rises as they all take a break. Dan comes back in shortly afterwards to give his verdict. 'It is all right,' he says. 'There is nothing. I wonder what is up with the bloody special, the police must be all asleep.'[44]

Shortly thereafter, Joe Byrne and Dan Kelly engage in a quiet but intense conversation with Ned. Dan, particularly, pushes the view that it might be time to pull out. Clearly, with the train still not here, something has happened and it may not be coming at all. They are all exhausted, they have an almost unmanageable number of prisoners to look after, and, with only a few hours of darkness left, why not gather their horses and go?

Ah, but Ned is not remotely interested. Leave once more, so they can be hunted once more, like wild dogs in the bush? No. No more running. This fight will be decided here. In Glenrowan. We have decided that this is where we are going to make our stand, so this is where we are going to make our stand.

Dan Kelly cedes with a surly nod of reluctant agreement.

—

Just after half past one in the morning, the special train from Melbourne starts to slow all but imperceptibly, slow, as the lights of Benalla Station appear in the darkness, way up ahead. At least their trip has been relatively fast, with the only mishap being a small delay when their locomotive had hit heavy iron railway gates just outside Craigieburn, closed because it is a Sunday night. Mercifully, though there was 'a crack like a bullet'[45] and the damage to the locomotive had been significant – including its entire braking system taken out – it had not prevented the train from proceeding and it had just kept rolling, going so fast it 'caused the carriage to oscillate very violently',[46] on the reckoning that the braking system on the guard's van could stop them regardless.

As the train pulls into Benalla, O'Connor finds Superintendent Hare and his seven troopers are there waiting on the platform, accompanied by one local volunteer, Charles Rawlins – all in heavy clothing, hats and scarves, even as they stamp their feet to guard against the penetrating cold. Their own train is on the next platform with seventeen horses, shanghaied for the occasion, loaded in their two luggage vans, and baggage packed.

Quickly now, Hare and O'Connor – with Sadleir also in attendance – closely consult as to what to do. It is suggested by one of the railway officers that they use the damaged train from Melbourne as pilot while its carriage can be attached to the carriages behind the Benalla engine. The proposal makes such sense it is quickly agreed to by them all, and the Melbourne engine soon has three red lights hung behind it, so the driver of the engine behind will be able to see it ahead. Senior Constable John Kelly, Hare's offsider, can take his six troopers and put them in the guard's van of the second train.

Before departure, Superintendent Hare has a quick word with the two engine drivers, telling them of his deep concerns about the exercise in which they are engaged. They must be on the lookout for torn-up rails, some kind of obstacle on the track or perhaps even an ambush. Yes, sir. There has also been the rumour that the Kellys have a powder keg and may have blown up the line – or maybe even intend to blow up the line with the train on it. It is with these specific fears in mind that Hare instructs young Constable Daniel Barry to strap himself to the front of the pilot engine and keep a lookout with his sharp eyes.

Mercifully for the young constable, the driver of the pilot engine, Henry Alder, refuses to allow any such thing on *his* train and, backed by the Benalla Stationmaster, Clement Stevens, tells Hare that it won't be necessary, as he will be able to see what is ahead from the cabin of the engine just as well as Constable Barry would from the front. And, just to be sure, Alder says, he will have his guard, Archibald McPhee, also keep his eyes peeled from just behind in the guard's van.

Finally, just before two o'clock, the train convoy – with thirty passengers and crew overall, together with the seventeen horses – leaves Benalla Station, bound for Beechworth, having only to pass through Glenrowan, some 14 miles away, and then Wangaratta some ten miles after that. Superintendent John Sadleir sees them off, and then goes back to bed, exhausted.

The mood of the officers and troopers on the train is mostly tired and tense – at the end of an exceedingly long and exhausting day, they are heading out in pursuit of proven police-killers – but also just a little exultant. They are many; the Kellys are few. After months stretching into years of being humiliated by the gang, it looks likely that there will now be a settling of accounts, as dangerous as that might be.

In the second train, Superintendent Hare gets into one compartment of the first-class carriage with the officer and the ladies, while the reporters have a compartment to themselves, and even the black-trackers – unaccustomed as they are – have a compartment nearly to themselves.

As they start off, Hare and O'Connor chat in the carriage, which pulls out just over a minute after the pilot engine. Superintendent Hare is particularly interested to know at what time Captain Standish had informed him of the situation.

'At half past seven,' O'Connor replies.

Hare is appalled and takes the younger man into his confidence. 'I never saw such a fellow as that Standish. He does not seem to care a single rush about the work. I told him hours before about it, and I begged him to go out and see you personally, as I knew it was a condescension on your part to come out to work again after the way he treated you.'

'Well, he never did . . .'[47]

They continue to chat lightly, a relatively easy thing to do because, while conversation between O'Connor and anyone had been difficult on the way up – so fast had the train been travelling, so loud the noise – now things are a lot slower and more cautious, and they poke along at not much more than 30 mph, though this does increase as they begin their run into Glenrowan, as it sits at the top of a small rise and the trains need something of a run-up.

Hare starts to feel sleepy now and, after apologising to O'Connor, carefully places his rifle in the luggage rack and then closes his eyes for a little nap.

—

At Glenrowan, resolution is wavering. In fact, after Mrs Reardon asks Dan Kelly whether she and her husband, James, can be allowed to go home with their eight children, Dan Kelly nods and says, 'You all can go . . .'[48]

As for Dan's burly bushranger brother, however, though Ned accepts that it might be the best thing to indeed let the prisoners go, he cannot resist putting on one more show. For even as the prisoners start to move towards the door – James Reardon scooping up one of his children, while old Martin Cherry, ever helpful, picks up another – it is Mrs Jones who stands in front of the door and says, 'Go back, and Ned Kelly will give us a lecture.'[49]

What?

'We will all be let go very soon . . .' she reassures them. 'You may thank me for it.'[50]

And lecture them he does. In the bar, Ned stands on a chair and holds court one more time for the road with the exhausted prisoners.

'The devil was in us,' Ann Jones later said. 'We had to want to hear the lecture and be listening and to be looking at the darling men . . .'[51]

The inn has been chaotically crowded since the women and children from the Stationmaster's house have come up, but even the smaller children somehow start listening when Ned speaks, so mesmerising are his cadences, so powerful his words. 'Reardon,' he starts in on the platelayer, 'do not you be so fond of getting out of your bed at night.

If you had a good horse, and I wanted it, I would take the horse and shoot you.'[52]

He then makes similar threats to Reardon's fellow platelayer, Sullivan, thinking he might be the same Sullivan, the New Zealand murderer, who had given Queen's evidence against some of his fellows to save his own dirty hide. The papers had been full of it. Advised by this Sullivan that he is no relation, Ned remarks, 'Them's the sort of dogs we want to catch. I would feel easy if I had them. The six black demons in Benalla and O'Connor and Hare.'

Now turning his attention to Bracken, he asks of those black demons – entirely unaware that they were preparing to go home – 'Are they good trackers?'

'I do not know how they would do here,' Bracken replies carefully, 'but they have got the name of being good trackers in Queensland.'

'Oh, bugger them,' Ned snorts dismissively. 'I could track an emu in Queensland myself.'[53] The bushranger goes on, conversationally now. 'Are there not 19 or 20 men in the force who are as great a rogues as myself?'[54]

Carefully now, Bracken agrees this is the case, and the bushranger seems satisfied with the answer.

Now, before letting them go – for he really is going to do just that – Ned decides to give his prisoners all fair warning. 'If any of you ever hear or see any one of us crossing the railway, or at any other place, and if the police should come and ask if you had seen any such party, you must say, "No; we saw nobody", and if I ever hear of any of you giving the police any information about us I will shoot you down like dogs. I do not mind a policeman doing his duty so long as he does not overdo it.'

Hugh Bracken can bear it no more. 'The police,' he says, 'are only earning an honest living. How, if you were an honest man, could you get on without them?'

Ned turns, faces Bracken and says, quite indignantly, for all the world as if he really means it, because he *does*, 'And am not I an honest man?'

'I'm damned if you are!' Bracken replies, to the laughter of nearly all.[55] For certainly the worthy Bracken is not laughing.

—

So it goes in the middle of the night.

No sooner has Tom Curnow arrived near his wife's mother's place out on the Benalla Road, than Isobel, holding her baby Muriel tightly to her, becomes hysterical once more, *insisting* they go home again before a gang member visits, and Curnow quickly agrees. Once they have her home again, Curnow says to his wife that he now realises it is too dangerous to try to warn the train and, with the firm promise that he will do nothing, at last he and his sister get his wife to agree to go to bed, as she is completely exhausted by the day's extraordinary events. It is just after two in the morning, she is very ill, and she has not slept for twenty hours!

Now, while his sister engages his wife's attention, Curnow slips outside and starts harnessing his horse, running a collar around its neck and a trace around its back legs. Come what may, he is convinced he must try to prevent the coming catastrophe and . . .

And what is that?

Cocking his ear, he listens again.

Is it . . .?

Is it . . . a *train* coming?

It is.

Forget the horse. Quickly grabbing the candle, scarf and matches, Curnow runs down into the small gully that separates his house from the railway line, and up the embankment that leads to the track proper. He runs along it towards the long straight stretch, which is where he knows he needs to be. With every step, the rhythmic rumbling of an approaching train in the far distance becomes louder – for the sound really does travel a long way on this freezing misty night – and there is no doubt it is coming from the direction of Benalla.

Quickly now, his hands shaking, Curnow lights the match. It takes! He holds it to the candle on this mercifully still night, with nary a breath of wind to blow out the flame, and now holds the red llama scarf up in front of the candle, hopefully providing a makeshift railway signal for both STOP and, more importantly, DANGER.

—

And still Ned is going on with his lecture.

'There was one bugger in Parliament,' he says, 'whom I would like to kill – Mr Graves.'[56]

'Why?' asks the fearless Bracken.

Clearly entirely unconcerned that he is making devastatingly damaging admissions before a respected officer of the law, Ned tells him. 'Because he suggested in Parliament that the water in the Kelly Country should be poisoned, and that the grass should be burnt. I will have him before long.'[57]

As to the former Premier Graham Berry, he, too, 'is no bloody good',[58] as he was guilty of giving the police altogether too much money for Ned's liking, all to capture him and his gang. 'As for Service, I know nothing of him. But they are all damned fools to bother their heads about parliament at all for this is *our* country.'[59] Not the politicians' country, not the police's country, but Kelly Country.

And then, once again, they think they hear something. Is *that* the sound of a train whistle? Again, Dan goes outside, this time for much longer, returning after five minutes to say, 'There is no sign of the special.'[60] Again Dan locks the front door after him and, closely observed by Hugh Bracken, paces over to the mantelpiece, lost in anxious thought. After tapping the key on that mantelpiece a few times, he then carelessly places the key by the clock, before being called away by Ned.

Carefully, quietly, amid all the confusion, Hugh Bracken now sidles up to the mantelpiece and takes the front-door key without the bushranger, or anyone else, for that matter, seeing him. He secretes it first in the pocket and then in the cuff of his trousers.

And then they hear it once more!

Out of the night comes the barest trace of a strange sound – is it a cock crowing, or perhaps a whistle?

As one, they all listen.

There it is again! Whistles! Short, sharp whistles!

Suddenly, the back door is thrown open and, coming from the breezeway, where he has been listening, Joe Byrne bursts in. 'The train is coming!' he roars.[61]

Ned Kelly could not be more pleased, saying to the prisoners, 'Here is the bloody special. Now we will show the bloody bobbies what we can do.'[62] For, oh yes, this is what they have been waiting for all along. 'You will see some play now, boys,' Ned roars. 'We will shoot them all!'[63]

Calling for total silence, Ned now listens closely in the full expectation that they will all shortly hear the train roar on through Glenrowan Station, on its way to Beechworth, only to tumble into the culvert just as they had planned, killing or maiming all the police and blacktrackers . . .

—

In the front of the cab, fireman Hugh Burch is furiously shovelling coal to keep the steam up for this long haul up the slope, while beside him driver Henry Alder is at the controls. Suddenly, though, about a mile and a half from Glenrowan Station, Alder and his guard Archibald McPhee spot something odd.

There! Way up ahead, in at least the rough direction that his train is heading, they see some kind of strange movement in the otherwise dark night, a curious . . . red . . . speck. It looks very much like a 'burning log in the bush'.[64]

But why on earth would a burning log be on the track before the train? It couldn't be. As it is in line with where the railway men know the curve commences, they assume that it really is burning somewhere ahead in the bush, but, the closer they get, the more it is obviously close to the line and . . . and even *on* the line.

And see there! A burning log does not move back and forth, as this red speck is doing.[65]

McPhee puts his head out the cabin window into the rush of freezing air and can 'distinctly see a whitish object with a light in front'.[66] Whatever it is, it is clearly human-inspired and out of the ordinary, and out of the ordinary means only one thing to railway men in the middle of the night: slow down. In fact, it really does mean STOP.

With the practised movement of a railway professional, the guard Archibald McPhee turns the wheel that will activate the brake in the guard's van – for the brake of the locomotive had of course been damaged in the accident at Craigieburn – while Alder gives off a few short blasts on his whistle as warning for the train behind.

For Thomas Curnow, still standing beside the railway line, furiously waving his lantern, it is horrifying. Here are hundreds of tons of metal and humanity hurtling towards their certain death, if the cab driver hasn't seen him! Has he . . .?

—

Steve Hart arrives from the Stationmaster's house with that man himself in tow. They have also heard the train, and Hart wants to get John Stanistreet up to the inn, away from any signalling system. The train has to keep going through.

So now all four bushrangers are straining their ears in the direction of the *clickety-clack*. And it is not long before they realise: the sound is diminishing. The train is slowing. The police must have been warned about what lies ahead!

The train is . . . slowing and yes . . . stopping.

They have been betrayed.

'By God . . .' Ned says loudly, before immediately identifying the only person released who is not already firmly in their camp, 'that bastard Curnow has deceived us.'[67]

—

Thomas Curnow sags with relief. For amid the roar of the engine, and the thundering of the train upon the tracks, the sound of screeching brakes is also now discernible, even as he notes that the shocking vision of the train looming ever larger has obviously slowed.

As the train passes him by at the pace of a fast jog, Archibald McPhee yells down to him, 'What's the matter?'

The guard can only just hear Curnow's reply as the schoolteacher shouts back at him, but it is chilling and unmistakable nevertheless: 'The Kellyssss . . .'[68]

Finally, mercifully, the locomotive comes to a halt and McPhee hops down . . . 'Hello, mate,' he repeats loudly, above the now shrill cry of the whistle. 'What is the matter?'[69]

—

When he first hears the sound of the whistle up ahead, the driver of the police train behind, John Bowman, immediately applies his own brakes, and there is a sudden surge of alarm in the carriage as men and equipment are thrown against each other. As the same happens to the horses, the air is filled with the screech of the outraged brakes, the curses of the troopers and the unearthly squeals of protest from the horses.

For his part, Superintendent Hare had just been snatching some precious sleep after all the excitement of the night, when his reverie at the entrance to the Land of Nod is now suddenly shattered and he is thrown violently forward. Instantly on his feet, he puts his head out of the window into the chilling night air and sees the three red lights of the pilot engine stopped ahead.

—

Up ahead, by that stopped first train in the middle of track, at twenty-five to three in the morning, Curnow's urgent words to McPhee tumble over each other in such a manner that sometimes one sentence has not quite finished before the next has begun – the precise thing he has frequently told his young students *not* to do. But this is different. This is life and death. The lives of the people on the train he has just stopped, and his death if he doesn't get back to his family in time. The frantic man explains the situation in no more than thirty seconds, the light from his candle giving his face an eerie, death's head appearance.

The track on the other side of Glenrowan has been torn up, he says, with the specific intent of murdering the police and the black-trackers . . . *The Kellys have taken over the town!* Where in the town they are, alas, Curnow does not specify.

But when McPhee tries to question Curnow – his words regularly interrupted by the driver of the pilot engine blowing short blasts on his whistle to warn the train behind that there is danger ahead – and mentions that the best thing will be to take the pilot engine slowly into Glenrowan Station, the schoolteacher is most insistent: 'No, no, don't you do that, or you will get shot.'[70]

But who *are* you, the guard wants to know, still thinking it might be a ruse. Curnow allows he is the local schoolteacher but is insistent on telling the guard one more thing before disappearing: please, please, please, do not tell anyone of my involvement in this. My own life and the lives of my family will be threatened. *Please!*

With this, Curnow takes his leave, ignoring the guard's pleas to talk to Superintendent Hare in the train behind, and quickly races back to his wife, desperate to get there before anyone might come to check on him. He finds her in a state of near nervous collapse, panic stricken by the train whistles and just knowing that her husband has been shot, and that the Kellys will shortly be coming for her and Cathy too. For his part, despite his calming words, Curnow is not sure that the last part might not soon come true, as he and his sister quickly take off his wet clothes to hide both them and the incriminating red scarf. Quickly all, to bed, as if we have been here all along!

—

Rapidly loading his rifle, and taking his key from his inside pocket to open the door of the first-class carriage, Superintendent Hare jumps down beside the tracks just in time to see the guard of the pilot train, holding a swaying lantern, heading back down the track to see him.

Archibald McPhee wastes no time in informing him about the man with the 'red handkerchief with a match at the back of it',[71] the warning about the line having been pulled up, and the Kelly Gang. And then, Superintendent, the man had just disappeared into the night, even though I begged him to see you before going.

At the news of the line being torn up, a chill moves through all of the troopers close enough to hear it, including Senior Constable John Kelly, who has just made his way forward. They had always known that the Kellys were murderous. But *this* murderous? There is no precedent for anything like it in the history of Victoria, or any other colony for that matter. If the Kellys had pulled it off, it really would have astonished the world.

Superintendent Hare now calls three of his best men to get down from the second train with their rifles loaded and at the ready, then together they walk down the line to the first train, where the fireman tells the same shocking story.

What to do?

After consultation – including with Senior Constable Kelly, who points out that the men would not be able to unload the horses where they are – Hare gives instructions. The pilot engine is slowly to move back and have its guard van connect to the second engine. All on the second engine are to be on guard and prepared for any emergency, as there is no telling what might happen. With his six best men, Hare then climbs onto the pilot engine and, with three troopers standing on each side of the engine gazing out to the left- and right-hand sides for trouble, he stands beside the driver Henry Adler as they carefully, at walking pace, shunt towards Glenrowan Station.

Inside their compartment of the first-class carriage of the second train, the four hyper-excited journalists – what a story! – take the seats they have been sitting on, and everything else they can find, including four big cushions, and put them up against the windows on the Glenrowan side of the train. Between them, they have just Joe Melvin's one small revolver, so they lock the doors of the carriage as added protection.

As to the ladies, in the next carriage along, they have just time to kiss darling Stanhope goodbye, and implore him to stay safe, before he heads off into the perilous night with Hare to do a man's work. Keep your head down.

On the pilot engine, Hare and his men eagerly strain their eyes, looking into the darkness. It is the driver, though, Henry Adler, who is looking most intently straight ahead and is the first one to cry out.

There! He swears he can see a man standing on the platform of Glenrowan Station, and they all strain their eyes and train their rifles accordingly, but as they proceed it is obvious that it was an apparition, because not only is that man not there, but no one is there. The whole place is eerily deserted, as the police special train that Ned Kelly has been waiting for all this time pulls into Glenrowan Station at twenty to three in the morning, some twenty-four hours later than the bush-ranger had been first expecting it.

—

In the back room of the inn, the four bushrangers quickly, if awkwardly, start to don their armour, strap themselves into it, and then help each other to put their long overcoats on. What is urgent now is for them to try to get down to the carriages and fire into them before the police have properly gathered themselves. Quick, lads, *quick!*

Ned and Joe finish first and go outside to gather their horses, with Ned, ever the leader, riding a little down the line to investigate what the situation is.

As to the prisoners, the question is are they still that? Perhaps they are free to go now? When the prisoner Tom Cameron is overheard suggesting this to platelayer James Reardon, however, young Jane Jones, still holding Dan Kelly's revolver, warns them not to leave without permission. It gets worse, for when Jane overhears young Tom Reardon suggest to Dennis Sullivan, 'Now would be a good time to escape,' Jane goes so far as to warn, 'If you attempt to escape, I'll tell Ned . . .'[72] Again, Cameron, particularly, must ask himself the question: *Just whose side are she and her mother on, anyway?*

There is little time to reflect on this, because, before the prisoners can make any move, Dan and Steve Hart have re-emerged from the back room, clad in their armour. There is a collective gasp from the prisoners as, for the first time, they sense just what this gang are capable of, what they are planning.

But if it is rounded metal that impresses, Ned Kelly and Joe Byrne are likely almost as stunned by what they see. For there, by the light of the moon, less than 200 yards away, they can now see – for a reason they don't quite understand – *two* locomotives coupled together and pulling several carriages towards Glenrowan Station. The train has its lights doused, giving it something of the aspect of a ghost train, and it is obvious that whoever is on it wants to present as little a target as possible to the bushrangers.

Quickly, Ned and Joe head back inside the inn and give the orders for every light to equally be doused – orders quickly acted on by Ann Jones, using jugs of water to douse the fire for good measure – as they all watch closely through the windows to see what the train will do. Will it continue on through Glenrowan Station, at which point it still might tumble into the culvert, or will it stop? There is the pervasive smell of kerosene in the air, coming from the doused lamps.

Ned goes outside to ride down the line again, to observe everything from as close as he can. It is, it has to be said, a beautiful wintry night, with the moon shining unusually brightly, the frost already forming, and the air so still and quiet that the tiniest sound from afar carries easily. Slowly, slowly, the train keeps *chug-chug-chugging* its way forward, now just 100 yards from the station. Is it stopping? No. Wait . . . yes, YES, it is stopping. And before all of their very eyes it does just that.

At this point, Ned Kelly is presented with a clear choice: fight or flee? For there is *still* time, even now, for the bushranger to acknowledge the truth of it, that his plan has failed, that the gang are now just four bushrangers up against a trainload of troopers and unlikely to survive. After all, they have horses and supplies, they are in Kelly Country and could easily evade their pursuers until dawn, at which point they could reassess their situation.

But that is the thing about Ned Kelly. He just doesn't have bowing to power in him. It is not in his nature.

Down at the station, Constable Charles Gascoigne is just helping to get the horses out of their carriage and onto the platform – no easy task, as the animals have been jolted to a sudden stop and can sense the extreme tension in the air, and so come out bucking and rearing – when he happens to gaze up from the station towards the silhouetted building that he knows to be the Glenrowan Inn. He almost fancies he can see a man there on horseback, watching them in the moonlight, but is not sure. Probably his imagination, but still he takes the precaution of telling Senior Constable Kelly, who immediately asks O'Connor to put two of his native police on guard on that side of the platform.

—

It is not Superintendent Hare's finest moment. Now surrounded by fourteen armed men – his own troopers, and the native police from Queensland – awaiting orders, he hesitates. The leader of the government forces in this crisis, he does not provide immediate leadership. Instead, he asks the one civilian present, Charles Rawlins – the volunteer from Benalla, a stock and station agent who knows the people of Glenrowan well – 'What had we better do?'[73]

Rawlins rises to the occasion. 'We are sure to hear of the Kellys at the railway gate, because of the horses having to cross,' he says. 'We will go down and see Stanistreet.'[74] Besides which, it may not even be necessary to wake him. As they had passed the Stationmaster's house, Rawlins mentions, he had seen a light burning within.

Excellent idea. Before going off together, however, Hare says to Rawlins, 'You are not armed, I will give you my revolver,' and even begins to give instructions on how it works, only for Rawlins to reply, 'It is a Webley, I know how to use it.' On consideration however, Rawlins adds, 'You can use the revolver better than I can, give me your double-barrelled gun.'

'No, I will stick to the gun,' Hare responds firmly.[75]

With that settled, Rawlins and Hare head off to the Stationmaster's house, in the company of three constables. Of the Stationmaster, there is no sign, but, from her bed, with her children beside her and the blanket pulled up over their eyes, his weeping wife – once she can be convinced to open the door, because they really are police – quickly tells them the lie of the land.

'The Kellys . . .' she sobs. 'They have taken my husband away and they are going to *kill* him; will you save him?'[76]

'How long since?' asks Mr Hare.

'Only five minutes since.'

'How many are there?' Rawlins asks.

'Forty,' she replies.[77]

The men hurriedly begin to say their goodbyes and utter their assurances that she and the children are now safe, so that they can get back to the station. This is at least partial confirmation of what Tom Curnow had previously told the train guard.

Of course, by now, the Kelly Gang have certainly fled, and the police will have to chase them through the night and into the next day, but it is still staggering that the police have been this close to them.

—

Inside the inn at this time, Constable Hugh Bracken has been well ahead of both Superintendent Hare and Ned Kelly, and, anticipating what is about to happen, quietly tells as many of the prisoners as he can trust to pass the message to the others. 'Lie down as flat as you possibly can on the floor, it is the only chance you have got.'[78]

Through the open windows, they soon hear the sound of whinnying horses being unloaded, the surest harbinger yet of the battle to come. For horses travel on trains only with police, and, if they are being offloaded, it not only means that the police are here but that they intend to stay. And if they intend to stay, it surely won't be long before they attack the Kellys in the inn, once they realise the bushrangers are still there. As everyone heeds Bracken's advice to lie on the floor, it is soon so packed that the only way they can manage to fit everyone in is to lie on their sides, while others head out to the slab hut at the back, where the kitchen and bedroom are, to see out the siege – if that is what this is going to be – the best they can.

In the confusion, Bracken takes his chance. After picking his way across the parlour, he retrieves the stolen key from the cuff of his trousers, deftly opens the front door in a manner that doesn't make a noise and quickly flits away. Yes, his primary sensation at this point is a deeply uncomfortable tingling down his spine, as he fears a shot ringing out in the night to bring him down, but there is nothing. Only thirty seconds later, running down the incline – and tumbling once in the dark rush, after jumping the fence – he arrives hatless, coatless and breathless, as Superintendent Hare and his men prepare to pursue the Kelly Gang on horseback, on the reckoning that by now they will have fled.

But Bracken puts them straight as he runs up, somehow managing to whisper and shout all at once to the first man he sees, Charles Rawlins, 'The Kellys are in Jones's, just going away; be quick, they will be off!'[79]

Ushered before Superintendent Hare, he repeats, 'They are here! They are here!' as now all the troopers turn to look at him. 'Over there – the Kellys – not five minutes ago,' Bracken gasps in a shouted whisper, while pointing to the Glenrowan Inn. 'Stuck us all up – the forty of them – quick, quick! . . . The Kellys are in Jones's! Surround the house, surround the house!'[80]

As one, all turn to gaze momentarily at the silhouette of the inn, its front thrown into deep shadow by the strong moonlight shining from high in the sky behind it, from just above Morgans Lookout.

Urgency is the key.

'For god's sake,' Bracken says, when no one has moved within a second of his utterances, 'take care or they will escape!'[81]

It is Hare who breaks the spell. 'Come on, boys! They are in Jones's Hotel!'[82]

It seems almost incredible to contemplate. Right here, right now, just a big stone's throw away, the most wanted gang in the whole continent awaits . . .

Chapter Fourteen

THE SIEGE BEGINS

If I hear any more of it I will not exactly show them what cold blooded murder is but wholesale and retail slaughter something different to shooting three troopers in self defence and robbing a bank.

Ned Kelly, giving fair warning eighteen months earlier in what would become known as the 'Jerilderie Letter'

Therefore put on the full armour of God, so that when the day of evil comes, you may be able to stand your ground, and after you have done everything, to stand.

The Bible, Ephesians 6:13

2.55 AM, 28 JUNE 1880, CRY HAVOC AND LET SLIP THE DOGS OF WAR!

'Come on, O'Connor,' Hare repeats, 'or . . . they will escape.'[1]

In a flash, Hare climbs onto one of the engine's running boards and gives his instructions, yelling above the racket caused by the horses rearing up, as the black-trackers, among others, try to get them under control.

Listen! You troopers are to follow me tightly. Do not fire unless they fire first. If they do, and anyone is wounded, that person is to be left to those who follow.

'O'Connor,' Hare now finishes, nodding towards where the black-trackers are still wrestling with the horses, 'are the men coming?'

'Come on, boys!' O'Connor roars at them. 'Come on!'[2]

And with that the horses are let free to gallop off towards Benalla in the moonlight, while four troopers and six black-trackers fall in behind Hare, all clutching their weapons tightly as they jog-trot towards the inn.

Sub-Inspector O'Connor is near the front, as is the volunteer Charles Rawlins, while bringing up the rear is the intrepid reporter from *The Argus*, Joe Melvin, the one journalist who has a weapon. Behind them, he leaves most of the other reporters building a wall of saddles on the southern end of the station, behind which they hope to have some minimal protection as they watch and record proceedings. (In the same spirit, in the first-class carriage, O'Connor's wife and sister-in-law stack up their dressing cases against the window for protection.)

To the journalists' left, they can see Senior Constable John Kelly also running up towards the inn with another two troopers, vaulting over the fence between the railway gate and the Stationmaster's house, and coming at it from a different angle. And who is this, now running back towards them? Oh, it is Joe Melvin, who has decided his place is not in the front line after all.

Melvin, with his colleagues thus, now watches closely, as in the 'dim, uncertain kind of light'[3] Hare remains easily distinguishable for his sheer height and bulk as he leads his men onwards.

—

From the inn, calmly watching the troopers come, three members of the Kelly Gang are standing in the deep shadow of the verandah, as their quarry moves quickly closer in the serious moonlight. For his part, the gang leader, Ned, is just a little way off, at the corner of the building, in shadow deep enough to go with the shadow on his brow, gazing intently. Not one of the bushrangers speaks a word.

Despite Superintendent Hare's initial prevarication, it is none other than he who takes the marginal lead of the main group and retains it even as Senior Constable Kelly's group now joins it.

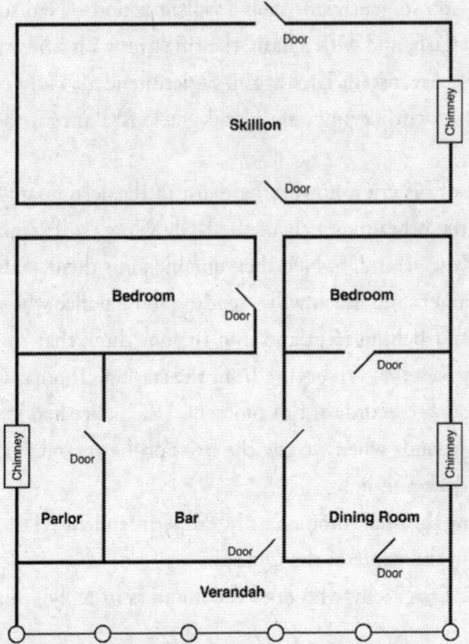

Floor plan of the Glenrowan Inn

Steady. Steady. Steady. Keep coming . . .

Coolly, Ned holds his Colt Revolving Rifle with his right arm directly out from his body, and with great difficulty – so heavy, awkward and cumbersome is all his armour – takes aim at the lead police officer, who is now just 40 yards away. He knows it is Superintendent Hare and is very pleased that the policeman has so presented himself. Here is a man who has been the bane of Ned's existence for much of the last two years.

Among those rushing beside Hare, it is Charles Rawlins who sees the figure and realises what is about to happen before it does. 'Look out!' he cries.[4]

Hare has just time enough to look up to see a dark figure in the lee of the inn, pointing a rifle at him with one arm, from about twenty yards away, when it happens.

Gently – oh so gently, for such a violent action – Ned squeezes the trigger. In a flash, and with a flash, the rifle fires with a fiery crack from the shadows. An instant later again, Superintendent Hare clutches his shattered left wrist, crying out, 'Good gracious! I am hit the very first shot.'[5]

The rest of his cries, however, are lost in the accompanying roar of guns from the other members of the Kelly Gang, still standing in the darkness of the verandah. Ned then quickly joins them as they all pick their own targets and fire at will – sending those police who can scrambling for cover behind trees and into the one ditch that runs through the Railway Reserve. Observing from the station, Thomas Carrington from the *Sketcher* records of this moment, 'The police had scarcely been gone a few seconds when we saw the front of the verandah of the hotel lit up with flashes of light . . .'[6]

Gathering himself momentarily, Superintendent Hare calls out, 'Surrender in the name of the Queen!'

And it is Dan Kelly who does the honours in reply: 'Surrender, be buggered!'[7]

This time, the chattering staccato gunfire from the bushrangers is more than matched by the unified volley of shots from the troopers. And now, from the darkness, the police can hear the bushrangers sneering at them, hooting, 'Come on, you bastards; the bloody police can't do us any harm.'[8]

What can they possibly mean by that? How could shooting at them not do them any harm? For it certainly has harmed the police leader. With the blood pouring from his wrist, Hare turns to Senior Constable Kelly, who must now formally take over command. Hare says, 'Kelly, surround the house, for God's sake, do not let them escape.' For good measure, he gives much the same order to the officer in charge of the Queensland black-trackers: 'Come on, O'Connor, the beggars have shot me – Bring your boys with you; surround the house.'[9]

Firing his gun one more time in the general direction of the Kellys, just on principle, Hare now takes action, even while using his right hand to grip his lift wrist tightly, almost as if his left hand will otherwise fall off. 'Rawlins, I am wounded,' he says. 'Take my gun and bag, they are no use to me, I cannot load again.'[10]

Rawlins grips it gratefully, at last with his hands on the rifle he had previously been denied.

Now turning back to Kelly, Hare says, 'Place the men under cover.'[11]

Senior Constable Kelly promises to do that, only begging Superintendent Hare to 'send up some ammunition'[12] when he gets back to the station.

Hare is just turning to go when a voice again rings out from the darkness. 'Surrender, you bloody dogs. You can't hurt us. Fire away.'[13]

One man, Constable Charles Gascoigne, is immediately galvanised. 'That is Ned Kelly's voice!' he cries.[14]

For his trouble, the insolence of the bushranger is answered with a tremendous volley from the police, occasioning a free-for-all as they continue to pour shots into Glenrowan Inn, while the four members of the Kelly Gang furiously fire shots back at them. In the midst of it all, strange sounds are heard, each one 'like the ring of a hammer on an anvil'.[15]

From the corner of the inn, Ned decides to break from his cover and walk a little down the hill, firing all the while in the direction of the flashes coming from the police, who are hiding behind whatever they can find, some behind trees, others behind the railway fence or in the ditch. Initially, he draws little return fire, as most of the police still have their heads down. Constable Gascoigne, however, sees the extraordinarily bulky figure coming down the hill and raises his .45 Martini-Henry rifle at it. So thick is the smoke from the previous volleys of shots on this extraordinarily still night that very few of the police can actually see Ned, but Constable Gascoigne can, meaning the figure can see him and . . . and now, sure enough . . . the man is turning towards him and raising his revolver.

Gascoigne gets his shot off first, to no effect, but the small sapling post he is hiding behind, about thirty yards from the hotel, is soon splintered with Ned's return fire. Bravely, Gascoigne keeps firing back

– still with no result – and now hears the bushranger yell, 'You bloody cocktails, you can't hurt me. I am in iron!'[16]

In response, so nervous is the constable as he fires at this figure – he is not sure who or what it is, only that it is firing at police – that both bullets miss his intended target, which is the bushranger's torso. One of Gascoigne's bullets, though, flies very low and hits Ned Kelly in his right foot, entering at his big toe and emerging at his heel, shattering bones as it goes. And another bullet is higher and passes first through Ned's bent left forearm and then his left upper-arm, whirling the bushranger around a little.

Yes, in the first actions of the battle, the two leaders of the opposing forces are each wounded badly.

Hit hard, and shocked that, for all his hard work in preparing the armour, he has still taken two bullets in his first serious clash while wearing it, Ned turns and, with great pain, staggering badly, disappears into the smoke and moonlit shadows.

And now, another cry rings out – this one from Joe Byrne. Despite Ned's claims that they can't be hurt, up on the verandah, Joe takes a bullet clean through his right calf.

—

Inside the inn, all is mayhem as the police bullets fly through the thin weatherboard walls and shred them into vicious whirling splinters, windows are shattered to shards, bottles in the bar explode, and in the cruel darkness the prisoners are screaming, the children are shrieking and crying, and all are praying, even as the bushrangers keep firing just yards away from them.

'This is all bloody Fitzpatrick's work!' Ann Jones is heard to cry out in the outhouse, as the bullets start to fly all around.[17]

Lying face-down on the floor in the bar, as the attack continues, her thirteen-year-old son, Jack, who had so happily been singing just a couple of hours earlier, suddenly stiffens and screams. A police bullet has come at a devilish angle, first hitting him in his left hip and then continuing up through his tiny body till it exits at his right armpit, causing him to start to convulse within seconds.

Suddenly, he manages to stand up and look around, before falling down and gasping in a piteous voice, 'Oh, God. Mother, dear mother, I'm shot!'[18]

One of the prisoners by the back door manages to call across the breezeway to tell Jack's mother the terrible news. Caring nothing for herself, she races into the bar, through the flying bullets, to find her bloodied son looking up at her. 'Oh, Mother, I am shot,' he repeats while trying and failing to rise by pulling himself up on her leg.[19]

Twenty yards away in the outhouse, Margaret Reardon is as yet untouched, despite the flying bullets all around, but she can hear the screams all right, and lies, weeping loudly, holding her baby tightly to her, trying to keep her body between her precious bundle and the gunfire.

Now, turning her son over, Ann Jones can see that he is entirely covered in blood, and, putting her hand on his body, she quickly finds the holes where his lifeblood is simply pouring out of him. White-faced, his eyes gaze up at his mother, speechlessly imploring her for help. Weeping, stricken, all she can do is tear off part of her apron and try to shove it in the huge hole in his hip to stop the blood.

Lying face-down nearby, old Martin Cherry looks to David Mortimer – who has his fingers in his ears, so as not to hear the screams of agony – and sees that the concertina player is in shock. He then nods to a young lad next to him and, amid all the weeping and loud praying for the Lord to help them, says, 'Come on, lad, we'll carry him in.'[20]

In the name of decency, both men do exactly that, and as gently as they can manage to lift the young lad and carry him out of the bar – his blood spattering their trouser legs – along the passage, across the breezeway and into the back building, where, with his mother's assistance, they get him into a corner, where the kitchen's chimney provides at least some protection. While his mother holds him, his sister Jane gets him a drink of water and a pillow for his head. Weeping, beside herself, covered in the blood of her son, Ann Jones can do nothing for the moment but continue to hold the two of them close and pray that the madness will soon end.

But it does not.

For, while Ann Jones stays huddling, cuddling her children next to the brick chimney, a ricochet strikes, creasing Jane's head. 'I am shot!' the girl cries, an instant before her mother cries too.[21] Jane, with panic in her eyes, turns to the Stationmaster, John Stanistreet, beside her, who manages to calm her a little by pointing out to her, sincerely, that it is nothing more than a very minor flesh wound, just above her ear, and the angle of entry is such that the bullet is visible right there, just beneath the skin. Together, Stanistreet and Ann Jones are able to remove the bullet, even if their hands are drenched in Jane's blood in the process.

One of the quarry workers, George Metcalf, is next to scream loudly in the dining room as a ricocheted bullet strikes him in the eye, giving him a grievous injury that immediately looks likely to be mortal.[22] At this point, the alarm in the room is not just the terrified type, felt by all the prisoners. For up on the mantelpiece a bullet hits the clock, which immediately springs to life, sounding loudly that the times are out of joint, until another bullet comes and ends its complaint.

—

It is now that a very brave quarry worker, Neil McHugh, takes one look at young Jack Jones and knows the boy will die unless he receives urgent medical attention. So, gently prising him away from his shattered mother, he picks up the grievously wounded Jack – the blood still pouring from the lad – and drapes him across his shoulders. With extraordinary courage, calling out as he goes, he walks out into the police barrage.

The first to see them is Constable Gascoigne, now behind a tree at the Benalla end of the inn, just ten yards from where Constable William Phillips is secreted behind another tree. Both can clearly determine that the new figure is a man with a child on his back and so hold fire, until another thought occurs.

'Gascoigne,' Constable Phillips calls softly, 'perhaps it is two of them clearing out. Come on and stop them.'[23]

Quickly, the troopers catch up to him as he reaches the rail gates, only convincing him to stop when they threaten to shoot him. Upon questioning, McHugh says something vague about 'armour', which means nothing to either trooper, but tells them there are thirty or forty prisoners in the house,

'Who is inside?' Phillips asks, referring to the bushrangers.

'Three, I think,' McHugh replies. 'There is one or two of them wounded. Look out in the morning, they will shoot you all out at daylight.'[24]

They let McHugh go to take young Jack to the empty house of platelayer James Reardon, where McHugh does his level best to save the young fellow's life, or at least stabilise it – while Gascoigne resumes his place at the Benalla side of the inn, and Phillips goes to the front of the house to wait his chance at getting a shot at the bushrangers.

—

Back in Stanistreet's home, the Stationmaster's terrified wife, Emily, is just trying to settle her weeping children when the door flies open and Senior Constable Kelly bursts in, looking for the ammunition that Charles Rawlins had apparently left there. In the confusion of everything, Kelly finds that Rawlins had brought the ammunition for the breech-loading guns that the constables used to use but don't any more.

And now, Mrs Stanistreet turns on him. 'You should not come here!' she says.

The policeman has little interest in that. 'For God's sake,' he says to her, 'go out of here! You will get shot here – take the children with you!'

'Where will I go?'

'Cannot you go over to McDonnell's?'[25]

'No, I will not go there,' she says in the manner of a woman who would under no circumstances be seen in such a den of thieves.

'Well, go out in the bush, towards Greta. There will be no danger there.'[26]

Mrs Stanistreet begins to gather her children up as Senior Constable Kelly races back to the front lines of what is now nothing less than a full-blown battle. In the heart of the shoot-out, journalist Joe Melvin has noted one group going particularly well. 'The trackers . . .' he records, 'stood the baptism of fire with fortitude, never flinching for one instant.'[27]

And so, too, are the journalists themselves going well. Far from merely observing, Joe Melvin and John McWhirter busy themselves sorting out 'the carbine and Martini-Henry ammunition and gave it out to the men as the messengers came to the station for it . . . Rawlins took the first lot and Senior Constable Kelly the next.'[28]

—

Meanwhile, Superintendent Hare, his legs now drenched in blood from the gushing wound in his hanging left wrist, has been escorted back first to the Stationmaster's house and then to the railway station itself by Rawlins. There, the artist for the *Sketcher*, Thomas Carrington, helped by the other journalists, quickly takes Mrs O'Connor's graciously proffered silk handkerchief and uses it to bind the Superintendent's wound. That good woman and her sister have now moved from the carriage to the heavier shelter provided by the station building, and, though worried sick about the safety of Stanhope, implore Superintendent Hare to not go back to the fight, so badly is he wounded. But he insists he must. Once his wound is bound, he asks Rawlins for his gun back.

'Surely you are not going back,' Rawlins remonstrates, 'let me have the gun.'

'I am going back,' Hare insists.[29]

As Hare painfully gets up, he gives orders for the train to go back to Benalla, so the officer in charge can be informed of what has occurred and send reinforcements, though his words are regularly interrupted by the relentlessly rumbling roar of gunfire rolling over them and on into the bush.

—

Down by the station, no sooner had the troopers hurried up towards the inn and the gunfight was underway than Constable Hugh Bracken had come to a sudden, terrifying realisation. By now, the failure of the special train to reach Wangaratta will have been noted, and the likelihood is that the Wangaratta authorities will send another train down the line to investigate. As it approached Glenrowan, it would roar to oblivion where the tracks had been torn up. Bracken realises that he must get to Wangaratta to warn them. And also bring back reinforcements. Notwithstanding that only twelve hours before he had been sick in his bed, has not slept since, and has just had bullets whistling around his ears, he now gathers in one of the horses, mounts it and gallops off down the line in the direction of Wangaratta.

—

Up in the inn, the Stationmaster John Stanistreet – now that he has managed to calm Jane Jones and her mother – has had *enough.* With the bullets continuing to fly, he feels his place is not with the Jones family but with his family. Standing up, he resolutely walks out of the kitchen to the backyard, where Dan, Steve and Joe are by the chimney, their rifles in their hands. In their armour and helmets, it is hard to tell which is which, but one of them says to him in a strangely metallic, echoey voice, 'If you go out, you'll be shot.'[30]

So be it. Stanistreet has had enough.

Mercifully, while fortune favours the brave, sometimes it positively blesses the foolhardy, for even though the firing is going on all around him from both sides, somehow the Stationmaster is able to emerge from the backyard of the inn and go down the path without being shot from in front or behind. When challenged by the police lines, he simply calls out in a voice of such affronted authority, 'Stanistreet, Stationmaster!'[31] that none of the troopers dares to shoot him. Once safely through the lines, he is quickly questioned by Senior Constable Kelly about the situation inside the inn and replies that there are 'about thirty or forty prisoners . . . lying on their faces . . . in the front room . . . [and] Mrs Jones's daughter and son have been wounded'[32] before he quickly moves on and heads straight back to his house, where it will immediately be his task to find his wife and children, who are strangely and worryingly absent.

—

Bit by bit, the police take up better positions, under Senior Constable Kelly's instruction, though with just seven troopers available beyond the black-trackers he has nowhere near enough of them to 'surround' the inn, as Hare had insisted must be done – most particularly as Kelly wants his men to stay in pairs for safety's sake.

Until reinforcements arrive, Senior Constable Kelly will just have to do the best he can, spreading his men in an arc to the south and west of the inn, effectively covering five o'clock to ten o'clock on the clock face, if the inn can be imagined as the centre of the dial. The most organised of these forces, and best protected, are the native police, as O'Connor has managed to place them in a well-protected ditch in the Railway Reserve only 50 yards from the inn, which allows them to shoot while exposing only a tiny part of their bodies to counter-fire.

After talking to Stanistreet, Senior Constable Kelly knows that all the prisoners are immobile on the floor, and so gives orders to his men to fire at every upright moving figure they can see, and generally to fire higher than waist level. 'It is fully expected that, in the darkness, the bushrangers will attempt to escape either by slinking away or coming out in the disguise of prisoners,' he tells his men.[33]

—

Of course, the night is filled with the flashes from the muzzles of many roaring guns, but suddenly the sky is filled with two enormous flashes, as from somewhere just behind McDonnell's Hotel two Chinese rockets are fired – a signal, perhaps, to sympathisers to rush to the aid of the gang? It will never be conclusively established, but there is no doubt that not a single shot is fired at police from behind their cordon and that whatever sympathisers might be there, none launch any attack in response to the rockets. The police, meanwhile, have no idea what the significance of the rockets is and just keep firing regardless, just as the Kelly Gang do.

Though it is at this point that Superintendent Hare briefly approaches the police lines once more, it is soon obvious to everyone, including himself, that he is in danger of collapse from loss of blood. When he does faint and is taken back down to the station, the ladies give him some precious sherry to revive him, and thereafter he is evacuated back to Benalla on the second engine – so quickly and in so much confusion that the ladies themselves are left behind – where those accompanying him can also send out cables for more police to come urgently. His last instruction before leaving is to ask a gentleman on the platform to pass on to his men that they must 'have a look out on the Greta side of the line to see that no assistance goes to the Kellys'.[34] For though no shots have yet been fired from sympathisers outside the police cordon, that is his great fear.

Finally, however, just as a thundering rain must inevitably fade to lighter rain, and then a sprinkle, and then a few scattered drops, and then nothing, there comes a curious lull in the battle, so suddenly quiet that Constable Gascoigne can even hear the bushrangers' horses at the back of the inn, pitifully whinnying.

Though nothing is said, let alone shouted, there is almost a tacit agreement from both sides to pause, to reassess, to determine the damage done and to work out how best to proceed from this point. Compounding the confusion is the thick smoke that engulfs the whole scene, as the smoke left over from so many guns blazing all at once has no breeze to shift it in this night of death and the deathly still.

It is only now, with the pause, that the police can hear for the first time the screams coming from the Glenrowan Inn, beseeching them, 'For God's sake, do not fire into the building, it is full of women and children!'[35]

It is now that Sub-Inspector O'Connor, despite having no authority over anyone other than his own black-trackers, takes the lead. 'Cease firing! Cease firing! Cease firing!' he calls, with a voice of command so crisp that no one chooses to challenge it.[36]

Once the firing has stopped, bar the odd sporadic shot, O'Connor sings out, 'Let the women out, let the women out!'[37]

The call is taken up by the men along the line, though with some adding their own twist. 'Lie down all who don't want to be shot,' one of the forward troopers calls shrilly, 'and make no attempt to leave the building till daylight or you will be shot, and we will fire high.'[38]

The first part of this command at least is clearly the way, and Rawlins, with his enormous, booming voice, calls out in support, 'Lie down, every one of you.'[39]

In a position of heavy cover, behind a tree up near the inn's verandah, Constable William Phillips now hears an extraordinary conversation take place between two of the bushrangers positioned close.

'Is that you, Joe?' a voice calls out.

'Yes, is that you, Ned?' another voice calls back. 'Come here.'

'Come here be damned. What are you doing there? Come with me and load my rifle. I'm cooked.'

'So am I. I think my leg is broke.'

'Leg be damned. You got the use of your arms. Come on. Load for me. I'll pink the buggers.'

'Don't be so excited; the boys'll hear us and it'll dishearten them.'

For a moment, Ned is quietened, as the reality of their situation seems to hit home. 'I'm afraid it's a case with us this time,' he returns rather disconsolately.

'Well, it's your fault; I always said this bloody armour would bring us to grief.'

But, despite the accusation, Ned suddenly feels a surge of confidence.

'Don't you believe it; old Hare is cooked, and we'll soon finish the rest.'[40]

The two then discuss exactly how they will do that, and they are soon joined by Steve and Dan. It is Ned's idea that he and Joe will head out now to do a long circuit and come out behind the police lines, while Steve and Dan attack from the front, killing the brutes in the crossfire. While Steve and Dan now go back into the inn to settle the prisoners down, Ned and Joe keep talking, the end result of which – likely due to Joe having been shot in the calf and being relatively immobile – is that Ned will go back out alone.

'I think Bracken has escaped!' Steve's voice suddenly rings out from inside the inn.

Bloody Bracken.

And so it goes. After giving some instructions to the three others that they must barricade the walls of the inn and the windows with whatever solid furniture they can get their hands on to stop the bullets, Ned leaves, while Joe limps back into the inn, cursing the wretched police who have done this to them all, most particularly bloody Bracken.

As for Ned, he is keen to get back to grips with the police, and, after slowly reloading his rifle once more and getting up, he heads out into the open, firing a shot at the first sign of a policeman he sees.

The weight! The discomfort. The sheer, crippling effort it takes to move around with the helmet and armour on, most particularly when you have been shot through the foot and arm and have already lost a fair amount of blood. Nevertheless, Ned is able to keep moving and get to his fine mare, Music, which he had left tethered some 100 yards east of the inn by a clump of trees in the paddock that adjoins it. And he would have got on her, too, bar the wave of weakness that suddenly breaks over him with such force that he is immediately obliged to sink to his knees. Removing his helmet, he takes off his skullcap and forlornly applies it to the wounds on his left arm. As to his right hand, upon examination he realises a bullet has taken away the ball of his thumb. He does not take off his right boot for fear of what he will find, and also because, whatever else, the leather is at least holding together what remains of his foot.

When he feels a little stronger, the sound of movement downhill – perhaps approaching police – galvanises him to get up, put his helmet back on and get moving once more, limping further up the hill – and no doubt leaving something of a snail-trail of blood as he half-drags his excruciatingly painful right foot behind him. When he finds another clump of trees and saplings higher up the hill, again he lowers himself to the ground, closes his eyes and soon floats from consciousness.

—

It is perhaps not surprising, given that the kookaburra is among the noisiest of Australian birds, that when the time comes for rest, a tranquil environment is their strong preference.

There are no kookaburras in the heavy bush that presses close to Glenrowan for the rest of this night. For never in the small town's existence has it ever known such uproarious noise, lasting for so long.

The police continue to fire indiscriminately at anything that moves and even things that don't. In all the confusion, and with the loss of Superintendent Hare, there is a woeful lack of organisation. Senior Constable John Kelly does his best, but instead of following a plan, concentrating on blocking off all means of escape while focusing on the possibility of getting a clear shot at the bushrangers that would not endanger the lives of the prisoners, there is . . . nothing. The police simply fire into the hotel at will. Given how close those on the train have come to losing their lives at the hands of this gang, none of them is disposed to mercy of any kind, and if prisoners happen to get hurt in the process, then that is just too damn bad.

A more experienced commander than Senior Constable Kelly might have organised for a group of his men to get close enough to the door of the hotel to rush inside and fight it out with the bushrangers – which would at least have the virtue of ending the siege quickly – but though the suggestion is made, neither that plan, nor any plan worthy of the name, is embraced.

Just keep firing, men!

And so they do, with the furious fusillades from both sides continuing, though it has to be said the firing from inside the inn seems to have diminished a little. Perhaps it is time to take a different tack?

'Come with me,' Senior Constable Kelly tells the man he respects as one of the best shots he has under his command, Constable James Arthur. For a great shot is what Senior Constable Kelly needs right now. Flitting quickly from tree to tree, the two policemen stay under as much cover as they can from the continuing fire coming from the inn, sometimes crawling along behind fallen logs. Finally, they reach their destination, the position where Senior Constable Kelly wants Constable Arthur to position himself, on the high ground about 100 yards from the north-western corner of the inn building. There is a tree there where Constable Arthur can get cover, while still being able to train fire on the inn. And yet the good constable – who all those years ago had earned Ned's respect by laughing at Constable Hall's cowardice – is just getting himself settled in, stooping down to get a look around the tree at the inn, and placing his hand on the ground as he does so, when he is startled by what he actually touches instead of wet earth.

For it is a six-chambered rifle, covered in blood. He is so astonished that for a moment he cannot speak, but then he gathers himself. 'Look here,' he whispers to Senior Constable Kelly.[41]

Both men are shocked.

'Look at this, too,' Constable Arthur says, pointing to a bloody skullcap and a pool of blood beside it, before drawing the obvious conclusion. 'My God, some of them have escaped.'[42]

Both policemen immediately cock their weapons and have them ready, almost sure that one of the gang must be near, perhaps watching them right now. Senior Constable Kelly is so nervous that he picks up the rifle for extra firepower, only to find that it is so thick with fresh blood that it sticks to his hand.

Quick enquiries with the nearest police confirm the gun and cap do not belong to one of them. That must mean it has come from one of the bushrangers. Has one of them been shot in the head? The worry is that, as it has been found at such a distance from the hotel, it seems likely that one of the gang really has got away through the thin police lines.

'I fear they have escaped,' Senior Constable Kelly says to Rawlins shortly afterwards, when that good volunteer is doing his rounds, handing out a fresh supply of cartridges. 'But, whatever happens, we must not fire into the house till we give the people inside time to get out, and they can't do that till daylight. I have told all the men to fire if they see anyone attempting to leave, to mind and fire high; if they keep down no one is likely to be injured.'[43]

—

Inside the inn, Ann Jones is hysterical with grief and rage over what has happened to her two children. She does, nevertheless, find the wherewithal to abuse Steve Hart, Dan Kelly and Joe Byrne, with whom she has previously been so friendly. 'Go! Go out! You cowards!' she screams at them. 'Go out and fight like men if you want to fight. Or run away, like curs if you are afraid! Go out of here. Do you want to see all my family murdered? Oh, you cowardly wretches!'[44]

And she is angry not just at them but also at the police who have done this to her son. Dazed, grief-stricken, covered in the blood of two of her children, she shrieks out at the troopers, 'Get up, you wretches, and die in the road yourselves! Don't lie down there in hiding! Stand up like men!'[45]

In the general mayhem and misery among the prisoners, it is David Mortimer who takes the lead, summoning up his courage to say to the bushrangers that surely they can now let the prisoners go?

Joe Byrne is not against it but points out, reasonably, that under the circumstances whoever opened the door and emerged would have every chance of being shot. This point is emphasised when one prisoner waves a white handkerchief out the window and it immediately attracts three shots, crashing in all around it, clearly aimed at it. That's what the police think of any attempt to surrender.

This notwithstanding, Ann Jones for one is determined to get herself and her remaining children out, come what may, and it is her completely fearless daughter who takes the lead. Holding a lighted candle, she goes to the outhouse and says, 'All women and children are to come out.'[46] Quickly, the women and children form up behind her and, only a few seconds afterwards, Jane, still bleeding from her head, opens the back door.

She has told her mother she will lead, as, 'I no longer care if I am killed. If my brother is going to die, I want to die with him.'[47] And so she now leads a group of predominantly women and children out through the backyard, ready to make a run for it, as the police hold their fire, wary as they are.

'Don't shoot! Don't shoot!' the women call, their hands in the air.

One entire family, however, the Reardons and their eight children, are deeply unlucky. Delayed by their seven-year-old daughter Kate suffering severe cramps from lying squashed up with all the other kids under the bed for too long, they emerge well behind the others, and are coming close to safety of the Stationmaster's house when the police suddenly hear male voices, the father talking to his older sons.

Treachery! It might be the Kelly Gang coming for them.

'Who comes there?' a trooper calls out.

'Women and children!' Margaret Reardon calls back.[48]

Wrong answer!

Or at least it seems to be, for she has no sooner said it than some of the troopers start to shoot.

Caught in no-man's-land, the family split up. Three of the younger children run forward to the police lines and safety; the rest of the family flee back inside the inn.

Mercifully, none of them is hit.

The battle goes on.

—

Something strange is going on. Up at Wangaratta, Sergeant Arthur Steele had been waiting patiently for the special train to arrive, wanting to have a few words with Superintendent Hare, and had already received a cable telling him it had left Benalla at five minutes past two that morning. But it is still not here.

Concerned when it is ten minutes late, at about five past three, he starts to walk down the track towards Benalla, hoping to perhaps hear the sound of the approaching train, knowing that at night the sound could carry for as far as seven or eight miles. But there is nothing, bar the rustle of the wind in the gum trees and the crickets playing their usual night symphony.

Or is there? For suddenly, in the crystal-clear night air, in the otherwise perfect silence now that he is removed from the movement at the station and the drowsy hum of the sleeping Wangaratta, Steele can hear something.

Shots! Yes, definitely shots, coming from his south, in the direction of Glenrowan. First a massive volley of shots, then rather more staccato shots. Whatever it is, it is something bad, and he immediately runs back to the station to tell the Stationmaster, Mr Laing, to get the Beechworth engine ready, while he would run up to wake the other troopers in the barracks. Then he must get a cable through to Superintendent Sadleir at his home in Benalla, to tell him there is '`heavy firing down the line`'[49] in the direction of Glenrowan.

He is just sending his last cable when he is suddenly summoned by the engine driver, Morgan, who makes an extraordinary claim. 'I think I hear a horseman coming on the sleepers,' he says.[50]

Steele cocks his ear but cannot hear a thing, so he walks away. But again he is summoned by the insistent Morgan. And now Steele can hear it too. It is coming from a long way off, but it is definitely the sound of galloping hooves, and Steele runs down the line towards it, straining to see in the dark.

And there he is. It is a man galloping along in the moonlight. Steele shouts to him. Constable Bracken recognises his voice and reins his horse in. The story comes pouring out. The Kellys are at Glenrowan. Quickly, Steele takes the constable's horse, instructing him to run the rest of the way, and races away to organise things. In short order, the station and the barracks are both a blur of activity, from the flashing of the Stationmaster's fingers on the cable key, sending messages dictated by Steele, to the special train pulling up to Wangaratta Station, to troopers checking their guns and their ammunition as they mount their steeds. The driver of the special train is, of course, advised of the break in the line and that he must be careful, as he heads off with two constables – Patrick Walsh and the man who had once been Lonigan's great friend, James Dwyer – while Steele rides off with five men, including the redoubtable Hugh Bracken, who is so exhausted he has to be helped into his saddle.

—

A bad dream? If only . . .

For, in Benalla, Superintendent John Sadleir is woken from his sound slumber by a young constable, who shoves a bunch of papers at him while spluttering out a story that Sadleir's groggy mind can't quite digest. But the five successive cables from Wangaratta instantly waken him – the train has not arrived; the train has arrived; sorry, cancel the last telegram; shots have been heard in the direction of Glenrowan; the Kellys, holed up with sixty prisoners in Glenrowan. Up and moving now, Sadleir and the constable immediately waken another thirteen police in the barracks, with orders that they must be ready to move out in fifteen minutes.

Shortly thereafter, the ailing Superintendent Hare arrives in Benalla on the special train, his mind reeling, still fresh from the fight. He barks at a man on the platform to assist him in getting to Dr John Nicholson's home. Nicholson answers the door slowly, but the sight of Hare's wound jolts him swiftly into action. He disappears into his bedroom to get changed, even as Hare yells from the front door that he needs urgent treatment, so that he can return to Glenrowan.

As soon as he is dressed, the doctor must come down to the telegraph office, where Hare will be dictating the cables that must be sent to Melbourne and every police station in the area, to advise them of what is happening in Glenrowan and what must be done.

By the time Dr Nicholson arrives at the police officer's side, only a few minutes later, Hare is again growing weak. Removing the tightly bound handkerchief that has been partly stemming the flow of blood from the wound, Dr Nicholson has as close a look as lantern light will allow. It is bad. Very bad. A severed artery is just the beginning of the damage done. This is what a left wrist looks like when it has been hit by a bullet – as opposed to the mere 'skin wound'[51] that he had found when he examined Fitzpatrick back in April 1878.

As experienced as he is, the good doctor is shocked by the damage the bullet has done, after passing 'obliquely in and out at the upper side of the joint, shattering the extremities of the bones, more especially of the radius'.[52] Far from giving Hare leave to return to the siege, Dr Nicholson is not even sure that the Superintendent won't have to lose his left hand.

At this point, Superintendent Sadleir arrives and Hare weakly tells him, 'Don't go without me, I shall be all right in a few minutes.'

Oh, no, you won't.

For, with the full backing of Dr Nicholson, Sadleir is firm. 'Don't be such a fool. You are a regular glutton. You have one bullet through you now, and I suppose you want more.'[53]

'I am determined to go back.'[54]

Of course you are. Of course you are. Still, have a little lie-down on this mass of postal bags, while the good doctor dresses your wound.

Superintendent Hare does so, and after urging Sadleir to 'hurry on'[55] and asking for some water, he suddenly passes out, which is useful.

For now, leaving Hare in the care of Benalla's Postmaster, Sadleir herds his nine troopers towards the special train, which, like an iron dragon in the moonlight, is already belching steam through its nostrils in its impatience to start. Alas – with more reports coming in of yet more wounded – the men must wait for a good ten minutes until Dr Nicholson arrives in the company of another Benalla doctor, Dr Hutchison. A tiny railway guard, Jesse Dowsett, who has packed his Railway Department-issued Breech Loader Colt revolver, is also on board, and in just minutes the now shuttling special train is racing back towards Glenrowan.

—

At Glenrowan, the firing at the inn goes on, the bullets tearing through the thin walls as women weep, men scream and . . . and . . . and lying on the floor of the kitchen out the back, one old man, Martin Cherry, suddenly groans fearfully. Out of the night, a bullet from the barrel of a police gun has hit him in the groin and travelled up into his abdomen. As Cherry continues to groan, massive internal haemorrhaging begins, and though those near him do what they can to ease his agonies, it is little enough, as the bullets continue to fly. Not far away, one of Cherry's fellow prisoners, John Larkins – who with others had been sheltering behind some stacked bags of oats – would report, 'The bullets came thick and fast like showers of hail.'[56] Despite that, Larkins crawls along the floor and gets to Cherry, easing him off one of the boys' beds in the back, where he had been when hit, and onto the floor, before covering him with a mattress in the forlorn hope that this might offer some protection.

—

And now they come in force. Sergeant Steele and his five troopers from Wangaratta arrive on horseback just after five o'clock in the morning, along the road that passes the rear of the inn, in the company of the worthy Hugh Bracken, who has of course returned to the fray.

The first trooper they see is Senior Constable Kelly, who begins to brief Steele – 'Hare is wounded, and one of the outlaws is gone'[57] – but something odd is going on. For Steele clearly wants no briefing, and he barely even registers the sound of the train arriving from Benalla. All he wants to know is where the Kelly Gang are – somewhere in that inn – for he wants to shoot them. And, if not them, anyone associated with them. Waving away the briefing, Steele – dressed for the occasion with his ever-present tweed jacket and hat and armed with his double-barrelled shotgun – runs up to the tree nearest to the inn and aims his gun at the back door, at which point the exasperated Constable

James Arthur, who has been watching the exchange between his two superiors, has to fiercely remonstrate, saying, 'Do not go up there, you will be shot . . .'[58]

So extraordinarily eager is Steele to start shooting at something, anything, he has placed himself in the firing line of other troopers behind him. Moreover, Steele has no interest in placing his own men anywhere, so eager is he to have a crack. Senior Constable Kelly thus places two of Steele's troopers in the most pressing gap, while the others sort themselves out.

Steele doesn't care. In the words of Constable Arthur, 'Steele seemed . . . excited. He fired from the tree when he was first there. He fired when I could see nothing to fire at . . .'[59]

—

Superintendent Sadleir, who now arrives with his troopers up from the station, is much more interested in what Senior Constable Kelly has to say, including the fact that to this point the police have not had enough men to properly surround the inn, and that the bushrangers inside are still firing heavily.

This last point is emphasised as, even while they are speaking, more firing comes from the inn, the bullets landing close enough to spray gravel up at their legs. As he would tell it afterwards, the report that Sadleir receives at this point is somewhat confused, as he is told by Senior Constable Kelly that, as well as dozens of prisoners on the floor, the Kellys have no fewer than thirty armed supporters inside the hotel with them, and even that 'breastworks from bags of horse-feed lined the wooden walls of the hotel'.[60]

Clearly they will need many more police on hand than they currently have. For the moment, Sadleir – who is now the senior man on site and takes over the whole operation – tells Kelly he can have the troopers he has brought with him from Benalla to place where he will, and that more troopers should already be on their way from Beechworth, before asking where O'Connor is.

'He is down there,' Senior Constable Kelly says, pointing to the distant ditch, 'in a hole.'

Still unsure, Sadleir commands, 'Take me down and show me where he is,'[61] and Kelly does just that.

Heading off, Sadleir turns to the troopers who have come with him and says, 'Come on, men, spread yourselves round the house and assist the others, walk three yards apart, so that you will not be a target for the outlaws to fire at you.'[62]

As Superintendent Sadleir and Senior Constable Kelly get within sight of O'Connor in the ditch, however, an odd thing happens. For when Sadleir says, 'Come here, O'Connor,' the Queenslander replies, 'No, you come here.'[63]

Stand-off.

And so Superintendent Sadleir turns to his underling, Senior Constable Kelly – the one who is not allowed to answer him back – and says, 'You go and place the men wherever you think they are required.'[64]

All put together, it will now be possible to complete something of a thin cordon around the Glenrowan Inn, even if there still remain gaps. Not that there is any sign that the bushrangers are intimidated, for all that. A brief consultation with O'Connor confirms for Sadleir what Senior Constable Kelly has told him. The inn is well fortified, and it would be very dangerous to storm it. And again, the point is well made.

But, first things first. To get a better picture of exactly what they are up against, Sadleir makes a very careful circuit of the inn, talking to the men as he goes. As he gets near the south-west corner, he finds young Constable Gascoigne. Because all is still in darkness, Sadleir is able to be right upon him before the young man is aware, but there is no fear in him. Rather, he is excited, for, as he tells his superior, he had been fired upon by Ned Kelly himself. He knows it was Ned, for he recognised his voice. Gascoigne tells Sadleir how he received some protection from a small tree, but there was a very strange thing. 'I fired at him point blank and hit him straight in the body. But there is no use firing at Ned Kelly; he can't be hurt. He has armour on.'[65]

'Armour?' Sadleir replies, amused. 'You must have made a mistake.'

'I did not make any mistake,' Gascoigne replies hotly. 'Edward Kelly and I have had several shots at each other at a short distance, about twenty-five yards. It is no use shooting at the hotel as the outlaws have armour on.'[66]

Even more bemused, Sadleir makes an encouraging comment regardless and moves on. Strange, these young constables, who can think the bushrangers now have armour on.

—

In the first flush of dawn, when four saddled horses are spotted tied up to the back door of the inn, they are summarily shot by Senior Constable Kelly and Constable Arthur, their animal screams haunting all those who hear them, adding to the sense of total desolation.

From now on, any of the Kelly Gang who wants to break through the cordon will have to fight his way through against police who now outnumber the lot of them by a factor of twelve to one.

And don't they know it.

For most of the police, now that they have got the Kelly Gang cornered, the opportunity to fire bullets in their general direction is simply too good to miss, no matter how devastating the consequences for those inside the inn. Of course, it does galvanise the prisoners who remain inside to try to get out of this death trap. Some of them now ask Dan Kelly if they can make an attempt to leave.

'You can go,' Dan replies dubiously, 'but I am frightened you will get shot. I do not begrudge your going if you can escape.'[67]

All the prisoners want to hear is that the bushrangers won't shoot them in the back, and some of them quickly open the front door in preparation for storming out . . . only to be sprayed with splinters of wood as shots come from all directions, but most particularly the ditch where O'Connor has his black-trackers.

Now it is O'Connor who takes the lead, calling out after the flurry of shots has faded, 'Who comes there?'

'Women and children!' comes the repeated reply,[68] but still the firing does not cease.

None of this shakes Margaret Reardon's resolution. Now the only woman left in the inn, she has had enough. Paralysed by fear throughout the night, with the coming of dawn through the shattered windows of the inn, some clarity has returned, and it has become obvious to her that, despite the debacle of the family's last attempt to get away, they must try again. Staying in this inn, with these outlaws, surrounded now by surely dozens of police who have already proved themselves uncaring when it comes to not killing or wounding innocents, is out of the question. This time, however, she will go without her husband, as she wants it to be absolutely clear that she is but a woman and, apart from her oldest son, Michael, who is seventeen and slight, and her sixteen-year-old son, Thomas, her brood are but children.

Once she approaches the back door with her children behind her, Dan Kelly approaches and gives firm advice. 'Mrs Reardon,' he says caringly, 'put out the children and make them scream, and scream yourself . . .'[69]

This time, the police must know from the start that it is a woman and children emerging, not armed bushrangers. There can be no question about one of the Kelly Gang being with them. Shortly, they are all formed up and ready to go, with Margaret holding the baby Bridget in her arms, and Michael right behind her with his terrified five-year-old sister, Ellen, clinging desperately to his left hand. True, the bushrangers give her a last-minute warning that she had better not go out as the police would certainly shoot her, but Margaret Reardon dismisses their concerns. 'Surely,' she replies, 'they can see that I am a woman.'[70]

The first clue the police cordon has as to what is about to happen is when a voice rings out from inside the inn: 'Don't shoot! Don't shoot! Woman and children coming out!'[71]

Just as she is about to head out the back door, Dan Kelly says to her, with obvious envy, 'If you escape . . .'

'What shall I do?'

'See Hare, and tell him to keep his men from shooting till daylight, and to allow all these people to go out, and that we shall fight for ourselves.'

And then she steps out, and amid the screams of her children as the police fire indiscriminately, she SCREAMS herself for the police to have mercy on them. 'I am only a woman, allow me to escape with my children!' she implores. 'The outlaws will not interfere with us – do not you!'[72]

Constable Arthur, for one, sees this and immediately makes the call. 'Don't fire . . . this is an innocent woman.'[73]

Sorry? Did someone say there's a group coming out of the inn where the bushrangers are and they are therefore fair game?

That, at least, seems to be the way Sergeant Steele hears it, for in response he roars at the small posse emerging, just twenty yards from his position, 'Put up your hands, or I will shoot you like a bloody dog.'[74]

For Margaret Reardon, who is holding her baby under her arm, putting her hands in the air is no easy thing, but she does the best she can, while Michael, who is still holding his toddler sister with his left hand, raises his right hand.

Sergeant Steele fires four times anyway, mercifully missing, narrowly and nearly, with two shots actually penetrating the baby's shawl, causing Mrs Reardon to cry out, 'Oh, you have shot my child.'[75]

Terrified, her son Michael calls to her, 'Mother, come back; you will be shot!'

But his mother will not hear of it, and replies, 'I will not go back; I might as well be shot outside as inside. I do not think the coward can shoot me.'[76]

Shrieking, Margaret pushes forward as fast as she can, determined that, come what may, she must either get herself and her baby away from the inn or die in the attempt, and she actually manages to get partial shelter behind a tree. For his part, Michael decides it would be nothing less than suicide, as a grown male, to follow his mother, and he jerks his baby sister around and rushes back towards the inn.

Sergeant Steele is just aiming to fire at Margaret Reardon again when Constable Arthur – regarded as one of the best shots in the whole district – roars at him, 'If you fire again, I'll bloody well shoot you myself.'[77]

Steele, with the madness of bloodlust upon him, appears in one manner not to hear, for he now calls out exultantly, and mistakenly, 'I've shot Mother Jones in the tits.'[78]

The news is not well received, with Constable Phillips instantly calling back, with dripping sarcasm, how very proud he must be to have such a feather in his cap.

A small parenthesis here. Oddly, Mrs Reardon's guardian, beyond Constable Arthur, proves to be one Jesse Dowsett, the railway guard who has just arrived on the train from Benalla and had positioned himself within 30 yards of the hotel, behind a fence that marks the border to the hotel's grounds. When he calls upon Mrs Reardon in a low voice to leave the shelter of the tree and come to him, she trusts his kind face and does just that, walking towards him. Once within reach, Dowsett grabs her and her baby, lifts them over the fence, and they are safe. Despite it all, the only injury is where a bullet has grazed baby Bridget's forehead. Close parenthesis.

Meanwhile, Sergeant Steele remains determined to bring down a prize, any prize, and – later claiming that the young man had not sufficiently held up his hands for his liking – squeezes off two shots at Michael Reardon while the young man is within just a few yards of the back door, still with his baby sister in one hand and his right arm raised up above his head. One bullet hits him in the shoulder and he collapses into the arms of his father, who had opened the door to grab his son and little Ellen to drag them both back inside.

Again, Steele is exultant. 'I've wounded Dan Kelly!' he cries.[79]

Inside the inn, all is madness, mayhem and maybe murder. 'You had better go out and surrender,' one of the prisoners suggests to Dan Kelly.

'We will never surrender,' Dan replies, 'but most likely we will leave directly.'[80]

—

Despite the withering comments of the troopers around him over the near-fatal shooting of baby Bridget and her older brother Michael, Steele remains unrepentant. For a reason the police officer can't quite fathom, he has a strong sense – at least the way he would tell it afterwards – that before this battle is over he would be confronting the Gang, and he is looking forward to it.

But he doesn't just want the Kelly Gang, he wants, specifically, Ned Kelly, and has even worked out the best way to do it. Recently, he has read about a notorious American outlaw, not unlike Kelly, who had survived for an extraordinarily long time despite being fiercely pursued and shot at – but who had finally been brought down by 'a double-barrelled gun, double loaded with buckshot'.[81] This, Steele knows, is consistent with the current practice of using shotguns and buckshot against train robbers in the United States, and it is with this in mind that he has brought with him a large stock of Australia's nearest equivalent of buckshot: large, leaden pellets known as 'swan drops'. To fire them, he has a double-barrelled shotgun now fully loaded with these drops.

Hopefully, if he can just get close enough to Kelly, he will be able to fire at him, and he feels strangely confident that he will be able to take him down.

—

Where is he? What is happening? In his small clump of trees, just 300 yards up the hill from the inn, Ned Kelly opens his eyes. It takes just a moment for it all to come back. The agony in his right foot, the wounds in his left arm. He is at Glenrowan and has been shot. The police are surrounding the inn, and his brother and mates are inside there.

What now? Fight or flight?

Of course, he must get back to the inn. Rising slowly, not much faster than the sun that will soon creep over the horizon, eventually Ned is upright and heading back down the hill to the hotel. As he goes, he can hear the odd crack of rifle fire both from police and from inside the inn and from the flashes of the police muzzles it is relatively easy to see where they are positioned. Sticking to the shadows, he has no difficulty in getting to the back door, where he is quick to call out, 'It's me, boys. It's Ned.'[82]

It is Joe who greets him first, his voice lighter for the fact that Ned has returned to them.

Ned's response is succinct. 'I'm shot. You can lick them. Keep your pluck up.'[83]

These two firmest of friends then part. Joe goes back into the bowels of the inn, while Ned goes to talk to Dan and Steve. As Joe heads back down the passage, he chats briefly to the prisoners in the big bedroom. When one of them asks if Joe can help them get away, he replies in kindly, if perhaps regretful, fashion, 'Stay where you are; you are a great deal better off than we are.'[84]

What Joe most feels like right now is a good, stiff drink, and it is with some purpose, thus, that he heads into the bar and fills a glass nearly to the brim with whiskey. Of course, he is standing in his heavy armour, while all around him the prisoners remain hugging the floor, trying to escape the shots that keep bursting through the walls. Allowing himself a moment of bonhomie in an otherwise totally desperate situation, Joe strikes a casual pose, lifting a foot onto the bar rail, preparing to propose a toast. As the apron of armour protecting his groin now digs into his thigh, he lifts it out of the way and returns to the toast. 'Many more years in the bush for the Kelly Gang,' he says,[85] before knocking his drink back with a single swig.

At this moment, a mighty volley of shots from the suddenly reinforced police rings out, and Joe, standing not too far from young Patrick Delaney and David Mortimer, suddenly staggers and whirls. A bullet has caught him in his unprotected groin, likely severing his femoral artery. The blood pours from him like an open tap at the bottom of a full tank – in such a large volume that, from ten yards away, James Reardon can hear 'the blood gushing'.[86]

Joe falls to the ground 'like a log',[87] without a word, and seconds later his glassy blue eyes, so blue, are staring unseeing at the ceiling.

In the face of the tragedy, Ned, who arrives on the scene only moments later, is surprisingly sanguine. 'We must make the best of it,' he says simply to the other two. 'My best friend is dead. I'll go out in the verandah, and challenge them . . .'[88]

And perhaps he does, or perhaps he doesn't. In the continuing roar of gunfire, shouting imprecations at the police in the middle of a volley is perhaps beside the point.

But when Ned comes back inside the shattered inn a short time later, he cannot immediately see either Dan or Steve. Perhaps they have escaped? And so he heads outside once more, aware that, with the dawn close, his cover of the night will soon be no more. As he goes, he inevitably passes close by many police, and by his later account, 'I could have shot them easily, and could have got away if I wished.'[89]

What does he do instead? This will ever after be the subject of speculation.

Perhaps he manages to stagger to a rendezvous point with sympathisers, where – shocked to find that Dan and Steve aren't there – he tells them that Joe is dead, that the situation is appalling and that the sympathisers must disperse, before fainting.

Or perhaps, weakened by loss of blood, sleeplessness and carrying 97 pounds of armour, he simply finds another quiet clump of trees and slips from consciousness. Either way, the siege of Glenrowan will have to proceed without him for a short time.

Though the firing from the inn seems to have diminished a little by this time, the fact that the encirclers still risk a bullet to the head is quickly and bloodily demonstrated when Trooper Jimmy takes a bullet across both eyebrows that slices him wide open. Not particularly troubled, the black-tracker drops down into the ditch for a moment before coming back up, firing five shots and calling out, 'Take that, Ned Kelly!'[90]

O'Connor and the other troopers laugh.

Try to kill us all in a train crash, will you? Then take that, fella!

—

And so it has come to this. Inside the inn, Dan Kelly and Steve Hart find themselves left with the corpse of Joe Byrne, left by Ned once more, surrounded by police and with no obvious way out. Somehow, it seems as though it is not just Joe who has the life gone out of him.

'What do we do now?' Steve Hart is heard to ask morosely of Dan, once they have returned to the bar.[91]

The reply goes unrecorded.

Shortly thereafter, some of the remaining captives ask the bushrangers where Ned is. They mumble that they do not know, that they suppose 'he is done'.[92]

—

Up the hill, in a grove of gum trees, Ned rallies his strength. Can he really leave his brother Dan and Steve alone inside the inn, surrounded by the police? He cannot. With his last remaining strength, just before seven o'clock, Ned raises himself and dons his helmet once more. With a supreme effort, he manages to stand and starts to move back towards the inn . . .

Chapter Fifteen

IT'S A BUNYIP

It looked for all the world like the ghost of Hamlet's father with no head, only a very long thick neck . . . It was the most extraordinary sight I ever saw or read of in my life, and I felt fairly spellbound with wonder, and I could not stir or speak.

Thomas Carrington of the Australasian Sketcher, describing what he saw at Glenrowan on the morning of 28 June 1880

6.50 AM, 28 JUNE 1880, GLENROWAN, A MONSTER FROM THE MIST

Yes, Constable Arthur could get closer to the inn, but he simply doesn't want to. He is possessed of a Martini-Henry rifle, 'as good at a hundred yards as at twenty',[1] and the danger in getting too close to the building is that the bullets might go right through the inn and hit someone on the other side. And so he stays 100 yards back, on the Wangaratta side, kneeling down behind a log not far from the spot where he had earlier found the rifle and skullcap. As he takes his sights along the barrel of his rifle, he is impatient for the sun to fully rise so he can get some warmth back into his bones.[2] For, good God, it is cold. In an effort to alleviate it a little, and at least to warm his lungs, he is just pausing to fill his pipe to have a smoke when he hears movement behind him. Turning, he can see something emerging from the bush, and he yells at him 'to keep back or you will be shot!'.

All Arthur hears in response is a 'rumbling noise'.[3]

Shocked, disbelieving, the worthy constable looks up to see the most extraordinary thing he has ever seen in his life – so staggering that his pipe immediately falls to the ground, and he stares, slack-mouthed. Steadily, the figure approaches, and, after first realising it is a man, Constable Arthur then thinks it must be 'some madman in the horrors who had put some nail keg on his head'.[4] Obviously, it is someone intent on storming the hotel under the protection of the headgear, so he sings out to him, 'Keep back, you damned fool!'[5]

But still the figure keeps coming . . .

It cannot be one of the Kelly Gang! They are all inside the inn, not attacking from the rear, surely. The shocked constable yells at the figure again, 'Keep back, or you will be shot!'[6]

But hark, for the figure speaks, albeit in an oddly metallic fashion. 'I could shoot you, sonny,' it says,[7] even as Constable Arthur sees that the figure is pulling back its oilskin coat, to reveal its right hand is holding a revolver, with its bloodied left hand coming up in support of it, and now . . . taking aim!

But the figure can't seem to lift its arm all the way, and the shot tears up the ground halfway between the two foes.

And, of course, many of the other police have now seen the figure too. Or have they?

In this first ghostly spectre of dawn, under the circumstances, it is not surprising that every bit of swirling mist, every emerging shadow, looks exactly like a bushranger coming at them, a harbinger of horror that quickly fades back into the mist, and now they are not sure if this is just one more. The true horror, however, is that this time, despite their earnest hopes, the figure is not their imagination and, all too suddenly, it has emerged from the mist and it really is a bushranger, or . . . or . . . or is it a MONSTER?

For there it is.

Coming at the police down the wooded slope that lies to the north of the inn is something that looks, as Sergeant Arthur Steele would later describe it, 'human, as to its clothes, but altogether inhuman as to its shape and general appearance'.[8] Slowly, cumbersomely, the figure keeps moving forward and it is now regularly firing at them from what appears to be a big revolver in its right hand.

Oh my Lord! After a sleepless night, in which the police have already and demonstrably narrowly escaped death, after all the shooting and all the screams, all the fears that have stalked their night with the promise that one lucky shot from the inn will see them breathe their last, now . . . *this.*

Still the figure keeps coming.

Is it even *human*?

'Ned Kelly at Bay' by Thomas Carrington. (From *The Australasian Sketcher*, 3 July 1880, courtesy Matt Shore)

In desperation, fearing the end, Arthur manages to quickly roll while still bringing his rifle to bear, aiming directly at the figure's head. The constable pulls the trigger, there is a mighty roar, and he has the grim satisfaction of seeing the figure's head instantly snap backward, but . . .

But still it keeps coming.

And now it is the monster's turn. For again the figure raises its two hands to fire, and again its revolver roars, hurling up a spume of dirt just a yard in front of Constable Arthur. Somehow, it seems, the beast does not have the strength to fire straight and is using all its energy just to stay upright.

Again, Constable Arthur fires, 'at a white mark, a slit in his helmet',[9] and the figure's head snaps back once more, but still it keeps staggering forward, firing back, but again mercifully missing.

'It appeared,' one of the police would later recount, 'as if he was a fiend with a charmed life.'[10]

(Not quite. Without the skullcap, there is no padding to protect Ned's head from the bullet hammer-blows on his helmet, and, unseen by his attackers, Ned's head begins to bleed, the blood trickling down his cheek and onto his neck.)

Constable Arthur fires a third shot, which misses entirely, and still the figure keeps moving, like a massive Frankenstein's monster in the Antipodes, the left leg forward first, and dragging the right one behind.

Cries ring out as the police continue firing, but all to no effect.

'My God, who is that?' railway guard Jesse Dowsett, who has rejoined the fray after taking Mrs Reardon to the station, calls to the man nearest him, Constable Patrick Healy.

'He is a madman!' comes one response.[11] And soon there are others . . .

'Look out, boys, he is the bunyip!'[12]

'You can't kill it!'

Dowsett's preliminary view, as he darts from tree to tree, trying to get close to the figure coming down the slope, is that it looks like 'a tremendous big blackfellow with something like a blanket on him'.[13] Noticing Senior Constable Kelly on his right, he shouts out, 'If you come here you can get a good shot at him.'[14]

From the railway platform, the artist for the *Australasian Sketcher*, Thomas Carrington, watches, mesmerised. He will later recount,

'Suddenly we noticed one or two of the men, with their backs turned to the hotel, firing at something in the bush. Presently we noticed a very tall figure in white stalking slowly along in the direction of the hotel. There was no head visible and in the dim light with the steam rising from the ground it looked for all the world like the ghost of Hamlet's father with no head, only a very long thick neck . . . The figure continued gradually to advance, stopping every now and then, and moving what looked like its headless neck slowly and mechanically round. Shot after shot was fired at it, but without effect, the figure generally replying by tapping the butt end of its revolver against its neck, the blows ringing out with the clearness and distinctiveness of a bell in the morning air. It was the most extraordinary sight I ever saw or read of in my life, and I felt fairly spellbound with wonder, and I could not stir or speak . . .'[15]

The Argus's Joe Melvin, right beside Carrington, is equally mesmerised, wondering how this is possible. 'He . . . walked coolly from tree to tree, and received the fire of the police with the utmost indifference, returning a shot from his revolver when a good opportunity presented itself.'[16]

From different angles now, Constables Healy and Montiford fire their own weapons, with an equal lack of results.

'Fire away, you buggers,' the figure laughs back at them. 'You cannot hurt me.'[17]

Ah, but Sergeant Steele might be able to. For though he also at first thought this figure was a tall black man wrapped in a rug, close observation has given him a clue. Amid the madness and terror of it all, he has heard something strange. Some odd . . . metallic sound.

There it is again.

As the police keep firing, Steele regularly hears first the blast from a gun, and then, an instant later, a small clinking sound. Could it be? Is that the explanation? Has this figure got some kind of metallic shield on? Vaguely, he recalls something Assistant Commissioner Nicolson told him a month earlier, about the stolen mouldboards, and the preposterous notion that they were being made into something like that.

Yes, that must be it. Perhaps not so preposterous after all. And now this extraordinary figure is lurching straight for Steele, continuing to tap its metal helmet with the butt of its revolver, even as – after being sure he can hear them yelling from the inn – he calls for Steve Hart and his brother Dan.

'Come out, boys, and we will lick the lot of them,' the figure yells, beckoning to the other two outlaws. 'Come out, and whip the lot of them. Oh, you bastards, we will put the daylight through you.'[18]

—

Down on the railway platform, Constable James Dwyer has been briefly with the journalists, watching the action, momentarily mesmerised, before he snaps out of it and determines that his place is in the fight. And yet, as he starts to run, one of the journalists, *The Daily Telegraph*'s George Allen, seizes him by the right arm and says, 'Do not, Dwyer, you may be shot . . .'[19]

Dwyer tears himself free with such force that he falls, but, once on his feet again, he starts running towards the action. The first man he sees, taking shelter behind a tree, is Constable Hugh Bracken. 'There,' Dwyer says, pointing with his finger at this monstrous figure, 'is Ned Kelly.'[20]

—

'Is it fate?' Steele would later rather vaingloriously record of his feelings as the figure lumbers closer. 'Is this Ned, come to settle the affair of our vendetta in person?' A strong sensation comes over him. A combination of a rising excitement and 'a creepy feeling about the roots of my hair'.[21]

Steele is chilled by the cold morning but is not sure if the shiver he feels now is because of that cold, or the simple wonder of seeing 'this ghostly apparition stand behind the lower part of a fallen tree, and quietly proceed to take pot shots at two or three of us with the queer-looking weapon that it carried'.[22]

And now the figure seems to be having more trouble holding its revolver steady, as it stops by a clump of three small trees and several fallen logs, about 100 yards north of the inn. Despite that, the bushranger seems to be enjoying it all. 'Come on, you bastards, you dogs,' he keeps laughing and yelling. 'You can't hurt me!'[23]

When his Colt revolver runs out of bullets, Ned is seen to take the bag that is over his shoulders and delve into it briefly. He walks a couple of yards into a clump of trees so he can kneel down to begin reloading, even as, seemingly from out of nowhere, his mare, Music, trots up to him – all saddled up and ready to be ridden – only to be shot for her trouble by the police, who are fearful that he might try to escape. Ned's lame hands fumble with his Colt, only to be so frustrated that he tosses it aside and takes out the Webley revolver that he had stolen from Lonigan back at Stringybark.

Steele is entranced as the bushranger keeps reloading. So entranced he neglects to do the obvious, which is to attack while he is powerless to shoot back.

As the exhausted Ned leans against the tree – mystified as to why his brother Dan and Steve Hart still have not rushed to help, and becoming deeply angered because of it – the railway guard, Jesse Dowsett, says to Senior Constable Kelly, who has just joined him on his right, 'Cannot you pot him off from there?'[24]

Senior Constable Kelly does his best but misses Ned on the first go, with the bullet clearly hitting the tree behind him, just to the right. The policeman fires again, and this time there is a reaction. 'By God, you have hit him on the hand!' the admiring Dowsett calls.[25]

Ned's weapon is knocked from his hand. That, alas, does not stop him, as he draws yet another gun from yet another holster, and he is suddenly up and walking towards them from the cover of the trees, right out into the open.

Dowsett holds his nerve, and runs even closer and ducks behind a big log, some three feet high, even as Ned Kelly continues his awkward advance. From this new position, the railway guard fires five shots at him, point blank, from a distance of a dozen yards. All for no result.

The bullets merely make a strange metallic sound, bouncing off 'like parched peas',[26] and the figure keeps coming.

'This must be the devil!' Dowsett cries out.[27]

Continuing to tap his helmet with his revolver, Ned jeers at them, 'You bloody dogs, you cannot shoot me.'[28]

What kind of man would not turn and run away at such a vision but stand and face it? A man like Dowsett. Noticing that Sergeant Steele is coming down towards the monster on the left, and Senior Constable Kelly on the right – and with the outlaw crippled but still advancing straight for him – Dowsett suddenly feels stronger. 'He must be mad,' he calls to the others, cheekily, 'he is ringing a bell to let us know where he is.'[29]

And, clearly, Dowsett for one is glad to know exactly where he is. For, despite it all, the humble and anonymous railway guard, who stands no taller than five feet four inches with his boots on, calls on the famous and mighty bushranger to give it all up, as Ned Kelly walks straight towards him. 'You had better surrender, old man,' he says bravely, like young David before Goliath with a mask on. 'Throw up your hands.'

'Never while I have a shot left,' Ned replies.[30]

This makes the young railway guard really angry. For now Dowsett approaches even closer and, from a distance where he simply cannot miss, shoots the figure in the head, asking rhetorically, 'How do you like that, old man?'[31]

But when the smoke from the shot clears, the figure is still standing, holding a revolver pointing back at Dowsett. 'How do you like this?' says Ned, as he fires back in turn,[32] and for the rest of his days Dowsett will never know how the bushranger missed him.

Down on the railway platform the journalists and others stand, entranced, watching the whole scene play out, regularly bursting out with exclamations of wonder.

'Look out, he's going to fire!'

'There he is behind that tree!'

'I can see him from here!'

'Look at little Dowsett, what a plucky fellow he is!'[33]

As the figure starts to shoot again, Steele, well out to Dowsett's left, starts to move in, while the firing from the other police goes on. Some shots clearly hit the figure, all for no result. (In fact, as Ned would later recount, 'It was just like blows from a man's fist receiving the bullets on my armour.'[34] And just as he had not fallen to the flailing fists of Wild Wright, so he does not fall now.)

Ned turns his whole body mechanically, slowly to the right, to see the advancing Steele, and laboriously lifts his revolver to fire at him. The policeman has to dive to the ground to dodge it.

'I felt the breath of the bullet,' Steele would later recount.[35] Desperate now, and shaken, the police sergeant fires his revolver again, for still no result, only the metallic clink again. By now, there are four police firing at close quarters, and though the figure reacts each time as though punched, it staggers back a step but it does not fall.

Now on his side on the ground, Sergeant Steele sees his chance. For there, beneath the fallen and dead white tree trunk behind which the outlaw is standing, he can clearly see his legs, and they look to be unprotected by armour. The clear thought of 'I win' surges through Steele. Lying over on his left side, with his small, round tweed hat still securely on his head, he aims his shotgun at those legs and squeezes the trigger.

There is a mighty roar, a flash of flame, a burst of smoke and the swan drops – small lead pellets the size of nail-heads – bursts forth. Immediately, there is a kind of strangled, tinny cry from the figure as it staggers a yard back. He must have hit him. But Steele certainly has not stopped him.

For now, Ned Kelly has turned and, after widening the stance of his legs to make sure he doesn't fall over, is taking careful aim at Steele once more. Steele rolls frantically just in time and now half-raises himself to put the right barrel of his gun at near point-blank range under the log, straight at the legs, and again pulls the trigger.

There is another cry, but still Ned does not fall. Though he has his pistol outstretched in his right hand, suddenly half the life seems to go out of him – he . . . can . . . no . . . longer . . . lift . . . his . . . arm . . .

horizontal – and the hand holding the pistol suddenly drops to his side.

Seeing what is happening, Senior Constable Kelly yells to Constable Bracken, who has followed up hard behind Jesse Dowsett, 'Come on, and we will rush him!'[36]

Steele immediately begins to do just that, using the tree on his left for cover and drawing his revolver as he runs. But now a strange thing happens. There is a groan, the monster lurches forward and then, in a strangled voice that sounds oddly hollow and metallic in the cylindrical iron helmet, cries out, 'That is enough I am done!'[37] before falling face up with a heavy crash behind the stump. He is bleeding from his hip, thigh and groin, where the last blast has hit him – but is still gripping his revolver tightly.

It is just on a quarter past seven on this misty morning before the dawn.

Running forward, Steele now leaps upon the fallen figure, as does Jesse Dowsett, while Senior Constable John Kelly is not far behind, running towards them. Still, Ned has one ounce of fight left in him, and with his horrifically bloodied right hand he tries to bring his revolver to bear on one of them, shooting blind back over his left shoulder, pulling the trigger just a split second after Dowsett grips his wrist to push the gun away.

The gun roars right beside Sergeant Steele's face, but again, despite the blast singeing his cheek and blowing his tweed hat from his head, the policeman has a miraculous escape. He grabs Ned's beard, which extends a long way under his helmet, the way another man might hold onto the reins of a bucking horse, even as Senior Constable Kelly crash-tackles into the lot of them, knocking them all off balance in his eagerness to get the helmeted head in a headlock. In the wild and muddy melee that follows, Dowsett gets his hands on the revolver and manages to cruelly twist it in such a manner that Ned's finger is strained to breaking point as the railway guard rips it off him.

The pistol, marked on the hilt with 'N.S.W.G.',[38] as in 'New South Wales Government' – for Ned had stolen it from Constable Devine at Jerilderie – still has three chambers loaded. With his gun gone, Ned gives up the uneven struggle, and it is Senior Constable Kelly who manages to wrench the helmet from his shoulders.

In one stunned moment, Ned's attackers can confirm for the first time just who they had been fighting, and it is Steele who gathers himself first to proclaim it. 'By heavens, it is Ned,' he exults.[39]

On the instant, a surge of savagery comes over Steele, who, after all, has already shown no compunction about firing at women and children and, to top it off, only seconds before has only narrowly escaped having his head blown off by the fallen figure before him. 'You bloody wretch,' he roars, as he takes aim at the bushranger's head with his revolver, 'I swore I would be in at your death, and I am!'[40] As Ned's left arm is held down by Jesse Dowsett, and his wounded right arm by the newly arrived Charles Rawlins, all the shivering, bloodied and bruised bushranger can do is to look up into that blackest of all black things in the world: the muzzle of a revolver pointed right at your head.

Ned will not plead for his life, but he does say, 'That's enough: I have got my gruel.'[41]

It is doubtful if Steele – whom Ned had once sworn to turn into soup – even hears him, so lost is he in this moment, a moment frozen in time, as the policeman steadies his aim and the three men on the ground brace themselves for the shot they know must come, one of them understanding his last moment on earth has arrived . . .

Appalled, Dowsett yells at Steele, 'Take the man alive – take him alive!'[42]

Constable Hugh Bracken, however, who has just arrived alongside the fallen Ned, goes one better. Stepping over Kelly, and protecting him with his own body, he brandishes his shotgun and says squarely at Steele, 'I'll shoot anyone who shoots him.'[43]

'Give me a chance,' Ned said then. 'Let me live as long as I can.'[44]

As the tension eases a little, Bracken adds, 'Do not shoot him; he never did me any harm. I am going to take his part.'[45]

Steele lowers his revolver, as many others now rush up.

And there is Ned Kelly. That bastard. The scene confronting Constable James Dwyer as he races up is an extraordinary one. There on the ground before him, wrapped in some kind of strange armour, is the man who, twenty months earlier, had killed three of his colleagues, including his dearest friend, Thomas Lonigan. Most conveniently, Kelly has his arms pinned and his legs spread-eagled, his groin vulnerable. The opportunity is just too good to miss, and this one is for Thomas . . .

'With something like a war whoop,' as it would later be described,[46] Dwyer races forward and aims the cruellest of kicks at Ned Kelly's testicles. Now, the last man who had attacked Ned Kelly in this part of the anatomy had died at Ned's hands not long afterwards, so in some ways Dwyer could count himself lucky. For, of course, instead of his swinging right foot striking soft testicles, it crashes into the armour of Kelly's groin-guard, composed of iron a quarter of an inch thick. Joe Byrne had gone down for being unprotected in those parts, but Ned would not. There is a loud clang, breaking the frozen moment, and Dwyer yells in excruciating pain, before hopping away like a demented and stricken kangaroo with a thorn in its paw.

Again relying on his saviour, Kelly twists his head to Constable Bracken and says, 'Bracken, save me; I saved you.'

'You showed little mercy to Sergeant Kennedy and Scanlan,' Constable Bracken says in reply.

'I had to shoot them,' the fallen bushranger responds, 'or they would have shot me.'[47]

And now the three intrepid journalists, McWhirter, Melvin and Allen, arrive, to find Ned still being held down by Senior Constable John Kelly, Steele, Dowsett and Rawlins. As shots ring out from the inn, and bullets start spurting up dirt, Senior Constable John Kelly asks McWhirter to pick up his rifle from the other side of the log where he has dropped it and to stand guard with Allen to 'keep a look-out to see that none of the outlaws came out again to fire'.[48]

Up on Morgans Lookout, the first direct rays of sun of the new day have hit, as below it Sergeant Steele and Senior Constable John Kelly now endeavour to remove Ned's extraordinary armour by unscrewing the various fastenings. It is hard going, and Sergeant Steele is soon obliged to borrow a pocket knife to cut many of the straps that hold it all together, in order to sufficiently loosen it, while the still heavily limping Dwyer heads off to the other side of the inn to tell Superintendent Sadleir and Sub-Inspector O'Connor what has occurred.

Ah, but Dwyer does not limp for long. For he is just passing on the low side of the inn when two shots ring out, both of which narrowly miss him, causing him to break into a dead sprint, to arrive breathless in front of Sadleir.

'Good God, Dwyer,' the stunned police officer says. 'Why are you going about in that reckless manner? You will be shot.'

'I came down, sir, to inform you of Ned Kelly's capture . . .'

'Are you sure?'

'Yes, sir,' Dwyer replies, pointing to the proof, 'for there is his blood on my hand and trousers.'[49]

'Who caught him first?'

'Sergeant Steele,' Dwyer pants out,[50] before giving rough details on what happened and how it happened, including a heartfelt apology for his own part in – I am terribly sorry, sir – trying to kick Ned Kelly in the balls.

The first part of Ned's coat of armour that had made him look so superhuman has just been removed when Dr Nicholson arrives on the scene. The good doctor would remember it ever afterwards. For there is Ned, sitting up, his helmet by his side, 'and a most extraordinary and pitiable object he looked. A wild beast brought to bay, and evidently expecting to be roughly used. His face and hands were smeared with blood. He was shivering with cold, ghastly white, and smelt strongly of brandy.'[51]

Even now, however, when Ned is at his lowest ebb, there remains some spirit to him, as, once Dr Nicholson starts to tend to the most dangerous of his wounds before his captors attempt to move him, he is stunned to hear the bushranger say to him, rather conversationally, 'This is the first time you had me as a patient, doctor.'[52] Dr Nicholson does not reply but keeps on working.

—

From inside the shattered inn, the equally shattered Dan Kelly and Steve Hart have been watching, appalled, as the policemen have surrounded Ned and finally brought him down, and they have been firing off the odd shot themselves when they can. Yes, they had heard Ned calling for them to come but . . .

But somehow, when it came to it, they lacked the will to do so. Now, however, that the police are all over Ned, the two start firing with fervour, with the enraged Dan even venturing from the cover of the building to take better aim. 'Fire away, you buggers,' he roars, still firing, 'you cannot kill me!'[53]

It is either the measure of a miracle or distance alone that no one is grievously hit, though one bullet from Dan raises a spurt of earth between Senior Constable Kelly and Sergeant Steele, and then another bullet hits the fallen tree, sending a splinter flying into Dr Nicholson's calf.

Of course, Dan's display draws extraordinarily heavy return fire from every policeman within coo-ee, and he is quickly forced to withdraw, the more so because, now that Steele has demonstrated that to bring one of these monsters down the key is to fire at the legs, the more canny of the police do that. Dan takes a bullet to the calf before getting back inside the inn, a shower of bullets raising splinters of wood all around the door frame as his bulk disappears through it.

—

And now Ned is helped to his feet, as although the pain for the fallen bushranger is excruciating with every movement he makes, every jolt he receives, there is nothing for the police to do but to remove him and themselves from the field of battle. His weight borne between the shoulders of Sergeant Steele and Constable Bracken, he is half-dragged, half-carried back towards the railway station, where it requires five troopers to lift him over the railway fence.

Quickly pushing ahead of them as they proceed are Senior Constable Kelly, Charles Rawlins and Dr Nicholson, carrying between them Ned's armour, and noting that – very oddly, for what can it mean? – some parts of it are marked with the name of *Hugh Lennon*,[54] the ploughmaker. Good Lord, but the armour is heavy, so heavy they wonder how Kelly could have stayed upright in it.

Ned Kelly is taken first to the guard's van to be more fully examined – under heavy guard – by Doctors Nicholson and Hutchinson, but this position has to be quickly abandoned as, from the inn, Dan Kelly and Steve Hart continue to rain fire upon them. The fact that Ned Kelly, without armour, is now in the environs they are firing on makes no difference to the bushrangers, leading to later speculation that there may even have been a death pact between them that if one of them were captured it was for the others to shoot him dead if possible.

Quickly, Ned is evacuated into the far more secure surrounds of Stanistreet's office in the station proper, where the bullets cannot penetrate. After Ned has been placed on a stretcher, and the madness and mayhem has receded a little, the doctors are able to get a better look at the bushranger, to first properly search him and then to strip off some more of his clothes, allowing them to determine just which of his many wounds is most serious.

'He was dressed in the dandy bushman style,' Thomas Carrington would later record, 'yellow cord pants, strapped with slate, cross-barred pattern cloth, riding boots with very thin soles and very high heels indeed; white Crimean shirt with large black spots; waistcoat same material as trousers; hair, jet black, inclined to curl, reddish beard and moustache, and very heavy black eyebrows – altogether a fine figure of a man, the only bad part about his face being his mouth, which is a cruel and wicked one.'[55]

Layer by layer, the clothes continue to come off, many of them courtesy of sharp scissors. And yet, what is this? Something curiously green? It is some kind of silk sash, which he has draped around his torso . . . It is about seven feet long and half a foot wide, with three-inch golden fringes at each end. Curious. Very curious.

Quietly, Dr Nicholson takes it off and tucks it away among his own effects. When Ned's pockets are searched by Senior Constable John

Kelly, he is found to have a silver Geneva watch, a lot of ammunition stuffed into a mustard tin and just threepence in his pocket – surely not all that is left of the thousands of pounds the Kelly Gang have stolen?

Senior Constable Kelly immediately asks Ned where Sergeant Kennedy's watch is.

'I cannot tell you,' he groans in reply, trembling in every limb. 'I would not like to tell you about it. I had to shoot Sergeant Kennedy and Scanlan for my own safety. I cannot tell you any more.'[56]

As to the armour itself, which is now sitting out on the station platform and drawing much attention, it is nothing if not impressive. No matter the number of bullets and pellets that had been fired at it, many of them from close range, none has penetrated. Close examination reveals three dints on the breastplate where bullets have hit, one on the shoulder plate and no fewer than five on the helmet – all of which, on the helmet, would likely have killed Ned had he not been wearing it. Also visible is 'the stain of sap from a green tree'.[57] Using the railway scales, the police work out that Ned's armour weighs 97 pounds.

All of this is noted down by the journalists, who now swarm around Ned, covering far and away the biggest story of their lives. And yet the journalists are not merely observers. Just as Joe Melvin had taken up a gun and fired at the Glenrowan Inn, so too do some of them now try to make Kelly more comfortable. John McWhirter cuts the boots from his feet,[58] and another gets a pillow for his head and roughly assists the extremely worried looking doctors, Nicholson and Hutchinson, to undress him.

That accomplished, the doctors wrestle with the key question: could a man survive so many wounds, such heavy loss of blood? Their preliminary survey finds Ned to have – beyond the two black eyes, a torn cheek from a helmet bolt, the ridge of his nose battered and many abrasions all over his body – two bullet wounds in his left arm and a bullet in his right arm, as well as no fewer than twenty-five weeping wounds, especially on the outer side of his right leg, caused by Sergeant Steele's swan shot.[59] Most of those pellets are still inside him. Not that it seems to worry Ned overly. There is also a bullet that has torn through his right foot and a slug that has 'entered the ball of the right thumb', causing a wound, which, Ned confesses to the doctor, is 'as painful as any of them, and prevented me holding my revolver'. For now, lying back, he says in quite a dream-like state, 'It was as good as Waterloo, wasn't it? As good as Waterloo . . .'[60]

The two doctors now assiduously set out to try to stabilise the bushranger, removing what pellets and slugs they can easily get to, before cleaning and suturing the wounds to stop the flow of blood. It is obviously extremely painful to the bushranger and yet, though he occasionally shifts uncomfortably and twice faints dead away, his only complaint – in the classic symptom of one who has lost a life-threatening amount of blood – is how his feet are frozen. In an effort to alleviate this, the reporters get a kerosene tin filled with water heated up, which they then place against Kelly's feet.

After fulfilling his other duties in ensuring that the cordon around the inn remains tight, Superintendent Sadleir now arrives and is immediately struck by 'the gentle expression on [Ned's] face. It was hard to think that he was a callous and cruel murderer'.[61] Ah, but 'the old spirit, half savage, half insane, was there notwithstanding', Sadleir would report, for not long afterward, even as the police officer is talking to him, 'there passed suddenly over his face a startling look of wild passion as he called me to send away the black bastard who was leaning over him'.[62]

The 'black bastard' in question? It proves to be merely a fireman who has been working on his engine, and has a blackened face because of it. Things calm when this is pointed out to Ned but flare again when Constable Dwyer enters.

'You cowardly dog, you kicked me when I was down!' Ned roars.

'*You* are the cowardly dog,' Dwyer replies, 'you killed my poor comrade.'

'Who was your comrade?'

'Poor Lonigan.'

'Look here, old man, when you were out there, did not you try to shoot me?'

'No.'

'Then,' says Ned, 'you had no business there.'[63]

At this point, Superintendent Sadleir interrupts to say that Dwyer had already apologised to him personally for having lost his temper, and he knows for a fact he is very sorry. And maybe he is . . .

'Will you have a drink of brandy, Ned?' Constable Dwyer asks, almost in a manner of making amends – as he had noticed the fallen bushranger looks wistfully at the bottle in his hands – and showing already that strange intimacy that oft evolves between those who capture and those who are captured. The brandy has come from Sub-Inspector O'Connor's wife, together with some sweet-cake for the brave troopers to share.

'Yes, please,' Ned replies, 'if you will give it to me.'

'Why would I not?'

'Put the glass to my lips, I cannot – my hands are tied.'

As Dwyer puts it to his lips, some of the brandy falls on Ned's big beard, and so thirsty is he after the morning's proceedings he lifts his handcuffed hands to his beard to allow him to suck a few more precious drops, before saying, 'Give me a bit of bread, I am very hungry.'[64]

Superintendent Sadleir sends Dwyer to get exactly that, together with more brandy from McDonnell's Hotel. When the constable returns promptly with scones and brandy, the once-was-bushranger is truly appreciative.

'Thanks, Mr Sadleir, this is more kindness than I ever thought to get . . .'

'You shall have every care and attention, Ned,' the police officer replies, as he puts yet one more pillow under his head, even as the doctors continue to dress his wounds. 'Do not irritate yourself. Keep yourself quiet.'[65]

There is another subject Sadleir wishes to address, however. 'Ned,' he says gently. 'The fate of the other two men [inside the inn] is certain, do you think if you sent a message up to them, they would surrender?'[66]

For this will save not only their lives but also the lives of the remaining prisoners and those of the police. And Ned does indeed consider the proposal for a few minutes. But on reflection . . . no. The outlaw is as flat out in his person as he is in his refusal. 'They will not mind what I say . . .' he says. 'The heart's gone out of them. They won't come out fighting like men . . . they're only boys . . . they'll stay in there until they're finished.'[67]

To Superintendent Sadleir, it sounds as if Ned simply doesn't particularly care what happens, as he is peppered with questions by all and sundry, and listlessly does his best to reply to them all.

Ned recounts that, 'When I saw my best friend dead, I had no more faith in them,'[68] and even goes on to refer to them as 'cowards'.[69] What appears to have affected him most is that neither one of them – let alone both – came out firing when he had been left to take on the police single-handed. 'Anyhow,' he says, 'I could have got away last night, for I got into the bush with my grey mare, and lay there all night. But I wanted to see the thing end.'[70]

And there is one thing Ned particularly wants to know. 'Why don't the police use bullets instead of duck-shot?' he asks, plaintively, in the manner of a man who feels very badly let down by having fallen to such an unmanly form of ammunition. 'I have got one charge of duck-shot in my leg.'[71] He goes on, 'I wanted to fire into the carriages, but the police started on us too quickly. I expected the police to come.'

Superintendent Sadleir: 'You wanted, then, to kill the people in the train?'

Kelly: 'Yes, of course I did. God help them, but they would have got shot all the same. Would they not have tried to kill me?'[72]

In this strangely convivial atmosphere, almost like a press conference – on this, the most profitable news day in the history of the colony – it is the train guard, Dowsett, who asks the question that most will ask, once the basic contours of what has happened become known. Why, once Ned had got beyond the police lines, and secured his horse, did he not mount up and ride away? Momentarily, Ned seems confused by the question, almost as if that option had never occurred to him, and he is amazed it could occur to anyone else. But his reply is gentle:

'A man would have been a nice sort of dingo,' he says, 'to walk out on his mates.'[73]

And so the conversation goes on.

Around nine o'clock, however, as Ned obviously begins to fade away, Dr Nicholson signals to the assortment of troopers and journalists in the room that it is time to go. For them, Ned is either a fascinating subject to write about or a captured criminal, but for Dr Nicholson he is his patient, and one who must rest.

By now, the morning sunshine has burned away the mist, and the inn is so visible you can even occasionally see the puffs of smoke coming from the bushrangers' guns, though for the most part they continue their sporadic firing from well back in the shadows, so as not to present an obvious target. The remaining bushrangers are now Superintendent Sadleir's focus. For if Ned is not going to help to get them out, Sadleir must find another way. One thing he knows he won't lack is manpower, as, with the railway line now repaired, the reinforcements come easily from both directions. With the latest arrivals from Beechworth, he now has a total of forty-six troopers in his cordon surrounding the inn – though he can't also help but notice that from everywhere else are now streaming dozens upon dozens of sightseers, locals who have heard what has happened and want to see the final chapter play out.

It is difficult because now, not only do Sadleir's men have to keep the remaining Kelly Gang members inside the police cordon, they also have to keep the crowd out. And here, of course, is the other factor he must contend with. There is a very real risk that a large group of sympathisers might attack the police lines and *break* the Kelly Gang out. This had certainly been Superintendent Hare's fear, warning before he left for Benalla about the Kellys receiving assistance from the Greta side of the line, and Sadleir has a strong sense now that the massing crowd is not with the police at all, but in fact sympathetic to the Kelly Gang at best, and in league with them at worst.

As to the journalists, they too had their fears, with Carrington later noting, 'We quite expected to be attacked from the rear, as there was a perfect nest of sympathisers on the opposite side of the line, in and about McDonnell's Hotel . . .'[74]

At least, Sadleir knows, he will not lack for advice and even orders on what to do. One of the new arrivals on the repaired line is Postmaster Cheshire, from Beechworth, along with his line repairer Mr Osborne, who has no sooner walked to the nearest telegraph pole than he has shinnied up it like the cat his boss's ancestors were surely named after. He splices an extension wire to it, which he then attaches to a small pocket instrument he has brought with him, and is instantly able to send and receive cables to Sydney and Melbourne. All 'amidst a storm of bullets'.[75]

From a small room in the station, Cheshire settles down to do exactly that, with police and railway communications taking precedence, while the reports of the journalists come next, and some 300 cables in total are sent over the next twelve hours, forming the base for the headlines and stories soon to be devoured across the country:

> DESTRUCTION OF THE KELLY GANG
> DESPERATE ENCOUNTER. NED KELLY CAPTURED-
> CHILDREN AND CIVILIANS KILLED AND
> WOUNDED
> (BY ELECTRIC TELEGRAPH)
> (BY OUR SPECIAL REPORTER)
> GLENROWAN, MONDAY NIGHT
> At last the Kelly Gang and the police have come within shooting distance, and the adventure has been the most tragic of any in the bushranging annals of the colony . . .[76]

In Melbourne, both Chief Secretary Ramsay and Captain Standish are suddenly able to tell Superintendent Sadleir what to do . . .

For his part, Sadleir has his own ideas, requesting from Standish that he organise to send a field artillery gun, with which they can blow the inn apart without risking police lives. He explains, in a cable sent at half past nine:

> Glenrowan, 28 June 1880. Weatherboard, brick chimney, slab kitchen. The difficulty we feel is that our shots have no effect on the corner, and there are so many windows that we should be under fire all the day. We must get the gun before night, or rush the place.[77]

After consultation with Colonial Secretary Robert Ramsay, Captain Standish accedes to this request and, as he must rush to the station to catch the special train about to depart, leaves the matter with Ramsay, who sends the order to the Garrison Artillery to have a cannon and crew able to fire it ready to leave on a second special train heading to Glenrowan.

At ten o'clock, the first special train leaves Spencer Street Station, bearing Captain Standish accompanied by Dr Charles Ryan, a doctor who happens to be Hare's cousin but who has been 'selected . . . on account of his experience in gunshot wounds',[78] gained in the Russo-Turkish War that had finished two years earlier. With them are a police sergeant with five troopers and enough ammunition to sustain a small war.

Also on board on this 'cold, grisly, winter's day',[79] just as Melbourne specialises in, is Julian Ashton of the local *Illustrated World News*. He has come at the invitation of Captain Standish but is stunned that 'all he talked about throughout the journey was whist'.[80]

Once it is confirmed at Glenrowan that the artillery will shortly be on its way from Melbourne, clearly, the most important thing is to get the remaining prisoners out of the inn before it arrives. And so, it is at Sadleir's behest that, just before ten o'clock, Charles Rawlins makes the call, less by virtue of any authority than the fact he has a voice 'like a bull',[81] and it now rolls towards the inn like a ball of dirty thunder:

> ALL THOSE INSIDE THERE HAD BETTER SURRENDER AT ONCE; WE WILL GIVE YOU TEN MINUTES

TO DO SO, AFTER THAT TIME WE SHALL FIRE VOLLEYS INTO THE HOUSE.[82]

Inside the inn, the call galvanises those who remain who are still capable of helping themselves. While the situation in the inn has been intolerable for the prisoners from the beginning, in the last hour, since the police reinforcements have arrived – all of whom seem to want to fire as many shots as they can at them – it has been an agony.

James Reardon has particularly suffered. While relieved at the escape of his wife and the rest of his children, he has tried to tend his shot oldest son, even while sitting with the two young ones squeezed between his knees 'expecting every minute to be shot'.[83] And for good reason . . . One bullet has come so close it has scraped the breast of his coat. In such circumstances, the call from outside is a miracle. They are going to be given another chance to get out of this living hell.

And it is now clear to all of them that the two bushrangers who remain will not try to prevent them leaving. In fact, Dan Kelly and Steve Hart seem to have just about forgotten all about them, and, standing tightly together in the passage, are obviously focused on their own fate. To one prisoner, these bushrangers, who have been awake for the better part of three days straight, look 'for all the world like two condemned criminals on the drop, waiting for the bolt to be drawn'.[84] They do, however, on prompting from Dave Mortimer, promise they won't fire on the prisoners from behind, and even shake hands with each man just before the attempt to escape is made. It has been a long night and they have got through it together.

—

And now, just after ten in the morning, it is Dave Mortimer who strides across the room, opens the front door a crack and waves a white handkerchief. As one, the police level their weapons, ready for anything – but, most crucially, they don't fire, as had happened five hours earlier.

And then it happens. Suddenly, the white handkerchief disappears and then, led by Dave Mortimer with his hands in the air, thirty prisoners burst forth, 'buzzing out like bees, running out from the front door in great confusion'[85] into the cold, wet day. The police take direct aim, just waiting for one of them to pull a trick, or a weapon from beneath their coats. At their back come the remains of the Reardon family, with the young and badly wounded Michael leading the way, and his father, James, directly behind him holding his toddler brother, William, and seven-year-old sister, Kate, by the hands.

'Don't fire!' all of them call. 'For God's sake, don't shoot us; don't, pray don't!'[86]

Even then, it is a close-run thing, with one constable pointing his rifle and saying, 'Let us finish this bloody lot.'[87] The horror, oh, the *horror*!

Desperate, scrambling, fearing on every instant that bullets will slam into him and his precious little children, Reardon gathers them in and charges to the drain . . . where one of the black-trackers cocks his rifle and points it at the platelayer's face . . . *No! Not here!* Shaking, breathless, Reardon runs once more, this time to the side of Superintendent Sadleir, where at last salvation lies.

Other prisoners have similar experiences and, fearing bullets from both front and back, race towards where Sadleir stands. Following shouted instructions, they throw themselves at his feet onto the cold, wet grass, while the police determine firstly that they are not armed and, secondly, that none of them is a bushranger, or one of their sympathisers.

'The faces of the poor fellows,' Joe Melvin of *The Argus* reports, 'were blanched with fear, and some of them looked as if they were out of their minds.'[88]

After questioning, most are immediately let go, as Rawlins knows at least half of them personally and is able to confirm their good character. The two McAuliffe brothers, however, are quickly arrested as Kelly sympathisers and placed in handcuffs, while the badly wounded Michael Reardon is rushed to Dr Nicholson to receive treatment.

The most significant information to come from the prisoners has been that, while Joe Byrne has been shot dead, Dan Kelly and Steve Hart are relatively uninjured, have their own suits of armour and are standing in the passage, still with their guns and plenty of ammunition. How to get them out and finish this, finally? Such is the subject of much discussion over the next few hours, both in Melbourne and at Glenrowan. Chief Secretary Robert Ramsay no sooner has an idea than he has cabled it to Hare at Benalla:

> Is it possible to construct a bullet-proof shield or screen of deals backed with hardwood? This mounted on a dray might enable the men to approach the house.[89]

Against the possibility that the siege will last until dark, the Chief Secretary also sends an emissary from his Melbourne office to enquire of Robert Ellery, the government astronomer and leading light of the colony's scientific community, if it might be possible to get the electric lights under which Carlton and Melbourne had played at the MCG in August of the previous year – a triumph that he was one of the driving forces behind – and 'proceed to Glenrowan by special train . . . so as to prevent the escape of the murderers'.[90]

No, Mr Ellery replies. It would take too long, and in any case the light thrown is so vivid it would cast such dark shadows that it 'probably would enable the bushrangers to escape rather than assist in effecting their capture'. Instead, he recommended, 'bonfires should be made round the building, which would lighten the space between them and it'.[91] This suggestion, too, is telegraphed by Ramsay to Superintendent Hare.

And now one of the troopers on the ground at Glenrowan has another idea. For, the thought just pops into Constable Dwyer's head, as he stands behind a tree at the northern end of the inn, observing the helmeted bushrangers moving around inside the house, *Why not put on Ned Kelly's armour and charge into the inn that way? He could get in close enough to work out where the danger lay, and draw fire upon himself, while other troopers could rush forward.* It is an interesting idea, with one enormous problem. Although the exceedingly strong Dwyer does actually manage to get parts of Kelly's armour on, with the help of a few locals standing on the station, there proves to be an enormous difference between that and actually walking with its weight upon you, let alone wielding a weapon. As he would later recount, 'the armour was so cumbersome and so heavy that I abandoned that idea'.[92] Dwyer had known Ned Kelly was strong, but he had not quite appreciated that his strength was that of three men, as he does now.

—

Extra! Extra! Special editions!

In both Melbourne and Sydney, the excitement is at fever pitch as every newspaper, especially those fortunate enough to have a journalist on site at Glenrowan, goes into overdrive, and ever-larger crowds flock around their headquarters to snatch the latest news off the presses. The first of the 'Extraordinary Issues', which are little more than telegrams sent from the scene and providing snippets of insight, hit the streets at eleven o'clock, and new ones come out every two or three hours thereafter for the rest of the day.

In Collins Street, Melbourne, outside the *Argus* office, near madness reigns as they devour Joe Melvin's every word. Tell everyone! The Kellys have struck again at Glenrowan, the siege is going on as we speak, Ned has already been taken, and . . . and . . . and he was wearing some kind of armour, that even covered his head. Never in the nigh on fifty years of the life of this town has such extraordinary news hit, and the people simply cannot get enough of it, buying every paper they can as successive editions come with the latest, always sensational, offerings. There are so many people outside the *Argus* office that Collins Street becomes impassable. Similar scenes are taking place outside the offices of *The Age* and *The Herald*, and in Sydney, and indeed in all the colonies around the country.

The Herald, being an afternoon paper, cashes in on this unprecedented day in print media. They are the first newspaper to run the big, fast-breaking story, in a full special edition, which is printed at half past three that afternoon:

> SPECIAL EDITION
> HERALD Office 3:30pm
> CAPTURE
> OF THE
> KELLY GANG
> TWO CHILDREN SUPPOSED TO BE SHOT DEAD
> DURING THE ENCOUNTER
> SUPERINTENDENT HARE AND SOME CONSTABLES
> WOUNDED
> NED KELLY SERIOUSLY WOUNDED
> A DESPERATE FIGHT[93]

Though the editorial concedes, 'The accounts of the doings received so far are meagre in the extreme,' the journalists at *The Herald* do their best to report the particulars of the story to the excited throngs that envelop their offices. 'Ned Kelly has three bullet wounds in him. Dr Nicholson does not consider any of them mortal. Police very plucky and game. The armour the gang have on is formed out of ploughshares.' As to what's set to come, the correspondent notes, 'now only Dan Kelly and Steve Hart are left and they must be shot or surrendered soon'.[94]

Never in the history of the Australian continent has one event garnered so much immediate attention, with detailed, blow-by-blow accounts buzzing down the line, live, almost as they happen. In London, the first reports of the capture of Ned Kelly make it to the streets on the same day it takes place.

—

In the meantime, back at Glenrowan, as the regular noon train from Melbourne pulls in, there is a stream of people getting off and a very few getting on. Ann Jones, together with her daughter Jane, and, most particularly, the grievously wounded Jack, carried on by stretcher, had left by train an hour earlier. They are on their way to Wangaratta Hospital, in the hope that Jack's life can be saved.

Getting off the train, among others, are a heavily armed Robert McBean, who had his gold watch stolen a decade earlier by Harry Power and young Ned, and has turned up here as a volunteer, Senior Constable Charles Johnston, who had previously been utterly disappointed with police inactivity after the Mansfield murders and the Euroa raid, and a Catholic priest – the Vicar General of the Catholic Church in Western Australia, in Victoria on a fund-raising expedition – Father Mathew Gibney, who had been on his way from Kilmore to Albury, only to happen upon the whole extraordinary scene. Of course, he offers to give whatever spiritual comfort he can to any who need it, including to the very Catholic Ned Kelly.

It takes the priest some time to make his way through the crowds of people and then the layer after layer of police that surround the stricken bushranger, but a man with a clerical collar has an authority all his own, coming from a higher order than even a police commissioner. Thirty minutes after arriving, thus, the good father is being ushered into the Stationmaster's office, where, there, amid myriad police, reporters and people unknown, lies the seriously stricken Ned, still being tended by Dr Nicholson, who is glad to see him.

For the medico now feels that, while he has done most of what he can for Ned's physical needs, death is still hovering close and it is the fallen bushranger's spiritual needs that most urgently require attention. It is with this in mind that Dr Nicholson once again uses his own authority to clear the room, this time including himself, and allows the bushranger to talk to the Catholic priest alone.

It is as well, for as soon as they are alone, Ned's first words are to ask Father Gibney 'to do anything you can towards preparing me for death'.[95]

'My son,' the priest begins as he leans over him, 'say, "Oh Jesus have mercy on me," and pray for forgiveness.'

Ned turns his head so that he is gazing straight into the priest's eyes and says quietly, 'It's not now I'm beginning to say that; I've done it for long before today.'[96]

As they speak, yet another thunderous volley of shots rings out, the loudest so far, as yet more reinforcements have arrived on the same train as Gibney and are eager to fire in even the general direction of the Kellys. (As there are no longer innocents inside the inn, and there are next to no shots, if any at all, coming from it, there is no reason for the police not to fire at will, and so they do – for many of them, it is the first time they have fired a shot in anger in their entire service, and now they are firing at the Kelly Gang! Even journalist Joe Melvin is seen to take his gun and bravely fire a few rounds at the inn.)

Both Father Gibney and Ned Kelly take pause, as they must, for the shooting is simply too loud for them to hear each other. What must it be like inside the inn, for those on the receiving end of such a ferocity of fire?

On that subject, once the shooting momentarily abates, the priest takes the opportunity to suggest that, as a priest, he might be the man to convince Ned's brother Dan and Steve Hart to peacefully give up. 'Do you think it would be safe for me to go up to the house . . .?'

In response, Ned says nothing for all of ten seconds, and then carefully replies, after due consideration, 'I would not advise you to go, they will certainly shoot you.'

'They would not shoot me if they knew I was a priest or a clergyman.'

'They will not know what you are, and they will not take time to think.'[97]

Father Gibney is not convinced and continues to feel that it is his duty to do something to help save these two men, God's children, who have wandered so far from the teachings of Jesus they were raised on. For the moment, however, satisfied that Ned has repented, the Father hears Ned's confession and then anoints him with holy oil, so that Ned can reconcile himself with his faith and his god. 'As I at first thought he was dying, I anointed him,' he records,[98] and before he leaves Ned's side he anoints him in the last sacrament of extreme unction.

Outside, things have fallen strangely quiet. By one o'clock, there is not even the odd pot-shot coming from the inn, no shouting, nothing but an eerie silence . . .

Of course, now in the middle of the day, it is impossible for those inside the inn to escape unseen – just as it is impossible for the police to get near the entrances without having to cross at least 50 yards of open ground, where they are likely to come under withering fire. In such a stand-off, it is to Father Gibney's amazement that there seems to be 'no sign of truce at any time offered; there was no signal given that the men might see, that they might have the idea their lives would be spared if they came out'. Nor could he get anyone interested in the idea, for 'there seemed to be an incessant feeding of anxiety in the mind of those men that were around'.[99]

The latter factor notwithstanding, still there are many troopers who wish to try their luck at storming the inn, led by the wretched Constable Harry Armstrong, who is now aware that he has become a byword for cowardice due to his failure to charge out of the bedroom at Aaron Sherritt's shack and confront his certain death.

Nevertheless, Sadleir is quick to tell Armstrong the same thing he tells all the volunteers. 'It is not time to rush yet; stand back and keep your ground.'[100]

As Sadleir later recounts, 'I was determined only that the outlaws, whom we held as rats in a trap, should be captured or destroyed without needlessly risking the life of one good man.'[101] After all, he reasons, 'When you have got a rat in a trap, you don't put your hand in the trap to pull it out.'[102]

In any case, on the direct orders of Chief Secretary Ramsay, a 12-pound Armstrong field gun leaves by special train from Melbourne at twenty past two, accompanied by Colonel Anderson and the twelve members of the Garrison Artillery who have hauled it there. See how the remains of the Kelly Gang cope with cannonballs flying at them and their inn.

Still, that gun will take a few hours to arrive, and up at Glenrowan the idea to rush the two surviving bushrangers persists. If not now, when? If not them, who? After all, once it is dark, a good deal of the police advantage will be lost, and if Ned could slip away in the night, last night, it is not out of the question that the same thing could be accomplished by the remaining bushrangers tonight.

As to what is actually happening inside the inn, no one knows, of course. The only thing obvious is that there is no more firing coming from there. This might be because the bushrangers are dead, that some of the police bullets have hit? Or it might be because they are conserving their ammunition for the big breakout they have planned.

As the afternoon wears on, yet more people continue to stream into Glenrowan from all parts. The atmosphere is rather like the opening night at a theatre, where there is standing room only, but no actual show. All that the watchers can see on this sunny afternoon is that fellow Sadleir, the local Superintendent in charge of policing in this area, puffing on his pipe as he talks to his police in one spot, before moving on and doing the same with the next pod of police, until he has completed the entire circuit of the inn.

From the inn itself, however, there is nothing, not the tiniest sound, nor the slightest sign of movement.

The same cannot be said for McDonnell's Hotel, on the other side of the railway tracks, where a roaring trade is going on. As the police note, a seemingly ever-greater congregation – if not conflagration – of noted Kelly sympathisers is gathering, most of them armed. Is something up? Will the mob turn on the police?

With so many armed troopers on hand, this remains unlikely, but so was four bushrangers encasing themselves in armour and holding sixty-two people prisoner.[103] All in all, it seems better to bring this whole thing to a conclusion before night falls, if only the police can find a way to do so without risking more of their own lives.

But how?

Senior Constable Charles Johnston – ever and always a man of action – has an idea, and now approaches Sadleir with it, while the Superintendent is chatting with O'Connor. Why not set fire to the inn? As Johnston explains to the Superintendent, if the police put up a heavy fusillade to keep the outlaws inside, and he approaches the inn from the south-western side, where the inn wall has no windows, he would be able to get right next to the wall unseen, and, with the right materials, be able to set fire to it and be able to get away before it is ablaze. The best part of the plan, he points out, is that, most propitiously, a light wind is blowing from that direction right now.

Puff, puff, puff on his pipe . . . each puff of smoke heading briskly north-east with the sudden breeze that has sprung up . . . Superintendent Sadleir considers it closely.

He does have some reservations, apparently not including the fact that the wounded Martin Cherry, who had been shot in the groin some ten hours before, is known to be in the inn somewhere. Firstly, Sadleir is not sure that the building – 'made of smooth, well-formed hardwood weatherboards, that did not offer a good surface to set fire to'[104] – would quickly catch alight. Secondly, why risk a forty-year-old man, married with several children – Johnston's wife had once been in the service of his family, and he liked her well – when there are so many younger, single constables available? After all, with so many holes in the walls from bullets, it was very likely anyone would be seen approaching by the bushrangers inside.

When the Superintendent expresses such doubts, however, saying, 'I will find a single man to do it, I will not send you,'[105] Johnston is as close to insistent as respect for Sadleir's rank will allow. It is *his* idea, and *he* wants to do it. (He is, after all, the same man who had told Sadleir *and* Hare, after the Brooke Smith debacle, 'If I am baulked again in the same way I will take the responsibility on myself, and go . . .'[106] He had meant it then, and he means it now.)

Sadleir reluctantly cedes, on strict condition that Johnston follows closely all of his instructions. First, he must get some kerosene and a small bundle of straw, all without letting the now large crowd know what he is about. True, it is a pity for Ann Jones that her inn will be burned to the ground, but, in the range of factors, that will simply have to be ignored. The Kellys have already killed three family men at Stringybark Creek, and Sadleir is loath to risk losing another one. Johnston hurries away to make his preparations.

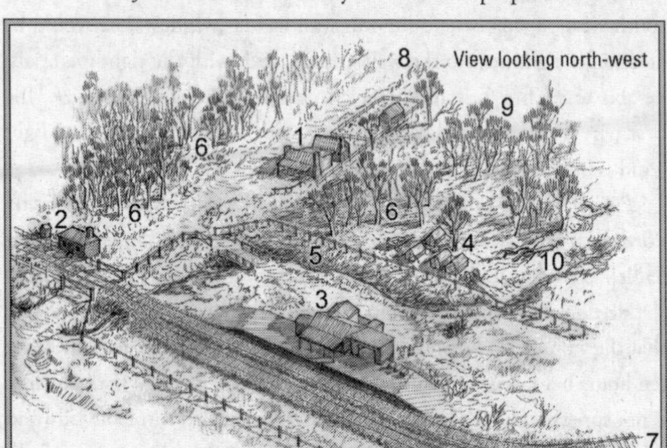

The scene at Glenrowan on the morning of 28 June 1880. 1) Ann Jones's Glenrowan Inn 2) Stationmaster's house 3) Glenrowan Railway Station 4) Railway workmen's tents 5) Boggy trench used as police shelter during siege 6) Police scattered throughout the bush 7) Railway line to Beechworth 8) Beaconsfield Pde north to Benalla/Wangaratta Road 9) Bush where Ned Kelly surprised police from the rear 10) Logs where Ned was finally taken. (Illustration by Bill Denheld)

And who is this, just arriving down the Greta road?

They are two striking-looking women, with a younger girl, all riding magnificent-looking horses, and they are accompanied by a couple of glowering men, one of whom seems to be pure bone and looks as though he'd sooner have a fight than a feed.

The older woman is wearing 'a black riding habit with red underskirt, and white [plumed] Gainsborough hat'.[107] It is the bee under her bonnet, however, that most quickly identifies her. For it is Maggie Skillion, the sister of the Kelly brothers, beside her sisters Kate and young Grace, with Wild Wright, and, not far behind, Dick Hart, Steve Hart's older brother.

While word of the siege has quickly spread throughout the district, it has moved even faster and more specifically to them at home in Greta, and they have reacted quickly.

—

So it is that, just before quarter to three on this now sultry afternoon, the police on the south-western side of the inn prepare to train sustained fire upon it, so that whatever outlaws are within will be forced to keep their heads down and stay inside.

As they do so, Senior Constable Johnston is concluding his preparations. He has already gathered a pile of dry hay – telling all and sundry that he needs it to feed the horses in the paddock by the railway – and after a long detour through the bush is still well outside police lines as he goes to get some kerosene from the railway station, when he is suddenly confronted by four men on horseback, heavily armed with rifles, revolvers and stares that could peel paint.

Who they are, and what they are about, he knows not – *the Four Horsemen of the Apocalypse?* – but it is clear they are not on his side of the equation. 'Did you see two horses, a grey and a brown, pass here recently?' Johnston asks quickly, displaying, as evidence that his intent is innocent, the hay he is carrying to feed them.[108]

No, they didn't. But Johnston can be glad his skin is *not* paint.

The main thing is that he is allowed to pass, being particularly pleased when he is out of their sight, and holding ever more tightly the kerosene and the matches.

—

And now, as Maggie Skillion approaches the police lines, Senior Constable Kelly takes the opportunity and asks her if she would assist the police by walking up to the inn and asking her brother to surrender.

Maggie reacts as if slapped across the face. 'I would sooner see them burn first!'[109]

They are interrupted by the sound of gunfire. For, following the plan, the troopers have fired three successive volleys at the two doors of the inn, ensuring that whoever is in there won't be poking their heads out, allowing Johnston the time he needs to do his work.

Arriving at the south-western wall, Johnston drops the hay in a pile and quickly douses it with kerosene – which is the key thing Dan Kelly had lacked two nights before, when the bushranger had tried to do the same thing to the Sherritt hut – before striking a match and dropping it onto the hay.

Nothing.

The match has fizzled.

He does it again.

Fa-fa-fa-FOOM. This time, the kerosene and then hay quickly burst into flame, and Johnston coolly turns and walks away. Now, whether the fire will take off from there is anyone's guess, but at least it is a start.

It is at this point that Father Gibney puts the question to Kate, 'Will you ask them to surrender?'

'Of course,' Kate replies enthusiastically. 'I'll go and see my brother.'[110]

And she would have done exactly that, but, as she runs towards the inn, she is intercepted by the police, who refuse her passage, and she must return to the good father's side. Though a man of God and on the side of law and order, he feels a rising fury at the police, so constantly thwarting any possibility of finding a peaceful resolution to the siege, and, with Maggie, heads off to find Sadleir . . . who is just a little worried.

Though the first burst of flame from the hay had been promising, it all seems to have died away. There is no visible fire, and just a little smoke. Is the whole thing just dying away?

But wait! There!

At first, it had seemed that the only smoke was coming from just where the hay had been lit, but suddenly it has appeared from beneath the eaves. The fire has caught.

As the crowd watch closely – they are now no fewer than a thousand strong – smoke soon starts billowing skywards. And then flames. From the western side of the inn, the people outside can see flames through the front window. It has caught. And with that south-westerly behind it, it is not going to take long to engulf the building.

A wail rings out.

It is Maggie Skillion charging forward and calling out, 'I will see my brother before he dies!'[111]

Not if the police can help it, she won't. Just as no one is allowed to break through the police cordon coming out of the inn, so too is no one allowed to break it going in, and she is quickly intercepted and stopped, even as her sister Kate cries out, 'My poor brother. My poor brother.'[112]

The two women embrace, unable to do anything and disbelieving that it has come to this. Now it is Kate who decides to try to breech the police lines, striding forth to be stopped by Sadleir.

'Kate Kelly, stop a minute,' he says. 'Where are you going?'

'I am going up to see Dan.'

'Will you induce them to surrender?'

'Surrender to you bloody dogs? No . . .'

'Stand back,' Sadleir replies, refusing her passage.[113]

As jets of flame sear through the many bullet holes in the roof, and the smoke billows ever higher, it is now obvious that whoever is in the inn has just minutes to get out, or they will be burned alive. Or dead.

The police begin to move in closer, though still using whatever trees are available for cover. Whatever else, it is obvious that the final scenes of the siege are about to take place. Watching closely, Father Gibney is appalled. 'My feelings,' he would later recount, 'revolted very much from the appearance it had . . . I said to myself, "These men have not five minutes to live. If they stop in they will be burned, and if they come out they will be shot." That was what decided me . . .'[114]

Urgently now, Father Gibney approaches Superintendent Sadleir and asks whether he may break the blockade and enter the hotel, to see if he can bring the bushrangers out alive.

Permission denied. Superintendent Sadleir won't hear of it.

The good father, however, feels he has the blessing of a higher authority still, and without another word he simply turns and starts striding towards the rising inferno.

'Stop!' the now exasperated Sadleir commands. 'If anybody is to go up, it is my place, and I beg you to go back.'[115]

Momentarily, Gibney appears to concede, taking three steps back towards the police officer, and Sadleir relaxes a little, but suddenly the priest whirls and is off once more, making the sign of the cross as he strides out – commending himself to his Lord and praying that if he falls his sins might be forgiven – before calling back over his shoulder, with force, 'I am not in the police service, I am going to do my duty, and there is no time to lose!'[116]

And as he proceeds to do exactly that, the crowd cheers, sounding to Gibney's ears 'as if I was going on a stage'.[117] A brave man doing his best to stop unnecessary bloodshed, he continues to stride forward. It all happens so quickly that, short of shooting him, there is no way of stopping him, and though hotly pursued by Sadleir and other police, to whom he has called, 'We must go on now,'[118] the priest is soon at the front door of a burning building that is thought to hold two murderous bushrangers.

With a lunge, Sadleir tries to grab the priest before he fully enters the hallway, but at this instant 'a great sheet of flame'[119] shoots between them, and, coughing, the policeman pulls back, certain that the priest has just uselessly sacrificed his life. The crowd is under the same impression, as they now cry out in horror, convinced they have just seen a brave man go to his death.

Inside the inn, Father Gibney pushes on, holding his crucifix high – a symbol of peace – even as he calls forth, 'I am a Catholic priest, and come to offer you your life.'[120]

There is no answer, bar the sound of roaring flames, cracking glass and falling, flaming timber.

'I am Father Gibney,' he roars again, now with rising desperation. 'For God's sake, speak to me.'[121]

Nothing, but silence.

Deathly silence?

It certainly feels like that, as, quickly now, and trying to shield his face with the inside of his coat from the smoke and heat, he walks through the dining room and through the open door on his left, leading into the bar. It is filled with smoke, though the gloom is pierced by the innumerable bullet holes in the roof, which let many shafts of sunlight in. The priest tries to go into the parlour at the far end of the bar, but as it is now a mass of flames, that is out of the question. He turns his back on the hungry flames to return to the dining room.

There!

There on the floor is a man, curled in almost the foetal position and unmoving. With blasts of heat all around, Gibney reaches down to touch him and instantly knows – Joe Byrne is the coldest thing in the building – that the man is dead and there is nothing to be done.

He hurries into the dining room and takes a door on the left that leads to a small bedroom. Realising there is no exit from that room, though, he comes back to the spot where Joe Byrne lies and where the fire is burning most violently. Terrified that he is to be caught in the flames, the priest blesses himself in the name of God and rushes towards the back along the hallway. He sees a door on his left and, again calling out, 'For God's sake, men, allow me to speak to you: I am a Roman Catholic priest!'[122] he steps into the small bedroom.

This time . . . there are two bodies. The 'two beardless youths',[123] Dan Kelly and Steve Hart, are lying closely by each other, with their feet towards the door and, bizarrely, their heads on makeshift pillows of rolled-up calico sacks that had previously held the suits of armour that now lie beside them. They are both 'very composed looking'.[124]

Again, the priest kneels down to lift a hand and is not at all surprised to find it cold and clammy, the unmistakable sign of death, just as the unseeing eyes of the second body, staring straight at the ceiling despite the thick and stinging smoke, make it obvious to this man of God that the other man, too, has gone to meet his maker – or worse.

Just what has happened here?

Gibney is firm in his view. He could not shake the feeling that they had only recently removed their armour then lain down and committed suicide. But how? That is far from clear, as neither man is covered in obvious blood. It is all more than merely passing strange. 'I concluded,' he would later recount, 'they lay in that position to let the police see when they found them that it was not by the police they died.'[125]

Alas, there is no time to investigate further. If Father Gibney does not leave within seconds, he risks dying too. The ravaging flames have now reached this back part of the inn, and, coughing furiously, the priest takes his leave through the rising smoke and heat, taking one backward glance at the two dead bushrangers lying so neatly before him.

Bursting through the back door with his hands raised – lest one of the many trigger-happy troopers take a shot at him – Father Gibney calls out, 'The men are all dead inside!'[126]

With that news, Constables James Dwyer and James Arthur, with Harry Armstrong – as desperate as ever to be seen leading the way – rush inside through the same back door that the priest has just exited, knowing they are safe from gunfire, but certainly not from the fire itself.

By now, it is impossible to get to Steve Hart and Dan Kelly quickly enough to retrieve the bodies – the whole room is ablaze – but, led by an almost demonically motivated Harry Armstrong, they do manage to grab the heavily armoured body of Joe Byrne, slightly scorched down the right side, and haul it out, even as the burning timbers begin to crash around them.

Meanwhile, other people have raced to the kitchen and bedroom out the back, where they know they will find Martin Cherry, hopefully still alive. He is, but he is covered in blood around his groin and down his legs, and is just barely holding on to life.

'Martin,' the bootmaker Thomas Dixon from Benalla says gently to his old friend, 'how are you?'[127]

'Oh, you know me,' Cherry whispers back, unseeing, clearly surprised.

He is dragged out – managing to gurgle out the words, 'Oh, don't hurt me,'[128] as they do so – just before the roof of the whole inn caves in at a quarter past three, with a roar of sparks and billowing plumes of smoke.

Even the most basic of examinations by the first troopers there reveals that Cherry is not long for this world, and with there being no chance of healing his body, steps are taken to soothe his soul. Father Gibney moves quickly. After making the sign of the cross, he administers the last rites . . .

Within a few minutes, Martin Cherry, born in Limerick, Ireland, fifty-eight years earlier, breathes his last.

As to what remains of the once proud Glenrowan Inn, it is now an inferno. True, there is some momentary alarm when shots are heard coming from inside – is there still someone alive after all? – but the onlookers realise this must be the explosion of the cartridges on the bushrangers as they burn. Mercifully, some genuine shots that ring out are from police revolvers, finally finishing the lives of some of the poor horses that have somehow still survived from being shot at dawn.

As one now, the people watching the event come as close to the burning building as they dare, or as the police will let them, most straining for at least a glimpse of the dead bushrangers. And there they are, Thomas Carrington noting that they 'could now be plainly seen amongst the flames, lying nearly at right angles to each other, their arms drawn up and their knees bent'.[129] Putting aside his horror, he sketches furiously, trying to capture the moment.

It is grisly, appalling, but mesmerising, and he is keenly aware that his every scratch of the pencil is recording a scene that will be talked about for years to come. Maybe even decades . . .

'Destruction of the Kelly Gang', drawn by Thomas Carrington during the encounter. (From the *Australasian Sketcher*, 3 July 1880, courtesy State Library of Victoria)

PART FOUR

RETRIBUTION

Chapter Sixteen

TRIALS AND TRIBULATIONS

He looked like a wild horse brought in from the hills.

James Ingram Jnr, a Beechworth local, who saw Ned as he was about to be taken from Benalla to Melbourne, the morning after he had been shot and captured

For my own part I do not care one straw about my life now for the result of the trial. I know very well from the stories I have been told of how I am spoken of, that the public at large execrate my name; the newspapers cannot speak of me with that patient toleration generally extended to men awaiting trial, and who are assumed according to the boast of British justice, to be innocent until they are proved to be guilty; but I do not mind, for I have outlived that care that curries public favour or dreads the public frown.

Ned Kelly

28 JUNE 1880, GLENROWAN, THE TWILIGHT DESCENDS, THE DARKNESS CLOSES IN

By four o'clock, there is nothing left of the inn, bar smoking ruins, two severely pockmarked brick chimneys, the lamp post, two iron bedsteads, a ravaged sewing machine and the signboard that still proudly boasts:

THE GLENROWAN INN
ANN JONES
BEST ACCOMMODATION[1]

As that accommodation still smoulders, smoke pouring through the bullet holes in the collapsed corrugated-iron roof, a group of police and journalists stand as close as they can to where the back entrance had been. Together, they are steadfastly gazing at the burning bodies of Dan Kelly and Steve Hart, their features now gone, their bodies moving in strange contortions as the muscles and tendons dry and contract in the heat.

Of course, under such circumstances, it takes some time before it is even remotely safe for anyone to venture into the ashes and still burning embers to retrieve what is left of the bodies. But, by just after four o'clock, this is done by the man of the moment, Senior Constable Johnston, who uses a long pole and forked stick to rake out the corpses. And now the charred remains of Dan Kelly and Steve Hart are removed on separate sheets of bark, and laid with Joe Byrne and Martin Cherry. The extremities of Kelly's and Hart's bodies have been destroyed, and there is nothing but their leg-bones, torsos and skulls that remain. The vision is sickening, with one observer noting, 'They presented a horrible appearance being roasted to a skeleton, black and grim reminding me of Old Knick himself.'[2] Their bodies are quickly covered.

As to their armour, that can come later, when it has cooled sufficiently to be handled. (Joe Byrne's pockets are at least searched, and among his effects is found a packet of poison. On his right hand is found the ring that had belonged to Constable Scanlan, and this is put aside to be given to his widow.) Upon Superintendent Sadleir's instructions, all four corpses are taken back to the railway station.

Through the fog of his pain, and the faintness of his hold on consciousness, Ned gradually becomes aware that he has visitors. Some more water and brandy helps to revive him. Though he remains under strict guard, his sisters are allowed in by Superintendent Sadleir to see him. The weeping sisters kiss their beloved brother on the cheek, as does Wild Wright's mute brother, Dummy, who has accompanied them. Kate sits at Ned's head 'with her arms around his neck . . . while the others were crying in a mournful strain at the state of one who, but the night before, was the terror of the whole colony'.[3] As the women gather themselves, a brief conversation ensues, although it is far from private as, together with the heavy guard, reporters have also been allowed in the room.

'I was at last surrounded by the police, and only had a revolver, with which I fired four shots,' Ned tells his family, at least the way Joe Melvin gives his account in *The Argus*. 'But it was no good. I had half a mind to shoot myself. I loaded my rifle, but could not hold it after I was wounded. I had plenty of ammunition, but it was no good to me. I got shot in the arm, and told Dan and Byrne so. I could have got off, but when I saw them all pounding away, I told Dan I would see it over, and wait until morning . . .'[4]

'It's a wonder,' Maggie says, 'you did not keep behind a tree.'

'I had a chance at several policemen during the night, but declined to fire . . . I got away into the bush, and found my mare, and could have rushed away, but wanted to see the thing out, and remained in the bush.'[5]

He adds that Music had followed him through the trees during all the firing and that he 'wouldn't care for myself if so long as my mare was safe'.[6]

Soon enough, however, it is time to go. The family has been allowed to see Ned, and talk to him, and that is enough. Besides which, there is another brother they must see, at least those who feel themselves strong enough.

It does not take long before the two older Kelly sisters have gathered as close as they can to the charred corpses, though the police initially keep them back. One look and Maggie doubles up as if hit in the stomach and emits the piercing wail of those for whom words cannot even begin to describe their pain. Her younger brother's remains are at least sprinkled now with the holy water of his sister's tears, as – while Wild Wright stands glowering – she continues 'howling loudly and lustily over the blackened bones',[7] as does Kate. (Young Grace has mercifully been kept back.)

The sisters' grief is a misery for all to behold as, between heart-rending wails, they 'cried bitterly, and repeatedly kissed the burnt bones of Dan'.[8]

As to Steve Hart's corpse, his brother Dick is a little more stoic, with his own emotions tending more towards anger that it should have come to this. It is his desire to claim the remains of his brother, on the spot, to take for burial by the family, but this request is firmly denied. Until an inquest can be held, they remain under the control of the Victorian Government.

In the end, however, Superintendent Sadleir reconsiders. The Kelly Gang have been destroyed, with three killed and the principal under lock and key. Against that, the town is seething with emotion, and Sadleir's forces are totally outnumbered by hundreds of armed sympathisers. Worse, for some reason, the railway line between Benalla and Glenrowan has been mysteriously blocked for the last two hours, and he and his men are feeling entirely isolated. What is most crucial right now is to calm the storm, and giving the bodies over to the families would help to achieve this. Sadleir thus tells Wild Wright that, in fact, the Kelly and Hart families have his blessing for the bodies to be taken by them. As Sadleir would subsequently report, 'This seemed to please them very much, as an unexpected favour.'[9]

The bodies are still being organised, however – wrapped in blankets so they can be properly transported with some minimum degree of dignity – when now, at half past five in the early evening, Sadleir must prepare himself, as the line has been cleared and the special train bearing Captain Standish and his entourage is now approaching Glenrowan Station.

As the great man alights on the platform, he is greeted by Superintendent Sadleir and Sub-Inspector O'Connor. And they really do greet him – glad to see him and to tell him the great news: the Kelly Gang are destroyed!

Strangely, however, the good captain is not nearly so warm in reply, and in fact when O'Connor puts out his hand, far from grasping it, pumping it and warmly congratulating him and Sadleir on their triumph, the Police Commissioner merely brushes fingers – and is equally diffident with Sadleir. It is almost as if the Commissioner feels slighted, offended, that the whole victory has taken place without him. Which can't be helped now. Standish's primary concern seems to be to find comfortable accommodation, and with that in mind he quickly turns his party around to head back to Benalla.

One thing before you go, however, captain. Sadleir mentions his decision to hand the corpses of Dan Kelly and Steve Hart to their families. 'Please do not interfere now,' Sadleir says with surprising presumption. 'Leave the matter as it stands.'[10]

'Certainly,' Captain Standish replies, within earshot of Sub-Inspector O'Connor, 'by all means, let them have them . . .'[11]

And so it is done. Not long after the train pulls out, the charred remains of the two dead bushrangers are taken by the families from the station to McDonnell's Hotel, where a small informal wake takes place, before a cart can be organised to take them on to Maggie Skillion's home in Greta. It is getting dark but still people are pouring in from all over the countryside. On receipt of the news that Dan and Steve have been burned, 'not one of the crowd there had the courage to lift the white sheet off the charred remains' until one man 'came up and struck a match – it being dark – pulling down the sheet and exposed all that remained of the 2 daring murderous bushrangers'.[12] The crowd around the body gasp collectively. Oh, the horror.

And yet, when suddenly word comes through that Superintendent Sadleir has changed his mind, the horror turns to outrage pure. Sadleir had received a cable from Captain Standish that – on safe reflection during his train ride to Benalla – it would be better to have the bodies available for a formal inquest, and his underling should see to it, and the police officer felt he had no choice but to follow orders and so advise the family. In response, Dick Hart is nothing if not upfront, passing a message back to Sadleir from McDonnell's Hotel, 'If you want the bodies back, you will have to fight for them.'[13]

—

The problem of retrieving the bodies will have to wait for the morrow – as soon after Sadleir has called for their return, the bodies are whisked away to Maggie Skillion's place, where they are laid out on the kitchen table.

The important thing now, for Sadleir, is to get Ned Kelly out of Glenrowan, which has no secure buildings to boast of, and where, despite the heavy police presence around him, there remains a real risk that there will be an armed uprising from the Greta mob, moving to free Ned by force of arms.

Normally, an accused criminal arrested under such circumstances would be placed in custody in the nearest police cells, until such time as a committal hearing could be held. No – on the reckoning that the captured bushranger's wounds are so severe that he needs specialised medical care that only a big city can offer, a place where the state has enough resources to keep him alive, before publicly killing him – far better to whisk him away to Melbourne Gaol, the most secure prison in all Victoria, where the Greta mob would be on alien turf and it would be out of the question for them to rescue him. For the night, however, Ned must first go to Benalla, which has a lock-up surrounded by a large, well-manned police barracks.

Upon arrival at Benalla, Ned, upon his stretcher, is taken under heavy guard to the lock-up, while, bizarrely, the body of Joe Byrne is placed in the adjoining cell.

AFTER MIDNIGHT, 29 JUNE 1880, WANGARATTA HOSPITAL, A BLACKER FATE STILL

On a small bed that nevertheless suddenly seems far too large for him, young Jack Jones is fading. His breaths are shallow and ever more spasmodic, as his mother and sister watch him closely by the flickering light of the lantern, quietly weeping as they hold a hand each. Sometimes, his breaths are like a lizard's tongue – frantic and light – at others like that of a dying dog in the sun, exhausted and long.

Now, just after midnight, the two types come together as the breathing becomes so shallow . . . *so* shallow . . . so very shallow . . . that at 12.46 am it stops altogether ________________________

THREE O'CLOCK IN THE MORNING, 29 JUNE 1880, BENALLA LOCK-UP, NED MAKES AN ADMISSION . . . OR DOES HE?

There are two reasons why strict orders are now enforced that Ned is not to be left alone under any circumstances. So fragile is his medical state that he must be monitored around the clock, with his every need catered for. And so devilish is he as a man that he must be prevented from taking his own life, to prevent justice having its day with him.

So it is that, at the beginning of his shift, in the wee hours, Senior Constable Kelly, in the presence of Constable Ryan, goes into Ned Kelly's cell to offer him milk and water.

Senior Constable Kelly cannot resist taking the opportunity. 'Ned,' he says gently, 'what about Fitzpatrick? Was his statement correct?'

'Yes,' Senior Constable Kelly and Constable Ryan will ever after *swear* he replied, also maintaining he was lucid, whatever his shallow grip on consciousness, 'it was I who shot him.'[14]

Four hours later, well after the sun has come up, Senior Constable Kelly escorts another visitor to Ned's cell. It is an odd thing for Constable McIntyre to go so quickly from the brightness of a fine spring day to the gloom of a small police cell, but at least he has no trouble in identifying a rather thin-looking Ned Kelly on his bunk. Which is more than can be said for Ned Kelly identifying him. 'Do you know this man?' Senior Constable Kelly asks the bushranger, pointing to McIntyre.[15]

'No,' Kelly replies, before correcting himself. 'It is Flood, is it not?'

'No. You took me for Flood the last time we met.'

'Oh, no, it is not Flood.'

'Do you remember the last time we met?'[16]

'Yes,' Kelly says, turning to Senior Constable Kelly and nodding towards McIntyre. 'He told me he would rather be shot himself than bring the other two men into it. He was afraid they were going to be shot.'[17]

McIntyre immediately feels great relief. He has achieved what he has come for – confirmation, in front of a reliable witness, that in no way had he been guilty of cowardice or of setting the other two up after Lonigan had been shot at Stringybark Creek, but in fact had been willing to sacrifice his own life rather than betray them.

The two also briefly discuss the circumstances of the death of Lonigan, with McIntyre continuing, 'When I held up my hands, you shot Lonigan?'

'No,' Ned answers. 'Lonigan got behind some logs and pointed his revolver at me. Did you not see that?'

'No, that is only nonsense.'[18]

For the first time, and despite his original accounts, McIntyre is maintaining that Kelly shot the constable in cold blood – but that is an aside. For now, McIntyre is able to ask another question that has long been troubling him. 'Why did you come near us at all, when you knew where we were?' he asks. 'You could have kept out of the way.'

'You would have soon found us out,' Kelly explains, perhaps ruefully, 'and if we didn't shoot you, you would have shot us. Our horses were poor, our firearms were bad, and we wanted to make a rise.'[19]

Though far from satisfied it is any kind of justification for the tragedy that has occurred, McIntyre at least feels it is some kind of explanation, and that is something.

One more time, however, McIntyre wishes to hear Kelly confirm the main thing he has come for. 'Did I show any cowardice?'

'No,' Kelly replies.[20]

(*Exeunt*, satisfied, Constable McIntyre and Senior Constable Kelly.)

8.30 AM, 29 JUNE 1880, GLENROWAN GLOWS

Sometimes in the undertaking business, it is just like this. When people want a certain kind of coffin and they want it immediately, and they have the money to pay, then you just have to work late to provide it. And when they suddenly want *two* such coffins, it can be an all-night job. It is a tired John Grant, thus, the Wangaratta undertaker, 'in a top hat fluttering with black ribbons',[21] who passes through Glenrowan on this early morning on his way to Greta. Behind him, on the cart, are two beautifully polished, freshly constructed coffins, with shining brass nameplates. As he passes by the ruins of the Glenrowan Inn, the remaining wisps of smoke mingle with the mist and float to the heavens.

MORNING, 29 JUNE 1880, THERE IS MOVEMENT AT THE STATIONS, FOR THE WORD HAS PASSED AROUND

At nine o'clock, it is time for Ned to take his leave of Benalla and be taken to Melbourne. Despite his criminal status, he will be taken in some semblance of comfort. The previous evening, Sergeant Whelan had instructed Constable Ryan to borrow a mattress, and the underling had obliged by asking Mrs Powell, who runs the Victoria Hotel with her husband, George.[22] Honoured, she has of course obliged, and so this morning Ned is placed on the mattress and, with a trooper at each corner, is carried slowly to a spring-cart.

He is then driven carefully to the railway station under a police escort of eight heavily armed troopers, with another trooper driving the cart. The curiosity of the townspeople is naturally excited and, as they strain to peep over the sides, the lucky and the tall catch a glimpse of the wounded Ned Kelly, 'formerly the terror of the district, but now reduced to the weakness of a child'.[23] On the platform, another police guard awaits, together with a heavily bandaged and rather pale Superintendent Frank Hare, surrounded by reporters.

Also waiting close by, the notably beautiful fifteen-year-old with the long, black hair, Kate Lloyd, Tom's younger sister, who is seen to be 'crying bitterly'.[24] As she approaches Ned, the crowd parts to let her through. How could they not, at the vision of such a stunningly beautiful girl, so very well dressed and so terribly distressed, coming forward? She must be Ned's sweetheart, I tell you.

Dabbing her eyes with a dainty handkerchief, she gets as close to Ned as allowed and leans over him, their eyes locking, both of them terribly moved, while now it is the turn of Superintendent Hare to look on, stony-faced.

A wounded Ned Kelly arrives in Melbourne, carried on a mattress. (From *The Illustrated Australian News*, 3 July 1880, courtesy Matt Shore)

And here is the train now, coming from the north, having gone gingerly over the newly repaired line that Ned and his prisoners had ripped up early on Sunday morning.

When it has come to a shuddering halt, Ned, entirely surrounded by wary policemen – their eyes darting back and forth like flies in a bottle – is placed in the guard's van, with half a dozen troopers and Dr Charles Ryan, whose job it is to get the prisoner to Melbourne Gaol alive. Also on board is the redoubtable Magistrate Alfred Wyatt, heading to Melbourne to ensure that the treatment of the prisoner remains within the law, having arranged with Standish and Sadleir to return by Thursday to conduct, in his capacity as district coroner, the inquest for Joe Byrne.

All aboard!

Miss Lloyd is seen to cry 'without restraint'[25] as the train pulls away from Benalla Station, taking Ned to his fate.

Almost as soon as the train has left, a curious train of events gets under way in Benalla. It begins with a macabre exercise at the Benalla Barracks, whereby the body of Joe Byrne is strung up against a door, so the photographer can do his work – and all the press men in the area are attracted to the spectacle.

Joe Byrne's body outside Benalla Police Station. (Photo by J. W. Lindt, courtesy State Library of Victoria)

Back in the day, Byrne had been a gloriously good-looking man of great strength and athleticism, piercing blue eyes and a smile never far from his lips. Some, especially the ladies, called him 'Sweet Birdie'.[26] Now, it seems, only the piercing blue eyes remain, staring in death from his sallow, gaunt face, complete with a grimace rather blackened by the smoke. His beard has been singed, while his arms are at grotesque angles just as they were when rigor mortis set in. His clothes have fared a little better, however, and his image will be preserved for posterity in his favourite collarless shirt, his tweed trousers and leather boots, and his blue coat – all of them, alas, covered in blood, as are his still-clenched fists of defiance. (Or, perhaps, his right fist is still clenched in the manner it was in, proposing a toast, when he was killed.)

As the photographer Arthur Burman takes his photo of the grisly scene, another photographer, J. W. Lindt, presses the shutter, taking a photo of Burman shooting Byrne's image. In that instant, Lindt's 'most famous single photograph'[27] is created.

Even as this is taking place, however, a quick, extremely quiet legal process is underway in the all but deserted Benalla Courthouse, uninterrupted by pesky pressmen. For, despite the promise made to Magistrate Wyatt that he would be the one to conduct the inquest in two days' time, in fact, that inquest now takes place, and is conducted by Captain Standish, assisted by his great friend, and fellow Melbourne Club member, Robert McBean JP. There are just three witnesses in the otherwise empty courthouse: two constables and quarry worker Alphonse Piazzi, who simply has to identify Byrne. All of them are pledged to secrecy as to the make-up of the proceedings, there is no medical evidence presented, of course no autopsy conducted, and within just minutes the verdict is delivered: Byrne had died through 'justified homicide . . .' and, 'The outlaw Joseph Byrne, whose body was before the Court and in the possession of the police, was shot by them whilst in the execution of their duty . . .'[28]

McBean will later sign the official record of Byrne's burial, listing Joe's occupation as '*OUTLAW*',[29] even though the act proclaiming them as outlaws had expired two days before his death.

In the words of *The Argus*, 'So quietly was the whole affair disposed of that no one was made aware of it.'[30]

—

Meanwhile, the train heads south, its very appearance causing enormous excitement as it makes its way. Through the strong combination of the bush telegraph and the electric telegraph, word spreads quickly that Ned is on this train, and at every stop through such places as Violet Town, Euroa, Longwood, Seymour and Kilmore, the train has not even come to a halt before people are pushing and shoving each other out of the way in their eagerness to get a look into the small windows of the guard's van.

And there he is! I saw him! I *saw* him, I tell you!

The big, bearded figure on the stretcher can even manage a wan wave when he is feeling strong enough, and it is noted that Ned's strength indeed seems to surge every time he has an audience. Between stops, when he has to make do with the much smaller audience of the guard of troopers, he is mostly in a trance-like state, though he occasionally makes small conversation, most particularly about what happened at Glenrowan.

As they pass through Donnybrook, however, he grows solemn. 'Look across there to the left,' he says to the trooper right beside him, nodding in the direction of the Big Hill at Beveridge. 'Do you see a little hill there?'

The guard nods, yes, he sees it.

'That is where I was born . . . Now, I am passing through it, I suppose, to my doom.'[31]

And that's enough now, Ned, for you must rest. Frequently, Dr Ryan checks his pulse to find it almost twice as high as normal, at 125 beats per minute, which he tries to bring down by administering the usual medicine: a mixture of brandy and water, heavy on the brandy and easy on the water.

With ever more alcohol loosening him, Ned tells Dr Ryan that he simply does not believe that Dan and Steve shot themselves. For 'they were "two bloody cowards", and hadn't enough pluck to kill themselves',[32] the opposite of Joe Byrne, who really was plucky. And now, of course, they are all dead while somehow, he, their leader, is still alive. This constant thought seems to bring on a certain moroseness, and Dr Ryan would even record that at one point Ned 'gave me the idea he wished to die'.[33] The train roars on . . .

—

Back at Benalla on this morning at eleven o'clock, it is time for an official police parade where, at Superintendent Sadleir's suggestion, Captain Standish can formally thank and congratulate the men who have finally brought Ned Kelly to justice. And yet, just after the men have formed up in their ranks, and he is about to address them, he notices something very troubling.

Black faces. This time, *real* black faces.

Stanhope O'Connor's Native Police have formed up with the white men! Talking loudly to Sadleir – for he refuses to speak to O'Connor personally – Captain Standish gives quick, firm instructions to have them removed immediately, and only after this is done does he begin.

And so the parade takes place, beneath leaden skies that look ready to burst. Captain Standish's speech is commendably brief, not because he is not inclined to loquaciousness, but because of the situation. Yes, they have destroyed the Kelly Gang, but just who else is out there, perhaps about to strike? A mood of menace hangs over the whole gathering, a sense that they have won a battle but the war goes on. Everywhere, stories of threats against everyone from Steele to Bracken to Johnston continue to circulate and – at the specific request of Chief Secretary Robert Ramsay – Thomas Curnow and his wife have been rushed to Melbourne for their own safety.[34]

—

Perhaps the only thing worse than the smell of rotting human flesh is the sickly sweet stench of the burned human flesh of someone you love, and it is that stench that fills the small slab hut of Maggie Skillion on the outskirts of Greta on this cold and misty morning. The coffins in which Dan and Steve will be interred, provided by the undertaker John Grant, who has now arrived at Maggie's house, are close to the best that money can buy – one marked '*Daniel Kelly, died 28th June 1880, aged 19 years*' and the other '*Stephen Hart, died 28th June 1880, aged 21 years*'[35]. They look fine, but still nothing can stop that *smell*, nor the heavy emotion in the heavily packed room.

And *still* they come, as 'the people seemed to flock from the gum trees',[36] striking up a cacophonous congregation of 200 wailing and groaning friends and family members all vying to see the grisly remains of Steve and Dan.

Soon enough, it gets out of hand, as some of them rush the hut, but Mrs Skillion, mistress and master of the realm, will have none of it. In a manner that would do Ned himself proud, she takes out a gun and threatens 'to blow out the brains of the first person that enters the house without permission'.[37] She then allows them to enter three at a time to see for themselves what the bastard police have done to her brother and his best friend, before they are ushered out.

When the time comes for Tom Lloyd to view the bodies, his response is instant, as he takes hold of Kate Kelly's hand, lifts his right arm to the heavens and swears 'a most dreadful oath that he would *never* leave their deaths unavenged'.[38] Shortly thereafter, he rides out of Greta, at the behest of Maggie Skillion, to plead with the police to release Joe Byrne's body into their custody.

For the crowd that Tom leaves in his wake, heady scenes continue as 'drink was brought over from Mrs O'Brien's Hotel, and they were all more or less in a state of intoxication'.[39] Not surprisingly under the circumstances, when Superintendent Sadleir's messenger arrives to inform the family that the police want the bodies back for an inquest, the answer is very simple: NO.

'We have got the bodies now,' an angry Dick Hart tells him straight, 'and we intend to stick to them.'[40]

What to do in the face of such defiance?

For it is obvious to Sadleir, once informed by his messenger of the situation, that the only way now to get the bodies back will be to do exactly as Dick Hart had challenged them to and send an enormous force of heavily armed troopers to Seven Mile Creek, to actually do battle for the bodies. This would entail having yet more dead bodies to deal with, and Sadleir is of the view that they would very likely include his own troopers. To the police officer, there seems little point in provoking an uprising of the Greta mob on such a macabre matter. After all, even beyond the report of the messenger, more troubling rumblings soon come in, to the effect that the Kelly sympathisers have all become drunk at the wake 'and are bouncing about armed, and threatening to attack the police'.[41]

To try to get the bodies under such circumstances is *madness*, and Sadleir knows it, but as Captain Standish is now insisting, he feels he has no choice and gives orders to Senior Constable Kelly to gather his men and prepare.

Also unsurprisingly, when Tom Lloyd rides into Benalla to formally request that Joe's body be handed over to him for burial by the Byrne family, the request is firmly denied. Lloyd can barely believe it and, trying a different tack, appeals to the authorities' good nature, begging them not to be too hard. He is clearly anxious as to what the next steps of the police will be, most particularly in regard to himself and other known sympathisers . . . 'What are you going to do with us now, Mr Kelly?' he asks of Senior Constable Kelly.

'Oh, I don't know, Tom,' the senior constable replies. 'You had better keep out of the way and behave yourself.'

'Oh! For God's sake don't interfere with us,' Tom Lloyd replies, with tears streaming down his face, his former oath of vengeance now seemingly forgotten. 'We have done you no harm. Be satisfied with the work you have already done and leave us and the poor girls in peace; our load is hard to bear.'[42]

—

On the train going to the south, it is now less Ned falling into morose silences than the troopers, as they head through the outer suburbs of Melbourne. No doubt, there will be big crowds, some of them Kelly sympathisers, and it is the troopers' responsibility to ensure that, whatever else happens, Ned Kelly is taken securely from the train to Melbourne Gaol.

At Spencer Street Station, a crowd of perhaps 4000 people has indeed gathered, so many that the authorities have taken the barricades usually used to hold back Melbourne Cup crowds and placed them on the platform that the Benalla train comes in on, to keep the people from falling on the tracks. Everyone, it seems, is pushing for even a glimpse of the most famous man in the land, and some have even hired drays, not for transport but simply to get higher for a better view.

In fact, however, most will be disappointed.

For that morning, Captain Standish had sent a telegram from Benalla to William Montfort Esq., his 'Officer in Charge of Police', giving orders that Ned be taken off the train at North Melbourne Station instead and placed in an ambulance that must be at the ready. 'Keep this dark so that there may be no crowd or public excitement,'

Standish had instructed. 'Let it be believed that he will go on to Melbourne.'[43]

—

For all that, there is still a crowd of many hundreds at North Melbourne Station when the train pulls in just before two o'clock, and it is only with the greatest difficulty that Ned can be conveyed on a stretcher to the wagonette that awaits.

'Although he looked at the crowd with some interest,' *The Argus* reports, 'all the look of bravado had gone. There was no demonstration of any sort made by the crowd, although the female section expressed commiseration for the worn-out, broken-down, and dejected appearance of one who had become known to them as a man of reckless bravery and of great endurance.'[44]

From the station, Ned is taken straight to Melbourne Gaol, just under two miles away, along a route lined with hundreds of people rushing out from factories, shops and homes, all equally desperate just to see him. The wagonette no sooner gets near the bluestone gateway of the gaol than, like a lazy frill-necked lizard before an errant mouse, the gates suddenly open wide and swallow the wagon whole, even before the 600- to 700-strong crowd there quite realise what is happening.

Yes, some had cheered, but so had they cheered every approaching wagon. Certainly, the police guard around it is heavy, but there is no sign upon it saying 'Ned Kelly lies within' and of course the wagon is totally enclosed so that no one can see inside. The gates slam shut behind it, the frill-necked lizard does not even burp, and once the wagon stops, Ned, still on his stretcher, is given over to the hands of the gaol Governor, Mr John Castieau. The Governor directs the prisoner to be carried to the gaol hospital, where he can be expertly cared for by the prison's principal medico, Dr Andrew Shields.

—

At Spencer Street Station, in the meantime, Superintendent Francis Hare is stunned at the reception he receives as he alights from the same train that has borne Ned Kelly. Yes, the thousands of people waiting there had been expecting to see Ned and are disappointed when he does not emerge, but there is Hare, all right, you can see it by his heavily bandaged wrist, now held in a sling. That is the man who led the attack on the Kelly Gang, who was felled in the battle but has lived to fight another day.

For his trouble, Hare is cheered to the echo – something he graciously acknowledges with a wave of his right hand as he walks through the adoring mass to get into the carriage that awaits, which takes him home to Richmond. (The next day, Hare will be whisked away to stay with his in-laws, the Clarke family, at Rupertswood Mansion in Sunbury, where his recovery can be in a secure environment. Not only will Dr Ryan attend him daily, but his father-in-law, Sir William Clarke, is quick to arm his servants, asking them to be on the lookout as Kelly sympathisers might come to shoot Mr Hare.)[45]

—

A visitor, for you, prisoner Kelly, as you lie on your bed in the gaol hospital, closely surveyed by doctors and guards alike. It proves to be Father James Aylward, from nearby St Patrick's Cathedral. Ned, though weak, receives the priest graciously, and they chat quietly for a few minutes, Father Aylward staying just long enough to assure himself that the captured bushranger will indeed live. Soon leaving the exhausted prisoner to rest, the good father must now go and have a far more difficult conversation.

In her small cell in the women's wing of Melbourne Gaol, Ellen Kelly, now a rather wizened woman of forty-eight years, looks up. Summoned from the laundry where she has been working, she finds she has an unexpected visitor, politely removing his hat as he enters her tiny, sweaty, darkened domain, which reeks of the sweet, tarry smell of carbolic soap. It is Father Aylward – a good friend of Father

Gibney's, who has given him a difficult task – and he has a grievously grave expression on his face . . .

Quietly, sorrowfully, the priest tells her the news. Dan . . . Dan has been killed in a siege at Glenrowan, as have Joe Byrne and Steve Hart. Ned is still alive, but is badly wounded, has been captured, and is in this same prison. The good father tells her he has just come from Ned, and her son is at least resting comfortably.

Though devastated, Ellen Kelly tells the priest that the news is not altogether surprising to her. Two nights earlier, she had had a strange dream that her boys had had a violent clash with the police and, in that case, too, her sons had lost badly.

But now let us pray. Together, the priest and the prisoner get on their knees and pray for the soul of the dear departed Dan Kelly.

Eternal rest grant unto them, O Lord, and let perpetual light shine upon them. May the souls of the faithful departed, through the mercy of God, rest in peace. Amen.

And now, Ellen Kelly asks that she be left alone with her grief, and not have to be sent back to the laundry.

And it is done. A short time later, the Governor of the Gaol, John Castieau – a career professional who believes in the exercise of punishment with a sensitivity to human frailty, 'justice tempered with mercy'[46] – comes to her cell and tells her she may take as much time off as she needs. As to seeing her boy, Ned, yes. As soon as he is judged strong enough, he personally will take her to see him.

—

The destruction of the Kelly Gang is not the only news in Victoria on this day. The Tenth Parliament of Victoria is dissolved and the next election is called for just a fortnight hence, on 14 July.

—

At Benalla on this Tuesday night, two men really have drawn the 'graveyard shift' to beat them all. For, very quietly, in a lost and lonely corner of Benalla Cemetery, guided by lantern light and a 'well-armed constable', the local undertaker inters Joe Byrne's body – wrapped only in a rough canvas shroud – in a pauper's grave. They are sure to leave no mark as to where he lies. Byrne is a criminal, not a martyr, and the authorities want no obvious point of congregation for those who will revere his memory.[47]

30 JUNE 1880, AT GLENROWAN, A DASTARDLY DUTY CALLS

The morning dawns cold, wet and miserable, and, after breakfast at Glenrowan Police Barracks, where Senior Constable John Kelly and five troopers had arrived late the night before, it is time. Following the formal orders of Captain Standish, who had safely returned to Melbourne the evening before, Senior Constable Kelly prepares to set off for Greta in the company of sixteen troopers to get the bodies of Dan Kelly and Steve Hart by force, so that an inquest can be conducted upon them.

The only hold-up is that Superintendent Sadleir appears not to have provided Coroner Bickerton and his clerk with the means to accompany them – no buggy, no horses – and soon enough the reason becomes apparent. Recognising the danger that the whole exercise would put his men in, the sensible Sadleir has made one last application to waive the need for an inquest, and by late morning the word comes through. A magistrate has granted a certificate authorising the burial of the bodies without an inquest.

Sanity has prevailed, and a certificate signed by local Justice of the Peace Mr A. Tone is issued,[48] allowing the family to have possession of the two bodies – meaning their burials may now proceed. The infinitely relieved Senior Constable Kelly and his men may stand down and return to their barracks.

It is as well. For early on this Wednesday afternoon, no fewer than eighty horsemen, most of them armed, form up outside Maggie Skillion's house as the coffins of the two dead heroes of the Kelly Gang are brought outside and placed on a cart, side by side in death as in life. These eighty men provide a mounted sentinel around the cart, while another eight wagonloads of the women and children come behind, and they all slowly make their way to Greta Cemetery and gather in a remote corner, where one large, deep hole has already been dug.

There, after local farmer and rate collector for the Oxley Shire Michael Bryan presides over an informal funeral, if not quite funeral ceremony, the earthly remains of those two firm friends to the end, Dan Kelly and Steve Hart, are finally laid to rest as a whipping wind freezes the mourners to their core. While everyone is deeply upset – including brother Jim, who has, in an odd twist of fate, just reappeared from three years' gaol in New South Wales – there is one standout, as reported in *The Argus*. 'Ettie Hart, sister of Steve, was, however, very excited, and fell into hysterics.'[49]

In a moment of strange symmetry, once the grave is filled – with Jim Kelly and Dick Hart asserting their rights as oldest brothers present to throw the first shovelfuls of sod upon the coffins – a local farmer is quick to bring his plough into play, having his horse drag it back and forth for half an acre around the grave, ensuring the burial site will remain secret. Thus the ploughshare accomplishes for Dan and Steve in Greta what it had not, ultimately, in Glenrowan – protection from interference with their person.

30 JUNE 1880, MELBOURNE, RUMOURS SWIRL

The word spreads like a bushfire with a southerly buster behind it. Kate Kelly has shot Sergeant Steele dead! Shot him down, as if *he* was the criminal!

Fortunately, there is no truth to it, but still it is so strong and prompts so many enquiries that John Sadleir must send a cable to Captain Standish:

> BENALLA, 12.10.
> No truth in the rumour about Steele. I have heard

from him half an hour since. There is a deal of ill blood, and I cannot reduce strength for a few days. JOHN SADLEIR. Superintendent of Police.[50]

And now, on this same afternoon at Melbourne Gaol, Ned has a new visitor. It is none other than his mother, Ellen. She is accompanied to Ned's cell by the Governor of the Gaol, John Castieau, already well known to them both, given his former tenure as the Governor of Beechworth Gaol for a decade before 1869, during which time it had become known as 'Castieau's Castle'.

Mother and son embrace and then sit and talk as the Governor remains quietly in the corner. Ned is communicative, his mother emotional, as for the first time she hears some detail of what her sons have done, and how it is that young Dan, Steve and Joe – whom Ned refers to collectively as 'my brave fellows'[51] – had come to die. In terms of his own deeds at Glenrowan, Ned speaks most fondly of his beloved grey mare, Music, telling his mother that, right to the end, she would have been strong enough to carry him away, even with his armour on, but she did not because, even though 'I could have escaped . . . I decided to see it out'.[52]

Beyond Glenrowan, Ellen is equally hungry for news of many others of their relatives that Ned has seen lately, while Ned, of course, asks how her life here has been. Before the discreet Governor Castieau gently mentions that the allotted time for their meeting, thirty minutes, will soon be up, Ellen Kelly beseeches her son to, as one paper would report, 'pay all respect and attention to the priest' who has been assigned to him by the gaol.[53] Sensing that perhaps his mother is fearful that he will take his own life, Ned puts her mind at ease, 'pointing out that he had numbers of opportunities of carrying out such an intention if he had felt any desire to do so'.[54]

And now it is time to go. Though Ellen Kelly is upset to be taken back to her cell before she has properly finished talking to her beloved son, she calms a little when Governor Castieau gently promises her that she will be able to visit him again, soon, when his health has improved.

2 JULY 1880, A LETTER TO THE EDITOR OF *THE ARGUS*

It is just one letter among many summing up the growing dissatisfaction with the way the police handled the final stage of the whole Kelly saga:

> Sir,—Now that the Kelly excitement is cooling, some of its features begin to excite comment. People are heard asking such questions as the following:—
>
> Why were the police permitted to fire into a slightly-built weatherboard house, which was well known to be crammed with men, women, and little children, killing and wounding indiscriminately? Again, who was it that permitted the police to burn the building when it was known that an innocent and helpless man lay there, and must be destroyed, and was in fact only saved by a civilian's pluck and humanity?
>
> Next, who was it that permitted the bodies of Daniel Kelly and Hart to be handed to a defiant pack of thieves and lawless vagabonds, whose sympathy and help had so long saved them from the gallows?
>
> Who allowed these bodies to be carted away before the inquest could be held? And why, when the tribe had got the bodies, and got drunk and insolent over them, did the authorities first claim them, and when denied and dared, recall their orders, and give these desperadoes best?
>
> If it was necessary to hold an inquiry upon Byrne, why was it unnecessary to have one over Hart and Daniel Kelly? What a farce it would be to hold one over Edward Kelly when he has been executed, and yet this has been the rule, and is the law.
>
> . . .
>
> Are there any Kelly sympathisers in the force, or are they simply muddle-headed and craven?
>
> —Yours, &c.
>
> July 1.
>
> GEO. S. GRIFFITHS[55]

For its part, a few days later, *The Ovens and Murray Advertiser* notes that 'the feeling is becoming general that the police were greatly to blame in connection with the attack on Jones's hotel, at Glenrowan. It is expected the Government will appoint a Royal Commission to institute an inquiry into the matter, together with the consideration of the general organization of the police force.'[56]

It is all but a small part of a growing outcry by public and press at the failings of the police in their pursuit of the Kellys, that it should have come to this.

10 JULY 1880, A HARBINGER OF HORROR APPEARS

The small item runs on page one of *The Ovens and Murray Advertiser*:

> **A NEW HANGMAN**.—Upjohn, a Ballarat fowl stealer, has been transferred to the Melbourne gaol. It is understood that Gately having cleared out to Sydney, will be succeeded in the post of hangman by this robber of hen-roosts. His first client in that case will, of course, be the murderer, Kelly. Such is fame; to defy the whole police force of the colony for twenty long months, and be finished by a miserable chicken-stealer.[57]

19 JULY 1880, IN MELBOURNE GAOL, FOR THE LOVE OF FAMILY

> The Hon,
> The Chief Secretary
> Sir,
> I beg most respectfully to request your permission to send for my sister Mrs Skillion to visit me at the Hospital of the above Gaol,

> to enable me to confer with her respecting the provisions of a Solicitor to prepare my Defence at my forthcoming trial and likewise for her to procure me the necessary clothing to appear thereat.
>
> I would also ask you to allow me to see my Mother. I have only seen her once.
>
> Your obedient Servant
>
> Edward Kelly X[58]

Across the bottom of it, Melbourne Sheriff Robert Rede, over whose desk the letter passes, writes a note saying:

> *Permission granted but special care must be taken as I have already verbally explained to the Governor of the Gaol.*[59]

22 JULY 1880, MELBOURNE, THIRD-TIME LUCKY FOR GRAHAM BERRY

No, it is not quite the overwhelmingly radical Assembly that formed in 1877, but it is a narrow majority for the Liberals of Graham Berry, who will now be Premier for the third time, and that is all that counts. Though Berry will not officially take over the reins as Premier for a couple of weeks, on this first day of sitting, no less than the radical Peter Lalor, the one-time hero of the Eureka Stockade, is selected for the role of Speaker.

30 JULY 1880, MELBOURNE, MAGGIE TAKES HER LOVE TO TOWN

The last time Tom Lloyd and Maggie Skillion had come to Melbourne, of course, it had been well observed by the police that their companion had purchased an inordinate amount of ordnance and weaponry

– which had subsequently disappeared. This time, however, there is no secrecy about what they want: legal firepower.

In the last month they have not been allowed to see or even communicate with Ned. Despite the promises that have been made and Sheriff Robert Rede apparently granting permission, it has not been possible to get Ned's instruction on how he wants his legal defence to be run. Now, however, it is a matter of urgency that they get this sorted. Ned's health has improved and he is deemed well enough to be taken in front of the Melbourne Police Court for his committal hearing on Monday. So Maggie and Tom have finally decided they must take matters into their own hands and engage someone of their own accord.

Their first meeting is with their first choice, David Gaunson, the radical member of the Legislative Assembly with a voice like a melody, who is interested in the case, nominally because as an ardent and outspoken opponent of capital punishment he sees it as his duty to place his legal skills at the service of Ned Kelly . . . but perhaps also because his instinct is always for publicity, and this case will be the most famous in the land. Alas, though he shows some interest, he declines to commit to it, so they must look elsewhere.

MORNING, 1 AUGUST 1880, SMUGGLING NED

It is time. Shortly before eight o'clock on this Sunday morning, another surprise plan is sprung on Ned Kelly. He is informed that today he will be going to Beechworth for his committal hearing, which will determine whether or not there appears to be a case in law for him to go to a full trial.

At half past eight, following a detailed plan, a wagonette arrives outside Melbourne Gaol to, once more, be quickly and quietly swallowed whole by the suddenly opening gates. Very few people are around to notice. Out of the wagonette now comes Ned's escort of four policemen: Sergeant Arthur Steele and Constables Hugh Bracken, Thomas McIntyre and Alfred John Faulkiner. Of them all, it is McIntyre who feels the most uncomfortable, as he is keenly aware that it is his testimony alone that will send Ned to the gallows, and he simply does not want to be around the murderer. Nevertheless, he has been told firmly by his superiors that 'you must not let your sensitivities interfere with your duty',[60] and so he does not.

And here is Ned now, on crutches, 'dressed cleanly and respectably [with] a pilot cloth coat, checked waistcoat, and corduroy trousers'[61] – his other clothes had been singed and then cut off by Doctor Nicholson after the siege – being escorted out of the prison by some warders and Mr Castieau.

No sooner does Ned catch sight of this escort than he reacts. 'I suppose you fellows are going to hang me,' he calls out. 'Here is McIntyre and I know he is going to do it.'

Notwithstanding that at least this is the first time that Ned has finally recognised him, without mistaking him for Flood, still McIntyre wishes that a hole would simply open up and swallow him whole. He tries to escape Ned's stare, but the bushranger is not going to let him off easily.

Nodding now to the rather comfortable-looking wagonette, he says, 'This is better than a wombat hole, eh, McIntyre?'[62]

McIntyre has the good grace to offer a feeble smile, and silence, though what he really wants to say is *'Et tu, Brute?'*[63] (For ever since that night, McIntyre's fate has been sealed. 'I left home every morning,' he would later recount, 'with full assurance that I would hear something about a wombat hole before I returned at night.'[64] Why, oh *why*, had he divulged that?)

Instead it is the Governor, as always kind yet stern in manner, who gently remonstrates with his prisoner. 'Now Kelly, your best game is to be quiet.'

'[Damn] it, ain't I always quiet?'

It is a fair point, but the fact that Ned is not really in the mood to be quiet on this morning shows a little later when the wagonette pulls up at Newmarket Station, a few miles out of Melbourne, where a special train – the authorities know that Ned loves special trains – will shortly arrive to take him and his guards to Beechworth. For, at the scenes of

Melbourne life going on all about him, so wonderfully removed from the unchanging vista of prison walls that he has known for the last month, Ned comes alive a little.

As they make their way into the station, Ned being carried on the hands of McIntyre and Faulkiner – as it is still too painful for him to walk far – the bushranger endeavours to attract the attention of some jockeys who are riding past the station as they exercise their horses. 'Bring those horses over here,' he calls, 'and Ned Kelly will show you how to ride them.'[65]

Sadly for Ned, though the jockeys engage in some good-natured banter with him, they don't realise that it really is Ned Kelly, and pass on. McIntyre, realising that Ned is somewhat deflated by the lack of reaction, tries to cheer him up, as they all wait on the platform for the train to arrive.

'There have been some extraordinary stories told about your shooting abilities,' he says. 'It was stated in a paper that you could gallop full speed alongside a fence and put a bullet into each post as you passed it.'

'So I can,' replies Ned a little more brightly, 'and no man is fit for the police force who couldn't do the same thing.'[66]

Sergeant Steele snorts in derision. 'Pooh! Pooh! That is nonsense. There was not one of you as good a shot as you pretended to be, and as for Hart, he was only a boy.'[67]

Leaning against the station building for support, Ned is suddenly enraged and, attempting to take off his coat, offers to fight Steele on the spot. Swearing at the trooper, he tells him straight out how much he regrets not having 'got you in the bush, when I would have showed you what I would do to you'.[68]

Steele, in response, remains remarkably unruffled, though he is careful not to accept Kelly's offer of a fight. Mercifully, the constables are able to restrain Ned, or at the least hold him upright and settle him down.

And here is the special train now, consisting only of an engine, carriage and guard's van. Ned is quickly bundled aboard the guard's van, where another four troopers await them all, and he is able to gratefully sink onto a chair, as his right leg cannot yet bear his weight. Only a couple of minutes later, the train pulls out and heads quickly north, roaring through all stations bar Seymour and Benalla, where there are quick stops.

For the most part, Ned is in good spirits, even singing several songs about the 'Bold Kelly Gang'. Sometimes, his spirits are high enough that he boasts about how hopeless the police had been. 'The idea of Hare, being a picked man, being sent up to catch me . . .' he begins, incredulously. 'I can tell you *every* place his party camped in the Warby Ranges, and who used to get up the horses.'

And nor is Hare's rival spared. 'What was Nicolson doing at Benalla,' he asks plaintively, 'pulling my friends into his office, and giving them money to do your lazy bastards' work? . . . The Government could have given them all the money they possess, and then they would not have sold me.'[69]

But there is also a fair measure of outrage apparent, not too far below the surface, as Ned asserts that he could never be hanged as to this day he had never seen a warrant, and is therefore illegally in custody.

As the train continues on and the Strathbogie Ranges rise up on the north-eastern horizon, Ned's eyes brighten a little and he says quietly, 'There they are; shall I ever be there again?'[70]

Watching him closely, even McIntyre is moved, recording that it could 'be plainly seen that, like Byrne, his aspirations were: "Give us our wildness and our woods, our huts and caves again . . ." Emotions which no other part of the country suggested, not even his birth place, seemed to flock upon him now, and he looked long and intently at them . . . Though his eyes were fixed on the rugged scenery before him his mind was reflecting upon scenes and events far beyond the limits of his vision.'[71]

When another familiar place comes into view, Ned says, 'Oh, this is Euroa. I know it and Scott of the Bank was the hardest man I ever had to deal with, he would not do a thing I wanted – He was an obstinate brute, but she wasn't a bad sort, I got on all right with her.'[72]

As they pass Glenrowan, of course, Ned gazes intently, and from the train points out the tree where he had been captured, as well as noting that 'a good man',[73] his great friend Joe Byrne, had died where the ashes of the inn still lie.

Sigh.

The train journey through his old haunts has stirred much nostalgia, as Ned now points to Constable Bracken, saying, 'There is a man I did not have heart to shoot . . .'[74]

When they pull into Beechworth Station at half past three, it is to be greeted by a crowd of a hundred people, who have once more been tipped off by the bush telegraph about Ned's imminent arrival. As the train slows, the crowd presses tightly in on the guard's van and there is some tension as the troopers on the platform, under the command of Superintendent Sadleir, force them back, so that Ned can be safely removed. With the eight troopers in the train tightly around him, Ned is lifted from the guard's van and rushed towards a heavily guarded van by the station, which is to rush him to Beechworth Gaol. There is just one small mishap when the hindquarters of the horse of Constable Alexander – one of the troopers hiding under the bed in Aaron Sherritt's shack that night, and now one of the station escort – comes close enough to Ned that he is able to give it a hefty kick.

With this accomplished, Ned soon finds himself once more in the familiar cells of Beechworth Gaol, which he had first entered some ten years before. As a new prisoner in the gaol, he is, of course, asked to strip off all his clothes. Ned agrees to all that but outright refuses to take off his pants. The warders look at Ned. Ned looks at the warders. He refuses. All right – you can keep your pants on.

—

And McIntyre? Where can he stay?

This proves to be a very sore point. For, instead of staying at the police barracks, which would be normal for an out-of-town constable,

McIntyre is told he is to sleep – for his own safety from sympathisers who likely want to kill him before the hearing – in the gaol, in the condemned cell opposite Ned's. Of course, McIntyre protests, but his superiors are firm. He is to stay in the gaol. In the condemned cell. Opposite Ned Kelly. And their cells lie in the shadow of the Beechworth Gaol gallows.

'Was this more than accident that we two men, the only survivors of the eight who met in Wombat forest, should be thus so peculiarly placed?' McIntyre would later pen his thoughts.

On arriving at his cell, Ned glances at the gallows and says, 'What a pity that a fine fellow like Ned Kelly should be strung up there.'[75]

FIRST WEEK OF AUGUST 1880, MAGGIE MANOEUVRES

Yes, Ned Kelly is known throughout the land as a strong man, but the Kellys also breed strong women in the image of Ellen. With both Ned and Ellen in gaol, leadership of the family's affairs has fallen to Maggie Skillion, and it is she, with Tom Lloyd, who has settled, for the moment at least, with the local William Zincke to defend Ned.

The ongoing concern in the days leading up to the hearing, now urgent, is to have visitation rights, and it seems that Zincke has at last gained them. Alas, when Maggie turns up at Beechworth Gaol on the Wednesday afternoon – to, among other things, give her brother a fresh change of underclothing – the gaol authorities point blank refuse to allow her in. So seriously do the authorities take their duty that even the undies themselves are refused access.

In deep consultation that night, Maggie and Tom Lloyd – who have become very close in the course of events over the last two years – decide on a new tack. Clearly a part of the problem here is that, although he is a newly elected member for the Ovens District on the Opposition side of politics, Zincke simply does not have the political clout they need. It would be better to try again to get David Gaunson, the ambitious Sydney-born thirty-four-year-old member for Ararat, who has already shown some interest in the case, to make the journey up to Beechworth and work with Zincke for Ned's defence. He is, after all, from the government's side of politics and known to be very close to the man who has once more become Premier and Chief Secretary this week, Graham Berry. Though not both a solicitor *and* a barrister like Zincke, he is clearly good on his feet and could represent Ned for the formality of the Beechworth hearing. For Gaunson, they know, as well as being a radical politician, has a long background as an attorney, and, most crucially – despite having attended the unveiling of the memorial for the Mansfield murders – has a strong sympathy for the Kelly case.

And yet, while Gaunson does indeed accept the offer cabled to him on Thursday morning, and informs them by return cable that he will catch the three o'clock train from Melbourne to Beechworth, the outraged Zincke resigns on the spot from the legal team. He had been happy to represent Kelly, but not with David Gaunson he won't.

With just hours to go, thus, before the hearing takes place, Ned Kelly's defence is thrown into the hands of one who is not prepared.

LATE NIGHT, 5 AUGUST 1880, BEECHWORTH, MIDNIGHT COUNSELLOR

And so come the key players in the legal theatre about to take place. After the train from Melbourne pulls into Beechworth Station late on this Thursday night, as well as Gaunson it disgorges the man with the most magnificent white moustache in the legal fraternity, Arthur Chomley, who had prosecuted Ellen Kelly two years before and will be assisting Chief Crown Prosecutor Charles Smyth. A third significant figure who arrives is Dick Hart, who, still mourning his brother Steve, is here on principle. While Hart makes his way to find Maggie Skillion and Tom Lloyd, Gaunson heads straight to Beechworth Gaol. Truly, what he would really like to do right now is have a very big drink – he is of the view that 'a man should get drunk once a month for the sake of his health',[76] and no one has ever accused him of not practising what he preaches – but for now this is more important.

The press is fully aware that one of the major reasons for Gaunson's engagement is the hope that he may be able to secure a private interview between the prisoner and his friends, and *The Argus* would report the meeting in that light: 'It is asserted that the Gang carried away a great deal more money from the banks they stuck up than was reported by the officials. There is no doubt the balance of the booty is planted, and that Ned Kelly is the only person alive who knows where the plant is concealed; hence the desire to have a private interview between him and his friends.'[77]

When Gaunson arrives at his client's cell just after midnight, escorted by the gaol's Governor, it is to find Ned asleep. Nevertheless, appreciating the urgency of the situation, and the stakes, Ned is more than happy to get up to have a meeting. In the quiet of the night, with only the stirrings of the other prisoners all around for competing sound, the two quietly talk for three-quarters of an hour – all of it monitored by the Governor, who remains there.

'All I want,' Ned tells his attorney with great forcefulness, 'is a full and fair trial, and a chance to make my side heard. Until now, the police have had all the say, and have had it all their own way. If I get a full and fair trial I don't care how it goes; but I know this – the public will see that I was hunted and hounded . . . from step to step; they will see that I am not the monster I have been made out. What I have done has been under strong provocation.'[78]

And, yes, he also wants his family to have visitation rights. 'I have been kept here like a wild beast,' he goes on, quietly. 'If they were afraid to let anyone come near me they might have kept at a distance and watched; but it seems to me to be unjust when I am on trial for my life, to refuse to allow those I put confidence in to come within cooey of me . . .'[79]

Gaunson promises to do all he can and takes his leave in the wee hours, arriving back at his hotel at half past one in the morning. At last, he can have a drink.

6 AUGUST 1880, THE COMMITTAL PROCEEDINGS BEGIN IN BEECHWORTH COURTHOUSE

And so they come. Hundreds of them. All hoping to get a prime position in the court, or at least just outside so that they might catch a glimpse of the most famous man in the land. It is the day of Ned Kelly's committal hearing, and the excitement of all of the populace, police and press is overwhelming.

At eight o'clock in the morning, before the crowd has properly gathered, Ned is brought from the gaol to the stone-walled courthouse inside a very small, covered wagonette. Still in chains, he is taken into the prisoners' room, where he consults once more with David Gaunson before the proceedings begin.

The court itself is packed 'to suffocation [point], the gallery being crowded with ladies, many of them being evidently sympathisers'.[80] *The Ovens and Murray Advertiser*, for one, is not happy with just who has turned up. Apart from the huge number of young women in the upstairs gallery, 'We regretted to see that such a large number of boys were allowed to be present; for instead of the prisoner being regarded as a thing to be condemned by all respectable members of society, he is being submitted to the public gaze, and made to appear – to the youthful mind at least – in the light of a hero of romance.'[81]

At last, at ten o'clock sharp, for those lucky enough to be inside, Kelly himself appears – it is *him*, it is really him! – dressed in 'a black coat, light trousers, and white shirt'.[82] He is carried into the room from his cell by two burly troopers, and once he has an audience the bushranger eschews their help and hops the rest of the way to the dock, where, at the request of Gaunson, a chair will soon be provided for him. As reported by *The Argus*, 'The prisoner . . . looked furtively round the court until his eyes fell on Mrs Skillion and Tom Lloyd, and then mutual signs of recognition passed between them. Mrs Skillion and Lloyd at first took seats at the attorneys' table, but before the proceedings commenced they shifted to the front seat in the body of the court, within a few feet of the prisoner.'[83]

Sitting in the front row of the public gallery is Superintendent

Sadleir, whereas – to the amazement of many – Captain Standish sits right beside Police Magistrate William Henry Foster. It will be Foster's claim that this is simply a matter of courtesy, but, with Standish taking that position, the scales of justice look lopsided from the beginning.

Just after ten o'clock, the true business of the day gets underway. After the legal preliminaries, including the charge that 'Edward Kelly, on the 26th day of October, in the year 1878, at Stringybark Creek, in the northern bailiwick, feloniously, wilfully, and of his malice aforethought, did kill and murder one Michael Scanlan [and Thomas Lonigan]'[84] – the two murders for which there is a witness – Mr Gaunson's first move is to apply for remand so that he can better acquaint himself with the facts of the case.

'Under the circumstances of the case,' Mr Foster says, 'I will grant a remand, but it will be for a very short period. I only do it in consequence of the serious nature of the case. I remand the prisoner until 2 o'clock this afternoon.'[85]

As quick as a flash, before Ned can be taken away, Maggie Skillion and Tom Lloyd step forward and try to touch hands with him, but they are quickly blocked by troopers. 'I've tried hard to see you,' Maggie tells her beloved brother. 'But they would not let me.'

'It looks,' Ned says regretfully to his favourite sister, 'as if they won't let me see you – good-bye.'

As the troopers now forcibly move her away, she calls out, 'Never mind, Ned, they are a lot of curs.'

'There's one native that's no cur,' Ned replies, 'and he will show them that yet.'[86]

—

At that appointed hour, when the court again gets underway, with Gaunson's request for a further adjournment quickly denied, the member for Ararat nevertheless warmly thanks the police magistrate for the recent adjournment, saying he has used the time to read as much as he can of the accounts of the murders in *The Argus*. However, he begs to advise that, as it has been utterly impossible for him to digest those reports in the time at his disposal, 'I am therefore, driven to beg Your Worship to remand the accused for a week, so that I might be able to consider carefully the defence that should be made on his behalf.'[87]

Gaunson also points out that, because of the premature order given by the former Chief Secretary, Robert Ramsay, and not rescinded by his successor, Graham Berry, who was sworn in just three days earlier, 'no person had been able to see the prisoner except professional gentlemen, and, in consequence, the prisoner has not had that fair opportunity of preparing his defence which the law entitled him to'.[88] He not only begs for remand, therefore, but also must respectfully request, one more time, that the order banning contact between Ned and his family be lifted.

In response, the man 'neath the white wig, wearing the black robes, Magistrate Foster, is firm. He does not believe sufficient case for remand has been made, and so they will proceed. And it is not within his province of operations to make an order for contact, so Gaunson will have to take that up with the government.

That settled, Charles Smyth now rises to begin the case for the prosecution. A man never more impressive than when on his feet in a courtroom, almost always speaking without notes, his large nose and calculating eyes give his visage a rather hawk-like appearance – while his full, grey beard shows that he is an *experienced* hawk, used to tearing criminals apart.

This, he says from the start, is a straightforward case, where the evidence is overwhelming, and the key witness for the Crown, Constable McIntyre, a man of impeccable character, was there when the murders occurred and saw it all from a distance of no more than 25 yards. In the first instance, the Crown will focus on the murder of Constable Lonigan, so he calls on Constable McIntyre now. That gentleman – while resolutely refusing to look anywhere in the direction of Ned Kelly – begins to relate his story, prompted along by the Crown prosecutor.

—

McIntyre tells of leaving Mansfield, of arriving at Stringybark Creek, of shooting at the parrots, of looking up to see Ned Kelly coming hard and yelling, 'Bail up!', and of course the story of poor Constable Lonigan being shot. As he gets to the part where the first of the fatal shots is fired, no one in the courtroom stirs – the horror, the *horror!* – and there is no doubt he comes across as a compelling, honest witness.

His key testimony is devastating for the case of Ned Kelly: 'I noticed the right-hand man of the party particularly, and saw his gun pointed directly towards my breast. I immediately held out my arms horizontally. As soon as I did so I saw the same man remove the gun a little towards his right hand and fire it, at Lonigan, who had started to run. Lonigan was standing on the opposite side of the fire to me, at a distance of ten or twelve feet. He was running towards a tree, and was about forty yards distant from the man who fired at him. I heard him falling immediately after the gun was fired. He had taken about four or five steps before he fell. I did not see him fall, but heard him breathing heavily and stertorously. The prisoner, Edward Kelly, was the man I alluded to as the "man on the right".'[89]

Again, in this most crucial of legal hearings, Constable McIntyre has made no mention of Lonigan attempting to shoot the bushranger, meaning that, to the court, it is as if Edward Kelly's intention had been to kill him from the first. In cold blood. (True, McIntyre does quote Dan as saying after the shooting, 'He was a plucky fellow, did you see how he caught at his revolver,'[90] but the point is not followed up.)

By five o'clock, McIntyre is just getting to the part where Sergeant Kennedy and Constable Scanlan are about to return, when Magistrate Foster adjourns the court for the day – and Ned is taken back to his cell at the gaol by a heavily armed guard of police.

And wouldn't you know it? That same 'large number of boys'[91] whom *The Ovens and Murray Advertiser* had identified as viewing Ned 'in the light of a hero of romance',[92] now run along behind Ned's wagonette as he, smiling, bunches his fist and points his finger as if it is a gun, and pretends to shoot them.

Back in the courthouse, Gaunson has the leave of Magistrate Foster to meet in the magistrate's chambers, where he again seeks permission to allow Maggie Skillion to visit her brother in his cell, and again the request is denied.

7 AUGUST 1880, COURAGE OR COWARDICE

On the Saturday morning, when court resumes, it goes as before, except that it is so cold that Ned is provided with an opossum rug to keep his legs warm – though when he sees an artist drawing his likeness, he pulls the rug up around himself, making clear that he does not care to be so depicted. For the most part, the bushranger is reserved, with a quiet demeanour, though on the rare occasions when the evidence seems to go his way, or Gaunson makes a successful objection, he is seen to smile and look over to Maggie, nodding.

One such occasion is when McIntyre admits to Smyth that, after Stringybark, 'I never saw the prisoner again until I saw him at Glenrowan on the 28th of June.'

Smyth asks, 'Had you any conversation with him then?'

This starts a line of questioning to which Gaunson objects a few times, stating at one point, 'At a time when the prisoner was prostrate and wounded these men fastened themselves on him to get information out of him that would incriminate him. It was a blackguard proceeding to go uninvited at such a time for the purpose of extracting evidence.'[93]

After all, had it really been necessary to interview a wounded and likely delirious prisoner so soon after his confinement, and had he been ordered to interview Kelly at the Benalla lock-up?

No, McIntyre responds. 'No one ordered me to interview the prisoner at the Benalla lock-up. I obtained access to the prisoner with Senior Constable Kelly . . . The prisoner was wounded, and was lying down. He was seemingly sane.'

And your whole account of the conversation was from memory, yes, queries Gaunson.

'Neither the senior constable nor I took any written notes of the conversation.'

Why, in your first report of the murders to Superintendent Sadleir, was there no mention of Ned Kelly as being the one responsible?

'If I did not state in that report that Edward Kelly was the man who shot Lonigan and Scanlan,' McIntyre responds carefully, 'I should have done so. I was at the time in a very excited state.'

Did you tell Ned Kelly that you believed that Fitzpatrick had perjured himself?

McIntyre vigorously denies it, but he does allow that, 'If [Fitzpatrick] possessed truthfulness, uprightness, and decency, I believe he would not have been discharged from the force.'[94]

Would McIntyre agree that it was solely on Fitzpatrick's evidence that Ellen Kelly had been placed in gaol for three years with an infant at her breast?

The constable cannot deny it.

And at least we can agree, constable, that *you* are a *coward*? That, at least, is the thrust of my learned friend's most probing question: 'Is it true that the instant Kennedy got off his horse [at Stringybark] you seized it and left him in the lurch?'

No, it is not true! He had not left Kennedy in the lurch at all! As a matter of fact, he had not even reached for the horse.

'The horse was restive and came towards me,' Constable McIntyre says defensively. 'No horse could stand still between two men firing at each other.'[95]

But you do accept, Constable McIntyre, that Kennedy was alive and with a gun in his hand, fighting for his life, at the time that you galloped away?

The constable cannot deny it.

And Constable Scanlan was also alive and armed?

'Yes . . .'[96]

Why on earth depart, then, when your companions needed you? 'Seeing Scanlan fall I expected no mercy, and therefore caught and mounted Kennedy's horse which was close to me.'[97]

Do you agree that a reward had been offered for the arrest of the Kellys 'dead or alive'?[98]

He cannot deny it.

Do you recall the prisoner saying, 'We don't want to take life, we only want your arms . . .'?

'No,' McIntyre replies, 'but I heard the prisoner say, "Fitzpatrick is the cause of all this."'

And did you agree?

'I cannot remember saying, "I know that," in answer to Kelly; but I will not swear I did not say so.'[99]

Did they at least have warrants, then, to arrest Ned and Dan Kelly?

'Kennedy may have had the warrant. I did not say in my examination in chief that we had no warrant. I had no warrant.'

Mr Gaunson: 'We had a row about plain clothes in Melbourne. I would like to know by what authority you scour the country in plain clothes, armed, and without warrants.'

Witness: 'I was acting under the instructions of Sergeant Kennedy . . .'[100]

On the issue of the heavy weaponry and bountiful ammunition they have with them, Gaunson is withering. 'You did not take a cannon with you?'

'No . . .' McIntyre replies, becoming ever more unsettled at this ongoing attack. 'We expected resistance.'[101]

Later, McIntyre will make a key admission: 'We had about twenty spare cartridges each. It is not usual to carry so much ammunition.'[102] But he will never allow that they were there from the beginning to kill the Kellys.

By the end of Gaunson's cross-examination, McIntyre is nothing less than a shattered man and is, as reported by the Melbourne *Herald*, 'suffering from such serious nervous excitement that he was several times nearly hysterical and during the adjournment had to be prescribed for.'[103]

And so it goes. As they head to the adjournment for lunch, Gaunson makes clear just how unimpressed he is with McIntyre's answers by saying, 'I will leave the witness to be turned inside out by a better man in the Supreme Court . . .'[104]

Of course, for the Sabbath, Ned can rest in his cell, but in the evening he has a meeting with Gaunson, who, among other things, conducts an interview with him on behalf of *The Age*.

'I do not pretend that I have led a blameless life,' Ned tells him, 'or that one fault justifies another, but the public in judging a case like mine should remember that the darkest life may have a bright side, and that after the worst has been said against a man, he may, if he is heard, tell a story in his own rough way that will perhaps lead them to intimate the harshness of their thoughts against him, and find as many excuses for him as he would plead for himself.'[105]

—

On the Monday morning, Ned has some new support, as Dick Hart is accompanied by his gorgeous sister Ettie, whom the bushranger has been sweet on. For it is noted that, while Ned seems to make some indecipherable sign at Dick, his signs to Ettie are all too decipherable . . . xxx . . . xxx . . . as the two blow each other kisses.

Over the next two days, there is a parade of witnesses, each essentially providing testimony that Ned Kelly has done exactly what he is accused of. Senior Constable Kelly is the final witness, on the Tuesday afternoon, testifying that, on the morning after Ned was captured, 'I visited the prisoner at 3 o'clock in the morning in the presence of Constable Ryan. I gave him a drink of milk and water. I then said to him, "Ned, what about Fitzpatrick; was his statement correct?" He said, "Yes, it was I who shot him."'[106]

Inevitably, Magistrate Foster delivers his judgment, and the prisoner, Edward Kelly, is committed to stand trial at Beechworth General Sessions, in nine weeks' time, on 14 October, for the murder of Constable Lonigan at Stringybark Creek. As is the custom, Magistrate Foster enquires whether the prisoner has anything to say . . .

Ned clearly wants to but is strongly motioned not to by Gaunson. With a heavy sigh, Ned agrees, saying only, 'If he wants me to say anything I'll very soon speak.'[107]

With his committal confirmed, of course the climactic moment has been reached, but as the prisoner is also charged with the murder of Constable Scanlan, in the next hearing many of the same witnesses give much the same evidence until late on Wednesday afternoon, when Ned is committed to stand trial for that murder, too.

The court is adjourned, at which point, to the amazement of the court, Kate Kelly, Ned's sister, evades the bailiffs and walks to the dock, close enough that Ned can lean over, clasp her delicate hands in his handcuffed ones and kiss her. Bless you, Kate. The two have just an instant to gaze at each other with enormous familial warmth before the troopers grab Ned, and the bailiffs grab Kate, to separate them.

Through all the proceedings, there has been no weakening of the Crown's outright refusal to allow the prisoner to see his family, though Gaunson has done his best.

—

On the Thursday morning, still under heavy guard, Ned is rushed to Wangaratta Station – thus circumventing the enormous crowd of sympathisers that has built up at Beechworth Station – and readied to head back to Melbourne Gaol on another special train. And yet, despite all the attempts at secrecy, the word has got out and a crowd of over 500 has gathered.

'Goodbye ladies,' Ned says tearfully, waving at two excited women on the platform, who wave their handkerchiefs at him. 'I shall never see you again.'[108]

The locomotive belches, the crowd falls first back and then quickly behind, and once more Ned leaves Kelly Country – his life again rolling backward as he wistfully gazes through the window at Glenrowan and Benalla, with all their attendant memories. As the reality of what likely awaits him starts to hit, as one more precious day starts to disappear with the journey, Ned remarks to Constable Bracken, 'If it is my fate to be hanged, I will be. I do not expect to get off.'[109]

26 AUGUST 1880, IN MELBOURNE GAOL, NED MOVES

Despite remaining in considerable pain, on this morning Ned is able to stand and even shuffle from the gaol hospital to his own solitary cell. His mood, not unexpectedly, is down. Despite his bravado in the court and seeming insouciance, it is a terrible thing to know that every sunrise brings him a day closer to facing his fate and there is no escaping . . . well, there is just no escaping.

MORNING, 18 SEPTEMBER 1880, CENTRAL CRIMINAL COURT, MELBOURNE, THE CROWN SHIFTS

Just like clockwork . . .

In a very slick legal manoeuvre, on this sunny Saturday that promises a blooming spring, the Crown prosecutor, Charles Smyth, makes application to Justice Redmond Barry in his chambers to transfer the trial of Edward Kelly from the Beechworth Circuit Court to the Central Criminal Court in Melbourne.

In short, the authorities know they have a much better chance of getting a Melbourne jury to hang Ned Kelly than they do a jury from Kelly Country, and so they want to move the trial to the city. Judge Barry is not long in agreeing with the Crown that, if the trial is held in Beechworth, 'efforts would be made to intimidate certain of the jurors on the jury'.[110] He therefore rules that the trial must be moved to Melbourne's Central Criminal Court.

—

And yet, there is further wheeling and dealing going on at the Crown Solicitor's Office as, on 22 September, Crown Solicitor Henry Gurner makes a curious suggestion in a letter to the new Attorney General, William Vale: 'I have the honor to suggest that it may be advisable, in the first instance, to only deliver Briefs to Counsel in one of the charges against the Defendant . . . that of shooting Constable Thomas Lonigan; subsequently if considered necessary, briefs can be sent in the other charge; that of shooting Constable Michael Scanlan.'[111]

The Attorney General approves the plan.[112] It is highly unorthodox, but it means that, on the off-chance they don't manage to get a guilty verdict against Ned for the murder of Lonigan, the Crown will have a second, separate chance in their prosecution of Scanlan. Nothing is to be left to chance. Ned Kelly *must* be hanged.

SEPTEMBER–OCTOBER 1880, WHAT TO DO WHEN YOU HAVE THE TASTE FOR CHAMPAGNE ON A BUDGET FOR BEER

Yes, there is a well-known admonition in Victoria at this time that all accused are 'innocent until proved Irish', and Ned is not only that but is also the most notorious criminal on the continent. But, despite that, Gaunson still has some hope that a guilty verdict against him is not a fait accompli.

After all, in the months after Ned was born, thirteen diggers from the Eureka Stockade were put on trial for their lives, charged with High Treason, and in the course of those trials it had been comprehensively proved that the five troopers who lay in their early graves only did so because of the actions of these men. And yet still no Victorian jury would convict any of them of the charges, as their defence had so cleverly proved – among other things – that there had been justification for their building the stockade and then defending themselves when the Redcoats had attacked them in such force in the early hours of 3 December 1854. And Judge Barry had presided over all but two of those cases.

In the case of Ned Kelly, Gaunson's best hope will be firstly to prove that Ned and his family had been unfairly maligned and then marginalised for many years; secondly that Ned had done nothing more than fight back against cruel injustices; and thirdly, specifically, that the four policemen at Stringybark Creek, who had arrived with leather straps specifically designed to carry dead bodies, were not there to merely execute warrants for the arrest of the Kelly Gang but to outright execute the gang. And Ned Kelly had done nothing but act in self-defence. If the defence could prove that final contention, there really might be a chance that a jury would refuse to convict him of cold-blooded murder.

But what skilled barrister – and a barrister it must be to appear before the Supreme Court – can they get to carry such an argument?

Herein lies the problem.

Though there are skilled and experienced barristers available, all of them are expensive, and of the many problems that the legal defence of Ned Kelly is facing at this time, the key one is an all but total lack of funds. For, despite the fears of the Crown that somewhere in the wilderness there lies a cache of ill-gotten gains that Ned will be able to use if given the chance to tell his family or supporters where it is, that is clearly not the case. Even though Ned is at last, finally, allowed to see Maggie on one occasion, no sudden flood of money appears.

And yet, so committed is the Crown to ensuring that the Kelly family remain poverty-stricken that, to Maggie's shocked amazement, when she tries to take out a mortgage on her mother's 88 acres at Greta, it is only to learn that the government has effectively confiscated that land. When David Gaunson had enquired at the Lands Department to find out how such a thing could possibly have occurred, a complicated saga emerges. Ellen Kelly had first obtained a selection under the *Amending Land Act 1865* and gone on to pay all the required rent over the next seven years' lease, borrowing some money on it from the Land Credit Bank.

'The bank subsequently sold her interest in the land to the prisoner's sister,' *The Argus* would explain, 'but the Lands Department on the application of the police had refused to grant a title to the ground.'[113]

It seems that the 'Black List' drawn up by Nicolson and Sadleir and handed over to the Lands Department over a year ago is still being kept on file, and indeed used. The bottom line is that, without having title to the land because of that police intervention, Maggie cannot borrow money against it to pay for a top barrister.

In fact, so poverty-stricken have the Kelly family now become that, after their immediate finances are exhausted, the only barrister they can afford is one Henry Bindon, who, though thirty-seven years old, has been practising for less than a year after struggling for a long time to get through his legal exams, and has not yet appeared before the Supreme Court, or even in a jury trial. But he does possess the most important qualification of all: he will accept just seven guineas a day in payment.

Though Bindon is effectively able to use the same manoeuvre that Gaunson used at the Beechworth committal hearing to get an adjournment on the grounds that he needs more time to master his brief – and because the family, frankly, Your Honour, is still hoping to raise funds for a better barrister than him – finally the date for the trial of Ned Kelly is settled for 28 October 1880 at the Melbourne Supreme Court before the Honourable Sir Redmond Barry KCMG, KB, the sixty-seven-year-old legend of the legal land who has been sitting on that court for the past three decades.

In the meantime, it is a measure of David Gaunson's commitment to the Kelly cause that, despite being unpaid, he still does all he can to prepare Bindon and to raise the money needed to get a better and more experienced counsel. The man they want is the legendary Hickman Molesworth, a barrister of sixteen years' experience, son of a Supreme Court Judge, and pillar of the Establishment, who has said he is available to represent Ned if the family can raise his fee of 50 guineas a day for the first two days and 10 guineas a day thereafter. But where can that money come from?

Gaunson's efforts include approaching the Crown for funds, on the grounds that, without such funds, Kelly cannot have a fair trial. In response, the Crown digs deep and grants seven guineas towards the cost of a counsel, and another seven guineas for a solicitor – enough to secure the services of Hickman Molesworth for about two hours and a top solicitor for four hours.

And so Henry Bindon it is to defend Ned, and Henry Bindon it will remain . . .

At least he is cheap.

Chapter Seventeen

ON TRIAL FOR HIS LIFE

> Let the hand of the law strike me down if it will, but I ask that my story might be heard and considered; not that I wish to avert any decree the law may deem necessary to vindicate justice, or win a word of pity from anyone. If my life teaches the public that men are made mad by bad treatment, and if the police are taught that they may not exasperate to madness men they persecute and ill-treat, my life will not be entirely thrown away.
>
> *Ned Kelly*

9 AM, 28 OCTOBER 1880, THE CENTRAL CRIMINAL COURT RESUMES

And so it begins.

All rise.

Courtroom scene from the Kelly trial. (From *The Illustrated Australian News*, 6 November 1880, courtesy State Library of Victoria)

Presiding in the Old Court House, which squats on the corner of Russell and La Trobe Streets, on this stiflingly hot morning is Justice Sir Redmond Barry. Yes, many think that because he has put Ellen Kelly in prison and is reputed to have said that, had Ned been brought to trial on the same charge, he would have sentenced him to twenty-one years, he should have disqualified himself from this case, but Judge Barry does not share this view, and that is all that counts.

Arriving ten minutes late, as he is the only legal official with the authority to do so, he is a man in his element, the most experienced trial judge in the colony – a highly venerated, elderly man of the law, all white wig, red robe and piercing stare from on high as he looks out from 'neath a gothic canopy that marks his authority over the packed courtroom filled with black-robed barristers wearing their (*sniff*) small grey wigs. Beyond them lies a packed public gallery, with every pew filled.

The jowly, pale Judge Barry, now exchanging stiff bows with the barristers before he takes his seat, is the embodiment of the Irish Protestant ascendancy, while – 'Calling Edward Kelly!' the court crier cries[1] – the powerful, hirsute, magnificent young man limping into the dock via a connecting passage from the gaol represents everything that is most dangerous about the Irish Catholics and the native-born generation of reprobates they have sired.

As Ned settles, the courtroom, almost as one – with the notable exception of Judge Barry himself, Crown Prosecutor Smyth and his offsider Arthur Chomley, who merely stare bleakly – practically holds its breath and leans forward to get a better look at the captured outlaw in the dimly lit surroundings. There he is. Ned stares back in turn. A man who can take on twenty-five troopers and not turn a hair is unlikely to be intimidated by this lot, and he makes that clear from the first. Given a dispensation to sit because of his injury, Ned takes his seat in the dock, resting pale and stern, 'looking like a selector in Sunday clothes'.[2]

After legal preliminaries, including Henry Bindon pleading for another adjournment on the grounds that he still hasn't had time to understand all the voluminous depositions taken in the case – request denied – it is time to get to the true business at hand, pursuing Kelly on the charge of murdering Lonigan.

And how does Edward Kelly plead?

'Not guilty,' Ned replies in a firm voice, more determined than defiant.[3]

After the jury has been empanelled, with both barristers challenging various candidates until twelve good men and true have been selected, the proceedings proper begin.

Crown Prosecutor Smyth now stands, looking every bit at home as Judge Barry in this domain, and outlines the case of the Crown – at some length. For, yes, while Ned Kelly is now only being prosecuted for the murder of Constable Lonigan – perhaps because that is the easiest one to prove, with Constable McIntyre's eyewitness account – Smyth does not confine his opening remarks to that murder. For good measure, my learned friend takes the court, and most particularly the jury, through the prisoner's whole sordid past, encompassing not just the horrendous murders at Stringybark but also the attempted murder of Fitzpatrick, the shocking murder in cold blood of Aaron Sherritt, the shoot-out at Glenrowan and Ned's attempt to cause the derailment of a train at the same place to murder a couple of dozen troopers and black-trackers.

The reporters scribble, the jury leans close, Smyth goes on at length – savouring his own words the way other men might savour a chocolate – and Ned glares balefully.

This man, Smyth says, indicating Ned, had boasted to a witness that he had stolen 200 horses, and yet 'had gone on to complain that the police would not let him live in peace!'[4]

But, if it pleases the court, it is time for the first witnesses.

Detective Michael Ward and Constable Patrick Day, Smyth's first two witnesses, affirm the circumstances in which the warrants for the arrest of Edward Kelly were issued – first for Horse Stealing and then for Attempted Murder of Constable Fitzpatrick. It is then time for the star witness.

Your Honour, we call on Constable Thomas McIntyre to take the stand. The Irish constable slowly, and seemingly reluctantly, comes forward and, as he enters the witness box, glances at Ned Kelly, who grimaces meaningfully at him. In response, McIntyre shakes his head softly, purses his lips and then whispers, 'I cannot help it, you placed me here.'[5] Composing himself, he now stares straight ahead at the jury, as Smyth invites him to recount what happened.

'In October 1878, I was stationed at Mansfield,' McIntyre begins, in a calm but sorrowful voice. 'On Friday the 25th[6] of the month, I left with Sergeant Kennedy and Constables Lonigan and Scanlan to search for the prisoner and his brother Dan, on a charge of attempting to murder Constable Fitzpatrick . . .'[7]

With gentle prompting from Smyth, he recounts firstly the mundane events of that day, and then the sudden, terrible attack, launched by 'four men, each armed with a gun, and pointing these weapons at Lonigan and me'.[8]

'Are any of those men present in the courtroom?' Smyth asks.

'Yes,' says McIntyre.

'Where?'

'Over there,' McIntyre replies, his finger now pointing straight at Ned Kelly, the way Kelly's gun had once pointed at Lonigan, for perhaps the same result.

'The witness,' Judge Barry's high-pitched voice breaks in, 'has identified the prisoner.'[9]

McIntyre's testimony goes on. 'The prisoner, who was one of the men, had the right-hand position, and he had his gun pointed at my chest. I, being unarmed, at once threw my arms out horizontally.'[10]

As one, the entire courtroom, this time including Judge Barry, leans in, eager to catch every word of this crucial testimony, while McIntyre continues to stare at the jury. Strangely, only Ned Kelly seems not to be hanging on every syllable. This is perhaps because he already knows what happens next, and knows it in excruciating detail, or perhaps he simply does not want to appear to be lending any of his own weight to this moment.

When it comes to the part where Ned actually fires at Lonigan,

McIntyre again changes his account from his original testimony, neglecting to mention – likely under pressure from his superiors – the key fact that Lonigan had been going for his own gun to shoot at Ned.

And now Ned is losing his nonchalance, no longer able to maintain a cool facade. Rather, the now-standing Ned grips the dock – a strong sense of wild power about him in this tight judicial environment – raises his right arm to the level of his shoulder and spits over it. It is a gesture, bush shorthand for *total contempt*, that he will repeat throughout the trial.

McIntyre goes on, however, detailing how, in exchange for Ned Kelly promising to spare the lives of Sergeant Kennedy and Constable Scanlan, he would attempt to persuade the two men to lay down their weapons on their return. 'About this time, half-past 5 or 6 o'clock,' the constable continues, 'Kennedy and Scanlan came up. The prisoner cried out, "Hush, lads! Here they come!"'[11]

Objection!

All eyes turn to the young counsel defending Edward Kelly.

Yes, Mr Bindon?

Henry Bindon objects to this whole line of testimony, as what is alleged to have happened to Constable Scanlan and Sergeant Kennedy has nothing to do with the alleged murder of Lonigan. Edward Kelly is not on trial for the murder of Kennedy and Scanlan, only Lonigan.

Objection overruled. Judge Barry agrees with Smyth's counter-submission that this evidence is admissible, 'to show the intent with which the first shot was fired'.[12] That is, 'whether or not Kelly had killed him in self-defence'.[13]

Please go on, constable.

McIntyre does, at some length, providing excruciating detail as to what happened when Kennedy and Scanlan returned, including the shots fired that brought down poor Scanlan, while he was still there.

Henry Bindon does his best in cross-examination to shake the testimony of McIntyre, but as he had stated to Judge Barry just a few hours earlier, he has not yet mastered his brief, to really know where to shake the constable. On this occasion, he could have highlighted the discrepancy between McIntyre's original account of the shooting of Lonigan, whereby Lonigan had been about to shoot Ned when he was shot himself, and this account, whereby Lonigan is shot in cold blood, but this crucial angle is completely ignored. The best Bindon can do is to show that McIntyre was not even sure of the legality of what they were doing.

'We went out with Kennedy to arrest the prisoner and his brother,' McIntyre says. 'I did not see the warrants for their apprehension. I can't swear that any of our party had a warrant. I knew of the warrants by the *Police Gazette*.'[14]

In the course of the cross-examination, McIntyre is keen, however, to justify his own actions in escaping, and says, 'When they were firing all round I thought no mercy would be shown to any of us. If I had known Kennedy would have fought I would not have left. I did not consider there was any opportunity for a fight.'[15]

And then Bindon is suddenly done, after just twenty questions, none of which has shaken Constable McIntyre and all of which have ignored the only issue that his client really has to go with – that he had shot Lonigan before Lonigan could shoot him as a matter of self-defence.

Personally, McIntyre is amazed to have been blessed with such a blundered cross-examination. As he would later recall, he had only been 'asked many questions that, not only seem to be but, are irrelevant to the case'.[16]

Because of Bindon's failure to properly cross-examine, there is no doubt the jury is left with the strong impression that Ned Kelly had simply shot Constable Lonigan down in cold blood. It is a performance perhaps excusable in such a junior barrister, but nevertheless manifestly inadequate counsel for charges of such life and death importance. For the moment, however, there is little enough time to reflect on this as the prosecution continues to roll out its witnesses, many of them from the sieges of Euroa and Jerilderie, testifying as to what Ned Kelly had admitted to doing when the Kelly Gang had held them as their prisoners.

George Stephens, who was locked up by the Kelly Gang when they held up Faithfull's Creek Station before Euroa, gives his compelling account of Ned admitting to him that he had shot Lonigan after the constable had pointed his revolver at Dan Kelly. 'I told Dan to cover Lonigan and I would cover McIntyre,' Stephens quotes Ned as recounting. 'I then called on them to "throw up their hands", and McIntyre immediately did so. Lonigan made for the log, and tried to draw the revolver as he went along. He laid down behind the log, and rested his revolver on the top of the log and covered Dan. I then took my rifle off McIntyre and fired at Lonigan, grazing his temple. Lonigan then disappeared below the log, but gradually rose again, and as he did so I fired again and shot him through the head.'[17]

Here, at least, is testimony that Lonigan had a gun and was going to use it, which is something. But still in Bindon's cross-examination he declines to bring this part of Stephens's testimony to the fore, and instead seeks to discredit him by focusing on the fact that he is a former policeman, who has been working as a paid informer against the Kellys and has been seeking to rejoin the force.

More minor witnesses follow, until the last witness for the day: James Gloster, the hawker held up at Faithfull's Creek Station. It had been noted of Gloster after the Euroa raid that, all of a sudden, he 'had plenty of money to pay cash for whatever he buys'. And, though he was suspected to be in cahoots with the Kellys by the local detective, Standish had written curtly to them:

> *I do not believe that Gloster has anything to do with the outlaws.*[18]

And so he takes the stand and gives similar testimony to Stephens, that Ned had admitted to shooting Lonigan and Sergeant Kennedy. 'He said,' Gloster recounts, quoting the prisoner, '"Lonigan ran to the log, and was trying to screen himself behind it when I fired at him. He fell. I was sorry afterwards that he didn't surrender. I did not wish to kill Lonigan, only to take their arms." He said that "Lonigan was struck in the head, and killed." He said, "People called it murder", but he had never murdered anyone in his life. I said, "How about Sergeant Kennedy?" He said, "I killed him in fair fight".'[19]

After Bindon's again ineffective cross-examination – though Gloster does allow of Ned's confessions, 'my impression was that he took the whole of the shooting on himself to screen the others'[20] – it has just gone six o'clock in the evening, and Judge Barry asks Crown Prosecutor Smyth if the case could be wrapped up on this very night if they keep pressing on.

'I am prepared to sit until midnight to clear it,' Judge Barry adds, clearly keener to get this whole thing out of the way than he is to examine every necessary nuance before finding a man guilty of murder. (And he is, too. The day before the trial had begun, Judge Barry had made arrangements for lighting the court with gas after dark. For, as the Melbourne *Herald* has noted that morning, 'it is understood the Judge will sit till midnight to get the trial finished as soon as possible. His Honour is averse to having the jury locked up during the race time.'[21] Nothing is to be allowed to interrupt his attendance at the Spring Racing Carnival.)

Your Honour, the Crown Prosecutor regrets to advise there are still eight witnesses to go, and so the case is adjourned until nine o'clock the following morning.

The jury is ushered out and taken to the Supreme Court Hotel, where they will be sequestered, while the prisoner is taken back to his tiny, cold cell at Melbourne Gaol to contemplate how the day's proceedings have gone for him.

Badly. But nothing he can say will convince his counsel to allow him to take over the questioning himself.

29 OCTOBER 1880, THE SECOND DAY OF PROCEEDINGS, IT GETS WORSE

Somehow, on this second day of the court proceedings, there is menace in the air. It is not just the ongoing heat, nor the humidity, nor the dust storm that has so suddenly blown in from the north. It is somehow a sense, at least for the Kelly camp – represented today by Tom Lloyd, a heavily veiled Maggie Skillion and Kate Kelly in the front-row seats in the gallery – that despite all their efforts Ned is inexorably approaching his legal end and there is little that can be done to stop it.

Certainly not by Henry Bindon, the youngish man with the dark, well-kept beard and plump, white flesh, always notable among his more withered and wiry sagacious colleagues. The standout feature, however, is his rather terrified expression as he sits behind his table, staring around with enduring wonder, realising that somehow he is representing the colony's most famous criminal in the trial of the century and they are losing badly. Ned himself seems to feel it, for even though on this day he is sporting a 'flowered silk handkerchief around his throat',[22] this sartorial touch does not overcome the slightly haunted look on his face as he stands in the dock.

The most compelling of the early witnesses on this day is Robert Scott, manager of the National Bank at Euroa. Along with other evidence, Scott recounts the conversation he had with Ned on their way back to Faithfull's Creek Station after the hold-up, and the bushranger's response to the question of who had shot Constable Lonigan. 'Oh, I shot Lonigan,' he faithfully reports as Ned's reply.[23]

At least, under cross-examination by Bindon, Scott acknowledges that 'the prisoner treated me and Mrs Scott well',[24] and 'had not used a single rude word before the ladies',[25] but the damage has been done. Yet one more respected loyal subject of Her Majesty the Queen has testified under oath that Ned Kelly has admitted to killing Lonigan.

And now comes the Jerilderie bank clerk, Edward Living. After going through how the Kellys came to take him prisoner and then rob the Jerilderie bank, Living recounts how he had talked to Kelly about what had happened to the policemen shot at Stringybark Creek, and that Kelly had acknowledged shooting them. 'The prisoner,' Living says clearly, while being careful not to look at the man in question, 'said, "The gun I shot the police with in the Wombat Hills was an old one but a good one, it would shoot round a corner."'[26]

Most interestingly, Living comes to his account of the attempt to have Ned's Jerilderie statement published. 'I then went with [the] prisoner and Constable Richards to the newspaper proprietor. He was not at home. [We] found his wife. He offered her a statement which as he said he wanted to have printed. She would not take it, [and so] he gave it to me.'[27]

It is at this point that assistant prosecutor Chomley attempts to introduce that letter as evidence.

'I object, Your Honour!'[28]

Anticipating this very objection, Smyth reaches out to his right to the defence counsel's table and deftly moves to put his hand on Bindon's shoulder to prevent him rising – acknowledging the truth before the court as he does so. 'As I understand it,' he says, 'the documents are not in fact in the hand-writing of the prisoner.'

Oh.

'I think,' Judge Barry says with some delicacy, 'the objection could be sustained . . .'[29]

Does Crown Prosecutor Smyth look relieved, as if this is his plan all along? Exactly that. Indeed, hadn't he remarked when tendering this same letter at Ned's committal hearing at Beechworth that he thought it inadmissible? Yes, the deft touch of an experienced lawyer.

For the Jerilderie statement, far more eloquent and privy to the facts of the case than Bindon, is the only means the defence has for Ned to put his case – that he is not a cold-blooded killer but had acted in self-defence – and now it has been ruled out by the inexperienced Bindon's own very-much-hoped-for objection.

(Henry Gurner, the Crown Solicitor, is not surprised. His lack of professional respect for Bindon is complete, and he would later describe him as 'a young member of the bar . . . who was furnished with an exceptional belief in his own capacity and a superlative contempt for all other members of the profession . . . Which he used freely and constantly to express.')[30]

At least on a day of all but unrelentingly black evidence for Ned Kelly, the redoubtable Jerilderie bank manager John Tarleton is able to provide a small ray of sunshine for the defence when he quotes Ned as telling him, 'It is all very well to say that we shot the police in cold blood. We had to do it in self-defence. I was driven to become an outlaw.'[31]

'Anything else he said?' Smyth asks.

'Kelly said that the police had persecuted him since he was a lad of fourteen, and it was not surprising he had turned outlaw.'[32]

Senior Constable John Kelly then gives an account of what happened at Glenrowan and, most importantly, corroborates Constable McIntyre's account of what Kelly had said to him and McIntyre in the cell at Benalla on the morning after Ned Kelly's capture, as to whether or not he had shot Constable Fitzpatrick. Senior Constable Kelly recalls asking Ned if Fitzpatrick's statement was correct, receiving the response, 'Yes, I shot him.'[33]

Bindon's cross-examination is as ineffective as ever and, when he retakes his seat, Ned Kelly is very annoyed and motions that he wishes to speak to him. Some furious whispering results, with Ned insisting that he wishes to cross-examine the senior constable himself. At first, he won't hear of Bindon's and Gaunson's protests that this is impossible, as it is simply not within the structure of court proceedings for an accused man who has counsel to take over the questioning. It is the senior man, Gaunson, who takes the lead, and insists that order and propriety be maintained, and finally Ned Kelly settles, glowering.

The penultimate witness for the prosecution is Sergeant Arthur Steele – for once without his tweed hat, to honour the formality of the proceedings. He gives a quick account of Kelly's capture before getting to the key testimony that Smyth wants him for.

'Was anything said about the police train that had been sent from Melbourne to Glenrowan?'

'I asked the prisoner what he intended to do if the police train was wrecked. He said he would shoot every bloody one that escaped.'[34]

One last question, sergeant. 'Did you mention Constable Fitzpatrick?'

'I did, sir, and Kelly said, "Oh, I shot him right enough."'[35]

Yes, Henry Bindon cross-examines Steele and is even able to make some headway in exposing his highly reckless – one might almost say murderous – behaviour during the siege of Glenrowan, but it is all rather beside the point. He is not on trial. Ned Kelly is. And Steele's testimony has further damaged him.

And now, finally, in the late morning, comes Dr Samuel Reynolds, who performed the post-mortem on the body of Thomas Lonigan. He describes the constable's wounds and confirms that he had been killed by the single shot to the right eye. 'That,' the good doctor says carefully, 'was the cause of death in a few seconds.'[36]

Alas, the most critical part of Dr Reynolds' post-mortem is not followed up. That is that he had extracted a bullet from Lonigan's right thigh – 'an ordinary revolver bullet'.[37] Not even McIntyre claimed that Ned shot a revolver at Lonigan, and the only explanation is that it came from the constable's own gun as he frantically withdrew it to fire at the bushranger, mistakenly shooting himself in the thigh instead. It is further evidence that could be used to prove Ned's version of what happened, which concurs with McIntyre's first account, but Bindon has neither the wit nor the wisdom, neither the experience nor the expertise, to pursue it.

With the conclusion of the testimony of this, his sixteenth witness, Smyth declares the case for the prosecution is concluded, at which point all look expectantly at Henry Bindon, who, momentarily, does nothing at all, apart from look rather stricken – which is what he has already been doing a great deal of over the last two days.

'Mr Bindon?' Judge Barry prompts.

As if awoken from a deep reverie, the prisoner's defence counsel responds that he wishes to be granted an adjournment of an hour, so as to determine whether he will call witnesses for the defence or not. As the request coincides with lunchtime, it is readily granted.

Of course, what Bindon would really like to do is to put Ned Kelly on the stand to explain his actions, to exert the power of his undoubted charisma on the jury, but in the colony of Victoria at this time, it is against the law for an accused person to give sworn evidence on his or her own behalf.

—

After lunch, when all are settled once more, again all eyes look to Bindon. What will he do?

'Your Honour,' the young barrister begins carefully, 'I wish to know whether His Honour would reserve a special case on the points I have objected to for the consideration of the Full Court.'[38]

'What points do you allude to?' His Honour asks,[39] mystified as to why on earth this upstart would want his own rulings to be reviewed by a panel of three Supreme Court Judges.

'All the transactions that took place after the death of Lonigan, which were detailed in evidence,' the very inexperienced barrister says very carefully.'[40]

For it is Bindon's contention, once more, that they should not have been admitted, as they were irrelevant to Ned's charge of having murdered Lonigan.

At this moment, Judge Barry reaches out and effectively slaps this junior counsel for the good of the law. For, as if explaining to a persistently recalcitrant child on his first day at school, His Honour points out 'that if an act were doubtful or ambiguous, or capable of two meanings, the conduct of the person before, at the time, or after the time of doing the act was admissible to show the motive and reason for his conduct. This evidence was admissible to show whether the shooting of Constable Lonigan were accidental or justifiable.'[41]

And that is that.

Defeated by the judge, deflated by his own inability to make his case, Bindon waves a legal white flag and begs to report, 'The defence will not call any evidence, *Your Honour*.'[42]

So be it. Judge Barry instantly softens, as this is precisely the result he has wanted. 'So be it,' he says. 'So be it.'[43]

It is time for the closing addresses, and Crown Prosecutor Smyth is quick to rise and begin, a legal master, going in for a practised kill that he knows he simply can't miss. 'Let me begin,' he says, 'by putting this question to you. Just what were the police doing in the Wombat Ranges when they were killed? The answer is that they were searching for an armed gang and, gentlemen, they had the full authority of the law to do so . . . That being so, they were entitled to the full protection of the law.'[44]

As to what happened there, well, there can be no doubt. 'I shall simply remind you from my notes of the evidence that [Constable McIntyre] gave. Constable McIntyre swore this, "I saw the prisoner move his rifle, bringing it in a line with Lonigan. Then he fired. I glanced round and saw the shot had taken effect on Lonigan. He fell to the ground. After a few seconds I heard him call out, 'Oh Christ, I'm shot.'" I again remind you, gentlemen, that evidence was not challenged . . .'[45]

Moving on now, the Crown Prosecutor gathers steam. 'A motive has been referred to. I will say this to you. When you find one man shooting down another in cold blood, do you really need to stop and enquire into his *motives*?'

Smyth's fist now pounds down into the table, by way of emphasis. 'I will tell you what the prisoner's motive was. It was one of malignant hatred against the police! He had been leading, as you know, a wild, lawless life.'[46]

Case closed! Well, there is more, but the essence of Crown Prosecutor Smyth's whole case is herein: the devastating account of Constable McIntyre, backed by the demonstrable proof that Ned Kelly is, and always has been, a bad man.

Can Ned Kelly's defence counsel make any headway against such a compelling case?

'Yes, Mr Bindon?' Judge Barry prompts the young barrister, though again in the manner of a man who does not actually want to waste any time at all.

Bindon stands and, for a moment, stares. This is the first time in his life he has addressed a jury, and he is frankly not sure where to start, but eventually he gets to it. 'The evidence is in one sense quite elaborate, but the bulk of it is quite extraneous matter.'[47] He goes on, 'Any crimes committed by the prisoner at Euroa, Jerilderie and Glenrowan are altogether irrelevant to what happened at Stringybark Creek. As to Stringybark Creek, you have but one witness. That one witness, McIntyre, has given a very well prepared account, constructed after the event. But at the time, McIntyre would have been in such a state of fear, that he could never have made the minute observations he claims to have made.'[48]

And think of the context in which the killings took place. 'The prisoner and his three mates,' he says, 'were following a lawful pursuit in the bush, when a party of men in disguise, fully armed – policemen in plain clothes, as they afterwards turned out to be – came upon them, and an unfortunate fracas occurred, in which Constable Lonigan lost his life.'[49]

Bindon goes on to encourage doubt in McIntyre's account and his credibility as a witness, while trying to bring out the softer side of Ned's character. 'The prisoner is not the bloodthirsty assassin the Crown Prosecutor has endeavoured to make out,' my something less than learned friend says, resolutely refusing to look at the jury while clutching the sheaf of papers on which he has taken copious notes. 'Both before and after the shooting of the police he showed that he had the greatest possible respect for human life, for he had many previous opportunities of assassinating policemen, if that was his desire, and at Euroa and Jerilderie he never harmed one of the persons who fell into his power.'[50]

Winding up to the crux of his argument, Bindon does not abuse the opposition's case; instead, he argues that it is dubiously perfect! 'McIntyre's statement showed such signs of deliberation and careful preparation that it ought to be received with suspicion.'[51]

'You, the jury, have an important and serious duty to discharge, and I urge you not to take away the life of a man on the prejudiced evidence of a single man.'[52]

'McIntyre said he saw the prisoner fire at Lonigan, but there is evidence of shots fired by others and to tell who fired the fatal shot is impossible. Only two men survived their fate, the prisoner and McIntyre. McIntyre's evidence is prejudiced and the prisoner's mouth is closed.'[53]

'Can you say that Edward Kelly was the man who alone murdered Lonigan? If you have the slightest doubts, I trust you will not find the prisoner guilty.'[54]

Bindon's final, earnest appeal is admittedly met with scattered applause from behind him, but a severe contrast is provided by the looks of indignation from the bench and scattered court officials.

Now, just gone five o'clock on this unseasonably warm, sleepy afternoon, it is, of course, nearly time for the jury to adjourn to discharge their duty. But, before they do so, Judge Barry has a few extra points he would like them to ponder, just in case any of them might be even *contemplating* finding the prisoner innocent.

He starts by outlining to the jury exactly what murder is, under the law. Extraordinarily, however, the hypothetical example he offers is almost identical to the Stringybark affair, as told by McIntyre.

He then moves on to the evidence of the case. 'Here, gentlemen, four constables went out to perform a duty. It was said they were in plain clothes. But with that they had nothing to do . . . These men were charged with a responsible and, as it turned out, a dangerous duty. And they were aware of that before they started. They went in pursuit of two persons who had been gazetted as persons against whom warrants were issued . . . And when in pursuit of those two persons therefore they had a double protection: that of the ordinary citizen and that of being ministers of the law charged with the administration of the peace of the country.'[55]

He brings home his point, as if he were Smyth's co-counsel for the prosecution. 'Whether they were in uniform or not, there was no privilege on the part of any persons to molest them as constables.'[56]

He continues to coach the jury for ten more minutes, telling them to 'be careful in considering the evidence of all the witnesses' and, 'it is for you the jury to say whether these witnesses had concocted the story or not'.[57]

The jury moves out of the courtroom, while everyone else, including Ned, remains sitting and waiting.

Sitting and waiting.

Just thirty minutes later, the jury shuffle back in, all of them suddenly interested in the pointy ends of their shoes – as practised barristers know, never a good sign for those hoping for an innocent verdict.

Sir Redmond Barry. (Courtesy State Library of Victoria)

Once they are settled, Justice Barry turns to the foreman, a dairyman by the name of Samuel Lazarus, who had been a digger around Ballarat at the time of the Eureka Stockade and knew better than most the barbarity authorities were capable of when they regarded people as criminals. Reading out the verdict, the craggy Lazarus, in his strong Liverpool accent, announces, 'Guilty.'[58]

Ned Kelly, who is standing in the dock at this point, gripping the rail, is seen to rock on his feet a little, almost as if suddenly buffeted by a gust of strong wind, perhaps created by the collective gasp from the rest of the courtroom.

Does the prisoner, the Clerk of the Court asks, have anything he'd like to say?

As a matter of fact, he does.

Rising, Ned addresses the judge, the jury and the assembly. 'Well, it is rather too late for me to speak now. I thought of speaking this morning and all day, but there was little use, and there is little use blaming anyone now. Nobody knew about my case except myself, and I wish I had insisted on being allowed to examine the witnesses myself. If I had examined them, I am confident I would have thrown a different light on the case. It is not that I fear death; I fear it as little as to drink a cup of tea. On the evidence that has been given, no jury-man could have given any other verdict. That is my opinion. But as I say, if I had examined the witnesses I would have shown matters in a different light, because no man understands the case as I do myself. I do not blame anybody – neither Mr Bindon nor Mr Gaunson; but Mr Bindon knew nothing about my case. I lay blame on myself that I did not get up yesterday and examine the witnesses, but I thought that if I did so it would look like bravado and flashness.'[59]

Which is as may be. But no words from Ned can alter the denouement.

For, after the traditional black square of cloth is placed upon his judicial wig, Judge Redmond Barry swivels to address the now convicted prisoner directly, even as the court crier calls out in his stentorian tones, demanding that the strictest silence now be observed, that this grave legal ritual may be observed with proper solemnity.

'Edward Kelly,' Judge Barry says portentously, a black storm about to break, 'the verdict pronounced by the jury is one which you must have fully expected.'

'Yes, under the circumstances,' Ned allows, equably.

'No circumstances that I can conceive could have altered the result of your trial.'

'Perhaps not from what you can now conceive, but if you had heard me examine the witnesses it would have been different.'

'I will give you credit for all the skill you appear to desire to assume.'

'No, I don't wish to assume anything. There is no flashness or bravado about me. It is not that I want to save my life, because I know I would have been capable of clearing myself of the charge, and I could have saved my life in spite of all against me.'

But His Honour will not hear of it. 'The facts are so numerous, and so convincing,' Judge Barry insists, 'not only as regards the original offence with which you are charged, but with respect to a long series of transactions covering a period of 18 months, that no rational person would hesitate to arrive at any other conclusion but that the verdict of the jury is irresistible, and that it is right. I have no desire whatever to inflict upon you any personal remarks. It is not becoming that I should endeavour to aggravate the sufferings with which your mind must be sincerely agitated.'

'No, I don't think that. My mind is as easy as the mind of any man in this world, as I am prepared to show before God and man.'

'It is blasphemous for you to say that,' His Honour retorts. 'You appear to revel in the idea of having put men to death.'

'More men than me have put men to death,' Ned says reasonably, 'but I am the last man in the world that would take a man's life. Two years ago, even if my own life was at stake, and I am confident if I thought a man would shoot me, I would give him a chance of keeping his life, and would part rather with my own. But if I knew that through him innocent persons' lives were at stake I certainly would have to shoot him if he forced me to do so, but I would want to know that he was really going to take innocent life.'

Yes, yes, yes. But, after dismissing Ned's further justifications and prevarications as so much nonsense, Judge Barry comes to his conclusion.

'The law will be carried out by its officers. The gentlemen of the jury have done their duty. My duty will be to forward to the proper quarter the notes of your trial and to lay before the Executive all the circumstances connected with your trial that may be required. I can hold out to you no hope, and I do not see that I can entertain the slightest reason for saying that you can expect anything. I desire to spare you any more pain, and I absolve myself from saying anything willingly in any of my utterances that may have unnecessarily increased the agitation of your mind. I have now to pronounce your sentence.'[60]

Whatever rustling, stirring, creaks there have been in the courtroom throughout the exchange between judge and prisoner now cease, as all there practically cease to breathe, let alone move, as they strain to catch every word.

'Prisoner at the bar, the sentence of the court is that you will be taken . . . to the place from whence you came,' Judge Barry begins gravely, now straining for a tone of legal detachment, 'and that you be taken thence at such time and to such place as his Excellency the Governor will direct, and that you then and there be hanged by the neck until you are dead . . .'[61]

There is a collective expiration of breath from the courtroom with the enunciation of those words, before Judge Redmond Barry follows up with the traditional pious plea, 'May the Lord have mercy on your soul.'

'I will go a little further than that,' Kelly calmly replies, 'and say I will see you there where I go.'[62]

'Remove the prisoner!' Judge Barry barks, the detachment now over.

And the warders would have, too, bar the fact that Ned raises his hand to forestall them a moment, and not one of them is inclined to insist.

Turning to Kate Lloyd in the gallery, Ned blows a kiss and says, 'Goodbye, you'll see me there . . .'[63]

With little further ado, Ned Kelly is led away, back to his cell in the gaol.

—

Outside the courthouse, a short time later, in La Trobe Street, a shattered Henry Bindon walks along, with Ned Kelly's words ringing in his ears, the words he had said to Judge Barry: *'Mr Bindon knew nothing about my case . . . Mr Bindon knew nothing about my case . . . Mr Bindon knew nothing about my case . . .'*[64]

Who can say that he was wrong? Not Bindon himself. Staggering to a stone bench in a quiet spot in the gardens in front of the Public Library – established in 1854 by Redmond Barry, who conceived of it as 'the people's university' – Bindon slumps down and, at least a little protected by the dusk, begins to weep.

—

At Melbourne Gaol, Ned's status has changed.

With the last possibility of innocence now torn from him, so too must he shed the regular clothing he has been wearing to this point and instead don the regulation plain, dark prison uniform. The prison blacksmith also rivets irons upon his legs, after first placing leather pads around his ankles to prevent chafing. (An extraordinary bit of humanity from a system that is planning an altogether different kind of chafing on another part of his body shortly.)

Ned is then taken to a particularly dingy cell in the old wing, which is nothing if not secure, with walls two feet thick, an inner door of iron bars and an outer one of solid iron. The outer door, however, is kept open and a lamp always kept lit inside. Around the clock, there will be one warder sitting there with the sole job of ensuring that Ned Kelly does nothing to rob the noose of its forthcoming pleasure.

In the meantime, it remains at Chief Secretary Graham Berry's insistence to Governor Castieau that Ned continues to be isolated from visitors, at least without Berry's written approval, and the same condition applies to letters that he wishes to send or receive. Nevertheless, the following morning, David Gaunson's brother, William, has an interview with Graham Berry and is able to persuade him to rescind the order.

Soon afterwards, Ned receives his first visitors. The party consists of two loyal friends, McAuliffe and Ryan, as well as his dear cousin Tom Lloyd, together with Miss McAuliffe, Miss Kate Lloyd and Maggie Skillion. The meeting is of 'a very touching nature'. Ned remains strangely stoic and calm, and expresses the hope that 'he would meet his doom in a proper manner; also that the result of his execution might lead to an investigation into the whole conduct and management of the police'.[65] The friends and family talk, and Ned becomes sad when conversation turns to his mother, as he says, 'I hope there is more justice shown in another world than has been shown to our family here.'[66]

They leave, with Maggie saying that Kate and Grace would be down to see him just as soon as she can get back up home to relieve them from caring for the children.

—

The Argus, for one, offers the now convicted criminal no sympathy, exulting on 30 October, 'It is now evident that no gang, however well armed, however desperate, and however fortunate, can escape the steady pursuit of the officers of justice, and with the execution of Edward Kelly we may hope will close the history of organised bushranging in Australia.'[67]

Besides which, the whole idea of bushranging does not sit well with a Melbourne that is then and there celebrating its arrival as one of the great cosmopolitan cities of the world. Since the beginning of October, the city has been hosting an International Exhibition, just as other great cities have done before it, including Sydney, London, Paris, New York and Philadelphia. All of those cities, and many, many more, have sent envoys and extensive exhibits to Melbourne for the occasion, just as many thousands of other visitors have arrived from all over the world, and now – after the years of preparation – never has the colony of Victoria been so proud.

Indeed, the grand Royal Exhibition Building, designed by architect Joseph Reed and constructed over the last eighteen months, is not just a building; it is a monument to Melbourne. With its tall dome, the imposing structure is the highest and most gracious building in the city, and is now packed, day in, day out. To add to the excitement, the Melbourne Spring Racing Carnival is reaching its climax – with the Melbourne Cup due on the coming Tuesday – and every evening Melbourne's fashionable set steps out, going to extravagant parties and revelling into the wee hours in their distinguished way.

Despite this colourful call to distraction, and notwithstanding the tremendous criticism he has received, David Gaunson is not ready to give up the fight. The people will demand clemency! And, what's more, they will abolish the death penalty! At Gaunson's initiative, a 'Reprieve Committee' is quickly formed, using the Robert Burns Hotel as their headquarters, and composed of such Kelly supporters as Gaunson himself, his brother William, Ned's sister Maggie Skillion, cousin

Kate Lloyd and noted phrenologist Archibald Hamilton, who is also Chairman of the Society for the Abolition of Capital Punishment.

Alas, the early signs for the committee are not good. Although Chief Secretary Berry grants William Gaunson, David's trusty brother and almost partner, an audience, and hears him out in his call for a reprieve, he does not go out of his way to give hope. Mr Berry says it is a matter for the Executive Council, who, upon meeting 'in a week's time from now', will set a date for the execution, and he, personally, cannot give an answer.

Clearly, what is needed is for public pressure to be whipped up and brought to bear, and it is with that in mind that the Gaunson brothers start to draft up a Petition for Reprieve, as well as to organise a public demonstration and a march to Government House for this Friday, 5 November.

In short order, the petition forms are printed and soon distributed at race meetings, watering holes and other congregations around town:

> PETITION for REPRIEVE
> To His Excellency the Governor-in-Council, -
> Your humble PETITIONERS (having carefully considered the circumstances of the case) respectfully pray that the Life of the CONDEMNED man, EDWARD KELLY, may be spared.[68]

3 NOVEMBER 1880, NED PENS ANOTHER LETTER

Ned Kelly wants to live. Though gratified by the pledges of his lawyers, family and friends to save him, he is not content to just leave it all up to them and has decided to write to the Governor of Victoria – the only man who can grant a reprieve at this late hour, by at least allowing more time for the legal process to examine the new evidence. Of course, because Ned's hands are badly wounded he can't write, but at least a friendly warder, William Buck, does agree to take down his words, and so, just as Joe Byrne had done for him two years earlier for the letter written at Jerilderie, Ned speaks slowly while every word is taken down.

Ned begins by putting forth the view that the trial would have had a different result if only he could have cross-examined the witnesses. As to the police he was accused of killing, the Governor should know, 'they sneaked out of the Town before day light disguised as diggers on a prospecting tour & camped at Stringybark that night. Some of the Party said they did not intend to bring one in alive which I can prove. Fitzpatrick I believe will swear on oath that they came to shoot me not to arrest me . . .'[69]

Ah, but you must be quick, Ned. For after the indulgent celebrations of the Melbourne Cup at Flemington the day before (the two-to-one favourite, Grand Flaneur, had come home first by a full length), the government has decided, and Ned has been told, that the Executive Council will meet this night to decide his fate, and so Ned composes the letter throughout the day, having it sent off to the Governor at sundown, in the hope it will reach him in time.

It does not.

For, early in the evening, the Executive Council meets at the Treasury Building and formally decides that Ned will be hanged . . . on the morning of Thursday 11 November.

Told later that night of the date of his forthcoming death by Governor Castieau, Ned comments rather wistfully, 'It is very short . . .'[70]

Chapter Eighteen

THE END IS HIGH

> The tendency which exists to regard a man with his hands imbrued in innocent blood as a modern ROBIN HOOD is much too prevalent in Victoria, and it requires to be sternly checked, and not encouraged.
>
> *The Argus*

5 NOVEMBER 1880, A GATHERING ON GUY FAWKES NIGHT

And from everywhere they come! Thousands of them. All assemble to support the notion that the death sentence of Ned Kelly should be commuted. In fact, there are so many that, while 4000 of them fit into the Hippodrome on Exhibition Street – the famous sporting venue, mostly used for equestrian shows and circuses – there are another 2000[1] outside, straining to hear every word they can. 'The larrikin class was strongly represented,' *The Argus* reported, 'and the majority of the women came from the neighbourhood of Little Bourke Street. There was, however, a large muster of ordinary working men, and many others who attended apparently out of curiosity.'[2]

Before the proceedings proper can begin, an obviously drunken woman – who for some reason has a seat on the central podium – stands and delivers, word for word, statements made by Ned Kelly to Judge Barry at the trial, stopping only to regularly wail at the pathos of it all, but soon enough the chair, the noted phrenologist Archibald Hamilton, calls the gathering to order. 'I am glad to act as chairman, not merely on behalf of Edward Kelly, but as an advocate for the abolition of capital punishment,' he declares, to warm applause. 'I call upon you to listen as if your own lives depended on the issue.'[3]

Just after eight o'clock, the meeting is underway.

From the stage, David Gaunson addresses the throng, beginning by saying that he wishes to hear no applause or dissent as he speaks to the motion, 'That this meeting, having considered all the circumstances of Edward Kelly's case, believes it is one fit for the exercise of the Royal prerogative of mercy, and therefore earnestly presses His Excellency the Governor in Council to favourably regard the prayer of this meeting, namely, that the life of the prisoner may be spared.'[4]

Immediately, despite his admonition, there is applause, together with a sole dissenting voice. 'What about the widows and orphans he has made?'[5]

Gaunson continues regardless, warming to the theme that Kelly had been the victim of many grave injustices, as had his mother, most particularly the unfounded accusation that the family had tried to murder Constable Fitzpatrick. Ellen Kelly had been gaoled for three years and a warrant issued for Ned's arrest, all on the word of a man shortly thereafter thrown out of the police force for perjury. He also insists, as he had done during the committal hearing at Beechworth, that Ned Kelly is anything but a cold-blooded killer and that he had only shot Constable Lonigan in self-defence.

Yes, friends!

Ned Kelly knew before the police arrived that they intended to 'shoot him and his brother down like dogs',[6] and it is for this reason, and this reason alone, that those constables were shot when they ventured to the spot in the ranges where the Kellys had erected a residence, to earn their lawful living panning gold, a spot far removed from anyone.

And why else would those constables have come to that spot, so heavily armed, carrying so much ammunition, if not for the purpose of shooting the Kelly Gang?

And so the gathering goes. There are other speakers, but it is Gaunson who makes the plea and sets the tone. His remarks are warmly received by the audience, and his discourse is regularly interrupted with cheering and cries of 'Hear, hear!' As to the people outside, there are admittedly quite a few who are severely out of temper at their exclusion and inability to hear, but, 'Superintendent Winch, with several troopers and foot police, succeeded in maintaining order.'[7]

Only just, however. Some of those outside regularly manage to light the fuses on fireworks aimed over the wall of the Hippodrome, meaning that at regular intervals, even as Gaunson speaks, 'large squibs came shooting over the battlements, and exploded amongst the gentlemen on the platform, with reports as loud as pistol shots'.

But, through it all, Gaunson continues, finishing with, 'To those who say justice should be meted out, I would reply, "Though justice be thy plea, consider this, that in the course of justice none of us shall see salvation. We do pray for mercy, and that same prayer doth teach us all to render the deeds of mercy."'[8]

He is met with thunderous applause, even as the crowd unanimously endorses the motion he has proposed, begging the Governor to spare poor Ned's life. It is decided to present the motion to His Excellency at half past ten the following morning.

Buzzing, with hope in their hearts that the life of Ned Kelly might be saved after all, they disperse and all head home to bed.

—

As to Ned in his prison cell for the condemned, this day he has dictated his second letter to the Governor, this one talking mostly of Glenrowan, and concluding with the solemn words of a man facing death:

> I should have made a statement of my whole career but my time is so short on earth that I have to make the best of it to prepare myself for the other world.[9]

And now, on his bunk, on this night as many nights, Ned sings himself to sleep, humming and mumbling the words to that well-loved hymn

'In the Sweet By and By':[10]

In the sweet by and by,
We shall meet on that beautiful shore;
In the sweet by and by,
We shall meet on that beautiful shore.

To our bountiful Father above,
We will offer our tribute of praise
For the glorious gift of His love
And the blessings that hallow our days.

6 NOVEMBER 1880, THE PRESS WEIGHS IN

The Argus, for one, is not impressed with the growing attempts to save the life of the murderer, pronouncing in its columns, 'For the credit of Melbourne, we regret to say that many thousands were present to express sympathy with one of the greatest ruffians ever consigned to the gallows. Of course, the action taken will have no effect upon the fate of the unhappy man, but it is truly lamentable that a crowd like that assembled last night could be got together for such a purpose.'[11]

As to the whole notion of the gang acting in self-defence, *The Argus* will not hear of it. Apart from everything else, 'Perhaps it will be contended that they acted in self defence when in cold blood they gave the *coup de grace* to poor KENNEDY as he lay wounded on the ground? But, of course, the "self defence" theory cannot be entertained for one moment, and had Mr GAUNSON had any regard for his public position, he would have told his audience so. It would be a very nice position of affairs if policemen could be justifiably killed on refusing to "bail up" at the bidding of the criminals of whom they were in search . . .'[12]

Gaunson is particularly pilloried by all and sundry for his role, with none more thunderous than the mighty *Age*: 'Mr David Gaunson, a chief expounder of law in Parliament, and a prominent leader at the justice seats in our courts, played the scandalous part that is reported of him on Friday. In violation of all public decency he organised a demonstration that he knew would attract the whole social scum of a large city like Melbourne in favour of arresting execution of justice upon the sole survivor of a cowardly gang of murderers.'[13] *The Age* reminds its readers that it is not just the city papers that are averse to the efforts of the reprieve movement, and reprints the strong opinions of regional newspaper the *MA Mail* to prove its point: 'The proper place for the Brothers Gaunson is on the drop by the side of the condemned man.'[14] *The Age* continues a few days later, 'It is not too much to say that the course pursued by the Gaunson brothers in reference to the case of the convict Kelly, will be execrated by right-thinking persons in every part of the globe.'[15] (Hold on to your hats, Bolivia.)

Nevertheless, the Governor of the colony, the Marquess of Normanby – a man of great diplomatic skill – does indeed receive the Gaunson brothers, in the company of anti-capital-punishment-campaigner Archibald Hamilton, a young politician by the name of J. P. T. Caulfield, and Kate Kelly, on this Saturday morning, 6 November, in the yellow drawing room that through heavy red curtains offers such splendid views of the Royal Botanic Gardens. Standing just off-centre from the massive two chandeliers overhead, His Excellency promises to report to the Executive Council, on the coming Monday, the motion for clemency that the large crowd has endorsed.

The good lord does feel bound to tell them, nevertheless, that 'The case has . . . already received careful consideration, and the decision arrived at was not come to without due care. I would be deceiving you and acting cruelly towards the condemned man if I held out any hope of mitigation.'[16]

But surely, Gaunson points out, 'it would be very undesirable to have an execution in our midst at this peculiar time, when all the nations of the earth are our visitors?'.

His Excellency does not appear to be much troubled by the prospect, whereupon David's brother, William Gaunson, begs to inform him that 'numerous and largely signed petitions for a reprieve are coming in, and the numbers which will come in will be something enormous if time is given'.[17]

Alas, His Excellency replies, 'this is not a case in which petitions can have any effect. The law has to be carried out, and if it is not, those who have the responsibility will have to answer to the country.'[18]

Desperate to get some sympathy out of the man, Hamilton then brings the very fetching Kate Kelly forward by the hand, explains that she is a sister of the condemned man and wonders if 'it might have some effect if she gets down on her knees before His Excellency and begs for mercy . . .'

The Governor has had enough. 'No, no,' he protests. 'I have a painful duty to perform, and I do not see that anything can be got by prolonging this interview.'[19]

They are shown the door, with David Gaunson particularly downcast. With the Governor's words ringing in his ears, a warning not to inflate the condemned man's hopes, as well as the savaging he has received from the colony's press, he decides to recede from the fight, and let his brother William take over the clemency campaign . . .

At least, however, the reprieve movement and its petition campaign goes on, with the likes of Jim Kelly and Wild Wright being particularly notable about Melbourne, collecting signatures. As *The Age* reports, 'Kate Kelly took up a position on the footpath outside St Francis's Church and requested signatures to a petition . . . A large number of weak-minded people, principally females, signed, but the good sense of the majority of those passing prevented them acceding to the reiterated requests. The members of St Patrick's Cathedral were much scandalised last evening by the rude intrusion of persons who came within the precincts of the building soliciting signatures for a petition praying for a commutation of the sentence of death passed on Edward Kelly, the bushranger. It is understood that the persons who were guilty of this indecorous importunity were instigated by Mr William Gaunson.'[20]

8 NOVEMBER 1880, THE MOB MOVES

The difference between a crowd and a mob? A crowd is broadly genteel, and is frequently composed of mere spectators at an event. Not a mob, though. They are more likely to be ruffians and tend to be active, even riotous, and oft with a heavy hint of menace – rather in the manner of the Greta mob.

This is a mob. No fewer than 200 strong and coming 'from the back slums of the city',[21] it descends on Melbourne's Town Hall this morning to demand – yes, *demand* – a reprieve for Edward Kelly, who, of course, is due to be hanged this Thursday.

The insolence! The outrage!

Led by the disgraceful William Gaunson, the wretches even have the impudence to enter the building, but mercifully the police just as quickly throw them out again. What now? Well, when Mrs Skillion, Kate Kelly, James Kelly and Wild Wright arrive, the whole lot, *The Argus* reports, 'set out for Government House with the unwashed-looking mob at their heels'.[22] Maggie has to turn back thanks to knee troubles, but the rest push on.

With the police hovering closely, the mob arrives at Government House. There William Gaunson is received by Captain Le Patourel, His Excellency's private secretary, who tells him that, although the Governor will not be receiving deputations, any petitions presented to him at the Treasury before two o'clock will be tabled at the meeting of the Executive Council at that hour.

At least a little satisfied with the progress, the mob then heads back to the Robert Burns Hotel in Lonsdale Street, where the tightest Kelly family and friends are staying. There, James Kelly and Wild Wright, who are visibly and loudly revered by the mob, effectively hold court, while the 'loafing-looking retinue . . . besiege the hotel, crushing through the passages and into the rooms in order to feast still further their morbid curiosity'.[24]

That afternoon, William Gaunson leads Mrs Skillion and Kate Kelly, backed by a mob now a thousand strong, to the Treasury Building to present their petition to the Executive Council – claiming it bears a staggering 32,434 signatures – and then wait to hear its decision.

The Argus, however, is not remotely impressed with the documents presented, and says so strongly: 'An examination of the petitions showed that they were signed principally in pencil, and by illiterate people, whilst whole pages were evidently written by one person.'[25]

And the Executive is not impressed either, as it is not long before Captain Le Patourel emerges to tell the prisoner's relatives, in the private room where they have been ushered, that 'The Executive determines to adhere to their decision – that the convict shall be executed on Thursday morning.'

Crushed, but not surprised, Maggie Skillion, Kate and James Kelly lead the mob back to the Robert Burns Hotel where, as the afternoon and then evening wear on, an ever bigger mob gathers, so big in fact that the members cannot all be accommodated inside at the bar and must spill onto Lonsdale Street.

Yes, things are now looking grimmer than ever for our Ned, but we have not given up hope.

When, at one point, James Kelly addresses the crowd from the door and proclaims, 'It is not all over yet,'[26] he is cheered to the echo. They still have more than two whole days until the hanging, and plans are already afoot for another mass meeting to be held the following evening on the Supreme Court Reserve, where, after a resolution is carried in favour of a reprieve, it can be presented to the Chief Secretary. In the meantime, Gaunson is sending out petitions all over the colony for signatures, which can also be presented. There is still hope!

EVENING, 9 NOVEMBER 1880, A CROWD GATHERS

And so they come, more than 1500 strong, to the approaches of the Supreme Court Reserve. For the call has gone out, and they have answered that call. They are the people who not only support commuting the sentence on Ned Kelly from death to life imprisonment but also still retain hope that something can be done.

But what's this? Between them and the grassy verge that lies by the

Supreme Court, there are a dozen armed police telling them to keep back and disperse, 'citing the authority of the law relating to the gaol, which forbids the assemblage of any large crowd of persons within its precincts'.[27]

Really? A dozen men think the people can be stopped?

Several cries go up from the back: 'Rush the ground!'[28]

Which is fine for those at the back. The problem is that those at the front, facing the armed police, are less inclined, and when no fewer than fifty police reinforcements arrive shortly afterwards, a potentially catastrophic clash is averted.

The thwarted crowd is just looking for new direction when the sound of horses approaching is heard, and another cry goes up. For it is none other than the irrepressible William Gaunson on the back of a cart, together with Wild Wright and Ned Kelly's siblings, Maggie, Kate and Jim, and they are all holding high the blazing torches that cast the familiar, flickering light that has marked the darkened faces of committed martyrs and revolutionaries alike through the ages.

After an unsatisfactory discourse with the police, who repeatedly refuse to answer him when he asks whether they are acting under orders in keeping them off the Supreme Court Reserve, William Gaunson now takes the lead, guiding the mob in a torch-led procession to a vacant block on the corner of Madeline[29] and Queensberry Streets in Carlton, where, in front of 2000 people, standing on the back of his cart, he reprises his brother David's theme of the previous Friday night at the Hippodrome, while also lambasting the press for its outrageous attacks on all those who have the simple human decency to seek a reprieve for Edward Kelly.

He proposes a motion that the meeting request the Chief Secretary to call the Executive Council together to again consider the Edward Kelly case, which is subsequently passed resoundingly – no fewer than a third of the people hold up two hands, so eager are they.

Now, Gaunson informs them, as Chief Secretary Berry has agreed to receive a deputation from this meeting at the Treasury on this night, he proposes they proceed to that august building at once.

Hooray! Yes, we will do that, and they soon fall in, to follow the cart with all its torch-bearers.

No fewer than 1500 people are soon gathered outside the Treasury, while the deputation consisting 'of three or four rough-looking men and three young women'[30] go inside to meet Berry in the Executive Council chamber.

Respectfully, but urgently, Gaunson tells Chief Secretary Berry what has happened at the meeting, and just how many signatures they have on their petition. 'We have 40,000 . . .' he assures the Chief Secretary. 'If time had been allowed, 500,000 signatures could have been obtained to save the man's life.' Furthermore, Mr Berry, it has leaked out that several members of the Executive Council had not been present when the case for Ned Kelly had been presented to them.

But Graham Berry will have none of it. 'I think that is a mistake. I believe the whole of the Ministers were present on the first occasion, and on the second not more than one, I think, was absent. That one was absent unavoidably, and it was well known that his opinion was in accord with the opinions of the other members.'

But surely Mr Berry will be interested that Patrick Quinn has come forward with new information about the intent of the police? That he has 'prepared an affidavit which he is willing to sign at once before the Chief Secretary as a justice of the peace . . .'?[31]

Gaunson begins to read out Quinn's unsigned affidavit to the Chief Secretary. Most crucially, it states that Senior Constable Strahan had said – two or three days before Strahan was shot – that, 'I'll shoot [Ned Kelly] down like a dog. I'll carry two revolvers, and one I'll place by his side, and swear he had it on him when I shot him.'[32]

This, of course, gives credence to Ned Kelly's key claim at the Stringybark trial that the killings were not cold-blooded murder, for he had only acted in self-defence and, if he had not killed the police, they would have killed him.

Suddenly, a man stands up to speak and, though he initially refuses to disclose his identity, finally admits that he is Patrick Quinn himself. 'I know all about the case from beginning to end,' he tells the Chief

Secretary. 'The case arose from the offer of a reward. The opinions of the people in the neighbourhood I come from is that a Royal Commission ought to be appointed.'

Patrick Quinn is assured that something will come of it and professes that he, for one, is more than willing to 'speak his mind openly and fearlessly on this matter'.

Graham Berry cannot budge on the issue of reprieve, and has the courage to come out and address the crowd. He tells them that 'every consideration has been given to the case, and no steps whatever have been taken by the Government to place any obstacles in the way of those who are acting to get a reprieve'. He adds that no new facts had been submitted, unless this latest statement by Quinn may be considered new. However, he argues, the time for the Quinn affidavit to have been presented was at the trial, not now, and that the trial itself had been 'patient'.

As to the petitions, he is sorry to tell the crowd that, while it is always a worthy exercise to present one's grievances to the Executive, they should know that the latest petitions were somewhat lacking, in that 'whole pages of them were written by the same hand'.

Nevertheless, and this is the key, he does commit to raising the matter once more with the Executive Council on the morrow, but feels bound to note that, personally, he 'could not hold out the slightest hope of any alteration'.[33]

But it is something. A shred of hope. The delegation leaves and, from the Treasury steps, informs the crowd outside of the result: the Executive will at least *consider* it once more. Hooray! It is what they have come for, and, with this assurance, the crowd quickly disperses.

MORNING, 10 NOVEMBER 1880, A LAST SHOT

With less than twenty-four hours to live, barring a miracle, Ned tries for that miracle, by dictating just one more letter to His Excellency the Governor of Victoria. As ever, he warms to the theme that he murdered no one at Stringybark. 'After my mother was convicted of aiding and abetting in shooting with intent to murder Constable Fitzpatrick I came back with the full intention of working a still to make whisky as it was the quickest means to obtain money to procure a new trial for my mother. I tried every legal means to obtain justice therefore you can see it never crossed my mind for revenge. If I had have went looking for the Police or shot them in any of the towns then there might have been some excuse for saying I shot them for revenge . . .

'Even to take the police evidence all through & the Two Years Career of me and my companions will show that we were anything but bloodthirsty and likewise in the whole of our Career we never ill used or maltreated women or child and always refrained from doing a cowardly act.'[34]

And there is more, much more, all of it either justification for what he had done or intended to show that, whatever else, he had not killed in cold blood: 'McIntyre's evidence shows that I had him covered when he threw up his arms and surrendered. So if my intention was to take life I should have shot McIntyre when I had him first covered.'

By letter's end, however, reality has returned to him. He clearly accepts that this letter will make no more difference than the other letters have done, and so he decides to make one last plea. 'There is one wish in conclusion I would like you to grant me, that is the release of my Mother before my execution as detaining her in prison Could not make any difference to the government now, for the day will come when all men will be judged by their mercy and deeds and also if you would grant permission for my friends to have my body that they might bury it in Consecrated ground.'[35]

At letter's end, Ned takes the quill from the warder, for the third and final time, and with his still severely injured hand, makes his tortured mark:

X

This final cross is darker and bolder than on his other letters, a sign of just how desperate he now is. The warder writes below it, 'Edward Kelly his mark'. It is done.

And, sure enough, the letter is presented to the Executive Council as it meets on the stroke of noon on this day. But the wheels of justice now have a momentum all their own, and the time for a reprieve has long since gone. The council's meeting is a short one and the vote is unanimous: Edward Kelly will hang at ten o'clock on the following morning.

—

In the distance, a heavy door is slammed, and now comes the steady sound of confident footsteps approaching – always a sign that it is a warder or official – echoing off the cold, stone floor and walls of the prison.

A visitor for you, Ned . . .

It is none other than the Governor of the gaol, John Castieau, who for this occasion adopts an even more gentle manner than usual for the brutal information he has come to impart.

As Ned listens closely, without either protest or noticeable emotion, the Governor softly tells him that the last avenues of appeal have been shut down, and that the legal machinery is now inexorably moving towards its end – his end. The Governor is sorry to inform Ned that tomorrow, 11 November, at ten in the morning, he will indeed be hanged by the neck until dead, as the sentence imposed by Judge Redmond Barry is carried out.

Yes, Governor. Thank you, Governor. Ned has always appreciated the respectful manner with which Castieau has treated him, and, in any case, he had expected precisely this news.

The Governor takes his leave and Ned is, for a short time, left alone on what will prove to be a singularly busy day.

That afternoon, Ned's last request is accorded. As it has long been his desire that his family and friends be able to have something of his to treasure after he has gone, on this sultry afternoon the official gaol photographer, Charles Nettleton, sets up his camera in the gaol courtyard, even as the manacled Ned is let out of his cell and shuffled towards him, taking up a position in the shade, just in front of the bluestone prison walls.

While the heavily armed warders keep a close watch, Ned does what he has effectively been doing all his life – he fronts up.

For the full-length portrait, the bushranger puffs out his chest and stares the camera right in the eye, even as he masks his crippled right hand by making a fist of it, and disguises his equally damaged left arm by holding onto a piece of rope tied to his leg irons.

The result is that he looks every inch Ned Kelly the proud bushranger and champion of his people – and not at all like the convicted murderer due to be hanged for his crimes before a day has passed. His whole demeanour marks a man who is, as *The Daily Telegraph* puts it, 'carrying out the desire of his friends and sympathisers that he should "die game".'[36]

For the second shot, Nettleton tightens his frame to a facial portrait, as, again, an extraordinarily serene and neatly coiffed-looking Ned Kelly, almost faintly amused as the sun overhead begins to sink towards his last sundown, gazes proudly like Moses upon his people as he shows them the Promised Land.

It is soon done.

Nettleton must race off to develop his shots – if the plates are not soaked in a solution of iron sulfate, acetic acid and alcohol in water within ten minutes, he will lose the images. (He has become known all over Melbourne for carrying 'his dark tent and equipment with him everywhere, a necessity in the days of the collodion process when plates had to be developed immediately after exposure'.[37] He has held this contract for the penal department for nigh on a quarter of a century, and as the special photographer for the government since 1854 he has seen Melbourne change from a town to a metropolis in precisely the span of Ned's short life.)

After a little while longer in the courtyard for Ned, it is time. Taking

Ned Kelly in chains, Old Melbourne Gaol. (Photo by Charles Nettleton, courtesy State Library of Victoria)

one last breath of fresh air, one last look at the blue sky, Ned shuffles back to the shadows and onwards to his cell, where he prepares to meet his last family visitors.

In the afternoon, his mother, Ellen, is brought from the female section of the gaol and ushered into his tight cell. The two embrace and quietly talk. Through it all, Ellen Kelly remains in control of her emotions as Ned speaks, and simply soaks up the vision and words of the

Portrait of Ned Kelly the day before he was hanged. (Photo by Charles Nettleton, courtesy Matt Shore)

son of whom she is so proud – a legend across the land, revered among the people who count, his people, their people – knowing, of course, that she will never see him alive again. Finally, however, she is told she must take her leave, and as the warders move in to move her out, she – at least as legend will have it – says her last words to him, the ones she has most come to say: 'Mind ye die like a Kelly, Son.'[38]

With a nod, Ned assures his mother he will do exactly that, and Ellen is whisked away and taken back to her own cell.

A couple of hours later, there is another family visit, as Ned's sisters Kate and young Grace arrive with his brother Jim. While Ned remains stoical and calm, Grace and Kate are quite the opposite in emotions. Just to see their beloved brother like this, caged like an animal and about to be executed like a rogue bull, deeply upsets them. After all, for what is he being executed? For standing up for his family and avenging the imprisonment of his innocent mother? For fighting back against the corrupt police? For being a leader to his people? For *what*? It is more than they can bear, and their tears flow freely together with the low cries of those trying to stifle sobs that just keep coming no matter what they do.

For his part, Jim is more controlled, aware that the last thing his condemned and beloved brother would want to see right now is anything resembling weakness on his part. It is okay for his sisters to weep, but it is unthinkable for him to do the same. He does, however, tell Ned that he only wishes he could have been with him and Dan as they made their last stand at Glenrowan.

Embracing his brother, Ned tells him that he is glad that he was not, as it is important that he has survived. Do you understand, Jim? It is now up to you to look after our mother and our sisters. *You*, Jim. You must stay strong for them. As reported in the *Kilmore Free Press*, 'Jim expressed himself that, so long as he lived, Ned should never die – that "he would be revenged".'[39]

After a final tearful embrace, his brother and sisters depart, and shortly afterwards Ned receives another final visit, from his cousins Tom and Kate Lloyd. Ned has one thing in particular he wants to say to Tom. 'Tom, near the head of the Rose River, line up the hill in front of you to the west and the rocks behind at the east and you'll find a place in the creek like a cattle crossing. Just as you come up out of the crossing, you'll find a hollow stump and there's a good saddle in it.'[40] This, apparently, is what remains of the great Kelly treasure thought to be out in the hills somewhere.

And yet, all too soon they are gone, too, the sounds of his cousins' steps fading away as they are taken down the worn stone corridors, then cut off as the iron door clangs shut behind them.

Still there are more visitors who come to see him, including Governor Castieau and his thirteen-year-old son, Godfrey, who have a few words. There is something about seeing such a young, innocent child that appears to affect Ned, and, before the two take their leave, Ned reaches his hand between the bars of his cell door to put it on young Godfrey's head and says, 'Son, I hope you grow up to be as fine a man as your father.'[41]

—

Outside the Robert Burns Hotel on this evening, at eight o'clock, no fewer than 4000 people are there with William Gaunson and others addressing the mob from an upper window. Shall we send a delegation to the Governor and demand Edward Kelly's life be spared?

We shall!

And if the Governor won't see us, we shall go to see the Chief Secretary.

As it happens, alas, when the delegation led by William Gaunson arrives at Government House, they are informed by Captain Le Patourel, 'His Excellency has fully considered the matter, and must positively decline any further interview.'[42]

After arriving then at Parliament House, at least the Chief Secretary receives a deputation led by William Gaunson and Archibald Hamilton, but Graham Berry is firm in defending the court's original sentence, adding that the Executive Council had already fully considered all the circumstances of the case. Yes, William Gaunson grants that this is so, and yet he takes another tack. In reference to the role of the Executive Council of Victoria, he says, 'laws are made one day; and repealed another day. The Executive Council after all only consists of nine mortal men. On this occasion, nine mortal men have refused to grant the prayer for mercy signed by more than 60,000 people in an incredibly short space of time.'

Upon hearing this, Berry promptly terminates the interview, saying, 'No good can be derived by further agitation; every latitude has been allowed the prisoner, and the jury having found him guilty he must suffer the extreme penalty of the law. [You] who are getting up this agitation are by no means friends of the condemned man or his family, for you are trying to raise false hopes which have no foundation . . . [Please] go back and disperse the crowd quietly.'[43]

Certainly, they go back to the hopeful crowd outside the Robert Burns Hotel, deflated and nearly defeated, but neither Archibald Hamilton nor William Gaunson can help himself. After Hamilton makes a speech attacking both the Governor and the Chief Secretary, William Gaunson attacks the press. Which is all fine as far as it goes, but the point remains, there is nowhere further to go. It is over.

The Age summed it up succinctly: 'The crowd, after listening for a time, quietly dispersed.'[44]

It is over.

—

Back in his cell, Ned's next visitor had been Dean Donaghy, official Catholic chaplain of the gaol, accompanied by Father Charles O'Hea, who both provide some spiritual comfort, with Father O'Hea personally promising Ned he will be with him on the morrow on the scaffold.

For his own last supper, Ned is allowed the finest meal that the gaol kitchen can provide – a large plate of roast lamb and peas, washed down by an entire bottle of claret.

And then, after much restless pacing, finally, at half past one in the morning, Ned goes to bed, or at least to bunk . . .

Understandably, sleep does not come easily, and to pass the time Ned is heard by warder William Buck to sing some of his favourite hymns, including his most beloved hymn of all, 'In the Sweet By and By'.

11 NOVEMBER 1880, COMETH THE DAY, COMETH THE HOUR

On this cloudy night of a slim moon, profound darkness envelops nearly all of Melbourne, as seemingly all the city awaits the morrow.

One small light, however, still dimly broods all night long.

Deep, deep in the heart of hulking Melbourne Gaol, the light in

Ned Kelly's cell shines on through what has been designated by the law to be the last night of his life, as he drifts in and out of sleep.

And so what does a man do as the sun rises on what he knows is to be the last morning of his life? The long-time warders at Melbourne Gaol have seen it all from the hundred prisoners already hanged within these walls. Some weep, some wail, most become incoherent in their panic.

Ned Kelly does none of these things.

At five o'clock on this morning, he does what he has been doing every morning for the last few weeks, as the warders observe him closely. He gets up. He stretches. He looks about.

And then he gets down on his knees and, after making the sign of the cross, prays to his Lord, who – he appears to think – he will soon be meeting.

He is calm and considered and prays softly for the next twenty minutes. He has, after all, known for a long time that this day is coming – certainly from the day of killing the policemen at Stringybark Creek, and perhaps from the day of first going bush after the arrest of his mother – and it is in no way a surprise to him. Nor to the press. Not for nothing had *The Ovens and Murray Advertiser* declared to the world in a headline, when Ned was just sixteen, that the young man was '**A CANDIDATE FOR THE GALLOWS**',[45] and now that candidate has been called forth.

Oddly, as the day dawns bright and ugly, Ned goes back to his bed for a little more sleep before the sleep eternal, and he remains the veritable eye of calm in the surrounding cyclone of activity and tension, an oasis of natural dignity while all around there is anxiety, anger and agonised emotions.

—

Outside Melbourne Gaol, the crowd begins to build from dawn, surging in numbers from half past seven onwards, carefully surveyed by armed troopers, some of whom are on horseback. No, there is nothing the crowd expects to see particularly – certainly not the hanging itself – but it is just something to be there, to be close. Broadly, it is the opinion of the afternoon paper, *The Herald*, that they are not ghouls so much as there in support. And nor are they just poor folk.

'The general sympathy which appeared to be felt for the condemned man,' the paper reports, 'was not confined to the lower orders alone, as the crowd which assembled around the gaol gates this morning testified . . . Women – many of them young, well-dressed and apparently respectable – were there mixing with the others.'[46]

Their numbers do not include any of the extended or immediate Kelly family members, as they have decided to stay together at the Robert Burns Hotel, while Maggie had left for home late the previous afternoon, preferring to be well away from the ghastliness of it all, and be with her children. Inside the hotel, the Kellys stay tightly together in the bar with their closest supporters, miserably counting down the minutes as they whisper to each other, while outside a crowd also builds.

As to Ellen Kelly, she works alone in the prison laundry, trying to keep busy.

—

As the bell of the Melbourne GPO, one mile to the south, strikes eight times to sound the hour, Ned again rises from his bunk and, as he grooms his moustache with his fingers, trying to put on a good face for the day ahead,[47] amazingly, he starts to sing. True, like his prayers, he does not do it so loudly that all of his words are necessarily discernible, but his warders at least recognise it as that song so beloved of so many in Kelly Country, and by no one more than the Kellys themselves, 'The Kelly Song':

Farewell to my home in Greta,
My loved ones fare thee well.
It grieves my heart to leave you
But here I must not dwell.[48]

Breakfast, prisoner Kelly?

Ned shakes his head. There is no big day planned ahead, and he is less in need of nourishment for his body than sustenance for his soul. It is with this in mind that, after his leg irons are taken off him at a quarter to nine, Ned receives the prison chaplain, Father Donaghy, and the good father takes Ned's confession.

'In the name of the Father, and of the Son, and of the Holy Spirit,' Ned begins, as he makes the sign of the cross. 'Bless me, Father, for I have sinned . . .'[49]

—

Just on nine o'clock, after giving confession, Ned is taken from the condemned cell in the old wing to the condemned man's cell that sits right alongside the gallows in the new main building. To get there, Ned must walk his last 50-odd yards in the open air, crossing the large internal courtyard, which boasts a small flowerbed outside the hospital ward. Such colour in the otherwise drab, grey surroundings immediately attracts Ned's attention.

'They look beautiful,' he says rather wistfully,[50] one of the few times he has betrayed any emotion. A sterner test is the handcart parked just outside the door to the old wing, which he knows is there to carry his body away to the 'dead-house'. Ned does not wince now. He remains composed. He is going to die like a Kelly.

The heavy, metal-lined wooden door of the new cell block is opened and the small group, with Kelly in the middle, still making his painful way forward on his injured foot, goes through into this cold and strange twilight world, where the light is filtered through windows surrounding the central tower and the dim skylights.

Carefully, walking straight ahead, passing through the middle point of the building, with the men's wing extending down to his right and the women's quarters along the bleak corridor off to his left, Ned and his retinue slowly climb the concrete staircase that leads to the gallows area. The other prisoners, though locked up in their cells, cock their ears, to hear every echoing footstep, every mumbled word, as this most notorious of men walks to his fate.

Ned Kelly steels himself and he and his entourage continue to shuffle forward along the noisy iron scaffolding, which veers slightly left around the empty central shaft of the building, which runs from the ground floor to the skylight above. It is in that central, open space on the ground floor, known as 'the gallery floor', that the audience will gather to witness his falling body come through the trapdoor.

Mercifully, there is little time for such thoughts.

Ned once again passes the two vast corridors filled with prisoners in their cells, the men now off to his left and the women off to his right. He can hear some of them, as they sporadically call out in defiance of the silence rule commanded of all prisoners when they are in this part of the gaol.

The small group finally come to the condemned cell, number 'M4', which is directly to the left of the gallows. It is not far past nine o'clock when they get there. And so it is here, in the condemned man's cell, a stone, cold cube, that he must wait out his final hour on this earth.

In the cell directly opposite M4, just beyond the dangling noose, sits the grey-haired, well-conditioned hangman, the chicken-stealer Elijah Upjohn. Upjohn is a fifty-eight-year-old ex-convict who, after being given his first gaol sentence at the age of eleven, was sent to Van Diemen's Land for stealing shoes in 1839. He has made his way into Melbourne Gaol via Ballarat, thanks to his own life of criminality. Upjohn's crimes have been as petty and numerous as Ned's have been serious and comparatively few.

—

Outside the main gates of the gaol, the crowd is now thick, several thousand strong, with more people joining all the time. Many are clutching the morning papers bearing the news of the execution, including the appointed hour.

Meanwhile, some twenty-seven official witnesses, 'privileged' folk – composed substantially of journalists, 'several constables and detectives, three or four medical men, a number of justices of the peace'[51] – start arriving, bearing the 'tickets', the printed documents of admission, which are carefully checked by the wardens on duty at the small 'wicket gate' contained within the enormous, main, iron-studded gates on Franklin Road. Their credentials confirmed, they are ushered inside, to gather in a small courtyard as they wait for the official party, Sheriff Robert Rede, Deputy Sheriff Louis Ellis and, of course, Melbourne Gaol Governor John Castieau.

—

Ned has not been in his cell long before Father O'Hea arrives. Looking at Ned Kelly now, about to meet his maker, the good father cannot help but remember the day, some twenty-six years ago, up Beveridge way, when he had cradled the infant Ned Kelly in his arms and intoned the holy words, imploring the Lord that this child be 'delivered from the corruption of sin, experience a relish for good works, and be delighted with the food of divine wisdom'.[52]

It seems extraordinary both that that gentle baby could have turned into the most feared and hunted criminal in the land, and that that feared and hunted criminal could, in turn, be this placid man kneeling before him, with such a short time left to live.

For another man in this situation, each tick of the clock would be like a slap to the face, if not a punch to the solar plexus. And yet, Ned had taken worse blows from Wild Wright and not flinched, and he does not flinch now, even as Father Donaghy and Father O'Hea administer the last rites of the Roman Catholic Church to him, with the former beginning, '*Through this holy anointing may the Lord in His love and mercy help you with the grace of the Holy Spirit . . .*'[53]

And now, just before ten o'clock, the official party needed for the high judicial process of a hanging arrive. The little man in his black uniform frockcoat is the Sheriff, Colonel Robert Rede, who had first come to the public's attention twenty-six years earlier, when he had been the commissioner in charge of the garrison at Ballarat during the time of the Eureka Stockade, the man who had taken the final responsibility for the murderous attack that had killed a couple of dozen diggers. With him is the more refined figure of the Governor of the gaol, John Castieau.

When everyone has arrived, the official party leads the way through the main gate, through the building housing the chapel, then out into the new cell block itself, coming in through a heavy door that brings them directly into the viewing gallery. Coming into the dull and gloomy chill of the building, they all shiver a little instinctively, and immediately look up, searching for . . . yes, there it is, right in front of each of them. The gallows.

As the Sheriff and the Governor proceed up the stairs, headed towards the condemned cell, the others of the party arrange themselves on the gallery floor. Some position themselves up on the stairs to make sure they get a good view, while gaol warders stand arranged on the side galleries.

All the while, a few muted calls of the locked-away inmates can be discerned through the thick doors of their tiny cells. The warders make no attempt to silence them on this particular occasion.

As they arrive on the platform together, just outside the condemned Ned's cell, and with just two minutes left before the clock strikes ten, the Sheriff and the Governor follow a strict legal protocol. For it is now Rede, the Sheriff of Melbourne – the man responsible for the execution of sentencing in this city – who turns to Governor Castieau and, in a voice capable of being heard by all witnesses, demands that the condemned felon Edward Kelly be brought forth so that his punishment may be administered.

'Colonel Rede, may I see the warrant?' Castieau replies in an equally clear voice,[54] as the journalists below furiously scribble down every word, every action.

Rede's hand is moving to his inside pocket even before Castieau has finished his demand, knowing that this is exactly what is expected. He hands the warrant to Castieau, and the Governor briefly scans the

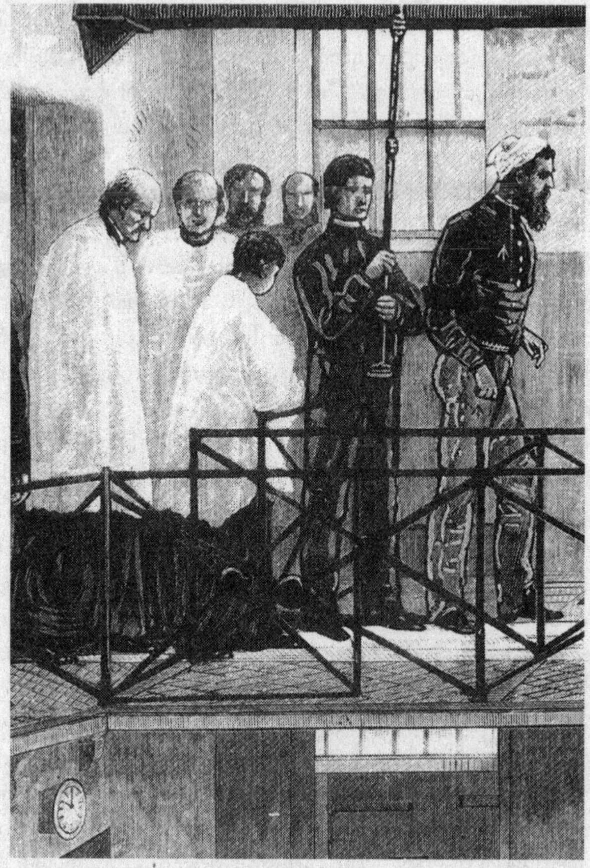

'Last scene of the Kelly drama: the criminal on the scaffold'. (From *The Australasian Sketcher*, 20 November 1880, courtesy Matt Shore)

words on the official government parchment, nods his head and bows to Rede, by way of acknowledgement that his warrant is in order.

Now the door of the executioner's cell, on the right-hand side of the gallows, opens and out comes executioner Upjohn, who briefly turns his head down on the audience. As he does so, an audible gasp comes from the witnesses. For, as they say, while beauty may be only skin deep, ugly goes clear to the bone, and, at first glance, Upjohn, who is carrying a heavy leather strap, appears to set new records in the field.

'Those who have seen [Upjohn's predecessor] Gately,' *The Herald* would comment, 'know how dreadfully forbidding were the miscreant's features. If it be possible, his successor is even more repulsive in appearance. He is an old man . . . but broad-shouldered and burly.'[55]

Closely shaved, with his white hair tightly cropped, he wears the prison attire, albeit in shirtsleeves, with no covering on his face and a notably brutal aspect about him. 'He has heavy lips and heavy features,' one reporter will pen, 'altogether the nose being the most striking and ugly. It is large in proportion, and appears to have a large carbuncle on the end. Altogether the man's appearance fully maintains the accepted idea of what a hangman should look like.'[56]

Following his own protocol, Upjohn now goes directly across to the doomed Ned's cell and enters. He neither looks at Ned nor speaks to him, but simply turns him and takes the leather strap to pinion his arms behind his back. (Come the time to swing, there is to be no possibility of the criminal trying to save himself by grabbing the rope.)

'There is no need for tying me,' Ned rebukes him gently,[57] as his wounded arm, like a cat with a thorn in its paw, instinctively flinches away from the executioner's endeavours, but Upjohn listens to the condemned man no more than he would a sack of potatoes that needs to be properly tied before being delivered to market, and continues to bind him up tightly. With the leather strap bound tightly above Ned's elbows, Upjohn puts a small, white nightcap on his head, though not yet over his eyes, and now they are ready for his last walk.

Preceded by the priests, one of whom is holding a crucifix and both of whom are loudly praying in Latin, Ned emerges from the cell, 'his jaunty air gone'[58] – reciting responses to the priests when they pause – and shuffles the five short steps to the noose, stopping at the spot that Upjohn has indicated, his feet right in the middle of the oblong in the floor formed by the trapdoor. Yes, there is a problem with one or both of his knees, as he is clearly limping, but he is resolute enough for all that.

As he comes to a halt, the witnesses are able to get their first good look at this, the most famous criminal on the continent. There he is, with his signature beard and whiskers and silk scarf around his neck, just as he had appeared on his last day in court.

While pale, Ned Kelly seems calm and in complete control. He does not shake – displaying neither fear nor fury – but is simply gazing resolutely forward, entirely expressionless. And that expression does not change even when he briefly looks down upon the witnesses, showing no particular interest – as if they are a train on an adjacent platform, a train he is not catching.

'Such is life,' he is reported to say,[59] in a low, rather unemotional tone.[60]

The noose.

The *noose.*

It dangles, languidly, from Upjohn's right hand.

Now, after the executioner steps forward to place the noose over Ned's head, Ned is seen to wince a little, before inclining his head slightly to make it easier for Upjohn. The rope is tightened around his neck and a doctor steps forward to check Upjohn's work, while the priests continue to loudly intone their prayers.

This is Upjohn's first hanging, and it must be done right. While the Americans have the knot at the back of the neck, often resulting in death by strangulation, the British system, which the colony of Victoria embraces, is to have the knot high up under the left ear. If positioned properly, and with sufficient drop in the rope, the snapping of the neck will kill the prisoner instantly. Of all the dark arts, it is the darkest.

It all seems to be in order, and the medical official, Dr Edward Barker, nods assent. Ned takes one last, longing look upwards towards the skylight, where lies the sun, fresh air, freedom and *life*, and then the white cap atop his head is drawn down over his face to form a hood, and the first of the darkness has closed in.

But wait . . .

Dr Barker has, after all, seen something amiss and begins to move forward to adjust the knot.

Alas.

Alas.

Alas.

He is too late.

With no ceremony, and seemingly no more emotion than a railwayman hauling on a lever to change some railway tracks – which this lever resembles – Upjohn steps back, half-turns and all in the one movement gives a hard yank on the trapdoor lever.

On the instant, the trapdoor clangs, Ned falls straight down and goes eight feet before coming to a stop with a horrifying jerk, his neck breaking in a split second. Waiting for exactly this sound, a howl of outrage, of extreme emotion, bursts forth from other convicts in the cell block. At least the way sad legend has it, in the laundry, where she is working, just near the gallows, Ellen hears both the clang of the trapdoor and the howls.

Down below, it appears that Ned is not yet dead, as, after spasmodic quivering of his limbs, which is simply caused by 'post-mortem involuntary contraction of the extensor muscles',[61] his knees come up towards his body several times, all of it lasting some ten seconds. Each time, his feet fall to perhaps four feet above the floor, as the witnesses continue to stare at his convulsing body at their level.

And then, after some four minutes that seem like an eternity – the one just begun, for Ned – there is nothing.

Nary a twitch. Just the body turning slightly as the rope lightly revolves.

He has died like a Kelly.

—

With the cries of the other prisoners now ebbing away, the only thing that can be heard are the muted prayers of the priests, rumbling on, rambling on.

Rumbling, rambling, rumbling, rambling on . . .

It is five past ten. In the words of *The Argus*, Ned's death 'was one of the most expeditious executions ever performed in the Melbourne gaol'.[62] No flashness, no bravado, just as Ned had lived.

Outside, it is less calm. When the distant bell of Melbourne's GPO had struck ten o'clock, the '4000 men women and children . . . nearly all of the lower orders . . . raised their eyes simultaneously to the roof of the gaol expecting to see a black flag displayed; but they looked in vain, for no intimation of the execution having taken place was given'.[63]

And yet, ask not for whom the bell tolls; it tolls for Ned. And with each successive tolling of the bell, the realisation sinks in and even 'the idlest, the most ignorant, the most dissipated realised at that moment the solemn fact that a fellow-creature had been passed from this world to the unknown in obedience to the just dictates of the outraged laws of his country . . .'[64]

Perhaps most affected is one woman, who falls to her knees and prays for the soul of Ned. As if in response to her plea, a strangely cold wind blows over the crowd, almost but not quite as bleak as the mood.

At the Robert Burns Hotel, where no one has spoken above a whisper for well over half an hour, it is Jim Kelly who glances at his watch and says, 'Ah, well, the poor devil is out of his misery anyhow by this time.'[65]

In response, Wild Wright is heard to mutter something unintelligible about the police, though the journalist who records the moment sagely notes, 'It was probably not of a laudatory nature.'[66]

—

After the legislated thirty minutes from the moment Ned dropped through the trapdoor, Dr Barker officially pronounces him dead.

'On removing the cap the face was found to be placid,' *The Argus* would report, 'and without any discolouration, and only a slight mark was left by the rope under the left ear. The eyes were wide open.'[67]

The dead bushranger's body is cut down, placed in the cart he had seen on the way in and taken to the prison's dead-house. Immediately, the police send a Notification of Execution to the City Coroner, stating that 'a prisoner of the Crown named Edward Kelly under sentence of death for murder was hanged at 10 am today in Melbourne Gaol'.[68]

The Coroner is now officially entitled to conduct a formal inquest on the deceased and does so. The inquest's jury of twelve men return a verdict that Ned had been 'judicially hanged, and that the provisions of the act for the private execution of criminals had been properly carried out',[69] while Governor Castieau, Deputy Sheriff Ellis and Dr Shields, the medical officer of the gaol, all provide written depositions corroborating this fact.

Alas, the request by Ned and his family that his body be given to the family for burial – for they wish to place him right beside Dan in the Greta Cemetery – has been firmly denied. Firstly, that is against the law, which stipulates that 'the body of every person executed for murder shall be buried within the precincts of the gaol in which he shall have been last confined',[70] and, secondly, because they have other things in mind for his cadaver.

It is for this purpose that, as arranged, the proprietor of the waxworks in Bourke Street, Maximilian Kreitmayer, now swiftly moves into action, taking a razor to the dead man's hair and beard. He then applies oil to the skin before pressing a plaster of Paris mould to his face and skull, in preparation for making a death mask, which he will charge the public money to view the following day.

And there is another purpose, too.

For, in the days that follow, the famed phrenologist Archibald Hamilton will examine the plaster-cast mask to pass learned judgement on the character of Edward Kelly. (Yes, that same man who had been a leading light on the Reprieve Committee, and Chairman of the Society for the Abolition of Capital Punishment – but this is too good an opportunity to miss!) By the reckoning of the 'science' of phrenology, by carefully studying the size and shape of the cranium, one could determine particularities of a person's character and mental abilities. In Hamilton's words, Ned's 'measurements to the phrenologist are remarkable. The head is scarcely of medium size for so big a man.'

And what does it all mean? Well, a lot, it seems, as the phrenologist goes through the various misgivings revealed to him by his tape measure, of the hanged man's character. He does concede that, 'It is no excuse for Edward Kelly's conduct to say that I could find many heads of as low a type as his in an hour's walk in Bourke Street, where the crowd is afloat which haunt the dens of infamy in that neighbourhood. But though the type is much more common than is generally believed, it differs from Kelly's in this, that there is not one head in a thousand of the criminal type so small in caution as his, and there are few heads among the worst that would risk so much for the love of power as is evinced in the head of Kelly from his enormous self-esteem. This self-esteem, combined with large love of approbation and hope, would often make him appear bright, dazzling and heroic to those who couldn't see through the veil which vanity threw around him. His love of family, his pride in the Kellys, is chiefly inspired by his self-esteem, and by the homage that was paid to his so-called courage and liberality.'

He also adds, 'He could take from the rich and give to the poor as long as the latter deferred to him as the cleverest man in the country.'[71]

—

The indignity of the phrenologist's words is yet a week away, however.

Though an official post-mortem is never recorded as being conducted on Ned's body, some time before his burial, his head is sawn off, to explore the effects of hanging, as authorities at the time are questioning whether death by hanging is indeed a humane and instant form of execution. Also in the name of medical research, his wounded arm is sawn open at the wrist and elbow, to examine how effective Dr Shields's treatments had been on Ned's wounds.

The next morning, the bodily remains of Ned Kelly are, in a quiet fashion, placed in a makeshift red-gum coffin, covered in shovelfuls of lime to speed up decomposition and placed in a six-feet deep grave that lies in a distant corner of the gaol yard, at the base of the western wall of the long, narrow graveyard between the women's exercise yard and the stone-breaking yard. A stone in the wall above his grave is marked with EK and a broad arrow.

Quickly and easily now, the shovelfuls of earth from the pile beside the hole are thrown down on the coffin, the first ones reverberating loudly on the wood, and in short order the grave is filled and the ground raked over.

Ned Kelly is gone.

But his legend will go on, as strongly as ever, thirteen decades after his death and well beyond.

Such is his life.

EPILOGUE

My brother Ned holds a very unique position among the great men of the world. Great men are proclaimed great almost exclusively by their friends, supporters, sympathisers and admirers; but you have proved that my brother, Ned Kelly, was proclaimed the greatest man in the world by his bitterest enemy.

Jim Kelly, in a letter from Greta West, written to J. J. Kenneally, an early Kelly author of great significance, December 1930

And so they took Ned Kelly and hanged him in the jail,
For he fought singlehanded although in iron mail.
And no man singlehanded can hope to break the bars;
It's a thousand like Ned Kelly who will hoist the flag of stars.

John Manifold

Just twelve days after Ned had been hanged, Sir Redmond Barry's long-term ill health overcame him and he dropped dead. Shades of 'I will see you there where I go . . .'?[1]

Perhaps. At the least, there was this: 'Although not constitutionally superstitious,' a doctor involved in the care of the famous judge declared, 'Barry was singularly affected by Kelly's words in the dock.'[2]

Whatever Ned Kelly's own dying thoughts on the prospect of Judge Barry joining him, there is no doubt that in, other realms of justice, Ned Kelly did have many of his wishes realised, starting with perhaps his most cogent one of all. In one of the condemned man's last talks with his family, just after he had been sentenced to death, Ned Kelly had expressed a hope that 'my execution might lead to an investigation into the whole conduct and management of the police'.[3]

And so it came to pass.

There were two broad reviews of police actions. A week after Ned's hanging, a Reward Board met for the first time to determine how the £8000 reward money should be distributed.[4] Advertisements were placed in the government gazettes of Victoria and New South Wales, as well as in the major daily and weekly newspapers of Sydney and Melbourne, inviting persons who considered themselves worthy to forward their claims to the board before the last day of 1880. Ninety-two people made applications for a share in the reward. Acting Chief Commissioner Charles Nicolson, along with Superintendents Hare and Sadleir, gave advice to the board and verification of claimants' statements. In addition, five people gave evidence at a hearing: the Honourable Robert Ramsay, Joe Melvin of *The Argus*, John McWhirter of *The Age*, George Allen of *The Telegraph* and the volunteer Charles Rawlins. After all claims were received, twenty-four claimants were eliminated first up. Among them was Constable Thomas McIntyre, upon whose sole testimony Ned had been sent to the gallows.

To the chagrin of Acting Chief Commissioner Nicolson, the largest amount of money, £800, went to Superintendent Francis Hare. The schoolteacher, Thomas Curnow, followed this, receiving an initial reward of £550. (Such were the rewards for risking your life to stop the train and save a couple of dozen lives.) After lodging a protest in 1881, Curnow was awarded an additional £450 in 1882 by the Chief Secretary's Department, bringing his total reward up to £1000.[5] From there, the bulk of the money went to the police officers, with Senior Constable John Kelly being awarded £377; Sergeant Arthur Steele with £290; and Constable Hugh Bracken £275, topped up by an extra allowance after he retired from the police force in 1882 of £29, 15 shillings a year, to compensate 'for special service and injury received in the destruction of the Kelly gang at Glenrowan'.[6] As to Superintendent John Sadleir, he received £240, while Charles Rawlins was awarded £137.

For his part in the siege at Glenrowan, railway guard Jesse Dowsett received £175, while Detective Michael Ward was awarded £100 due to his 'connection with the employment of [Aaron Sherritt]'.[7] Acting Chief Commissioner Nicolson received not a penny, and nor did any money go to anyone on the spy network he had set up – something manifestly unfair, most particularly in the case of the Diseased Stock Agent, the selector and schoolteacher from the Greta district named Daniel Kennedy.[8]

As to Constable Johnston, who had been so active in the pursuit and instrumental in finally finishing the siege, he was awarded just £98.

And the Queensland black-trackers? They were given the relatively paltry sum of £50 each, for the simple reason that 'it would not be desirable to place any considerable sum of money in the hands of persons unable to use it', and even then the money was not given to them directly but to the Victoria and Queensland governments, 'to be dealt with at their discretion'![9] Sub-Inspector Stanhope O'Connor was disgusted, though his own award was relatively generous at £237.

In 1994, the descendants of two of the Aboriginal constables, Jack Noble and Gary Owens, or 'Barney', issued a writ against the Victoria and Queensland governments in the Queensland Supreme Court for a total of $84 million. The figure of $42 million each was arrived at 'based on compound interest calculated at 12 per cent', together with 'pecuniary damages for suffering caused by the with-holding of the reward money'.[10] The following year, the court dismissed the claim, with Justice John ruling 'the descendants were not proper plaintiffs because they were not the executors of the trackers' estates'.[11] The plaintiffs announced they would appeal, with action 'stayed until further notice' in April 1999. The matter remains in the Queensland Court of Appeal, as it is yet to be established, among other things, whether the claimants have the legal standing to sue on behalf of the estates.

The second, and far more important, review of the Kelly outbreak came shortly afterwards. On 7 March 1881, the Governor of Victoria, the Marquess of Normanby, signed the order for a Royal Commission 'to enquire into the circumstances preceding and attending the Kelly outbreak . . .' as well as 'report upon the present state and organization of the police force'.[12]

The Royal Commission started taking evidence on the morning of 23 March at the Treasury, at the top of Collins Street, and the first witness was Captain Standish, who had retired from his position six months earlier, on the last day of September of the previous year. It proceeded for the next six months, over sixty-six sittings – including in Greta, Glenrowan, Benalla, Beechworth, Sebastopol and Wangaratta – with a further sixty-five witnesses answering 18,289 questions[13] as the commissioners tried to get to the bottom of exactly what had happened, and most particularly why it had happened.

At the end, in October 1881, the commissioners released their findings, which included many recommendations, but most crucially:

- Censured Commissioner Frederick Standish, ruling that his conduct 'was not characterized either by good judgment or by that zeal for the interests of the Public Service which should have distinguished an officer in Captain Standish's position. The Commission attribute much of the bad feeling which existed amongst the officers to the want of impartiality, temper, tact, and judgment evinced by the Chief Commissioner in his dealings with his subordinates.'[14]
- Called for Superintendent Francis Hare, Assistant Commissioner Charles Hope Nicolson and Inspector Alexander Brooke Smith to retire, particularly criticising the man notable for his 'indolence and incompetence',[15] Brooke Smith, for not following up hard on the sighting of the Kelly Gang in Wangaratta on 3 November 1878. 'Upon no other occasion throughout the pursuit,' it recorded, 'from the murders at the Wombat to the final affray at Glenrowan, was there presented a more favourable prospect of capturing the Gang.'[16]
- Cited Superintendent John Sadleir for 'several errors of judgment while assisting in the pursuit of the Kelly Gang; that his conduct of operations against the outlaws at Glenrowan was not judicious or calculated to raise the police force in the estimation of the public . . . Your Commissioners therefore

recommend that Superintendent Sadleir be placed at the bottom of the list of superintendents.'[17]

- Criticised Sergeant Arthur Loftus Maule Steele for his failure to go after the Kelly Gang at Wangaratta on 4 November 1878, despite having 'a large body of well-armed troopers under his command, then actually engaged in the search for the outlaws . . . There can be little doubt, that, had he exhibited judgment and promptitude on that occasion, he would have been the means of capturing the Gang, and preventing the loss of life and the enormous expenditure of money incurred subsequently in the extermination of the outlaws. Your Commissioners therefore recommend that Sergeant Steele be reduced to the ranks.'[18]

This does not happen, and, even in 1882, when another inquiry is held specifically to determine whether Steele did or did not 'fire deliberately at Mrs Reardon and other persons imprisoned in the hotel at Glenrowan',[19] he was found not guilty of all charges. One thing that helped was the 310 citizens from Wangaratta, twenty-three from Yackandandah and twelve from Chiltern who signed a petition in support of him. (Later, James Whitty and the Moyhu Stock Protection Society would present him with an engraved sword, to mark their appreciation of his work in capturing Kelly. The sword is now in the National Museum in Canberra. The inscription on the sword reads, *'Presented to Sergeant Steele, Victoria Police by the Moyhu Stock Protection Society as a testimony of the high esteem they entertain of his services during the recent outbreak, Wangaratta, 1880.'*)

All four constables in the hut the night Aaron Sherritt had been shot were, in the view of the commission, 'guilty of disobedience of orders and gross cowardice',[20] only alerting police sixteen hours after the event, and should be sacked. By this time, Harry Armstrong had already left the police force and gone to America, but the commission recommends that the other three be dismissed – and they are.

Detective Michael Ward was criticised for 'misleading his superior officers upon several occasions', and it was recommended that 'Detective Ward be censured and reduced one grade'.[21]

The commission also condemned the process of continually remanding the sympathisers, asserting that such remands 'did violence to people's ideas of the liberty of the subject; they irritated and estranged probably many who might have been of service to the police; they failed to allay apprehensions of further outrages on the part of the gang, or to prevent them from obtaining the requisite supplies; they crippled the usefulness of officers who had been called away from active duty . . . to attend the Petty Sessions at Beechworth . . . and what was of more significance, the failure of the prosecutions led the public to believe that the conduct of affairs was mismanaged'.[22]

A key recommendation of the committee was, 'That immediate steps be taken by the Government to arm the mounted police of the Colony with Regulation Pattern Martini-Henry carbines, that the entire force be instructed in their use of the weapon by means of regular drill and periodical target practice and a reasonable quantity of ammunition shall be served out to each man for such practice.'[23]

And Alexander Fitzpatrick did not escape censure. He was criticised for being a very indifferent character in the force, from which he was ultimately discharged. And, make no mistake, the Royal Commission concluded, 'Fitzpatrick's conduct, however justified by the rules of the service, was unfortunate in its results . . .'[24]

And yet, if the Fitzpatrick episode was the catalyst for the terrible events that followed, it was equally obvious to the Royal Commissioners that the root cause went far deeper than a lying wastrel of a constable. In the course of the inquiry, both Superintendent John Sadleir and Inspector William Montfort pointed out that a key problem was the enormous sense of grievance many of the Irish selectors felt over the lack of justice accorded to them, most particularly when it came to access to new land being opened up.

Inspector Montfort was particularly frank in his testimony: 'A great deal of the difficulty with these men would be got over if they felt they were treated with equal justice – that there was no "down" upon them.

They are much more tractable if they feel that they are treated with equal justice.'[25]

Even Captain Standish had realised that it was Fitzpatrick who had much to answer for, and said so to the Royal Commission: 'I believe these outrages would never have happened if it had not been for the shooting of Constable Fitzpatrick, and the consequent anger and indignation of the Kellys at their mother having received that severe sentence, and at their associates having received the sentence of six years.'[26]

Much the same point was made to Mounted Constable Robert Graham, the next man appointed to Greta after the siege of Glenrowan. In a chat with Ned Kelly's uncle, Tom Lloyd Snr, the old man laid it on the line for him. 'The Kellys wanted ground,' he told Graham. 'Now, the sympathisers wanted land, and, if they could be guaranteed access to that land, they would get rid of the few troublemakers and hotheads remaining in the district.'[27] If the rest of the police force had been 'more like Graham', Lloyd later said to his son, 'and less like Fitzpatrick, there never would have been a Kelly Outbreak.'[28]

—

There is no doubt that had Captain Standish not already retired, he would have been obliged to stand down, but in any case the principal is that he has indeed been held accountable for his shoddy and dishonest management of the whole outbreak and his reputation was publicly destroyed in the short time that remained to him. For, in the face of it all, Captain Standish receded to the Melbourne Club, in much the same manner as his grip on sanity receded. Some habits died hard, however, as the *Australian Dictionary of Biography* records that, in 1882, Captain Standish 'was involved in what was for many years a cause célèbre when he was almost thrown out of the window of the Melbourne Club by one Colonel Craigie Halkett, whom he had addressed by a provocative nickname'.[29] Colonel Halkett did *not* like to be called 'Jumbo', and he'd be *damned* if he'd let the blighter get away with it!

His health failing, his spirit ailing, Captain Standish eventually died in the Melbourne Club at half past five on 19 March 1883, aged fifty-eight. 'He was,' according to *The Argus*, 'suffering from disease of the heart and of the liver, and there were also indications of softening of the brain. The immediate cause of death was disease of the heart, aided by a general breakup of the system.'[30]

In looking back on his career, and his ineffectiveness at the time of the Kelly outbreak, the paper commented, 'It is evident now that at that time Captain Standish was suffering from the disease which subsequently developed itself unmistakably.'[31]

—

Superintendent Hare and Assistant Commissioner Nicolson fared better, as although both did indeed resign from the police after the Royal Commission released its findings, they were both reinstated as Superintendents by Cabinet pending their appointment as stipendiary police magistrates – a role that both went on to fill with some aplomb.

Hare would go on to spend a good deal of time writing his memoirs. *The Last of the Bushrangers: An Account of the Capture of the Kelly Gang* was published in London in 1892, allowing him to give his own, frequently self-serving, account of his role in the Kelly outbreak.

—

As to Sub-Inspector Stanhope O'Connor, his superiors in Queensland seemed to take a surprisingly dim view of his efforts and, two weeks after the siege of Glenrowan, the Queensland Police Commissioner wrote to him in singularly bald terms, 'I regret exceedingly that, so far as I can judge from the very meagre information contained in your report, and the more fully detailed accounts given by newspaper correspondents, I am unable to find any cause for congratulation . . .'[32]

In high dudgeon, O'Connor resigned shortly afterwards, intending to join the Victoria Police Force – at least this would bring his wife back close to her family – but in the fallout from the Royal Commission this plan was shelved. They moved to Melbourne regardless, where the polished O'Connor forged a successful career at the Melbourne Stock Exchange. He died in St Kilda on the first day of spring 1908, aged sixty.

—

Hugh Bracken was judged as one of the few men in the Victoria Police Force who came out of Glenrowan with his reputation improved. The commission stated flatly it 'approves of the action taken by Constable Bracken when imprisoned by the Kelly gang in Mrs Jones's hotel, at Glenrowan, and recommend him for promotion in the service'.[33]

For some reason, Bracken was not called upon to give evidence at the Royal Commission, and many in the community asked why, one man writing a letter to *The Argus*: 'Why was Constable Bracken – one of the most important witnesses – never called, while men, some of whom bear unreliable characters in the force, were brought forward?'[34]

For the sake of his and his family's safety after his role in the siege of Glenrowan and the attendant publicity – he received many threats on his life – Constable Hugh Bracken requested and received a transfer, firstly to the Richmond Training Depot, followed by a subsequent transfer to the police barracks at Wallan.

Alas, he remained haunted by the events at Glenrowan – something likely exacerbated by the frequently expressed views of his police colleagues that he should not have prevented Steele shooting Ned, who had, after all, shot three police officers – and in 1883 he suffered a nervous breakdown, occasioning his discharge from the force.

Happiness was not to be his, and even less so after his first wife died in March 1884, and his second wife just ten years later. Finally, it all became too much, and on Friday morning, 23 February 1900, at his home in Wallan, Hugh Bracken put a gun to his head and pulled the trigger, killing himself instantly, with the *Argus* reporter from Kilmore commenting, 'the suicide evidently being of a most deliberate nature'.[35]

Vale, Hugh Bracken.

—

Like Hugh Bracken, Tom Curnow and his wife, Isobel, were keen to move away from Glenrowan once the siege was over. Curnow received special treatment from the government, being granted leave with full pay and going to stay with his parents in Ballarat until a transfer could be sorted out by the Education Department.

Upon arrival in Ballarat, Curnow was treated as a public celebrity, with *The Ballarat Star* noting on 3 July 1880, 'Mr Curnow was the hero of quite an ovation on Friday, his intelligent bravery at Glenrowan recognised by the 400 or 500 people at the corner.'[36] This unplanned holiday came to an end when he was 'appointed as a "special assistant" to State School 33, Dana Street, Ballarat'.[37]

The first official recognition of Thomas Curnow's actions at Glenrowan did not come from the Reward Board but from the Victorian Humane Society. In July 1881, the society honoured Curnow with their second-highest award – a silver medal presented to him by the Governor in front of 2000 people, a great honour for an ordinary citizen – 'for great bravery and imminent risk to his life incurred in generously signalling an approaching train with police'.[38]

Curnow remained on the staff of State School 33 in Ballarat for nearly twenty-seven years, achieving a record as a 'steady reliable and earnest teacher',[39] before retiring on 30 June 1915. He died in Ballarat just before Christmas 1922, aged sixty-seven, with his gravestone only bearing the name 'Ginge Curnow'. There is no Victorian Education Department annual award in his name for service to the public above and beyond the call of duty, but there should be.

Funnily enough – or perhaps just another twist typical of the Kelly story – the man appointed to replace Curnow as the schoolteacher at Glenrowan was none other than local Greta selector and schoolteacher Daniel Kennedy, who had taught the likes of the Lloyds and McAuliffes at the Greta Common School years ago.[40] Indeed, he is the very same Daniel Kennedy well known to the police as the Diseased Stock Agent.

—

Thomas McIntyre continued his career in the police force until, a month after giving evidence to the Royal Commission, he retired, in September 1881.

In 1900, eager to set the record straight – or at least the record as he would like it to be – McIntyre also wrote a book, subsequently to remain unpublished, *A True Narrative of the Kelly Gang*, where he once more put down an account to indicate that Lonigan had been shot in cold blood.

'I knew it was Ned Kelly,' he wrote, 'as soon as I looked at him, seeing that he had me fairly and deadly covered, without the slightest tremor in the rifle. I wanted that rifle lowered before I attempted to get my firearms and accordingly threw out my arms horizontally. Immediately I did so Ned Kelly shifted the muzzle of the gun to the right and without taking it from his shoulder shot at Lonigan who had started to run partly towards and partly down the creek putting his hand down as if to get his revolver. He had no time to open the case and must have been looking over his right shoulder when he was shot in the right eye by Ned Kelly.'[41]

Of all his accounts, this, frankly, is the most ludicrous. It would have us believe that Ned Kelly could not only hit a moving target in the right eye at a distance of 40 yards but that Constable Lonigan also looked back over his shoulder at a gunman while trying to get away from him. As passionate Kelly researcher Michael Ball has pointed out to me, 'Well, Ned did say that "this gun could shoot around the corner" but this really is taking things too far.'

There is no doubt that McIntyre's experience with the Kellys all but defined him, as he noted in his memoirs: 'The Kelly gang created a cloud which cast a shadow over my life.'[42] He went on, 'My experience during the two years of the Kelly outbreak was not a bed of roses without any thorns to mortify the flesh. I believe I was foolishly sensitive. If I had been wise I would not have lain awake night after night fretting about what I could not help. In October 1878, I was 161 lbs in weight, in October 1880 I was 143 lbs, and spitting blood.'[43] If only he hadn't mentioned hiding in the wombat hole. *Why* had he done that? The question gnawed at him every day.

'It ruined his life, the Stringybark Creek episode, according to my mother,' his grandson, Howard Humffray, later told *The Age*.[44]

Thomas McIntyre moved to Ballarat and spent the rest of his days writing poetry, a good deal of it about the Victoria Police, and including his experience in the Kelly trials. And yet, though he had been the key witness for the prosecution, he ended up forging a strong friendship with the man who had tried to shake his testimony in the committal hearing, David Gaunson. In the final lines of his memoirs, McIntyre wrote, 'Before closing I would like to thank my friends, especially several gentlemen to whom I am greatly indebted for their support at a critical period of my life, amongst them I would like to mention the name of Hon. D. Gaunson, Kelly's solicitor, in whom I found a courteous gentleman and a staunch friend. I desire to inform these gentlemen that although they may think me ungrateful I desire to plead to that charge; NOT GUILTY.'[45]

McIntyre died in Ballarat in 1918, aged seventy-two.

—

Though the Royal Commission rewarded Constable Charles Gascoigne, who had performed so well at Glenrowan, with £137, he was dismissed from the Victoria Police in 1882, 'allegedly because of comments he made suggesting the Kelly Outbreak could be explained in part by the behaviours and attitudes of the police themselves'.[46] No matter, he went on to become a very successful miner and died in 1927, aged seventy-three. As an aside, it is interesting to note that, as the siege ended, Gascoigne gathered in one of Ned Kelly's shoulder plates that had been shot off and, after first hiding it in his saddlebag, then secreted it in a nearby creek, from where he later retrieved it as a souvenir. It re-emerged in 1970 when sold by his niece to a collector,[47] and then again in 2001 when it was sold to the State Library of Victoria for $202,750.

—

Sergeant Michael Kennedy's widow, Bridget, never moved from the house next to Mansfield Police Station at 102 High Street, and never remarried. One thing she always hungered for was the return of her husband's gold watch, and, via a local publican, she let it be known that there was £10 to anybody who could provide it. One day, a girl in her middle teens, later found to be Ned's cousin, turned up at the hotel to say she had come for the £10 and, sure enough, promptly handed the watch over when the money was paid to her.[48] It was soon in Mrs Kennedy's possession, and she treasured it for the rest of her days. She died on 3 November 1924 at the age of seventy-five and is buried in the same grave as her husband at Mansfield Cemetery.

Sergeant Kennedy's son, Michael, and grandson, Michael, also served with great honour in the Victoria Police Force. On the occasion of the centenary of the Stringybark Creek killings, grandson Senior Constable Michael Kennedy was present, bearing the famous gold watch that Ned Kelly had stolen from the slain police officer. He said of the Stringybark tragedy, 'Some of my family feel bitter but I've read a fair bit about what happened and I see it as just unfortunate . . . I realise that in those days things were tough for people like the Kellys. It would be hard to just sit back and see the rich getting richer and the poor getting poorer.'[49]

—

Despite the recommendation of the Royal Commission that John Sadleir be placed on the bottom rung for promotion, he remained in the police force until his retirement in 1896, at which point he was second only in rank to the Police Commissioner. Upon retirement, Sadleir, too, penned his memoirs, *Recollections of a Victorian Police Officer*, published in 1913.

Most interestingly, it gave his account of what McIntyre had told him three days after Lonigan's shooting at Stringybark Creek: 'Lonigan was sitting on a log, and on hearing the call to throw up his hands, he put his hands to his revolver, at the same time slipping down for cover behind the log on which he had been sitting. Lonigan had his head above the level of the log and was about to use his revolver when he was shot through the head.'[50]

Sadleir died at his home, Orwell, in Kooyong Road, Elsternwick, on 21 September 1919. He was eighty-six years old.

—

Henry Bindon's legal reputation was trashed after his performance in the Kelly case, and for the next decade he could only pick up crumbs of legal work. He became paralysed with a terrible illness in 1891 and died two years later.

—

In large part because of his support for Ned and his lack of support for capital punishment, David Gaunson lost his seat of Ararat in 1881. He was re-elected regardless in 1883 and, over the next twenty-five years, alternated between legal and political careers – continuing to manage his ongoing double act of respectable public life while forging dubious ties with infamous characters. He served as legal adviser to Madame Brussels, keeper of Melbourne's most famous brothel, and to the Licensed Victuallers' Association. In the mid-1890s, he also represented John Wren, infamous financier and gambling entrepreneur, as one of his clients – before dying in early January 1909, aged sixty-two.

—

Wild Wright – my favourite Kelly character after Ned, incidentally – did not die as I thought likely for saying 'Men first, dogs come last!' once too often. Instead – after being arrested one more time for the road, along with Jim Kelly, in September 1881, for Horse Stealing – he first found work as a horseman with Wirth's Circus and then as part of a boxing troupe. Later in life, he moved to the Northern Territory, where in 1911 he contracted malaria and died at Newcastle Waters Station, aged sixty-two. His son, Jack Wright, became a noted Geelong VFL footballer, 1902–06.

—

Harry Power was finally released from prison in February of 1885, and it is said he went to work at a property, Bald Hill Station, owned by Sir William Clarke and his wife, Janet.

Later, Power went to work as a guide on the hulk *Success*, showing people where the prisoners – of which he had been one – used to be quartered. Alas, later that same year, after he had declined to travel to Sydney with the *Success*, and likely fled 'from Melbourne to avoid the influenza epidemic',[51] in November 1891 his body was found in the Murray River, near Swan Hill, and he appeared to have died from drowning. There was no indication of what had happened. The last of the gentleman bushrangers was gone, aged 71.

—

Francis Hare died, in 1892, in the same place in which he had recuperated from his wounds after the siege: Rupertswood Mansion, in Sunbury. After being laid low with diabetes for all of three months, much of it spent in a private hospital, he appeared to have recovered enough that he sought a change of air, and, given that his wife was Lady Clarke's aunt, the offer was made for him to have a spell at Rupertswood, which he happily accepted. He was doing well until Friday 8 July, when he collapsed into a comatose state, before dying the next day, aged sixty-one.

—

Charles Hope Nicolson died in 1898 at the age of sixty-nine, at his home in South Yarra, after a short illness described as 'rheumatism of the heart'.[52] He had been working as a police magistrate right up until the last few days before he died, 'a duty which he discharged with credit and honour', according to *The Argus*.

'In all controversy as to the incidents of the Kelly epoch,' the paper went on, 'and even when unfairly attacked – he maintained always a manly and dignified silence.'[53]

—

Detective Michael Ward went on to great prosperity, working as a private detective for a Melbourne agency, which he co-owned. He died on 27 August 1921 in Carlton, aged seventy-five.

—

Maggie Skillion's relationship with her husband, Bill, did not survive his time in prison, and she took up with the man she became so close to while they did all in their power to support the Kelly Gang – her first cousin, Tom Lloyd. The two went on to have eleven children together, and were sure to name their first boy, born in 1882, Ned. Maggie lived until 1896, dying of rheumatic gout at just thirty-nine. Within three years, Lloyd married Steve Hart's second youngest sister, Rachel, with whom he had six children. He died in 1927, aged sixty-nine.

—

Kate Kelly came to a sad end. After marrying a blacksmith by the name of William Foster in 1888, she moved to Forbes in New South Wales and, after giving birth to six children, of whom three died in their infancy, ended up drowning in the Forbes River in 1898 in mysterious, if not suspicious, circumstances. It was likely suicide, five months after the birth of her sixth child, and she was buried in Forbes Cemetery, spending eternity just a few yards from Ben Hall.

After the death of those two beloved older daughters, it was Ellen Kelly who came to the fore to raise their children, with the great help of her faithful son, Jim. (Following Kate's death, it was Jim who drove a cart all the way to Forbes to collect Kate's three surviving children and bring them back to Eleven Mile Creek.) One of those children, Fred, would die in action in the First World War and is now buried near Villers-Bretonneux. His reported last words to the army padre who held him as he died were, 'Kiss me, Granny,'[54] a likely indicator of just how close he became to his mother's mother, the mighty Ellen Kelly.

—

As to many of the other characters in the Kelly saga, some of the most fascinating information as to what happened in their lives came to light just over three decades after Ned was hanged, when a journalist for the Sydney *Sun*, Brian William Cookson – a superb writer – journeyed to Victoria, and tracked down and interviewed all the major players who were willing to talk.

Alexander Fitzpatrick was found by Cookson living in Hawthorn, Victoria. His reputation had been damaged by his dismissal from the force in 1880, and what was left of it had been destroyed by the Royal Commission the following year. It was not something that would be healed by time.

When Cookson interviewed him, Fitzpatrick was quick to complain, 'For years afterwards I had to stand up and defend myself against unjust accusations. Even in theatrical productions, I have been libelled . . .

'The startling and dramatic nature of the events that followed upon the incident that I was connected with focused attention upon me. The easily gullible public, as curious as children, and ever hungry for pitiable gossip, listened greedily to any tale at that time, and my position was most unenviable. But I can always say this: I did my deed, fairly and squarely, though I was then little more than a lad.'[55]

And yet, as Cookson pointed out, Fitzpatrick never sued for libel or slander.[56] He most vociferously denied all allegations that he had tried to interfere with Kate Kelly.

'In the name of commonsense, was it likely, when I told them that I had come to arrest Dan Kelly, that they would permit me to be even friendly towards Kate Kelly! They all showed me bitter dislike from the time that I rode up. Their whole attitude to the police force was one of intense hostility. It was only natural that they should try and blame me for causing the trouble that led to the gang defying the law. One of the proofs that I acted the straight part came from Ned Kelly himself. When he stuck up the bank at Jerilderie the question was put to him while he was talking with some of the townspeople, "What about Fitzpatrick?" Ned answered, "If he had done what they say he did the country would not have been big enough to hold him." Ned Kelly clearly meant that if I had molested his sister Kate he would have shot me no matter where he found me.'[57]

And yet, he clearly bore Kelly no rancour, saying of him, among other things, that he would have made a first-class soldier. 'Ned Kelly rises before me as I speak,' he told Cookson. 'Considering his environment, he was a superior man. He possessed great natural ability, and under favourable circumstances would probably have become a leader of men in good society, instead of the head of a gang of outlaws.'[58]

If the corollary to the 'Only the good die young' theory is that 'Many a bad man makes old bones', Alexander Fitzpatrick was the long-living proof, as he lived for nearly five decades after the events that made him famous in some quarters, infamous in others, and died in 1924, aged 68.

—

Arthur Steele was found in much better circumstances, happily and healthily living in retirement at Wangaratta.

'His house, a commodious, well-shaded one, is at once pointed out to the visitor. It is on the top of the river bank. Below, the King and

Ovens rivers merge into one sluggish stream. Sergeant Steele occupies his leisure a good deal in farming. He is as keen as ever on horses – he always did love a good horse – and he finds agriculture an agreeable and profitable pastime.'[59]

And his memories of Glenrowan?

Oddly enough, he was not disposed to discuss it, on the grounds, 'It has all been told so often.' (No! Never enough!)

'But, all the same,' Steele went on, 'I may as well say that my success was owing to my using a shot gun instead of a rifle or pistol. It was no use trying to reach a vulnerable place in that man's armour with a bullet. Shot was the stuff for that job; good big shot. And that's what I got him with at last.'[60]

Strangely enough, a man whom Steele spends a good deal of time with in his old age is the one-time Jerilderie bank accountant and now fellow Wangaratta local Edward Living. The two would frequently talk of the Kelly years, Living's daughter Sylvia would report to author Ian Jones, 'as though it was terribly important to them'.[61]

Arthur Steele died in Wangaratta on 9 February 1914, aged seventy-six.

—

Most bitter in her recollections was Ann Jones, then seventy-seven years old and, strangely enough, still living in Glenrowan, in a small cottage within a stone's throw of where the Glenrowan Inn once stood.

She was unwell, and very weak, but rallied to put forth her thoughts . . .

'I well remember Kelly coming to my place that dreadful night,' she told Cookson in her quavering voice. 'It was raining, and very wet. He took me and my dear little girl away, and locked my two little boys up in a room by themselves. He made me turn the key – said he would shoot me if I refused to do everything that he told me. I begged him to lock myself and my daughter in my own room, but he wouldn't . . .

'When my dear little boy was hit he stood up, looked round, and then fell down. "Oh, God," he cried, in such a piteous voice, "Mother, dear mother, I'm shot!" . . .

'My boy died. Died miserably and without help. And my brave little girl, who was wounded herself, never got over it . . . She died not long after . . . Oh, dear! Oh, dear!

'They shot my dear innocent brave children – oh! The cowards! And we got no compensation! Nothing at all.'

Exhausted with the strain of her narrative, Cookson recounted, the old woman lay back upon the pillow, weeping bitterly. Broken, exhausted, she then bade him farewell. 'I shall not be long here,' she moaned. 'Soon I shall see my dear murdered children again! Good-bye! God bless you for letting me shake the hand of an Englishman in this accursed place.'[62]

Emerging from the darkened cottage into refreshingly bright sunshine, Cookson wondered how she could bear to live so close to the spot 'where the unfortunate woman had seen her boy slain, and where her own life had been wrecked'. And yet, as he also noted, 'she is not alone in the exemplification of the weird, inexplicable fascination for the place where the light had gone out of her life. Only a few miles away that other old woman is draining out the bitter dregs of a ruined life in sight of the place in which she had known the only happiness of her life and close by to where her sons met their shocking, if well-deserved, fate.'[63]

—

He was referring to Ellen Kelly, whom he finds some days later, now living in 'a small cottage, fenced, and with some pretence at a garden about it',[64] with some of Kate's kids still with her and, of course, her ever faithful son Jim, just a mile and a half from the old place at Eleven Mile Creek. Cookson's portrait of Ellen Kelly when she emerges, is arresting.

'An ancient woman, of aspect so forlorn as to suggest most strongly a life not only devoid of hope for the future, but weighed down with some great, overpowering sorrow of the past,' he recorded. 'Her frame was spare and poorly clad; the wrists and hands were as scant of flesh as the talons of an eagle, the thin shoulders, stooping with the weight of years and of lifelong tragedy, giving but feeble support to a head upon which the freckled skin was drawn as tight as parchment upon a drum. The thin, wan face was almost devoid of expression – save that one of hopeless grief and despair that was frozen upon it.'[65]

Ah, but when she speaks of her dead sons there is expression all right, and plenty of it, most particularly when Cookson opens his remarks by floating the theory that her son Dan and Steve Hart had not perished in the Glenrowan Inn at all but had been seen alive and well in South Africa – an absurd theory that in recent times had done the rounds.

'The old woman started violently. "What!" she cried tremblingly. "Dan not dead! No! It's a lie." And the aged head was bowed upon a meagre breast. "It's a lie," she murmured. "Dan is not alive. Dan is dead – dead – dead. What!" she exclaimed, clutching at the rough table for support. "Don't I know that he's dead? Haven't I proof of it all these weary years? Do you think I don't know? I tell you Dan's dead and gone, many years ago."'[66]

Does she have proof of that?

'The old woman's stern, gaunt face,' Cookson told his readers, 'had become once more impassive in its pitiful expression of frozen despair. She was looking out of doors – out to where the rain was still steadily drenching the half-flooded countryside – gazing, with the rapt air of one who beholds a vision afar off, at something invisible to all save her. Then she spoke, slowly and abstractedly.

"Dan is dead. No one knows it better than I do. Yes; I have the proof. Look!" and she turned to *The Sun* representative, and in a voice that, though feeble, was almost a scream, exclaimed: "If Dan Kelly was alive all these years, wouldn't he have come to me? Would he let me want and go hungry, as I have done? Would he have seen me ending my life in this misery and done nothing to help me? Wouldn't he have told Jim?"'[67]

Thirty years on, she had no doubts as to the root cause of the whole outbreak. 'People blame my boys for all that has happened,' she told the intrepid journalist. 'They should blame the police. They were at the bottom of it all. We were all living so happily at the old homestead. We were not getting too rich, but were doing all right. The trouble began over a young constable named Fitzpatrick. That was in April 1878. He came to our place over there and said he was going to arrest Dan. He started the trouble. He tried to kiss my daughter, Kate. He had no business there at all, they tell me – no warrant or anything. If he had, he should have done his business and gone . . .

'Oh, you can't imagine what I suffered. You can't understand what it means, to us poor people in the bush, to be taken away from all that we have – our children. But they took me away, and I had to stay in prison for years. And for nothing – for nothing at all. Because I never touched that constable – his name was Fitzpatrick – at all. I had no part in his being hurt. That was all his own fault. I declare this to you now, declare it before the God I shall soon see, and by my hope of salvation after a life of dreadful trouble, that I did nothing to Fitzpatrick. It was all untrue. And they tore me away from my children and shut me up in prison for years . . . That was the beginning. The police are to blame for everything that happened afterwards.'[68]

—

As Ellen became ever more frail, it was Jim who continued to care for her with noted tenderness. In 1923, when another journalist, this one from *Smith's Weekly*, journeyed to find them both, Jim was nothing if not caring in his attitude to his mother.

'My chief concern,' he told the journalist when Ellen was out of hearing, 'is to look after the poor old soul. She has been a great mother to us all, and the least I can do now is to make her happy.'

Ellen felt equally warmly about Jim, telling the journalist when her son was out of hearing in turn, 'Jim is just wonderful, a fine son! I want him to go down to Wangaratta. He could earn a good living there as a bootmaker. But he won't leave me . . .'[69]

Ned remained a presence in their lives, with the facial portrait taken the day before he was hanged prominently displayed. With her walking stick, the old and fragile woman pointed to the photo of her powerful, robust son, now in his grave for over forty years, and said, 'Ned was a great son. He was the only dark one of the family. All the rest were red-headed. They took after their father. But poor Ned was black like meself.'

She paused, and nodded towards Ned's photo once more: 'Ned would have made a great general in the war.'

Another pause.

'A great general, no matter what side he had been on.'[70]

Ellen Kelly died at Greta West just a few weeks later, on 27 March 1923, at the age of ninety-one, with Jim of course at her side. She was buried in Greta Cemetery. She had borne twelve children, outlived her first husband, Red, by nearly sixty years and outlived all but five of her children.

As to Jim Kelly, he stayed living in the same house for the rest of his days, never marrying – 'How could I give any woman my last name?' he would say[71] – and finally died, as a respected figure of his community and the patriarch of his wider family, in 1946. He was eighty-seven.

—

The longest lived of all the Kelly siblings was the second youngest of them, John, who was the second child of the union between Ellen and George King, born in March 1875. Too young to personally remember anything but a whisper of the events that made his brothers infamous, John went on to lead a peripatetic life that included, after a long stint as a 'world champion' stockwhip cracker, stunt rider and rope spinner with Wirth's Circus, serving with the mounted section of the Western Australia Police Force. John Kelly, Regimental number 880, became a probationary constable on 12 March 1906, and a second-class constable from 1 August of the same year. Though he only stayed a couple of years, before returning to the circus, he served with honour, and went on to travel the world as before, doing stunt-riding and whip-cracking with Barnum & Bailey's Circus. He enlisted in the Australian Army and served on the Western Front, rising to the rank of sergeant, and then became an instructor at the El Caballo Blanco riding school in Argentina, finally dying in Buenos Aires in 1956, aged eighty-one.

As to the longest lived of the members of the Kelly Gang, that was Joe Byrne's youngest sister, Ellen. Born on 7 February 1871, she made it all the way to the 1960s. In 1964, the author Ian Jones found her living in the Mercy Hospital in Albury and was stunned at her clear resemblance to her brother, killed eighty-four years earlier. He interviewed her several times over the following few weeks, recording her family's oral history of Joe, and it was as well, for she died soon after he began, on 5 August 1964, aged ninety-two.

—

Of all those involved in the Kelly siege at Glenrowan, not surprisingly, the last person left standing was Bridget Reardon, the tiny baby carried in her mother's arms from the Glenrowan Inn, while Sergeant Steele fired at them – with two bullets penetrating her shawl. She never moved far from the scene of the action, marrying and raising four children, finally dying in Benalla in 1966 aged eighty-six.[72] Her brother Michael, who was shot by Steele, carried the bullet in his shoulder until his own death in 1942.

—

And Ned himself?

Of course, he was long deeply mourned – perhaps by no one so much as Steve Hart's younger sister, Ettie. Details on her relationship with Ned are scratchy at best, though it was certainly the view of the police in the lead-up to the siege of Glenrowan that, wherever she was, Ned was unlikely to be far away, and she was definitely a supportive figure to him throughout his imprisonment, committal hearing and trial. As Ned's hanging approached, Ettie based herself with the rest of the Kelly family at the Robert Burns Hotel, and was active in both the Reprieve Committee and in collecting signatures for the petition.

She deeply mourned his death at the time and, seemingly, ever afterwards. She eventually married some three years later one of Ned's good friends, John Williams. Ettie and her husband, John, with their two children, became one of the most prosperous and successful farming families in North-Eastern Victoria, eventually settling in Rutherglen, where their magnificent country estate and elaborate mansion, Olive Hills, can still be seen today.

Most interestingly, in her scrapbook, now in the possession of her great-great-grandson Paul O'Keefe of Sydney's Northern Beaches, there is a poem in her hand that appears to have been written by her. Its words seem to fit one who is still mourning her lost love, Ned Kelly, gone to be with her brother Steve Hart:

Oh we will not weep
for those that sleep
beneath the shady
mould for they lofted
rest on Jesus' breast and
triumph the last sound

Like Brother you have gone
To the home of your rest
Where suffering can no
Longer harm you but
If it pleases God with
His endless joys to choose
You.[73]
Esther 'Ettie' Hart, 1861–1926

—

Beyond personal memories, however, Ned's *legend* lived on. For there was something about his story that not only fascinated his fellow Australians at the time but has continued to absorb every generation that has followed. In 1906, one of the *world's* first feature films, *The Story of the Kelly Gang*, made in Victoria, played in the Athenaeum in Melbourne. As commented by *The Argus*, 'the best scene is the attempt to wreck the special train beyond Glenrowan by tearing up the metals and sleepers. The next good picture is the capture of Kelly. For those who have only read highly-coloured accounts of the career of the gang and their doings the biography will give a very good idea of the last of the Victorian bushrangers.'[74]

The film was very popular – in fact, so much so that, with so many other films on bushranging subsequently coming out, in 1912 both Victoria and New South Wales passed laws against further such films being made, for fear that the Kellys and criminality were being romanticised. (God forbid.)

Nevertheless, there have been many Kelly films since, including two mass-release feature films: *Ned Kelly*, starring Mick Jagger, in 1970, and *Ned Kelly*, with Heath Ledger in the lead role, in 2003. Neither enjoyed major box-office success.

And, of course, there have been the books, of which this one is merely the latest. The most outstanding of the secondary sources, in my view – and to which I acknowledge the debt of this book – are *The Complete Inner History of the Kelly Gang*, J. J. Kenneally (1929); *Ned Kelly: Australian Son*, Max Brown (1948); *Ned Kelly: A Short Life*, Ian Jones (1995); *The Fatal Friendship: Ned Kelly, Aaron Sherritt and Joe Byrne*, Ian Jones (1992); *I Am Ned Kelly*, John Molony (1980); *Ned Kelly: The Authentic Illustrated History*, Keith McMenomy (1984); *The Ned Kelly Encyclopaedia*, Justin Corfield (2003); *The Kelly Outbreak 1878–1880*, John McQuilton (1979); *The Trial of Ned Kelly*, J. H. Philips (1987); *A True Narrative of the Kelly Gang*, Thomas McIntyre (1902); and *The Kelly Gang: The Outlaws of the Wombat Ranges (The Mansfield Pamphlet)*, G. W. Hall (1879).

In the world of the arts, Ned has been a frequent and famous subject, never more so than in the series of twenty-seven iconic paintings by Sidney Nolan interpreting the life and times of Ned Kelly, using the tale to explore themes of injustice, love and betrayal, while capturing the Australian countryside.

Beyond books, films and paintings, however, Ned lives on as a cultural phenomenon, a figure beloved by many, reviled by a few, with his image frequently showing up as a tattoo, often on the torsos and arms of hard men in trouble with the law. The phrase 'As game as Ned Kelly' is a high compliment in the popular vernacular.

In my last book, on the Eureka Stockade, I treasured a quote from one Paul Murphy, founder of Eureka's Children, who said, 'Whenever you see the Eureka flag, whether it's farmers in Mildura, soccer fans or on building sites, it simply means "I'm pissed off with whoever's in charge",'[75] and the image of Ned as a tattoo has a similar feel about it, with perhaps the addendum that it also states, 'And I am actively fighting against it.'

As to what happened to Ned himself, therein lies a staggering and convoluted tale, littered with rumours, intrigue, crime, politics and law, featuring farmers, policemen, relatives of Ned and even a stripper from New Zealand – all of it leaving the truth of the matter very difficult to determine. In recent times, even after a decade of archaeological, forensic and historical examination, which has laid many old myths to rest and uncovered many truths, mysteries continue to surround Ned's bones – most particularly his skull.

—

For just under fifty years, Ned's corpse lay with other executed criminals inside the walls of Melbourne Gaol, which was closed in July of 1924, with a portion of the buildings and land set apart for educational purposes. In early 1929, excavations were commenced for the foundations of additions to the Working Men's College, and the remains of those criminals were quickly unearthed. The quicklime, which was supposed to have aided in the quick decomposition of the remains, had not quite done its job. It was recorded that the workmen and onlookers were most fascinated, and 'unpleasant happenings occurred, it being alleged that graves were rifled and bones carried away as souvenirs'.[76]

As for Ned's remains, the most comprehensive contemporary newspaper report had it that, on 12 April 1929, after finding 'a stone marked "E.K." and bearing the imprint of the broad arrow',[77] the workmen came on to Ned's coffin.

'The bones were found when the lip of a steel shovel tore the lid from the rough wooden coffin in which Kelly's body was buried. The coffin was five or six feet below the additional level of the gaol yard. Immediately the discovery was made there was a rush to the grave. The bones, which were remarkably well preserved, were taken by the workmen to be kept as mementos. H. Lee, the contractor of Richmond, secured the skull. There was a complete set of teeth on the upper jaw. Morbid souvenir hunters removed most of the bones.'[78]

To save embarrassment, the authorities were said to have retrieved most of the bones from the looters, though the whole affair was rather haphazard. It was decided that the bodies would be exhumed and reburied in the yard of the Penal Establishment at Pentridge in Coburg, around six miles north of the Melbourne Gaol. Among the remains of forty-seven men moved to Pentridge and reinterred into three mass graves was Ned. (The irony being that the last time Ned had left Pentridge, he had said, 'I would rather face the gallows than go to gaol again.'[79] In the case of Pentridge Gaol, curiously, he had now done both.)

Pentridge remained in operation as a prison until 1997, when it was sold to private developers, by which time the precise location of the graveyard and Ned's remains had been forgotten. A series of excavations, overseen by Heritage Victoria, were conducted from 2006, and two of the three mass graves from 1929 were quickly discovered, though the third one 'containing the remains of 15 more men, probably including Kelly'[80] was not found until February 2009.

Given the historical significance, and the popular and political interest in the remains of Ned Kelly, the Victorian Institute of Forensic

Medicine (VIFM) moved quickly, but another mystery was unfolding – concerning the head of Ned.

There is no official documentation from the day after Ned's execution, and before his burial, saying that a post-mortem was carried out on his body. Many authors and journalists have relied on a short report by a 'gossiping correspondent'[81] in the *Bendigo Independent* published on 19 November 1880, asserted that, after Kreitmayer took the mould of Ned's head for the death mask, his 'body was at the mercy of science – a group of doctors and students. The head was sawn off and the brain removed – a pointless atrocity that has been common knowledge for many years. The brain would be given some spurious scientific value, preserved in a jar; the head, stripped of flesh, would be kept purely as a curio, supposedly as a paper weight on the table of some minor government official.'[82] The newspaper report states that the 'skull was taken possession of by one gentleman, and it is probable that he may hereafter enlighten us upon the peculiarities of the great criminal's brain'.[83]

This scenario has proved difficult to verify. Researcher Helen Harris located records that document enquiries refuting the *Bendigo Independent*'s claims that Kelly's body was subject to an autopsy by medical students after his execution. An example of this evidence is a letter from the prison Governor, John Castieau, stating that there was no truth to the dissection rumours.[84] I might add that my own principal researcher, Libby Effeney, also looked far and wide, long and strong, for 'official' documentation recording such an occurrence, but found no evidence to back up the sole claims of the *Bendigo Independent*.

To add to these muddied waters, there goes the story that back in 1929, when the remains of Ned had been discovered at the old Melbourne Gaol site, the foreman on the site secured what he thought was Ned's skull. This skull eventually found its way to Colin Mackenzie, the first director of the Australian Institute of Anatomy in Canberra. The institute made a cast of the skull and then turned it over to the National Trust in 1972, which put it on display in the museum of the Old Melbourne Gaol, next to Ned's death mask. In 1978, the skull, which had at some point been labelled 'E. Kelly', was stolen.

(Everyone still with me? God bless you, tree people, I am singing for you, too.)

Tom Baxter, a farmer from Western Australia, emerged in 1999 to say that he was in possession of the skull of Ned Kelly, the very one stolen from the Melbourne Gaol Museum, yet did not want to hand it over for examination. In 2008, Heritage Victoria reached out to Mr Baxter, who, without saying how he came into possession of it, agreed to return the skull on 11 November 2009, 129 years to the day after Kelly's execution.

The VIFM analysed the Baxter skull, comparing it with the replica that had been made at the Institute of Anatomy, and all the images matched up. 'They also located a tooth – kept by the grandson of a workman present at the 1929 exhumation – and it fit perfectly.'[85] Furthermore, they compared a CT scan of the skull with the CT scans of the death masks of some, though not all, of the men executed at Melbourne. 'These comparisons eliminated all but two men: Frederick Deeming, a serial killer who was suspected of having been Jack the Ripper, and Ned Kelly.'[86] And so the mystery is, at the least, narrowed down! This could be Ned's skull.

But was it? Let the forensics continue . . .

In September of the following year, 2010, the coroner was satisfied that a clear history of the excavation site at Pentridge had been established, thereby determining that no inquest was required to be performed on the unidentified remains. With that, the team at the VIFM worked in conjunction with an Argentine Forensic Anthropology Team, running mitochondrial DNA (mtDNA) tests on the remains found at Pentridge (they tested thirty left clavicles, to be precise), the Baxter skull and a sample from a Melbourne high-school teacher, Leigh Olver, who is the living great-grandson of Ned's little sister Ellen.

The tests found that the mtDNA from Mr Olver was a match to a set of remains that were found in the third mass grave in 2009. There was no match, however, with the Baxter skull. The Baxter skull turned out to match another set of remains that are in fragmentary condition, and hypothesised to be Deeming, who is thought to have been buried close to Kelly.

Of all the remains exhumed from the mass graves, it turns out that Ned's were among the most intact. 'They were missing only a few cervical vertebrae, some small bones, and the skull, except for a palm-sized fragment.'[87] Though the mtDNA tests are conclusive enough, this small fragment lends further proof that the complete Baxter skull is not Ned's, and that the stories of Ned's body being targeted by trophy hunters in 1929 are unlikely. Furthermore, the bones showed unmistakable evidence of Kelly's injuries from the shoot-out at the Glenrowan Inn, which matched the injuries documented by Dr Shields after Ned's arrest.

The question still remains: was Ned's head sawn off, as Jones claims? Almost certainly. Upon examination, the skull fragment found with the Kelly remains 'came from the back of his cranium, and shows saw marks across the top and down the sides. The cuts clearly continue on the cervical vertebrae below. This tells us that a physician had explored the remains of Kelly with more than his eyes. In that era, authorities were concerned with whether hanging was indeed an instantaneous, humane form of execution.'[88] It has been hypothesised by the forensics team that the saw marks found on Ned's remains are evidence of at least a limited autopsy being conducted on his body, probably to examine the effect of execution on the interior back half of the neck. However, still no official government record of this has come to light.

With the current evidence, it is impossible to establish what happened to the rest of Ned's skull, or, indeed, if he had been buried with or without it. Perhaps, as Ian Jones postulated, some minor government official used it as a paperweight in 1880, or perhaps it sits on a pool-room shelf somewhere, or perhaps it is long gone, decomposed many years ago.

Thanks to many people's hard work, what we do know is that the back of his skull was sawn open after his execution, that he was buried at old Melbourne Gaol and exhumed in 1929, and that most of his remains were not taken by trophy hunters but were reinterred at

Pentridge. The rest, at this point in history, is open for interpretation.

What to finally do with his remains, however?

Well, the last words of Ned's final letter to the Governor, which he dictated to Warder Buck on 10 November 1880, just a day before he faced the gallows, expressed two wishes. The first was that his mother be released before his execution, and his final wish was that 'you would grant permission for my friends to have my body that they might bury it in consecrated ground'.[89]

And so, finally, on 1 August 2012, 132 years after Ned Kelly was killed, the Victorian Attorney General Robert Clark issued a new exhumation license so that Ned's remains could be returned to the Kelly family.

Ned's family chose to indeed bury him in consecrated ground, at Greta Cemetery, where his mother, Ellen, and brother Dan also rest.

On 20 January 2013, in an episode that made front-page news around the country, Ned was buried in an unmarked grave in the consecrated ground of Greta Cemetery, his coffin encased in concrete to deter looters.

The publicity surrounding Ned's reburial prompted yet one more wave of analysis as to whether Ned was a good man or a bad man. It is a question that has divided the nation since Ned's demise. In the course of researching this book, I found myself with my principal researcher Libby Effeney in Glenrowan in early May 2013, and we visited the dining room of the Glenrowan pub, where there is a replica of Ned's armour. I had just finished trying on the helmet when a couple of kids came in, a seven-year-old lad and his five-year-old sister.

'Do you know who this is?' I asked.

'Ned Kelly!' they replied in happy unison.

'Was he a good man or a bad man?'

'Bad man!' cried the little boy, even as, at exactly the same time, his sister shouted with conviction, 'Good man!'

It is much the same answer that two halves of the Australian population have given since, frequently, and with just as much certainty.

And even when it comes to experts on the subject, the division remains. The greatest Kelly writer of them all, Ian Jones, wrote in his iconic book of Ned, 'Perhaps he was the only real Robin Hood who has ever lived,' while a Victorian journalist I admire, who worked on the ABC/Channel 4 documentary *Outlawed: The Real Ned Kelly*, Christopher Bantick, in January 2013, decried the ongoing mythologising of Kelly as a hero, asserting that our most famous bushranger was, in fact, 'psychotic and dangerous'. 'How he has been excused,' Bantick went on, 'from planning mass murder at Glenrowan is an interesting example of distorted historical revisionism. The Glenrowan incident was by any measure a calculated bloodbath of Port Arthur proportions.'[90]

Both views have ample echoes throughout the generations, with Malcolm Ellis's view in the *Bulletin*, 31 December 1966, being a particular standout when he described Ned Kelly as 'one of the most cold-blooded, egotistical, and utterly self-centred criminals who ever decorated the end of a rope in an Australian jail'.[91]

For what it's worth, I disagree – and am far closer to the Jones end of the equation. (And I note with acidity that, while Stanhope O'Connor is generally well remembered for his place in the Kelly saga, he is a man who led a party of his native troopers to massacre thirty-two innocent Aboriginal men at Cape Bedford in 1879 – still with barely a word of criticism to this day!)

Ned Kelly was not born bad, and nor did he choose criminality out of some whimsical, evil desire to break the law. In another environment, he really would have made a first-class soldier, if not officer . . . if not General. He was born to a sea of troubles, and really did take arms against them. And horses. And whole towns . . .

He was both a product of his times and an extraordinary product thereof, an Australian creation forged in wrought iron, whose deeds and misdeeds have *no* parallel in human history. He was an exceptional man, and my own hope, cited on the opening pages – to use Ned's own words quoted at the beginning of the book – is that the public in judging a case like Ned's 'should remember that the darkest life may have a bright side, and that after the worst has been said against a man, he may, if he is heard, tell a story in his own rough way that will perhaps lead them to intimate the harshness of their thoughts against him, and find as many excuses for him as he would plead for himself'.[92]

Vale, Ned Kelly.

You were a one-off.

You were an Australian original.

Mate, we remember you.

NOTES AND REFERENCES

CHAPTER ONE: BORN A KELLY

1. There is endless speculation as to Ned's date of birth, with some experts believing it to be as late as June 1855, and many believing he was born in Wallan Wallan. Referring to a number of other records, I have surmised that the account I give here is the most accurate.
2. I have described the Kelly hut that was said to have been built in 1859 and still stands at Beveridge today. The precise layout and structure of the Kelly hut at Beveridge in 1854 is unknown, but I presume it would have been made of the same materials and have a similar design.
3. Hall, p. 7.
4. Buckley, p. 192. It is my assumption that this was the ritual used.
5. Brown, *Australian Son*, p. 14
6. *Kilmore Free Press*, 11 May 1865, p. 4.
7. Ibid.
8. Ibid.
9. *Kilmore Free Press*, 1 June 1865, p. 4.
10. *The Sydney Morning Herald*, 30 March 1865, p. 4.
11. *Kilmore Free Press*, 13 April 1865, p. 2.
12. Bottle, p. 181.
13. *Kilmore Free Press*, 13 April 1865, p. 2.
14. Ibid.
15. *The Sydney Morning Herald*, 10 February 1865, p. 4.
16. King, p. 119.
17. Ibid.
18. Clune, *The Kelly Hunters*, p. 50. Frank Clune records this as a saying used throughout the colony at this time when stock theft was common. Anyone looking for his 'strayed' or 'lost' animal would likely find it being preserved in a neighbour's brine cask, no longer identifiable.
19. Jones, *Ned Kelly: A Short Life*, p. 25.
20. Clune, *The Kelly Hunters*, p. 51.

21. Ibid., p. 53.
22. Jones, *Ned Kelly: A Short Life*, p. 17.
23. Ibid., p. 22.
24. Lake and Kelly, p. 88.
25. Burgoyne, p. 38.
26. Clune, *The Kelly Hunters*, p. 53.
27. Burgoyne, p. 18.
28. *The Ovens and Murray Advertiser*, 19 April 1879, in McQuilton, p. 7.
29. Clune, *The Kelly Hunters*, p. 53.
30. *Victoria Police Gazette*, 6 June 1867, p. 224.
31. This was the usual phraseology used by judges at the time.
32. The regulations under the *Grant Act 1865* were designed to blunt squatters' tactics that allowed them to take up all the prime land. Under the previous two Acts, a person could select land and then purchase it within a short period of time. A seven-year lease, however, made swift alienation of land more difficult. Like the Acts before it, the squatters found various ways to subvert the intention of this Act.
33. Moyal, p. 17.
34. Though sometimes spelt as Skilling, in police documents he is Skillion, and that is what I have gone with.
35. Though his real name was Henry Johnstone, his bushranger name was Harry Power, and to avoid confusion I have used that throughout.
36. *The Argus*, 10 March 1877, p. 4.
37. Ibid.
38. Ibid.
39. Dickens, 'Great Expectations', *All the Year Round*, No. 84, 1 December 1860, p. 169, www.djo.org.uk/all-the-year-round/volume-iv/page-169.html.
40. Hare, p. 94.
41. Clune, *The Kelly Hunters*, p. 65.
42. *The Ovens and Murray Advertiser*, 30 October 1869, p. 4.
43. Ibid., 19 June 1869, p. 2.
44. Sadleir, pp. 281–2.
45. *The Ovens and Murray Advertiser*, 19 October 1869, p. 2.
46. Ibid., 30 October 1869, p. 4.
47. Ibid., 19 October 1869, p. 2.
48. Clune, *The Kelly Hunters*, p. 65; *Bendigo Advertiser*, 18 June 1904, p. 6, NLA Trove online resource: http://trove.nla.gov.au/ndp/del/article/89879429.
49. *Bendigo Advertiser*, 18 June 1904, p. 6, NLA Trove online resource:

http://trove.nla.gov.au/ndp/del/article/89879429.
50. Based on *The Ovens and Murray Advertiser*, 30 October 1869, p. 4 (reported speech changed to direct speech).
51. Ibid.
52. *Benalla Ensign*, 29 October 1869, p. 2, NLA Trove online resource: http://trove.nla.gov.au/ndp/del/article/66837804.
53. Based on *Benalla Ensign*, 29 October 1869, p. 3, NLA Trove online resource: http://trove.nla.gov.au/ndp/del/article/66837804 (reported speech changed to direct speech).
54. *The Ovens and Murray Advertiser*, 30 October 1869, p. 4.
55. Based on *Benalla Ensign*, 29 October 1869, p. 3, NLA Trove online resource: http://trove.nla.gov.au/ndp/del/article/66837804 (reported speech changed to direct speech).
56. Jones, *Ned Kelly: A Short Life*, p. 35.
57. *Benalla Ensign*, 6 May 1870, p. 2.
58. Ibid., 18 March 1870, p. 2.
59. Ashmead, p. 17.
60. Based on *Benalla Ensign*, 18 March 1870, p. 2 (reported speech changed to direct speech).
61. Ibid.
62. Ibid.
63. Standish, p. 593.
64. Sadleir, p. 71.
65. *The Ovens and Murray Advertiser*, 24 May 1870, p. 2.
66. Sadleir, p. 267.
67. Haldane, p. 58.
68. *Benalla Ensign*, 1 April 1870, p. 2.

CHAPTER TWO: TROUBLED TIMES

1. C. H. Nicolson, 7 September 1881, Royal Commission on the Police Force of Victoria, SLV, Q.16861, p. 624.
2. *The Argus*, 10 March 1877, p. 4, NLA Trove online resource: http://trove.nla.gov.au/ndp/del/article/5915473.
3. Hare, p. 94.
4. Jones, *Ned Kelly: A Short Life*, p. 42.
5. *Benalla Ensign*, 6 May 1870, p. 2.
6. Ibid.
7. Ibid.
8. *The Ovens and Murray Advertiser*, 10 May 1870, p. 2.

9. *Benalla Ensign*, 6 May 1870, p. 2.
10. C. H. Nicolson, 7 September 1881, Royal Commission on the Police Force of Victoria, SLV, Q.16861, p. 624.
11. Hare, p. 93.
12. C. H. Nicolson, 7 September 1881, Royal Commission on the Police Force of Victoria, SLV, Q.16861, p. 624.
13. Ibid.
14. Ibid.
15. *Benalla Ensign*, 13 May 1870, p. 2.
16. F. A. Hare, 5 April 1881, Royal Commission on the Police Force of Victoria, SLV, Q.1586, p. 93.
17. C. H. Nicolson, 7 September 1881, Royal Commission on the Police Force of Victoria, SLV, Q.16861, p. 624.
18. Ibid.
19. Ibid.
20. Sadleir, p. 161.
21. *Kyneton Observer*, 4 June 1870, p. 2.
22. *The Argus*, 10 March 1877, p. 4, NLA Trove online resource: http://trove.nla.gov.au/ndp/del/article/5915473.
23. Hare, p. 64.
24. F. A. Hare, 5 April 1881, Royal Commission on the Police Force of Victoria, SLV, Q.1589, p. 93.
25. Ibid.
26. C. H. Nicolson, 7 September 1881, Royal Commission on the Police Force of Victoria, SLV, Q.16861, p. 624.
27. F. A. Hare, 5 April 1881, Royal Commission on the Police Force of Victoria, SLV, Q.1589, p. 93.
28. *The Brisbane Courier*, 20 December 1890, p. 6. NLA Trove online resource: http://trove.nla.gov.au/ndp/del/article/3507773.
29. Ibid.
30. Ibid.
31. Clune, *The Kelly Hunters*, p. 75.
32. Hare, p. 71.
33. F. A. Hare, 5 April 1881, Royal Commission on the Police Force of Victoria, SLV, Q.1589, p. 93.
34. C. H. Nicolson, 7 September 1881, Royal Commission on the Police Force of Victoria, SLV, Q.16861, p. 624.
35. Sadleir, p. 163.
36. C. H. Nicolson, 29 March 1881, Royal Commission on the Police Force of Victoria, SLV, Q.955, p. 44.

37. *Benalla Ensign*, 10 June 1870, p. 2.
38. E. Kelly, Letter to Sergeant James Babington, 28 July 1870, PROV, VPRS 937, P0, Unit 272, seen online at PROV, http://prov.vic.gov.au/whats-on/exhibitions/ned-kelly/the-kelly-story/the-kelly-family/ned-kelly-to-sergeant-babington.
39. *The Argus*, 5 August 1870, p. 5, NLA Trove online resource: http://trove.nla.gov.au/ndp/del/article/5827938.
40. Ibid.
41. E. Kelly, Jerilderie Letter, February 1879, SLV, MS 13361, p. 1.
42. Police Magistrate's Notebooks, Wangaratta, 10 November 1870, PROV, VPRS 1503, P0, Unit 4.
43. E. Kelly, Jerilderie Letter, February 1879, SLV, MS 13361, p. 4.
44. Ibid.
45. Based on ibid. (reported speech changed to direct speech).
46. *The Ovens and Murray Advertiser*, 12 November 1870, p. 3.
47. Ibid.
48. Ibid.
49. Based on ibid. (reported speech changed to direct speech).
50. Police Magistrate's Notebooks, Wangaratta, 10 November 1870, PROV, VPRS 1503, P0, Unit 4.
51. *The Ovens and Murray Advertiser*, 12 November 1870, p. 2.
52. E. Kelly, Jerilderie Letter, February 1879, SLV, MS 13361, p. 7.
53. Coffey, p. 46.
54. Ibid., p. 69.
55. Jones, *Ned Kelly: A Short Life*, p. 57.
56. Ibid.
57. Kenneally, p. 84.
58. Based on E. Kelly, Jerilderie Letter, February 1879, SLV, MS 13361, p. 6, http://slv.vic.gov.au/our-collections/treasures-curios/jerilderie-letter (reported speech changed to direct speech).
59. Hall to Superintendent Barclay, 22 April 1871, PROV, VPRS 937, Unit 413, pp. 2–3.
60. *The Ovens and Murray Advertiser*, 5 August 1871, p. 3.
61. Ibid.
62. McIntyre, Section 4, p. 60.
63. E. Kelly, Jerilderie Letter, February 1879, SLV, MS 13361, pp. 8–9.
64. Ibid., p. 9.
65. Ibid.
66. Ibid., p. 10.
67. Ibid.

68. Jones, *Ned Kelly: A Short Life*, p. 59.
69. Based on E. Kelly, Jerilderie Letter, February 1879, SLV, MS 13361, p. 10 (tense changed).
70. Jones, *Ned Kelly: A Short Life*, p. 59.
71. Hall to Montfort, 20 April 1871, PROV, VPRS 937, Unit 413.
72. Dr McRea to Standish, 15 May 1871, PROV, VPRS 937, Unit 413.
73. *The Ovens and Murray Advertiser*, 2 May 1871, p. 4.
74. Ibid., 4 May 1871, p. 2.
75. Ibid., 5 August 1871, p. 3.
76. Ibid.
77. Ibid.
78. Ibid.
79. Based on ibid. (reported speech changed to direct speech).
80. Ibid.
81. McQuilton, p. 81.
82. Allen, p. 91.
83. *The North Eastern Ensign*, 22 November 1872, p. 2, NLA Trove online resource: http://trove.nla.gov.au/ndp/del/article/70739718?searchTerm=%22Ellen%20Kelly%20and%20Jane%20Graham%22&searchLimits=sortby=dateAsc.
84. E. Kelly, Jerilderie Letter, February 1879, SLV, MS 13361, p. 13.
85. Ibid.
86. *Benalla Ensign*, 22 April 1873, p. 2.
87. Ibid., 4 March 1873, p. 3.
88. Kenneally, p. 84.
89. Jones, *Ned Kelly: A Short Life*, p. 68. A full-length photograph of Ned Kelly in his boxing outfit was taken that day. It surfaced in the 1960s and remains one of only two full-length studies of Ned that are known to exist.
90. Ibid., p. 69.

CHAPTER THREE: WORKING FOR THE MAN

1. Brown, p. 34.
2. Based on *The Ovens and Murray Advertiser*, 21 December 1878, p. 4 (reported speech changed to direct speech).
3. Ashmead, p. 1.
4. Ibid., p. 23.
5. Benalla Petty Session Cause List Book, 23 October 1871, PROV, VPRS 1874, Unit 4.

6. *The North Eastern Ensign*, 8 November 1872, p. 2.
7. Ibid., 22 November 1872, p. 2.
8. Arrests and Convictions of the Quinns, Kellys and Lloyds, Royal Commission on the Police Force of Victoria, Appendix Ten, p. 699.
9. Corfield, p. 316.
10. *Frankston Standard Leader*, 4 February 2013, p. 15. The story of how the two came to meet comes from the work of researcher Steve Jager, who has drawn from oral history of the Frankston area.
11. F. C. Standish, 23 March 1881, Royal Commission on the Police Force of Australia, SLV, Q.182, p. 10.
12. *Daily Southern Cross*, 3 November 1876, p. 2.
13. Ibid.
14. Ibid.
15. Ibid.
16. *Mercury*, 10 October 1876, p. 3.
17. *The Ovens and Murray Advertiser*, 3 October 1876, p. 2.
18. Ibid., 5 August 1876, p. 2.
19. McQuilton, p. 30.
20. Murray, p. 33.
21. *The Argus*, 12 December 1878, p. 5, NLA Trove online resource: http://trove.nla.gov.au/ndp/del/article/5924398.
22. P. Mullane, 20 July 1881, Royal Commission on the Police Force of Victoria, SLV, Q.13530, p. 489.
23. McMenomy, p. 81.
24. Ibid., p. 60.
25. E. Kelly, Jerilderie Letter, February 1879, SLV, MS 13361, p. 16.
26. *The Wangaratta Dispatch*, 17 February 1877, p. 2.
27. E. Kelly, Jerilderie Letter, February 1879, SLV, MS 13361, pp. 16–17.
28. *The Wangaratta Dispatch*, 3 March 1877, p. 3.
29. *The Ovens and Murray Advertiser*, 1 March 1877, p. 3.
30. Based on ibid. (reported speech changed to direct speech).
31. *The Wangaratta Dispatch*, 3 March 1877, p. 3.
32. Brown, pp. 42–3.
33. *The Ovens and Murray Advertiser*, 2 March 1877, p. 3.
34. E. Kelly, Jerilderie Letter, February 1879, SLV, MS 13361, p. 15.
35. Ibid., pp. 15–16.
36. *Kilmore Free Press*, 11 May 1865, p. 4.
37. *The Ovens and Murray Advertiser*, 21 December 1878, p. 4.
38. Ibid., 17 March 1877, p. 2.
39. E. Kelly, Jerilderie Letter, February 1879, SLV, MS 13361, p. 16.

40. Hare, p. 170.
41. Ibid., p. 171.
42. Clune, *The Kelly Hunters*, p. 71.
43. C. H. Nicolson, 29 March 1881, Royal Commission on the Police Force of Victoria, SLV, Q.1020, p. 46.
44. Ibid., p. 47.
45. Ibid.
46. Ibid.
47. Kenneally, p. 18.
48. *Victoria Police Gazette*, 26 September 1877, p. 257.
49. E. Kelly, Jerilderie Letter, February 1879, SLV, MS 13361, p. 16.
50. Clune, *The Kelly Hunters*, p. 123.
51. Hall, p. 26.
52. *Australian Town and Country Journal*, 14 August 1880, p. 9.
53. Ibid.
54. Hall, p. 26.
55. What follows is my assumption, based on Kelly's account of the pain he suffered, and my own consultation with medical experts.
56. *The Age*, 9 August 1880, p. 3.
57. *The Ovens and Murray Advertiser*, 2 October 1877, p. 2.

CHAPTER FOUR: A SIGNIFICANT VISIT

1. Ibid., 11 December 1877, p. 4.
2. Based on ibid.
3. Ibid., 27 November 1877, p. 2 (reported speech changed to direct speech).
4. *The Wangaratta Dispatch*, 24 October 1877, p. 2.
5. Ibid., p. 3.
6. E. Kelly, Jerilderie Letter, February 1879, SLV, MS 13361, p. 18.
7. Deakin, p. 13.
8. Geoffrey Bartlett, 'Berry, Sir Graham (1822–1904)', *Australian Dictionary of Biography*, Vol. 3, http://adb.anu.edu.au/biography/berry-sir-graham-2984.
9. Deakin, p. 16.
10. Ibid.
11. Sadleir, p. 180.
12. Ibid.
13. *Victoria Police Gazette*, 20 March 1878, p. 78.
14. 'Second Progress Report of the Royal Commission of Enquiry into the

Circumstances of the Kelly Outbreak, 1881', Royal Commission on the Police Force of Victoria, p. x.

15. J. Whelan, 13 May 1881, Royal Commission on the Police Force of Victoria, SLV, Q.5945, pp. 235–6.
16. A. Fitzpatrick, 6 July 1881, Royal Commission on the Police Force of Victoria, SLV, Q.12812, p. 463.
17. Warrant to Apprehend Dan Kelly, 5 April 1878, in Regina vs Ellen Kelly, William Williamson and William Skillion, Kelly Historical Collection, PROV, VPRS 4966, P0, Unit 1, Item 4.
18. *Australian Town and Country Journal*, 14 August 1880, p. 9, NLA Trove online resource: http://trove.nla.gov.au/ndp/del/article/70946696.
19. Based on E. Kelly, Jerilderie Letter, February 1879, SLV, MS 13361, p. 22 (reported speech changed to direct speech).
20. *Australian Town and Country Journal*, 14 August 1880, p. 9, NLA Trove online resource: http://trove.nla.gov.au/ndp/del/article/70946696.
21. E. Kelly, Jerilderie Letter, February 1879, SLV, MS 13361, p. 23.
22. *Australian Town and Country Journal*, 14 August 1880, p. 9 (interview with Ned Kelly, Beechworth, Sunday, 9.30 pm, original: 'There is Ned coming along by the side of the house'), NLA Trove online resource: http://trove.nla.gov.au/ndp/del/article/70946696.
23. J. Whelan, 13 May 1881, Royal Commission on the Police Force of Victoria, SLV, Q.5947, p. 236.
24. I have based this account on Fitzpatrick's subsequent testimony together with James Whelan's account of what was said, both in police reports and at the Royal Commission.
25. Deposition of A. Fitzpatrick, 17 May 1878, in Regina vs Ellen Kelly, William Williamson and William Skillion, Kelly Historical Collection, PROV, VPRS 4966, P0, Unit 1, Item 4.
26. *The Ovens and Murray Advertiser*, 10 October 1878, p. 3.
27. Ibid.
28. A. Fitzpatrick, 6 July 1881, Royal Commission on the Police Force of Victoria, SLV, Q.12822, p. 463.
29. Ibid.
30. Ibid.
31. *The Argus*, 22 May 1878, p. 10, NLA Trove online resource: http://trove.nla.gov.au/ndp/del/article/5933379.
32. Ibid.
33. Ibid.

34. Ibid.
35. Deposition of A. Fitzpatrick, 17 May 1878, in Regina vs Ellen Kelly, William Williamson and William Skillion, Kelly Historical Collection, PROV, VPRS 4966, P0, Unit 1, Item 4.
36. Ibid.
37. Ibid.
38. Ibid.
39. Regina vs Ellen Kelly, William Williamson and William Skillion, Kelly Historical Collection, PROV, VPRS 4966, P0, Unit 1, Item 4, pp. 4–5.
40. Ibid.
41. McQuilton, p. 63.
42. A. L. M. Steele, 31 May 1881, Royal Commission on the Police Force of Victoria, p. 319.
43. Ibid.
44. *The Ovens and Murray Advertiser*, 18 April 1878, p. 2.
45. Statement of Strahan, 27 September 1878, in Regina vs Ellen Kelly, William Williamson and William Skillion, Kelly Historical Collection, PROV, VPRS 4966, P0, Unit 1, Item 4.
46. Kenneally, p. 37.
47. Statement of A. L. M. Steele, 17 May 1878, Regina vs Ellen Kelly, William Williamson and William Skillion, Kelly Historical Collection, PROV, VPRS 4966, P0, Unit 1, Item 4.
48. M. E. Ward, 3 May 1881, Royal Commission on the Police Force of Victoria, p. 160.
49. Ibid.
50. Ibid.
51. *Federal Standard* (Chiltern), 25 May 1878, p. 2.
52. Ibid.
53. M. E. Ward, 3 May 1881, Royal Commission on the Police Force of Victoria, SLV, Q.3040, p. 160.
54. Ibid.
55. *The Ovens and Murray Advertiser*, 6 June 1878, p. 2.
56. McIntyre, Section 1, p. 4.
57. E. Kelly, Jerilderie Letter, February 1879, SLV, MS 13361, p. 30.
58. J. Sadleir, 7 April 1881, Royal Commission on the Police Force of Victoria, SLV, Q.1738, p. 105.
59. Superintendent Sadleir to Captain Standish, 29 August 1878, in Royal Commission on the Police Force of Victoria, SLV, Q.1755, p. 107.
60. McIntyre, Section 1, p. 7.
61. Ibid.

62. *The Argus*, 12 December 1878, p. 5.
63. A. L. M. Steele, 31 May 1881, Royal Commission on the Police Force of Victoria, SLV, Q.9133, p. 331.
64. This account is based on an interview with Paul O'Keefe, the grand-nephew of Steve Hart.
65. *The Ovens and Murray Advertiser*, 10 October 1878, p. 3.
66. Ibid., p. 5.
67. Ibid., p. 3.
68. Ibid.
69. Ibid.
70. Statement of A. Fitzpatrick, 22 May 1878, in Regina vs Ellen Kelly, William Williamson and William Skillion, Beechworth Court of Assize, PROV, VPRS 4966, P0, Unit 1, Item 4.
71. *The Ovens and Murray Advertiser*, 10 October 1878, p. 3.
72. Ibid.
73. Kenneally, p. 38.
74. Ibid., p. 42.
75. *The Argus*, 14 October 1878, p. 7.
76. *The Ovens and Murray Advertiser*, 15 October 1878, p. 3.
77. Kenneally, p. 44.
78. *The Ovens and Murray Advertiser*, 15 October 1878, p. 3.
79. Hall, p. 15.
80. *The Ovens and Murray Advertiser*, 12 October 1878, p. 4
81. Kenneally, p. 37.
82. A. Wyatt, 13 April 1881, Royal Commission on the Police Force of Victoria, SLV, Q.2275, p. 131.
83. *The Argus*, 10 August 1880, p. 7, NLA Trove online resource: http://trove.nla.gov.au/ndp/del/article/5961325.
84. Based on Williamson to Inspector Green, 29 October 1878, Appendix 13, Royal Commission on the Police Force of Victoria, p. 702 (reported speech changed to direct speech).
85. *The Ovens and Murray Advertiser*, 21 December 1878, p. 4.
86. A. Wyatt, 13 April 1881, Royal Commission on the Police Force of Victoria, SLV, Q.2327, p. 133.
87. Ibid.
88. Ibid., p. 131.
89. Sadleir to Pewtress, 18 October 1878, Royal Commission on the Police Force of Victoria, p. 106.
90. J. Sadleir, 7 April 1881, Royal Commission on the Police Force of Victoria, SLV, Q.1742, p. 106.

91. *The Argus*, 10 November 1880, p. 6, NLA Trove online resource: http://trove.nla.gov.au/ndp/del/article/5983081.

CHAPTER FIVE: STRINGYBARK CREEK

1. J. Sadleir, 7 April 1881, Royal Commission on the Police Force of Victoria, SLV, Q.1741, p. 106.
2. J. Kelly, 18 May 1881, Royal Commission on the Police Force of Victoria, SLV, Q.7978, p. 299.
3. Ibid.
4. Hall, p. 27.
5. J. Sadleir, 7 April 1881, Royal Commission on the Police Force of Victoria, SLV, Q.1752, p. 10.
6. Ibid., p. 106.
7. McIntyre, Section 1, p. 6.
8. J. Sadleir, 7 April 1881, Royal Commission on the Police Force of Victoria, SLV, Q.1752, p. 106.
9. Based on *The Argus*, 30 October 1878, p. 6, NLA Trove online resource: http://trove.nla.gov.au/ndp/del/article/5919040 (reported speech changed to direct speech).
10. McIntyre, Section 1, p. 11.
11. J. Sadleir, 7 April 1881 (Kennedy to Sadleir), 16 August 1878, Royal Commission on the Police Force of Victoria, SLV, Q.1741, p. 105.
12. J. Sadleir, 7 April 1881 (Sadleir to Kennedy), 10 August 1878, Royal Commission on the Police Force of Victoria, SLV, Q.1738, p. 105.
13. J. Sadleir, 7 April 1881 (Kennedy to Sadleir), 16 August 1878, Royal Commission on the Police Force of Victoria, SLV, Q.1741, p. 105.
14. McIntyre, Section 1, p. 12.
15. Ibid., p. 13.
16. Hall, p. 24.
17. McIntyre, Section 1, p. 16.
18. Ibid., p. 15.
19. Ibid.
20. *The Argus*, 23 June 1877, p. 9.
21. Ibid., 10 March 1877, p. 4, NLA Trove online resource: http://trove.nla.gov.au/ndp/del/article/5915473.
22. The alternative version of this, of course, is that Ned Kelly came across their tracks. I have gone with this version principally because it was the conclusion of the Royal Commission after examining all the evidence, that Sergeant Kennedy 'not only divided his party, but allowed

McIntyre to fire off his rifle at some birds, thus attracting the Kellys to the spot'.

23. E. Kelly, Jerilderie Letter, February 1879, SLV, MS 13361, p. 33.
24. Ibid., p. 14, http://slv.vic.gov.au/our-collections/treasures-curios/jerilderie-letter.
25. Ibid., pp. 30–1. Ned Kelly's and Thomas McIntyre's accounts of how many guns the Kellys had in their possession on this day are different. My best reckoning is that of Ian Jones, that they had two large guns and a pocket revolver.
26. Ibid.
27. McIntyre, Section 1, p. 17.
28. Ibid.
29. E. Kelly, Jerilderie Letter, February 1879, SLV, MS 13361, p. 33.
30. McIntyre, Section 1, p. 17.
31. *South Australian Register*, 7 August 1880, p. 5, NLA Trove online resource: http://trove.nla.gov.au/ndp/del/article/43152058?searchTerm=Have%20you%20got%20any%20firearms&searchLimits.
32. McIntyre, Section 1, p. 17.
33. Ibid., Section 2, p. 19.
34. Statement of Thomas McIntyre in Edward Kelly Capital Case File, Kelly Historical Collection, Part 2, Crown Law Department, PROV, VPRS 4966, P0, Unit 2, Item 10, p. 13.
35. Ibid.
36. *The Argus*, 7 August 1880, p. 8, NLA Trove online resource: http://trove.nla.gov.au/ndp/del/article/5983525?searchTerm=%22why%20should%20we%20have%20poison%22&searchLimits=l-title=13.
37. McIntyre, Section 1, p. 18.
38. Ibid., Section 2, p. 19. In his interview with *The Age*, 9 August 1880, Kelly specifically denied that he had said this.
39. *The Argus*, 7 August 1880, p. 8, NLA Trove online resource: http://trove.nla.gov.au/ndp/del/article/5983525.
40. *The Sydney Morning Herald*, 7 August 1880, p. 6, NLA Trove online resource: http://trove.nla.gov.au/ndp/del/article/28387582.
41. *The Sydney Morning Herald*, 12 November 1878, p. 7, NLA Trove online resource: http://trove.nla.gov.au/ndp/del/article/13423088.
42. McIntyre, Section 1, p. 18.
43. Ibid., p. 17; Victoria Police website, www.police.vic.gov.au/content.asp?Document_ID=10583.
44. *The Australasian Sketcher*, 23 November 1878, p. 129, NLA Trove

online resource: http://trove.nla.gov.au/ndp/del/printArticlePdf/60622471/3?print=n.
45. *The Sydney Morning Herald*, 12 November 1878, p. 7, NLA Trove online resource: http://trove.nla.gov.au/ndp/del/article/13423088.
46. *Australasian Post*, 9 February 1961, p. 22.
47. Deposition of Thomas McIntyre, 31 October 1878, Kelly Historical Collection, Part 5, Miscellaneous Records, PROV, VPRS 4969, P0, Unit 1, Item 23, p. 7.
48. Based on E. Kelly, Jerilderie Letter, February 1879, SLV, MS 13361, pp. 38–9 (reported speech changed to direct speech).
49. *The Argus*, 7 August 1880, p. 8, NLA Trove online resource: http://trove.nla.gov.au/ndp/del/article/5983525.
50. McIntyre, Section 2, p. 19.
51. Ibid., Section 1, p. 18.
52. *The Argus*, 7 August 1880, p. 8, NLA Trove online resource: http://trove.nla.gov.au/ndp/del/article/5983525.
53. Ibid., 19 August 1880, p. 1S, NLA Trove online resource: http://trove.nla.gov.au/ndp/del/article/5959395.
54. *The Age*, 9 August 1880, p. 3.
55. Ibid.
56. Ibid.
57. McIntyre, Section 1, p. 23.
58. Ibid.
59. Edward Kelly Capital Case File, Kelly Historical Collection, Part 2, Crown Law Department, PROV, VPRS 4966, P0, Unit 2, Item 10, p. 23.
60. Ibid., pp. 23–4.
61. McIntyre, Section 2, p. 24.
62. Ibid.
63. *The Age*, 9 August 1880, p. 3.
64. *The Argus*, 30 October 1878, p. 6, NLA Trove online resource: http://trove.nla.gov.au/ndp/del/article/5919040?searchTerm=%22We%20will%20handcuff%20you%22&searchLimits=l-title=13.
65. McIntyre, Section 2, p. 23.
66. *The Argus*, 30 October 1878, p. 6, NLA Trove online resource: http://trove.nla.gov.au/ndp/del/article/5919040.
67. McIntyre, Section 1, p. 22.
68. Ibid., Section 2, p. 22.
69. Ibid.
70. *The Argus*, 9 August 1880, p. 6, NLA Trove online resource: http://

trove.nla.gov.au/ndp/del/article/5978894?searchTerm=%22But%20you%20cannot%20blame%20us%20for%20anything%20Fitzpatrick%20has%20done%22&searchLimits=.

71. Edward Kelly Capital Case File, Kelly Historical Collection, Part 2, Crown Law Department, PROV, VPRS 4966, P0, Unit 2, Item 10, p. 30.
72. Ibid.
73. *The Argus*, 29 October 1878, p. 5, NLA Trove online resource: http://trove.nla.gov.au/ndp/del/article/5918902?searchTerm=%22shoot%20no%20man%20if%20he%22&searchLimits=l-title=13.
74. McMenomy, p. 79.
75. Ibid.
76. Kenneally, p. 73; McMenomy, p. 107.
77. *Yea Chronicle*, 23 August 1900, p. 3, NLA Trove online resource: http://trove.nla.gov.au/ndp/del/article/59950873.
78. *The Argus*, 13 December 1878, p. 5, NLA Trove online resource: http://trove.nla.gov.au/ndp/del/article/5924588.
79. *The Sydney Morning Herald*, 10 August 1880, p. 5, NLA Trove online resource: http://trove.nla.gov.au/ndp/del/article/13465796.
80. *The Sydney Morning Herald*, 13 December 1878, p. 5, NLA Trove online resource: http://trove.nla.gov.au/ndp/del/article/28392421?searchTerm=%22Let%20me%20alone%20to%20live,%20if%20I%20can%22&searchLimits=l-title=35.
81. *The Argus*, 13 December 1878, p. 5, NLA Trove online resource: http://trove.nla.gov.au/ndp/del/article/5924588?searchTerm=%22No,%20I%20forgive%20you,%20and%20may%20God%20forgive%20you%20too%22&searchLimits=sortby=dateAsc.
82. Hare, p. 104.
83. E. Kelly, Euroa Letter, 14 December 1880, PROV, VPRS 4966, P0, Item 3, p. 13.
84. Ibid., p. 12.
85. Constable McIntyre's First Report of Police Murders by Kelly, 28 October 1878, Kelly Historical Collection, Police Branch, PROV, VPRS 4965, P0, Item 317.
86. McIntyre, Section 2, p. 29.
87. Ibid.
88. T. Meehan, 20 September 1881, Royal Commission on the Police Force of Victoria, SLV, Q.17647, p. 667.
89. Ibid., p. 668.
90. McIntyre, Section 2, p. 30.

91. 'Report of Constable McIntyre of the Murders Committed at Stringybark Creek', PROV, VPRS 4966, Consignment, P0 Unit 1, Item 1, p. 9, http://prov.vic.gov.au/whats-on/exhibitions/ned-kelly/the-kelly-story/string-bark-creek/report-of-constable-mcintyre-of-the-murders-committed-at-stringy-bark-creek.
92. *The Argus*, 28 October 1878, p. 5, NLA Trove online resource: http://trove.nla.gov.au/ndp/del/article/5918768?searchTerm=%22and%20others%20left%20now%20on%20horseback%20to%20scour%20the%20country%22&searchLimits=l-title=13.
93. McIntyre, Section 1, p. 32.
94. Gillison, p. 71.
95. McIntyre, Section 1, p. 32.
96. Deposition of Thomas McIntyre, 29 October 1878, Kelly Historical Collection, Part 5, Miscellaneous Records, PROV, VPRS 4969, P0, Unit 1, Item 23, p. 7.
97. *The Argus*, 5 November 1878, p. 6, NLA Trove online resource: http://trove.nla.gov.au/ndp/del/article/5919925.

CHAPTER SIX: AFTER STRINGYBARK

1. Despite *The Argus* saying she was in Pentridge, Ellen Kelly was in fact in Melbourne Gaol at this time.
2. *The Argus*, 28 October 1878, p. 5.
3. Based on F. C. Standish, 23 March 1881, Royal Commission on the Police Force of Victoria, SLV, Q.7, p. 1 (reported speech changed to direct speech).
4. *The Argus*, 29 October 1878, p. 5.
5. *Supplement to the Victoria Government Gazette*, No. 111, 28 October 1878, p. 2599.
6. *The Argus*, 29 October 1878, p. 5, NLA Trove online resource: http://trove.nla.gov.au/ndp/del/article/5918902?searchTerm=%22The%20sorrow%20felt%20for%20the%20death%20of%20Scanlan%20is%20universal%20throughout%20the%20district%22&searchLimits=sortby=dateAsc.
7. Ibid., 30 October 1878, p. 6, NLA Trove online resource: http://trove.nla.gov.au/ndp/del/article/5919040?searchTerm=%22unless%20they%20wanted%20to%20get%20shot%22&searchLimits=sortby=dateAsc.
8. *Mirror* (Perth, Western Australia), 1 August 1953, p. 8, NLA Trove online resource: http://trove.nla.gov.au/ndp/del/article/75736469; *The*

Argus, 30 October 1878, p. 6, NLA Trove online resource: http://trove.nla.gov.au/ndp/del/article/5919040.

9. *The Argus*, 31 October 1878, p. 10, NLA Trove online resource: http://trove.nla.gov.au/ndp/del/article/5919220?searchTerm=%22morning%20for%20using%20threatening%20language%22&searchLimits=sortby=dateAsc.
10. Ibid., 4 November 1878, p. 6, NLA Trove online resource: http://trove.nla.gov.au/ndp/del/article/5919758?searchTerm=%22in%20his%20race%20for%20life%20he%20fell%20from%20horseback%22&searchLimits=.
11. Based on ibid., 21 November 1878, p. 5, NLA Trove online resource: http://trove.nla.gov.au/ndp/del/article/5921848?searchTerm=%22I%20had%20tracked%20the%20Kellys%20and%20their%20horses%20from%20the%20camp%22&searchLimits= (reported speech changed to direct speech).
12. Ibid., 30 October 1878, p. 4, NLA Trove online resource: http://trove.nla.gov.au/ndp/del/article/5919088.
13. *Gippsland Times*, 1 November 1878, p. 3, NLA Trove online resource: http://trove.nla.gov.au/ndp/del/article/62025619?searchTerm=%22Business%20is%20entirely%20suspended%20at%20Mansfield%22&searchLimits=.
14. Sadleir, p. 186.
15. *The Argus*, 30 October 1878, p. 6, NLA Trove online resource: http://trove.nla.gov.au/ndp/del/article/5919040.
16. Based on *The Argus*, 30 October 1878, p. 6, NLA Trove online resource: http://trove.nla.gov.au/ndp/del/article/5919040 (reported speech changed to direct speech).
17. Sadleir, p. 185.
18. Ibid., p. 186.
19. Ibid.
20. J. Sadleir, 6 September 1881, Royal Commission on the Police Force of Victoria, SLV, Q.16659, p. 610.
21. Sadleir, p. 186.
22. Ibid., p. 190.
23. Based on J. Sadleir, 7 April 1881, Royal Commission on the Police Force of Victoria, SLV, Q.1736. p. 105 (reported speech changed to direct speech).
24. Sadleir, p. 191.
25. *The Argus*, 31 October 1878, p. 8, NLA Trove online resource: http://trove.nla.gov.au/ndp/del/article/5919293?searchTerm=%22murdere

rs%20who%20are%20still%20at%20large%22&searchLimits=sortby=dateAsc.

26. Ibid.
27. *Victoria Government Gazette*, No. 114, 1 November 1878, p. 2779.
28. Ibid., No. 113, 30 October 1878, p. 2777.
29. C. H. Chomley, *Yea Chronicle*, 20 September 1900, p. 2, NLA Trove online resource: http://trove.nla.gov.au/ndp/del/article/59950948.
30. *Australasian Sketcher*, 23 November 1878, p. 135.
31. McMenomy, p. 89.
32. *Australasian Sketcher*, 23 November 1878, p. 135, NLA Trove online resource: http://trove.nla.gov.au/ndp/del/article/60622461.
33. *The Argus*, 1 November 1878, p. 5.
34. McIntyre, Section 2, p. 27.
35. Sadleir, p. 187.
36. Ibid.
37. *The Age*, 30 October 1878, p. 3.
38. Parliamentary Debates Legislative Council and Legislative Assembly, 1878, Vol. 1, Melbourne, John Ferres, p. 1593.
39. *The Argus*, 1 November 1878, p. 4, NLA Trove online resource: http://trove.nla.gov.au/ndp/del/article/5919484?searchTerm=%22passed%20through%20all%20its%20stages%20with%20applause%22&searchLimits=.
40. Rickards, p. 128.
41. Ibid., p. 129.
42. Based on ibid. (reported speech changed to direct speech).
43. H. Bracken (Volunteer), Letter, Kelly Historical Collection, Police Branch, PROV, VPRS 4965, P0, Item 159, p. 1.
44. This is consistent with the Catholic ritual at the time for graveside services.
45. *The Mansfield Courier*, 2 November 1878, p. 2.
46. Rickards, p. 129.
47. *Yea Chronicle*, 20 September 1900, p. 2, NLA Trove online resource: http://trove.nla.gov.au/ndp/del/article/59950948.
48. Jones, *Ned Kelly: A Short Life*, p. 131.
49. Ibid.
50. M. Twomey, 8 September 1881, Royal Commission on the Police Force of Victoria, SLV, Q.17403, p. 656.
51. Based on H. Laing, 22 July 1881, Royal Commission on the Police Force of Victoria, SLV, Q.13960, p. 508 (reported speech changed to direct speech).

52. Based on ibid. (tense changed).
53. Based on A. L. M. Steele, 31 May 1881, Royal Commission on the Police Force of Victoria, SLV, Q.8856, p. 320 (reported speech changed to direct speech).
54. Based on ibid., p. 321 (reported speech changed to direct speech).
55. Based on ibid. (reported speech changed to direct speech).
56. H. Laing, 22 July 1881, Royal Commission on the Police Force of Victoria, SLV, Q.13961, p. 509.
57. M. Twomey, 8 September 1881, Royal Commission on the Police Force of Victoria, SLV, Q.17417, p. 656.
58. J. Sadleir, 7 April 1881, Royal Commission on the Police Force of Victoria, SLV, Q.1764, p. 107.
59. Sadleir, p. 196.
60. J. Sadleir, 7 April 1881, Royal Commission on the Police Force of Victoria, SLV, Q.1767, p. 107.
61. Ibid.
62. C. H. Nicolson, 24 March 1881, Royal Commission on the Police Force of Victoria, SLV, Q.366, p. 16.
63. Andrew Lemon, 'Inventing the Melbourne Cup', *The La Trobe Journal*, No. 88, December 2011, p. 10, www.slv.vic.gov.au/latrobejournal/issue/latrobe-88/t1-g-t2.html.
64. C. H. Nicolson, 24 March 1881, Royal Commission on the Police Force of Victoria, SLV, Q.389, p. 17.
65. *The Argus*, 8 November 1878, p. 6, NLA Trove online resource: http://trove.nla.gov.au/ndp/del/article/5920305?searchTerm=&searchLimits=l-publictag=Mansfield+Murders.
66. Sadleir, p. 197.
67. Ibid.
68. *Australasian Sketcher*, 3 July 1880, p. 150.
69. *The Argus*, 8 November 1878, p. 6.
70. Ibid.
71. C. H. Nicolson, 24 March 1881, Royal Commission on the Police Force of Victoria, SLV, Q.405, p. 17.
72. J. Sadleir, 7 April 1881, Royal Commission on the Police Force of Victoria, SLV, Q.1798, p. 109.
73. Ibid.
74. Ibid.
75. Ibid., Q.1848, p. 110.
76. Based on C. H. Nicolson, 24 March 1881, Royal Commission on the Police Force of Victoria, SLV, Q.405a, p. 17 (reported speech changed to direct speech).

77. J. Sadleir, 7 April 1881, Royal Commission on the Police Force of Victoria, SLV, Q.1842, p. 110.
78. Ibid., Q.1848, p. 110.
79. *The Sydney Morning Herald*, 9 November 1878, p. 7, http://news.google.com/newspapers?nid=1301&dat=18781109&id=7dthAAAAIBAJ&sjid=R5EDAAAAIBAJ&pg=7216,5400648.
80. Ibid., Q.12387, p. 445.
81. Ibid., Q.12391, p. 445.
82. C. Johnston, 28 June 1881, Royal Commission on the Police Force of Victoria, SLV, Q.12411, p. 446.
83. Ibid.
84. E. Kelly, Jerilderie Letter, February 1879, SLV, MS 13361, pp. 51–2.
85. C. Johnston, 28 June 1881, Royal Commission on the Police Force of Victoria, SLV, Q.12421, p. 446.
86. Ibid., Q.12465, p. 447.
87. Ibid., Q.12467, p. 447.
88. C. H. Nicolson, 7 September 1881, Royal Commission on the Police Force of Victoria, SLV, Q.16896, p. 631.
89. C. Johnston, 28 June 1881, Royal Commission on the Police Force of Victoria, SLV, Q.12500, p. 448.
90. C. H. Nicolson, 7 September 1881, Royal Commission on the Police Force of Victoria, SLV, Q.16899, p. 632.
91. Based on C. Johnston, 28 June 1881, Royal Commission on the Police Force of Victoria, SLV, Q.12495, p. 448 (reported speech changed to direct speech).
92. Hare, p. 210.
93. Threatening letter received by Monk, Kelly Historical Collection, Part 1 Police Branch, PROV, VPRS 4965, P0, Unit 3, Item 235. After its author, a local called Walter Lynch, was sentenced, Monk received more threatening letters in March and April of 1879. There were investigations and then he was even shot at.
94. *The Argus*, 16 November 1878, p. 8, NLA Trove online resource: http://trove.nla.gov.au/ndp/del/article/5921233?searchTerm=%22for%20an%20order%20adjudging%20the%20Kellys%20and%20the%20two%20unknown%20men%20to%20be%20%22&searchLimits=.
95. Ibid., 10 November 1880, p. 6, NLA Trove online resource: http://trove.nla.gov.au/ndp/del/article/5983081.
96. P. Quinn, Royal Commission on the Police Force of Victoria, SLV, Q.17716, pp. 670–1.
97. Hare, p. 96.

98. *The Sunday Times* (Perth), 19 April 1914, p. 2, NLA Trove online resource: http://trove.nla.gov.au/ndp/del/article/57823264.
99. Based on *The Age*, 13 November 1878, p. 3 (reported speech changed to direct speech).
100. *Bendigo Advertiser*, 14 November 1878, p. 3.
101. Based on Parliamentary Debates, Legislative Council and Legislative Assembly, 1878, Vol. 1, p. 1793 (reported speech changed to direct speech).
102. Based on ibid. (reported speech changed to direct speech).
103. Based on ibid. (reported speech changed to direct speech).
104. Deakin, p. 79.
105. Jones, *Ned Kelly: A Short Life*, p. 132.
106. Hare, p. 177.
107. Sadleir, p. 201.
108. Ibid., p. 205.
109. Ibid.

CHAPTER SEVEN: EUROA

1. Scott, p. 1.
2. Hare, p. 113.
3. Statement of William Fitzgerald, 20 September 1880, Kelly Historical Collection, Part 5, Miscellaneous Records, PROV, VPRS 4969, P0, Unit 1, Item 17.
4. Ibid.
5. Hare, p. 114.
6. Ibid., p. 115.
7. *The Argus*, 10 August 1880, p. 7, NLA Trove online resource: http://trove.nla.gov.au/ndp/del/article/5961325.
8. Ibid., 12 December 1878, p. 6.
9. Ibid.
10. Ibid., 10 August 1880, p. 7.
11. Ibid., 12 December 1878, p. 6, NLA Trove online resource: http://trove.nla.gov.au/ndp/del/printArticlePdf/5924398/3?print=n.
12. Ibid.
13. Ibid., 20 February 1923, p. 7.
14. Hare, p. 116.
15. Ibid., p. 117.
16. Ibid.
17. *The Argus*, 20 February 1923, p. 7.

18. Ibid., 10 August 1880, p. 7, NLA Trove online resource: http://trove.nla.gov.au/ndp/del/article/5961325.
19. Ibid.
20. Ibid.
21. Ibid.
22. Ibid., p. 5.
23. E. Kelly, Euroa Letter, 14 December 1880, PROV, VPRS 4966, P0, Item 3, pp. 8–9.
24. Ibid., p. 15.
25. *The Argus*, 11 August 1880, p. 6, NLA Trove online resource: http://trove.nla.gov.au/ndp/del/article/5971588.
26. Hare, pp. 120–1.
27. *The Argus*, 11 August 1880, p. 6, NLA Trove online resource: http://trove.nla.gov.au/ndp/del/article/5971588?searchTerm=%22report%20you%20to%20your%20superior%20officer%22&searchLimits=sortby=dateAsc.
28. Statement of Henry Dudley, Queen vs Edward Kelly: Murder File, Kelly Historical Collection, Part II, Crown Law Department, PROV, VPRS 4966, P0, Unit 1, Item 2.
29. *The Age*, 13 December 1878, p. 3.
30. *The Argus*, 11 August 1880, p. 6, NLA Trove online resource: http://trove.nla.gov.au/ndp/del/article/5971588.
31. Statement of Henry Dudley in Edward Kelly Capital Case File, Kelly Historical Collection, Part 2, Crown Law Department, PROV, VPRS 4966, P0, Unit 2, Item 10, p. 58, http://wiki.prov.vic.gov.au/index.php/Ned_Kelly_Trial:_Capital_Case_File_and_report_to_the_Governor.
32. *The Argus*, 11 August 1880, p. 6, NLA Trove online resource: http://trove.nla.gov.au/ndp/del/article/5971588.
33. Ibid., 14 December 1878, p. 8.
34. Robert Scott to Chief Manager, 13 December 1878, Kelly Historical Collection, Part 1, Police Branch, PROV, VPRS 4965, P0, Unit 3, Item 165, p. 2.
35. *The Argus*, 12 December 1878, p. 5, NLA Trove online resource: http://trove.nla.gov.au/ndp/del/article/5924398.
36. Hare, p. 125.
37. Ibid.
38. Scott, p. 2.
39. Ibid., p. 3.
40. Ibid., pp. 3–4.
41. Ibid., p. 4.

42. Hare, p. 125.
43. *The Age*, 11 August 1880, p. 3.
44. Scott, p. 3.
45. *The Argus*, 12 December 1878, p. 5.
46. Scott, p. 3.
47. Hare, p. 127.
48. *North Queensland Register*, 1 October 1990, p. 32, NLA Trove online resource: http://trove.nla.gov.au/ndp/del/article/82340128?searchTerm=%22by%20no%20means%20the%20ferocious%20ruffian%20she%22&searchLimits=.
49. Scott, p. 4.
50. Ibid., p. 5.
51. Ibid.
52. Brown, p. 92.
53. Sadleir, p. 203.
54. Ibid.
55. Hare, p. 130.
56. Ibid.
57. *North Queensland Register*, 1 October 1900, p. 31, NLA Trove online resource: http://trove.nla.gov.au/ndp/del/article/82340142?searchTerm=%22not%20even%20neglect%20such%20refinements%20as%22&searchLimits=.
58. Hare, *The Last Bushrangers*, p. 128
59. *The Argus*, 12 December 1878, p. 5.
60. Scott, p. 6.
61. Ibid., p. 7.
62. Ibid., p. 12.
63. Ibid., p. 9.
64. *The Argus*, 12 December 1878, p. 5.
65. Ibid., 11 August 1880, p. 6, NLA Trove online resource: http://trove.nla.gov.au/ndp/del/article/5971588.
66. Ibid., 12 December 1878, p. 5.
67. Ibid.
68. Ibid., 11 August 1880, p. 6, NLA Trove online resource: http://trove.nla.gov.au/ndp/del/article/5971588.
69. Ibid., 12 December 1878, p. 5.
70. A. Wyatt, 12 April 1881, Royal Commission on the Police Force of Victoria, SLV, Q.2127, p. 123.
71. Ibid., Q.2135, p. 123.
72. Ibid., Q.2142, p. 124.

73. Scott, p. 13.
74. Hare, p. 130.
75. *The Argus*, 20 February 1923, p. 7, NLA Trove online resource: http://trove.nla.gov.au/ndp/del/article/1877492?searchTerm=&searchLimits=l-publictag=Kelly+Gang.
76. A. Wyatt, 12 April 1881, Royal Commission on the Police Force of Victoria, SLV, Q.2153, p. 125.
77. Chomley, p. 79.
78. *The Age*, 13 December 1878, p. 3.
79. A. Wyatt, 12 April 1881, Royal Commission on the Police Force of Victoria, SLV, Q.2172 and Q.2162, p. 125.
80. Ibid., Q.2163, p. 125.
81. Ibid., Q.2166, p. 125.
82. *The Argus*, 12 December 1878, p. 5.
83. Ibid.
84. Sadleir, p. 205.
85. Scott, p. 12.
86. Sadleir, p. 207.
87. C. H. Nicolson, 24 March 1881, Royal Commission on the Police Force of Victoria, SLV, Q.551, p. 23.
88. Hare, p. 138.

CHAPTER EIGHT: AFTER EUROA

1. *The Argus*, 12 December 1878, p. 6.
2. Ibid., 11 December 1878, p. 5.
3. *The Age*, 11 December 1878, p. 3.
4. Ibid., 12 December 1878, p. 3.
5. *The Herald* (Melbourne), 11 December 1878, p. 3.
6. Ibid.
7. Ibid., 14 December 1878, p. 2.
8. *Australasian Sketcher*, 21 December 1878, p. 11.
9. *The Herald* (Melbourne), 12 December 1878, p. 3.
10. F. C. Standish, 23 March 1881, Royal Commission on the Police Force of Victoria, SLV, Q.25, p. 2.
11. Hare, p. 93.
12. Ibid., p. 95.
13. Ibid., p. 140.
14. *The Herald* (Melbourne), 14 December 1878, p. 2.
15. *Queenslander*, 21 June 1879, p. 790.

16. Second Progress Report of the Royal Commission of Enquiry into the Circumstances of the Kelly Outbreak, 1881, p. xv.
17. Scott, p. 14.
18. Chief Commissioner of Police Standish to Chief Secretary Berry, 13 December 1878, PROV, VPRS 4969, P0, Unit 1, Item 18, Record 4.
19. McMenomy, p. 136.
20. S. O'Connor, 30 March 1881, Royal Commission on the Police Force of Victoria, SLV, Q.1104, p. 51.
21. Based on *The Argus*, 30 October 1880, p. 8 (reported speech changed to direct speech).
22. Ibid., http://trove.nla.gov.au/ndp/del/article/5919758.
23. J. Sadleir, 13 April 1881, Royal Commission on the Police Force of Victoria, SLV, Q.2490, p. 139.
24. E. Kelly, Euroa Letter, 14 December 1880, PROV, VPRS 4966, P0, Unit 1, Item 3, p. 17.
25. Captain Standish and Superintendent Hare in Charge of the Pursuit, Victoria Police Commission, Second Progress Report of the Royal Commission of Enquiry into the Circumstances of the Kelly Outbreak, 1881, p. xvi.
26. The Queensland Trackers, Victoria Police Commission, Second Progress Report of the Royal Commission of Enquiry into the Circumstances of the Kelly Outbreak, 1881, p. xvi.
27. Sadleir, p. 268.
28. S. O'Connor, 29 March 1881, Royal Commission on the Police Force of Victoria, SLV, Q.1093, p. 50.
29. P. Mullane, 20 July 1881, Royal Commission on the Police Force of Victoria, SLV, Q.13519, p. 488.
30. E. Kelly, Euroa Letter, 14 December 1880, PROV, VPRS 4966, P0, Unit 1, Item 3, p. 2.
31. Ibid., p. 16.
32. *The Argus*, 18 December 1878, p. 6.
33. E. Kelly, Euroa Letter, 14 December 1880, PROV, VPRS 4966, P0, Unit 1, Item 3, p. 2.
34. Ibid., pp. 7–8.
35. Ibid., p. 9, http://prov.vic.gov.au/whats-on/exhibitions/ned-kelly/the-kelly-story/euroa/edward-kelly-gives-statement-of-his-murders-of-sergeant-kennedy-and-others-and-makes-other-threats.
36. Ibid., pp. 15–16.
37. Chief Commissioner of Police Standish to Chief Secretary Berry, 18 December 1878, PROV, VPRS 4969, P0, Unit 1, Item 18, Record 2.

38. *The Herald* (Melbourne), 18 December 1878, p. 3; reprinted in *The Ovens and Murray Advertiser*, 19 December 1878, p. 2.
39. Staggeringly, that condition remained in place until 1950.
40. *The Argus*, 27 December 1878, p. 4.
41. Ibid., 5 June 1879, p. 4, NLA Trove online resource: http://trove.nla.gov.au/ndp/del/article/5945794.
42. Ibid.
43. Ibid., 27 December 1878, p. 4.
44. Ibid.
45. Deakin, p. 15.
46. *Punch* (Melbourne), 'The History of the Berry Ministry and How it Made Victoria a Fine Country for the Working Man', p. 39.
47. J. Sadleir, 12 April 1881, Royal Commission on the Police Force of Victoria, SLV, Q.2065, p. 120.
48. *The Ovens and Murray Advertiser*, 14 January 1879, p. 2.
49. *The Herald* (Melbourne), 4 January 1879, p. 3.
50. Based on *The Age*, 9 January 1879, p. 2 (reported speech changed to direct speech).
51. *Benalla Standard*, 7 January 1879, p. 2.
52. Earp, p. 11.
53. *The Ovens and Murray Advertiser*, 14 January 1879, p. 2.
54. *The Argus*, 20 January 1879, p. 6, NLA Trove online resource: http://trove.nla.gov.au/ndp/del/article/5929032?searchTerm=%22prevails%20throughout%20the%20district%22&searchLimits=l-title=13.
55. *Benalla Standard*, 1 April 1879, p. 3.
56. F. A. Hare, 5 April 1881, Royal Commission on the Police Force of Victoria, SLV, Q.1522, p. 90.
57. Ibid.
58. Reported Appearances of the Kelly Outlaws, Appendix 5, Royal Commission on the Police Force of Victoria, p. 690.
59. *The Advertiser* (Adelaide), 23 September 1911, p. 8, NLA Trove online resource: http://trove.nla.gov.au/ndp/del/article/5315858?searchTerm=%22woman%20come%20out%20to%20get%20water%22&searchLimits=.
60. *The Ovens and Murray Advertiser*, 18 January 1879, p. 4.
61. *Corowa Free Press*, 17 January 1879. The page number is unclear on the photocopy kindly provided by Ian Jones.
62. One Who Was There, 'The Kelly Raid on Jerilderie', in Lundy, p. 66.
63. *The Ovens and Murray Advertiser*, 14 January 1879, p. 2.
64. Ibid.

65. Ibid.
66. *The Argus*, 20 January 1879, p. 6.
67. Ibid.
68. *The Ovens and Murray Advertiser*, 21 January 1879, p. 3.
69. Ibid.
70. Bowman to O'Loghlen, Kelly Historical Collection, Part 3, Chief Secretary's Office, PROV, VPRS 4967, P0, Unit 1, Item 8.
71. Ibid.
72. Ibid.
73. Ibid.
74. Hare, p. 193.
75. Ibid., pp. 193–4.
76. *The Herald* (Melbourne), 27 January 1879, p. 2.
77. McMenomy, p. 109.
78. *The Argus*, 10 November 1880, p. 6, NLA Trove online resource: http://trove.nla.gov.au/ndp/del/article/5983081. NB: Mid-January is an estimate only of when this scene occurred.
79. Sadleir, p. 206.
80. S. O'Connor, 30 March 1881, Royal Commission on the Police Force of Victoria, SLV, Q.1221 and Q.1223, p. 60.
81. Ibid.
82. Sadleir, p. 207.
83. Hare, p. 140.
84. Ibid.
85. F. A. Hare, 31 March 1881, Royal Commission on the Police Force of Victoria, SLV, Q.1270, p. 63.
86. Kenneally, p. 81.
87. Hare, p. 141.
88. F. A. Hare, 31 March 1881, Royal Commission on the Police Force of Victoria, SLV, Q.1270, p. 63.
89. Ibid.
90. Ibid.
91. Ibid.
92. Hare, p. 158.
93. Ibid.
94. F. A. Hare, 31 March 1881, Royal Commission on the Police Force of Victoria, SLV, Q.1270, p. 63.
95. Hare, p. 158.
96. Ibid.
97. Sadleir, p. 207.

98. Hare, p. 141.
99. F. A. Hare, 31 March 1881, Royal Commission on the Police Force of Victoria, SLV, Q.1274–5, p. 63.
100. *The Herald* (Melbourne), 7 February 1879, p. 3.
101. Ibid.

CHAPTER NINE: JERILDERIE

1. *The Herald* (Melbourne), 18 February 1879, p. 3.
2. Ibid.
3. McCarthy, p. 12.
4. *The Herald*, (Melbourne), 18 February 1879, p. 3.
5. One Who Was There, 'The Kelly Raid on Jerilderie', in Lundy, p. 70.
6. Ibid.
7. Ibid.
8. Ibid., p. 71.
9. Ibid.
10. Shaw, p. 48.
11. One Who Was There, 'The Kelly Raid on Jerilderie', in Lundy, p. 71.
12. Based on ibid. (reported speech changed to direct speech).
13. Ibid.
14. Ibid., p. 72.
15. Kenneally, p. 146.
16. NB: I have cleaned up some of the spelling and punctuation of the quotes from the Jerilderie Letter that follows, as I have Ned reading it, and it is his spoken word that I am trying to capture, not his written word to merely record.
17. E. Kelly, Jerilderie Letter, February 1879, SLV, MS 13361, pp. 24–6.
18. Ibid., p. 27.
19. Ibid., p. 29.
20. Ibid., pp. 50–1.
21. Ibid., pp. 42–3.
22. Ibid., p. 56.
23. Ibid., p. 19.
24. Ibid., p. 56.
25. *The Herald* (Melbourne), 19 February 1879, p. 3.
26. One Who Was There, 'The Kelly Raid on Jerilderie', in Lundy, p. 74.
27. Ibid.
28. *The Herald* (Melbourne), 12 February 1879, p. 3.
29. Ibid.

30. Ibid.
31. Ibid.
32. One Who Was There, 'The Kelly Raid on Jerilderie', in Lundy, p. 76.
33. *The Herald* (Melbourne), 12 February 1879, p. 3.
34. *The Age*, 12 February 1879, p. 3.
35. One Who Was There, 'The Kelly Raid on Jerilderie', in Lundy, p. 76.
36. *The Age*, 12 February 1879, p. 3.
37. Ibid.
38. Ibid.
39. *The Ovens and Murray Advertiser*, 13 February 1879, p. 2.
40. Ibid.
41. One Who Was There, 'The Kelly Raid on Jerilderie', in Lundy, p. 77.
42. *The Argus*, 11 August 1880, p. 6, NLA Trove online resource: http://trove.nla.gov.au/ndp/del/article/5971588.
43. One Who Was There, 'The Kelly Raid on Jerilderie', in Lundy, p. 78.
44. Hare, p. 148.
45. One Who Was There, 'The Kelly Raid on Jerilderie', in Lundy, p. 81.
46. Ibid.
47. Ibid., p. 80.
48. *The Argus*, 12 February 1879, p. 6.
49. One Who Was There, 'The Kelly Raid on Jerilderie', in Lundy, pp. 83–4.
50. *The Ovens and Murray Advertiser*, 13 February 1879, p. 2.
51. *The Age*, 12 February 1879, p. 3.
52. *The Argus*, 12 February 1879, p. 6, NLA Trove online resource: http://trove.nla.gov.au/ndp/del/article/5932022.
53. Ibid.
54. Ibid., 11 August 1880, p. 6, NLA Trove online resource: http://trove.nla.gov.au/ndp/del/article/5971588.
55. *The Herald* (Melbourne), 12 February 1879, p. 3.
56. Ibid.
57. *The Sydney Morning Herald*, 26 January 1935, p. 13, NLA Trove online resource: http://trove.nla.gov.au/ndp/del/article/17137438.
58. Ibid.
59. One Who Was There, 'The Kelly Raid on Jerilderie', in Lundy, p. 87.
60. Ibid., p. 85.
61. Ibid., p. 87.
62. *The Sun* (Sydney), 7 September 1911, p. 9.
63. *The Herald* (Melbourne), 18 February 1879, p. 3.
64. One Who Was There, 'The Kelly Raid on Jerilderie', in Lundy, pp. 89–90.

65. This directly contradicts Ned's other statement that Victoria couldn't hold a man who touched Kate, and that Fitzpatrick had never molested his sister.
66. This speech is an amalgam of two reports, from *The Herald* (Melbourne), 18 February 1879, p. 3, and *The Age*, 12 February 1879, p. 3.
67. One Who Was There, 'The Kelly Raid on Jerilderie', in Lundy, p. 89.
68. *The Age*, 12 February 1879, p. 3.
69. *The Argus*, 12 February 1879, p. 6, NLA Trove online resource: http://trove.nla.gov.au/ndp/del/article/5932022.
70. *The Age*, 12 February 1879, p. 3.
71. *The Argus*, 12 February 1879, p. 6, NLA Trove online resource: http://trove.nla.gov.au/ndp/del/article/5932022.
72. One Who Was There, 'The Kelly Raid on Jerilderie', in Lundy, p. 90.
73. Based on *The Bathurst Free Press and Mining Journal*, 2 February 1893, p. 4, NLA Trove online resource: http://trove.nla.gov.au/ndp/del/article/62181863 (reported speech changed to direct speech).
74. *The Age*, 12 February 1879, p. 3.
75. Jones, *Ned Kelly: A Short Life*, p. 164.
76. Lundy, p. 95.
77. Gribble, *The Leisure Hour*, 'A Day with Australian Bushrangers', p. 196.
78. Ibid.
79. *The Herald* (Melbourne), 18 February 1879, p. 3. The Melbourne *Herald* actually has Hart and Ned shouting this together. But because Hart has already left, that is not possible. And it is far more in keeping with Ned's rather exuberant make-up than Hart's rather dour approach.
80. Based on ibid. (reported speech changed to direct speech).
81. *The Argus*, 11 February 1879, p. 5, NLA Trove online resource: http://trove.nla.gov.au/ndp/del/article/5931845.
82. *The Sydney Morning Herald*, 11 February 1879, p. 5, NLA Trove online resource: http://trove.nla.gov.au/ndp/del/article/28391918.
83. *The Advertiser* (Adelaide), 7 October 1911, p. 15.

CHAPTER TEN: AFTER JERILDERIE

1. *The Ovens and Murray Advertiser*, 13 February 1879, p. 2.
2. Sadleir, p. 208.
3. Hall, p. 71.
4. Colonial Secretary of New South Wales Sir Henry Parkes to Acting Chief Secretary Sir Bryan O'Loghlen, 14 February 1879, Kelly

Historical Collection, Part III, Chief Secretary's Office, PROV, VPRS 4967, P0, Unit 1, Item 12.

5. *The Ovens and Murray Advertiser*, 20 February 1879, p. 2.
6. Ibid., 11 February 1879, p. 3.
7. Ibid.
8. Ibid.
9. Ibid., 18 February 1879, p. 3.
10. Ibid.
11. Hare, p. 159.
12. Based on F. A. Hare, 31 March 1881, Royal Commission on the Police Force of Victoria, SLV, Q.1276, p. 64 (reported speech changed to direct speech).
13. F. A. Hare, 31 March 1881, Royal Commission on the Police Force of Victoria, SLV, Q.1276, p. 64.
14. Ibid., Q.1277, p. 64.
15. Ibid., Q.1278, p. 64.
16. Ibid.
17. Ibid.
18. Hare, p. 165.
19. Ibid.
20. F. A. Hare, 31 March 1881, Royal Commission on the Police Force of Victoria, SLV, Q.1279, p. 65.
21. One Who Was There, 'The Kelly Raid on Jerilderie', in Lundy, p. 105.
22. E. Kelly, Jerilderie Letter, February 1879, SLV, MS 13361, pp. 54–6.
23. F. C. Standish, 23 March 1881, Royal Commission on the Police Force of Victoria, SLV, Q.47, p. 4.
24. Standish to Seymour, 15 February 1879, Kelly Historical Collection, Part 4, Kelly Reward Board, PROV, VPRS 4968, P0, Unit 2, Item 62, p. 3.
25. Seymour to Standish, 17 February 1879, Kelly Historical Collection, Part 4, Kelly Reward Board, PROV, VPRS 4968, P0, Unit 2, Item 62, p. 4.
26. Standish to Seymour, 17 February 1879, Kelly Historical Collection, Part 1, Police Branch, PROV, VPRS 4965, P0, Unit 5, Item 393, p. 50.
27. Hare, p. 165.
28. F. A. Hare, 31 March 1881, Royal Commission on the Police Force of Victoria, SLV, Q.1280, p. 65.
29. Ibid.
30. Hare, p. 321.
31. Ibid., p. 192

32. Ibid.
33. Ibid., p. 169.
34. *The Argus*, 21 February 1879, p. 6, NLA Trove online resource: http://trove.nla.gov.au/ndp/del/article/5933126.
35. Based on F. A. Hare, 5 April 1881, Royal Commission on the Police Force of Victoria, SLV, Q.1501, p. 85 (reported speech changed to direct speech).
36. Browne, p. 27.
37. Renowned historian Henry Reynolds estimates that as many as 20,000–30,000 Aboriginal people were killed by similar actions in Queensland in the nineteenth century.
38. *The Inquirer and Commercial News* (Perth), 11 May 1881, p. 1S.
39. *The Herald* (Melbourne), 4 March 1879, p. 3.
40. *The Sun* (Sydney), 4 September 1911, p. 10.
41. Hare, p. 186.
42. Ibid.
43. F. A. Hare, 31 March 1881, Royal Commission on the Police Force of Victoria, SLV, Q.1284, p. 66.
44. Hare, p. 187.
45. Ibid., p. 190.
46. F. A. Hare, 31 March 1881, Royal Commission on the Police Force of Victoria, SLV, Q.1284, p. 66.
47. Hare, p. 190.
48. F. A. Hare, 31 March 1881, Royal Commission on the Police Force of Victoria, SLV, Q.1284, p. 66.
49. Ibid.
50. Ibid.
51. Jones, *Ned Kelly: A Short Life*, pp. 182–3.
52. Lowe, p. 35.
53. Ibid., p. 36.
54. Standish to Hare, 18 June 1880, Hare Papers, the University of Melbourne Archives, Accession 79/78, Francis Hare Papers, No 22.
55. Ibid.
56. F. C. Standish, 23 March 1881, Royal Commission on the Police Force of Victoria, SLV, Q.47, p. 4.
57. *The Ovens and Murray Advertiser*, 22 March 1879, p. 5.
58. F. A. Hare, 31 March 1881, Royal Commission on the Police Force of Victoria, SLV, Q.1320, p. 72.
59. *Bendigo Advertiser*, 2 July 1879, p. 3, NLA Trove online resource: http://trove.nla.gov.au/ndp/del/article/88214139.

60. Ibid.
61. Ibid.
62. Sadleir, p. 219.
63. Ibid.
64. Hare, p. 205.
65. Ibid., p. 227.
66. Sadleir, pp. 215–16.
67. Ibid., p. 216.
68. Based on McMenomy, p. 146 (reported speech changed to direct speech).
69. *The Argus*, 2 July 1880, p. 7, NLA Trove online resource: http://trove.nla.gov.au/ndp/del/article/5982850.
70. Nicolson to Secretary of Lands, 19 March 1879, Kelly Historical Collection, Part 1, Police Branch, PROV, VPRS 4965, P2, Unit 4, Item 177.
71. Secretary of Lands to Nicolson, 24 March 1879, Kelly Historical Collection, Part 1, Police Branch, PROV, VPRS 4965, P2, Unit 4, Item 177.
72. List of Suspected Persons in the North-East District, Kelly Historical Collection, Part 1, Police Branch, PROV, VPRS 4965, P2, Unit 4, Item 177.
73. *The Ovens and Murray Advertiser*, 24 April 1879, p. 2.
74. Standish to O'Loghlen, 22 April 1879, Kelly Historical Collection, Part 3, Chief Secretary's Office, PROV, VPRS 4967, P0, Unit 1, Item 12.
75. Jones, *Ned Kelly: A Short Life*, p. 186.
76. Assistant Commissioner of Police Nicolson to Secretary of Lands, 7 May 1879, Kelly Historical Collection, Part 1, Police Branch, PROV, VPRS 4965, P2, Unit 4, Item 177.
77. Ibid.
78. Tanner's Land Refused, 16 June 1879, Kelly Historical Collection, Part 1, Police Branch, PROV, VPRS 4965, P2, Unit 4, Item 196.
79. Hare, pp. 172–3.
80. *The Sun* (Sydney), 28 August 1911, p. 9.
81. *Benalla Standard*, 1 April 1879, p. 3.
82. Hare, p. 202.
83. Ibid., p. 199.
84. *The Argus*, 6 August 1880, p. 6, NLA Trove online resource: http://trove.nla.gov.au/ndp/del/article/5980120.
85. Detective Report, 14 June 1879, Kelly Historical Collection, Part 1,

Police Branch, PROV, VPRS 4965, P0, Unit 4, Item 342, p. 2. This young man will later prove to be sympathiser Mick Nolan.

86. Report: Surveillance of Mrs Skillion, Kelly Historical Collection, Part 1, Police Branch, PROV, VPRS 4965, P0, Unit 4, Item 342.
87. Detective Report, 14 June 1879, Kelly Historical Collection, Part 1, Police Branch, PROV, VPRS 4965, P0, Unit 4, Item 342, p. 2.
88. Ibid., 5 June 1879, p. 4, NLA Trove online resource: http://trove.nla.gov.au/ndp/del/article/5945794.
89. Ibid., 18 June 1879, p. 7.
90. Deakin, p. 21.
91. *The Argus*, 18 June 1879, p. 7.
92. Deakin, p. 21.
93. *The Argus*, 18 June 1879, p. 7.
94. F. A. Hare, 31 March 1881, Royal Commission on the Police Force of Victoria, SLV, Q.1282, p. 65.
95. Hall, p. 72.
96. With thanks to my friend Warren Fahey, of Warren Fahey's Australian Folklore Unit, www.warrenfahey.com. This nursery rhyme was first published in 1879.
97. Hare, p. 207.
98. Ibid., pp. 224–5.
99. Ibid., p. 226.

CHAPTER ELEVEN: NICOLSON TAKES OVER

1. Based on J. Sadleir, 12 April 1881, Royal Commission on the Police Force of Victoria, SLV, Q.2041 and Q.2042, p. 119 (reported speech changed to direct speech).
2. Sadleir, p. 216.
3. Mr Nicolson Resumes Charge of the Pursuit, Victoria Police Commission, Second Progress Report of the Royal Commission of Enquiry into the Circumstances of the Kelly Outbreak, 1881, p. xviii.
4. F. C. Standish, 23 March 1881, Royal Commission on the Police Force of Victoria, SLV, Q.52, p. 4.
5. Mr Nicolson Resumes Charge of the Pursuit, Victoria Police Commission, Second Progress Report of the Royal Commission of Enquiry into the Circumstances of the Kelly Outbreak, 1881, p. xviii.
6. C. H. Nicolson, 7 September 1881, Royal Commission on the Police Force of Victoria, SLV, Q.16901, p. 633.
7. C. H. Nicolson, Memo to the Melbourne Chief Commissioner of

Police, Benalla, 19 May 1880, in C. H. Nicolson, 25 March 1881, Royal Commission on the Police Force of Victoria, SLV, Q.915, p. 40.

8. C. H. Nicolson, 7 September 1881, Royal Commission on the Police Force of Victoria, SLV, Q.16903, p. 634.
9. Mr Nicolson Resumes Charge of the Pursuit, Victoria Police Commission, Second Progress Report of the Royal Commission of Enquiry into the Circumstances of the Kelly Outbreak, 1881, p. xviii.
10. *The Argus*, 5 July 1879, p. 7.
11. *The Ovens and Murray Advertiser*, 5 July 1879, p. 4.
12. *The Argus*, 5 July 1879, p. 7.
13. Kenneally, p. 109.
14. *The Argus*, 18 February 1880, p. 1, NLA Trove online resource: http://trove.nla.gov.au/ndp/del/article/5974995. My thanks to Sharon Hollingsworth for this reference.
15. *The Ovens and Murray Advertiser*, 16 September 1879, p. 2.
16. Ibid., p. 217.
17. *The Argus*, 26 November 1880, p. 6.
18. Ibid., 10 August 1880, p. 7, NLA Trove online resource: http://trove.nla.gov.au/ndp/del/article/5961325?searchTerm=%22go%20out%20and%20try%20to%20come%20across%20the%20Kellys%22&searchLimits=l-title=13.
19. Nicolson to Standish, 10 November 1879, Royal Commission on the Police Force of Victoria, SLV, Q.16233, p. 591.
20. C. H. Nicolson, 25 March 1881, Royal Commission on the Police Force of Victoria, SLV, Q.841, p. 36.
21. Ibid., Q.842, p. 37.
22. *Supplement to the Victoria Government Gazette*, 24 December 1879, No. 648, p. 75.
23. Ibid., p. 76.
24. *The Ovens and Murray Advertiser*, 29 July 1879, p. 2.
25. Jones, *The Fatal Friendship*, p. 148.
26. *The Ovens and Murray Advertiser*, 9 March 1880, p. 3.
27. Ibid.
28. Ibid.
29. *Bendigo Advertiser*, 13 March 1880, p. 3, NLA Trove online resource: http://trove.nla.gov.au/ndp/del/article/88882076.
30. Statement of Stanhope O'Connor, 29 March 1881, Royal Commission on the Police Force of Victoria, SLV, Q.1092, p. 50.
31. *The Argus*, 5 March 1880, p. 4.
32. F. C. Standish, 23 March 1881, Royal Commission on the Police Force of Victoria, SLV, Q.57, p. 4.

33. Based on *The Argus*, 21 September 1881, p. 7, NLA Trove online resource: http://trove.nla.gov.au/ndp/del/article/5982927 (reported speech changed to direct speech).
34. McIntyre, Section 6, p. 89.
35. Reported Appearances of the Kelly Outlaws, Appendix 5, Royal Commission on the Police Force of Victoria, p. 694.
36. C. H. Nicolson, 25 March 1881, Royal Commission on the Police Force of Victoria, SLV, Q.771, p. 34.
37. Reported Appearances of the Kelly Outlaws, Appendix 5, Royal Commission on the Police Force of Victoria, p. 694.
38. Report of Sergeant Whelan, 19 October 1879, Kelly Historical Collection, Part 1, Police Branch, PROV, VPRS 4965, P0, Unit 6, Item 456, p. 1.
39. *Victoria Police Gazette*, 20 September 1879.
40. *The Argus*, 23 April 1880, p. 7, NLA Trove online resource: http://trove.nla.gov.au/ndp/del/article/5982947.
41. F. C. Standish, 23 March 1881, Royal Commission on the Police Force of Victoria, SLV, Q.71, p. 5.
42. Second Progress Report of the Royal Commission of Enquiry into the Circumstances of the Kelly Outbreak, 1881, p. x, http://cat.lib.unimelb.edu.au/record=b2308044.
43. Corfield, p. 165.
44. CCP Standish, 10 May 1880, Kelly Historical Collection: Miscellaneous Papers, PROV, VPRS 4969, P0, Unit 1, Item 30, Record 3, p. 3.
45. Kenneally, p. 124.
46. Hare, p. 232.
47. Based on F. A. Hare, 1 April 1881, Royal Commission on the Police Force of Victoria, SLV, Q.1429, p. 77 (reported speech changed to direct speech).
48. Based on ibid. (reported speech changed to direct speech).
49. Ibid.
50. Ibid.
51. Ibid.
52. Ibid., Q.16537, p. 605.
53. C. H. Nicolson, 29 March 1881, Royal Commission on the Police Force of Victoria, SLV, Q.933, p. 42.
54. Based on ibid. (reported speech changed to direct speech).
55. F. C. Standish, 23 March 1881, Royal Commission on the Police Force of Victoria, SLV, Q.76, p. 6.

56. C. H. Nicolson, 7 September 1881, Royal Commission on the Police Force of Victoria, SLV, Q.16903, p. 634.
57. Ibid., 25 March 1881, Royal Commission on the Police Force of Victoria, SLV, Q.755, p. 33.
58. Ibid., 29 March 1881, Royal Commission on the Police Force of Victoria, SLV, Q.941, p. 43.
59. Ibid., Q.943, p. 43.
60. F. C. Standish, 23 March 1881, Royal Commission on the Police Force of Victoria, SLV, Q.76, p. 6.
61. C. H. Nicolson, 29 March 1881, Royal Commission on the Police Force of Victoria, SLV, Q.945, p. 43.
62. Mrs Sherritt Snr, 20 July 1881, Royal Commission on the Police Force of Victoria, SLV, Q.13184, p. 476.
63. F. C. Standish, 30 August 1881, Royal Commission on the Police Force of Victoria, SLV, Q.15849, p. 576.
64. C. H. Nicolson, 25 March 1881, Royal Commission on the Police Force of Victoria, SLV, Q.798, p. 35.
65. Based on Mrs Sherritt Snr, 20 July 1881, Royal Commission on the Police Force of Victoria, SLV, Q.13184, p. 476 (reported speech changed to direct speech).
66. Mrs Sherritt Snr, 20 July 1881, Royal Commission on the Police Force of Victoria, SLV, Q.13184, p. 476.
67. S. O'Connor, 30 March 1881, Royal Commission on the Police Force of Victoria, SLV, Q.1110, p. 52.
68. C. H. Nicolson, 25 March 1881, Royal Commission on the Police Force of Victoria, SLV, Q.800, p. 35.
69. *The Argus*, 2 August 1880, p. 6, NLA Trove online resource: http://trove.nla.gov.au/ndp/del/article/5976545.
70. Standish to Nicolson, Note, 28 May 1880, in F. A. Hare, 1 April 1881, Royal Commission on the Police Force of Victoria, SLV, Q.1436, p. 78.
71. Sadleir, p. 220.
72. Hare, p. 233.
73. Sadleir, p. 216.
74. *The Argus*, 22 May 1880, p. 5, NLA Trove online resource: http://trove.nla.gov.au/ndp/del/article/5976950.
75. Kenneally, p. 98.
76. Hare, p. 234.
77. Based on J. Sherritt, 4 August 1881, Royal Commission on the Police Force of Victoria, SLV, Q.15115, p. 548 (reported speech changed to direct speech).

78. Based on Hare, p. 234 (reported speech changed to direct speech).
79. M. E. Ward, 28 July 1881, Royal Commission on the Police Force of Victoria, SLV, Q.14160, p. 516.
80. Based on Hare, p. 235 (reported speech changed to direct speech).
81. Based on Report of Constable Bracken, 24 September 1880, in Queen vs Ann Jones, Kelly Historical Collection, Part 1, Police Branch, PROV, VPRS 4965, P0, Unit 2, Item 137 (reported speech changed to direct speech).
82. Ibid. (reported speech changed to direct speech).
83. *The Argus*, 20 July 1880, p. 6, NLA Trove online resource: http://trove.nla.gov.au/ndp/del/article/5953860; F. A. Hare, 5 April 1881, Royal Commission on the Police Force of Victoria, SLV, Q.1498, p. 84.
84. M. E. Ward, 28 July 1881, Royal Commission on the Police Force of Victoria, SLV, Q.14160, p. 516.
85. F. A. Hare, 5 April 1881, Royal Commission on the Police Force of Victoria, SLV, Q.1516–18, pp. 89–90.
86. Sadleir, p. 222.
87. Based on ibid. (reported speech changed to direct speech).
88. Ibid.
89. Affidavit of Francis Hare, 16 September 1881, Royal Commission on the Police Force of Victoria, p. 674.
90. F. A. Hare, 5 April 1881, Royal Commission on the Police Force of Victoria, SLV, Q.1516–18, pp. 89–90.

CHAPTER TWELVE: A PLAN INTERRUPTED

1. This is the spelling used in most sources, including *The Argus* (22 July 1881), *Freeman's Journal* (18 February 1999), *North Queensland Register* (22 October 1900) and *The Ovens and Murray Advertiser* (13 March 1861).
2. *The Argus*, 1 July 1880, p. 6, NLA Trove online resource: http://trove.nla.gov.au/ndp/del/article/5982611.
3. *The Ovens and Murray Advertiser*, 1 July 1880, p. 2.
4. *The Argus*, 1 July 1880, p. 6, NLA Trove online resource: http://trove.nla.gov.au/ndp/del/article/5982611.
5. *South Australian Register*, 5 July 1880, p. 5, NLA Trove online resource: http://trove.nla.gov.au/ndp/del/article/43154144.
6. *The Argus*, 1 July 1880, p. 6, NLA Trove online resource: http://trove.nla.gov.au/ndp/del/article/5982611.
7. *The Age*, 1 July 1880, p. 3.

8. Armstrong's first name is given as Henry in official documents but he was commonly known as Harry.
9. H. Armstrong, 21 June 1881, Royal Commission on the Police Force of Victoria, SLV, Q.12137, p. 433.
10. *The Argus*, 6 August 1880, p. 6, NLA Trove online resource: http://trove.nla.gov.au/ndp/del/article/5980120.
11. *The Age*, 1 July 1880, p. 3.
12. *The Argus*, 1 July 1880, p. 6.
13. *The Age*, 1 July 1880, p. 3.
14. Ibid., p. 2.
15. Ibid., p. 3. Again, I have altered the quote slightly to accommodate Wicks's thick German accent.
16. W. Duross, 4 May 1881, Royal Commission on the Police Force of Victoria, SLV, Q.3638, p. 180.
17. Ibid., Q.3649, p. 180.
18. *The Argus*, 1 July 1880, p. 6, NLA Trove online resource: http://trove.nla.gov.au/ndp/del/article/5982611.
19. Ibid., 28 June 1880, p. 5.
20. E. Barry, 20 July 1881, Royal Commission on the Police Force of Victoria, SLV, Q.13389, p. 483.
21. *The Argus*, 1 July 1880, p. 6.
22. W. Duross, 4 May 1881, Royal Commission on the Police Force of Victoria, SLV, Q.3657, p. 180.
23. *The Age*, 1 July 1880, p. 3.
24. W. Duross, 4 May 1881, Royal Commission on the Police Force of Victoria, SLV, Q.3657, p. 180.
25. *The Age*, 1 July 1880, p. 3.
26. *The Argus*, 1 July 1880, p. 6, NLA Trove online resource: http://trove.nla.gov.au/ndp/del/article/5982611.
27. E. Barry, 20 July 1881, Royal Commission on the Police Force of Victoria, SLV, Q.13396, p. 484.
28. *The Argus*, 28 June 1880, p. 5, NLA Trove online resource: http://trove.nla.gov.au/ndp/del/article/5983167.
29. Ibid., 1 July 1880, p. 6, NLA Trove online resource: http://trove.nla.gov.au/ndp/del/article/5982611.
30. Mrs Sherritt Jnr, 21 July 1881, Royal Commission on the Police Force of Victoria, SLV, Q.13803, p. 498.
31. T. Dowling, 5 May 1881, Royal Commission on the Police Force of Victoria, SLV, Q.4210, p. 193.
32. *The Age*, 1 July 1880, p. 3.

33. Ibid.
34. E. Barry, 20 July 1881, Royal Commission on the Police Force of Victoria, SLV, Q.13393, p. 483.
35. H. Armstrong, 21 June 1881, Royal Commission on the Police Force of Victoria, SLV, Q.12153, p. 434.
36. *The Argus*, 2 July 1880, p. 7, NLA Trove online resource: http://trove.nla.gov.au/ndp/del/article/5982850.
37. Ibid., 1 July 1880, p. 6, NLA Trove online resource: http://trove.nla.gov.au/ndp/del/article/5982611.
38. E. Barry, 20 July 1881, Royal Commission on the Police Force of Victoria, SLV, Q.13408, p. 484.
39. *The Argus*, 1 July 1880, p. 6, NLA Trove online resource: http://trove.nla.gov.au/ndp/del/article/5982611.
40. Ibid.
41. Ibid., 29 June 1880, p. 5, NLA Trove online resource: http://trove.nla.gov.au/ndp/del/article/5975546.
42. Based on ibid., 1 July 1880, p. 6 (reported speech changed to direct speech).
43. H. Armstrong, 21 June 1881, Royal Commission on the Police Force of Victoria, SLV, Q.12158, p. 434.
44. E. Barry, 20 July 1881, Royal Commission on the Police Force of Victoria, SLV, Q.13404, p. 484.
45. *The Age*, 1 July 1880, p. 3.
46. *The Argus*, 1 July 1880, p. 6, NLA Trove online resource: http://trove.nla.gov.au/ndp/del/article/5982611.
47. Donald G. Sutherland to his parents, 8 July 1880, MS 13713, Box 4243/4.
48. Hare, p. 253.
49. Amory, p. 423.
50. In 1939, one of the workers, John C. Lowe, wrote an account of this event. According to this, it was an Italian man whom Piazzi was sharing a tent with who was sleeping with the woman at this time.
51. Account of J. C. Lowe, 1939, original manuscript held by Thomas Lowe of Yarrawonga, published in the *Benalla Ensign*, 18 and 25 June 1997.
52. Ibid.
53. Mrs Smith (née Jones) to Chief Commissioner Chomley, 9 May 1893, PROV, VPRS 4965, P0, Unit 3, Item 147, p. 5.
54. Based on *The Argus*, 5 December 1881, p. 10 (reported speech changed to direct speech).

55. *The Argus*, 5 December 1881, p. 10, NLA Trove online resource: http://trove.nla.gov.au/ndp/del/article/11525752.
56. Ibid., 29 June 1880, p. 6, NLA Trove online resource: http://trove.nla.gov.au/ndp/del/article/5975546.
57. F. A. Hare, 5 April 1881, Royal Commission on the Police Force of Victoria, SLV, Q.1477, p. 81.
58. *The Argus*, 29 June 1880, p. 6.
59. Ibid.
60. Ibid.
61. *The Sydney Morning Herald*, 30 June 1880, p. 6, NLA Trove online resource: http://trove.nla.gov.au/ndp/del/article/13463179.
62. J. Reardon, 14 May 1881, Royal Commission on the Police Force of Victoria, SLV, Q.7607, p. 276.
63. Ibid.
64. Ibid.
65. *The Advertiser* (Adelaide), 23 September 1911, p. 8, NLA Trove online resource: http://trove.nla.gov.au/ndp/del/article/5315858.
66. Based on *The Sydney Morning Herald*, 30 June 1880, p. 6, NLA Trove online resource: http://trove.nla.gov.au/ndp/del/article/13463179 (reported speech changed to direct speech).
67. J. Reardon, 14 May 1881, Royal Commission on the Police Force of Victoria, SLV, Q.7608, pp. 276–7.
68. Based on ibid. (reported speech changed to direct speech).
69. *The Argus*, 29 June 1880, p. 6, NLA Trove online resource: http://trove.nla.gov.au/ndp/del/article/5975546.
70. Ibid.
71. *The Sydney Morning Herald*, 30 November 1880, p. 7, NLA Trove online resource: http://trove.nla.gov.au/ndp/del/article/13480554.
72. Ibid.
73. Ashmead, p. 51.
74. Ibid.
75. *The Argus*, 1 July 1880, p. 6, NLA Trove online resource: http://trove.nla.gov.au/ndp/del/article/5982611.
76. Based on H. Armstrong, 21 June 1881, Royal Commission on the Police Force of Victoria, SLV, Q.12162, p. 435 (reported speech changed to direct speech).
77. H. Armstrong, 21 June 1881, Royal Commission on the Police Force of Victoria, SLV, Q.12162, p. 435.
78. T. Curnow, 20 September 1881, Royal Commission on the Police Force of Victoria, SLV, Q.17597, p. 663.

79. Ibid.
80. Ibid.
81. Ibid.
82. Ibid.
83. T. H. Cameron, letter to his brother, Glenrowan, 8 July 1880, Mitchell Library, AK25/CY3268, frames 1–22.
84. T. Curnow, 20 September 1881, Royal Commission on the Police Force of Victoria, SLV, Q.17597, p. 664.
85. Based on ibid. (reported speech changed to direct speech).
86. Shaw, p. 88.
87. T. Curnow, 20 September 1881, Royal Commission on the Police Force of Victoria, SLV, Q.17597, p. 664.
88. *The Sun* (Sydney), 5 September 1911, p. 9.
89. T. Curnow, 20 September 1881, Royal Commission on the Police Force of Victoria, SLV, Q.17597, p. 664.
90. Ibid.
91. Ibid.
92. *The Argus*, 26 November 1880, p. 6, NLA Trove online resource: http://trove.nla.gov.au/ndp/del/article/5952385.
93. Ibid., 28 June 1880, p. 5.
94. Ward to Standish, 27 June 1880, Kelly Historical Collection, Part I, Police Branch, PROV, VPRS 4965, P0, Unit 1, Item 33.
95. T. Curnow, 20 September 1881, Royal Commission on the Police Force of Victoria, SLV, Q.17597, p. 664.
96. Ibid.
97. Based on ibid. (reported speech changed to direct speech).
98. Ibid.
99. Hare to Standish, 27 June 1880, Kelly Historical Collection, Part 1, Police Branch, PROV, VPRS 4965, P0, Unit 1, Item 33, p. 2.
100. J. Sadleir, 14 April 1881, Royal Commission on the Police Force of Victoria, SLV, Q.2751, Q.2754 and Q.2759, p. 147.
101. Sadleir, p. 223.

CHAPTER THIRTEEN: GLENROWAN DANCES

1. Anon., 'The Wild Colonial Boy', lyrics in Steward and Keesing, p. 39–40.
2. J. Kelly, 18 May 1881, Royal Commission on the Police Force of Victoria, SLV, Q.8028, p. 300.
3. Ibid., Q.8029, p. 300.

4. Ibid., Q.8030, p. 300.
5. A. L. M. Steele, 31 May 1881, Royal Commission on the Police Force of Victoria, SLV, Q.8994–5, pp. 325–6.
6. J. Sadleir, 14 April 1881, Royal Commission on the Police Force of Victoria, SLV, Q.2759, p. 147. Spelling of 'Millewa' changed to avoid confusion.
7. Ann Jones to Montfort, Kelly Historical Collection, Part 1, Police Branch, PROV, VPRS 4965, P0, Unit 1, Item 63, p. 3.
8. Letter of Captain Standish to Sub-Inspector O'Connor, Appendix 2, Royal Commission on the Police Force of Victoria, p. 682.
9. Hare to Standish, Kelly Historical Collection, Part 1, Police Branch, PROV, VPRS 4965, P0, Unit 1, Item 33, pp. 3–5.
10. T. Curnow, 20 September 1881, Royal Commission on the Police Force of Victoria, SLV, Q.17597, p. 664.
11. Ibid.
12. Ibid.
13. S. O'Connor, 30 March 1881, Royal Commission on the Police Force of Victoria, SLV, Q.1114, p. 53.
14. Ibid.
15. Ibid., Q.1115, p. 53.
16. F. A. Hare, 5 April 1881, Royal Commission on the Police Force of Victoria, SLV, Q.1501, p. 84.
17. T. Curnow, 20 September 1881, Royal Commission on the Police Force of Victoria, SLV, Q.17597, p. 665.
18. Ibid.
19. *Mercury*, 2 July 1881, p. 3.
20. Statement of Jane Jones, Kelly Historical Collection, Part 3, Chief Secretary's Office, PROV, VPRS 4967, P0, Unit 3, Item 60, p. 17.
21. Shaw, p. 100.
22. Frank Bell to John Wood, 11 September 1880, in Adam-Smith, p. 172.
23. Hare, p. 260.
24. T. Curnow, 20 September 1881, Royal Commission on the Police Force of Victoria, SLV, Q.17597, p. 665.
25. Claims Lodged with the Kelly Reward Board: Constable Hugh Bracken, Kelly Historical Collection, Part 4, Kelly Reward Board, PROV, VPRS 4968, P0, Unit 1, Item 1, p. 10.
26. Ibid.
27. *The Argus*, 29 June 1880, p. 6, NLA Trove online resource: http://trove.nla.gov.au/ndp/del/article/5975546.
28. Ibid.

29. Claims Lodged with the Kelly Reward Board: Constable Hugh Bracken, Kelly Historical Collection, Part 4, Kelly Reward Board, PROV, VPRS 4968, P0, Unit 1, Item 1, p. 11.
30. Ibid., p. 12.
31. Ibid.
32. *The Argus*, 30 June 1880, p. 6, NLA Trove online resource: http://trove.nla.gov.au/ndp/del/article/5952870.
33. Claims Lodged with the Kelly Reward Board: Constable Hugh Bracken, Kelly Historical Collection, Part 4, Kelly Reward Board, PROV, VPRS 4968, P0, Unit 1, Item 1, p. 13.
34. Hare, p. 261.
35. Ibid.
36. Claims Lodged with the Kelly Reward Board: Constable Hugh Bracken, Kelly Historical Collection, Part 4, Kelly Reward Board, PROV, VPRS 4968, P0, Unit 1, Item 1, p. 13.
37. T. Curnow, 20 September 1881, Royal Commission on the Police Force of Victoria, SLV, Q.17597, p. 665.
38. Ibid.
39. Anon., 'Farewell to my Home in Greta', lyrics in Steward and Keesing, pp. 48–9. 'Collected by Max Brown from Mrs Barry, of Beechworth, Victoria, and said to have been sung about 1879. Obviously it purports to be a dialogue between the bush ranger Ned Kelly and his sister Kate.'
40. Mrs Jones to Montfort, Kelly Historical Collection, Part 1, Police Branch, PROV, VPRS 4965, P0, Unit 1, Item 63, p. 4.
41. *The Argus*, 26 November 1880, p. 6, NLA Trove online resource: http://trove.nla.gov.au/ndp/del/article/5952385.
42. T. H. Cameron, letter to his brother, Glenrowan, 8 July 1880, p. 2.
43. Based on T. Curnow, 20 September 1881, Royal Commission on the Police Force of Victoria, SLV, Q.17597, p. 665 (reported speech changed to direct speech).
44. Claims Lodged with the Kelly Reward Board: Constable Hugh Bracken, Kelly Historical Collection, Part 4, Kelly Reward Board, PROV, VPRS 4968, P0, Unit 1, Item 1, p. 14.
45. *The Argus*, 29 June 1880, p. 5, NLA Trove online resource: http://trove.nla.gov.au/ndp/del/article/5975546.
46. Ibid., 5 July 1880, p. 6, NLA Trove online resource: http://trove.nla.gov.au/ndp/del/article/5983068.
47. S. O'Connor, 30 March 1881, Royal Commission on the Police Force of Victoria, SLV, Q.1116, p. 53.
48. *The Sydney Morning Herald*, 30 November 1880, p. 7, NLA Trove

online resource: http://trove.nla.gov.au/ndp/del/article/13480554.
49. Ibid.
50. J. Reardon, 14 May 1881, Royal Commission on the Police Force of Victoria, SLV, Q.7622, p. 277.
51. Mrs Jones to Montfort, Kelly Historical Collection, Part 1, Police Branch, PROV, VPRS 4965, P0, Unit 1, Item 63, p. 3.
52. J. Reardon, 14 May 1881, Royal Commission on the Police Force of Victoria, SLV, Q.7628, p. 277.
53. Claims Lodged with the Kelly Reward Board: Constable Hugh Bracken, Kelly Historical Collection, Part 4, Kelly Reward Board, PROV, VPRS 4968, P0, Unit 1, Item 1, p. 15.
54. *The Argus*, 30 June 1880, p. 6, NLA Trove online resource: http://trove.nla.gov.au/ndp/del/article/5952870.
55. Ibid.
56. Ibid.
57. Ibid.
58. Ibid.
59. Claims Lodged with the Kelly Reward Board: Constable Hugh Bracken, Kelly Historical Collection, Part 4, Kelly Reward Board, PROV, VPRS 4968, P0, Unit 1, Item 1, p. 16.
60. Ibid.
61. J. Reardon, 14 May 1881, Royal Commission on the Police Force of Victoria, SLV, Q.7628, p. 277.
62. Claims Lodged with the Kelly Reward Board: Constable Hugh Bracken, Kelly Historical Collection, Part 4, Kelly Reward Board, PROV, VPRS 4968, P0, Unit 1, Item 1, p. 17.
63. *The Argus*, 30 June 1880, p. 6, NLA Trove online resource: http://trove.nla.gov.au/ndp/del/article/5952870.
64. McPhee, Letter to the Kelly Reward Board, Kelly Historical Collection, Part 5, Miscellaneous Records, PROV, VPRS 4969, P0, Unit 1, Item 19, p. 4.
65. Ibid.
66. Ibid.
67. *Windsor and Richmond Gazette*, 5 January 1889, p. 9, NLA Trove online resource: http://trove.nla.gov.au/ndp/del/article/72558543.
68. T. Curnow, 20 September 1881, Royal Commission on the Police Force of Victoria, SLV, Q.17597, p. 666.
69. McPhee, Letter to the Kelly Reward Board, Kelly Historical Collection, Part 5, Miscellaneous Records, PROV, VPRS 4969, P0, Unit 1, Item 19, p. 4.

70. Hare, p. 264.
71. F. A. Hare, 5 April 1881, Royal Commission on the Police Force of Victoria, SLV, Q.1501, p. 86.
72. Sullivan Statement in Queen vs Ann Jones, Kelly Historical Collection, Part 1, Police Branch, PROV, VPRS 4965, P0, Unit 2, Item 137.
73. Charles C. Rawlins, 11 March 1881, Kelly Reward Board, Minutes of Evidence, Q.49, p. 4.
74. Ibid.
75. Ibid.
76. Ibid.
77. *The Argus*, 21 July 1880, p. 6, NLA Trove online resource: http://trove.nla.gov.au/ndp/del/article/5979698.
78. M. Reardon, 8 June 1881, Royal Commission on the Police Force of Victoria, SLV, Q.10551, p. 379.
79. Charles C. Rawlins, 11 March 1881, Kelly Reward Board, Minutes of Evidence, Q.49–50, p. 4.
80. Based on *The Argus*, 5 July 1880, p. 6, NLA Trove online resource: http://trove.nla.gov.au/ndp/del/article/5983068; and J. Kelly, 18 May 1881, Royal Commission on the Police Force of Victoria, SLV, Q.8052, p. 301 (quotations conjoined).
81. S. O'Connor, 30 March 1881, Royal Commission on the Police Force of Victoria, SLV, Q.1116, p. 53.
82. Based on *The Argus*, 20 July 1880, NLA Trove online resource: http://trove.nla.gov.au/ndp/del/article/5953860 (reported speech changed to direct speech).

CHAPTER FOURTEEN: THE SIEGE BEGINS

1. S. O'Connor, 30 March 1881, Royal Commission on the Police Force of Victoria, SLV, Q.1116, p. 53.
2. Ibid., pp. 53–4.
3. T. Carrington, 7 June 1881, Royal Commission on the Police Force of Victoria, SLV, Q.10028, p. 361.
4. *The Argus*, 21 July 1880, p. 6, NLA Trove online resource: http://trove.nla.gov.au/ndp/del/article/5979698.
5. D. Barry, 17 May 1881, Royal Commission on the Police Force of Victoria, SLV, Q.7380, p. 284.
6. T. Carrington, 7 June 1881, Royal Commission on the Police Force of Victoria, SLV, Q.10033, p. 362.
7. Douthie, p. 119.

8. *Bendigo Advertiser*, 30 June 1880, p. 2, NLA Trove online resource: http://trove.nla.gov.au/ndp/del/article/88885410.
9. J. Kelly, 18 May 1881, Royal Commission on the Police Force of Victoria, SLV, Q.8093–4, p. 302.
10. C. C. Rawlins, 15 June 1881, Royal Commission on the Police Force of Victoria, SLV, Q.11588, p. 411.
11. *The Argus*, 29 June 1880, p. 5, NLA Trove online resource: http://trove.nla.gov.au/ndp/del/printArticlePdf/5975546/3?print=n.
12. J. Kelly, 18 May 1881, Royal Commission on the Police Force of Victoria, SLV, Q.8106, p. 302.
13. *The Argus*, 21 July 1880, p. 6, NLA Trove online resource: http://trove.nla.gov.au/ndp/del/article/5979698.
14. F. A. Hare, 5 April 1881, Royal Commission on the Police Force of Victoria, SLV, Q.1506, p. 87.
15. *Australasian Sketcher*, 17 July 1880, p. 166, NLA Trove online resource: http://trove.nla.gov.au/ndp/del/article/60622528.
16. C. Gascoigne, 2 June 1881, Royal Commission on the Police Force of Victoria, SLV, Q.9677, p. 350.
17. *The Sydney Morning Herald*, 30 November 1880, p. 7, NLA Trove online resource: http://trove.nla.gov.au/ndp/del/article/13480554.
18. *The Advertiser* (Adelaide), 23 September 1911, p. 8.
19. Douthie, p. 102.
20. Ibid., p. 19.
21. *South Australian Register*, 10 July 1880, p. 1S.
22. George Metcalf did in fact die of that wound, less than four months later.
23. W. Phillips, 9 June 1881, Royal Commission on the Police Force of Victoria, SLV, Q.1311, p. 402.
24. Ibid.
25. J. Kelly, 18 May 1881, Royal Commission on the Police Force of Victoria, SLV, Q.8123, p. 302.
26. Ibid.
27. *The Argus*, 29 June 1880, p. 5, NLA Trove online resource: http://trove.nla.gov.au/ndp/del/article/5975546.
28. J. McWhirter, 7 June 1881, Royal Commission on the Police Force of Victoria, SLV, Q.10331, p. 372.
29. Ibid., Q.10314, p. 371.
30. *The Argus*, 29 June 1880, p. 5.
31. J. McWhirter, 7 June 1881, Royal Commission on the Police Force of Victoria, SLV, Q.10317, p. 371.

32. Ibid., Q.10317–18, p. 371.
33. *The Argus*, 6 July 1880, p. 7, NLA Trove online resource: http://trove.nla.gov.au/ndp/del/article/5955606.
34. Based on John McWhirter, 21 March 1881, Kelly Reward Board, Q.144, p. 9 (reported speech changed to direct speech).
35. C. C. Rawlins, 15 June 1881, Royal Commission on the Police Force of Victoria, SLV, Q.11651, p. 413.
36. S. O'Connor, 29 March 1881, Royal Commission on the Police Force of Victoria, SLV, Q.1119, p. 54. I have taken the liberty of adding exclamation marks, as in modern usage that better conveys what happened, I think.
37. S. O'Connor, 29 March 1881, Royal Commission on the Police Force of Victoria, SLV, Q.1119, p. 54.
38. *The Argus*, 21 July 1880, p. 6, NLA Trove online resource: http://trove.nla.gov.au/ndp/del/article/5979698.
39. Ibid.
40. Ibid., 21 September 1881, p. 7, NLA Trove online resource: http://trove.nla.gov.au/ndp/del/article/5982927.
41. Ibid., 2 July 1880, p. 7, NLA Trove online resource: http://trove.nla.gov.au/ndp/del/article/5982850.
42. J. Kelly, 18 May 1881, Royal Commission on the Police Force of Victoria, SLV, Q.8164, p. 303.
43. *The Argus*, 21 July 1880, p. 6, NLA Trove online resource: http://trove.nla.gov.au/ndp/del/article/5979698.
44. *The Advertiser* (Adelaide), 23 September 1911, p. 8.
45. Ibid.
46. M. Reardon, 8 June 1881, Royal Commission on the Police Force of Victoria, SLV, Q.10584, p. 379.
47. *The Advertiser* (Adelaide), 23 September 1911, p. 8.
48. M. Reardon, 8 June 1881, Royal Commission on the Police Force of Victoria, SLV, Q.10590, p. 379.
49. A. L. M. Steele, 31 May 1881, Royal Commission on the Police Force of Victoria, SLV, Q.8998, p. 326.
50. Ibid.
51. *The Ovens and Murray Advertiser*, 10 October 1878, p. 5.
52. *The Argus*, 2 July 1880, p. 7, NLA Trove online resource: http://trove.nla.gov.au/ndp/del/article/5982850.
53. Hare to Standish, 2 July 1880, Royal Commission on the Police Force of Victoria, Appendix 3, p. 688.
54. Hare, p. 273.

55. J. Sadleir, 14 April 1881, Royal Commission on the Police Force of Victoria, SLV, Q.2764, p. 148.
56. *The Ovens and Murray Advertiser*, 14 August 1880, p. 8.
57. J. Arthur, 9 June 1881, Royal Commission on the Police Force of Victoria, SLV, Q.11219, p. 400.
58. Ibid.
59. Ibid., Q.11142, p. 398.
60. Sadleir, p. 228.
61. J. Kelly, 18 May 1881, Royal Commission on the Police Force of Victoria, SLV, Q.8186, p. 304.
62. J. Dwyer, 1 June 1881, Royal Commission on the Police Force of Victoria, SLV, Q.9407, p. 339.
63. J. Kelly, 18 May 1881, Royal Commission on the Police Force of Victoria, SLV, Q.8187, p. 304.
64. Ibid.
65. Based on Sadleir, p. 230, and C. Gascoigne, 2 June 1881, Royal Commission on the Police Force of Victoria, SLV, Q.9679, p. 350 (quotations conjoined).
66. Based on C. Gascoigne, 2 June 1881, Royal Commission on the Police Force of Victoria, SLV, Q.9679, p. 350 (reported speech changed to direct speech).
67. J. Reardon, 14 May 1881, Royal Commission on the Police Force of Victoria, SLV, Q.7655, p. 278.
68. Ibid., Q.7693, p. 277.
69. Ibid., Q.7665, p. 278.
70. *The Argus*, 28 March 1882, p. 9, NLA Trove online resource: http://trove.nla.gov.au/ndp/del/article/11536188.
71. Ibid., 21 July 1880, p. 6, NLA Trove online resource: http://trove.nla.gov.au/ndp/del/article/5979698. It is my assumption that this call was made from the following quotation: 'This was in answer to a request from a man who cried from inside that the place was full of women and children.'
72. M. Reardon, 8 June 1881, Royal Commission on the Police Force of Victoria, SLV, Q.10617, p. 380.
73. J. Arthur, 9 June 1881, Royal Commission on the Police Force of Victoria, SLV, Q.11126, p. 397.
74. M. Reardon, 8 June 1881, Royal Commission on the Police Force of Victoria, SLV, Q.10619, p. 380.
75. Ibid., Q.10624, p. 380.
76. Ibid., Q.10632, p. 380.

77. Shaw, p. 187.
78. J. Arthur, 9 June 1881, Royal Commission on the Police Force of Victoria, SLV, Q.11126, p. 397.
79. Clune, *The Kelly Hunters*, p. 166.
80. McMenomy, p. 180.
81. *The Sunday Times* (Perth), 19 April 1914, p. 2, NLA Trove online resource: http://trove.nla.gov.au/ndp/del/article/57823264.
82. Shaw, p. 181.
83. *The Ovens and Murray Advertiser*, 1 July 1880, p. 2.
84. Shaw, p. 181.
85. S. O'Connor, 30 March 1881, Royal Commission on the Police Force of Victoria, SLV, Q.1142, p. 55.
86. J. Reardon, 14 May 1881, Royal Commission on the Police Force of Victoria, SLV, Q.7673, p. 278.
87. Ibid.
88. *The Ovens and Murray Advertiser*, 1 July 1880, p. 2.
89. *Bendigo Advertiser*, 1 July 1880, NLA Trove online resource: http://trove.nla.gov.au/ndp/del/article/88885439.
90. *The Argus*, 30 June 1880, p. 6, NLA Trove online resource: http://trove.nla.gov.au/ndp/del/article/5952870.
91. Shaw, p. 183.
92. J. Reardon, 14 May 1881, Royal Commission on the Police Force of Victoria, SLV, Q.7678, p. 279.

CHAPTER FIFTEEN: IT'S A BUNYIP

1. James Arthur, 9 June 1881, Royal Commission on the Police Force of Victoria, SLV, Q.11160, p. 398.
2. NB: The timetable for the final shootout between Ned and the police varies wildly in most contemporary accounts, with only broad agreement that from first shot to last it took around thirty minutes.
3. James Arthur, 9 June 1881, Royal Commission on the Police Force of Victoria, SLV, Q.11160, p. 398.
4. Ibid., Q.11183, p. 399.
5. *The Argus*, 2 July 1880, p. 7, NLA Trove online resource: http://trove.nla.gov.au/ndp/del/article/5982850.
6. James Arthur, 9 June 1881, Royal Commission on the Police Force of Victoria, SLV, Q.11160, p. 398.
7. *The South Australian Advertiser*, 10 July 1880, p. 2S, NLA Trove online resource: http://trove.nla.gov.au/ndp/del/article/30804003.

8. *Sunday Times* (Perth), 19 April 1914, p. 2, NLA Trove online resource: http://trove.nla.gov.au/ndp/del/article/57823264.
9. James Arthur, 9 June 1881, Royal Commission on the Police Force of Victoria, SLV, Q.11162, p. 398.
10. Hare, p. 285.
11. *The South Australian Advertiser*, 2 July 1880, p. 5, NLA Trove online resource: http://trove.nla.gov.au/ndp/del/article/30803692.
12. Ibid.
13. Jesse Dowsett to Traffic Manager, 2 July 1880, Kelly Historical Collection, Part 5, Miscellaneous Records, PROV, VPRS 4969, P0, Unit 1, Item 1, p. 16.
14. Jesse Dowsett, 8 June 1881, Royal Commission on the Police Force of Victoria, SLV, Q.10916, p. 389.
15. *Australasian Sketcher*, 17 July 1880, p. 167, NLA Trove online resource: http://trove.nla.gov.au/ndp/del/article/60622528.
16. *The Argus*, 29 June 1880, p. 5, NLA Trove online resource: http://trove.nla.gov.au/ndp/del/article/5975546.
17. McHugh, p. 307.
18. James Dwyer, 1 June 1881, Royal Commission on the Police Force of Victoria, SLV, Q.9451, p. 341.
19. Ibid.
20. Ibid.
21. *Sunday Times* (Perth), 19 April 1914, p. 2, NLA Trove online resource: http://trove.nla.gov.au/ndp/del/article/57823264.
22. Ibid.
23. Shaw, p. 204.
24. *The Argus*, 1 July 1880, p. 6.
25. Based on ibid. (in the original, there is a blank, which I have inferred should be 'God').
26. Jesse Dowsett, 8 June 1881, Royal Commission on the Police Force of Victoria, SLV, Q.10919, p. 389.
27. *The Argus*, 1 July 1880, p. 6.
28. Ibid.
29. *Illustrated Australian News*, 17 July 1880, p. 115, NLA Trove online resource: http://trove.nla.gov.au/ndp/del/article/60094218.
30. *The Argus*, 1 July 1880, p. 6, NLA Trove online resource: http://trove.nla.gov.au/ndp/del/article/5982611.
31. Ibid.
32. Ibid.
33. Ibid., 2 July 1880, p. 7, NLA Trove online resource: http://trove.nla.gov.au/ndp/del/article/5982850.

34. Hare, p. 288.
35. *Sunday Times* (Perth), 19 April 1914, p. 2, NLA Trove online resource: http://trove.nla.gov.au/ndp/del/article/57823264.
36. *The Argus*, 11 August 1880, p. 6, NLA Trove online resource: http://trove.nla.gov.au/ndp/del/article/5971588.
37. A. L. M. Steele, 31 May 1881, Royal Commission on the Police Force of Victoria, SLV, Q.9038, p. 328.
38. Jesse Dowsett, 8 June 1881, Royal Commission on the Police Force of Victoria, SLV, Q.10926, p. 390.
39. *The Argus*, 1 July 1880, p. 6, NLA Trove online resource: http://trove.nla.gov.au/ndp/del/article/5982611.
40. Jesse Dowsett, 8 June 1881, Royal Commission on the Police Force of Victoria, SLV, Q.10934, p. 390.
41. Dowsett to Traffic Manager, 2 July 1880, PROV, VPRS 4969, P0, Unit 1, Item 1.
42. Jesse Dowsett, 8 June 1881, Royal Commission on the Police Force of Victoria, SLV, Q.10934, p. 390.
43. Based on *The Argus*, 12 August 1880, p. 6, NLA Trove online resource: http://trove.nla.gov.au/ndp/del/article/5957112 (reported speech changed to direct speech).
44. Jesse Dowsett, 8 June 1881, Royal Commission on the Police Force of Victoria, SLV, Q.10940, p. 390.
45. Shaw, p. 207.
46. John McWhirter, 7 June 1881, Royal Commission on the Police Force of Victoria, SLV, Q.10351, p. 373.
47. *The Argus*, 11 August 1880, p. 6, NLA Trove online resource: http://trove.nla.gov.au/ndp/del/article/5971588.
48. John McWhirter, 7 June 1881, Royal Commission on the Police Force of Victoria, SLV, Q.10354, p. 373.
49. James Dwyer, 1 June 1881, Royal Commission on the Police Force of Victoria, SLV, Q.9480–2, p. 342.
50. Based on James Dwyer, 1 June 1881, Royal Commission on the Police Force of Victoria, SLV, Q.9482, p. 342 (reported speech changed to direct speech).
51. *The Argus*, 2 July 1880, p. 7, NLA Trove online resource: http://trove.nla.gov.au/ndp/del/article/5982850.
52. Carrington, p. 21.
53. James Dwyer, 1 June 1881, Royal Commission on the Police Force of Victoria, SLV, Q.9473, p. 342.
54. *The Age*, 30 October 1880, p. 5.

55. Carrington, p. 21.
56. *The Argus*, 29 June 1880, p. 5, NLA Trove online resource: http://trove.nla.gov.au/ndp/del/article/5975546.
57. Ashmead, p. 43.
58. John McWhirter, 7 June 1881, Royal Commission on the Police Force of Victoria, SLV, Q.10386, p. 374.
59. Based on *The Argus*, 2 July 1880, p. 7 (tense changed).
60. McMenomy, p. 183.
61. Sadleir, p. 238.
62. Ibid.
63. Jesse Dowsett, 8 June 1881, Royal Commission on the Police Force of Victoria, SLV, Q.10942, p. 390; *The Argus*, 12 August 1880, p. 6, NLA Trove online resource: http://trove.nla.gov.au/ndp/del/article/5957112.
64. James Dwyer, 1 June 1881, Royal Commission on the Police Force of Victoria, SLV, Q.9482, p. 343.
65. Ibid.
66. Ibid.
67. Shaw, p. 214.
68. James Dwyer, 1 June 1881, Royal Commission on the Police Force of Victoria, SLV, Q.9486, p. 343
69. Ibid., Q.9487, p. 343.
70. *The Argus*, 29 June 1880, p. 6, NLA Trove online resource: http://trove.nla.gov.au/ndp/del/article/5975546.
71. Ibid.
72. Ibid.
73. Shaw, p. 215.
74. *The Argus*, 5 July 1880, p. 6.
75. Ibid., 30 July 1880, p. 6.
76. Ibid., 29 June 1880, p. 2.
77. *The Age*, 29 June 1880, p. 3.
78. Ibid., p. 7, NLA Trove online resource: http://trove.nla.gov.au/ndp/del/article/5975535.
79. *The Sydney Morning Herald*, 25 January 1934, p. 13.
80. Ibid.
81. Sadleir, p. 235.
82. *The Argus*, 5 July 1880, p. 6, NLA Trove online resource: http://trove.nla.gov.au/ndp/del/article/5983068.
83. James Reardon, 14 May 1881, Royal Commission on the Police Force of Victoria, SLV, Q.7669, p. 278.
84. *The Argus*, 5 July 1880, p. 6, NLA Trove online resource: http://trove.nla.gov.au/ndp/del/article/5983068.

85. John Sadleir, 14 April 1881, Royal Commission on the Police Force of Victoria, SLV, Q.2829, p. 150.
86. *The Argus*, 5 July 1880, p. 6.
87. James Reardon, 14 May 1881, Royal Commission on the Police Force of Victoria, SLV, Q.7670, p. 278.
88. *The Argus*, 5 July 1880, p. 6.
89. Ibid., 29 June 1880, p. 7, NLA Trove online resource: http://trove.nla.gov.au/ndp/del/article/5975535.
90. Ibid.
91. Ibid.
92. James Dwyer, 1 June 1881, Royal Commission on the Police Force of Victoria, SLV, Q.9520, p. 344.
93. *The Herald*, 28 June 1880, p. 2.
94. Ibid.
95. Based on *The Argus*, 19 July 1880, p. 7, NLA Trove online resource: http://trove.nla.gov.au/ndp/del/article/5964748 (reported speech changed to direct speech).
96. *Daily Telegraph*, 29 June 1880, p. 3.
97. Rev. M. Gibney, 28 June 1881, Royal Commission on the Police Force of Victoria, SLV, Q.12302, p. 441.
98. Ibid.
99. Ibid.
100. John Sadleir, 14 April 1881, Royal Commission on the Police Force of Victoria, SLV, Q.2879, p. 153.
101. Sadleir, p. 229.
102. Fitchett, p. 44.
103. James Reardon, Royal Commission on the Police Force of Victoria, SLV, Q.7607, p. 276.
104. John Sadleir, 14 April 1881, Royal Commission on the Police Force of Victoria, SLV, Q.2865, p. 152.
105. Ibid.
106. Charles Johnston, 28 June 1881, Royal Commission on the Police Force of Victoria, SLV, Q.12500, p. 448.
107. *The Argus*, 29 June 1880, p. 6, NLA Trove online resource: http://trove.nla.gov.au/ndp/del/article/5975546.
108. Ibid., 10 August 1880, p. 7, NLA Trove online resource: http://trove.nla.gov.au/ndp/del/article/5961325.
109. John McWhirter, 7 June 1881, Royal Commission on the Police Force of Victoria, SLV, Q.10405, p. 374.
110. *The Herald* (Melbourne), 19 July 1880, p. 2.

111. Hare, p. 292.
112. Shaw, p. 264.
113. Stanhope O'Connor, 30 March 1881, Royal Commission on the Police Force of Victoria, SLV, Q.1183, p. 56.
114. Rev. M. Gibney, 28 June 1881, Royal Commission on the Police Force of Victoria, SLV, Q.12310, p. 442.
115. Stanhope O'Connor, 30 March 1881, Royal Commission on the Police Force of Victoria, SLV, Q.1184, p. 57.
116. Rev. M. Gibney, 28 June 1881, Royal Commission on the Police Force of Victoria, SLV, Q.12312, p. 442.
117. Ibid., Q.12318, p. 442.
118. Stanhope O'Connor, 30 March 1881, Royal Commission on the Police Force of Victoria, SLV, Q.1189, p. 57.
119. Sadleir, p. 237.
120. Rev. M. Gibney, 28 June 1881, Royal Commission on the Police Force of Victoria, SLV, Q.12314, p. 442.
121. Ibid.
122. Ibid.
123. *New Zealand Tablet*, Rōrahi VII, Putanga 382, 13 Hereturikōkā 1880, p. 17.
124. Rev. M. Gibney, 28 June 1881, Royal Commission on the Police Force of Victoria, SLV, Q.12318, p. 442.
125. Ibid.
126. Ibid., Q.12321, p. 442.
127. *The Argus*, 1 July 1880, p. 6, NLA Trove online resource: http://trove.nla.gov.au/ndp/del/article/5982611.
128. Ibid.
129. Ibid., 5 July 1880, p. 6, NLA Trove online resource: http://trove.nla.gov.au/ndp/del/article/5983068.

CHAPTER SIXTEEN: TRIALS AND TRIBULATIONS

1. McMenomy, p. 163.
2. Donald G. Sutherland to his Parents, 8 July 1880, MS 13713, Box 4243/4. 'Old Knick' was the spelling used by the author, Donald Sutherland.
3. Ibid.
4. *The Argus*, 29 June 1880, p. 6, NLA Trove online resource: http://trove.nla.gov.au/ndp/del/article/5975546.
5. Ibid.

6. Based on Donald G. Sutherland to his Parents, 8 July 1880, MS 13713, Box 4243/4 (prepositions changed).
7. *The Argus*, 5 July 1880, p. 6, NLA Trove online resource: http://trove.nla.gov.au/ndp/del/article/5983068.
8. *The Herald* (Melbourne), 29 June 1880, p. 3.
9. John Sadleir, 14 April 1881, Royal Commission on the Police Force of Victoria, SLV, Q.2875, p. 153.
10. Ibid.
11. Stanhope O'Connor, 30 March 1881, Royal Commission on the Police Force of Victoria, SLV, Q.1180, p. 56.
12. Donald G. Sutherland to his Parents, 8 July 1880, MS 13713, Box 4243/4.
13. *The Argus*, 1 July 1880, p. 6.
14. Ibid., 11 August 1880, p. 6, NLA Trove online resource: http://trove.nla.gov.au/ndp/del/article/5971588?searchTerm=%22it%20was%20I%20who%20shot%20him%22&searchLimits=sortby=dateAsc.
15. *The Age*, 9 August 1880, p. 3.
16. Ibid.
17. *The Argus*, 9 August 1880, p. 6, NLA Trove online resource: http://trove.nla.gov.au/ndp/del/article/5978894.
18. *The Age*, 9 August 1880, p. 3.
19. Ibid.
20. *The Argus*, 9 August 1880, p. 6, NLA Trove online resource: http://trove.nla.gov.au/ndp/del/article/5978894?searchTerm=%22Did%20I%20show%20any%20cowardice%22&searchLimits=.
21. Jones, *Ned Kelly: A Short Life*, p. 246.
22. Report of Constable Ryan, 16 July 1881, Kelly Historical Collection, Part 1, Police Branch, PROV, VPRS 4965, P0, Unit 2, Item 109. When Mrs Powell received her mattress back all bloodied and dirty, she demanded and received 10/ in compensation from the Victoria Police.
23. *The Argus*, 30 June 1880, p. 6.
24. *The Australian Pictorial Weekly: An Illustrated Newspaper*, 10 July 1880, p. 38.
25. *The Argus*, 30 June 1880, p. 6, NLA Trove online resource: http://trove.nla.gov.au/ndp/del/article/5952870.
26. *The Herald* (Melbourne), 30 June 1880, p. 3.
27. Graeme Johanson and Shar Jones, Design and Art Australia Online: www.daao.org.au/bio/john-william-lindt/biography.
28. *The Argus*, 30 June 1880, p. 6, NLA Trove online resource: http://trove.nla.gov.au/ndp/del/article/5952870.

29. Castles, p. 69.
30. *The Argus*, 30 June 1880, p. 6, NLA Trove online resource: http://trove.nla.gov.au/ndp/del/article/5952870.
31. *Australian Town and Country Journal*, 10 July 1880, p. 6, NLA Trove online resource: http://trove.nla.gov.au/ndp/del/article/70945462.
32. *The Argus*, 30 June 1880, p. 6, NLA Trove online resource: http://trove.nla.gov.au/ndp/del/article/5952870.
33. Ibid.
34. Ramsay to Standish, 29 June 1880, Kelly Historical Collection, Part 1, Police Branch, PROV, VPRS 4965, P0, Unit 1, Item 46.
35. *The Argus*, 30 June 1880, p. 6, NLA Trove online resource: http://trove.nla.gov.au/ndp/del/article/5952870.
36. *The Herald* (Melbourne), 30 June 1880, p. 3.
37. Ibid.
38. Ibid.
39. Ibid.
40. *The Age*, 1 July 1880, p. 3.
41. Based on *The Argus*, 1 July 1880, p. 6, NLA Trove online resource: http://trove.nla.gov.au/ndp/del/article/5982611 (tense changed).
42. *The Herald* (Melbourne), 30 June 1880, p. 3.
43. Standish to Montfort, 29 June 1880, Twenty-four Assorted Telegrams Relating to Glenrowan Outrage, Kelly Historical Collection, Part 1, Police Branch, PROV, VPRS 4965, P0, Unit 1, Item 46, p. 9.
44. *The Argus*, 30 June 1880, p. 6, NLA Trove online resource: http://trove.nla.gov.au/ndp/del/article/5952870.
45. Dr Ryan's bill was some four hundred and fifty guineas for the government, and overall some 600 pounds was spent upon surgical attendance of Mr Hare. The government, however, questioned the payment of four guineas for the treatment of a black-tracker wounded in the head at Glenrowan (Chomley, p. 154).
46. Castieau, p. viii.
47. There was much secrecy and misinformation around the inquest and burial of Joe Byrne. For example, Sadleir says, 'The body of Byrne was buried at 4 o'clock on Tuesday afternoon in the Benalla cemetery, and was not claimed by any one' (Sadleir's Report, 1 July 1880, Royal Commission on the Police Force of Victoria, SLV, Q.2880, p. 153). Standish says, 'Byrne's body was also brought down, and photographed there the next morning without my knowledge. An inquest was held on Byrne, and I instructed him to be buried straight off in the Benalla cemetery' (F. C. Standish, 23 March 1881, Royal Commission on the

Police Force of Victoria, SLV, Q.77, p. 6). While *The Argus* of 30 June 1880 and *The Ovens and Murray Advertiser* of 1 July 1880 both reported that Joe's body was returned to his friends: 'The body was subsequently handed over to the friends of the outlaw, who were waiting in Benalla to receive it, and they conveyed it to Greta.' I have followed Ian Jones's thesis from *The Fatal Friendship*, p. 194.

48. Ibid.
49. *The Argus*, 2 July 1880, p 7, NLA Trove online resource: http://trove.nla.gov.au/ndp/del/article/5982850.
50. Sadleir to Standish, 30 June 1880, Twenty-four Assorted Telegrams Relating to Glenrowan Outrage, Kelly Historical Collection, Part 1, Police Branch, PROV, VPRS 4965, P0, Unit 1, Item 46, p. 7.
51. *The Daily Telegraph*, 1 July 1880, p. 3.
52. Ibid.
53. *The Argus*, 1 July 1880, p. 6, NLA Trove online resource: http://trove.nla.gov.au/ndp/del/article/5982611.
54. Ibid.
55. Ibid., 2 July 1880, p. 7, NLA Trove online resource: http://trove.nla.gov.au/ndp/del/article/5982799.
56. *The Ovens and Murray Advertiser*, 6 July 1880, p. 2.
57. Ibid., 10 July 1880, p. 1.
58. Request of Prisoner Edward Kelly to be Allowed an Interview with his Mother and Sister, Kelly Historical Collection, Part 3, Chief Secretary's Office, PROV, VPRS 4967, P0, Unit 1, Item 28, p. 2.
59. Ibid.
60. Based on McIntyre, Section 6, p. 98 (reported speech changed to direct speech).
61. *The Age*, 2 August 1880, p. 3.
62. McIntyre, Section 6, p. 98.
63. Ibid.
64. Castles, p. 44.
65. McIntyre, Section 6, p. 99.
66. Ibid.
67. Ibid.
68. Based on ibid. (reported speech changed to direct speech).
69. A. J. Faulkiner, 11 May 1881, Royal Commission on the Police Force of Victoria, SLV, Q.5492–3, p. 225.
70. *Bendigo Advertiser*, 3 August 1880, p. 3, NLA Trove online resource: http://trove.nla.gov.au/ndp/del/article/88636559.
71. McIntyre, Section 7, p. 100.

72. Scott, p. 19.
73. *Bendigo Advertiser*, 3 August 1880, p. 3, NLA Trove online resource: http://trove.nla.gov.au/ndp/del/article/88636559.
74. Ibid.
75. McIntyre, Section 7, pp. 101–2.
76. Phillips, p. 18.
77. *The Argus*, 6 August 1880, p. 6, NLA Trove online resource: http://trove.nla.gov.au/ndp/del/article/5980120.
78. *The Age*, 7 August 1880, p. 5.
79. Ibid.
80. *The Illustrated Australian News*, 28 August 1880, p. 154.
81. *The Ovens and Murray Advertiser*, 7 August 1880, p. 4.
82. *The Argus*, 9 August 1880, p. 6, NLA Trove online resource: http://trove.nla.gov.au/ndp/del/article/5978894.
83. Ibid., 7 August 1880, p. 8, NLA Trove online resource: http://trove.nla.gov.au/ndp/del/article/5983525.
84. Ibid.
85. Ibid.
86. Ibid.
87. Based on ibid. (reported speech changed to direct speech).
88. Based on ibid. (reported speech changed to direct speech).
89. *The Ovens and Murray Advertiser*, 7 August 1880, p. 5.
90. *The Argus*, 7 August 1880, p. 8, NLA Trove online resource: http://trove.nla.gov.au/ndp/del/article/5983525.
91. *The Ovens and Murray Advertiser*, 7 August 1880, p. 4; Jones, *Ned Kelly: A Short Life*, p. 262.
92. *The Ovens and Murray Advertiser*, 7 August 1880, p. 4.
93. *The Age*, 9 August 1880, p. 3.
94. For the sake of structure here, I have slightly altered the order of McIntyre's answers, bringing together two responses on Fitzpatrick.
95. *The Argus*, 9 August 1880, p. 6, NLA Trove online resource: http://trove.nla.gov.au/ndp/del/article/5978894.
96. Phillips, p. 17.
97. *The Argus*, 9 August 1880, p. 6, NLA Trove online resource: http://trove.nla.gov.au/ndp/del/article/5978894.
98. Ibid.
99. *The Age*, 9 August 1880, p. 3.
100. Ibid.
101. Ibid.
102. Ibid., 12 August 1880, p. 3.

103. *The Herald* (Melbourne), 9 August 1880, p. 3.
104. *The Argus*, 9 August 1880, p. 6, NLA Trove online resource: http://trove.nla.gov.au/ndp/del/article/5978894.
105. *The Age*, 9 August 1880, p. 3.
106. Ibid.
107. *The Age*, 11 August 1880, p. 4.
108. Jones, *Ned Kelly: A Short Life*, p. 267.
109. Based on *The Age*, 13 August 1880, p. 3 (reported speech changed to direct speech).
110. Ibid.
111. With particular thanks to Charlie Farrugia, Senior Collections Adviser at the Public Record Office Victoria, for his generous help in finding this fresh material. Law Department Correspondence 80/4493, Inward Registered Correspondence, PROV, VPRS 266, P0, Unit 339.
112. Registers of Inwards Correspondence, PROV, VPRS 251/P, Unit 37, pp. 257–8.
113. *The Argus*, 16 October 1880, p 8, NLA Trove online resource: http://trove.nla.gov.au/ndp/del/article/5956030.

CHAPTER SEVENTEEN: ON TRIAL FOR HIS LIFE

1. This was established practice at the time.
2. Brown, p. 206.
3. Phillips, *The Trial of Ned Kelly*, p. 35.
4. Ibid., p. 36.
5. McIntyre, Section 7, p. 104.
6. *The Argus* reported that McIntyre said the party left on Friday the 23rd. The correct date is Friday 25 October 1878.
7. *The Argus*, 29 October 1880, p. 6, NLA Trove online resource: http://trove.nla.gov.au/ndp/del/article/5955087.
8. Ibid.
9. Phillips, p. 40.
10. *The Argus*, 29 October 1880, p. 6, NLA Trove online resource: http://trove.nla.gov.au/ndp/del/article/5955087.
11. Hall, p. 46.
12. *The Argus*, 29 October 1880, p. 6.
13. Phillips, p. 42.
14. *The Argus*, 29 October 1880, p. 6.
15. Ibid.
16. McIntyre, Section 7, p. 105.

17. *The Argus*, 29 October 1880, p. 6.
18. Police Report of Senior Constable James Gill, 13 October 1879, Kelly Historical Collection, Part 1, Police Branch, PROV, VPRS 4965, P0, Unit 4, Item 256, p. 1.
19. Based on Phillips, p. 54, and *The Argus*, 29 October 1880, p. 6 (quotations conjoined).
20. *The Argus*, 29 October 1880, p. 6.
21. *The Herald* (Melbourne), 28 October 1880, p. 3.
22. Brown, p. 207.
23. *The Argus*, 30 October 1880, p. 8.
24. Ibid.
25. Phillips, p. 56.
26. Edward Kelly Capital Case File, Kelly Historical Collection, Part 2, Crown Law Department, PROV, VPRS 4966, P0, Unit 2, Item 10, p. 79.
27. Ibid., pp. 79–80.
28. Phillips, p. 59.
29. Ibid.
30. Ibid., p. 78.
31. Based on *The Age*, 30 October 1880, p. 5 (reported speech changed to direct speech).
32. Phillips, p. 59.
33. *The Argus*, 30 October 1880, p. 8.
34. Phillips, p. 65.
35. Ibid.
36. Edward Kelly Capital Case File, Kelly Historical Collection, Part 2, Crown Law Department, PROV, VPRS 4966, P0, Unit 2, Item 10, p. 95.
37. *The Argus*, 30 October 1880, p. 8.
38. Based on *The Argus*, 30 October 1880, p. 8, NLA Trove online resource: http://trove.nla.gov.au/ndp/del/article/5977228 (reported speech changed to direct speech).
39. *The Age*, 30 October 1880, p. 5.
40. Ibid.
41. *The Argus*, 30 October 1880, p. 8, NLA Trove online resource: http://trove.nla.gov.au/ndp/del/article/5977228.
42. Phillips, p. 71.
43. Ibid.
44. Ibid., p. 72.
45. Ibid., p. 73.

46. Ibid., pp. 74–5.
47. *The Argus*, 30 October 1880, p. 8.
48. Phillips, pp. 76–7.
49. *The Argus*, 30 October 1880, p. 8, NLA Trove online resource: http://trove.nla.gov.au/ndp/del/article/5977228.
50. Ibid.
51. *Bendigo Advertiser*, 30 October 1880, p. 1S, NLA Trove online resource: http://trove.nla.gov.au/ndp/del/article/88639356.
52. *The Argus*, 30 October 1880, p. 8.
53. Phillips, p. 77.
54. *Bendigo Advertiser*, 30 October 1880, p. 1S.
55. *The Argus*, 30 October 1880, p. 8.
56. Ibid.
57. Based on *The Argus*, 30 October 1880, p. 8 (reported speech changed to direct speech).
58. Edward Kelly Capital Case File, Kelly Historical Collection, Part 2, Crown Law Department, PROV, VPRS 4966, P0, Unit 2, Item 10, p. 96.
59. *The Argus*, 30 October 1880, p. 8, NLA Trove online resource: http://trove.nla.gov.au/ndp/del/article/5977228.
60. Ibid.
61. Phillips, p. 100.
62. *The Argus*, 30 October 1880, p. 8, NLA Trove online resource: http://trove.nla.gov.au/ndp/del/article/5977228.
63. *The Daily Telegraph* (Melbourne), 30 October 1880, p. 5.
64. Phillips, p. 101.
65. *The Ovens and Murray Advertiser*, 2 November 1880, p. 4.
66. Based on ibid. (reported speech changed to direct speech).
67. *The Argus*, 30 October 1880, p. 6, NLA Trove online resource: http://trove.nla.gov.au/ndp/del/article/5977281.
68. Petitions for Reprieve, Kelly Historical Collection, Part 2, Crown Law Department, PROV, VPRS 4966, P0, Unit 3, Item 1.
69. Ned Kelly to Governor, 3 November 1880, in Edward Kelly Capital Case File, Kelly Historical Collection, Part 2, Crown Law Department, PROV, VPRS 4966, P0, Unit 2, Item 10.
70. *The Daily Telegraph* (Melbourne), 4 November 1880, p. 3.

CHAPTER EIGHTEEN: THE END IS HIGH

1. I have used the estimates of *The Argus* newspaper. *The Age* estimated

2600 persons inside the Hippodrome and 5000–6000 people in the streets outside.

2. *The Argus*, 6 November 1880, p. 8, NLA Trove online resource: http://trove.nla.gov.au/ndp/del/article/5956473.
3. Based on ibid. (reported speech changed to direct speech).
4. Ibid.
5. Ibid.
6. Ibid., p. 6, NLA Trove online resource: http://trove.nla.gov.au/ndp/del/article/5956523.
7. Ibid., p. 8, NLA Trove online resource: http://trove.nla.gov.au/ndp/del/article/5956473.
8. Ibid.
9. Edward Kelly to Governor of Victoria, in Edward Kelly Capital Case File, Kelly Historical Collection, Part 2, Crown Law Department, PROV, VPRS 4966, P0, Unit 2, Item 10.
10. *Independent* (Bendigo), 12 November 1880, p. 2.
11. *The Argus*, 6 November 1880, p. 6, NLA Trove online resource: http://trove.nla.gov.au/ndp/del/article/5956523.
12. Ibid.
13. *The Age*, 9 November 1880, p. 3.
14. Ibid., 6 November 1880, p. 5.
15. Ibid., 9 November 1880, p. 3.
16. Based on *The Argus*, 8 November 1880, p. 7, NLA Trove online resource: http://trove.nla.gov.au/ndp/del/article/5972534 (reported speech changed to direct speech).
17. Ibid.
18. Ibid.
19. Ibid.
20. *The Age*, 8 November 1880, p. 2.
21. *The Argus*, 9 November 1880, p. 6, NLA Trove online resource: http://trove.nla.gov.au/ndp/del/article/5982507.
22. Ibid.
23. Ibid.
24. Based on ibid. (tense changed).
25. Ibid.
26. Ibid.
27. Ibid., 10 November 1880, p. 6, NLA Trove online resource: http://trove.nla.gov.au/ndp/del/article/5983081.
28. Ibid.
29. This is the former name of what is now the top end of Swanston Street.

30. *The Argus*, 10 November 1880, p. 6, NLA Trove online resource: http://trove.nla.gov.au/ndp/del/article/5983081.
31. Based on ibid. (reported speech changed to direct speech).
32. Ibid.
33. Ibid.
34. Edward Kelly to Governor of Victoria, 10 November 1880, Edward Kelly Capital Case File, Kelly Historical Collection, Part 2, Crown Law Department, PROV, VPRS 4966, P0, Unit 2, Item 10.
35. Ibid.
36. *The Daily Telegraph* (Melbourne), 11 November 1880, p. 3.
37. J. Gittins, 'Nettleton, Charles (1826–1902)', *Australian Dictionary of Biography*, Vol. 5, http://adb.anu.edu.au/biography/nettleton-charles-4289.
38. *Kilmore Free Press*, 18 November 1880, p. 4.
39. Ibid.
40. Jones, *Ned Kelly: A Short Life*, p. 286.
41. Ibid., p. 285.
42. Based on *The Age*, 11 November 1880, p. 2 (tense changed).
43. Ibid. (tense and personal pronouns changed).
44. Ibid.
45. *The Ovens and Murray Advertiser*, 4 May 1871, p. 2.
46. *The Herald* (Melbourne), 11 November 1880, p. 2.
47. *Kilmore Free Press*, 18 November 1880, p. 4.
48. Anon., 'Farewell to my Home in Greta', lyrics in Keesing and Stewart, p. 48.
49. Based on Catholic practice.
50. *The Herald* (Melbourne), 11 November 1880, p. 2.
51. *The Argus*, 12 November 1880, p. 6.
52. Buckley, p. 192. It is my assumption that this was the ritual used.
53. Based on Catholic practice.
54. *The Argus*, 12 November 1880, p. 6.
55. *Australian Town and Country Journal*, 13 November 1880, p. 14, NLA Trove online resource: http://trove.nla.gov.au/ndp/del/printArticlePdf/70949712/3?print=n.
56. Ibid.
57. *The Argus*, 12 November 1880, p. 6, NLA Trove online resource: http://trove.nla.gov.au/ndp/del/article/5982177.
58. Ibid.
59. *The Herald* (Melbourne), 11 November 1880, p. 2.
60. An alternative version of his last words, as the rope was being placed

around his neck, is, 'Ah well, I suppose it has come to this . . .' as reported in *The Argus*, 12 November 1880, p. 6.

61. *Independent* (Bendigo), 12 November 1880, in Jones, *Ned Kelly: A Short Life*, p. 288.
62. *The Argus*, 12 November 1880, p. 6, NLA Trove online resource: http://trove.nla.gov.au/ndp/del/article/5982177.
63. Ibid.
64. *The Herald* (Melbourne), 17 November 1880, p. 2.
65. Ibid.
66. Ibid.
67. *The Argus*, 12 November 1880, p. 6, NLA Trove online resource: http://trove.nla.gov.au/ndp/del/article/5982177.
68. Kelly Inquest File, PROV, VPRS 24, P0, Unit 411, File [18]80/938.
69. Ibid.
70. *Criminal Law and Practice Statute 1864*, Part IX, ss. 315, in *Victoria Government Gazette*, No. 233, 10 June 1864, p. 613, www.austlii.edu.au/au/legis/vic/hist_act/tclaps1864316.pdf.
71. *The Herald* (Melbourne), 18 November 1880, p. 2.

EPILOGUE

1. *Australasian Sketcher*, 6 November 1880, p. 299, NLA Trove online resource: http://trove.nla.gov.au/ndp/del/article/60622639.
2. Cowen, p. 12.
3. Based on *The Ovens and Murray Advertiser*, 2 November 1880, p. 4 (reported speech changed to direct speech).
4. The Reward Board had been appointed under an Order in Council dated 19 July 1880, but they deemed it advisable to postpone their meetings until Ned Kelly's fate had been decided.'
5. Pryor, p. 33.
6. Ibid.
7. Kelly Reward Board: Report of the Board and Minutes of Evidence, 1880–1881, R. S. Brain, Acting Government Printer: Melbourne, p. iii.
8. L. J. Pryor, 'The Diseased Stock Agent', *Victorian Historical Journal*, Vol. 61, No. 4, Issue 236, December 1990, pp. 243–69.
9. 'Report of the Board appointed to enquire into and report upon the proper mode of distributing the rewards offered for the capture of the Kelly Gang', *Victorian Parliamentary Papers*, Session 1, 1880–81, p. iv.
10. *The Daily Telegraph*, 2 February 1996, p. 25.
11. *The Age*, 13 September 1997, p. A8.

12. Victoria Police Commission, 5 July 1881, Royal Commission on the Police Force of Victoria, Appendix 20 (Minutes of Proceedings at Meetings Held by the Royal Commission on Police), p. 714.
13. It is often recorded that 17,789 questions were asked at the 1881 Royal Commission. However, at some stage throughout the process of drafting the Minutes of Evidence, the numbering of the questions dropped back 500 units; Question 7774 is recorded as followed by Question 7275. I have accounted for this error.
14. 'Second Progress Report of the Royal Commission of Enquiry into the Circumstances of the Kelly Outbreak, 1881', Royal Commission on the Police Force of Victoria, p. iv.
15. Ibid., p. v.
16. Ibid., Appendix VII, p. xiii.
17. Ibid., p. v.
18. Ibid., pp. v–vi.
19. *The Argus*, 3 March 1882, p. 6, NLA Trove online resource: http://trove.nla.gov.au/ndp/del/article/11533788.
20. 'Second Progress Report of the Royal Commission of Enquiry into the Circumstances of the Kelly Outbreak, 1881', Royal Commission on the Police Force of Victoria, p. vi.
21. Ibid., p. v.
22. Ibid., p. xv.
23. Ibid., p. iv.
24. Ibid., p. x.
25. William B. Montfort, Royal Commission on the Police Force of Victoria, Appendix 1 (Evidence Taken behind Closed Doors), Q.29, p. 680.
26. Captain F. C. Standish, 23 March 1881, Royal Commission on the Police Force of Victoria, SLV, Q.181, p. 10.
27. Ian Jones, 'Kelly – the Folk Hero', in Cave, p. 178.
28. Jones, *Ned Kelly: A Short Life*, p. 299.
29. J. S. Legge, 'Standish, Frederick Charles (1824–1883)', *Australian Dictionary of Biography*, Vol. 6, http://adb.anu.edu.au/biography/standish-frederick-charles-4632.
30. *The Argus*, 20 March 1883, p. 6, NLA Trove online resource: http://trove.nla.gov.au/ndp/del/article/8505153.
31. Ibid.
32. D. T. Seymour, Letter to Stanhope O'Connor, Brisbane, 15 July 1880, in Royal Commission on the Police Force of Victoria, p. 453.
33. 'Second Progress Report of the Royal Commission of Enquiry into the

Circumstances of the Kelly Outbreak, 1881', Royal Commission on the Police Force of Victoria, p. vi.
34. *The Argus*, 11 February 1882, p. 10.
35. Ibid., 26 February 1900, p. 9, NLA Trove online resource: http://trove.nla.gov.au/ndp/del/article/9050435.
36. *The Ballarat Star*, 3 July 1880, p. 4.
37. Pryor, p. 22.
38. Annual Report of Victorian Humane Society, 1881, in Pryor, p. 26.
39. Pryor, p. 48.
40. L. J. Pryor, 'The Diseased Stock Agent', *Victorian Historical Journal*, Vol. 61, No. 4, Issue 236, December 1990, pp. 243–69. Though it is said that Daniel Kennedy even taught Dan Kelly at the Greta Common School in 1868, no official documentation has been found to verify this quite probable claim.
41. McIntyre, Section 1, p. 17.
42. McMenomy, p. 83.
43. McIntyre, Section 7, p. 112.
44. *The Age*, 18 October 2005, p. 7.
45. McIntyre, Section 7, p. 113.
46. Shaw, p. 297.
47. K. Oldis, 'The True Story of the Kelly Armour', *The La Trobe Journal*, Spring 2000, No. 66, pp. 38–48.
48. B. W. Cookson, 'The Kelly Gang from Within', in *The Sun* (Sydney), 14 September 1911.
49. *The Age*, 27 October 1978, p. 4.
50. Sadleir, p. 187.
51. *The Advertiser* (Adelaide), 9 November 1891, p. 5.
52. *The Argus*, 1 August 1898, p. 7, NLA Trove online resource: http://trove.nla.gov.au/ndp/del/article/9844892.
53. Ibid.
54. Jones, *Ned Kelly: A Short Life*, p. 300.
55. *The Sun* (Sydney), Cookson, 23 September 1911, p. 4.
56. Ibid.
57. Ibid.
58. Ibid.
59. Ibid., 3 September 1911, p. 9.
60. Ibid.
61. Jones, *Ned Kelly: A Short Life*, p. 300.
62. *The Sun* (Sydney), Cookson, 2 September 1911, p. 4.
63. Ibid.

64. Ibid., 28 August 1911, p. 4.
65. Ibid.
66. Ibid.
67. Ibid.
68. Ibid.
69. *Smith's Weekly*, 7 April 1923, p. 9.
70. Ibid.
71. Interview with Steve Hart's grand-nephew, Paul O'Keefe, 13 April 2013.
72. All information on the Reardon children supplied by Jeanine Grieg.
73. Poem from Esther Hart's scrapbook (courtesy of Paul O'Keefe, Ettie Hart's great-great grandson.)
74. *The Argus*, 27 December 1906, p. 5, NLA Trove online resource: http://trove.nla.gov.au/ndp/del/article/9663171.
75. *The Age*, 27 October 2008, p. 1.
76. Inward Registered Correspondence III, PROV, VA 475, Chief Secretary's Department, File [19]29/W 4499.
77. *The Morning Bulletin*, 13 April 1929, p. 9, NLA Trove online resource: http://trove.nla.gov.au/ndp/del/article/54649831.
78. Ibid.
79. Brown, p. 34.
80. Samir S. Patel, 'Final Resting Place of an Outlaw', *Archaeology*, Vol. 65, No. 5, September/October 2012, http://archive.archaeology.org/1209/features/ned_kelly_bones_australia_old_melbourne_gaol.html.
81. *Bendigo Independent*, 19 November 1880, p. 2.
82. Jones, *Ned Kelly: A Short Life*, p. 289.
83. *Bendigo Independent*, 19 November 1880, p. 2.
84. Register of Letters and Memos Sent (Outward Correspondence) (VA 724 Victoria Police), PROV, VPRS 676, P0, Unit 25 and Memorandum Books (VA 724 Victoria Police), PROV, VPRS 676, P0, Unit 72, pp. 389, 408.
85. Samir S. Patel, 'Final Resting Place of an Outlaw', *Archaeology*, Vol. 65, No. 5, September/October 2012, http://archive.archaeology.org/1209/features/ned_kelly_bones_australia_old_melbourne_gaol.html.
86. Ibid.
87. Ibid.
88. Ibid.
89. Edward Kelly to Governor, 10 November 1880, Edward Kelly Capital Case File, Kelly Historical Collection, Part 2, Crown Law Department, PROV, VPRS 4966, P0, Unit 2, Item 10.

90. *The Australian*, 18 January 2013, www.theaustralian.com.au/national-affairs/opinion/let-us-not-cry-for-ned-kelly/story-e6frgd0x-1226556115776.
91. *The Bulletin*, 31 December 1966, p. 9.
92. *The Age*, 9 August 1880, p. 3.

BIBLIOGRAPHY

INITIALS USED

ML The Mitchell Library, Sydney
NLA National Library of Australia, Canberra
PROV Public Record Office Victoria, Melbourne
SLV The State Library of Victoria, Melbourne

BOOKS

Adam-Smith, P., *Romance of Australian Railways*, Rigby, Adelaide, 1973

Allen, N., *Ellen: A Woman of Spirit*, Network Creative Services, Melbourne, 2012

Amory, M. (ed.), *The Letters of Evelyn Waugh*, Penguin, London, 1982

Blackmore, R. D., *Lorna Doone*, Sampson Low, Son & Marston, London, 1869

Bottle, W. J. M., *Datas: The Memory Man (By Himself)*, Wright and Brown, London, 1932

Boxall, G., *History of the Australian Bushrangers* (Third Edition), T. Fisher Unwin, London, 1908

Brown, M., *Ned Kelly: Australian Son*, Angus & Robertson, Melbourne, 1980

Browne, S., *A Journalist's Memories*, Read Press, Brisbane, 1927

Buckley, T., *The Catechism of the Council of Trent*, Alois (trans.), George Routledge & Co., London, 1852

Burgoyne, A., *Memories of Avenel*, Halstead Press, Sydney, 1955, http://handle.slv.vic.gov.au/10381/182023

Carrington, T., *Ned Kelly: The Last Stand* (facsimile edition), Lothian Books, Melbourne, 2003

Castieau, J. B., *The Difficulties of My Position: The Diaries of Prison Governor John Buckley Castieau*, National Library of Australia, Canberra, 2004

Castles, A. C., *Ned Kelly's Last Days: Setting the Record Straight on the Death of an Outlaw*, Allen and Unwin, Sydney, 2005

Cave, C. F., *Ned Kelly: Man and Myth*, Cassell Australia, Melbourne, 1968

Chomley, C. H., *The True Story of the Kelly Gang of Bushrangers*, Fraser and Jenkinson, Melbourne, 1920

Clarke, M., *Clarke of Rupertswood 1831–1897: The Life and Times of William John Clarke*, Australian Scholarly Publishing, Melbourne, 1995

Clune, F., *The Kelly Hunters: Impartial History of the Life and Times of Edward Kelly, the Ironclad Outlaw*, Angus and Robertson, Sydney, 1954

Ned Kelly's Last Stand: The Life and Times of Australia's Ironclad Outlaw, Angus and Robertson, Sydney, 1962

Coffey, B., *The Brackens*, Bill Coffey, South Melbourne, 1990

Coles, J. C., *The Life and Christian Experience of John Cowley Coles*, M. L. Hutchison, Melbourne, 1893

Cookson, B. W., *The Kelly Gang From Within (Articles Written by Cookson and Compiled by Brian McDonald)*, Australian History Promotions, Sydney, 2005

Corfield, J., *The Ned Kelly Encyclopaedia*, Thomas C. Lothian, Melbourne, 2003

Cowen, Z., *A Touch of Healing, 1977–1982, Vol. 2*, University of Queensland Press, Brisbane, 1986

Deakin, A., *The Crisis in Victorian Politics 1879–1881: A Personal Retrospect*, Melbourne University Press, Melbourne, 1957

Dean, G. and K. Passey, *The Bushranger Harry Power: Tutor of Ned Kelly*, Victorian Bushranger Enterprises, Melbourne, 1991

Douthie, J., *I Was at the Kelly Gang Round-up*, Network Creative Services, Melbourne, 2008

Ellis, S. E., *A History of Greta*, Lowden Publishing Co., Kilmore, Victoria, 1972

Fitchett, W. H., *Ned Kelly and his Gang*, Fitchett Brothers, Melbourne, 1925

Gill, K. F., *Edward 'Ned' Kelly: The Historical Record 1820–1893*, Kelvyn F. Gill, Melbourne, 2012

Gillison, J., *A Colonial Doctor and his Town*, Cypress Books, Melbourne, 1974

Haldane, R., *The People's Force: A History of the Victoria Police*, Melbourne University Press, Melbourne, 1986

Hall, G. W., *The Kelly Gang: The Outlaws of the Wombat Ranges (The Mansfield Pamphlet)*, self-published, Mansfield, 1879

Hare, F., *The Last of the Bushrangers: An Account of the Capture of the Kelly Gang* (facsimile edition), The Naval and Military Press, London, 1894

Harvie, J. C., *The Convict Hulk 'Success': The Story of Her Life, and the Lives of Those Who Filled Her Cells: A Relic of the Past, Interesting Reminiscences*, Spectator Publishing Co., Melbourne, 1891

Jones, I., *The Fatal Friendship: Ned Kelly, Aaron Sherritt and Joe Byrne*, Lothian Books, Melbourne, 2003

The Friendship that Destroyed Ned Kelly: Joe Byrne, Lothian Books, Melbourne, 1992

'Kelly – the Folk Hero', in C. F. Cave, *Ned Kelly: Man and Myth*, Cassell Australia, Melbourne, 1968

Ned Kelly: A Short Life, Lothian Books, Melbourne, 2003

Keesing, N. and D. Stewart, *Old Bush Songs and Rhymes of Colonial Times*, Angus and Robertson, Sydney, 1957

Kenneally, J. J., *The Complete Inner History of the Kelly Gang and their Pursuers*, The Kelly Gang Publishing Company, Melbourne, 1980

King, J. A., *'Mad Dan' Morgan Bushranger*, Phillip Mathews, Sydney, 1976

Lake, M. and F. Kelly (eds), *Double Time: Women in Victoria (150 years)*, Penguin, Melbourne, 1985

Lewis, W., S. Balderstone and J. Bowman, *Events that Shaped Australia*, New Holland Publishers, Sydney, 2006

Lowe, P., *Hunters and Trackers of the Australian Desert*, Rosenberg Publishing, Sydney, 2002

Lundy, H. C., *Jerilderie 100 Years*, Jerilderie Shire Council, Jerilderie, New South Wales, 1958

Manifold, J., *The Death of Ned Kelly and Other Ballads*, Favil Press, London, 1941

Mansfield, P., *Graham Berry: Geelong's Radical Premier*, Geelong Historical Society: Geelong, 2006

McCarthy, F. D., *New South Wales Aboriginal Place Names and Euphonious Words*, V.C.N. Blight, Government Printer, Sydney, 1963

McHugh, E., *Bushrangers: Australia's Greatest Self-Made Heroes*, Penguin Books, Melbourne, 2011

McIntyre, T. N., *A True Narrative of the Kelly Gang*, Sections 1–7, Victoria Police, Melbourne, 2006, www.police.vic.gov.au/content.asp?Document_ID=10583

McMenomy, K., *Ned Kelly: The Authentic Illustrated History*, Hardie Grant Publishing, Melbourne, 2001

McNicoll, R., *Number 36 Collins Street*, Allen and Unwin, Sydney, 1988

McQuilton, J., *The Kelly Outbreak 1878–1880*, Melbourne University Press, Melbourne, 1987

Molony, J., *I Am Ned Kelly*, Allen Lane, Melbourne, 1980

Moyal, A., *Clear Across Australia: A History of Telecommunications*, Nelson, Melbourne, 1984

Murray, J., *Larrikins: 19th Century Outrage*, Landsdowne Press, Melbourne, 1873

Phillips, J. H., *The Trial of Ned Kelly*, The Law Book Company Limited, Sydney, 1987

Pryor, L. J., *Thomas Curnow*, privately published, Melbourne, 1986

Punch (Melbourne), *The History of the Berry Ministry and How It Made Victoria a Fine Country for the Working Man*, J. McKinley and Co, Melbourne, 1879

Rickards, E. C., *Bishop Moorhouse of Melbourne and Manchester*, Murray, London, 1920

Sadleir, J., *Recollections of a Victorian Police Officer*, Penguin, Melbourne, 1973

Scott, S., *The Kelly Gang at Euroa*, Popinjay Australian Publications, Woden, Australian Capital Territory, 1989

Shaw, I. W., *Glenrowan: The Legend of Ned Kelly and the Siege that Shaped a Nation*, Macmillan, Sydney, 2012

Woodham-Smith, C., *The Great Hunger: Ireland 1842–49*, Hamish Hamilton, London, 1962

CORRESPONDENCE

Anonymous Letter to Monk, PROV, VPRS 4965, P0, Unit 3, Item 235

Bowman to O'Loghlen, PROV, VPRS 4967, P0, Unit 1, Item 8

Bracken, H. to Standish, PROV, VPRS 4965, P0, Item 159

Cameron, T. H., Letter to his brother, Glenrowan, 8 July 1880, ML, AK25, Microfilm: CY3268, frames 1–22

Chief Commissioner of Police Standish to Chief Secretary Berry, 18 December 1878, PROV, VPRS 4969, P0, Unit 1, Item 18

Chief Secretary's Department, File [19]29/W 4499, Inward Registered Correspondence III, PROV, VA 475

Dowsett to Traffic Manager, 2 July 1880, PROV, VPRS 4969, P0, Unit 1, Item 1

Hall to Montfort, 20 April 1871, PROV, VPRS 937, Unit 413

Hall to Supt Barclay, 22 April 1871, PROV, VPRS 937, Unit 413

Hare to Standish, 27 June 1880, PROV, VPRS 4965, P0, Unit 1, Item 33

Jones, A. to Montfort, PROV, VPRS 4965, P0, Unit 1, Item 63

Kelly, E., Euroa Letter, 14 December 1880, PROV, VPRS 4966, P0, Item 3

Kelly, E., Jerilderie Letter, February 1879, SLV, MS 13361

Kelly, E. to Sergeant James Babington, 1870, VPRS 937, P0, Unit 272
Law Department Correspondence 80/4493, Inward Registered Correspondence, PROV, VPRS 266, P0, Unit 339
McRea to Standish, 15 May 1871, PROV, VPRS 937, Unit 413
Nicolson to Sadleir, 1 May 1879, PROV, VPRS 4965, P2, Unit 4, Item 177
Nicolson to Secretary of Lands, 19 March 1879, PROV, VPRS 4965, P2, Unit 4, Item 177
7 May 1879, VPRS 4965, P2, Unit 4, Item 177
O'Loghlen to Sir Henry Parkes, 17 February 1879, PROV, VPRS 4967, P0, Unit 1, Item 12
Palmer to Ramsay, 27 June 1880, in Reports and Correspondence: Services Required by Queensland Trackers, PROV, VPRS 4965, P0, Unit 5, Item 393
Ramsay to Standish, 29 June 1880, PROV, VPRS 4965, P0, Unit 1, Item 46
Register of Inward Correspondence, PROV, VPRS 251, P0, Unit 37
Register of Letters and Memos Sent, Outward Correspondence, VA 724 Victoria Police, PROV, VPRS 676, P0, Unit 25
Sadleir to Standish, 30 June 1880, in Twenty-four Assorted Telegrams Relating to Glenrowan Outrage, PROV, VPRS 4965, P0, Unit 1, Item 46
Scott to Chief Manager, PROV, Kelly Historical Collection, Part 1, Police Branch, VPRS 4965, P0, Unit 3, Item 165
Scott, A. G., Letters of Scott 'Moonlight' and Rogan Written while Awaiting Execution in Darlinghurst Gaol (4/825.2), State Records NSW, NRS906, Special Bundles (Colonial Secretary),1880, Microfilm copy SR Reel 2868, photocopy (COD291)
Secretary of Lands to Nicolson, 24 March 1879, PROV, Kelly Historical Collection, Part 1, Police Branch, VPRS 4965, P2, Unit 4, Item 177
Seymour to Standish, 17 February 1879, PROV, VPRS 4968, P0, Unit 2, Item 62
Smith, Mrs (née Jones) to Chief Commissioner Chomley, 9 May 1893, PROV, VPRS 4965, P0, Unit 3, Item 147
Standish to Hare, 18 June 1880, Hare Papers, the University of Melbourne Archives, Accession 79/78, Francis Hare Papers, No. 22
June 1880, Hare Papers, the University of Melbourne Archives, Accession 79/78, Francis Hare Papers, No, 25
Standish to Montfort, 29 June 1880, in Twenty-four Assorted Telegrams Relating to Glenrowan Outrage, PROV, VPRS 4965, P0, Unit 1, Item 46

Standish to O'Loghlen, 22 April 1879, PROV, VPRS 4967, P0, Unit 1, Item 12
Standish to Seymour, 15 February 1879, PROV, VPRS 4968, P0, Unit 2, Item 62
17 February 1879, PROV, VPRS 4965, P0, Unit 5, Item 393
Sutherland, D. G. to his parents, 8 July 1880, SLV, MS 13713, Box 4243/4
Ward to Standish, 27 June 1880, PROV, VPRS 4965, P0, Unit 1, Item 33

DIARIES, MEMOIRS, JOURNALS

Ashmead, J. W., *The Thorns and the Briars: A True Story of the Kelly Gang*, SLV, MSPA PA, Box 55, 1922
Earp, L., *Ned Kelly Story: Condensed from Joseph Ashmead's Biography*, SLV, PA 02/28, Box 55, 1939

GOVERNMENT PUBLICATIONS

Parliamentary Debates Legislative Council and Legislative Assembly, Victoria, 1878, Vol. 1, John Ferres Government Printer, Melbourne, SLV, LTOM 1, V33
New South Wales Government Gazette
Victoria Government Gazette
Victoria Police Gazette

JOURNAL ARTICLES

Dickens, C., 'Great Expectations', *All the Year Round*, No. 84, 1 December 1860, Dickens Journals Online: www.djo.org.uk/all-the-year-round/volume-iv/page-169.html
Gribble, J. B., 'A Day with Australian Bushrangers', *The Leisure Hour*, 1885
Holland, A., 'After Glenrowan: Some Recent Findings on the Provenance of the Kelly Gang Armour', *The La Trobe Journal*, No. 69, Autumn 2002, SLV website: www.slv.vic.gov.au/latrobejournal/issue/latrobe-69/t1-g-t7.html
Lemon, A., 'Inventing the Melbourne Cup', *The La Trobe Journal*, No. 88, December 2011, SLV website: www.slv.vic.gov.au/latrobejournal/issue/latrobe-88/t1-g-t2.html
Monash, J., 'Cabbages and Kings', *Table Talk*, 18 April 1929
'Noble and McBride vs State of Victoria and State of Queensland – Case Summary', Australian Indigenous Law Reporter,

2000, 5:1, www.austlii.edu.au/cgi-bin/sinodisp/au/journals/AUIndigLawRpr/2000/2.html

Oldis, K., 'The True Story of the Kelly Armour', *The La Trobe Journal*, No. 66, Spring 2000, SLV website: www.slv.vic.gov.au/latrobejournal/issue/latrobe-66/t1-g-t4.html

Patel, S., 'Final Resting Place of an Outlaw', *Archaeology*, Vol. 65, No. 5, September/October 2012

Pryor, L. J., 'The Diseased Stock Agent', *Victorian Historical Journal*, Vol. 61, No. 4, Issue 236, December 1990

Smith, J., 'Archaeological Investigations of Prisoner Burials at the Old Melbourne Gaol and Pentridge Prison', *Provenance: The Journal of Public Record Office Victoria*, No. 10, 2011, http://prov.vic.gov.au/publications/provenance/provenance2011/losing-the-plot

Wright, B., 'In Pursuit of the Kelly Reward: An Examination of Applicants to Join the Hunt for the Kelly Gang in 1879', *Provenance: The Journal of Public Record Office Victoria*, No. 10, 2011, http://prov.vic.gov.au/publications/provenance/provenance2011/pursuit-of-the-kelly-reward

NEWSPAPERS AND PERIODICALS

The Advertiser (Adelaide)

The Age

The Argus

Australasian Post

Australasian Sketcher with Pen and Pencil (Melbourne)

The Australian

The Australian Pictorial Weekly: An Illustrated Newspaper

Australian Town and Country Journal

The Ballarat Star

The Barrier Miner

The Bathurst Free Press and Mining Journal

Bell's Life (Sydney)

Benalla Ensign and Farmer's and Squatter's Journal (also known as *The North Eastern Ensign*)

Benalla Standard

Bendigo Advertiser

Bendigo Independent

The Brisbane Courier

The Bulletin

The Cornwall Chronicle
Corowa Free Press
Daily Southern Cross
The Daily Telegraph (Melbourne)
The Daily Telegraph (Sydney)
Echo (Sydney)
Euroa Advertiser
Federal Standard (Chiltern)
Frankston Standard Leader
Freeman's Journal
Gippsland Times
The Herald (Melbourne)
The Illustrated Australian News
The Illustrated World News
Independent (Bendigo)
Jerilderie Gazette
Kerang Times and Swan Hill Gazette
Kilmore Free Press
Kyneton Observer
The Mansfield Courier
The Mansfield Guardian
Mercury (Hobart)
Mirror (Perth, Western Australia)
The Morning Bulletin
New Zealand Tablet
The North Eastern Ensign (also known as *Benalla Ensign and Farmer's and Squatter's Journal*)
North Queensland Register
The Northern Territory Times and Gazette
The Ovens and Murray Advertiser
Queenslander
Smith's Weekly
The South Australian Advertiser
South Australian Register
The Sun (Sydney)
The Sunday Times (Perth)
The Sydney Morning Herald
The Wangaratta Dispatch
The Wangaratta Dispatch and North-Eastern Advertiser
Windsor and Richmond Gazette
Yea Chronicle

REPORTS AND PAPERS

Account of J. C. Lowe, 1939, original manuscript held by Thomas Lowe of Yarrawonga

Benalla Petty Session Cause List Book, 23 October 1871, PROV, VPRS 1874, Unit 4

Bracken, Hugh, Claim Lodged with the Kelly Reward Board, PROV, VPRS 4968, P0, Unit 1, Item 1

Detective Report, 14 June 1879, PROV, VPRS 4965, P0, Unit 4, Item 342

Fitzgerald, W., Statement, 20 September 1880, PROV, VPRS 4969, P0, Unit 1, Item 17

Francis Hare Papers, the University of Melbourne Archives, Accession 79/78, http://gallery.its.unimelb.edu.au/imu/imu.php?request=multimedia&irn=5937

Gill, Senior Constable James, Police Report of 13 October 1879, PROV, VPRS 4965, P0, Unit 4, Item 256

Jones, J., Statement, PROV, VPRS 4967, P0, Unit 3, Item 60

Kelly, E., Request of Prisoner Edward Kelly to be Allowed an Interview with His Mother and Sister, PROV, VPRS 4967, P0, Unit 1, Item 28

'The Kelly Historical Collection', PROV, VPRS 4965 to VPRS 4969

Kelly Inquest File, PROV, VPRS 24, P0, Unit 411, File [18]80/938

'Kelly Reward Board: Report of the Board and Minutes of Evidence, 1880–1881', R. S. Brain, Acting Government Printer, Melbourne

List of Suspected Persons in the North-East District, PROV, VPRS 4965, P2, Unit 4, Item 177

McIntyre, T., Deposition, 31 October 1878, PROV, 4969, P0, Unit 1, Item 23

First Report of Police Murders, 28 October 1878, PROV, VPRS 4965, P0, Item 317

Report of the Murders Committed at Stringybark Creek, VPRS 4966, P0 Unit 1, Item 1

McPhee, Claim Lodged with the Kelly Reward Board, PROV, VPRS 4969, P0, Unit 1, Item 19

Memorandum Books (VA 724 Victoria Police), PROV, VPRS 676, P0, Unit 72

Ned Kelly Capital Case File, PROV, VPRS 4966, P0, Unit 2, Item 10

Petitions for Reprieve, PROV, 4966, P0, Unit 3, Item 1

'Police Commission: Minutes of Evidence taken before Royal Commission on the Police Force of Victoria, together with appendices; presented to both houses of Parliament by His Excellency's Command' (facsimile edition), Heinemann Royal Commission, Melbourne, 1968, SLV, RARELTF 351.74 V666M

Police Magistrate's Notebooks, Wangaratta, 10 November 1870, PROV, VPRS 1503, P0, Unit 4

'Progress Report of the Royal Commission of Enquiry into the Circumstances of the Kelly Outbreak, 1881', Royal Commission on the Police Force of Victoria, R. S. Brain, Acting Government Printer: Melbourne

Queen vs Ann Jones, PROV, VPRS 4965, P0, Unit 2, Item 137

Queen vs Edward Kelly, Murder File, PROV, VPRS 4966, P0, Unit 1, Item 2

Regina vs Ellen Kelly, William Williamson and William Skillion, PROV, VPRS 4966, P0, Unit 1, Item 4

Report of Constable Ryan, 16 July 1881, PROV, VPRS 4965, P0, Unit 2, Item 109

Report of Sergeant Whelan, 19 October 1879, PROV, VPRS 4965, P0, Unit 6, Item 456

'Second Progress Report of the Royal Commission of Enquiry into the Circumstances of the Kelly Outbreak, 1881', Royal Commission on the Police Force of Victoria, J. Ferres, Government Printer, Melbourne

Standish, 10 May 1880, PROV, Kelly Historical Collection, Miscellaneous Papers, VPRS 4969, P0, Unit 1, Item 30

Tanner's Land Refused, 16 June 1879, PROV, VPRS 4965, P2, Unit 4, Item 196

WEBSITES

All Down Under: http://alldownunder.com/index.html

Australasian Legal Information Institute: www.austlii.edu.au

Australian Dictionary of Biography: http://adb.anu.edu.au

Design and Art Australia Online: www.daao.org.au

Eleven Mile Creek: http://elevenmilecreek.blogspot.com.au

Iron Icon: www.ironicon.com.au

Iron Outlaw: www.ironoutlaw.com/index.html

Kelly Gang: www.kellygang.asn.au

Public Record Office Victoria: http://prov.vic.gov.au

State Library of Victoria: www.slv.vic.gov.au

Trove, National Library of Australia: http://trove.nla.gov.au

University of Melbourne, University Library Digital Repository: http://repository.unimelb.edu.au/10187/10631

Victoria Government Gazette: http://gazette.slv.vic.gov.au

Warren Fahey's Australian Folklore Unit: www.warrenfahey.com
The Western Australia Police Historical Society Inc.: www.policewahistory.org.au/HTML_Pages/Ned.html

INDEX

Aboriginal people, 26–7
black-trackers, 58, 364–5, 369–71, 374–5, 377–8, 384, 399, 400, 408, 424–5, 430, 472, 478, 483–4, 488, 501, 515, 603, 696
Kulin nation, 27
land wars, 26–9
massacre of, 370, 726
Adair, William, 85
Ah Fook, 37–41, 79, 117
Ah On, 109
Alder, Henry, 498, 499, 504, 505, 508
Alexander, Constable Robert, 429, 438, 442, 462, 620
Allen, George, 487, 553, 559, 695
Allen, Paddy, 371, 403
Allwood, Constable James, 199
Anderson, Colonel, 577
Anderson, Constable, 252
anti-death penalty campaigners, 658–66, 691, 707
Hippodrome rally, 661–3, 665
armour, 409–12, 419, 427–9, 529, 539–40, 550, 552, 561, 572–3
mouldboards stolen for, 409, 411, 419, 552
replica, 725
taken as souvenir, 705
Armstrong, Constable Harry, 429, 438, 441–3, 445, 447, 460, 462–3, 466, 577, 586, 698
Armstrong, Magistrate Henry, 85
Arthur, Constable James, 82, 476, 531, 538, 540, 542, 548–51, 586
arts, portrayed in, 719–20
Ashmead, Joseph, 97
Ashton, Julian, 569
attempts to save Ned's life, 658–71
anti-death penalty campaigners, 658–66, 691
petition for reprieve, 659, 665, 667–71, 678
Reprieve Committee, 658–9, 691, 718
Australian Institute of Anatomy, 722
Avenel 11–26
Aylward, Father James, 608–9

Babington, Sergeant James, 56, 59, 65

Baird, Constable, 159
Ball, Michael, 704
Balwoski, Joseph, 51, 55
bank robberies
  Euroa, 266–77, 288, 355
  Jerilderie, 329–53, 355
  planning, 248–9, 252
Bantick, Christopher, 726
Barker, Dr Edward, 688, 690
Barry, Constable Daniel, 476, 498
Barry, Edmund, 404
Barry, Ellen, 404, 435, 438–46
Barry, Ellen 'Belle' *see* Sherritt, Belle
Barry, Judge Redmond, 30, 150–4, 368, 633, 634, 636, 639–56, 661, 673, 694
Baumgarten, Gustav, 117, 122–4
Baumgarten, Margaret, 223
Baumgarten, William, 117, 122–4, 154, 223
Baxter, Tom, 723
Becroft, Frank, 257, 266, 267, 274, 283
Beechworth
  committal hearing at, 624–32
  conveying Ned to, 616–21
  Court, 109, 150–1, 307–10, 359
  Gaol, 72–5, 83, 86, 90, 128, 154, 310, 379, 612, 620, 621
  pursuing Kelly Gang, 230–6
Bell, Frank, 487
Bell, Constable William, 122–3
Benalla Barracks, 600–1
Benalla Courthouse, 40, 54–5, 143, 601
Benalla Police Station, 38, 40, 51, 134, 158, 597, 603
Berry, Graham, 125–7, 204, 205, 212, 246, 247, 288, 290, 292, 298–301, 386–8, 405, 407, 503, 615, 622, 626, 657, 659, 669–71, 678
Beveridge Catholic Church and School, 11
Bickerton, Coroner, 610
Bindon, Henry, 636, 638, 641–56, 707
birth, 4, 6, 728
'Black List', 381, 635
black-trackers, 364–5, 369–71, 374–5, 377–8, 384, 399, 400, 408, 424–5, 430, 472, 478, 483–4, 488, 501, 515, 603, 696
Blundell, Mr, 382
body/remains, 691–2, 720–6
  burial at Melbourne Gaol, 692, 724
  death mask, 691, 722
  DNA testing, 723–4
  head sawn off, 692, 722, 724
  reburial at Pentridge, 721, 724
  remains dug up, 720–1, 724
  return to Kelly family, 725
  skull, 721–3
Boles, Charles, 167

books about Kellys, 704, 719, 726
Booth, Edward, 268
Bowen, Sir George Ferguson, 100, 127
Bowman, John (barrister), 151, 152, 308, 309
Bowman, John (train driver), 487, 506
Bracken, Amelia, 413
Bracken, Constable Hugh, 76, 220–1, 233, 604, 616, 620, 632, 702
  escorting Ned to Beechworth, 616, 620
  Glenrowan, 413, 426–7, 430, 454, 470, 474, 484–92, 495, 501–3, 512–14, 525, 529, 534–5, 537, 553, 557–9, 561, 702
  reward, share of, 695
  Royal Commission, 702
  suicide, 702
Bracken, Mrs, 492
Bradley, Edward, 267–8
Brooke Smith, Inspector Alexander, 130, 228, 229, 236–40, 402, 697
Brown, Frederick, 84
Brown, G. Wilson, 12
Brown, Detective Joseph, 140
Brussels, Madame, 707
Bryan, Michael, 611
Buck, William, 659, 679, 725
building new family house, 124–5
Bullock Creek, 102, 103, 145–6, 150, 157–8, 160, 191
Burch, Hugh, 504
burial
  Greta Cemetery, 725
  Melbourne Gaol, 692, 724
  Pentridge Gaol, 721, 724
Burkes Holes sawmill, 97, 101, 303
Burman, Arthur, 601
bushrangers
  Greta mob labelled, 121
  Hall, Ben, 13–14, 111, 179, 213, 356
  Morgan, Mad Dan, 14–17, 197, 356
  Ned learning about, 49
  Power, Harry, 33–7, 44–66, 708
Byrne, Andrew, 108–10, 124
Byrne, Catherine, 235, 314, 373, 404
Byrne, Denny, 235, 438
Byrne, Ellen, 717
Byrne, Joe, 106–7, 109, 111–13, 124, 128, 141, 142, 146–7, 174, 179–85, 248, 250, 314, 366–7, 384, 416, 427–9, 432, 438–48, 600–3, 717
  armour, 410, 428
  body strung up, 600–1
  burial, 610
  death, 545–7, 572, 585, 592, 620
  Faithfull's Creek, 257, 263, 265, 266, 271–8, 281
  Glenrowan, 456, 465, 467, 486, 488, 492, 495, 497, 504, 509, 510, 520, 525, 528–9, 532, 545–7

inquest, 600–2
Jerilderie, 321, 323, 326, 329–36, 342–4, 350
killing Sherritt, 440–1
letter writing, 259–61, 265, 327, 659
on the run, 224, 225, 246, 248, 314–16, 448
request for body of, 605–6
Sherritt and, 106, 235–6, 316, 367, 402, 422–3, 438–41
Sherritt hut, 438–47, 466
Stringybark Creek, 174, 179–83, 185, 191, 201
Byrne, Margaret, 106, 234, 236, 293, 314, 359, 365–8, 371–3, 383, 404, 416, 426, 427
staking out house of, 365–8, 371–3, 377, 413, 429, 438
Byrne, Patrick, 235

Cameron, Don, 246–7, 296–9
Ned's letter to, 296–9, 327
Cameron, Tom, 465, 495, 509, 510
Canny, Constable, 476
Carrington, Thomas, 487, 518, 524, 548, 551–2, 562, 567, 587–8
Casement, David, 262
Castieau, Godfrey, 677–8
Castieau, John, 66, 607, 609, 612, 617, 657, 660, 673, 677–8, 684, 685, 691, 722
Caufield, J. P. T., 665
Cherry, Martin, 461, 500, 521, 537, 579–80, 592
Cheshire, Postmaster, 568
Chesterfield, Lord, 451
childhood, 6–23
becoming man of the house, 20–33, 35
bravery, 21–3, 26
poverty, 7, 10
saving drowning child, 21–3
Chomley, Arthur, 151, 153, 622, 638, 646
Clarke, Janet, 708
Clarke, Sir William, 608, 708
Clune, Frank, 320
committal hearing, 624–32
Condell, Sergeant, 13
Considine, Mr, 463
Cookson, Brian, 710–16
Cox, Charlie, 330–1, 335, 337
Cox, Mrs, 336
Curnow, Cathy, 463–4, 470, 487, 493, 496, 507
Curnow, Isobel, 463–4, 470, 480, 487, 493, 496, 507, 604, 703
Curnow, Muriel, 502
Curnow, Thomas, 463–4, 467–70, 474, 477, 480–93, 496, 502–7, 512, 604, 695, 703
Cuthbert, Henry, 218

Davidson, Inspector, 13
Davidson's Hotel, Jerilderie, 320, 322
Day, Constable Patrick, 118, 639

Deakin, Alfred, 125, 126, 247, 387
death by hanging, 682–90
death mask, 691, 722
Deeming, Frederick, 723, 724
Delaney, Catherine, 227
Delaney, Daniel, 302
Delaney, John, 463–6
Delaney, Patrick, 545
Devine, Senior Constable George, 321–6, 332, 337, 345, 347, 349, 351, 557
Devine, Mary, 322, 324–9, 337, 345, 349, 351
Dickens, Charles, 44
Dinning, William, 145
Diseased Stock Agent *see* Kennedy, Daniel
divided public opinion, 725–7
Dixon, James, 90
Dixon, Thomas, 586
Donaghy, Father Dean, 679, 682, 684
Donald (tracker), 58, 63, 364
Dowling, Constable Thomas, 429, 438, 443, 444, 446
Dowsett, Jesse, 536, 543, 551, 554–9, 566, 695
Doxey, Constable John, 18, 19
Duckett, Mr, 462
Dudley, Henry, 262–3, 265, 280
Dunne, Peter, 343–4, 352
Duross, Constable William, 429, 438, 439, 440
Dwyer, Constable James, 535, 553, 558–60, 564–5, 572–3, 586
Effeney, Libby, 722, 725
Eleven Mile Creek, 30–2, 36, 43, 50, 67, 75–6, 88, 97, 317, 377
    police guarding, 317–18, 377, 383
Ellery, Robert, 572
Elliott, William, 335, 336
Ellis, Louis, 684, 691
Ellis, Malcolm, 726
Eureka Stockade, 6, 27, 125, 126, 615, 634, 685, 720
Euroa, 250–86, 288, 355, 619

Faithfull's Creek station, 252–84, 643
family poverty, 7, 10, 635
farewells to family, 675–7
Farrell, John, 110, 111, 116, 128
Faulkiner, Constable Alfred, 616, 618
Felons Apprehension Act 1865 (NSW), 14, 16
Felons Apprehension Act 1878 (Vic), 212–13, 218, 225, 242, 301, 308, 309, 386, 403
    cessation of, 436
films about Ned, 719
first arrest, 40–2
first imprisonment, 72–4
Fitchett, William Henry, 250, 287, 434
Fitzgerald, Mrs, 253–5, 265, 266, 278
Fitzgerald, William, 253–6
Fitzpatrick, Constable Alexander, 99, 117–22, 130–42, 151–6, 182, 183, 203, 241, 241, 259,

261, 273, 296, 415–16, 520, 536, 629–31, 647, 710–11
cause of whole saga, 122, 520, 630, 699, 700, 715
Cookson's interview with, 710–11
death, 711
dismissal from police, 415, 629, 662, 710
fateful visit to Kelly home, 130–41, 318
Ned accused of attempt to murder, 138, 142, 145, 345, 639, 662
Royal Commission, 699, 710
Flood, Constable Ernest, 89, 95, 172, 182, 249, 280, 597
Ford, Dr, 57, 58
Ford, Thomas, 25
Foster, Fred, 710
Foster, Magistrate William, 307, 308, 358, 380, 625–7, 631
Foster, William, 709
Frankston, 98–9
Frost, Bill, 43, 90

Garrison Corps, 291–2, 396, 569, 577
Gascoigne, Constable Charles, 476, 511, 519–23, 527, 539–40, 705
Gately (hangman), 614, 687
Gaunson, David, 247, 616, 621–31, 634, 636, 647, 654, 657–9, 662–6, 669, 705, 707
Gaunson, William, 657–9, 665–70, 678–9
Gibbons, Robert, 488
Gibney, Father Mathew, 575–7, 582–7, 609
Gibson, Thomas, 14
Gill, Mrs, 340–1
Gill, Samuel, 306, 323, 326, 337–40, 363, 398, 399
Glenrowan, 239–40, 389, 412–14, 448–588, 591
criticism of police at, 613–14
dance at, 474–5
death of Dan and Steve, 585–8, 592
death of Joe, 545–6
Inn, 401, 412, 452, 459, 463, 469, 516–87, 591
letter to *The Argus* about, 613
Ned injured, 520, 528, 544, 546, 563–4
Ned taken, 557–67
Police Barracks, 430, 484–5, 610
sabotaging railway, 454–8, 482
setting fire to Inn, 581–7
siege, 516–73
Gloster, James, 257–9, 263, 264, 266, 643–4
gold sluicing operation, 147, 157
Gorman, Stationmaster, 277
Gouge, Ann, 274
Gouge, Bill, 252
Gould, Ben, 67–70, 267, 301
Gould, Rev William, 90
Governor of Victoria, 665, 667, 678, 679, 696

Ned's letters to, 659–60, 663, 671–2
Graham, Constable Robert, 145, 700
Grant, John, 598, 604
grave
dug up, 720–1, 723
Greta Cemetery, 725
Melbourne Gaol, 692, 720, 724
Pentridge Gaol, 721, 724
Graves, James Howlin, 247, 503
Gray, Bill, 37, 42
Greta, 26–30, 65, 68, 102–4, 114–15
Greta Cemetery, 75, 611, 691, 716, 725
Greta mob, 104–12, 115, 121, 139, 142, 158, 160, 174, 384, 412, 449, 596, 605
Gribble, Reverend, 335, 348–50
Griffiths, G. S., 613
Gunn, Alex, 37, 38, 75–8, 85, 86, 89
Gunn, Ellen, 75
Gunn, Yeamann, 39
Gurner, Henry Field, 243, 633, 646

Hackett, Judge, 109
Halkett, Colonel Craigie, 700
Hall, Ben, 13–14, 111, 179, 213, 356, 710
Hall, Constable Edward, 69–71, 78–85, 89, 228, 531
Hamilton, Archibald, 659, 661, 665, 666, 678–9, 691
hanging, 682–90
crowds outside gaol, 680–1, 683
family denied body, 691
farewells to family before, 675–7
last words, 688
official witnesses, 683–4
photographed before, 674
Hanlon, John, 363
Hare, Superintendent Francis, 46, 53–64, 66, 239, 241, 245, 290, 291, 295, 309–10, 312–16, 319, 320, 336, 352, 354, 358–72, 375, 377, 382–4, 389–91, 396, 399, 403, 404, 608, 695, 701, 708
death, 708
Glenrowan, 416–18, 422, 424–32, 471–84, 498, 499, 506, 508, 511–19, 524, 526, 527, 530, 533, 535, 537, 567, 599
memoirs, 701
Ned's opinion of, 618
reward, share of, 695
Royal Commission, 697, 701
subsequent career, 701
Harkin, Hugh, 338–9
Harkin, Sergeant, 224
Harris, Helen, 722
Hart, Dick, 149, 384, 412, 580, 594, 595, 605, 611, 622, 631
Hart, Ettie, 412, 413, 611, 631, 717–18
Hart, John, 302
Hart, Julia, 426
Hart, Nicholas, 150

Hart, Rachel, 709
Hart, Richard *see* Hart, Dick
Hart, Steve, 105, 116, 139, 149–50, 157, 291, 367, 384, 410, 432, 618, 718
 body, 594, 595, 604, 605, 610, 613
 death, 585, 592, 594, 603
 Euroa, 266–70, 274, 275
 funeral, 610–11
 Glenrowan, 448, 450, 451, 455, 457, 459, 464, 477, 480, 505, 510, 525, 529, 547, 561, 562, 570, 572, 576, 585
 Jerilderie, 321, 323, 326, 330–6, 339, 343, 347, 350
 on the run, 224, 227, 248, 321, 323
 rumour that still alive years later, 714
 Stringybark Creek, 174, 179, 180, 183, 191
Harty, Francis, 153
Hayes, Constable, 297
Healy, Constable Patrick, 551, 552
Hester, Dr James, 82
Hippodrome rally, 661–3, 665
Hollows, Herbert, 487
horse stealing, 21, 29, 36–7, 43, 49, 67, 77–84, 98, 101, 107, 111–13, 116, 128, 639
 Minnie, 344–5, 348, 350
 re-branding, 112–13, 123
Horwood, Constable, 164
Humffray, Howard, 705
Hutchison, Dr, 536, 562, 563
hymn, favourite, 663–4, 679

Ingram, James Jnr, 591

Jagger, Mick, 719
James, Senior Constable Frank, 230
Jefferson, Henry B., 342–3, 347–8, 351–2
Jeffrey, Robert, 128
Jerilderie, 306, 320–53
John, Justice, 696
Johnson, William, 98
Johnston, Senior Constable Charles, 236–41, 285, 286, 575, 578–9, 581–2, 592, 604
Jones, Ann, 401, 412, 426, 427, 452–4, 457, 459, 460, 463, 468, 477, 484, 486, 493, 495, 500, 510, 521, 522, 525, 532, 575, 579, 596, 712–13
Jones, Ian, 717, 719, 722, 724, 726
Jones, Jack, 474, 493, 494, 520–3, 532, 575, 596, 712–13
Jones, Jane, 453, 454, 457, 484, 486, 495, 509, 510, 521, 522, 525, 532–3, 575, 596, 713
justice (lack of)
 Ned's view, 48, 112, 163, 259–61, 296–9, 311, 327–9, 591, 637
 police, from, 48, 260, 699–70

Keating, Vincent, 230, 231
Kelly, Alice, 132, 138, 141, 155, 244

Kelly, Annie, 5, 11, 24, 36–8, 42, 75, 88–9, 172
Kelly, Dan, 9, 24, 65, 67, 90, 96, 98, 101, 105, 106, 109, 128–39, 142, 143, 146, 150, 151, 156, 165, 213, 283, 290, 367, 406, 432
  body, 594, 595, 604, 605, 610, 613
  death, 585, 592, 593, 603, 609
  Euroa bank robbery, 266, 267, 273, 274
  Fitzpatrick incident, 131–9, 142
  funeral, 610–11
  Glenrowan, 456, 459–61, 467, 469, 470, 474, 477, 481, 486, 495, 497, 500, 503, 510, 518, 525, 529, 540, 543, 547, 561, 562, 570, 572, 576, 585
  grave, 611, 725
  Jerilderie, 321, 323, 326, 329–31, 339, 347, 350
  on the run, 213, 224, 248, 257, 314–16, 359
  rumour that still alive years later, 714
  Sherritt hut, 434, 441, 442, 445–7, 466
  Stringybark Creek, 172, 174–8, 183, 185, 192, 627, 643
Kelly, Ellen (nee Quinn), 5–12, 20, 24, 25, 30, 32, 37, 43, 51, 54, 58, 65, 67, 81, 89–91, 97–8, 114, 122, 132–47, 150–8, 358, 621, 713–16
  Cookson's interview with, 713–16
  death, 716
  farewell to Ned, 675–6
  forfeiture of selection, 381, 635
  gaoled on false charge, 143–7, 150–7, 243, 259, 261, 368, 416, 629, 662
  Melbourne Gaol, 157, 244, 608–9, 621, 675, 681, 689
  Ned trying to get justice for, 259, 261, 311, 327, 358
  offences, 25, 54, 97–8, 151
  raising grandchildren, 710, 713
Kelly, Ellen (sister), 90, 132, 723
Kelly Gang, 178, 198, 201, 204, 211, 213, 216–18, 223–30, 239, 242–6, 253–588
  books about, 704, 719, 726
  Euroa, 250–86, 288, 355
  films about, 719
  gentility, 289
  Glenrowan, 448–588
  Jerilderie, 329–53, 355
  legal status, change of, 436
  press coverage *see* press coverage
  public admiration, 356, 426–7
  reward for, 205, 213, 225, 292, 315, 357–8, 408, 695–6
  songs about, 356, 389, 494, 681

supporters *see* Kelly sympathisers
Kelly, Grace, 24, 88, 132, 292, 580, 593, 657, 676
Kelly, James 'Tipperary Jim', 10, 30, 151
Kelly, Jim, 9, 24, 67, 89–90, 98, 101, 115–16, 243, 611, 666–9, 676–7, 690, 694, 710, 713, 715–16
Kelly, John (brother), 716–17
Kelly, John 'Red', 4–12, 17–20, 23–5, 56, 87, 90, 103, 716
Kelly, Senior Constable John, 163–5, 411–12, 475, 498, 508, 511, 516, 518, 519, 523–26, 530–2, 537–40, 551, 554–63, 581, 597–8, 605–6, 628, 631, 647, 695
Kelly, Kate, 9, 24, 88, 132, 140, 144, 244, 292, 317–19, 376, 383, 404, 406, 413, 428, 580, 582, 583, 592, 593, 605, 611, 632, 645, 657, 665–9, 676, 709–11, 715
Kelly, Margaret 'Maggie' *see* Skillion, Maggie
Kelly, Mary Jane, 5
Kelly sympathisers, 355–6, 388–90, 400, 605, 658
  arrest and trial, 301–10, 699
  committal hearing, at, 624
  demanding reprieve, 667–71
  discharge from gaol, 379–81
  funding defence of, 305, 307
  Glenrowan, in, 412–13, 426, 461, 496, 578, 594
  Reprieve Committee, 658–9, 691, 718
Kenneally, J. J., 694, 719
Kennedy, Bridget, 164, 189, 208, 211, 214, 219–22, 706
Kennedy, Daniel 'Denny', 400–1, 418–19, 431–2, 471, 484, 696, 703
Kennedy, Detective Douglas, 223–4
Kennedy, John Thomas, 164, 189
Kennedy, Michael (grandson), 706
Kennedy, Michael (son), 706
Kennedy, Sergeant Michael, 148, 159, 163–70, 174, 182–90, 194, 196, 197, 200, 204, 206, 208–22, 255, 259, 265, 415, 427, 437, 491, 559, 563, 629, 641–4, 706
Kershaw, 495
Kilfera Station, 42, 54, 58
Kilmore Free Press, 12, 14, 16, 677
King, George, 90, 91, 112, 116, 118, 132, 716
Kirkham, Constable, 476
Kreitmayer, Maximilian, 691, 722
Kyneton, 55, 59, 64

Laing, Henry, 227–9, 534
Lalor, Peter, 126, 615

land wars, 6, 26–9, 300, 386–7
Larkins, John, 456, 537
last confession, 682
last request, 673, 725
last rites, 684
last supper, 679
last words, 688
lawlessness of family, 4–5, 10, 19, 26, 54, 97–8
Lazarus, Samuel, 653
Le Patourel, Captain, 667, 668, 678
Ledger, Heath, 719
Lee, H., 721
legend, 719–20, 726
Legislative Council (Vic), 27, 125–6, 218, 299–300, 386
letters from Ned
  to Cameron, 296–9, 327
  to Gill, 327–9, 362–3, 398
  to Governor of Victoria, 659–60, 663, 671–2
  to O'Loghlen, 310–11
  to Sadleir, 259–61, 298
Lindsay, David, 134, 137, 152
Lindt, J.W., 601
Living, Edward, 331–6, 340–1, 344, 363, 645, 712
Living, Silvia, 712
Lloyd, Bridget, 406
Lloyd, Jack, 9, 10, 26, 34, 48, 54, 57–62, 68, 71, 129, 131, 302
Lloyd, Jane (nee Quinn), 9, 26, 30
Lloyd, Kate (Miss), 406, 599, 600, 656, 657, 659, 677
Lloyd, Kate (nee Quinn), 9, 26, 30
Lloyd, Mary, 368
Lloyd, Tom Jnr, 9, 30, 68, 96, 104, 111, 112, 147, 191–3, 385–6, 605–6, 615, 616, 621–2, 625, 645, 657, 677, 709
Lloyd, Tom Snr, 9, 26, 35, 303–5, 308, 700
Longmore, Francis, 47
Lonigan, Maria, 166, 219, 283
Lonigan, Constable Thomas, 98, 118–20, 124, 159, 166, 169–71, 174–80, 191, 194, 196, 199, 206, 210, 217, 218, 222, 255, 265, 275, 283, 297, 298, 345, 415, 559, 564, 598, 626–7, 640–51, 704
Lyall, Andrew, 253
Lynch, Walter, 243

McAuliffe brothers, 413, 461, 571, 657
McAuliffe, Miss, 657
McBean, Robert, 42–8, 51, 54–6, 58, 143–4, 575, 602
McCall, Constable, 429
Macauley, William, 256–7, 266, 278, 281–3
McColl, John, 194
McCormick, Catherine, 67–71, 73, 267
McCormick, Jeremiah , 67–71, 73, 267
McCulloch, Sir James, 57, 64, 420
McDonnell, Hanorah, 481

McDonnell, Paddy, 460
McDonnell's Hotel, Glenrowan, 412, 449, 460, 523, 578, 595
MacDougall, Robert, 262, 263, 265, 271, 282
McDougall, Thomas, 344, 349
McElroy, John, 359, 368, 369
McFarland (barrister), 368–9
Machell, Robert, 99–101
McHugh, Neil, 522–3
McInerny, Constable, 39
McIntyre, Constable Thomas, 159, 165–97, 199, 207, 208, 213, 215, 217–18, 255, 311, 376, 597–8, 704–6
  escorting Ned to Beechworth, 616–21
  memoirs, 704–5
  Ned's committal hearing, 626–9
  Ned's trial, 639–43, 647, 648, 650–2
  reward denied to, 695
  Stringybark Creek, 165–97, 199, 215, 217–18, 255, 672, 704, 706
Mackenzie, Colin, 722
Mackie, James, 332, 348
McMonigle, John, 97, 101, 303, 307, 359
McPhee, Archibald, 499, 504, 505, 506, 508
Macpherson homestead, 15
McRea, Dr, 82
McWhirter, John, 487, 524, 559, 563, 695
Maginness, William, 119
Magor, Constable, 429
Manifold, John, 694
Mansfield, 74–8, 148, 158–60, 168, 242–3
  aftermath of murders, 204–6, 210–11, 214, 221–2
  Kennedy's funeral, 221–2
  memorial to policemen, 414–15
  murders *see* Stringybark Creek murders
  Police Camp, 302–3
Marquess of Normanby, 665, 667, 696
Mary the Larrikin, 321
Meehan, Constable Thomas, 194
Melbourne Central Criminal Court, 633
Melbourne Club, 45, 47, 99, 288, 478, 482, 700
Melbourne Cup, 232
Melbourne Gaol, 66
  burial in grounds of, 692, 724
  conveying Ned to, 596, 599–603, 606–7, 632
  Ellen in, 157, 244, 608–9, 612, 681, 689
  Ned in, 608, 612, 614–16, 633, 657, 673–80
  remains dug up at, 720–1, 724
Melvin, Joe, 234, 487, 509, 516, 524, 552, 559, 563, 571, 576, 592, 695
Metcalfe, George, 522
Miller, Robert, 302, 303, 308
Mills, Senior Constable, 373
Molesworth, Hickman, 636

Monash, John, 341–2
Monash, Louis, 341
Monk, Ted, 197, 199, 200, 207–8, 210, 215, 241–3
Montfort, Sergeant William, 48, 58, 61, 62, 81–2, 416, 606, 699
Montiford, Constable, 552
Moorhouse, Bishop James, 219, 221, 222
Morgan (engine driver), 534
Morgan, Mad Dan, 14–17, 197, 356
Morgan, Phillip, 18, 19
Mortimer, David, 463, 464, 474, 485, 488, 489, 495, 521, 532, 545, 570, 571
mouldboards stolen for armour, 409–12, 419, 552
Mount Battery Station, 35
Mount Killawarra, 96
Moyhu Races, 405–8
Murdoch, James, 83, 85
Murphy, Paul, 720
Murray, John, 55, 59
Music (Ned's horse), 477, 529, 554, 593, 612
mythologising Ned, 719–20, 726

Nettleton, Charles, 674
Newland, George, 74–6, 83–5, 196
newspaper stories *see* press coverage
Nicholson, Dr John, 135, 137, 151–3, 375, 535–6, 560–3, 567, 571, 574, 575, 617
Nicolson, Assistant Commissioner Charles, 52–65, 98, 113–14, 131, 138, 204, 205, 209, 231–9, 244–5, 280, 283–6, 290, 293, 316, 378–81, 395–403, 407, 412–25, 430–2, 476, 552, 618, 635, 695, 697, 701, 709
Noble, Constable Jack, 696
Nolan, Sidney, 720

O'Brien, Bridget, 401
O'Connor, Louisa, 399, 424, 483, 486, 488, 516, 524, 565
O'Connor, Sub-Inspector Stanhope, 369–71, 375, 399–400, 407, 422–4, 471, 478, 479, 482–3, 486, 488, 498–500, 509, 511, 515–16, 518, 524, 526, 528, 538, 540, 546, 560, 578, 594–5, 603, 696, 701–2, 726
O'Donoghue, Cornelius, 462
O'Hea, Father Charles, 7, 12, 17, 86, 679, 684
O'Keefe, Pual, 718
Oliver, Captain Hamilton, 375
O'Loghlen, Sir Bryan, 212, 300, 309, 357, 363, 380, 386
  Ned's letter to, 310–11
Olver, Leigh, 723
Osborne, Mr, 568
Owens, Constable Gary, 696

Parkes, Sir Henry, 357
peacocking and dummying, 103, 108, 110
Pentridge Gaol, 33, 45, 49, 86–7, 157

buried at, 721, 723, 724
Perkins, Henry, 302
Perkins, Mrs, 201
petition for reprieve, 659, 665, 667–71, 678
Pewtress, Sub-Inspector Henry, 148, 158, 194–7, 199, 208, 210, 215, 221, 242–3
Phillips, Constable William, 476, 522, 523, 528, 543
photographs, 674, 676, 716
phrenology, 691–2
Piazzi, Alphonse, 451–2, 602
plaster cast of head, 691
police
 brutality, 80–1, 98, 119, 297
 guarding Kelly house, 317–18, 377, 383
 incompetence, 238, 246, 250, 288–9, 312–13
 murders *see* Stringybark Creek murders
 Ned's view of, 95, 238, 246, 250, 296–8, 311, 327–8, 465
 reward, share of, 695–6
 Royal Commission, 694–5, 696–702
police informants, 400–2, 413, 430–2
 Jones, 401, 412
 Kennedy, 400–1, 418–19, 431, 471, 484, 696, 703
 Quinn, 159–60, 244–5, 312, 402
 reward not given to, 696
 Sherritt, 235–6, 313–16, 319, 359–62, 365–8, 382, 402, 403, 416, 422–3, 425–6, 696
 Stephens, 401
Powell, George, 599
Powell, Mrs, 599
Power, Harry, 33–7, 44–66, 97, 102, 107, 112, 142, 145, 290, 575, 708
 Ned as apprentice, 36–7, 45–50, 102, 111
 Ned blamed for informing on, 64–5, 72, 83, 84
 newspaper interview, 112, 171
 pursuit and capture, 45–64, 81, 233, 361, 416
Power, Walter, 96
press coverage, 573
 The Age, 363, 487, 573, 631, 664–6, 679
 The Argus, 171, 196, 203, 204, 206, 304, 363, 386, 407, 487, 573, 592, 602, 607, 611, 623–5, 658, 661, 664, 667, 668, 690
 Australasian Sketcher, 215, 265, 289, 487, 551, 588
 Benalla Ensign, 42, 47, 51, 55, 64
 Bendigo Independent, 722
 Bulletin, 726
 Daily Telegraph, 487, 674
 Euroa Advertiser, 250, 287
 Jerilderie Gazette, 306
 Kilmore Free Press, 677
 Kyneton Observer, 59
 Melbourne *Herald*, 289,

298, 318, 371, 573–4, 630, 644, 681, 687
Ovens and Murray Advertiser, 40, 41, 42, 47, 51, 73, 83, 85, 121, 301, 304, 305, 320, 355, 357, 398, 400, 406, 614, 624, 627, 680
Sydney Morning Herald, 236
Prout Webb, Katherine, 482, 486, 488, 516, 524
Prout Webb, Thomas, 400, 482

Quinlan, John, 15, 16
Quinn, Ellen *see* Kelly, Ellen
Quinn, James, 5, 6, 30, 59
Quinn, Jimmy, 10, 26
Quinn, Mary, 30, 60
Quinn, Patrick, 156, 159–60, 244–5, 312, 402, 670–1

Ramsay, Robert, 407, 414–21, 424, 479, 482–3, 568, 569, 572, 577, 604, 626, 695
Rankin, James, 337–9, 347–8
Rats' Castle, 228–30, 265
Rawlins, Charles, 498, 511–13, 516, 517, 519, 523, 524, 528, 532, 558, 559, 561, 569, 571, 695
Reade, Albert, 307, 308
Reardon, Bridget, 455, 541, 543, 544, 717
Reardon, Ellen, 541, 543
Reardon, James, 455–9, 464, 500–1, 509, 543, 570, 571
Reardon, Kate, 533, 571
Reardon, Margaret, 455–7, 500, 521, 533, 541–3, 551, 698
Reardon, Michael, 455, 465, 541–4, 571, 717
Reardon, Thomas, 541
Reardon, William, 571
Rede, Sheriff Robert, 615, 616, 684–6
religion/faith, 12, 86, 575–6, 679, 680, 682, 684
favourite hymn, 663–4, 679
last confession, 682
last rites, 684
remains *see* body/remains
Reprieve Committee, 658–9, 691, 718
reward for Kelly Gang, 205, 213, 225, 292, 315, 357–8, 408
distribution of, 695–6
Reynolds, Alec, 487, 489
Reynolds, Edward, 468, 488, 489
Reynolds, Hillmorton, 488
Reynolds, Dr Samuel, 196, 199, 648
Richards, Constable Henry, 294, 321, 323, 326, 330, 337, 339–40, 344–8, 351, 646
Robert Burns Hotel, 385, 658, 667, 668, 678, 679, 681, 690, 718
Robertson JP, Mr, 303
Rosier's gun shop, 385–6
Rowe, Dr John, 36–7
Royal Commission, 694–5, 696–702
Rule, Richard, 91, 97, 101

Rutherford, George, 15
Ryan, Anne, 25
Ryan, Constable, 159, 163, 597, 599, 631
Ryan, Dr Charles, 569, 600, 603, 608
Ryan, Joseph, 153
Ryan, Timothy, 230, 237, 657

Sadleir, Superintendent John, 39, 64, 127, 147–9, 158, 164, 166, 168, 203, 205, 209–11, 221, 228, 230–6, 239, 249, 280, 283, 284, 295, 301, 303, 307, 308, 312, 313, 316, 355, 369, 377, 379, 381, 395, 407, 706–7
  after Glenrowan, 594–6, 600, 603, 605, 610, 611, 620
  'Black List', 381, 635
  Glenrowan, 421–6, 430–2, 471–3, 498, 499, 534–6, 538–40, 560, 564–8, 571, 577–9, 582–4
  memoirs, 706–7
  Ned's letter to, 259–61, 265, 298
  reward, share of, 695
  Royal Commission, 697–8, 699
  subsequent career, 706
Sambo, Corporal, 369, 370, 375, 430
Sandiford, Rev Samuel, 164, 221
Saunders, James, 91, 97, 101
saving drowning child, 21–3
sawmill jobs, 91, 96, 97, 101
Scanlan, Constable Michael, 159, 164–6, 170, 174, 182–5, 191, 194, 196, 197, 199, 206, 210, 218, 222, 238, 255, 265, 415, 559, 563, 592, 629, 641
Scanlan, Father, 221, 222
schooling, 11–12
Scott, George, 273
Scott, Reverend, 399
Scott, Robert, 266, 268–70, 272, 274–5, 278, 282, 284, 289, 619, 645
Scott, Susy, 268, 270–4, 278, 289, 619, 645
Service, James, 407, 436, 503
Seymour, Mr D. T., 295
Shaw, Fanny, 268, 272, 274, 291, 292
Shelton, Dick, 21–3
Shelton, Esau, 23
Sherritt, Aaron, 105–6, 109, 111–13, 124, 142, 201–2, 225, 230, 234–6, 382–4, 402–4, 416, 434–5, 438–41
  Byrne and, 106, 235–6, 316, 367, 402, 422–3, 434, 438–41
  courting Kate Kelly, 383–4, 404
  informant, 235–6, 313–16, 319, 359–62, 365–8, 382, 402, 403, 416, 422–3, 425–6, 695
  marriage to Belle, 404, 421
  shooting of, 440–1, 449, 456, 460, 461, 466, 468, 471, 475, 698

staking out Byrne house, 365–8, 371–3, 403
Sherritt, Anne, 421–2, 429
Sherritt, Belle, 404, 421, 423, 425, 434, 435, 438–43, 446, 460
Sherritt, John, 421, 425
Shields, Dr Andrew, 607, 691, 692, 724
Shoebridge, Senior Constable Edward, 163, 232
Sinclair, Farmer, 408–9
Skillion, Bill, 33, 38, 42, 88, 90, 124, 132, 135–8, 141–3, 147, 150, 152–5, 157, 243, 709
Skillion, Maggie (nee Kelly), 8, 11, 24, 33, 88, 141, 144, 243–4, 292, 376, 377, 383–6, 398, 404, 406, 428, 657, 658, 667–9, 681, 709
after Glenrowan, 580–3, 593, 595, 604–5, 614–16
attempts to save Ned's life, 658, 667–9
children, 709
Ned's trial, 621–2, 625, 628, 635, 645
police guarding house of, 413, 426, 430
Smith, John Thomas, 293, 399, 471
Smith, Louisa *see* O'Connor, Louisa
Smith, Patrick, 66
Smyth, Charles, 99, 117, 130, 416, 622, 626, 628, 633, 638–41, 644, 646, 649–50
Sparrow, Henry, 215
squatters, 6, 8, 14, 19, 27–9, 102–3, 107–8, 386
Standish, Captain Frederick, 45–8, 52–8, 64, 82, 99–101, 113, 114, 127, 203–5, 220, 231–6, 243, 281, 284, 288, 290, 292–3, 295, 298, 301, 307–10, 315, 363–5, 374–8, 380–1, 391, 396, 399, 407, 414–25, 453, 471–2, 475, 478–9, 482–4, 488, 499, 568, 569, 594–5, 600, 602–6, 610, 611, 624, 643, 697, 700, 701
Stanistreet, Emily, 454, 480, 512, 523–4
Stanistreet, John, 389, 453–4, 458–9, 463, 464, 480–2, 505, 511, 522, 523, 525–6
Stawell, Sir William Foster, 243
Steele, Sergeant Arthur, 105, 115, 129, 138–41, 150, 152, 159, 160, 163, 180, 182, 228, 229, 240, 241, 244, 246, 604, 611, 711–12
Cookson's interview with, 711–12
escorting Ned to Beechworth, 616, 618
Glenrowan, 476, 533–8, 542–4, 549, 552–61, 712, 717
Ned's trial, 647–8
picture of, 129
reward, share of, 695
Royal Commission, 698
Stephens, George, 253–5, 263, 271, 401, 642–3

Stevens, Clement, 475, 476
Stock Protection Societies, 165, 328, 363, 698
The Story of the Kelly Gang film, 719
Stowe, Constable John, 122–3
Strahan, Senior Constable Anthony, 129, 130, 140, 144, 159–60, 167, 172, 182, 232, 234, 235, 244, 312, 670
Stringybark Creek murders, 169–93
  aftermath, 204–6, 210–11, 214, 221–2
  centenary, 706
  expiry of warrants for, 436
  memorial, 414–15
  Ned on trial for, 624–32, 637–56
  Ned's account, 255, 259, 265, 275, 297–9, 559, 563, 670–2
Sullivan, Dennis, 455, 457, 458, 501, 510
supporters *see* Kelly sympathisers
sweethearts
  Ettie Hart, 413, 631, 717–18
  Kate Lloyd, 599, 600, 656, 657

Tanner, Mary, 193
Tanner, William, 193, 381
Tarleton, John, 331–6, 346, 348, 646–7
Tennant, Mr, 253
Thom, Constable Hugh, 114, 115, 159, 163
Thomas, William, 55
Thompson, Mr, 84
Thomson, Mr C.G., 369
Tierney, Father, 404
Tone, Mr A., 610
trial, 637–56
  bias of judge, 638
  committal hearing, 624–32
  defence, 616, 621–3, 634–6
  Ned's address, 653–4
  sentence, 655–6, 673
  transfer to Melbourne Central Criminal Court, 633
Trooper Jimmy, 369, 430, 546
Twomey, Constable Michael, 229

Upjohn, Elijah, 614, 683, 686–9

Vale, William, 633
Vandenberg, Henry, 247–8
Vandenberg, Mary, 226–7, 248
Victoria Hotel, Everton, 226, 247
Victorian Institute of Forensic Medicine, 721–3

Walsh, Senior Constable Patrick, 228, 535
Wangaratta, 227–30
  Police Court, 70–3, 82–4
Ward, Detective Michael, 142–4, 149, 244, 246, 285, 297, 301, 316, 359–62, 371, 383, 400–3, 412, 422, 423,

425, 429, 438, 466–9, 476, 639, 695, 698–9, 709
Watt (telegraph-line repairer), 275–6, 278, 283
Whelan, Sergeant James, 39–40, 42, 50, 117, 118, 130, 131, 134–6, 151, 281, 285, 413, 599
whiskey distilling, 5, 147, 157, 672
Whitty, James, 107–11, 116, 123, 124, 128, 698
Wicks, Anton, 435–9, 442, 444–7, 461
Williams, John, 718
Williamson, Brickey, 78, 112, 124, 132, 135, 137, 138, 141, 143, 150, 152, 154, 155, 157, 381
Wills, Magistrate Alfred Currie, 41, 70, 83
Wilson, Samuel, 340
Winch, Superintendent, 663
Wombat Ranges, 102, 149–50, 166, 168
Woodham-Smith, Cecil, 3
Woods, John, 377
Wren, John, 707
Wright, Bridget (nee Lloyd), 91, 112
Wright, 'Dummy', 77, 206, 207, 211, 212, 592
Wright, Isaiah 'Wild', 76–8, 81, 83–6, 91–4, 124, 149, 156, 165, 192, 206–7, 211, 212, 302, 358–9, 380, 398, 406, 684, 690, 707–8
  Ned beating in fight, 91–4, 96, 107, 121, 556
  supporting Ned, 580, 593, 594, 666, 667, 669
Wright, Jack, 708
Wyatt, Magistrate Alfred, 155–7, 276–83, 358–9, 600, 601

Younghusband, Isaac, 253

Zincke, William, 143, 151, 307, 308, 437, 621–2